ESSENTIAL TORAH

ESSENTIAL TORAH

*A Complete Guide
to the Five Books of Moses*

GEORGE ROBINSON

Schocken Books, New York

Copyright © 2006 by George Robinson

All rights reserved. Published in the United States by Schocken Books,
a division of Random House, Inc., New York, and in Canada
by Random House of Canada Limited, Toronto.

Schocken Books and colophon are registered trademarks of Random House, Inc.

Library of Congress Cataloging-in-Publication Data

Robinson, George, [date]
Essential Torah : a complete guide to the five books of Moses / George Robinson.
p.   cm.
Includes bibliographical references and index.
ISBN 0-8052-4186-8
1. Bible. O.T. Pentateuch—Criticism, interpretation, etc.   I. Title.
BS1225.52.R63 2006   222'.1061—dc22   2005040174

www.schocken.com

Printed in the United States of America
First Edition
2   4   6   8   9   7   5   3   1

The great existentialist of the Hasidic movement, Rabbi Menachem Mendl of Kotzk, once wrote:

> If you wish for your children to study Torah, study it yourself in their presence. Otherwise they will not study Torah themselves, learning only . . . to instruct their children to study.

In the course of working on this book, I had the honor of studying for several years with three women who took the words of the Kotzker Rebbe to heart. This book is dedicated to them and to their children, with gratitude for teaching me and learning with me:

THE BLESSING FOR TORAH STUDY

ברוך אתה ה' אלקינו מלך העולם
אשר קדשנו במצותיו וצונו לעסוק בדברי תורה.

Blessed are You, *Adonai* our God, Ruler of the universe, who sancti-
fies us by Your commandments and commanded us to study words
of Torah.

May the words of Torah, *Adonai* our God, be sweet in our mouths
and in the mouths of all Your people so that we, our children and all
the children of the House of Israel may come to love You and study
Your Torah for its own sake. Blessed are You, *Adonai,* who teaches
Torah to Your people Israel. Blessed are You, *Adonai* our God, Ruler
of the universe, who chose us from among all peoples by giving us
Your Torah. Blessed are You, *Adonai,* who gives the Torah.

CONTENTS

ACKNOWLEDGMENTS

The Kotzker Rebbe said, "Some people wear their faith like an overcoat. It warms only them, but does not benefit others at all. But others light a fire and also warm others." I have been fortunate to sit by the fire of many good people in writing this book.

First and foremost in inspiring many of the thoughts contained here are my dear *khevruta,* my partners in Torah study to whom this book is dedicated, Connie Heymann, Elizabeth Lorris Ritter, and Patricia Dorff. They were also kind enough to offer their insights and experience for the final chapter. Their husbands—John Muller, Barry Ritter, and Danny Heuberger—and their children—Katherine Muller, Tina and David Ritter, and Benjamin and Claire Heuberger—were patient enough to let me steal some of their time. Many thanks also to others who participated in our study sessions—Susan Leopold, Sheldon Koy, Donna Smiley, and Steve Meltzer.

As was the case with its predecessor, *Essential Judaism,* many of the ideas between this book's covers got their first airing at Beth Am, the People's Temple, and my gratitude to the members of that congregation, living and dead, is enormous. So, too, is my debt to the members of Hebrew Tabernacle, which has become a home to Beth Am and to me. Many of the commentaries in the second half of this book had their first life as *derashot* delivered before those two congregations, and my special thanks go to Rabbi Margaret Moers Wenig, Rabbi Tamar Malino, Rabbi Karen Kaplan, Rabbi Stephen Berkowitz, and Rabbi Scott Weiner, and to Cantors Michael Kruk and Rebecca Fletcher, at whose pulpits—and on whose shoulders—I have been privileged to stand.

The eight students—Allison Ancowitz, Abraham "Ace" Bouchard, Michael Herson, Elana Leopold, Tina Ritter, Joshua Rotbert, Daniel Saez, and Gabriel Salzman—in the class on Torah that I co-taught with Rabbi Wenig, Gerson Goodman, and Edith Rubino in 1998–99 were the first people to watch me take the first childlike steps in *Khumash* that I had attempted since I was not much older than they. The passages on Torah cantillation were helped immeasurably by the contributions of Margot Fein and Connie Heymann. The chapter on Torah study benefited enormously from the rabbis and scholars who contributed their insights; I thank them for their time and the gift of their experience. Thank you to Israel Moshe Sandman for the citations regarding the physical dimensions of a *sefer Torah;* to Joy Weinberg and Hilary Ziff of *Reform Judaism* magazine for combing their library for several articles; to Nina Nesher, my very patient occasional Hebrew tutor; and to Molly Rubinstein, for sharing her insights into Yosef and his brothers.

My team of staunch supporters, friends, and allies that helped make writing *Essential Judaism* such a pleasant experience stood by me again for this book. Connie Heymann once again vetted the manuscript as a first reader—she could hardly be called a naive informant anymore, given her own enormous knowledge. Rabbi Margaret Moers Wenig continues to be not only a good friend and spiritual counselor but also a source of sound advice whose wisdom got me through several difficult points on this journey. Marsha Melnick is quite simply a rock; if everyone in publishing was as generous and caring as Marsha, you'd never hear an author complain again.

When we began shopping the proposal for this book, Marsha asked me, "How would you feel about Schocken?" My reply was emphatic: "How would I like to be published by the press that was founded for the express purpose of bringing out books by Martin Buber and Franz Rosenzweig? Is 'honored' strong enough?" Had I known then what a wonderful experience it would be to work with Altie Karper and, for a time, Susan Ralston, I would have been even more forceful in expressing my pleasure. For anyone writing a book on a Jewish subject, Schocken and its staff are a dream come true. Rabbi S. David Sperling read the book with a thoroughness at which I can only marvel. He caught numerous errors in Hebrew, Aramaic, and English, in fact and in interpretation. I am deeply indebted for his extraordinary effort.

My mother, Barbara Robinson, went through a spiritual search not unlike my own; it led her in a different direction, but she has been a genuine inspiration to me on my own path. Her activism in her church has been a shining example of what it means to be a giving part of a faith community, and my admiration, love, and respect for her have contributed to the making of this book.

The process of writing *Essential Torah*, to my dismay, proved to be almost as drawn out as the work on its predecessor. Needless to say, I couldn't have gotten through it without the support of many people, family, friends, and colleagues too numerous to mention by name. Special thanks are due to Rob Goldblum, Gary Rosenblatt, and the staff of *Jewish Week;* Bob Leiter, Carin Smilk, and the staff at *Inside Magazine* and the *Jewish Exponent;* and Gail Zimmerman at the *Detroit Jewish News.* I never missed a deadline (that I can recall) but sometimes I've been a little hard to find, for which I apologize.

Throughout the conception and writing of *Essential Torah,* only one person has been utterly indispensable to me. I will merely reiterate the praise I offered in my previous book and say that Margalit Fox is the best friend and partner I could hope for and a thousand times better than I deserve.

George Robinson
New York, NY, August 2006

I am frequently asked by non-Jews, "What do Jews believe in?" Having long since given up trying to come up with a snappy one-sentence answer, I usually say, "Jews believe in the Written Torah and the Oral Torah." This is a reply that, as you might expect, raises more questions than it answers.

And that suits me down to the ground. What could be more Jewish than asking questions about sacred texts? It's what Jews have done for millennia. It is the heart of what Torah is all about.

And it's why I wrote this book. My previous book, *Essential Judaism: A Complete Guide to Beliefs, Customs, and Rituals,* was an attempt to address basic questions about the practice of the Jewish religion, with a little history and folklore thrown in on the side. When I finished the book, I had the nagging feeling that I had given short shrift to an important subject area, the sacred texts that guide and (intermittently) govern Jewish belief.

This book is my attempt to address that imbalance and to clarify my one-sentence answer to the question of Jewish belief. Of course, as you will learn in the pages to follow, there probably isn't any one thing that *all* Jews believe, and while I say that Jews believe in the Written and Oral Torahs, it might be more accurate to say that most Jews believe in most of the Written and Oral Torahs, some Jews believe in all of the Written and Oral Torahs, and some Jews don't believe in the Written and Oral Torahs other than to acknowledge their existence as part of Jewish history.

We live in a time of extremes in both faith and skepticism, and Jews are not exempt from either.

That said, one must acknowledge that the Written Torah—the Hebrew Bible, but particularly the first five books, the "Five Books of Moses"—is one of the foundation stones of Western culture. The three great Abrahamic faiths—Judaism, Christianity, and Islam—grow out of this text. Much of Western skepticism is a reaction against this text. A firsthand knowledge of the Hebrew Bible, also called the *Tanakh* (an acronym derived from the Hebrew name of its three component parts: *Torah,*

Nevi'im/Prophets, *Ketuvim*/Writings), is an essential part of a well-rounded education.

But for Jews it is more. For many, it is the word of God directly passed on to Moshe on Mount Sinai. It is the basis of the Jewish religion and, because of the all-encompassingly quotidian nature of that religion, of Jewish daily life. Taken in tandem with the Oral Torah, the vast literature that grew out of the Written Torah as commentary and codification, these texts tell a Jew what to eat, when to pray, how to conduct business, even when to have conjugal relations. (For those of us who are not more stringent in our religious lives, the texts are frequently honored more in the breach than the observance, but that doesn't diminish their importance.)

To some extent, the structure of this book is similar to that of its predecessor. As I did in *Essential Judaism*, I begin with the Torah as ritual object and part of the liturgy. This is where an ordinary Jew (and, for that matter, a non-Jew) is most likely to first encounter Torah. Understanding its place in prayer and ritual observance is a good way to begin to grasp its literal centrality to Judaism.

Chapter 2 offers an overview of the themes and literary structures that run throughout the Five Books of Moses. Without some sense of these overarching concerns, it is all but impossible to discuss the text in some meaningful way. As the excellent contemporary Bible scholar Richard Elliott Friedman has observed, you can read any of the Torah's stories in isolation, but if you do so, you are missing the layers of meaning that are available when you know the whole book.

The question that inevitably follows directly from such knowledge is "Who wrote this book?" Chapter 3 is dedicated to answering that question. As will become obvious quickly, there is no definitive answer, but there certainly is an abundance of theories.

Despite, or because of, its authorship, the Torah is a text that speaks to us through a web of gaps, dislocations, contradictions. It is multivocal and polysemous, with the result that commentary designed to fill in those lacunae and resolve those paradoxes abounds. Indeed, with the exception of a few schismatic groups (notably the Karaites and Samaritans) who have rejected Rabbinic Judaism, almost all Jews accept to some degree the writings of the rabbis who created normative Judaism through the Talmud and the sages who have produced Torah commentary up to and including the present day. Chapter 4 is an attempt to get this veritable ocean of commentary and elaboration into a teaspoon.

It is my firm belief (already stated in *Essential Judaism*) that Jewish feminism is one of the most significant forces for change in Jewish thought since the founding of the State of Israel. Yet women have a difficult relationship to Torah. Since the 1960s, Jewish women have won a hard-earned place at the table of Torah scholarship, raising often painful questions about their place in the Jewish community. In Chapter 5, I try to explicate some of their ideas. Although this book is primarily intended as a reference work, I will readily admit that I am not only sympathetic to Jewish feminist scholarship, but deeply moved and impressed by it. It is the single most energizing set of texts I read while writing this book. They represent an exciting rethinking of Judaism that I believe will benefit us all.

Regardless of one's denominational affiliation (or lack thereof), there are passages in the Torah that make us wince. Extreme violence, slavery, and Jewish triumphalism at its least attractive are but a few of the problematic themes that one encounters. Chapter 6 is an attempt to place these issues in a context that will allow us to read them with understanding, if not sympathy.

One of the most satisfying aspects of the publication of *Essential Judaism* has been the adoption of the book by conversion classes and other classes in basic Jewish belief and practice. My secret hope for the book was that it would help fuel the revival of a spiritual Judaism that I saw already occurring in the Reform movement and in the rapid growth of Jewish Renewal. This book will, I hope, find a similar readership, and to that end, I include a chapter on how to study Torah. I asked many experts how they study Torah, but I also sat down with a group of "ordinary" Jews—the women I study with—to find out what they have gained from what is, at the time of this writing, five years of Torah study.

The second half of the book is an attempt to apply practically some of the lessons of the first part. Here you will find essays on each of the fifty-four Torah portions, as well as brief overviews of each of the five books. I have tried to draw upon as wide a range of commentaries as possible, in the hope of giving you a sampling of the many flavors of Torah scholarship available. But, ultimately, these essays are my own response to the Torah. I hope they will lead you to other commentaries and to conclusions of your own.

As for the question "How should I study Torah?" the answer that motivates much of this book is the advice that I. I. Rabi, the Nobel laureate in physics, received from his mother every day when he left for grade school. She would hand little Isidore his lunch and tell him, "Ask good questions."

That is what Torah is all about.

A NOTE TO THE READER

There are several widely used transliteration systems for both Hebrew and Aramaic, but I have tried to follow my own ears as much as possible when using Hebrew and Aramaic terms. In particular, I have transliterated the gutteral letter *Khaf* with the letters *kh* throughout, and not with the more familiar *ch*, so that readers cannot mistake the pronunciation for the Anglo-Saxon pronunciation of *ch*.

When he revived Hebrew as a modern language in Palestine toward the end of the nineteenth century, Eliezer Ben-Yehuda chose Sephardic pronunciation over Ashkenazic, with the result that the State of Israel uses the Sephardic pronunciation and, following their lead, the Reform movement in the United States does the same. That's what I learned, so that's what I have used.

I have translated non-English terms the first time they appear and occasionally thereafter. When in doubt, check the glossary.

Throughout this book I have scrupulously avoided gendered language when referring to the Deity. God is beyond gender, and the use of gendered "God-talk" bothers me for a number of obvious reasons. Consequently, I have not even used words like Lord or King, preferring *Adonai* (admittedly, a Hebrew word meaning "our Lord" and a gendered one at that) and gender-free English terms. (The only exceptions occur where I am quoting someone else.)

Almost all biblical figures are referred to by their Hebrew names throughout the book. Thus Moses will usually appear as Moshe, Aaron as Aharon, Cain and Abel as Kayin and Hevel, and so on. I hope this gives readers who are approaching the Torah for the first time some idea of the sound and poetry of the original Hebrew.

Similarly, I have referred to the books of the Hebrew Bible by their Hebrew names. To simplify your reading a little, here are the books in the order in which they appear:

TORAH (FIVE BOOKS OF MOSES, KHUMASH, PENTATEUCH)

Bereishit/Genesis
Shemot/Exodus
Vayikra/Leviticus
B'midbar/Numbers
Devarim/Deuteronomy

NEVI'IM (PROPHETS)

NEVI'IM RISHONIM (THE EARLY PROPHETS)
Yehoshua/Joshua
Shoftim/Judges
Shmuel Aleph/I Samuel
Shmuel Bet/II Samuel
Melakhim Aleph/I Kings
Melakhim Bet/II Kings

NEVI'IM AKHARONIM (THE LATER PROPHETS)
Yeshayahu/Isaiah
Yirmiyahu/Jeremiah
Yekhezkel/Ezekiel

TREI ASAR (THE TWELVE MINOR PROPHETS)
Hosheya/Hosea
Yoel/Joel
Amos/Amos
Ovadyah/Obadiah
Yonah/Jonah
Mikhah/Micah
Nakhum/Nahum
Kabakuk/Habakkuk
Zefanyah/Zephaniah
Haggai/Haggai
Zekharyah/Zechariah
Malakhai/Malachai

KETUVIM (THE WRITINGS)

Tehillim/Psalms
Mishlei/Proverbs
Iyov/Job

KHAMESH MEGILLOT (THE FIVE SCROLLS)
   Shir Ha'Shirim/Song of Songs
   Rut/Ruth
   Eikhah/Lamentations
   Kohelet/Ecclesiastes
   Ester/Esther
Danyel/Daniel
Ezra/Ezra
Nekhemyah/Nehemiah
Divrei Hayamim Aleph/I Chronicles
Divrei Hayamim Bet/II Chronicles

All dates in this book are given as B.C.E. (Before the Common Era) or C.E. (Common Era). Jews do not recognize Jesus as the Son of God, so "Anno Domini," or, "in the year of our Lord," is inappropriate. Personally, I find it heartening to see that this usage has been adopted in many highly visible places, including some of our nation's most prestigious newspapers. If that's what people deride as "political correctness," you can put me down as an avid fan.

ESSENTIAL TORAH

1

A TREE OF LIFE . . .

The Torah in Practice

It's early morning, probably a Monday or a Thursday—a market day in ancient Jerusalem—and, although it is autumn, the weather is warm and dry. But then, the weather is usually warm and dry in Jerusalem in the month of Tishri. The year is 444 B.C.E., and most of the Jews gathering near one of the gates of the city have been back in Judah for only a few years. They have returned at last from *galut/exile* in Babylon at the behest of the great Persian kings: first Cyrus, who conquered Babylonia, and now his successor, Artaxerxes, ruler of the most formidable empire in the Middle East. It was Artaxerxes who sent the priest and scribe Ezra (a direct descendant of Moshe's brother Aharon) back to Judah "to regulate Judah and Jerusalem according to the Law of your God, which is in your care" (*Ezra* 7:14). Now Ezra is going to fulfill that pledge.

Someone has erected a wooden tower at the square before Jerusalem's Water Gate and the people have been gathering for some time, milling about, waiting to hear a man read from a document that they have all heard about but, in all probability, have neither read nor had read to them. Let an eyewitness tell what happens next.

All the people gathered themselves together as one man into the broad place that was before the water gate; and they spoke unto Ezra the scribe to bring the book of the Law of Moses, which the LORD had commanded to Israel. And Ezra the priest brought the Law before the congregation, both men and women, and all that could hear with understanding, upon the first day of the seventh month. And he read therein before the broad place that was before the water gate from early morning until midday, in the presence of the men

and the women, and of those that could understand; and the ears of all the
people were attentive unto the book of the Law. . . .

And Ezra opened the book in the sight of all the people—for he was above
all the people—and when he opened it, all the people stood up. And Ezra
blessed the LORD, the great God. And all the people answered: "Amen,
Amen," with the lifting up of their hands; and they bowed their heads, and
fell down before the LORD with their faces to the ground. . . . And [the eld-
ers] read in the book, in the Law of God, distinctly; and they gave the sense,
and caused them to understand the reading.

(*Nekhemyah* 8:1–3, 5–6, 8; 1917 Jewish Publication Society trans.)

Ezra read from the cool of first light that day into the blistering heat of
midday. No one stirred from his place. The next day he did the same and
the listeners were as rapt in their attention as before.

And so it began.

What is this book, this Law of Moshe, so powerful that the men and
women who listened to it "fell down . . . with their faces to the ground"
upon hearing it read aloud?

In a word, it is the Torah.

WHAT IS THE TORAH?

The Torah, as contemporary Bible scholar James L. Kugel has written, is
the "single term that might summon up the very essence of Judaism . . .
[yet] it is an idea that defies easy summary." As Kugel notes, the Hebrew
word itself, *torah*, went through a complex evolution and is used in several
quite disparate ways.

The first time the word occurs in the Hebrew Bible is in *Shemot* 12:49:
"There shall be one Torah for [both] you and for the stranger that dwells
in your midst."

Teaching? Law? Each is used by translators. Each fits.

Like almost all Hebrew words, *torah* has a three-letter root, which it
shares with the verb *horah* (a different word from the familiar circle dance
of the same name, which is Roumanian in origin), meaning "teach." (See
"A Quick Introduction to the Hebrew Language," page 7.) Literally, *torah*
is a teaching.

This theory of the derivation of the word, while consistent with its uses
and meanings, is not universally accepted. Philologists have long debated

the origins of the word *torah*. Some have suggested that it is not derived from *horah* but is, rather, a formation influenced by other ancient Near Eastern words like the Akkadian *tertu*, meaning "oracle." Another theory posits *torah* as a derivation from the Hebrew *yarah*, meaning "to cast," as in lots that are used to predict the future.

Faced with this uncertainty, all we can do is focus on how the word's usage evolved and what it has come to mean to us. As noted above, *torah* is often used to mean a teaching, law, or precept. For example, the rules governing Nazirites—men and women who dedicated periods of their lives to God by vowing to abstain from cutting their hair and consuming intoxicants, Samson being the most famous example—can be found in a section of *B'midbar*/6, which is often referred to as the *torah* of the Nazirite. Colloquially, a teaching by a contemporary rabbi may be called a *torah*, too.

For our purposes, the most salient meaning of the word *torah* is the Pentateuch (from the Greek meaning "five pieces"), that is, the first five books of the Hebrew Bible. It is the first of the three scriptural divisions whose initials form the acronym that gives the Hebrew Bible its other name, *TaNaKh* (for *T*orah, *N*evi'im/the Prophets, *K*etuvim/the Writings). The Pentateuch is also called the Five Books of Moses for their putative author, and is often referred to as a *Khumash*, from the Hebrew word for "five."

This is the meaning of *torah* that is most often encountered in popular Jewish writing and, for reasons that will become apparent shortly, the meaning with which most Jews are familiar.

The Pentateuch, or Torah, consists of:

1. Genesis/*Bereishit*, also called *Sefer Ha'Yetzirah/the Book of Creation*
2. Exodus/*Shemot*, also called *Sefer Ha'Ge'ulah/the Book of Redemption*
3. Leviticus/*Vayikra*, also called *Torat Kohanim/Instructions of the Priests*
4. Numbers/*B'midbar*, also called *Khumash Ha'Pekudim/the Book of the Censuses*
5. Deuteronomy/*Devarim*, also called *Mishneh Torah/the Repetition of the Law*

The Hebrew name of each book is derived from the first significant word of each book: *Bereishit/Beginning*, *Shemot/Names*, *Vayikra/And He Called*, *B'midbar/In the Wilderness*, and *Devarim/Words*. The commonly used names—Genesis and so on—are derived from Greek and reflect the content of the books. *Bereishit* recounts the Creation, the origins of humanity, and the origins of the Jewish people; *Shemot* tells the story of the departure of the Jews from bondage in Egypt, the Revelation on Mount Sinai, and the beginning of the Hebrews' time in the desert; *Vayikra* is a compendium of laws; *B'midbar* continues the story of the Israelite wanderings in the desert, enumerates the twelve tribes, and sets down additional laws; and *Devarim* repeats the laws mentioned in the previous three books (hence its Greek name Deuteronomy, "second law"), prepares the Israelites for entry into the Promised Land, and ends with the death of Moshe.

As we will see throughout the remainder of this book, the Torah—the Pentateuch—is the heart of Judaism, whether one is Orthodox or Reform or anything in between. The "laws and precepts" on which Judaism—and by extension, Christianity and Islam—is based are to be found in the Torah.

But the meaning of the Torah is not transparent.

It's actually anything but. The Torah is often frustratingly opaque, and to base one's conduct on its prescriptions and proscriptions alone would be difficult at best. As time passed, the Jews moved farther away from the origins of this sacred text. Their language underwent the evolutionary changes that are inevitable in a living tongue, and the meaning of original passages of Torah became obscured. In many cases, the laws are presented in the narrative by implication and inference, and must be teased out by various hermeneutic methods. There are also passages that seem infuriatingly incomplete. For example, Moshe tells the Israelites that they can eat meat from animals that have been slaughtered in the manner that God has prescribed. But the description of that slaughtering method is nowhere to be found.

When the Jews of Judah heard Ezra read from the sacred *Torat Moshe/Torah of Moses*, they were overwhelmed with the desire to follow its teachings, but there were plenty of those teachings they simply couldn't understand, even with the elders trying to explain them. Ezra, tradition says, convened a great body of scholars (either 85 or 120, depending on the source), called the *Knesset Ha'Gedolah/Great Assembly*, to interpret and adjudicate matters of Torah. Convened sometime between 539 and 332 B.C.E., *Knesset Ha'Gedolah* included many men who could read and write (a rarity in those days), and they were entrusted with the task of bringing order out of a chaos of texts, rulings, and customs.

But it was believed that by writing down the rulings of the rabbis, the Great Assembly would be undermining the importance of the Torah, a

Written Law that they had been empowered only to clarify. What they developed was, by contrast, an Oral Law. The distinction between Written Torah and Oral Torah has persisted to this day, with the Written Torah, or *Torah she'b'ktav*, referring to the Pentateuch. The postbiblical books that constitute Oral Torah, *Torah she'ba'al peh* (literally, "Torah from the mouth"), include such key texts as the Mishnah and the Gemara, collectively known as the Talmud, the centerpiece of Rabbinic Judaism. We'll examine this distinction at much greater length in Chapter 4.

To contemporary Jews, the Written Torah and the Oral Torah are equal parts of one whole. Although their view of the status of Oral Torah and the *halakhah/the body of Jewish religious law* that is derived from it, will differ depending on what branch of Judaism they come from, all will tell you that Written Torah and Oral Torah together constitute Torah. And they will go farther and tell you that their teachings, the teachings of their teachers, their teachers' teachers, and so on, going back in an unbroken chain of tradition that begins at Sinai where God gave Moshe the Tablets of the Law, is all considered to be Torah, the living and constantly evolving body of Jewish knowledge, thought, and practice. Used in that sense, one could say Torah is being made every day.

And so it is.

But for our purposes, we will define Torah a bit more narrowly (or this book could never be completed), focusing on the Five Books of Moses— *Torah she'b'ktav*—and their central role in Jewish thought and practice.

A QUICK INTRODUCTION TO THE HEBREW LANGUAGE

The Torah is written in Hebrew (Biblical Hebrew, to be exact, but the distinctions between Biblical, Mishnaic, and modern Hebrew, while significant, are irrelevant for our purposes). A certain basic knowledge of the language will prove useful in understanding certain important facts about the Torah.

The Hebrew language has twenty-two letters, a chart of which may be found below. (It should be added that there are five letters that have distinctive forms when they appear at the end of a word.) Each of these letters has a single sound (a few of them appear to have the same sound; the exact sounds of these letters have been lost to history) and functions as a consonant. As we will see later, the "pointing," called *nikudot,* that represents vowel sounds was a later addition to the Torah (and is not present in the Torah scrolls). There are no capital letters in Hebrew.

Hebrew is a gendered language, with all nouns categorized as either masculine or feminine. Adjectives, adverbs, verbs, plurals, and possessives all must agree in gender with a given noun, depending on the context.

Each letter of the Hebrew alphabet has a numerical value. In fact, in the Hebrew text of the Torah in almost all *Khumashim* the chapter and verse numbers are given in Hebrew. There is a form of Bible interpretation based on the numerical values of Hebrew words that is called *gematria,* and many commentators with their feet planted firmly in Jewish mysticism will talk about these numerical values at length.

Most Hebrew words (verbs in particular) are based on three-letter roots. (There are a very few verbs that are exceptions to this rule, having two or four letters in their root.) As we will see quite frequently, a great deal can be learned about a word's meaning by examining its root and seeing what other words are derived from that root. For example, consider the words derived from the three-letter root *lamed-mem-dalet* (l-m-d), the root of the verb *lilmod/to study.* (The infinitive form in Hebrew always begins with *l'/to.*) Some of the other words that are derived from that root include *talmid/a male student, talmidah/a female student,* and a word we will encounter many times, the Talmud, that central work of Rabbinic Judaism, whose name obviously refers to the practice of study that is so dear to Jewish hearts. (In fact, a Hebrew grade school will sometimes be called a *talmud Torah,* i.e., a place for Torah study.)

The Hebrew Alphabet

א	aleph	ח	khet	ם	mem sofit
ב	bet	ט	tet	נ	nun
ב	vet	׳	yud	ן	nun sofit
ג	gimel	כ	kof	ס	samekh
ד	dalet	כ	khof	ע	ayin
ה	hei	ך	khaf sofit	פ	pei
ו	vav	ל	lamed	פ	fei
ז	zayin	מ	mem	ף	fei sofit

צ	tzadi
ק	kuf
ר	resh
שׁ	shin
שׂ	sin
ת,ת	tav

THE TORAH SCROLL

The first time that a Jew encounters the Torah is almost invariably in a synagogue, as a hallowed scroll—a physical object and the subject of a highly specific ritual, *Seder Kri'at Ha'Torah/the Service for the Reading of the Torah*. Let's take a closer look at a *sefer Torah/Torah scroll*.

The Torah scroll is a throwback to an earlier literary epoch; it is literally a scroll, wound onto two long wooden rods at each end. The first question that should pop into anyone's mind is why, in this age of e-books and hypertext, Jews still read their sacred texts from a scroll. The first answer, of course, is that it is traditional; Jews have been reading from *sifrei Torah* (plural of *sefer Torah*) for over two and a half millennia. The Torah scroll has been written by hand by scribes for that same period of time, and still is today. At the same time, reading from a scroll long after the invention of bound books was another way for Jews to distinguish themselves and their religious practices from those of Christians, Muslims, and pagans. Finally, reading from scrolls produced in pretty much the same manner as those read by Jews as far back as the fifth century B.C.E. connects contemporary Jews to the unbroken continuity of their history.

As befits a sacred text and an object used in religious rites, the creation of the *sefer Torah* is governed by a complex set of regulations, mainly dating from the Mishnaic and Talmudic eras (between the second and sixth centuries C.E.). Every element of the *sefer Torah*, from its physical dimensions to the parchment on which it is written to the ink and the quill with which it is written, is prescribed by *halakhah*.

Consider the size of a Torah scroll. In the Talmud tractate *Bava Batra* of the Babylonian Talmud, it is written:

> Our Rabbis have taught: One must not make a Torah scroll either with its length greater than its circumference, or its circumference greater than its length. They inquired of Rabbi [as Yehudah Ha'Nasi was known]: The dimensions of a Torah scroll are how much? He replied: When using gevil-parchment, six handbreadths; when using klaf-parchment, I do not know the dimensions.[1]

A minor tractate of the post-Talmudic period, called *Sefer Torah*, adds that the height and circumference of the scroll "must be exactly alike." Tractate *Sefer Torah* gives the scribe considerable leeway in how he writes the text on a panel of parchment; the panel "must contain not less than three columns nor more than eight," so the size of a finished Torah scroll may vary somewhat. Most *sifrei Torah* are between eighteen and twenty-two inches high. The basis for this is post-Talmudic. The *Shulkhan Arukh/ Prepared Table*, Rabbi Joseph Caro's medieval codification of *halakhah*, states that each of the Tablets of the Law that Moshe brought down from Sinai was six *tefakhim* high and six wide; a *tefakh* is a measurement equivalent to the width of a man's palm, estimated at about three and a half inches, giving a total of approximately twenty-one inches.

Each panel of parchment will contain forty-two lines of text, with a three-inch margin at the top, a four-inch margin at the bottom, and two-inch margins on the left and right (leaving ample room for the scribe to sew the panels together with sinew or animal hair). Most modern Torah scrolls are written in 245 columns of forty-two lines each. It takes an expert scribe about a year on average to complete a single Torah scroll, although some scribes write faster than others.

PAPER, PEN, AND INK

One does not write the words of sacred texts on just any paper lying around, with whatever media come to hand. The rules governing the parchment on which a *sefer Torah* is written, and the pen and ink with which it is written, are many and very specific. Within the parameters set by the rabbis, though, an interesting process of evolution has taken place, allowing for a certain degree of change over the past two millennia in both the materials and the processes by which they are prepared.

The *k'laf/parchment* on which the Torah scroll is written, the hair or sinew with which the panels of parchment are sewn together, and the quill pen with which the text is written all must come from ritually clean—that is, kosher—animals. Thus, the skin from which the parchment is derived must come from an animal that chews its own cud and has cloven hooves—a cow, ox, lamb, or goat are all acceptable. And the bird whose feather provides the *sofer/scribe* with a *kulmus/quill pen* must also be kosher—a chicken, goose, duck, pigeon, or turkey. A scribe may never use tools made of "base metals," for these are associated with implements of war.

That much hasn't changed in two thousand years.

However, some of the materials have changed to meet changed circumstances in the Diaspora or new technologies.[2]

For example, in Talmudic times (a bit less than two thousand years ago) animal hides designated for use in producing parchment for *sifrei Torah* were treated with salt and barley flour and then soaked in the juice of gall-nuts. Today, however, a more effective method of treating the hides has been devised. After two days of soaking in clear water, the hides are immersed for seven days in limewater, which separates the hair from the skin and makes the skin more pliable. The old method produced a parchment having one usable side; with the new method, either side can be used. However, tradition dictates that the inner side be the one written upon. To determine which is the inner side, a *sofer* will wet the skin and allow it to curl; the side that bends backward is the correct side. (A single sheet of parchment is called a *yeriah;* the average Torah scroll will be made of fifty *yeriot,* with between three and eight columns of writing on each.) One thing has not changed: the scribe must choose the hides carefully, using only the finest quality available. After all, this is a *sefer Torah,* and it should last two hundred years or more.

In Talmudic times, *soferim* would write with reed or willow pens. The reed had a symbolic significance that resonated powerfully in an age in which the great rabbis urged Jews to be "soft like the reed rather than stiff like the cedar." The willow pens were derived from willows that had been used as part of the *Arbah Minim/Four Species* that are held and shaken as part of the rituals of the festival of Sukkot; when the festival was over, *soferim* would separate out the willow branches and turn them into pens for writing Torah scrolls. But reeds and willows are not readily available throughout the world, and as the Jews were scattered across the globe, other, more accessible alternatives had to be found. Hence the use today of quill pens. (Sephardic scribes still use reeds whenever possible.)

Like the other components of a *sefer Torah,* the *d'yo/ink,* too, has undergone changes over time, while still conforming to basic strictures.

The ink with which a Torah scroll is written must be solid black, very durable, and not indelible. Two thousand years ago a *sofer* would hold a container over a flame of olive oil and then scrape the accumulated carbon from the surface of the vessel, mix it with honey, oil, and gallnuts (used for their tannic acid) to create his writing fluid. Today, however, the ink used is a compound of gallnuts, gum arabic, and copper sulfate, to which some scribes add vinegar and alcohol. The mixture is boiled and then strained.

Here's one recipe for kosher ink given in a manual for *soferim* called *Khasdei David* (as reported by Mordechai Pinchas, an English scribe, on his excellent Web site at http://www.bayit02.freeserve.co.uk/index.html):

Ingredients:
  3 grammes of gumy rabik (gum arabic)
  3 grammes of afatsim (gallnuts)
  1 gramme of kankantum (vitriol—i.e. iron or copper sulphate)
  Quarter of a litre of water
Crush the gallnuts into a fine powder (basically this is tannic acid). Mix all the ingredients together. Cook on an open flame until the residue is left. Strain out the larger lumps of gallnut. Leave for 6 months to turn black. Use as ink!

Before the *sofer* can begin the laborious task of copying the sacred text, there is one final bit of physical preparation to be done. Taking a ruler and a *sargel*, a stylus that looks like a small carpenter's awl (but that has a reed point—no base metals, remember), he will score the individual sheet of parchment to be used with forty-three thin parallel lines that stretch nearly the width of the sheet, and two vertical lines that demarcate the left and right margins. In this way the scribe ensures that the lines of text will be straight and equally spaced, and that they will begin and end at the same point on each line.

COMMANDMENT 613: TO WRITE A *SEFER TORAH*

The final *mitzvah* prescribed in the Torah is that every Jew should write a Torah scroll. In practice this is not feasible, and completing a letter of a newly written scroll as part of a *siyum* is considered the fulfillment of this *mitzvah* (see page 21). But where in the Torah is this injunction stated?

In *Devarim* 31:19, *Adonai* tells Moshe, "Now write for yourselves this Song and teach it to *B'nei Yisrael* that they might recite it, so that this Song will serve as My witness for [them]." Of course, the plain-sense meaning of this sentence is that Moshe is to write down and teach to the Israelites one small part of *Sefer Devarim*, and that the commandment to write it down was directed to Moshe (and possibly also to Yehoshua as his successor, as Maimonides interprets it).

However, the Talmud says otherwise. In Tractate *Sanhedrin*, Rabbah says, "Even though a person may have inherited a scroll of the Torah from his ancestors, it is nevertheless a commandment for one to write his own, as the verse states, 'Now, write for yourselves this Song.' " In Tractate *Menakhot*, this ruling is further amplified, closing with Rav Sheshet's statement, "[O]ne who corrects even a single letter in a defective scroll is likened to one who has written the entire scroll." Later sages, chief among them Maimonides, will elaborate on this theme, but it is clearly the intent of the rabbis that every Jew should put quill pen to *k'laf* at least once.

THE WORK BEGINS

The physical preparations are virtually complete. But this is not an ordinary copying job, and there are spiritual preparations to be made as well. Before his workday begins, the *sofer* will immerse himself in the *mikveh/ritual bath*. Just before he goes to his worktable, he will perform the ritual of handwashing. At last the writing itself may begin. The *sofer* sharpens his quills, cutting a writing point that will allow him to move smoothly between broad and narrow lines. Then he tests the quill and ink by writing the name Amalek, and then crossing it out. The original Amalekites were a Sinaitic tribe who treacherously attacked *B'nei Yisrael/the Children of Israel* in the desert, after the Exodus from Egypt. In *Devarim* 25:19, God instructs *B'nei Yisrael* to blot out their name forever (but also to remember the terrible sins of the Amalekites). Since that time, Amalek has been the traditional name applied to the most deadly and ferocious of the enemies of the Jewish people, from Haman to Hitler.

Then the scribe murmurs, "I am writing the Torah for the holiness of the Torah and the name of *Ha'Shem* for the holiness of God's name," and the work begins.

What that work consists of is the most painstaking copying. One does not sit down to write a Torah scroll casually. Not a single letter—not even a *yud*, the smallest letter in the Hebrew alphabet, barely more than half a pen stroke—can be written from memory. As he writes, the scribe will read each word aloud to double-check the accuracy of his work. The *sofer* works from a *tikkun*, a special copy of the *Khumash*, from which he copies the text onto his sheets of parchment. Like the scroll itself, the *tikkun* has 248 pages (corresponding to the sheets of parchment in the average *sefer Torah*) with forty-two lines per page. And like the scroll that the *sofer* is creating, the *tikkun* has neither vowel markings, punctuation, nor paragraph breaks.

Like the materials that go into a *sefer Torah*, the lettering also is governed by certain rules. Each letter stands alone, with blank space on all four sides. The space between letters of a word is prescribed (a hair's breadth); likewise the space between words (the width of a small letter). Between lines there must be the space of the height of a line, and between each of the Five Books there must be the space of four lines.

There are three styles of script in which a *sefer Torah* may be written: the *Beit Yosef/House of Joseph*, used by Ashkenazic scribes; the *Ari*, used by most Hasidic scribes and named for the great sixteenth-century mystic, Isaac Luria, known as the *Ari/Lion;* and the *Vellish*, generally used by Sephardic scribes. Each of these three is a version of *ketav Ashuri/ Assyrian writing*, a script that developed from Aramaic writing and was picked up by the Jews during the Babylonian exile in the sixth century B.C.E. The primary difference between the Sephardic and Ashkenazic scripts is that the latter is somewhat thicker and may therefore require an extra penstroke or two to execute a letter; the *Vellish* is also somewhat more rounded. (And there are even variations within the three main styles. For example, scribes who are Lubavitcher Hasidim use a slightly different form of the *Ari*.) Whatever script is used, letters must be clearly, crisply formed so that there is no confusion between them; with letters that closely resemble one another—*dalet* and *resh*, for example—this is a real concern. Traditionally, the test for recognizability is that a child of average intelligence can tell what the letter is.

Tradition dictates many other elements in the writing of a Torah scroll. For example, *soferim* will begin almost every column of a *sefer Torah* with a word that begins with the letter *vav*. The basis of this custom is rather unusual. In *Shemot* there is a description of the curtains that adorned the *Mishkan/Tabernacle* that the Israelites built to house the tablets on which the Ten Commandments were written; these curtains were held up by twenty *amudim/pillars*, each topped with a silver band with *vavim/hooks* (sing., *vav*). At some point a *sofer* saw the reference to the *vavim ha'amudim/ hooks on the pillars* and took it as a sign that each column—*amud*—of the Torah should be topped by a hook, a *vav*.

It is also traditional that the scribe arrange his writing so that six specific words from the Torah appear within the first line at the top of a column of text: *Bereishit/Beginning* (from *Bereishit* 1:1), *Yehudah/Judah* (from *Bereishit* 49:8), *Ha'Ba'im/the One who comes* (from *Shemot* 14:28), *Sh'mor/Observe* (from *Shemot* 34:11), *Mah/How* (from *B'midbar* 24:5) and *Ve'a'ida/I will call forth as witnesses* (from *Devarim* 31:28). Each of these words represents a significant concept in Judaism. *Bereishit*, the word that opens the Torah, establishes God as the Creator, the First Cause of all things. *Yehudah* indicates that the tribe of Judah will be the root of the Davidic line of kings of Israel. *Ha'Ba'im* refers to God's role as the Protector of *B'nei Yisrael*. *Sh'mor*, an order to the Israelites from God to "observe" the commandments, refers to the renewal of God's Covenant with the Israelites as Moshe descends from Sinai with the second set of tablets. *Mah* is the first word of the passage, *Mah tovu ohalekha Ya'akov/ How lovely are your tents, Jacob*, words of praise spoken by the Gentile prophet Balaam, instead of the curse he was supposed to place upon the Israelites (it is also one of the opening passages of the morning service). *Ve'a'ida* is the word by which Moshe calls forth heaven and earth as witnesses to the eternal nature of the Covenant.

Shirat Ha'Yam/the Song at the Sea, the passage in *Shemot* 15 in which Miriam and the Israelite women sing of God's great miracle of the parting and closing of *Yam Suf/the Sea of Reeds* and destruction of *Pharoah/ Pharaoh* and the Egyptian army, is another passage that receives special treatment in *sifrei Torah*. Because the waters formed two "walls" protecting the Israelites as they crossed over, the Song itself is written in a pattern that looks like a brick wall. *Shirat Ha'Yam* occupies exactly thirty lines of text; the first line is full, but the next line is divided in thirds with two open spaces, followed by a line divided in two with an open space, which is followed by a line in thirds, a line in two, and so on. (Similarly, Moshe's final speech to the Israelites, known as the Song of Moshe and found in *Devarim* 32, is written in a unique style, covering seventy lines, each with a space in the middle.)

Sometime in the ninth century C.E., scribes decided that the Torah's text would be more attractive to the eye if it were justified on both the left and right margins. The result was one more peculiarity of Torah calligraphy, the extending of some letters horizontally to fill out a line. The letters that most frequently receive this treatment are *tav, resh, he, dalet, lamed,* and the final *mem.* Apparently these letters were selected because they are the easiest to widen laterally.

There is another feature of the lettering for a *sefer Torah* that is found nowhere else in Hebrew, a kind of ornamentation called *taggin* (from the Aramaic word *tag,* meaning crown). *Taggin* are found on seven of the letters (*shin, zayin, tet, ayin, tzadi, gimel,* and *nun*). A *tag* looks a little like the letter *zayin,* a thin line extending vertically upward with a thickening at the top; on the seven letters that sport them, they are found atop the left-hand side of the letter in threes, with the middle one slightly taller than the others, creating a stylized crown. The first letter of the Torah, the *bet* in *Bereishit,* is uniquely decorated with four *taggin.*

WHERE OLD TORAH SCROLLS GO TO DIE

Clearly, Judaism does not prohibit writing the Name of God per se, but it does prohibit erasing or defacing a Name of God. Consequently, observant Jews avoid writing any Name of God casually for fear that the written Name might later be defaced, obliterated, or destroyed accidentally or by one who does not know better. The commandment not to erase or deface the Name of God is derived from *Devarim* 12:3–4. In verse 3, *B'nei Yisrael* are told that when they conquer the Promised Land, they must destroy all things related to the idolatrous religions of that region and must utterly destroy the names of the local deities. Immediately afterward, in verse 4, they are commanded not to do the same to their God. From this, the rabbis inferred that we are commanded not to destroy any holy thing, and not to erase or deface a Name of God.

Given that stricture, it follows that one does not dispose of an old, *possul/invalid sefer Torah* by just any means. Rather, these scrolls are treated with great reverence. One option is for papers with the Name of God, including Torah scrolls, to be kept in a *genizah,* a storeroom in a synagogue designated specifically for this purpose. Practices regarding both the *genizah* and the final disposition of its contents have differed historically from community to community. As Elkan Adler has noted:

> Most ancient synagogues had genizot. That of Feodosia in the Crimea is an alcove on the ground floor at the back of the ark, approachable from the outside of the building by a hole so small as only to admit of the entrance of a very small boy. . . . At Bokhara the genizah is in the roof, but disused copies of scrolls of the Law are walled up by stucco in arched alcoves surrounding the interior of the building. At Teheran it is in an underground cellar, so damp that papers turn to pulp in a few weeks. . . . In a secret chamber in the eaves of the roof of one of the chapels of the ancient synagogue at Aleppo . . . is the genizah of that famous city. . . . Its contents are periodically removed, and are taken solemnly to the Jewish cemetery. Their burial is locally supposed to induce a downfall of rain. At Rustchuk, burials of "shemot" take place every ten years, when a sermon is delivered, followed by a banquet, and the right of burying each sack is sold as a *mitzvah;* one month later a stone is laid over the place of burial, and inscribed as the genizah of the year in question. . . . In the Orient generally, shemot are from time to time deposited temporarily in some corner or cupboard of the synagogue, often below the ark or "almemar." When the collection grows too big, or when some special occasion arises, such as a drought, the papers are solemnly gathered up and carried off to the "bet khayyim" and buried there with some ceremony. With this custom is associated the far older practice of burying a great or good man with a "sefer" which has become "pasul" (unfit for use through illegibility or old age). In Morocco, in Algiers, in Turkey, and even in Egypt, such paper interments continually occur.

As we will see in Chapter 3, the *genizot* have become a remarkably rich resource for scholars studying the history of Jewish communities and of the sacred texts.

TO ERR IS HUMAN

Needless to say, even the best *soferim* are only human. Mistakes will creep into the work of the most diligent artisan. The three most common errors are:

- dittographic: a word is written twice where it actually occurs only once in the text;
- haplographic: where two identical letters or words occur, one is omitted;
- homoioteleutonic: where a phrase occurs twice in close proximity, the scribe inadvertently copies from the second passage, thereby omitting the words that occur in between.

For small errors—for instance, a single wrong letter—the scribe will scrape out the incorrect text with a sharp piece of glass or similar non-metal implement and write the correct letter. But when an error involves a significant amount of text, he will have to discard the entire *yeriah* and begin that section again, possibly losing as much as three columns of work in a single disastrous blow. It is not hard to see why *Keset Ha'Sofer* (a manual for scribes) forbids *soferim* to work after midnight!

Scribal errors fall into two categories, major and minor. Minor errors are easily corrected or, in rare cases, do not alter the meaning of a word or passage. For example, the omission of a thin letter like a *vav*, which essentially is a single pen stroke, can be remedied by the insertion of the letter (or its removal where it is superfluous). Similarly, some letters can be easily fixed by either shortening or extending them—a final *nun* can be made from a *vav* by lengthening it at the bottom, or the reverse can be done by scraping away the longer part. On rare occasions, a transposition of letters may not even change the meaning; as Alfred Kolatch points out, if *kesev* is incorrectly written as *keves*, there is no damage done because both words mean "lamb."

Major errors, however, involve a significant change or loss of meaning. The most serious of these concerns either the omission or misspelling of one of the seven names of God that occur in the Torah—*YHVH, Adonai, El, Eloah, Elohim, Shaddai,* and *Tz'vaot.* It is not permissible to erase the Name of God, so this error can be corrected only by rewriting the entire *yeriah.* That's why a scribe takes special care—and says, "I am writing the Name of God"—each time he writes one of the seven Names. Other major errors include the omission of a full-width letter, which would require squeezing the entire word in such a way that it would be messy and possibly illegible, and misspelling a word in a way that alters the meaning of a sentence.

The rabbis disagreed on how many errors must be found in a scroll before it is declared *posul/invalid.* Some experts hold that if three errors are found in a column the scroll may not be used; others say four. If a *sefer Torah* is found to be *posul*, it is buried in a cemetery just like a person. (See "Where Old Torah Scrolls Go to Die," page 16.) However, the common practice today, given that a new *sefer Torah* may cost as much as $60,000, is to remove and replace the defective *yeriah*. A scroll is also considered *posul* if there is a tear in a sheet that extends through two lines of text; such a tear may be mended either by sewing or by the use of a glued patch on the reverse side. However, if the tear goes through three or more lines of text, the page must be replaced before the Torah may be used again. Excessive wear that leads to problems of legibility may cause a scroll to be declared invalid.

For most *soferim* today, a large part of the workday consists of checking, correcting, and repairing older *sifrei Torah*. A scribe may find himself called to a synagogue to check through all their *sifrei Torah;* he will roll (literally) through each scroll looking for blots, tears, holes, and fading. If a scroll is in good condition, the process takes about an hour, but it is tedious and physically tiring. If he finds errors in the scroll that must be corrected for it to be kosher, the scribe has thirty days in which to make the corrections, during which time the scroll may not be used for public reading. If a scroll is found to be *posul*, the scribe will usually tie the *gartel/belt* that is customarily tied around the scroll itself around the fabric mantle that covers the scroll to indicate that it is not to be used.

When a *sofer* has completed the writing of a Torah scroll, he must go through a similar process of checking for errors. While it is still a series of unconnected parchment sheets, the Torah will be proofread a minimum of three times. Today, this process is usually done at least in part by computer. The computer is more reliable than human beings in catching actual textual errors like misspellings and misplaced or missing words, but a human reader is needed to catch smaller, subtler problems like tiny breaks or flaws in the letters. Today, many *soferim* will also do computer checks of older scrolls upon request.

Even when the writing and the proofreading are completed, the *sofer*'s job is not done yet. He now has about fifty completed sheets of parchment, but they aren't a *scroll* until he sews them together. The *yeriot/parchment sheets* are sewn together with *giddin*, a special thread made from the dried veins of a kosher animal. Usually, the *giddin* comes from the hindquarters of the animal, which Jews are forbidden to eat, but *giddin* can also be made from tendons taken from the foot muscles. As Mordechai

Pinchas explains, "The sinew is extracted, then bashed until the threads inside are released. These are then stretched and spun. A single ball of *giddin* should suffice for a whole Torah."

The actual sewing of the *yeriot* is one of those rare processes for which there are no specific rules, although scribes should be careful not to sew too close to the edge of sheets because this would both limit their flexibility and make it easier for tears to occur. Pinchas notes, "This stuff is pretty tough and it is quite an effort to pull it through the parchment."

With the sheets sewn together, the *sofer* now has an object that is recognizably a scroll, but it still isn't ready for use in a synagogue. Quite simply, it would be impossible to handle this scroll without, well, handles. The scribe will now attach, with *giddin,* the ends of the scroll to rounded dowels made of maple wood. These poles are called the *atzei khayim/trees of life* (sing., *eitz khayim*). The name is derived from *Mishlei* 3:17–18, in which it is written that the Torah "is a tree of life to all who cling to it," a passage that occurs in the liturgy for the reading of the Torah. The handle has several components. At the top and bottom of each pole are wooden discs that allow the Torah to be rolled while resting on a flat surface; these may be highly decorative. Below the bottom disk there is a handle; above the top disk is a finial often ornately carved and sometimes partly made from ivory. (When a *sofer* works on an older scroll, he will remove these handles to make it easier to work with the parchment.)

Although the scribe's job is just about done, he will usually leave a few letters in outline form. They will be filled in shortly as part of a ritual called *Siyum Ha'Torah/(Celebration of) the Completion of the Torah.* When a synagogue receives a new Torah, it is a major moment in the congregation's spiritual life and one that should be celebrated with great joy. The new scroll will be presented to the congregation under a *khupah/canopy,* just as a bride is presented at a wedding. Two older scrolls will be taken from the *aron ha'kodesh/holy ark* and brought under the *khupah* to "greet" their new sibling. Then the older scrolls are returned to the ark and the new scroll is placed on the *bimah/reader's desk* and opened to its last section. Then members of the congregation, usually with their hands guided by the *sofer,* fill in the outlined letters, thereby completing the *sefer Torah.*

In doing this, these Jews are fulfilling the 613th and final commandment given in the Torah, that a Jew should write a Torah scroll. (See "Commandment 613: To Write a *Sefer Torah*" on page 12.) In the Talmud it is written that "he who corrects even one letter of a *sefer Torah* is regarded as if he had written the entire Torah himself." Given the arduous nature of the job of the *sofer*, filling in one letter is as close as most of us are likely to come to accomplishing this, but the task is a holy one, and fortunate is the Jew who gets the opportunity to fulfill it.

The scroll now completed, the congregation will sing and dance with joy (giving time for the ink to dry). Then the scroll is rolled to its middle and closed, dressed, and placed in the ark. Over the next four Sabbaths, this scroll will be used for the weekly Torah reading, a sort of breaking-in process. And now it is one of a highly esteemed family. (As such, it will be adorned with appropriately regal vestments; see "A Well-Dressed Torah" below.)

Once it is part of the daily life of the congregation, a *sefer Torah* will be read from publicly much as Ezra's original scroll was read on that market day in Jerusalem two and a half millennia ago. But much has changed since 444 B.C.E. and, as we will see, the rituals surrounding the reading of the Torah have become more complex and richer.

A WELL-DRESSED TORAH

The rabbinic codes of Jewish law encourage us to enhance the beauty of a *mitzvah*. Rabbinic law requires us to light Hanukah candles. How much nicer it is if we use a really beautiful *hanukiyah/Hanukah candelabrum*.

The same is true of the Torah, only more so. With the destruction of the Temple in Jerusalem, which meant an end to the role of the *kohanim*, the Torah became a surrogate not only for the Temple itself but also for the priests, in the sense that the elaborate garments of their office (described in great detail in *Sefer Vayikra*) were adapted for clothing the scrolls containing the sacred text.

When we see a fully clothed and ornamented *sefer Torah* today it is easy to understand the correspondences. The mantle that covers the scroll, called the *me'il*, is the equivalent of the priestly robe; the belt that holds the scroll closed under the mantle, called the *khittul* or *mappah* in Hebrew or the *gartel* in Yiddish, corresponds to the girdle of the priestly robe; the crown or *keter* that sits atop the *atzei khayim* of the Torah when it is fully ornamented are obviously equivalent to the priest's headdress, and the breastplate that adorns the Torah is modeled on the breastplate that the priests wore.

Other ornaments have a less obvious relationship to the priestly garments, but are just as traditional. The *yad/hand*, the pointer used by the person reading the Torah, ends in a hand with pointing index finger. On some Torah scrolls in place of a *keter* there are *rimonim/pomegranates*, elaborate silver ornaments shaped like the eponymous fruit and adorned with small bells, like those on the hem of the priestly robes.

The *sefer Torah* is ornamented differently in the Sephardic tradition. Instead of the mantle, breastplate, *keter*, or *rimonim*, the *sefer Torah* will be enclosed in an elaborately carved wooden case called a *tik*. The scroll is never taken out of this case, but is read from in an upright position.

SEDER K'RIAT HA'TORAH/SERVICE
FOR THE READING OF THE TORAH

This is where almost all Jews first encounter the Torah as both ritual object and sacred text, in the section of the prayer service called *Seder K'riat Ha'Torah*.

To understand and to visualize the Torah service, you first have to be familiar with the layout of the synagogue interior. At the front of any synagogue is the *aron ha'kodesh* (often called the *heikhal/sanctuary* by Sephardic Jews), a cabinet or closet that is usually attached to the wall and in which the Torah scrolls are kept. Almost all of these repositories have doors, often ornately decorated; in Ashkenazic synagogues, most have a *parokhet/curtain* in addition to the doors. The *aron* traditionally is situated so that the congregation prays facing it and facing Jerusalem, site of the original Temple—the eastern wall in western countries, the western wall in eastern countries. (In Jerusalem, one faces toward the Western Wall, the last remaining portion of the Temple.)

Above the ark is the *ner tamid/perpetual light*, which burns in perpetuity (although in the modern world of electricity, one reluctantly makes allowances for changing lightbulbs and power outages). In the Temple in Jerusalem, it was the responsibility of the *Kohanim/priests* to tend the *ner tamid*, which burned only pure olive oil consecrated for this purpose. The

most famous story concerning the *ner tamid,* of course, is that of the miracle that occurred after the Maccabees reclaimed the Temple from the
forces of Antiochus; although there was only enough oil to burn for a single day, the priests lit the lamp anyway and the oil lasted for eight full days,
an event commemorated by the celebration of Hanukah. Regardless, the
pale flickering light of the *ner tamid* serves as a metaphor both for the
extraordinary spectacle of fire and fury in which the Torah was given at
Sinai and of the perpetually watchful presence of the Almighty in our
daily lives.

The prayer service is conducted from an elevated platform, the *amud,*
on which a reading table is placed (the *bimah*); in traditionally observant
congregations the *bimah* may be in the middle of the sanctuary, but in
Reform, Reconstructionist, and most Conservative congregations today it
is on the *amud* in front of the sanctuary, right in front of the *aron.*

The Torah is read (or chanted; see "Torah Cantillation" on page 31)
aloud in the synagogue on Shabbat, Monday, Thursday, and on Festivals,
almost always as part of the *Shakharit/Morning* service. (There are a few
exceptions, most notably the *Minkhah/Afternoon* services for Shabbat and
for Yom Kippur, which consist in large part of the Torah service.) *Seder
K'riat Ha'Torah* is a self-contained unit, or "rubric," as scholars of liturgy
call them, that comes after the *Sh'moneh Esreih/Eighteen Benedictions,* the
standing prayer that is also called the *Amidah,* one of the key elements in
the morning service. A minyan, or prayer quorum of ten adult Jews, is
required for *Kri'at Ha'Torah.* ("Adult" means anyone who has reached the
age of *bar* or *bat mitzvah.* Reform, Reconstructionist, and egalitarian conservative congregations count women toward a minyan; Orthodox congregations do not.) If a quorum is not present, the prayer service proceeds,
but everyone prays individually, and the Torah is not read.

As Lawrence A. Hoffman has noted,[3] the Torah service has three essential functions. The first is a practical one: it represents an opportunity for
the study of a key sacred text; such study is a significant component of
Jewish worship, particularly for the traditionally observant. Second, reading the Torah has a ritual function, replacing the animal sacrifices and
other offerings that could be presented only at the Temple in Jerusalem.
Finally—and to my mind the most satisfying—*Seder K'riat Ha'Torah*
serves a powerful symbolic function. It is a reenactment of the Giving of
the Law at Sinai, an attempt to recapitulate Revelation and to renew it
every three days. At Passover we are instructed to believe that we were
among the Israelites freed from bondage by God, and we thank God for

performing that miraculous deliverance every morning; with *Seder K'riat Ha'Torah,* we are allowed symbolically to partake of the next step on the journey through the Wilderness, to receive and accept Divine Revelation at Sinai, and what could possibly be more important than that?

Much as the morning service is composed of self-contained units like *Seder K'riat Ha'Torah,* the Torah service itself contains several component parts. Briefly, there are five such sections to the Torah service, each of which, in turn, contains several different prayers:

1. Removing the Torah from the Ark
2. Reading the Torah/the *Aliyot*
3. The *Haftarah*
4. Prayers for the Community
5. Returning the Torah to the Ark

Let's examine each in turn.

1. REMOVING THE TORAH FROM THE ARK

The Torah service is primarily an affirmation of God, an acknowledgment of the greatness of the Creator and, to the extent the Torah itself is mentioned, it is as a recognition of the Torah as an identification with God, a unity in which the Torah is the Word of the Ineffable made manifest on earth. This is abundantly clear from the liturgy for removing the Torah from the ark.

After the *Amidah* is completed, the rabbi and the *khazan/cantor* approach the ark and the congregation rises. Two prayers are said or sung, *Ein Kamokha* and *Av Ha'Rakhamim:*

Ein Kamokha
There is no deity like you, *Adonai.* And no works like Yours. Your dominion is a dominion for all times. And Your sovereignty is for all generations. God is Ruler; God has always ruled; God will always rule. God will grant strength to the people. God will bless the people with peace.

Av Ha'Rakhamim
Author of mercy, bestow Your goodness on Zion. Rebuild the walls of Jerusalem. For it is in You alone we put our trust, our Sovereign, high and exalted God, *Adonai* eternal.

The ark is opened to reveal the *sifrei Torah*. The *khazan* sings or chants *Vay'hi binsoa:*

> With the moving of the ark, Moshe would say, "Arise, *Adonai*, scatter your enemies, those who hate you will flee from you. For out of Zion will come forth Torah and the word of *Adonai* from out of Jerusalem. Blessed is the One who gave Torah to the people Israel in holiness.

The tone of the liturgy shifts subtly here from an affirmation of God's greatness to an affirmation of *Adonai*'s mercy. On festivals that fall on a weekday, the next prayer that will be recited is *Adonai, Adonai*, a catalog of the thirteen attributes of God's mercy, taken from *Shemot* 34:6–7. If you are counting, note that the repetition of *Adonai* is taken to refer to two separate aspects of the Divine mercy, the forgiving of sinners before they sin and after they sin. (It is telling, though, that the liturgy omits one item from the biblical text, that God punishes sinners "unto the third and fourth generations.")

> *Adonai, Adonai,* God merciful and gracious, endlessly patient, exceedingly kind and truthful, preserving kindness unto the thousandth generation, forgiving iniquity, transgression and sin, cleansing.

The next two prayers are also reflections on God's compassion, albeit more indirectly so, focusing on God's hearkening to our prayers.

> *Y'hyu*
> May the words of my mouth and the meditations of my heart be acceptable to you O God, my Rock and my Redeemer.

> *Va'ani Tefilati*
> I offer my prayer to You, *Adonai*, at this time. God in your great mercy answer me with Your saving truth.

In most Orthodox congregations, *Va'ani Tefilati* will be followed by *B'rikh Sh'mei*, a lengthy passage in Aramaic that is drawn from the medieval masterpiece, *Sefer Ha'Zohar/The Book of Splendor*, the central work of Jewish mysticism. Reform prayer books and the Israeli Conservative movement's prayer book completely omit this, whereas the Reconstructionist and Conservative siddurim give only excerpts and offer alternative readings to be inserted in its place. In essence, *B'rikh Sh'mei* is a recapitulation and reaffirmation of both God's enormous power and the Eternal's all-encompassing mercy. Clearly, the more rationalist streams of Judaism were uncomfortable with the more mystical elements of this passage. However, the final two sentences, known as *Bei Ana Rakhitz*, are usually sung in Ashkenazic Orthodox synagogues and even in many liberal ones.

The Torah is now taken from the ark. The rabbi or cantor will either hold it or give it to a congregant chosen for the honor of carrying the scroll. The Torah should always be held with the right hand, on the right-hand side of the body; the right-hand side is identified with both physical and spiritual strength, as in the passage from *Shemot* 15:6, "Your right hand, O *Adonai*, glorious in power."

The rabbi, the cantor, and the person chosen for the honor of carrying the Torah now turn to face the congregation and the cantor sings the *Sh'ma:*

Sh'ma Yisrael, Adonai Eloheinu, Adonai Ekhad.
Hear, O Israel, *Adonai* is our God, *Adonai* is One.

and the congregation repeats it in response. The cantor then sings:

Ekhad Eloheinu, gadol Adoneinu, kadosh Shemo.
Our God is One, great is our God, God's name is holy.

And once more the congregation echoes the cantor. In most congregations, the trio on the *bimah* then turns to face the ark and bows as the cantor says:

Gadlu L'Adonai itie, u'neromemah Shemo yakhdav.
Proclaim God's greatness with me, and let us exalt the Name of God together.

There is a pleasing internal echo in these last two statements, with *gadol Adoneinu / great is our God*, echoed by *gadlu L'Adonai / God's greatness*. (Two additional notes here on choreography: the Torah-bearer should lift up the *sefer Torah* a little at the end of each of these three verses; in Sephardic congregations, *hagbah*, which we will encounter shortly, occurs here rather than at the end of the Torah reading.)

Once more the trio turns, but this time they step down from the *bimah* and begin the procession around the congregation with the Torah, called a *hakafah (pl., hakafot)/circuit(s)*. As they walk through the aisles, members of the congregation will reach out to touch the Torah itself with the fringes of their prayer shawl, with their prayer book, or with their fingers, then kiss the fringes, book, or fingers. Occasionally someone may even lean over and kiss the covered scroll itself. As the *hakafah* goes on, the congregation will sing:

L'Kha Adonai
Unto You *Adonai* are greatness, strength, and glory, and everything
    on earth.
Unto You *Adonai* are dominion and sovereignty over [earth's] rulers.
Let us exalt *Adonai* and bow before the footstool of God.
Let us exalt *Adonai* and bow at the holy mountain of God,
For *Adonai* our God is holy.

It is important to note that the Torah is carried into the very midst of the worshippers, into the community itself. At Sinai, the holy mountain alluded to in *L'Kha Adonai*, all 600,000 *B'nei Yisrael* saw and heard the awesome majesty of the Revelation, from the smallest child to the oldest woman and man, from the least enlightened Jew to Moshe, God's greatest prophet. Torah is not the exclusive property of anyone. It belongs to all. The *hakafah* affirms this in the most direct way possible, allowing—indeed, encouraging—all of us to show our love of God's greatest gift.

In this same vein, Rabbi Elie Munk has a trenchant observation based on the architecture of the traditional synagogue, in which the *bimah* is in the center of the congregation rather than elevated at the front of the sanctuary. Munk writes:

There is an essential difference between the reading of the Torah and the other prayers. The latter are the call of Israel to its God—whereas the reading of the Torah represents the message of [the Eternal] to [God's] people. Hence for the recital of the other prayers the *shaliakh tzibur*, the messenger of the congregation, stands in front of it, to submit the requests of the community to [God]. But the reading of the Torah is performed on the *bimah* in the midst of the congregation, from an elevated position, as if God had gathered the people in assembly . . . to proclaim [the Divine] will to them.

This elevation has practical and linguistic ramifications that we will touch on momentarily.

2. READING THE TORAH

Now the reading of the *parashah/Torah portion* itself begins. On Monday and Thursday mornings and for the Shabbat afternoon *Minkhah service,* only a portion of that week's *parashah* will be read and three *aliyot* will be given. On Sabbath mornings, in most synagogues, the entire *parashah* (or *sidrah;* these terms are used interchangeably) for the week will be read and seven *aliyot* will be given, as well as a *maftir/completer* who will also read the prophetic reading for that given service, called the *haftarah.* (The *haftarah* will be either a reading from one of the books of the *Nevi'im* that has been specified for that Torah portion, or one associated with a special event on the ritual calendar. For a complete list, see "*Parashiyot* and *Haftarot* of the Annual Reading Cycle" on page 42 and "Special Readings for the Festivals" on page 48.)

An *aliyah,* the singular form of *aliyot,* literally means "an ascending or going up." To be "called to the Torah," that is, to be called up to the *bimah* to read the blessing for the reading of the Torah, is to receive an *aliyah,* to be an *oleh* (m.) or *olah* (f.).[4] As suggested by Rabbi Munk's observation mentioned earlier, the calling "up" is both literal (in most modern synagogues) and figurative. Indeed, the nomenclature carries such a powerful moral charge that the Zionist movement has expanded the original definition of *oleh* from "one who journeys to Jerusalem from another city within *Eretz Yisrael/the Land of Israel*" to "one who emigrates permanently from a foreign country to *Eretz Yisrael.*" Perhaps, in the context of the Torah service, to receive an *aliyah* has the unmistakable echo of Moshe being called up to Mount Sinai by God to receive the original Revealed Word. (For information on the order in which people are called to the Torah over the course of the reading, see "Rules Governing *Aliyot,*" page 35.)

Originally, the *oleh* was expected not only to chant the blessings for the reading of the Torah but to chant his designated portion of the *parashah* as well. Today, with diminished Hebrew literacy and diminished expertise in chanting the Torah with the proper cantillation, the rule rather than the exception in most congregations, only a *bar* or *bat mitzvah* will be expected to read all or most of his or her *parashah* from the *sefer Torah.* There are still many Jews who have learned to *leyn* Torah (as the Yiddish phrase has it), and most congregants find it particularly satisfying when a layperson like themselves chants perfectly from the week's *parashah*. It is a skill that is important to have, and learning to read from the Torah should be widely encouraged.

What happens when someone is "called to the Torah"?

In many congregations, the *olim* are called to the Torah by a ritual functionary called the *gabbai* (the word is derived from the Hebrew for "to collect," possibly a reference to a mostly abandoned practice of auctioning off or selling *aliyot* as a way of supporting the congregation). Whether it is the *gabbai*, the *khazan*, or the *ba'al koreh* who calls them, the ritual is the same. The person who invites them up to the *bimah* will do so for the first *aliyah*, which goes to a *kohein* (i.e., a member of the priestly caste, descendant of Aharon, the first *kohein* and brother of Moshe), by saying, "*Ya'amod [Hebrew first name] ben [Hebrew first name of the father] v'[Hebrew first name of the mother], ha'kohein/Let [first name], son of [father] and [mother], the kohein, come forth.*"[5] (For a woman the formula is the same, except that the female form of the verb is *ta'amod*.) The second *aliyah* goes to a *levi*, a member of the Israelite tribe of Levi, whose function in the First and Second Temples was to assist the *kohanim* with Temple services and maintenance. Each subsequent *aliyah* begins in the same way, with the number of the *aliyah* substituted for the designation of *kohein* or *levi*. For example, if I am called for the fourth *aliyah*, the *gabbai* would say, "*Ya'amod Gedalyah ben Yoel v'Basha, rivi'i.*"

The *oleh* (fem. *olah*) should make his way to the *bimah* by the most direct route possible, moving with alacrity. Technically (if not literally) speaking, it is still the *oleh* who is reading the Torah, so he will recite the blessings that precede and follow the reading of the portion. First, though, he touches the *tzitzit/fringes* of his *tallit/prayer shawl* to the place in the scroll at which the reading will begin, then he kisses the *tzitzit*. It is absolutely forbidden to touch the parchment and ink of the scroll itself; if the *oleh* is not wearing a *tallit* (which will depend on the *minhag/custom* of the congregation), he may use the *tzitzit* of the person reading Torah, the *yad/pointer*, or a handkerchief set aside specifically for this purpose. When this ritual has been completed, the reader will roll the scroll closed. The *oleh* then firmly grasps the *atzei khayim* and recites in a voice that can be heard by the entire congregation,[6] "Praise *Adonai*, to whom our praise is due." The congregants reply, "Praise *Adonai*, to whom our praise is due now and forever." The *oleh* then says:

> Blessed are You *Adonai,* our God, Sovereign of the universe, who chose us from all peoples by giving us the Torah. Blessed are You *Adonai,* Who gives the Torah.

Notice the shift from the past tense of the first sentence to the present tense of the second; revelation happens every day, and the Torah is always renewed.

The *oleh* steps back and the *ba'al koreh* reads the portion while a *shomer/guardian* (usually the *gabbai*) reads along silently to make sure there are no errors. The *oleh* should stand attentively beside the reader, if possible reading along quietly with him, so that the blessing will not have been "said in vain." When the reading is completed, the *oleh* touches the *tzitzit* (or their surrogate) to the point in the scroll where the passage ends, kisses them, and the the scroll is rolled shut. Again, the *oleh* grasps the staves and recites loudly:

> Blessed are You *Adonai,* our God, Ruler of the universe, who has given us a Torah of truth, implanting within us eternal life. Blessed are You *Adonai,* Who gives the Torah.

In most congregations, at this point the *shaliakh tzibur/prayer leader* will offer special blessings for the *oleh,* depending on the situation. Most commonly, the prayer leader will offer a *Mi shebeirakh,* a blessing for either the general health and well-being of family members or for a specific person who is ill (as requested beforehand by the *oleh*), or one of the special blessings for *b'nei mitzvah,* for honored scholars, or for those who have recently survived a life-threatening situation. The last (called *bentching gomel* in Yiddish) is an exchange of blessings between the *oleh* and the congregation, with the *oleh* thanking God for Divine protection and goodness, and the congregation replying with the wish that God may continue to do so. (The Talmud requires a minyan for reciting the *gomel* blessing, but given that it is part of the Torah service, which requires a minyan as well, this seems only logical.)

After the *Mi shebeirakh* is recited, the *oleh* moves to the right-hand side of the *bimah* (the previous *olah* resumes her seat). It is traditional that there always be at least three Jews present on the *bimah* during the actual reading of the Torah, and the presence of the previous *oleh* fulfills that tradition. When someone has completed an *aliyah,* she should return to her seat quietly but not quickly; the reason for the easy saunter is that it should not look like being called to the Torah is such a burden or trauma that one runs from the experience. As the *olah* returns to her seat, it is customary to say, *"Yasher ko'akh"* to a male or *"Yasher ko'klukh"* to a female, which roughly means, "May your power be increased," a nice Jewish way of saying "Job well done." The appropriate response is *"Barukh tihiyeh,"* which roughly means "May you be blessed."

On Shabbat and Festival mornings, the final *aliyah* is followed by a half-*Kaddish,* used here as a punctuation to set off a section of the service from the one that follows. Then the *maftir* is called and follows the same procedures but is responsible for only the last two or three verses of the *parashah.*[7] The *maftir's* real job begins shortly after, as we will see momentarily.

The reading of *parashat ha'shavua/Torah portion for the week* completed, the *gabbai* now calls to the *bimah* the *hagbah* and *golel,* congregants with the jobs of holding the Torah aloft for the entire congregation to see and of dressing the scroll, respectively. In Sephardic congregations, *hagbahah* precedes the reading of the Torah and, since the scroll is enclosed in an ornate wooden cabinet called a *tik, g'lilah,* the dressing of the scroll, is rather more perfunctory. In Ashkenazic practice, these two rituals are performed after the *maftir* finishes the Torah portion but before the *haftarah* is read.

TORAH CANTILLATION

The Torah was never merely read. Almost from the very beginning, it was chanted, or sung. In most synagogues, the public reading is done by the rabbi, the cantor, or a *ba'al koreh* (or *ba'al kr'iah*)/*master of the reading,* a layperson trained in cantillation, or liturgical chanting.

Torah scrolls are written in "unpointed" Hebrew, that is, without vowels, punctuation marks, or any indication of the melodies to which the text is chanted. In the post-Talmudic period, systems of notation were developed from previously existing oral traditions; the notation system, called *t'amim* (sing. *ta'am*), served three purposes. First, it showed the reader how to accent the words; second, it divided the verses correctly; and finally, it transmitted to the reader the melodic patterns used in chanting the text. The most important system of *t'amim* was developed by the Masoretes of Tiberias in the ninth and tenth centuries C.E. The Masoretic text became recognized as the standard version of the Hebrew Bible, together with the cantillation marks that it included. There are twenty-eight different markings, each with its own melodic significance; fifteen of these markings are written over the words to which they refer, a dozen under them, and one in between words.

Given that a Torah scroll is written with neither punctuation, vowel markings, nor *t'amim*, how does a person preparing to read Torah learn the *parashah?* Like a *sofer*, a prospective *ba'al koreh* will work with a book called a *tikkun*. The one used by a *ba'al koreh* is called a *tikkun l'kora'im* and it gives, in parallel columns, both the unpointed version found in the *sefer Torah* and the Masoretic version with all its markings. *Ba'alei Kri'ah* generally will practice with the Masoretic text until they are so familiar with it that the contents of the unpointed version will be readable to them; the melodies may very well be an aid to memorization. In earlier times, a *somekh/prompter* would help out with an elaborate series of hand signals called cheironomy, indicating the appropriate cantillation. Today, the prompter will usually stand by the *ba'al koreh* and simply correct any errors that would change the meaning of the text.

Although the *t'amim* are used throughout the world, the tunes they represent differ from community to community. For example, the *nusakh/musical mode* used to chant Torah and *haftarah* by the Yemenite community, one of the oldest systems of cantillation in Judaism, differs significantly from the one used by the Sephardic Jews of North Africa.

There are eight major musical traditions:

- Southern Arab Peninsula. The oldest known tradition of Torah cantillation and probably as close as you can get to the style used in Babylonia in the seventh century C.E., because the notation system is probably based on the one used there. Used by Yemenite Jews.
- Middle Eastern. Another old tradition, also probably derived from the Babylonian system. Used by Jews from Iran, Bukhara, Kurdistan, Georgia, and northern Iraq.
- Near Eastern. Also called Eastern Sephardic, this musical tra-

dition has been strongly influenced by Arabic *maqam* modes. The most commonly used non-Ashkenazic style in contemporary Israel, it was used by Jews in the Balkans, Turkey, Syria, central Iraq, Lebanon, and Egypt.

- North African. An interesting admixture that draws on African pentatonic scales, particularly in communities farther away from the Mediterranean. Used by Jews in Libya, Tunisia, Algeria, and Morocco.
- Italian. One of the only traditions in which cheironomy is still used. Used by Jews in Rome and in the Roman Jewish community of Jerusalem.
- Sephardic. More properly called western Sephardic, this is the style of the original Spanish and Portuguese Jews.
- Western European Ashkenazic. Medieval in origins, the style was first recorded in cantorial manuals of the nineteenth century. Predominantly used by Jews in Germany, France, England, and Ashkenazic communities of the Netherlands.
- Eastern European Ashkenazic. Evolved from the Western European Ashkenazic, it is the dominant style of Ashkenazic cantillation in Israel and the Anglophone Jewish world today.

Within each of these eight modes, one can find many regional variations as well. Moreover, there are different musical modes within each of the main traditions for specific holidays and different books of the Bible. For example, each of the five *Megillot* has its own *trop*, or melody. *Shirat Ha'Yam*, the passage of poetry in *parashat Beshalakh* that the Israelites sing after the miracle of *Yam Suf*, has a distinctive *trop*, chanted on *Shabbat Shirah*, as does the reading of the Ten Commandments. There is a separate and unique *trop* for the reading of the Torah on the High Holy Days as well. Finally, the *haftarah* is chanted to a melody of its own, with the reader working from the Masoretic text.

Being asked to perform *hagbahah* is a great honor, but one that, unlike the others, requires a certain degree of physical strength and dexterity. To do it properly one must, by grasping the ends of both wooden poles, raise the *sefer Torah* while it is still opened and with at least three columns of text showing, then turn in all directions—right, left, back, and finally front—so that the entire congregation can see it. (One small useful trick is to use the edge of the reading table to lever the scroll to an upright position before lifting.) If one is unsure of their ability to control the scroll when it is aloft, there is no disgrace in respectfully declining the offer to perform this honor. Dropping the *sefer Torah* is one of the worst faux pas I can imagine committing in a synagogue, and the custom in such event is for the congregation to fast for forty days (just the daylight hours, and people can, alternatively, give money to charity), so the person who perpetrates this gaffe will make himself highly unpopular.

While the scroll is held aloft, the congregation should be trying to see the letters of the sacred text; they then bow and recite in Hebrew, "This is the Torah that Moshe placed before the Children of Israel, from the Mouth of *Adonai* to the hand of Moshe." In this simple ritual, we affirm not only our certainty in the Torah itself (and our celebration of it), but our place in the continuity of Jewish history: "*This* is the Torah" dictated by God to Moshe at Sinai and presented to *B'nei Yisrael* who were present at that solemn moment and who, in turn, handed it down through generations to us. Elsewhere in this book we will examine at great length the actual processes of the composition of the Torah and its transmission to the Jewish people and beyond, but as an article of faith, expressed in our worship service, we accept the notion of—at the very least—Divine inspiration in the writing of the text and an unbroken line of tradition that has brought it to use today.

As the *hagbah* sits down with the Torah, the *golel* or *golelet* (fem.), comes over to dress it. She will tie or buckle the now rolled-up scroll with a *gartel,* place the mantle over it, and replace the *yad,* the breastplate, and the *keter / crown* or *rimonim* (finials often in the shape of a pomegranate). (For details regarding the ornamentation of the Torah, see "A Well-Dressed Torah" on page 21.) *G'lilah* is one of those rare ritual tasks that can be entrusted even to a child (properly supervised), a lovely way to communicate directly to him the love and respect that Jews have always had for these ancient texts.

(On two of the festivals, Simkhat Torah and Shavuot, the Torah and *Seder K'riat Ha'Torah* take on added significance. See "Two Holidays for Torah" on page 52.)

RULES GOVERNING *ALIYOT*

Being an *oleh* is an honor, and there is an order of priority for the giving of *aliyot*. The first *aliyah* in a traditionally observant synagogue will be given to a *kohein*, and the second will be given to a *levi*. The next five will be given to a *yisrael*, that is, any Jew who doesn't fall into the first two categories. A worthy Talmud scholar is customarily given a favored position in the list, usually *shlishi* (third). The *maftir* can be given to a *kohein, levi,* or *yisrael*. In rare cases where additional people are called to the Torah above the usual number (for example, when many relatives of a *bar* or *bat mitzvah* are present in the synagogue), the additional *aliyot* may be given to a *kohein* or *levi*. The purpose of this elaborate pecking order, which dates back to antiquity, was to avoid disputes within a community, and it is still followed out of a sense of tradition. When no *levi'im* are present, the *kohein* who had the first *aliyah* takes the second *aliyah* as well. (Incidentally, if someone says to the person assigning honors that he is a *kohein*, his word is sufficient.)

People celebrating life-cycle events also are recognized with *aliyot*, in the following order:

1. A wedding on that day (at a weekday service);
2. A wedding in the coming week (at a Shabbat service);
3. A *bar* or *bat mitzvah;*
4. Someone celebrating the birth of a child;
5. A wedding in the previous week (at a Shabbat service);
6. *Yahrzeit / anniversary of the death of a family member* on that Shabbat or during the week;
7. The parent of a male child whose *b'rit milah / circumcision ceremony* falls during the coming week; the *mohel* performing said ceremony; the *sandek*, who holds the baby during the ceremony (at a Shabbat service).

On Festivals, it is the custom to give *aliyot* to people who have made significant contributions to the well-being of the congregation (and not just monetary ones!).

It was once the custom to auction off *aliyot* as a way of raising funds for the synagogue. However, in the nineteenth century the Vilna Gaon discouraged the practice because he felt it made the reading of the Torah appear to be a commercial enterprise.

Mourners do not read from the Torah during the first week of bereavement, so they cannot be called to the Torah during that time. But if no *kohein* or *levi* is present, a *kohein* or *levi* who is in mourning may be called for the appropriate *aliyah* on Shabbat. Any mourner, on the other hand, may serve as *hagbah* or *g'lilah*, since neither of these honors involves reading from the Torah.

The number of *aliyot* varies depending on the occasion of the reading, as follows:

three *aliyot* on weekday mornings, minor fast days, and *Tisha B'Av;*
four on *Rosh Khodesh* (the first day of the Hebrew month) and *Khol Ha'Mo'ed,* the intermediate days of Sukkot and Pesakh;
five on Festivals;
six on Yom Kippur;
seven on Shabbat mornings (but only three for Shabbat afternoon service).

3. READING THE *HAFTARAH*

What is the *haftarah* and why do we read it?

Contrary to what might seem obvious to an English speaker, *haftarah* and *torah* have completely different Hebrew roots, so they are not linguistically related. However, the Hebrew root from which *haftarah* is derived is one with which we are already familiar, *fei-tav-resh* (f-t-r), the same root as *maftir* (or *maftirah* for a woman), from the verb meaning "to complete." The *haftarah*, one might say, is the reading that completes this segment of the service, much as the *maftir*, who not coincidentally is the one who reads the *haftarah*, is the reader who completes it, as well as completing the reading of the *parashah*.

The *haftarot* are all derived from the books of the *Nevi'im*. There are many explanations for this practice, but the most commonly given version is that during the reign of the Hellenizing tyrant Antiochus Epiphanes in the second century B.C.E., the reading of Torah was banned along with numerous other ritual practices and, until the Maccabees rid the Land of Israel of his rule, reading from *Nevi'im* was a way of circumventing that edict. Other historians suggest that the choice of the prophetic texts was a rebuke to the Samaritans, who rejected not only the post-Pentateuchal books but also the writings of the rabbis during the early years of the Second Temple.

Whatever the reason for reading the *haftarot*, the passages were chosen for their resonance back to the Torah portion with which they are linked, although sometimes the connection may be a bit obscure or oblique. Others are related to specific periods or events in the ritual calendar; for example, the *haftarot* during the three-week period of semi-mourning leading up to the somber observance of Tisha B'Av are prophecies of rebuke for the backsliding *B'eni Yisrael*, while the seven readings that occur after that observance and that lead up to the Days of Awe are known as the *haftarot* of consolation, giving comfort to the suffering people in the wake of the destruction of the Temple.

In an ideal world, the *haftarah* would be read from a parchment scroll like the Torah itself, but the practice today is to read it from a printed book. If possible, the book should be a complete Hebrew Bible rather than a *Khumash* with just the *haftarot* included. In any case, the *haftarah*'s text will be pointed, that is, it will include punctuation and the *nikudot*, the marks that indicate vowels. Like the reading of the Torah portion, the *haftarah* reading requires the presence of a minyan and, also like the Torah, the *haftarah* should be chanted rather than read, if possible. However, the *haftarah* is chanted to a different *trop*. (See "Torah Cantillation" on page 31.)

Before beginning the reading of the *haftarah*, the *maftir* pronounces a blessing that thanks God for the benefits of the prophets:

> Blessed are You *Adonai* our God, Ruler of the universe, who has chosen good prophets and loved their words, spoken in truth. Blessed are You *Adonai*, who chooses the Torah, Moshe Your servant and Israel Your people, and prophets of truth and righteousness.

After the congregation replies, "Amen," the *maftir* reads the passage. As is the case with a reading from the Torah, if the entire selection is not read, a minimum of ten verses is required. Then the *maftir* concludes by reciting a series of four blessings, each with a different theme: God's faithfulness, the rebuilding of Zion, the coming of the Messiah from out of the House of David, and gratitude for the gift of the Sabbath.

4. PRAYERS FOR THE COMMUNITY

At this point, with the scroll(s) still visible, we ask for the blessings of God, whose Presence is indicated by the surrogate presence of the *sifrei Torah*. The first two prayers in this section are occasionally referred to by the same name, *"Yekum Purkan/May salvation arise,"* and each opens,

> May salvation arise from heaven, grace, kindness, and compassion, long life, abundance, and help from heaven, healthy bodies, perfect light, progeny who live and endure and who never abandon or treat lightly the wisdom of the Torah.

However, from this point the two prayers diverge considerably. The first, rather startlingly, goes on to petition—in the present tense—on behalf of the Jewish leaders of antiquity, heads of the Talmudic academies and *yeshivot* of Babylonia. The second seeks blessings for members of the congregation itself. From its outset, the Reform movement felt that the first version of *Yekum Purkan,* expressing its concern for communities and institutions that had long ceased to exist, was an anachronism and inimical to their beliefs; it was dropped from their prayer books in this form, frequently to be replaced by a more universalist prayer for good government, peace, and harmony. Similarly, in the past half-century Reform and Reconstructionist siddurim have added to the second *Yekum Purkan* the phrase "and with the rebuilding of the State of Israel."

The two versions of *Yekum Purkan* are followed by a communal *Mi shebeirakh* prayer for the congregation that is indicative of the esteem in which the institution of the synagogue is held. It is a prayer for "those who dedicate synagogues for worship, and those who enter them to pray, and those who provide candles for light, and wine for *Kiddush* and for *Havdalah,* and food for guests and charity for the poor, and all who faithfully occupy themselves with the needs of the public." Since the establishment of the State of Israel, Reform, Reconstructionist, and Conservative prayer books have added prayers for the protection of the Jewish state, which are placed here as well. Many Orthodox congregations also recite the prayer at this point in the service, although it does not appear in most Orthodox prayer books.

The prophet Jeremiah/Yirmiyahu urged the Jews to seek the welfare of the city in which they lived, even in exile. To that end, we now pray for the

leaders of the country in which the congregation resides, a prayer called
Ha'Noten t'shuah/The One who grants salvation. The actual text of this
prayer will vary slightly from nation to nation; in the United States it will
be made for "the president and vice president" but obviously a different
wording would be used elsewhere. (In some congregations, this prayer is
followed by another *Mi shebeirakh*, this one for the soldiers of the Israel
Defense Force.)

Twelve or thirteen times a year, these prayers will be followed by a special blessing, the *Birkat Ha'Khodesh/the prayer for the new month.* Judaism
uses a lunar calendar, with the beginning of each month marked by the
new moon. On the Sabbath immediately preceding the new moon, called
Shabbat Mevarekhim, we pray for God to grant us a good month, "one of
blessing and goodness for us." In traditional prayer books, these wishes
are usually specific to the individual and the Jewish people, but liberal
siddurim have extended them in a more universalistic manner to all humanity. (As *Rosh Khodesh*, the observation of the new month, has gained
in popularity among many American Jews, particularly those of a feminist
persuasion, new rituals surrounding its observation have burgeoned. For
more information, you might start with my book, *Essential Judaism.*)

The final prayer of this section of the Torah service, *Hazkarat Nishmot
Ha'Kedoshim,* offers a commemoration of Jewish martyrs throughout history. In the nineteenth century, more liberal Jewish prayer book editors
were upset by the text of this prayer, which calls loudly for God's vengeance for "his servants' spilled blood," and concludes with a harsh quote
from *Tehillim* about those nations who persecute Jews: "He judges the
nations, filling [their lands] with bodies, crushing heads across the land."
Reform prayer books deleted the prayer; the Conservative prayer book
deletes that last sentence.

5. RETURNING THE TORAH TO THE ARK

Seder K'riat Ha'Torah has the shape of a bell curve. It starts with the
many prayers and blessings before removing the *sefer Torah* from the ark,
prayers that we previously characterized as an affirmation of God, an
acknowledgment of the greatness of the Creator, and a recognition of the
Torah as the Word of the Holy One made manifest on earth. As the service continues, it rises to a crescendo with the *hakafah* and the actual reading of the *parashah*, the emotional and theological high points of this
sequence. Then there is a gradual decrescence, ending with a series of

blessings and prayers that accompany the returning of the Torah scrolls to the ark, a sequence that serves in tandem with the opening section to bookend those peaks. Not surprisingly, the final movement of the Torah service is a series of reaffirmations of those first stated principles, an echo of the opening section.

This final section of the Torah service begins with *Ashrei*, a lengthy prayer proclaiming the joy of following God and the greatness of *Adonai*. After opening with lines drawn from elsewhere in the Psalms, this hymn includes the entire text of Psalm 145. Psalm 145 is a particularly esteemed passage of scripture, a lengthy alphabetical acrostic that is also recited as part of the opening sections of the *Shakharit* and *Minkhah* services. In Tractate *Berakhot* the rabbis say that one who recites Psalm 145 three times a day is guaranteed a place in *Olam Ha'Ba/the World to Come;* one who prays at all the services on a day on which Torah is read has discharged that duty for the day.

From here the remainder of this part of the service moves quickly. The prayer leader raises up the *sefer Torah* and the congregation stands, singing:

Let them praise the name of *Adonai*, for God's name is exalted.

The majesty of God is above the heavens and earth. The Eternal One is the strength of the people, the praise of the faithful, the Children of Israel, who are dear to God. Hallelujah!

These hymns are followed by the recitation of Psalm 29, generally believed to be one of the oldest psalms, a paean to God as an overwhelming force, "whose voice can break trees."

Finally, the Torah is placed back in the the ark, and the congregation recalls once more the ark in motion in the desert with a prayer that begins as follows:

And with [the ark's] coming to rest, he [Moshe] would say: *Adonai,* You who are the myriad thousands of Israel. . . .

The Torah service then closes with what is perhaps the most familiar passage contained in it, and one of the most enduring metaphors used to describe the Torah, *Eitz Khayim/Tree of Life:*

It is a tree of life to those who hold fast to it and happy are those who support it. Its ways are ways of pleasantness and all its paths are peace. Return us to You, *Adonai,* that we may return. Renew our days as of old.

The curtains of the ark are drawn closed and *Seder K'riat Ha'Torah* is completed.

A DOUBLE PORTION

According to the Talmud, the entire Torah must be read within a year, with no *parashiyot* omitted. A little elementary arithmetic suggests a problem in the annual cycle of the reading of the Torah: there are fifty-two weeks in the secular year but there are fifty-four *parashiyot*. This situation is exacerbated when you consider that when a festival falls on Shabbat a special Torah portion is read, rather than the designated *parashah* for that week (see "Special Readings for the Festivals," page 48). How can this problem be resolved?

The answer is quite simple—double up some of the *parashiyot*. Here are the seven pairs that are traditionally permitted. Although it is rare that all seven will be found in a single calendar year, at least two are guaranteed to turn up annually.

Shemot:	*Vayak'heil–Pekudei*
Vayikra:	*Tazria–Metzora*
	Akharei Mot–Kedoshim
	Behar–Bekhukotai
B'midbar:	*Khukat–Balak*
	Matot–Ma'asei
Devarim:	*Nitzavim–Vayeilekh*

During a leap year, which adds four weeks to the Jewish calendar— the month of *Adar Sheini/Adar II*—some of the doubled *parashiyot* are detached and read on separate *Shabbatot*. The Jewish leap year will occur seven times in a cycle of nineteen years.

PARASHIYOT AND HAFTAROT
OF THE ANNUAL READING CYCLE

Bereishit	*Bereishit* 1:1–6:8	*Yeshayahu* (Isaiah) 42:5–43:11 (42:5–21)*
Noakh	" 6:9–11:32	*Yeshayahu* 54:1–55:5 (54:1–10)
Lekh Lekha	" 12:1–17:27	*Yeshayahu* 40:27–41:16
Vayeira	" 18:1–22:24	*Melakhim Bet* (II Kings) 4:1–37 (4:1–23)
Khayei Sarah	" 23:1–25:18	*Melakhim Aleph* (I Kings) 1:1–31
Toledot	" 25:19–28:9	*Malakhi* 1:1–2:7
Vayeitzei	" 28:10–32:3	*Hosheya* 12:13–14:10 (11:7–12:12)
Vayishlakh	" 32:4–36:43	*Hosheya* (Hosea) 11:7–12:12 (*Ovadiah* 1:1–21)
Vayeishev	" 37:1–40:23	*Amos* 2:6–3:8
Miketz	" 41:1–44:17	*Melakhim Aleph* 3:15–4:1
Vayigash	" 44:18–47:27	*Yekhezkel* (Ezekiel) 37:15–28
Vayekhi	" 47:28–50:26	*Melakhim Aleph* 2:1–12
Shemot	*Shemot* 1:1–6:1	*Yeshayahu* 27:6–28:13; 29:22–23 (*Yirmiyahu* [Jeremiah] 1:1–2:3)
Va'era	" 6:2–9:35	*Yekhezkel* 28:25–29:21
Bo	" 10:1–13:16	*Yirmiyahu* 46:13–28
Beshalakh	" 3:17–17:16	*Shoftim* (Judges) 4:4–5:31 (5:1–31)
Yitro	" 18:1–20:23	*Yeshayahu* 6:1–7:6; 9:5–6 (6:1–13)

*Parentheses indicate the *haftarah* according to the Sephardic custom.

Mishpatim	"	21:1–24:18	Yirmiyahu 34:8–22; 33:25–26
Terumah	"	25:1–27:19	Melakhim Aleph 5:26–6:13
Tetzaveh	"	27:20–30:10	Yekhezkel 43:10–27
Ki Tisa	"	30:11–34:35	Melakhim Aleph 18:1–39 (18:20–39)
Vayak'heil	"	35:1–38:20	Melakhim Aleph 7:40–50 (7:13–26)
Pekudei	"	38:21–40:38	Melakhim Aleph 7:51–8:21 (7:40–50)
Vayikra	Vayikra	1:1–5:26	Yeshayahu 43:21–44:23
Tzav	"	6:1–8:36	Yirmiyahu 7:21–8:3; 9:22–23
Shemini	"	9:1–11:47	Shmuel Bet (II Samuel) 6:1–7:17 (6:1–19)
Tazria	"	12:1–13:59	Melakhim Bet 4:42–5:19
Metzora	"	14:1–15:33	Melakhim Bet 7:3–20
Akharei Mot	"	16:1–18:30	Yekhezkel 22:1–19 (22:1–16)
Kedoshim	"	19:1–20:27	Amos 9:7–15 (Yekhezkel 20:2–20)
Emor	"	21:1–24:23	Yekhezkel 44:15–31
Behar	"	25:1–26:2	Yirmiyahu 32:6–27
Bekhukotai	"	26:3–27:34	Yirmiyahu 16:19–17:14
B'midbar	B'midbar	1:1–4:20	Hosheya 2:1–22
Naso	"	4:21–7:89	Shoftim 13:2–25
B'ha'alotekha	"	8:1–12:16	Zekharyah 2:14–4:7
Shelakh	"	13:1–15:41	Yehoshua 2:1–24
Korakh	"	16:1–18:32	Shmuel Aleph (I Samuel) 11:14–12:22
Khukat	"	19:1–22:1	Shoftim 11:1–33
Balak	"	22:2–25:9	Mikhah 5:6–6:8
Pinkhas	"	25:10–30:1	Melakhim Aleph 18:46–19:21

Matot	"	30:2–32:42	Yirmiyahu 1:1–2:3
Ma'asei	"	33:1–36:13	Yirmiyahu 2:4–28, 3:4 (Yirmiyahu 2:4–28, 4:1–2)
Devarim	Devarim 1:1–3:22		Yeshayahu 1:1–27
Va'etkhanan	"	3:23–7:11	Yeshayahu 40:1–26
Eikev	"	7:12–11:25	Yeshayahu 49:14–51:3
Re'eih	"	11:26–16:17	Yeshayahu 54:11–55:5
Shoftim	"	16:18–21:9	Yeshayahu 51:12–52:12
Ki Tetzei	"	21:10–25:19	Yeshayahu 54:1–10
Ki Tavo	"	26:1–29:8	Yeshayahu 60:1–22
Nitzavim	"	29:9–30:20	Yeshayahu 61:10–63:9
Vayeilekh	"	31:1–30	Yeshayahu 55:6–56:8
Ha'azinu	"	32:1–52	Shmuel Bet 22:1–51
V'Zot Ha'Berakhah	"	33:1–34:12	Yehoshua 1:1–18 (1:1–9)

HOW *SEDER K'RIAT HA'TORAH* EVOLVED

In a sense, we are now back at the Water Gate in Jerusalem with Ezra. Except that this public reading of the Torah was not the first recorded in Jewish history; in fact, Moshe instructs the Hebrews to read the Torah or—more likely—specific parts of *Devarim* every seven years. Despite those hoary historical precedents, *Seder K'riat Ha'Torah* is one of the more recently developed parts of the Jewish liturgy, probably post-Talmudic in origin.

The earliest references to the practice of reading the Torah in public may be found in the book itself. In *Devarim* 31:10–13, a ritual called *Hak'hel* is prescribed in which the king calls together *Am Yisrael/the People Israel* every seventh year at Sukkot to hear him read from sections of *Sefer Devarim*. The passages usually read at this time were from the beginning of the book up to *Devarim* 6:9, followed by *Devarim* 11:13–21, finishing with *Devarim* 14:22 to the end of chapter 28. For many commentators, this ritual is considered a significant *mitzvah/commandment* for both readers and auditors, albeit one that can be performed only every seven years. Some have said that it is nothing less than a reenactment of receiving the Torah at Sinai, the seminal event in Jewish history.

The next encounter we have with a public reading of the Torah is the one with which this chapter began, that day in Jerusalem on which Ezra brought together the Jews of the city to hear the Law. But like *Hak'hel,* this seems to be an isolated example of the practice and one that does not correspond to contemporary rituals. It is important to note, though, the choice of location for this event—the city gates. In both biblical and non-biblical literature we find that the city gates were an important gathering place and focus of community activity, the marketplace for the city, and, frequently, the place at which royalty would hold court. Gradually, the synagogue would take on some of these roles, and it is hard not to wonder if the Torah reading wasn't a catalyst for that transition, which apparently took place sometime between the First and Second Temples. (Was the Torah read in the Temple in Jerusalem? We don't know for sure, but there is some speculation to that effect.)

According to Talmudic sources, it was Moshe himself who prescribed the reading of the Torah on Shabbat, and Ezra or the prophets who added the weekday morning readings. (Maimonides ascribes the entire reading schedule to Moshe.) Why those days? The rabbinic explanation, found in a *baraita/noncanonical passage of Mishnah,* is drawn from a typically oblique reading of the Torah itself. In *Shemot* 15:22 we are told "And [*B'nei Yisrael*] went three days in the wilderness and found no water." The rabbis said that water really meant the Torah, because it is written elsewhere, "All those who thirst come to the water." Therefore, since the newly freed Hebrews went as much as three days without hearing Torah, they were exhausted. Hence, the prophets or elders said that the Torah should be read every three days and prescribed the additional readings for weekday mornings. A more likely and practical explanation is that Monday and Thursday were market days in Jerusalem, and would be the most likely to provide a larger listenership.

When did the practice begin? The discussion of it that takes place in Tractate *Bava Kama* of the Babylonian Talmud suggests a fairly early date. *Encyclopaedia Judaica* argues that since the Septuagint (the Greek translation of the text made on behalf of the Greek Jews of Egypt at the behest of Ptolemy II) was written for use in such readings, the practice can be safely dated to the first half of the third century B.C.E. Both Josephus and Philo refer to the regular readings as "an ancient practice" and there is reference to it in the New Testament. Experts believe that the growth of the synagogue as an institution is at least partly linked to the practice of the public reading of Torah, and some of the most intriguing evidence regarding the Torah reading can be found in discussions of the ancient synagogue.

What we know about the ancient synagogue is a fascinating and often frustratingly fragmented mix of archaeology, period texts, and educated speculation. The historical record is frequently inconclusive or mute. Given that the first known prayer books date from the ninth century C.E., it is well-nigh impossible to trace the exact development of the Torah service itself with any certainty.

Ezra's public reading of the Torah marks the beginning of a sea change in Jewish thought and practice: a shift from the Temple, the sacrifices, and the powerful *kohanim* to the synagogue, prayer, and rabbinic valorization of text and text study. Indicative of that shift, as Steven Fine has noted, is a major change in the rabbinic attitude toward the *sifrei Torah* themselves. In the Second Temple period, the Torah began for the first time to be considered a sacred object per se. Fine says, "[With] the priestly urim and tumim[8] oracles gone . . . and direct prophesy on the wane, the scroll came to be treated as an oracular document from which God's will could be discerned." The emphasis in Jewish life now shifts from the Tabernacle and Temple to the Torah, with the relationship of Jews to the sacred text becoming their most important connection to the Divine. References to "holy books" and "sacred law" date from after this period. This treatment of these objects even extends to non-Jews like Ptolemy II, who prostrates himself before the completed Septuagint (hardly something that the Pharoah who dueled with Moshe would have done).

We will never know when the first synagogues were founded, but many historians infer that this shift to text-as-sacred-object is a prerequisite both to the creation of the synagogue as an institution and to the rise of Rabbinic Judaism, which took the interpretation of such texts as its focus and raison d'être (as we will see in Chapter 4). At any rate, the resulting innovation, in which textual study became an integral part of worship and every bit as important as prayer, was and still is unique in Western religions. And while the Temple stood in Jerusalem, it was the primary function of the synagogues, with prayer apparently taking second place.

On the other hand, judging from the textual evidence, the ancient synagogues still deferred to the Temple. In Tractate *Megillah* it is prescribed that the synagogue be oriented toward Jerusalem and the Temple: "The doors of the synagogue are built on the eastern side, for thus we find in the Tabernacle, for it is said: 'Before the Tabernacle toward the east, before the tent of meeting eastward.' " With the synagogue set up this way, the congregants are facing the ark, and toward the east, that is, Jerusalem.

However, archaeological evidence suggests a slightly more ambivalent attitude in the aftermath of the destruction of the Temple. Fine reports that, while most of the Palestinian synagogues of the fourth century C.E. were aligned to Jerusalem, such an alignment was not universal and "a number of synagogues had their shrines on a wall other than the one aligned with Jerusalem." His explanation for this disparity is intriguing:

> This phenomenon seems to reflect the tension in ancient Judaism that God is in His Temple, yet is everywhere. Instructively, this tension and its architectural ramifications can be sensed in synagogues of the medieval and modern periods. While the standard codes of Jewish law all legislate that the synagogue interior be aligned toward the Torah shrine on the Jerusalem wall of the synagogue, the reality is far more complex in even the most Rabbinically oriented medieval and early modern communities. Alignment toward Jerusalem is an ideal in these sources, though in many cases not an architectural reality.

But even the if the architects and builders paid only lip service to the alignment of Torah and Temple, the textual emphasis should remind us that for Jews both ancient and modern the Torah is a link to Sinai that has more than a merely symbolic nature. As we will see repeatedly, the words we say during *hagbahah* are to be understood as a powerful metaphorical truth: "This is the Torah that Moshe placed before the Children of Israel, from the Mouth of *Adonai* to the hand of Moshe."

At the same time, the Torah service is also a reminder of the reading by Ezra that day in Jerusalem, although probably not by conscious design. The wooden stand from which he read to the assembled Israelites is evoked by the *bimah* and *amud* found in contemporary synagogues. Similarly, the *aron ha'kodesh* in a modern synagogue bears more than a family resemblance to ones that can be seen in ancient mosaics representing its forebears of a previous millennium.

Not surprisingly, the worship practices of the Second Temple–era synagogues are not without similarity to our own, as is attested to by Philo and Josephus. Of course, much of what we take for granted as contemporary ritual practice dates back to before the fall of the Second Temple, the public reading of the Torah being chief among them. The reading of the *haftarot* is prescribed in the Talmud and Tosefta (an auxilliary compilation of Oral Law that postdates the Mishnah). The number and priority of *aliyot* was debated at length by the rabbis of the Mishnaic period.

But with the destruction of the Second Temple those practices, now so much more important in sustaining the Jewish people in exile, evolved gradually into our own. Interestingly, though, there was a split between the Jewish community that remained in Palestine after 70 C.E. and the leading Diaspora community of Babylonia. That split is reflected, of course, by the existence of not one but two Talmuds, the *Bavli* (Babylonian) and *Yerushalmi* (Jerusalem or Palestinian). But the division is also manifested in a major difference in ritual practice: in Palestine the Torah was read over a three-year cycle, while the Babylonian Jews (and by extension, most of the Jews in *galut*) read the Torah in its entirety each year. (The exact nature of the triennial cycle of readings is unclear today, but there are contemporary counterparts.)

If we were miraculously dropped into a second century C.E. congregation in the Diaspora, we would probably recognize many of the practices in *Seder K'riat Ha'Torah* as identical to our own. What would undoubtedly resonate most powerfully for us is the centrality of the Torah to the beliefs and rituals of these Jews who were born two millennia before us. And that brings us to an obvious and unavoidable question: What is it about this book—these five books, if you prefer—that has maintained its hold over the Jewish people for more than two thousand years? What makes the Torah important today?

To answer that question, we must proceed to a discussion of the content of the Torah.

SPECIAL READINGS FOR THE FESTIVALS

THE FIVE *MEGILLOT*

The five *megillot/scrolls* are books of the *Tanakh* that are associated with specific holidays of the Jewish calendar. Each book is read on a specific day as part of the prayer service for that particular holiday.

Sukkot:	*Kohelet* (Ecclesiastes)
Purim:	*Ester* (Esther)

Pesakh:	*Shir Ha'Shirim* (Song of Songs)
Shavuot:	*Rut* (Ruth)
Tisha B'Av:	*Eikhah* (Lamentations)

In addition, there are prescribed Torah and *haftarah* readings for each of the Festivals.

ROSH HASHANAH

First Day:	*Bereishit* 21:1–34, *B'midbar* 29:1–6
Haftarah:	*Shmuel Aleph* 1:1–2:10
Second Day:	*Bereishit* 22:1–24, *B'midbar* 29:1–6
Haftarah:	*Yirmiyahu* 31:1–19

YOM KIPPUR

Morning:	*Vayikra* 16:1–34, *B'midbar* 29:7–11
Haftarah:	*Yeshayahu* 57:14–58:14
Afternoon:	*Vayikra* 18:1–30
Haftarah:	*Yonah* 1:1–4:11, *Mikhah* 7:18–20

SUKKOT

First Day:	*Vayikra* 22:26–23:44, *B'midbar* 29:12–16
Haftarah:	*Zekharyah* 14:1–21
Second Day:	Same as first day
Haftarah:	*Melakhim Aleph* 8:2–21
First Day *Khol Ha'Mo'ed:*	*B'midbar* 29:17–25
Second Day *Khol Ha'Mo'ed:*	*B'midbar* 29:20–28
Third Day *Khol Ha'Mo'ed:*	*B'midbar* 29:23–31
Fourth Day *Khol Ha'Mo'ed:*	*B'midbar* 29:26–34
Shabbat Khol Ha'Mo'ed:	*Shemot* 33:12–34:26 and *B'midbar* 29:17–25, 23–29 or 26–31, depending on whether it is first, third, or fourth day of *Khol Ha'Mo'ed*
Hoshanah Rabbah:	*B'midbar* 29:26–34
Haftarah (for all of Khol Ha'Mo'ed):	*Yekhezkel* 38:18–39:16

SHEMINI ATZERET

Torah:	*Devarim* 14:22–16:17, *B'midbar* 29:35–30:1
Haftarah:	*Melakhim Aleph* 8:54–9:1

SIMKHAT TORAH

Torah:	*Devarim* 33:1–34:12, *Bereishit* 1:1–2:3, *B'midbar* 29:35–30:1
Haftarah:	*Yehoshua* 1:1–18

HANUKAH

First Day:	*B'midbar* 7:1–17
Second Day:	*B'midbar* 7:18–29
Third Day:	*B'midbar* 7:24–35
Fourth Day:	*B'midbar* 7:30–41
Fifth Day:	*B'midbar* 7:36–47
Sixth Day:	*B'midbar* 7:42–47
Seventh Day:	*B'midbar* 7:48–59 (if *Rosh Kodesh, B'midbar* 7:48–53)
Eighth Day:	*B'midbar* 7:54–8:4
Hanukah on *Rosh Khodesh:*	*B'midbar* 28:1–15, plus appropriate reading for sixth or seventh day
Shabbat Hanukah:	Regular Shabbat reading, plus reading for day of Hanukah on which it falls
Haftarah:	*Zekharyah* 2:14–4:7
Second Shabbat of Hanukah:	Regular Shabbat reading (always *Miketz, Bereishit* 41:1–44:17), plus *B'midbar* 7:54–8:4
Haftarah:	*Melakhim Aleph* 7:40–50
Shabbat Rosh Khodesh: 28:1–15, plus reading for day of	Regular Shabbat reading, *B'midbar* Hanukah on which it falls

PURIM

Torah:	*Shemot* 17:8–16

PESAKH

First Day:	*Shemot* 12:21–51, *B'midbar* 28:16–25
Haftarah:	*Yehoshua*, 3:5–7, 5:2–6:1, 6:27
Second Day:	*Vayikra* 22:26–23:44, *B'midbar* 28:16–25
Haftarah:	*Melakhim Bet* 23:1–9, 21–25
Shabbat Khol Ha'Mo'ed Pesakh:	*Shemot* 33:12–34:26, *B'midbar* 28:19–25
Haftarah:	*Yekhezkel* 37:1–14
Seventh Day:	*Shemot* 13:17–15:26, *B'midbar* 28:19–25
Haftarah:	*Shmuel Bet* 22:1–51
Eighth Day:	*Devarim* 15:19–16:17 (if on Sabbath, *Devarim* 14:22–16:17)
Haftarah:	*Yeshayahu* 10:32–12:6

SHAVUOT

First Day:	*Shemot* 19:1–20:23, *B'midbar* 28:26–31
Haftarah:	*Yekhezkel* 1:1–28, 3:12
Second Day:	*Devarim* 15:19–16:17 (if on Sabbath, *Devarim* 14:22–16:17)
Haftarah:	*Kabakuk* 2:20–3:19

YOM HA'ATZMAUT

Torah:	*Devarim* 7:12–8:18
Haftarah:	*Yeshayahu* 10:32–12:6

TISHA B'AV

Morning:	*Devarim* 4:25–40
Haftarah:	*Yirmiyahu* 8:13–9:23
Afternoon:	*Shemot* 32:11–14, 34:1–10
Haftarah:	*Yeshayahu* 55:6–56:8

Readings are the same on other fast days as well.

TWO HOLIDAYS FOR TORAH

There are two festivals on the Jewish ritual calendar in which the Torah has a particularly central place. Simkhat Torah, which celebrates the completion of the year's reading of the Torah, begins on the night of 22 Tishrei, which is usually sometime in October. Shavuot, which commemorates the Giving of the Torah at Sinai, begins on the night of 6 Sivan, which is usually sometime in June.

SIMKHAT TORAH

Simkhat Torah festivities center on the reading of the Torah. A congregation will perform seven *hakafot* at the beginning of *Seder Kri'at Ha'Torah*, during which congregants will carry, as they circle the *bimah*, all of the Torah scrolls that the synagogue owns, while they chant an acrostic prayer similar to the *ana Adonai hoshea na* passage of *Hallel*. Each *hakafah* will be followed by lively singing and dancing with the scrolls. The children of the congregation participate eagerly, marching with the adults, carrying little flags or miniature Torah scrolls of their own.

After the seventh *hakafah*, the first of the day's two Torah readings is chanted. (Many congregations read from the Torah at the evening service on this holiday, regardless of whether they will hold a morning service the next day. In congregations in which the holiday is celebrated at night, this will be the only time all year that the Torah is read as part of the evening service.) *Devarim* 33–34 is the story of the death of Moshe, the end of the Five Books of Moses. In the morning service, everyone in the congregation receives an *aliyah*. Different congregations do this in different ways. In progressive synagogues, group *aliyot* will be given to "all the adult males," "all the firstborn," "all the adult females," and whatever other categories the rabbi or *gabbai* can devise to include everyone. In other synagogues, many scrolls will be read from simultaneously and/or the passage from *Devarim* will be repeated over and over until everyone has received an *aliyah*. In all congregations, one *aliyah* will be reserved for *kol ha'ne'arim/all the youngsters*, with all the children coming to the *bimah* to recite the blessings, while four adults hold up a *tallit* over the children, a canopy that combines love and tradition. The *aliyah* for the last section of the passage from

Devarim is a special honor, and the person who receives it is called *khatan Ha'Torah/the bridegroom of the Torah*. The recipient of the first *aliyah* for the second reading—the beginning of *Bereishit*—is called *khatan Bereishit/the bridegroom of the Beginning*. It is also a great honor. When the final section of *Devarim* is completed, the custom is for the congregation to chant, *Khazak, khazak, v'nit khazeik/Be strong, be strong, and let us strengthen one another*. This chant (which is then repeated by the reader) is offered every time a book of the Torah is completed in synagogue, but it seems to carry an additional fervor on Simkhat Torah.

Simkhat Torah is a time of joyous public displays. There literally is dancing in the streets of many Jewish communities, a spectacle well worth seeing in the Hasidic sections of Brooklyn, on Manhattan's Upper West Side, and in the Orthodox neighborhoods of Jerusalem. For some the holiday is also a splendid opportunity to overindulge, which led outstanding rabbinical authorities like the Khofetz Khaim to caution that it is not appropriate to drink to excess on this day.

SHAVUOT

It seems ironic that the sole account of Shavuot in the Torah refers only to the agricultural basis of the holiday—the celebration of the harvesting of the first fruits of the yearly planting cycle. And it is doubly ironic, because Shavuot is the only major festival mandated in the Torah solely on an agricultural basis, despite the fundamental importance of the Giving of the Law, which is the other event commemorated on this holiday. The name Shavuot means "weeks," a reference to the fact that the holiday marks the conclusion of the counting of the seven weeks of the Omer period, which begins on the second night of Pesakh.

Outside of Israel, there are few vestiges today of the agricultural beginnings of Shavuot, although in Israel it is a significant festival on secular *kibbutzim*. The custom of decorating the synagogue with flowers and plants, the practice of marking the holiday with a dairy (i.e., nonmeat) meal, and the inclusion of the *megillah* of *Rut* in the synagogue service are the primary reminders of its agrarian provenance.

Today, Shavuot primarily celebrates the most important moment in the Covenant between God and the Jews: the giving of the Torah to Moshe and its acceptance by the newly freed Hebrews at Sinai. Not surprisingly, Shavuot has come to be dedicated to the idea of Torah study and Jewish education. One custom that traditional Jews still observe is an all-night study session held on the first evening of the festival, called *tikkun leil Shavuot*. This custom, which had its beginnings in the community of kabbalists centered around sixteenth-century Safed, is designed to prepare Jews for "receiving" the Torah again on Shavuot.

In keeping with the theme of Jewish education, Shavuot has traditionally been the time when many Conservative and Orthodox Hebrew high schools marked graduation. The newest observance associated with the holiday is the Reform movement's Confirmation ceremony, reaffirming the participation of high school–age teens in Judaism and Jewish scholarship. It is also at this holiday that many congregations of all denominations consecrate their younger Hebrew school students, urging them to study their tradition and live in it.

Liturgically, the major addition for Shavuot, besides the usual Festival prayers, a *Yizkor* service, and the reading of *megillat Rut*, is the *Akdamut* prayer, which is recited at the morning service in Ashkenazic congregations. *Akdamut* is a forty-four-verse acrostic that glosses the Ten Commandments while offering praise to God and the Creation. Sephardic congregations read a special *ketubah/marriage contract*, in recognition of the "marriage" of God and the Jewish people that receives its consummation with the giving of the Torah.

NOTES

1. During the Talmudic period, there were three types of parchment used in the creation of Torah scrolls, *tefillin*, and *mezuzot*. *Gevil* was made of the whole animal hide, stripped of its hair, and was thick and none too pliable. *K'laf* and *doksostos* were thinner parchments that were made by splitting the *gevil* into layers, with the *k'laf* being the outer layer, next to the hair, and the *doksostos* the inner layer. *K'laf* was the preferred writing surface. Today, however, it is possible to stretch the hide thin enough for it to be used without splitting, and *k'laf* has come to mean the parchment so made.

2. One thing that hasn't changed yet but may in the near future is who may be a scribe. Under *halakhah*, women are not permitted to act as *soferim STAM*, that is, scribes who write *sifrei Torah*, *tefillin*, and *mezuzot*. However, they are permitted to make *giddin* and ink, and to prepare quills. According to some decisors, they may even write a *megillat Ester/scroll of [the book of] Esther*. The reasoning behind this restriction is that if you are not permitted to read from the text as a *ba'al koreh*, you are not allowed to write it. Interestingly, in Israel women are permitted to write *mezuzot* because the placement of a *mezuzah* on one's doorposts is a *mitzvah* that women are bound to fulfill just as men are.

Although (as a female Reform cantor pointed out to me) under *halakhah* women are not permitted to serve as rabbis or cantors or *ba'alei kr'iah*, the Reform, Reconstructionist, and Conservative movements have rejected that position and it is probably only a matter of time before these movements produce their first female *soferim*. (At least two major medieval halakhic decisors—Rabbenu Asher ben Yechiel and Rabbi Yitzchak Alfasi—hold that a woman *is* permitted to write a Torah.) It should also be noted that for a long time, a scribe had to be right-handed (the side of the body associated with the strength of God), and that is no longer the case. So change is possible, even within the strictures and structures of *halakhah*.

3. The discussion of the Torah service that follows owes a great deal to Rabbi Hoffman's excellent *My People's Prayer Book, Vol. 4: Seder K'riat Ha'Torah*. This series, published by Jewish Lights, provides a superb overview of the entire siddur and is highly recommended.

4. Women are called to the Torah in Reform, Reconstructionist, and egalitarian Conservative congregations. It is not the custom for them to be given *aliyot* in Orthodox synagogues.

5. The Reform movement has dropped all references to the priestly and levite castes; hence there is no special recognition of either *kohanim* or *levi'im* in their calling of *olim*.

6. In Sephardic congregations, it is customary, before saying the blessing for the reading, for the *oleh* to express thanks to the congregation for the honor of being called to the Torah by saying *"Adonai imakhem/May Adonai be with you,"* to which they respond, *"Adonai yivarekhekha/May Adonai bless you."* After the reading is completed, but before the blessing after the reading, he will say, *"Emet torateinu k'doshah/In truth our Torah is holy."*

7. On festivals or *Shabbatot* that fall on *Rosh Khodesh*, the first day(s) of the new month, the *maftir* reads *B'midbar* 28–29 (from a second *sefer Torah* rolled to the appropriate place) rather than the closing verses of the week's Torah portion. This passage describes the sacrifices that were to be performed on festivals and *Rosh Khodesh*, now replaced by the reading of this passage, just as the other sacrifices were replaced by prayer and Torah study.

8. The *urim* and *tumim* were objects (of uncertain design) described in *Shemot* 30, which were used by the priests in the First Temple to determine the will of God. See my commentary on *parashat Tetzaveh* on page 379 for more information.

2

MORE THAN HISTORY,
MORE THAN LAW

An Overview of the Torah

What I want to achieve is an understanding on our part that the Bible is not just a book of the past. It is far more than that; it is a book of the present and future. In all times, in all periods, in crisis as well as in success, man may find his problems and anxieties defined in this Book of Books.

—Rabbi Joseph Soloveitchik

Bereishit bara Elohim et ha'shamayim v'et ha'aretz. V'ha'aretz hayitah tohu va'vohu. . . . / In the beginning, God created the heavens and the earth. And the earth was chaos and void.

In the fall, after the High Holy Days have passed, as the eight days of Sukkot draw to a close with Simkhat Torah, Jews throughout the world begin once again the ancient cycle of Torah readings. On *Shabbat Bereishit,* the first Sabbath after Simkhat Torah, the words that open the sacred text are repeated. Once more we read *parashat Bereishit,* the same old story of the Creation, the forbidden fruit, the expulsion from *Gan Eden / the Garden of Eden.*

We do this just as Jews have done for more than two millennia, whether as part of an annual or triennial cycle, reading the same text, forever unchanged. No one knows for certain when this practice became a regular part of Jewish worship, but whichever historians you follow, the Jews have been over this ground several thousand times.

Why?

Why reread the same text every year, in the same order, with the same *haftarot*? To the best of my knowledge, Judaism is the only one of the Western faith traditions that does this, that keeps on doing it.

Of course, there are many answers.

The first and most obvious one is that the Torah is a text of incredible richness and inexhaustible complexity. Like *The Iliad* and *War and Peace* and *Don Quixote*, it is a book that reveals new facets every time one reads it. The first-century rabbi Ben Bag-Bag counsels in *Pirkei Avot/sayings of the Fathers,* "Turn it and turn it again, for everything is in it." When my Torah study group was meeting regularly, we read through the *parashiyot* three times in three years, and we found something new each time. As we will see repeatedly in this book, the *Khumash* is an inexhaustibly rich text that has produced thousands of pages of commentary.

But isn't that also true of the works of Shakespeare? We love Shakespeare but we don't let his writings govern our lives. One could argue that by reading the Torah portions each week, we are linking ourselves to more than two millennia of Jewish tradition, which is a fine thing in and of itself. But how is this different from having a seder, building a *sukkah,* putting *mezuzot* on our doors? Of course, there is an answer that combines these two arguments: that we study the Torah because it is the basis for much of what is considered Western morality, that it is a more pivotal text to our civilization than *Hamlet,* that it contains the roots of Judaism, Christianity, and Islam. This is all true, but I'm rather uncomfortable with that notion; it reminds me of a famous exchange between a journalist and Gandhi. "What do you think of Western civilization?" asked the journalist. To which Gandhi replied, "I think it would be a good idea."

I can conceive of another explanation, which synthesizes the previous three arguments for studying Torah and reading the weekly *parashiyot.* This kind of Torah study does more than situate us in the flow of Jewish history, take us on a rewarding intellectual journey, and allow us to see where the Western world came from. To study Torah a week at a time, year after year, is to be immersed in the beginnings of our people, to experience anew each year the Creation, the Expulsion, the Flood, the Exodus from *Mitzrayim/Egypt,* the Revelation at Sinai, the Wandering in the Wilderness, and the preparations for crossing over into *Eretz Yisrael.* We do this both as individuals hearing these stories, reading them ourselves, exploring the commentaries and creating our own, and as part of the community that was shaped by this experience.

In the morning blessings Jews pray that they will experience Creation anew each day. In going through the cycle of Torah readings they do the same thing with the entire story of the origins of their people—indeed, of all humanity. The *haggadah,* the text of the Passover seder, tells us to consider ourselves as having been present at the Exodus from Mitzrayim/ Egypt; reading the *parashiyot* of *Sefer Shemot* every year allows us relive it. Rabbi Nakhman of Bratzlav wrote, "Attempt to go through all of our sacred texts in the course of your lifetime. You will then have visited every place in the Torah." Let us now consider some of those places.

STORIES AND MEANINGS

We know the stories.

We know about the Creation, about Adam and Khavah/Eve and the serpent and the Expulsion from *Gan Eden,* about the wrath of Kayin/Cain and the murder of Hevel/Abel, about Noakh/Noah and the Flood, and about the Tower of Babel. We have heard about the Patriarchs and Matriarchs: about Avraham and Sarah, Hagar and Yishmael/Ishmael, the binding of Yitzkhak/Isaac, Ya'akov/Jacob usurping Eisav's/Esau's birthright and blessing, Yosef/Joseph and his brothers. We have been told about the baby Moshe in the bulrushes, the burning bush, the duel with the Egyptian magicians and the hardness of Pharoah's heart, the Ten Plagues and the first Passover, the parting of the *Yam Suf* and the fiery revelation at Sinai.

Even if one has never read the Torah—in Hebrew or any other language—the stories it contains are almost too familiar. They are among the principal metals out of which Western literature has been forged. A list of literary works that draw on the Torah for their subject matter or inspiration would be longer than the Torah itself.

But if the only contact we have had with the first five books of the Bible is through its literary descendants, no matter how noble, then we don't really know what is *in* the Torah, for several reasons. First, the stories as told in the Torah itself are frequently quite different from the way we may remember them or have experienced them in other books. So it behooves us to go back to the originals. Second, the Torah is more than just the stories; it is also the complex web of themes that underpin them, as well as the poetry and the laws that are contained within them. And more than that, it is the way in which the stories are told, how the poetry and laws are structured. As Judah Goldin has written in a similar context, "The way the table is set is as important as the food. . . . [P]atterns of presentation are not to be detached or erased from passages quoted. Form is not immaterial or an afterthought."

Finally, and for our purposes perhaps most important, in going back to the original material and then reading forward to understand it, we are reading the Torah (and by extension the rest of the Hebrew Bible) in a way that may be unfamiliar to most of us, reading it in the context in which it was written and for many hundreds of years interpreted—reading it Jewishly. (Ideally that would mean reading it in Hebrew, but realistically, we will have to rely on translators who can do that for us.) To do that we will not only revisit the Torah's own text but, in subsequent chapters, also examine how it has been read by successive generations of Jewish commentators.

First we must deal with the text itself. Our purose here is not to recapitulate the stories the Torah tells; that kind of reading you should do for yourself. Rather, let's examine the basic themes of the book and the ways in which it works as a text. Of necessity, we will focus almost exclusively in this chapter on the Pentateuch. Remember, however, that Jewish sacred texts never stop with the individual book in hand; there are always commentaries, commentaries on commentaries, and so on, that enrich our understanding of the Hebrew Bible. We will deal with that rich, dense forest of Jewish Bible scholarship at length in later chapters.

IN THE BEGINNING, GOD

Why, the rabbis asked, does the Torah begin with the Creation? After all, they argued, the central function of the Torah is to outline the *mitzvot/ commandments* God gives to Israel. The book should begin, like *Aseret Ha'Dibrot/the Ten Sayings, Commandments*, with "I, *Adonai*, am your God." Or, as Rabbi Yitzkhak says, referring to the first *mitzvah* mentioned in *Sefer Shemot*, "The Torah should have begun with 'This month shall be [the first month]. . . .' "

Elsewhere in this book I argue that *Sefer Bereishit* may be read as a lengthy precredit sequence to the main story of the Torah, the deliverance from Egypt, the Revelation at Sinai, the giving of the *mitzvot*, and the events in the desert that lead up to the entrance of the Israelites into the

Promised Land. There are many explanations given by the classical commentators for the structure of the *Khumash,* and we will touch on some of
them later. But, at the risk of seeming flippant, there is an essential reason
for beginning in the beginning: it introduces us immediately to the protagonist of the book, the one "character" who is present throughout.

God.

In his excellent book *The Way into Encountering God in Judaism,* Dr.
Neil Gillman delineates the central trajectory of the Torah into three succinctly chosen words: Creation, Revelation, and Redemption. Those three
certainly sum up the relationship between God and humanity. Jonathan
Levenson boils the Hebrew Bible down to the connection between Sinai
and Zion: the Giving of the Law and the Revelation of God at the mountain, and its relationship to the promise of the Land and a Messianic Age.
In other words, Creation, Revelation, Redemption, again. The difference
is one of emphasis, but both scholars are essentially correct.

Whichever version of the central ideas of the Torah one picks (and
there are plenty more if these don't thrill you), it always boils down to the
relationship between God and humankind. The evolving nature of that
relationship is the core of the Torah.

That should come as no great surprise. The Torah itself begins with
God the Creator, preparing for the Creation. It ends with an encomium to
Moshe as the greatest prophet of God. Throughout the entire text, as we
shall see, there is a movement from the Eternal One to humanity and back
again. But in the Torah all things begin with God, including the book
itself. After all, the opening words of the Torah are "*Bereishit bara Elohim/
In the beginning of God's creating . . .*"[1]

Rabbi Adin Steinsaltz has said that Kabbalah, the central tradition of
Jewish mysticism, is the true Jewish theology. For those of us who know
little Kabbalah, that statement may seem utterly baffling. After all, what is
the Torah, with all its discussion of God and man, if not theology?

But, in fact, there is a significant omission from the Torah: there is no
description of God, no enumeration of God's properties and capacities,
hence no theology in the conventional sense of that word, which is, to paraphrase one dictionary definition, "the science which treats God, God's
attributes and God's relations to the universe." In the Torah, God is a
given, an axiom from which everything else, literally, proceeds. It will fall
to the great medieval mystics to attempt to derive a real Jewish theology.

What, then, is the God of the Torah?

Any statement that one can make about God based on the Five Books of Moses can be countered by another statement from elsewhere in the text that seems to be diametrically opposed to the first one. Thus God is compassionate, merciful, "abundant in goodness and truth," "slow to anger," and yet also "a jealous God" who punishes "unto the third and fourth generations." God is just, yet there are punishments in the Torah that defy our understanding and horrify our modern sensibilities; the destruction of Sedom/Sodom and Aurora/Gomorrah, the *Akeidah/Binding of Yitzkhak,* the deaths of Nadav and Avihu all come immediately to mind.

Clearly, God has many aspects and attributes. In fact, God is known by many names in the Torah, and they often are a reflection of the many-sided nature of the Divine. (See "The Names of God," page 63.) The simplest way to get to the heart of the matter is to lay out briefly what we actually do know about God from the Torah itself, keeping in mind the dictum of a Jewish sage who said, "If I could describe God, I would *be* God." It is also important to keep in mind that much of what we "know" about God comes from later sources than the Torah: post-Pentateuchal biblical writings, postbiblical materials, and, most frequently, the liturgy, which, understandably, speaks of God often. These materials—and the Torah itself—speak of God in anthropomorphic terms, a regrettable necessity. The most we can hope to understand is a tiny fragment of the immensity of the Divine. Giving God human traits is a way of shaping that understanding so that it fits into a recognizable cognitive grid. God, the Torah tells us, created humans in the Divine image; in order to comprehend even a small part of the Godhead, we reverse the process. Robert Ingersoll wrote, "If the elephant had a god it would have four legs and a trunk." Whether or not one shares Ingersoll's disbelief, certainly we can agree that we inevitably personalize God in an image that we can understand, hence an anthropomorphic image. But like the parable of the blind men with the elephant, each of us individually and all of us collectively cannot possibly fathom the complexity of the Infinite.

Given that daunting proviso, what can we learn of *Adonai* from the Torah?

Let's start at the literal beginning, repeating the first sentence of the Torah: *Bereishit bara Elohim et ha'shamayim v'et ha'aretz/In the beginning, God created the heavens and the earth.*

God is the One who creates the universe and, as we proceed through the seven days of Creation, everything in it. The syntax of the first sentence makes it clear that God preexists Creation. God's existence is axiomatic; the Creator is somehow outside of Creation, having no beginning (and by implication, no end).

Does God create ex nihilo, out of nothing? The medieval Jewish philosophers thought so but the Torah is more ambiguous on this question. One can read the opening of *Bereishit* to say that God created the world out of *tohu v'vohu*, chaos and formlessness, or void, or nothingness. But this nothingness isn't exactly nothing; it's a something of some kind. The medieval thinkers were understandably troubled by this reading, because it suggests that *tohu v'vohu* might share some preexistence with God.

It is an argument that might seem like medieval hairsplitting—how many angels can dance on the head of a pin if God is playing the music?—but it does matter for at least one significant reason. The Creation myths of the Ancient Near East echo (or more likely are echoed by) the opening of the Torah. As Bruce Feiler notes in *Walking the Bible*, the Sumerians had a Creation myth in which the world was first a primeval sea that was "split into a vaulted heaven and a flat earth." Babylonian cosmology was predicated on one god, Marduk, killing another god, Tiamat, who was represented as a watery chaos; he cuts her in two, thereby creating earth and sky, then he "creates, in succession, light, the firmament, dry land, heavenly lights, animals and man." Then Marduk rests and celebrates.

Needless to say, this has a familiar ring. But there are important differences. First, in premonotheistic Creation stories the gods themselves are usually given origins. And they are also given human emotions. The gods of the Ancient Near East (and of Greece and Rome, for that matter) are less like *Adonai* than a bunch of Marvel Comics superheroes, bundles of neuroses who are jealous of one another, who lust after mortals and have sex with them, and who commit astonishing acts of avarice and violence for depressingly mundane reasons.

The God of the Torah is, as some commentators have remarked, more abstract. *Adonai*'s emotional states are referred to occasionally—God is angry, jealous, moved, and so on—but there isn't any of the explicit and richly wrought personification of the polytheistic texts. And God is One and Only One. The anthropomorphism with which we render the Eternal is more a function of our inability to cope with the Infinite than a reflection of an actual theological understanding of God as a large, irritable human being.

And that leads us to another, even more powerful difference between God and the gods. For all the anthropomorphizing of *Adonai*, the Creator acts for very different reasons than Zeus and Marduk; whereas the entire action of the Trojan War grows out of petty jealousies and fits of pique of the residents of Olympus, the stories in the Torah are motivated by God's ethical considerations, by the necessity to punish evil and reward good as God sees them. There are 217 cultures around the world that have a story about a deluge that covers the world, according to Charles Sellier and David Balsiger, but the Torah's version is one of the only ones in which the flood is caused as punishment for mankind's evil.

That's why we call it "ethical monotheism."[2]

THE NAMES OF GOD

In his edited edition of James George Frazer's *The Golden Bough*, Theodor Gaster notes, "In primitive thought, the name of a person is not merely an appellation, but denotes what he is to the world outside of himself—that is, his 'outer' as distinguished from his inner being. Thus, the 'name of God' in the Bible is His outward manifestation in the world. . . ." Not surprisingly, given the plethora of Divine attributes, God has many Names in the Hebrew Bible and in Jewish liturgy, and those names are multiplied by the inexactitude of the translator's art. (As we will see in Chapter 3, the appearance of God's various appellations provided an important clue to the scholars seeking the identity of the authors of the Torah.)

The Holy One tells Moshe, "I revealed Myself to Avraham, to Yitzkhak and to Ya'akov as *El Shaddai*, but My Name *Adonai* I did not make known to them" (*Shemot* 6:3). In the Bible and the Talmud, God has many Names: *El / The Strong One, El Shaddai / God Almighty, El Olam / God Everlasting, El Khai / The Living God, El Elyon / God Most High, Elohim / God, Adon / Lord, Adonai / Lord, Adonai Tzva'ot / Lord of Hosts, Abir / The Strong, Kedosh Yisrael / Holy One of Israel, Melekh / The Ruler, Tzur Yisrael / Rock of Israel.* Some of these are proper names; others are epithets or circumlocutions used to designate God. Rabbi Ronald H. Isaacs identifies seventeen different names in the Bible alone, some of them derived from Canaanite names for their many gods.

The sages of the Talmudic period believed that there were seven names of God in the Torah, each of which referred to a specific aspect of the Divine. For example, *YHVH* is the proper name of God, a name so sacred that it is not vocalized. This name occurs almost six thousand times in the *Tanakh*. *Elohim* refers to the aspect of God that is discerning and judging (because it is a plural, it suggests the multifarious nature of God as well). *Adonai*, meaning Lord, is the way in which the *YHVH* Tetragrammaton (Greek, meaning "four letters") is vocalized; in this form it always refers to the Almighty and also appears in the alternate spelling *Adon*, which may occasionally refer to a human sovereign. *El*, a name of Canaanite origin also used to refer to pagan gods, is often used as a combining form to invoke God in place names like Bet-el. *El Shaddai*, the Mighty One, is the God who inspires awe. The sages also pointed to *Elo'ah*, a poetical form, and *Tzva'ot*, meaning hosts, as other names for the Deity found in the Pentateuch.

For non-Jews, the most familiar Name derived from the Hebrew Bible is probably Jehovah, a mistransliteration of the four-letter Name, *Yud-He-Vav-He*, referred to in Hebrew as the *Shem Ha'Meforash*. This Name is considered too sacred and too powerful to be vocalized. The Tetragrammaton is frequently shortened to *Yah (Yud-He)*, *Yahu*, or *Yeho (Yud-He-Vav)*, especially when used in combination within names or phrases, as in *Yehoshua* (meaning "the Lord is my Salvation"), *Eliyahu* (meaning "my God is the Lord"), and *Halleluyah* ("praise the Lord"). A traditionally observant Jew will not vocalize any of God's Names outside the context of prayer. Thus, in an Orthodox songbook, one will find *Elokeinu* for *Eloheinu/Our God*, *Adoshem*, or, most commonly, *Ha'Shem/The Name*, for *Adonai*.

Progressive Jews have brought their own set of concerns and strictures to the naming of the Supreme Being. God has no gender in conventional human terms, but gendered God-talk has historically implied a valorization of God's masculine attributes. Reform, Reconstructionist, and some Conservative siddurim will avoid using gendered names for God, discarding Lord or King in favor of *Adonai*, Ruler, or Sovereign (as, in fact, I have done throughout this book).

Many traditionally observant Jews will not write the vernacular equivalent of the sacred names, preferring G-d or L-rd (although other no less traditional Jews deride this practice because these words are English, not Hebrew, and therefore *not* true names of God). This practice, however, has different roots from the ban on uttering *Shem Ha'Meforash,* the proscribed sacred Name. Contrary to popular belief, this practice does not come from the commandment not to take God's Name in vain. In Jewish thought, that commandment refers solely to oath taking, and is a prohibition against swearing by God's Name falsely or frivolously (the word normally translated as "in vain" literally means "for falsehood"). Incidentally, this is why observant Jews serving on juries or testifying in court will affirm rather than swear.

Judaism does not prohibit writing the Name of God per se, as we have seen in Chapter 1. But it does prohibit erasing or defacing a Name of God. Consequently, observant Jews avoid writing any Name of God casually because of the risk that the written Name might later be defaced, obliterated, or destroyed accidentally or by one who does not know better. This prohibition applies only to Names that are written in some permanent form. Recent rabbinical decisions have held that typing on a computer is not a permanent form of writing; thus it is not a violation to type God's Name into a computer and then backspace over it or cut and paste it, or to copy and delete files with God's Name in them. However, once you print the document out, it becomes "permanent."

In its recounting of the Creation, the Torah makes God's uniqueness and Infiniteness fairly explicit. God and the world are distinct. The processes of nature are caused by God. Indeed, the very idea of "nature" is Greek in origin, not Jewish. (As we shall see shortly, even those nonnatural events that we call "miracles" are considered in Jewish thought to be part of the process.) And the verb used here, *bara,* is associated only with God's acts of Creation. A similar verb, *oseh,* is used for human creations and for some of God's creations. So God's creating is clearly of a different order than that of humanity.

Although Orthodox congregations recite Maimonides' thirteen articles of faith, Judaism is not, by and large, a creedal religion. However, there is one key prayer, the *Sh'ma,* taken from *Sefer Devarim,* that states most emphatically one of the central tenets of the Jewish understanding of God: *"Sh'ma Yisrael Adonai Eloheinu Adonai ekhad/Hear, O Israel, Adonai [alone] is God, Adonai is One."* The unity and singularity of God, the uniqueness and oneness of the Holy One is a key message of the Torah and of virtually every text that follows from it. There is no other deity, no other creator, and as *Aseret Ha'Dibrot / The Ten Commandments* forcefully remind us, we are to have no other gods before the One God.

That said, what can we actually *know* about God?

A part of the answer can be found in another famous passage of the Torah, the Holiness Code, a lengthy set of commandments given by God to *B'nei Yisrael* in *Vayikra,* punctuated repeatedly by the admonishment, "You shall be holy because I, *Adonai,* your God, am holy." (We will examine the related concept, that humanity is created "in the image of God," momentarily.)

What must we do to be holy like God? If we look at this list, we can discern some of the traits of the Deity, ones that we, as humans, can emulate. Yet, surprisingly, much of the Holiness Code is occupied with concerns about interpersonal behavior: you shall not hate your brother in your heart; you shall surely rebuke your neighbor; you shall not take vengeance; you shall not bear a grudge; you shall not stand idly by the blood of your neighbor; you shall not steal; you shall not go about as a talebearer; the stranger who dwells among you shall be as one born to you and you will love him as yourself; you shall love your neighbor as yourself. (Some of these are familiar from the *Aseret Ha'Dibrot* and, indeed, the Holiness Code recapitulates and expands on the Ten Commandments considerably.)

The *mitzvot* of the Holiness Code are given randomly by design. No commandment is privileged over any other; there is no prioritization, no compartmentalization. The result, as Everett Fox notes, is that the Holiness Code reads holiness into all the aspects of daily life. There is seemingly no aspect of our life into which the *mitzvot* do not extend, just as there is no area of Creation in which God is not present. Consequently, if we are to be holy, we must acknowledge and welcome the spiritual element into even our most ordinary and material concerns. And in that way, we become like God, whose realm is everywhere, who is concerned with everything and, tellingly, everyone.

Yet in so many ways we are not like God and cannot hope to be like God, as the Torah also reminds us frequently. God is immensely powerful; God is the one who creates the world with an utterance, who flushes the earth clean of corruption with a deluge, who reduces the cities of Sodom and Gomorrah to ash, who visits ten extraordinary plagues upon Egypt and allows the Hebrews to walk dry-shod through the parted *Yam Suf.* This God is the familiar author of miraculous "deeds and wonders" to whom we pray every day.

IN SEARCH OF THE MIRACULOUS

For the fundamentalist Christian, the words of the Bible are to be understood literally. For even the most traditionalist of Jews, however, a literal reading of the Torah, the *peshat/plain meaning* of the text, is only one of several ways of reading the text and, for many of the Orthodox, not even the most important one. The *Tanakh* is only a starting point for understanding God in Jewish thought, and this is nowhere more obvious than in the interpretation of nonnatural phenomena, what we colloquially describe as "miracles." For the fundamentalist Christian, if God made the rules, that is, the laws of nature, then God can change or abrogate them as well. When God suspends the laws of gravity or alters the motion of bodies in space—the parting of the *Yam Suf/Sea of Reeds* by Moshe *in parashat Beshalakh*, for example, or the sun refusing to set at Gibeon in *Sefer Yehoshua*—that is within the realm of God's powers.

For the classical Jewish commentator, however, such "miracles" are hardwired into the system. In *Pirkei Avot*, the rabbis list ten things that God created just before the first Sabbath: 1) "the mouth of the earth" that swallowed the rebellious Korakh and his followers; 2) "the mouth of [Miriam's] well" that kept the Israelites supplied with water in the Wilderness; 3) "the mouth of the she-ass" that spoke to Balaam; 4) "the rainbow" that God showed Noakh as a sign of the pledge not to destroy the earth again; 5) "the manna"; 6) "the staff" that Moshe used to perform wonders; 7) "the *shamir*," a miraculous worm that cut the stones for the Temple; 8) and 9) "the letters" and "the writing" inscribed upon the Tablets that Moshe brought down from Sinai; and 10) the Tablets themselves. What this passage tells us is that many of the events that seem miraculous to humanity were provided for in the original act of Creation, that God had foreseen these eventualities and created the means by which events unfolded. So what we see as a series of miracles is nothing more than the workings of God's natural laws.

Intriguingly, as Yair Zakovich demonstrates at length, the Bible doesn't have a word that means "miracle," strictly speaking. The word *nes*, which is usually translated as "miracle" and will be familiar to anyone who has celebrated Hanukah, takes on that meaning only in postbiblical texts. Other words, such as *gedolot/great deeds* and *n'fla'ot*, which Zakovich says take in all God's works, the miraculous included, are used more infrequently. Clearly the concept of the "miracle" is a more complex one in the Torah itself than most of us imagine.

It is important to remember that ordinary human beings can perform magic in the Torah. Pharoah's advisers, after all, can transform their staffs into snakes, just as Moshe does. When Balak hires Balaam to put a curse on the Israelites, he does so because Balaam has a proven track record of working wonders. Wonder-working clearly is not even dependent on belief in the One God.

The Torah makes this point explicitly in *Devarim* 13:2–4: "If a prophet arises among you who gives a sign or wonder, and the sign or wonder comes to pass, but he desires to lead you into idolatry, you shall not hearken to that prophet, for *Adonai* your God [is testing] you whether you truly love *Adonai* your God." Miracles do not prove a religious truth; they can be performed on behalf of and by idolators and pagans.

Similarly, one cannot build faith in God on such a shaky foundation as the miraculous, as we learn when *B'nei Yisrael* are wandering in the Wilderness. When Moshe sends out the spies and they return with negative reports about Kina'an/Canaan, all but Yehoshua/Joshua and Kalev/Caleb appear to have forgotten that God has promised the land to them. These are men who have seen the miracles of manna and the pillars of fire and smoke, yet they don't trust in the power of the Almighty. Their faith is weak because it is predicated on the old principle, "What have you done for me lately?" When God stops manifesting the Divine Presence through miracles, they are unable to sustain belief. As Rabbi Pinchas Lipner writes, "The lack of faith on the part of the spies and the nation resulted from the fact that they had not achieved their faith by working on it or by struggling with it. . . ."

God may reveal the Divine Presence through the miraculous, but it is not miracles to which we must aspire, or for which we should hope. We were created "in the image of God" but we are not gods.

But what does it mean to be created in the image of God?

IN THE IMAGE OF GOD

When God decides to create the first man, the Creator tells the *malakhim/angels* (or *messengers*) that he will be created *"b'tzelem Elohim/in the image of God,"* a decision that has weighty consequences for us as human beings.

After all, God does not create any other creatures in this manner, that is, by themselves, one at a time, and in the image of the Creator. There is a presumption throughout the rest of the Torah and all the texts that follow that being created in the image of God carries with it a powerful charge of responsibilities. The entire Holiness Code is predicated on this presumption. Indeed, much of what we understand as human morality proceeds from the notion that we, created in God's image, must live by *imitatio dei/imitation of God*, imitating God in our behavior. "The fact that it has been revealed to us that we are made in [God's] image gives us the incentive to unfold the image and in so doing to imitate God," Martin Buber writes.

This is where the ethical part of "ethical monotheism" comes in. The notion is introduced, with the story of the Expulsion from *Gan Eden*, that behavior is judged and either rewarded or punished. God repeatedly warns the Hebrews in the Wilderness that failure to observe the commandments and strictures placed upon them in the Revelation at Sinai and henceforward will result in terrible chastisements. But the faithful observance of the commandments—the *mitzvot*—will be rewarded with the full bounty of the earth and sky, that is, rain in abundance and in season, resulting in successful farming, grazing, and life. (See "Water in Its Time" on page 70.)

From the first breach of God's commandments—the eating of the fruit of the tree of knowledge of good and evil—dire consequences are threatened. But God softens that threatened judgment, exchanging exile for a promised death. (Of course, the eating of the fruit and the Expulsion from *Gan Eden* do introduce mortality into human existence, so God's original sentence is not revoked, merely postponed.) Exile will become one of the running themes in the Torah: exile from *Gan Eden;* Kayin's enforced wanderings; Noakh's being cast adrift on an endless sea; Avraham's marching orders spoken by God; and the intricate dance of home/exile/home that is the story of the Patriarchs, slavery in Egypt, the Exodus, and the arrival at the border of Kina'an. It is with this last departure, the one that ends the Torah, that the book brings to fruition an elaborate set of connections between exile as punishment, God's Revelation of the true contract (i.e., the *mitzvot*), and the final redemption of *B'nei Yisrael*.

WATER IN ITS TIME

The Sinai Peninsula gets an average of forty millimeters of rainfall per year, about an inch and a half, and this is not all that atypical for the region. Needless to say, water is a scarce and valuable commodity in the Middle East. Understandably, water, rain, dew, and wells all figure prominently in the Torah.

Consider the case of Yitzkhak. He is seen throughout his brief time in *Sefer Bereishit* as a somewhat passive figure. His one significant proactive moment comes when he reopens the wells his father dug that were closed by the Philistines. Those wells represent a claim to greatness for both father and son; their digging is a selfless act that benefits any human being traveling in the desert. After all, it was the probability of death by thirst that led Hagar to place Yishmael out of her sight so that she wouldn't see him die, and it was a messenger of God who showed her the spring that mysteriously bubbled up near the child. In rocky, sandy desolation, water truly must seem heaven-sent.

Similarly, one of the wonders that Miriam bestows upon the Israelites as they wander in the Wilderness is her well, which follows them wherever they go. When she dies, the well ceases producing water and the Israelites are plunged into mourning for more reasons than the loss of a matriarchal figure.

Indeed, many of the disputes that dog Moshe and Aharon as they lead their people through the Sinai Desert center on water—or more accurately, a lack of water. There is the incident of the bitter waters of Marah and two separate incidents in which Moshe brings forth water from rocks, the latter of which will result in God barring him from entering Kina'an. And what is it that God promises the Israelites if they keep the *mitzvot?* Rain and dew in their proper time, a necessity for any agricultural society but doubly so for one that chooses to plant in an arid landscape.

Two of God's first acts in the Torah are to separate earth from water and day from night. God requires of us many acts of separation, small-scale versions of the great divisions that mark the Creation story. Throughout *Sefer Vayikra,* we are given detailed commandments regarding the separation of the pure from the impure, the permissible from the proscribed, the sacred from the quotidian. Consider some of the most basic tenets of Judaism:

- *Kashrut*—The dietary laws set apart certain animals that we are prohibited from eating. The prohibitions are generally based on certain taxonomic distinctions. For example, we can eat only animals that chew their own cud and have cloven hooves. Animals that do not qualify in one of these categories are forbidden. When faced with an animal that seemingly doesn't fit into one of the taxonomies available to them, the rabbis generally would prohibit eating it. Hence, the lobster, which lives in the water yet walks, which seems to be seafood yet has neither scales nor gills, falls between categories and therefore is not to be eaten. Even the highly arcane rules governing *sha'atnez/the mixing of wool and linen,* are derived from a similar separation of categories (see "*Sha'atnez:* The Mysterious *Mitzvah*" on page 72).
- *Ritual purity*—The consumption of blood, which the Torah considers to be the carrier of life, is to be avoided. So the rules governing ritual kosher slaughtering are designed to prevent us from consuming blood, and the priests who must be ritually pure are not permitted contact with the dead. Menstruating women and women who have recently given birth are considered ritually impure. (But see Chapter 5, "Hearing Silenced Voices: Women and the Torah.")
- *Havdalah*—The ceremony that marks the end of the Sabbath or a Festival specifically thanks God for separating sacred time from ordinary time. Indeed, the rules governing Shabbat may be seen as an elaborate series of rituals, prohibitions, and permissions designed to emphasize the division between the holy and the quotidian.

So when we observe Shabbat, we are not only emulating God in taking the seventh day for rest, we are also behaving *imitatio dei* by acknowledging that there are two different kinds of time that are marked off from one another.

How else can we be holy like the Holy One?

As the Holiness Code clearly tells us, we must love mercy and do justice. The Prophets will amplify these commandments to emphasize the social action component of Jewish practice in the later books of the Hebrew Bible. After them, other sages will speak of *tikkun olam/repairing the world,* doing whatever can be done by human means to speed the redemption of a flawed and unredeemed world. Hillel, most famously, will boil it down to one sentence, "That which is hateful to you, do not do to others," and will tell an unbeliever that this is the entire Torah, "the rest is commentary, go and study."

But if the world is unredeemed and we are, most certainly, imperfect, we will err in many ways, some inadvertent, others deliberate. Right from the start, Adam and Khavah make a terrible decision and it leads to the first of many exiles, this one from *Gan Eden.*

SHA'ATNEZ: THE MYSTERIOUS MITZVAH

In *Vayikra* 19:19 Jews are forbidden to wear clothing made from a mixture of wool and linen or to sow their fields with a mixture of two species of seeds. They are also prohibited from mating different species of animals and from yoking them together (behind a plow, for example). It takes no great imagination to understand the prohibitions regarding animals; it would be cruel to yoke together animals that greatly differ in size and strength, since one of them is going to get dragged along, perhaps even choked.

But the linen-and-wool ban is mystifying. Rashi, the great medieval Bible commentator, admits that he cannot find an explanation for it. Still, even today Orthodox Jews will submit garments for a *sha'atnez* test to make sure that they do not contain this forbidden mixture.

Edward L. Greenstein, a former professor of Bible at the Jewish Theological Seminary who is now teaching at Tel Aviv University, offers a possible answer. In the initial act of creation, God established categories, classes of things, species. Greenstein cites Joseph Bekhor Shor, the twelfth-century Bible commentator and a student of Rashi's, who suggested a ban on all hybrids: "Do not sow your orchard with two kinds [of seed], lest the sum of the seed which you have sown and the produce of the orchard become consecrated." In short, by combining or cross-breeding species, humans usurp the act of Creation by making something that the first Creator didn't.

EXILE

The first time that God speaks to Avraham, who will be the first propo-
nent of monotheism, the first of the Patriarchs, and, by extension, father
of the Jews, the Holy One says, "Go forth from your land, from your
birthplace, and from your father's home to the land that I will show you."
In short, go into exile to perform a task for me.

Avraham is not the first human to be sent into exile. On the contrary,
exile occurs so frequently in the Torah that one has a nagging suspicion
that it is the assigned portion of all humanity, to be ripped up from one's
roots and to wander the face of the earth. Adam and Khavah are expelled
from *Gan Eden,* Kayin is condemned to wander the earth, Noakh and his
family are literally set adrift on a raging sea, and the builders of the Tower
of Babel are scattered across the globe.

And the litany of exiles doesn't end with Avraham. Indeed, alone
among his antecedents, Yitzkhak lives his life in his home and dies there.
But Ya'akov and Eisav, Yosef and all his brothers, and, over the next four
hundred years, their descendants, the Hebrews, are forced into or born
into exile. (The repeated patterns of sin, exile, and reconciliation with
God underline quite artfully the thematic/religious message of the Torah.
As we shall see later in this chapter, they do so in highly complex and brilliantly worked-out narrative structures.)

One could argue that nomadism is mankind's lot. Bruce Chatwin
erected an entire theory of human history around the tension between the
desire to wander and the urge to sink roots. Blaise Pascal said that man's
greatest tragedy was "his inability to sit quietly in a room."

But Judaism is unique in making exile an article of religious doctrine.
Galut is at once punishment—Adam and Khavah, Kayin, the builders at
Babel, Moshe fleeing after his murder of the Egyptian taskmaster—and a
step toward revelation and redemption. If the first man and woman are
not ejected from *Gan Eden,* then the entire history of humanity cannot
take place. If Noakh does not find himself adrift in the ark, the human
race will not survive. God's command to Avram to *"lekh lekha / go forth"* is
the necessary prelude to his discovering monotheism for himself and
beginning to spread its teachings. Ya'akov must flee his home to go to
Haran before he can be vouchsafed the vision of the ladder, the promise of

the Covenant, the wives with whom he will found a nation. And Yosef, his favorite son, must be sent into slavery in Egypt so that his brothers and father can survive the famine. Finally, it is only when they are in the wilderness of Sinai that the Israelites are privileged to receive the Revelation at the mountain that is the heart of the Covenant—the *mitzvot* and all they entail. And the revelations of the desert come with an explicit warning that the Israelites will transgress again and be scattered to the four corners of the earth once more.

This pattern, which runs throughout the Torah, continues in Jewish thought long after the events in the first five books of the *Tanakh* have concluded. The destruction of the First Temple and the Babylonian exile are a prelude to the Israelites rediscovering the Torah and the commandments. And traditionally observant Jews believe that it will only be with the ingathering of the exiles from the four corners of the earth that the Messianic Age will finally be made possible.

God has made promises to humanity and to *B'nei Yisrael,* and those promises, made to us in exile, call for a quid pro quo of sorts. Walter E. and Fay Sand Reed titled their book on the Torah *Contract with God,* and that is, indeed, what the Patriarchs, Moshe, and the Israelites secured. That contract, the Covenant, is the center of all Jewish thought. Its culmination is the end of exile and the end of its concomitant—human mortality. When the Messianic Age arrives, even death will be reversed and suspended forever.

THE COVENANT(S)

In fact, God makes several Covenants with humanity over the course of the Torah (and at least one more significant one with King David later in the Hebrew Bible). As the successive Covenants are stated, the number of human participants narrows. Thus, we move from an initial agreement between God and Adam and, by implication, all humanity, to a second one between God and Noakh, taking in those who adhere to seven basic laws (see "The Noahide Laws" on page 77). Then God makes a promise to Avraham that will extend to his offspring, the twelve tribes that will spring from the loins of Ya'akov, that is, *B'nei Yisrael.* In this way, by the time the Israelites witness God's Revelation at Sinai and accept the Covenant by saying "We will do and we will hear," God's Covenant has become the property of an entire nation. Of course, they are required to do something in return for the promise of *Eretz Yisrael,* but we will come to that part of the bargain shortly. The later pledges do not supersede the earlier ones—in Jewish thought one needn't be a Jew to be a righteous person.

Not surprisingly, the Covenant between God and *B'nei Yisrael* as stated in the Torah has its roots in the legal practices of the Ancient Near East. As we will see in greater detail later in this chapter, the language of the Covenant is not all that different from that of more mundane legal documents of the time and region. (Is this an indicator that God is not the author of the Torah? Perhaps God merely chooses to address humanity in language it will understand. Regardless, this is an issue we will delve into at great length in Chapter 3.)

A key element in the rites that secured a Covenant in the Ancient Near East was an exchange of blood between vassal and suzerain. By mingling their blood, the vassal pledged to fulfill certain obligations specified in the language of the Covenant; the sovereign implicitly promised his protection to his subjects. God and Avraham make a similar exchange of promises in *Bereishit* 17. God promises that Avram will father a mighty nation that will endure for generations to come, secure in the Covenant, and that the Almighty will deliver to his offspring the land of Kina'an. In return, Avram takes on a new name—Avraham—that is a signifier of his changed status and, more important, circumcises himself, his sons, and his servants, and pledges that his offspring will continue to observe the rite of circumcision down through the ages.

Hence, with the rite of circumcision, the Covenant is sealed with a drawing of blood.[3] Yet this is not merely a vestigial remnant of the old ritual mingling of blood. Rather, it means that the fact of the Covenant is inscribed on the very flesh of a Jewish man from his eighth day of life. And the use of circumcision as a metaphor elsewhere in the *Tanakh* serves as a powerful reminder of the importance of this ritual. When Moshe tries to beg off the task of leading the Hebrews out of bondage, he tells God (manifested in the burning bush) that he is, according to most translations, "slow of speech." But the literal meaning of the phrase used is that he has "an uncircumcised tongue." When Moshe in his final speech to *B'nei Yisrael* tells them of God's promises, he says that when the Covenant is fulfilled, "Then *Adonai* your God will circumcise your heart and the hearts of your offspring so that you will love *Adonai* your God with all your heart and soul" (*Devarim* 30:6). A similarly metaphorical use of circumcision to mean removing an obstruction in one's heart occurs several times in the prophetic writings as well.

What makes the Covenant between God and the Israelites so powerful? God's pledge, for all the threats that it contains regarding humanity's failure to live up to its part of the bargain, represents nothing less than an acceptance of humanity as it is—flawed, ambivalent, even downright bad. (What does God pledge to Noakh? That the Eternal will never again destroy the earth and its inhabitants by flood because of the wrongdoing of human beings.) God places the "yoke of the *mitzvot*" upon humanity, and that is a not inconsiderable burden, yet the Almighty also recognizes that this burden cannot be fulfilled. Moreover, God has given us free will. As Arnold Eisen deftly notes, "A moral God who seeks a moral world, *[Adonai]* has created humanity free to disobey."

Although that disobedience usually takes negative forms, human will can also call on the Supreme Being to examine Divine morality. Avraham can bargain for the lives of the people of Sodom—fifty righteous ones? Forty? Ten?—and Moshe can negotiate with God to keep the Israelites alive in the desert, even when their sins are terrible.

Eisen expresses what he calls the simultaneous "terror of the *brit* . . . and its comfort" in powerful terms:

> The awesome creator of mankind is brought into the human camp, demanding a degree of ethical and ritual purity that mere mortals are hard pressed to achieve. Yet the *mysterium tremendum* is thereby rendered accessible and, to a degree, comprehensible. Israel cannot penetrate the fire and cloud of God's presence, but the people can know what God wants of them. Even more remarkably they can rest confident that God will submit to the seeming indignity of human conversation. [God] will negotiate, with Abraham, over the destruction of Sodom, and agree, after the pleading of Moses, to pardon the transgressions of Israel.

There is, then, another concomitant to the bargain. We are not expected to be blameless. We are supposed to observe the *mitzvot* (to which we will turn momentarily). But when we fail, there is still the opportunity for repentance. If you trace the behavior of God toward humanity in the Torah, it is not hard to find examples of stern punishments meted out swiftly; but it is equally easy to cite examples of punishment mitigated. If the concept of *teshuvah/repentance or returning to God* is primarily post-biblical in its articulation in Jewish thought, the roots of it—and the roots of God's forgiveness—are already present in the Almighty's decision not to kill Adam and Khavah, to protect Kayin in his exile, to permit the Israelites to survive the desert despite the sin of the *Eigel Zahav / Golden Calf* and to grant them the land that was promised. Even the threat of future expulsion so darkly held over their heads at the end of *Sefer Devarim* is accompanied by the promise of free will: "Choose life, that you and your offspring may live." (But see "Free Will or Not?" on page 78.)

The Covenant with the Israelites, while of paramount importance, is only exclusive to the extent that the human signatories follow the *mitzvot*. More than that, it is not God's only Covenant with humanity. The Covenants with Adam and Noakh still are in force and, as we see in chapter 2 of *Sefer Devarim,* even the promise of land is not given solely to the Israelites. As Maimonides puts it, "Know that the Lord desires the heart, and the intention of the heart is the measure of all things. This is why, our sages say, the pious among the Gentiles have a share in the world to come. There is no doubt that everyone who ennobles the soul with excellent morals and wisdom based on faith in God certainly belongs to the ones of the world to come."

We are all offspring of the Creation, sons and daughters of Adam and Khavah. Yet the Israelites are chosen to receive a special Covenant, one that places a unique set of demands upon them, the *mitzvot*.

THE NOAHIDE LAWS

In God's Covenant with Noakh in the aftermath of the Flood, the Creator extracts certain promises from him. The seven precepts to which Noakh agrees became known as the Noahide laws. Non-Jews are encouraged to follow these guidelines. They are:

1. Do not murder.
2. Do not steal.
3. Do not worship false gods.
4. Do not practice sexual immorality.
5. Do not eat the limb of an animal before it is killed.
6. Do not curse God.
7. Set up courts and bring offenders to justice.

FREE WILL OR NOT

Does humanity have free will? Given the omnipotence and omniscience of God, does it make sense to say yes? The Torah doesn't give a clear-cut answer to these questions, with the result that Jewish thinkers have been debating them ever since.

Clearly, God is the supreme actor in human history, but it would seem that humans have some degree of agency as well. God's reaction to the building of the Tower of Babel suggests that this human act was contrary to the desires of the Almighty; hence it became necessary for God to thwart this nefarious plan. Obviously, with the emphasis of the story of the Exodus from Egypt so heavily on persuading Pharoah to free the Hebrew slaves from bondage, there must be some concept of human will at work in the text.

Yet how did the Hebrews come to be in Egypt? They are there by God's design, at the end of the elaborate working out of Yosef's story. The implication here, almost but not quite stated in the text itself, is that God has a plan that surpasses not only human understanding but also human life expectancy. And the Hebrews will be in Egypt for four hundred years while God does not respond to their cries of agony.

Still, the Hebrews in the Wilderness continually disappoint not only Moshe but God as well. Does God intend the incident of the Golden Calf? Why does the Eternal permit Moshe to argue many times against God's intentions to punish the Israelites? These stories suggest a God who permits independent human action. And Moshe's instructions to the Hebrews at the end of his life—"Choose life that you and your offspring may live"—clearly presumes a degree of choice.

Ultimately, we cannot unravel this dilemma, whether we draw solely on the Torah or have recourse to later texts. Perhaps the best answer is something I said jokingly to a rabbi after a congregational discussion on just this topic: "If you knew you didn't have free will, would it make you act any differently?"

THE *MITZVOT*

What are *mitzvot* (sing., *mitzvah*)? The word is usually translated as "commandment," although it also has come to mean "good deed" colloquially. If you want a dictionary definition, then a *mitzvah* is an act having a religious significance, commanded to humanity by God through the medium of the Torah. That is putting it drily, defining one of the central concepts of Judaism without capturing any of its resonance, its nuance. Rabbi Arthur Lelyveld has written, "The word Mitzvah, writ large and uttered reverently, means an act which I perform because God requires it of me." Rabbi David Hartman takes it a step further: "The mitzvot are not abstract demands implied by a Platonic form or a Kantian categorical imperative; they are demands made by a personal will and presuppose a personal relationship to God."

In short, the *mitzvot* are the other end of God's deal with the Israelites, the obligation that comes with Revelation and the promise of *Eretz Yisrael*. Although the rabbis who counted up the *mitzvot* enumerated in the Torah, coming up with the number 613, include several commandments that appear in the Torah before the Revelation at Sinai ("Be fruitful and multiply" generally being considered the first), the bulk of them are given at Sinai and in the Wilderness, given directly by God or through Moshe. (A few are inferred, such as the *mitzvah* of writing a Torah scroll.)

What is the purpose of the *mitzvot*? This is the subject of much analysis and debate among Jewish thinkers. Certainly they help forge a community out of the quarrelsome tribes of Israel (as we shall see momentarily), giving them a commonality of mission to go with their shared desires. Even today, some of the most fundamental religious requirements of Judaism help reinforce our sense of belonging to an extended family—communal prayer, comforting the bereaved, rejoicing with bride and groom, visiting the sick.

Yet at the same time, the *mitzvot* also set the Hebrews apart from other peoples. Indeed, one of the principal themes of the second half of the Torah is creating a distinction between the monotheistic *B'nei Yisrael*, "a nation of priests," and their pagan neighbors. Many of the *mitzvot* that seem baffling to us—the strictures governing the cutting of hair and beards, the prohibition against tattoos, even some of the rules governing sexual conduct—have their roots in an attempt to distinguish the conduct of the Israelites from that of idolators whose worship practices included tattooing, ritual-related tonsorial and facial hairstyles, and even human sacrifice.

As we have seen, the notion of separation runs throughout the Torah, almost from God's first act in *Bereishit*. God separates day from night, waters from waters, waters from the heavens, and so on. Similarly, many of the *mitzvot* are about separations between sacred and profane—the Sabbath from the rest of the week, permitted foodstuffs from prohibited, permitted behaviors from forbidden. Taken in that thematic context, many of the more obscure elements of *halakhah*—for example, the dietary laws or the prohibition regarding mixing linen and wool—make a bit more sense. Indeed, there are whole volumes dedicated to making sense of the *mitzvot*, explaining their etiology and purpose.

There are, on the other hand, at least a few Jewish thinkers who believe that "making a bit of sense" of the *mitzvot* is entirely alien to God's intentions. The most eloquent and occasionally strident of them is Yeshayahu Leibowitz, the brilliant scientist and Torah scholar who is perhaps better known for his controversial positions in defense of human rights in the Middle East and his denunciation of the Israeli occupation of the West Bank and Gaza. In a startling and impressively reasoned essay, Leibowitz has argued that "every reason given for the mitzvot that bases itself on human needs . . . voids the mitzvot of all religious meaning."

Leibowitz argues that if the *mitzvot* "are the expression of philosophic knowledge, or if they have any ethical content, or if they are meant to benefit society, or if they are meant to maintain the Jewish people," all of which are traditional explanations for them, then "he whom performs them serves not God but himself, his society or his people." Thus a tradesman who fulfills the *mitzvah* of not using false weights because of a sense of ethical commitment to fair dealing with his customers has decentered the meaning of the commandment from serving God to serving other human beings. There is no Kantian categorical imperative operating here (and Leibowitz specifically dismisses Kant for his atheism); the imperative is to serve God.

Consequently, in Leibowitz's interpretation, one fulfills the *mitzvot* to serve God and only to serve God. The *mitzvot* are an expression of God's will; to follow them is to follow God's will in service of that will. It is this, he argues, that makes Judaism a concrete faith "grounded in a complex of well-defined religious deeds and ritual practices." For him, only a strict adherence to the letter of the law serves God. Yet he also says that the Torah "is divine, not human," and therefore no one can fulfill the commandments perfectly.

What is missing from Leibowitz's equation, I think, is a key aspect of the role of free will, granted by God. We have not only the will to reject the *mitzvot,* which Leibowitz would readily acknowledge, but also the will, indeed, the desire and necessity, to interpret the *mitzvot.* All too frequently, the *mitzvot* as outlined in the Torah are obscure, abstruse, even opaque. The rabbinic sages began to interpret the *mitzvot* in the Mishnah and Gemara, and continued doing so in subsequent commentaries on the Talmud and, in commentaries on those commentaries. In other words, Jews have for hundreds of years been reading, rereading, and reinterpreting the *mitzvot* in an attempt to understand the will of the Eternal, to make the commandments make sense for an always-changing world. Without getting into a lengthy wrangle over changing standards in *halakhah* and the degree to which it binds us today, there is certainly a proliferation of understandings of the *mitzvot,* and that growth was and remains something of a necessity.

Whether one accepts Leibowitz's understanding of the *mitzvot* or not (and reading him, you really begin to understand the phrase "yoke of the *mitzvot*" as a daunting kind of self-willed bondage), this last point is obviously true. And it takes us back to one of our initial premises, that the God of the Torah is finally unknowable by human beings. Maimonides says that even a perfect individual who fulfills all the *mitzvot* possible (keeping in mind that many of them were predicated on the existence of the Temple in Jerusalem and therefore have no force today) would still be prevented from achieving complete oneness with God; that person's failing would be that she is a human, mortal, and therefore grounded in the material world, "an intelligence grounded in matter." Ultimately, whatever our reasons for performing *mitzvot,* we may serve God but never see or understand God.

However, if I may be permitted one small aside, it is in the *mitzvot* that we can find the answer to the question with which this chapter opened: Why do we read the Torah over and over? When Ezra read the Torah to the Israelites in 444 B.C.E., the people clamored for more; reading the Torah aloud to them was a way of reaffirming the Covenant (and fulfilling one of the *mitzvot*). When we sit in synagogue and hear the Torah read on Shabbat, on Monday, and on Thursday, we, too, reaffirm the Covenant.

FROM ONE MAN TO A FAMILY, FROM A FAMILY TO TWELVE TRIBES

The initial unit of humanity in the Torah is the single individual, Adam. Of course, God gives Adam a partner, Khavah, almost immediately, and they quickly become the first family, giving birth to Kayin and Hevel. And, as we have seen already, the Covenant goes through several variations as the human parties to this contract with God grow in number. The initial version of the contract may be between God and all humanity, but with the advent of Avram/Avraham, it becomes more specifically a contract with a family and then with a single nation (albeit a nation without a home).

Similarly, the focus of the Torah itself shifts from the seeds of all humanity—first Adam, then Noakh and his children, who are, after all, a second starting point for the human race—then to a single family, the Patriarchal/Matriarchal line, before turning its attention to *Am Yisrael.*

As a result, one of the key motifs in the Torah—and one of the few that doesn't directly involve God for the most part—is the interactions of family units. Those family units are invariably dysfunctional.

The desire to have a family, to perpetuate not only the human race but one's own lineage, is strong, perhaps rooted as much in the necessities of a primitive agrarian and pastoral economy as in some primal need to propagate the species or to fulfill God's very first commandment to humans, "be fruitful and multiply." As a result, the recurring theme of barrenness (Sarah's, Rivkah's, Rakhel's) takes on a tremendous force—economic, tribal, and personal. To not have children is to be as good as dead (Bereishit 30:1) and, consequently, threats to the well-being of children carry a particularly intense terror.

So it is painfully ironic that, although family is a crucial reality in the Torah, crucial enough for God to enjoin us to honor our parents, it is also a site of terrible conflict, including direct threats of violence and actual murder. Kayin kills Hevel, ending the first sibling rivalry. Firstborn sons are repeatedly divested of their hereditary rights: Yishmael, Eisav, Re'uven, Menasheh. In an age in which primogeniture is a general rule, this is pretty radical stuff, almost as radical as the idea of worshipping a single, invisible deity. To undermine the rights of the firstborn would seem to go hand in hand with rejecting paganism. Yet the Patriarchs are, for the most part, not very successful parents. But for all the parental missteps—

playing favorites among offspring being only the most glaring—and frat-
ricidal rage, the familial tensions are ultimately resolved peaceably, if not
always happily. Perhaps God's disposal of Kayin's case, another punishment of exile, served as a cautionary tale.

So Yishmael and Yitzkhak come together to bury Avraham alongside
his wife. Ya'akov and Eisav embrace by the banks of the Yabok. Yosef's
brothers do not kill him, and he reciprocates later by not seeking revenge
for their crimes against his person. Blood unites, a very important idea
in a world of tribal cultures. Perhaps it is this very quality—the ability
to put aside even murderous rage and draw together as a family—that
God sought when he chose Avraham and his descendants to receive the
Covenant and to grow into His chosen nation.

At the same time, it also points to an aspect of the Creator that is frequently invoked as a metaphor in the liturgy of all the major Western faith
traditions—God as Supreme Parent. All of the members of my Torah
study group are parents (except me), and each of them responds instinc-
tively to the idea that God acquires parenting skills as the story in the Book
unfolds. Over and over we see God doling out praise, comfort, and encour-
agement on the one hand, and then scolding and punishing on the other.
It is as if the Eternal One knows that the parental role is one that humans
can understand and appreciate, a facet of the Ineffable that is somehow
comprehensible to us. So it is that in the course of Ya'akov's heartbreak-
ingly sad lifetime, a lifetime littered with tragedy, loss, and moral uncertainty, God appears to him on four occasions, at those moments when he
most needs to have his sense of mission, of the Covenant, renewed and
bolstered. When the flesh-and-blood parents of the Torah are unable to
ease the fears of their children, some One greater does.

FROM RABBLE IN ARMS TO A NATION OF PRIESTS

It is one of the questions that irks casual readers of the Torah: Why do we
have to suffer through the long description of the building of the *Mishkan*
that runs through five *parashiyot* of *Sefer Shemot*? This *Popular Mechanics*
lesson in sanctuary building makes for rather drab reading, particularly
given how repetitive it becomes. For example, we are treated to two successive enumerations of the contributions of each of the twelve tribes,
even though their donations are identical in the smallest detail.

Yet one could argue that this seemingly endless digression is actually central to the second half of the Torah. The description of the *Mishkan* is separated from the account of its construction by one of the most painful narrative incidents in the Wilderness journey, the manufacture of the Golden Calf. The actual building and dedication of the *Mishkan* can be seen as an elaborate atonement for that terrible transgression, and it is an atonement in kind, collecting gold and other goods from the Israelites to create an object whose purpose is religious in nature. Where the Golden Calf is a disastrous attempt to find an idolatrous substitute for the invisible *Adonai,* the *Mishkan* is an enormously elaborate glorification of the Eternal One.

More than that, though, the building of the *Mishkan* is an activity that draws on the gifts and the labors of everyone in the encampment and forges a nation-in-formation out of a rebellious, obstreperous rabble. The Torah does not use words lightly, and the extraordinary detail with which this episode is recounted serves to underline the communal nature of the contributions and the efforts. Slowly, with the construction of this glorious Tabernacle, the Israelites are also constructing themselves. As human labor transforms nature's raw materials into something else, something new, so these acts of human labor transform the laborers into something they haven't been before—a community. And because the goal of this project is, finally, the exaltation of God, it is the logical first step on the road to becoming what the Creator has told them they will be, "a nation of priests" consecrated to God.

The Israelites are, after all, not much more than an enormous dysfunctional family, several generations of the offspring of the sons and grandsons of Ya'akov. But they must be welded into a nation of free men and women from a band of ex-slaves who live in the ambivalent mixture of fear of the future and the desire to return to Egypt and bondage. The last half of the Torah is about this transformation, begun with the *Mishkan* and carried out through tests of will and endurance in the Wilderness.

At the end of the Torah, the Israelites are a nation that has defended itself successfully against hostile neighbors, survived thirst and hunger, and worked together for shared goals. They are ready to accept the fruits of the Covenant, to enter the land God has promised to them, and to conquer it for themselves.

HOW THE STORY IS TOLD

For the religious believer of whatever denomination of Judaism, the themes and stories contained in the Torah are what make it a living document after all these centuries. For the nonbeliever who recognizes it as a great literary work, the book lives on because it is brilliantly structured and written. In truth, both are right, and that combination of form and content is what makes the Torah compelling, a book that we reread every year with renewed interest.

A story is more than the summation of its plot and themes. The meaning of a story is inseparable from how it is told. Andrew Sarris, who was my primary mentor when I was beginning to write about film, offers the slightly tongue-in-cheek example of two film versions of the story of Little Red Riding Hood. "If the story . . . is told with the Wolf in close-up and Little Red Riding Hood in long-shot, the director is concerned primarily with the emotional problems of a wolf with a compulsion to eat little girls. If Little Red Riding Hood is in close-up and the Wolf is in long-shot, the emphasis is shifted to the emotional problems of vestigial virginity in a wicked world."[4] One could also tell the story from the point of view of Granny, focusing on the vulnerability of the elderly, or the Woodsman, in a version that could be either an allegory of Labor and Capital or a meditation on the hardships of self-employment. You get the joke.

But it's not really a joke at all. Form and content are not so easily separated and, as we shall see in the remainder of this chapter, narrative choices in the Torah have a tremendous impact on our understanding of the text. Indeed, the highly elliptical nature of biblical narrative to the major body of Jewish texts that are devoted to the interpretation of the Torah.

More than that, studying narrative structure gives us an entrée into understanding the Torah in a way that doesn't require access to the vast library of Jewish commentary (which we will get to later). It can even make the text somewhat more transparent to a reader who has little or no Hebrew (a definite handicap, but not utterly disabling). It's a bit like deciphering a novel or a film set in a culture we don't know well; we can still understand the relationships and the basic plot, although there are nuances that a native of that culture would immediately "get" that we will miss.

Think for a moment of the Torah as a motion picture. The narrative line of this movie is relatively linear; there are no flashbacks or flashforwards, strictly speaking. However, there are frequent hints of events to come, foreshadowings of disaster and triumph. And there are even more frequent reminders of events that have already taken place, promises made, deeds done or undone, old enmities unhealed.

Time in the Torah is somewhat elastic, as in the movies. There are cascades of events that are compressed into a few sentences. For example, the genealogies that are used almost as punctuation throughout *Sefer Bereishit* work as transitions in which whole generations are dealt with in a blur of births, deaths, and life spans; they are like those montage sequences in older films in which calendar leaves are blown away, or a series of newspaper headlines appear, giving us several months' worth of information in a few seconds. As Franziska Bark puts it, "The genealogies function to gather up time until the story has reached the protagonist of a narrated event." Then there are the individual story arcs within each book, which can be extraordinarily detailed. The story of Yosef and his brothers is the length and complexity of a novella, with enough psychological verisimilitude for a nineteenth-century novel (albeit with a lot less sociological and historical detail).

In a sense, the manipulations of time in the Torah are a reflection of the contrasting nature of time as experienced by God and by humanity. For God, as the psalmist has it, a thousand years are but as the blink of an eye. For humanity, a thousand years are the life spans of a dozen generations. The Torah, from both necessity and art, gives us a certain double perspective, allowing us to see the events as they unfold in linear fashion, yet placing them in a literally cosmic time frame, from Creation to an implied redemption. At the same time this double perspective recapitulates the tension that runs through the entire Torah (indeed, the entire *Tanakh*) between God's omnipotence and human free will. Time always moves forward inexorably but not steadily, and we have cause to ponder what has gone before and what will come after.

In the Talmud, the rabbis suggest that there is no past or future in the Torah, no chronology, as if everything were always happening all at once, and many of the classical commentators build on that idea in interesting and often startling ways. Yet there is a linear movement of time in the

Torah and it is this movement, as manipulated by the author(s)/editor(s), that gives the book much of its force. Of course, we watch as the Patriarchs and Matriarchs grow from children to adults, from vigor to senescence, and we are moved. But more than that the Torah is structured around a dense thicket of internal echoes and allusions that draw us back and shove us forward in the story, all the more so with each successive reading of the text, when we know what will happen and how it is depicted.

The text itself is almost never judgmental. The author(s)/editor(s) almost never moralize. But one can feel their disapproval and approval powerfully through their use of those allusions and echoes. For example, as Bruce Feiler points out in his book *Abraham,* the text uses the same verb meaning "to afflict" to describe Sarai's treatment of Hagar and the Egyptians' abuse of the Israelites. Similarly, when Hagar flees from Sarai it is to the Wilderness of Shur, the first stop the Israelites make after crossing the *Yam Suf.* Or, to offer a favorite example of my own, the Hebrew word for Noakh's boat, *teivah,* appears only one other time in the Torah, when it is used to indicate the basket in which Moshe is placed when he is set adrift in the Nile. In each of these three cases, the intent and moral position of the narrator is implicit but utterly clear.

The pattern of echoes and allusions frequently extends well beyond single words. As Robert Alter notes, "Parallel acts or situations are used to comment on each other in biblical narrative." Alter points out in his seminal 1981 book, *The Art of Biblical Narrative,* that there is an entire category of scenes that are prescribed by literary conventions, the biblical equivalent to the cinematic showdown on a western street or the flight to the "green world" in Shakespearean comedy. Given the conventional nature of these recurring type-scenes, as they are called, every deviation from formula, every element that differentiates them from one another, should be examined with special interest.

Here is a particularly telling example from Alter. In the Patriarchal chronicles and in the story of Moshe, there is a type-scene involving the betrothal of the "hero." It generally involves an encounter at a well between the soon-to-be fiancée and a young male stranger, with the stranger being brought home to meet the family, leading to an engagement. This type-scene occurs three times in the Torah, when Avraham's servant seeks a wife for Yitzkhak, when Ya'akov encounters Rakhel, and when Moshe meets Tzipora/Zipporah.

In each of these three scenes, a young man (or his surrogate in the case of Yitzkhak) goes to a foreign land and encounters a beautiful young woman at a well. Water is drawn in such a way as to establish a bond between the male stranger and the young woman, which is followed by an excited rush home (expressed in a headlong tumbling series of terse verbs). Hospitality is extended, a bargain is struck, and a betrothal takes place. But while all three scenes fit this basic template, each differs from the other two in telling ways.

From the very start, the initial version of this scene stands apart from its two successors in an obvious way: the male seeking a woman is not the groom-to-be but a servant of the future father-in-law. So we know implicitly that Yitzkhak is passive, either unable or unwilling to take action for himself. One senses from the dialogue in which Avraham instructs the servant—later tradition calls him Eliezer, so we will do the same—that the boy/man is overprotected.

Eliezer stations himself near the well toward evening and waits for the local females to come and draw water. Rivkah turns up, waters his camels, and identifies herself. Eliezer gives her jewelry, she runs home, her brother Lavan comes out to welcome the stranger, brings him home and feeds him, and a betrothal is negotiated.

What also separates this scene from the two that follow is that Rivkah is the only woman in the three versions who actually draws water for the stranger. In fact, as Alter notes, she is a churning vessel of activity, the subject of eleven verbs of action and one of speech in her brief introductory scene. In this respect, her first appearance and its contrast with Yitzkhak's absence anticipates the trajectory of their marriage, with Rivkah not only participating in but engineering the scheme to secure Ya'akov his aging father's blessing. Lavan's appearance in this first version of the scene also offers a hint of his later behavior. When he sees how his sister has been festooned with jewelry by this mysterious stranger, his eyes light up like a slot machine hitting the jackpot.

How apt, then, that the second version of this type-scene involves Ya'akov, Lavan's nephew, and will lead to a series of reversals for the younger man that are clearly intended to represent payback for his treatment of Eisav and Yitzkhak. Even the scene itself presents Ya'akov with tests that Eliezer is spared. Unlike the servant, he comes empty-handed, with only his staff and the clothes on his back. The well he finds is not in the town but in the fields (appropriate to the story of his servitude to Lavan, with its complicated series of intrigues involving animal husbandry and agricultural wealth), and its mouth is covered by a stone that he must remove, much as he will later have to wrestle with the mysterious stranger by the banks of the Yabok.

At the same time, as Alter writes, this is a more personal story than the first type-scene, with Ya'akov smitten by Rakhel's beauty and almost immediately resolved to marry her. By contrast, we know nothing about Rivkah's appearance or, in the final version of this type-scene, Tzipora's either.

What about Moshe's encounter at the well? This version is the "most compact," Alter points out. Unlike his predecessors in the Patriarchal chronicles, Moshe has not been sent specifically in search of someone—he is fleeing a probable manslaughter charge. And unlike the two previous versions of the scene in which endogamy—marriage within the tribe—is the result, Moshe will find a Midianite bride. Aptly enough, unlike Eliezer and Ya'akov's, his greeting is less than cordial; he must fight off a group of male shepherds, defending the seven daughters of Yitro at the well, before drawing water for their flocks. The scene underlines his alienness—he is, after all, an Israelite raised as an Egyptian prince—as well as his quick temper and willingness to engage in fisticuffs. And when he is given Tzipora in marriage, little is made of the choice of daughter. We can see here how a creative author can take a scene dictated by the literary convention and, by creating subtle variations within it, make each repetition of that scene carry enormous thematic and psychological weight. And this is an example of biblical narrative at work for which a reader doesn't need any knowledge of Hebrew at all!

Here is another example of how narrative structure in the Torah can convey additional meaning. Depending on how you read his motives, Ya'akov either tricks his brother into selling him the birthright for a bowl of lentil stew and some bread, or Eisav is so uncaring that he unthinkingly agrees to the sale. Ya'akov, with the aid or at the behest of his mother, Rivkah, then tricks his bedridden, aged father, Yitzkhak, into giving him the blessing intended for the firstborn Eisav, again using food as the catalyst for the deception. But when Ya'akov flees to Haran in anticipation of his brother's deadly rage, the tables are turned on him by Lavan, who is, significantly, Rivkah's brother. Just as Yitzkhak was tricked in bed, so is Ya'akov, when Lavan gives him the wrong sister—his daughter Leah, instead of the previously agreed-upon daughter, Rakhel (anticipating the "bed trick" beloved of Greek comedy and Shakespeare). When Ya'akov confronts his uncle with the deception, Lavan tells him, "It is not the custom here to marry the younger daughter before the elder," which can only be read as an ironic and biting thrust at Ya'akov the trickster, who did his older brother out of his inheritance. (Yitzkhak and Leah are also linked by references to their "tender" eyes.) Finally, Ya'akov will get the last laugh, after a fashion, by manipulating the mating habits of Lavan's sheep to his own economic advantage, a distinct echo of his use of the goatskin to deceive Yitzkhak into giving him the firstborn's blessing. When all is said and done, this story has a structural complexity and richness that Balzac would envy.

But when we factor in the linguistic elements, it becomes even denser. To do that we need to add a little Hebrew. One of the key methods by which the Torah achieves its literary effects is through the use of word-play, and the story of Ya'akov offers an excellent example.

Ya'akov gets his name because he comes out of Rivkah's womb grabbing his brother's heel, *akev* in Hebrew. But as a verb, the three-letter root of the word, *ayin-kof-vet,* means "to overreach," with a strong negative connotation. And a related word, *akov,* which rhymes with Ya'akov, means "deceitful" or "crooked." So the name could be translated correctly as "he will deceive."

A more than faint aroma of unfair dealing clings to Ya'akov throughout the first half of his story, integrally related to his striving to get ahead of his brother, literally from birth. But after he has undergone his terrible trials with Lavan and his life-altering confrontation with the stranger at the River Yabok (another deliberate echo of his name), Ya'akov is given a new name, Yisrael, meaning "one who has striven with God," and his old trait is given a new, and much more positive, connotation. Only then can he finally make his piece with Eisav and move on with his life and mission. (Significantly, as Connie Heymann pointed out to me, from now on Ya'akov/Yisrael is known by both names and becomes a real, multidimensional personality, with the wordplay of those names enriching our appreciation of his many facets.)

Such wordplay occurs throughout the Torah, adding a rich linguistic subtext to the narrative and frequently conferring different levels of meaning on the stories. Many commentators have remarked that the Hebrew Bible is laconic in its narration, never using two words when one will do, with the result that every word has considerable weight. But it is also repetitive in many places. This seeming contradiction is, in reality, no contradiction at all. The repetitions are as much a part of the way that biblical narrative works as is the wordplay.

Perhaps the best example of the creative use of repetition is found in the use of the *leitwort/lead-word,* a device first remarked on by Martin Buber and Franz Rosenzweig in the course of their monumental work of translating the *Tanakh* into German in the 1920s. Buber writes:

> A *Leitwort* is a word or word-root that recurs significantly in a text, in a continuum of texts, or in a configuration of texts; by following these repetitions, one is able to decipher or grasp a meaning of the text, or at any rate, the meaning will be revealed more strikingly. The repetition, as we have said, need not be merely of the word itself but also of the word-root; in fact, the very difference of words can often intensify the dynamic action of the repetition.

The story of Ya'akov is one of the best examples of *leitworter* at work over a sustained stretch of text, with the punning parallel of *berakhah/blessing* and *bekhorah/birthright* a central structuring device. Ironically, a translator may choose to disguise the presence of a *leitwort* in Hebrew in the interests of readability, replacing the repeated word with synonyms for the sake of variety and thereby violating the structural integrity of the text.

What makes repetition such an effective device is the way it draws attention to variation; after all, if we are used to reading a phrase, any deviation from that familiar phrase stands out immediately. This is nowhere more obvious, or more important, than in another frequently used device in the Torah, "contrastive dialogue," as Alter has called it.

Dialogue in the Hebrew Bible is a major source of narrative information, frequently moving the story forward more than the narration does. Yet the strictures governing dialogue in the *Tanakh* are considerable and, for reasons of convention, fairly rigid. Dialogue scenes involving more than two characters (or one character speaking with a collective represented as a single voice) are very rare. Characters speak, as Alter observes, in "the decorum of normative literary Hebrew, allowing only the most fragmentary and oblique indications of a personal language, of individual ticks and linguistic peculiarities." Consequently, differentiation between characters is conveyed through contrast.

Returning again to the story of Ya'akov, look at the scene in which Eisav sells the birthright to him. When Eisav asks for the stew, he uses a verb associated with the feeding of animals and cannot even name the food he seeks, calling it "that red, red stuff." By contrast, Ya'akov is almost legalistically precise, telling his brother in the imperative verb form, "First sell me your birthright. . . . First swear to me. . . ." As Alter points out, unlike his brother, Ya'akov doesn't use the particle-word *na*, which suggests a certain deference, and he doesn't specify that it is to him that the birthright will go until almost the very end of his offer.

The disparity in their modes of speech is telling. On the one hand, Eisav is clearly ill-suited to be the bearer of the birthright. He is all appetite, and it comes out in his inarticulate, almost vulgar use of the language. Ya'akov is future-oriented in a way that his more impulsive brother is not and, hence, the right son to carry on the Covenant. Yet at the same time there is something not entirely seemly about his bargaining and his contractual logic; it will come back to haunt him when he attempts to make a deal with Lavan.

As we can see from even this brief survey of literary devices at work in the Torah, this is a book whose meaning is conveyed and enriched by a thrilling economy of means and a dazzling array of linguistic and narrative effects. Even when read in translation by someone with no Hebrew at all, its power certainly can be appreciated. But there is another aspect of the Torah, its function as a legal text, that moves us out of the realm of story, theme, and character and into another kind of literature altogether.

THE TORAH AS LEGAL DOCUMENT

Edward L. Greenstein has written, "The Bible encompasses a variety of genres: stories, hymns, proverbs, prayers, laws, prophetic speeches, and more. Yet the particular religious worldview of the Bible cuts across these diverse materials, organizes them, and gives them unity." This is nowhere more apparent than in the Torah's treatment of the laws handed down, not only at Sinai, although that is where the bulk of their transmission occurs, but throughout the *Khumash*. Legal material is frequently integrated into the narrative, as in the first commandment that God gives to humanity, "Be fruitful and multiply," or in the almost covert way that the *mitzvah* of *bikur kholim/visiting the sick* is slipped into the story of Avraham, when God comes to see him while he is recuperating from being circumcised.

Of course, the latter case is a good example of Rabbinic Judaism reading backward to the Torah text to find a legal injunction from God to humanity, but this isn't the sleight of hand that it initially seems to be. On the contrary, it is also an example of precisely the phenomenon of which

Greenstein writes, the pervasiveness of the Torah's understanding of God and humanity filtering into matters both simple and complex, mundane and sacred. As the rabbis explain in the Gemara, if we are to be "like God" in whose image we are created, then we must behave like God, who visits the ailing Avraham, who clothes Adam and Khavah, and so on. So if the laws we find in the Torah are interwoven with the stories, the proverbs, and the poetry, it is not by mistake.

Although the sages find 613 *mitzvot* in the Torah, one could hardly call the book a law code. It isn't comprehensive enough to merit that description. A list of what is missing from the Torah's legal passages would be many times longer than the Torah itself. In fact, as we will see in Chapter 4, there is a substantial body of Jewish writing on *halakhah* that grew out of precisely those lacunae, the halakhic midrashim. (Their narrative counterpart is the aggadic midrashim, which responds to similar gaps in the stories.)

More than that, as we have already noted in discussing the Holiness Code, the *mitzvot* are given in a seemingly haphazard order. One can discern many themes at work in them (as we have already) and even find some common threads running through parts of the Torah devoted exclusively to legal material. But more often than not the overall order is frankly baffling.

Greenstein has a wonderful thesis about the legal material found in the Torah. He notes that the word *torah* itself, while often translated as "law," might more properly be rendered in English as "teaching." Then he adds, "The laws of the Torah are one of its means of teaching; they are the specific behaviors by which God inculcates his ways—what we call values—in his human creatures. If we are to understand these values, we must read the laws, in a sense, as a sort of body language that outwardly symbolizes something of much deeper significance."

This function of the *mitzvot* helps to explain why the laws are not given in a more systematic and complete way, are not given as a law code per se. The legal passages are, as Greenstein says, "selective, illustrative, paradigmatic." And when the Hebrews finally conquered *Eretz Yisrael*, the Torah was not used as the nation's legal code. If it had been, there would have been no need for the public reading Ezra staged in 444 B.C.E., because everyone would have had at least some familiarity with the text, which was clearly not the case. Rather, the purpose of the laws was, as Greenstein says, "to instill abstract values through concrete acts."

With this understood as their purpose, we can see why it was given to the Levites to pass along the teachings (in *Devarim* 33:10), and why there is so much more emphasis on issues of ritual purity than on, say, traffic codes or rules governing the sale of produce. And we can see why the Torah takes for granted that the Hebrews will know how to ritually slaughter an animal (the details of which will not be spelled out until after the Talmudic period), yet gives us the procedures for making a sacrifice in the Tabernacle in copious (not to say downright numbing) detail.

In that respect, the Torah's role as legal document reminds me of a famous remark of Chief Justice John Marshall's, calling upon his brother justices to "remember it is a Constitution we are expounding here." Human legal codes are designed to be constantly updated to meet changing circumstances and mores, taking into account everything from a new stop sign at the corner of Overlook Terrace and 187th Street to the rising economic weight of the Internet. A constitution, however, is supposed to last. It is supposed to say something more fundamental and unchanging about our values as a nation. If you consider how few times in the past two and a quarter centuries the United States Constitution has been amended, it's obvious that the Founding Fathers built well.

The Torah—whether the work of God or of human authors inspired by God—should, if anything, exist on an even higher plane. If you are looking for a systematic elucidation of Jewish ritual law, you turn to Joseph Caro's *Shulkhan Arukh* and its many successors, and to the hundreds of thousands of pages of rabbinic responsa written since the Talmud; they read more like law codes and they incorporate the Jewish equivalent of two millennia of case law.

But the Torah, while it certainly contains plenty of "laws," is about something deeper and more fundamental. Even in its most legalistic passages, it is a book about the values that should follow from being made *b'tzelem Elohim*.

THE POETRY OF THE TORAH

The Hebrew Bible contains some of the greatest poetry in Western literature, most notably in the *Tehillim*. With a few important exceptions, though, the poetry of the *Tanakh* falls outside our purview, coming as it does after the Torah. The exceptions, however, are glorious ones, particularly the Song at the Sea, sung or spoken by *B'nei Yisrael* after the destruction of Pharoah's army at *Yam Suf.*

The poetic passages of the Torah have a few things in common worth noting. As in other multiform works of literature, the poetry usually occurs in a moment of heightened emotion, when characters have no other way of expressing their intense feelings but to burst into song, so to speak. (The passages of Torah that are most explicitly poetic are often referred to as songs, as in *Shirat Ha'Yam* or Moshe's song of farewell.)

Biblical poetry in both the Torah and subsequent parts of the *Tanakh* is unrhymed. There are frequent examples of assonance at line endings, but given the repetitive nature of Hebrew pronouns, that is more unavoidable than deliberate. As Perry Yoder observes, the basic structural unit of Hebrew biblical verse is the line, which is usually divided into two parts linked by a caesura. The poetry tends to be strongly metrical, but scholars have argued for centuries about the organizing principal at work in Hebrew prosody. The likeliest description of this kind of verse is "free rhythm."

NOTES

1. There are many ways to translate this phrase—and any other in the Torah, for that matter. But the participial form ("in the beginning of God's creating"), although awkward, is probably as close to an English equivalent as you can get for a construction that has no English equivalent.

2. In point of fact, "ethical monotheism" is a Greek construction and quite postbiblical. As Rabbi Arnold Jacob Wolf observes, the role of Moshe and the relationship of the Israelites to God "cannot be captured in the Greek notion. . . . It requires categories of its own." He argues that Torah and Moshe "cannot be captured in any non-Jewish schema," a conviction that obviously I share or I wouldn't have written this book.

3. It is highly significant, I think, that when a circumcised male adult converts to Judaism, he not only immerses himself in the waters of the *mikveh,* but also must undergo a pinprick at the point of his penis where circumcision has taken place. Thus he undergoes the same symbolic and real bloodletting as a newborn Jewish boy.

4. Andrew Sarris, *Interviews with Film Directors* (New York: Bobbs-Merrill, 1967).

3

BLACK FIRE ON WHITE FIRE

The Writing of the Torah

The Torah is not an artifact of nature, a product of the universe; the
universe, on the contrary, is a product of the Torah. . . . Jews adhere to
signs because reality innately is constituted as linguistic for them.

—Susan Handelman, *The Slayers of Moses:*
The Emergence of Rabbinic Interpretation
in Modern Literary Theory

The Torah is, as we have already seen, a remarkable document, whether
read as a literary text, a philosophical and theological text, a legal code, or
a unique combination of all three. And no matter which of several theories
of the composition of the Torah one accepts as correct, the author or
authors of this book must have been quite special as well. Confirming or
determining the identity (or identities) of the author has led scholars on a
search that has spanned centuries. Our study of that search will take us
through not only the Torah itself but through most of the other books
of the *Tanakh,* a trip that will encompass the post-Pentateuchal history
of the Jewish people up to the destruction of the Second Temple and
beyond.

But not just yet, because the earliest opinion about the identity of the
author (or perhaps Author) of the Torah involves an answer that stands
outside of historical time. The Jewish mystics tell us that God wrote the
Torah in black fire on white fire, and that the Torah existed before the
world itself. You can't get much further outside of human history than that.

THE TRADITIONAL VIEW

Avot, the tractate of Mishnah usually translated as Sayings (or Ethics) of the Fathers, begins, "Moshe received the Torah from Sinai and transmitted it to Yehoshua, Yehoshua to the Elders, the Elders to the Prophets, and the Prophets transmitted it to the Men of the Great Assembly."

Simply put, this is the traditional view of the creation of the Torah, that it was dictated to Moshe by God on Mount Sinai over the forty days and nights that he spent there, communing with the Almighty. Rabbi Judah David Eisenstein writes, "The traditional belief is that [the Five Books of Moses] were all written by Moshe under the inspiration of God, and that every statement in the Masoretic text is, therefore, to be considered of divine origin, and hence absolutely true." (For a brief discussion of the Masoretic text and men who produced it, see "Men of Tradition," page 126.)

In what textual evidence is this belief grounded? As we will see in the next chapter, rabbinic commentary frequently finds ways of filling in lacunae in the Torah's text that explain (or explain away, if you are of a cynical turn of mind) the gaps in the narrative or legal passages under examination, and certainly there are plenty of postbiblical texts invoked to bolster the claim of Moshe's authorship as a scribe of the Divine. But there are also what appear to be clues in the Torah itself that point readers toward the Mosaic identity of the author.

We may accept the lengthy sections of *Sefer Devarim* that recount Moshe's farewell address as his composition and that represent a significant portion of that book. In *Devarim* 31 there are references to a scroll written by Moshe that was kept in the ark. As we have already seen, Moshe also instructs the Israelites to read the Torah aloud every seven years, and there is the implied duty of writing a Torah. So there are a few indicators of Moshe's writings in the book itself.

But there is nothing in those texts to indicate that the Torah under discussion is the entire Pentateuch and, as we know, the word *torah* frequently refers to a specific teaching rather than the entire *Khumash*.

We must look to postbiblical texts for the doctrine that Moshe is the author of the entire Five Books that bear his name. That doctrine is first enunciated in the Talmud and attributed to an older *baraita* (a rabbinic statement dating from the period of the Mishnah but not included in the Mishnah itself). There it is stated that "Moshe wrote his own book and the section concerning Balaam. . . . Yehoshua wrote his own book and [the last] eight verses of the Torah." The idea behind the latter statement, obviously, is that Moshe couldn't have written the story of his own death; as his successor, Yehoshua was the logical choice to complete the Torah. (One minor point jumps out from the passage of Talmud above. Why is reference made to the story of Balaam specifically? Moshe does not appear in this episode, so apparently the rabbis felt it necessary to underline his ostensible role as narrator.)

Elsewhere in the Talmud the question is raised: "Is it possible that Moshe, while still alive, would have written, 'So Moshe . . . died?' " R. Yehudah offers the opinion that the final verses of the Torah were written by Yehoshua, as noted above, but this means that the Torah scroll would have been incomplete when Moshe commanded, "Take this Book of Torah." The rabbis could not accept the idea that Moshe would knowingly proffer an imperfect Torah to B'nei Yisrael. R. Shimon had a plausible explanation: "Up to this passage, the Holy One dictated and Moshe repeated the words and wrote them out, but from this passage on, the Holy One dictated, and Moshe wrote them down with tears in his eyes."

This, then, is the traditional understanding of Moshe's lengthy sojourn on Mount Sinai, that for forty days and nights he took the Divine dictation that would become the Torah. (However, as the late Emil Fackenheim observed, "Even Orthodox tradition does not reduce human reception to such extreme passivity. Why, in that case, would there be any need for a Moses to receive the Torah?") And this was the Torah that was revealed with God's appearance to the men, women, and children who stood at the base of the mountain. For the traditionally observant, these phenomena are inextricably linked—the theophany at Sinai, the Giving of the Law, and Moshe as "Israel's great scribe," to use R. Eleazar the Elder's phrase.

The tradition of Mosaic authorship seems to have been supported by later biblical texts as well as the Talmud. In Ezra, Nekhemyah, and Divrei Hayamim, the last three books of the Tanakh, repeated reference is made to the "Torah of Moshe" and the "Book of Moshe." When Ezra reads to the people on that all-important day in Jerusalem, he reads from "the scroll of the Torah of Moshe." (Of course, as we have already seen, the exact meaning of those phrases is ambiguous—are we talking about the entire Pentateuch or some segment of it?)

The ascription of authorship of the Torah to Moshe has obvious effects. If the book is the product of the greatest prophet and scribe taking down the words of God, it must, perforce, be flawless, and it carries the enormous weight and force that only the Word of the Eternal can have. But, as the TV ads say, there's more. Tradition says that Moshe not only took down the Written Torah—the Pentateuch—but also was given the Oral Torah, the laws eventually set down in the *Mishnah,* during those days and nights on Sinai.

In fact, there is an even more extreme position taken by some, called the "maximalist position," by the great Talmudist David Weiss Halivni. This position, stated in the Palestinian Talmud by R. Yehoshua ben Levi, argues that all subsequent Jewish texts relating to the Torah—the rest of the *Tanakh,* Mishnah, Gemara, halakhic rulings and writings, *tosefot, haggadot,* "even what an astute disciple will, in the future, say in the presence of his master"—were given to Moshe at Sinai.

This position leaves me quite speechless. At this extreme, the entire element of human creativity, indeed of human will itself, is dissolved in a sea of Holy Omniscience that renders all future efforts at the study and interpretation of Torah utterly superfluous. That said, it must be noted that the maximalist position carried considerable weight in the medieval period, the most exhilaratingly creative time in the history of Jewish Bible commentary.

The promulgation of the idea that Moshe was the sole author of the Pentateuch—we will suspend discussion of subsequent texts for now—is a comparatively late development, considering that the Mishnah was not completed until the middle of the third century C.E., almost seven hundred years after Ezra read the Torah in Jerusalem. But it was an idea that would go unchallenged for another millennium.

CRACKS IN THE FACADE

It would take a while before objections to the idea of Mosaic authorship of the Torah would be raised publicly. But the seeds of concern were already planted in the book itself. Could Moshe have written this sentence from *B'midbar* 12:3: "Now the man Moshe was very humble, more than any other man on the face of the earth." As Richard Elliott Friedman observes, "[O]ne would not expect the humblest man on earth to point out that he is the humblest man on earth." And there is the disputed matter of the recounting of Moshe's death and burial.

One can explain away all these problems, as the rabbis tacitly did, by saying that Moshe was merely the vehicle for a Divinely authored text. But such an answer merely begs a series of questions that only grow more insistent as we examine the text itself more closely.

Such an examination reveals a text that contains not only multiple retellings of the same story, called "doublets" (two Creations, three versions of the naming of Be'ersheva, etc.), but significant anachronisms, contradictions, and inconsistencies. To cite only a few:

- In *Shoftim* 18 we learn that the city of Laish was renamed Dan shortly after the death of Shimshon/Samson. But in *Bereishit* 14:14 Avraham and his 318 retainers go after the men who kidnapped his kinsman and pursue them "as far as Dan."
- In *Yehoshua* 14 we are told that Kiryat Arba was not renamed *Khevron/Hebron* until the Israelite conquest of Kina'an. Yet in *Bereishit* 23, we are told about the renaming.
- In *Bereishit* 36:31 we read, "These are the kings who reigned in the land of Edom before there reigned any king over *B'nei Yisrael.*" Shaul/Saul, the first Israelite king, did not ascend to the throne until three centuries after the death of Moshe.
- In *Bereishit* 12:6–7 the narrator, in the course of describing Avraham's situation in the land, notes in an aside, "The Canaanites were then in the land." The implication is, of course, that they are no longer there, that is, that the Israelite conquest of Kina'an has taken place. There is a similar passage in *Bereishit* 13:7.
- *Bereishit* 11:31 has Avraham living in Ur of the Chaldeans, but the Chaldeans did not exist as a people until well after Avraham's lifetime.
- In his final testament to his sons, Ya'akov says to Yehudah, "The scepter shall not depart from Yehudah nor the ruler's staff from between his feet as long as men come to Shiloh." If this is a reference to the city of Shiloh as a temporary resting place for the *Mishkan*, it's a bit premature, since the *Miskhan* didn't come to Shiloh until after Moshe's death and the conquest of Kina'an.
- There are several passages in the Torah that refer to a phenomenon lasting "until this day." For example, in describing the naming of Be'ersheva in *Bereishit* 26:33 the text says that such is its name "until

this very day." Such a wording suggests that the author is writing considerably later than the events in question.

- There are numerous inconsistencies in the text, suggesting either error or, possibly, more than one author. For example, in the rebellion at Pe'or, the women who seduce the Israelites are first called Moabites, then Midianites. Mount Sinai and Mount Horeb are used almost interchangeably to designate the mountain at which the Israelites received the Torah.

This list is far from exhaustive. But it is sufficient to implant doubts about Moshe's authorship of the Torah. Factor into this equation the reality that only *Devarim* ascribes authorship to Moshe, and even that attribution is limited to specific sections of the book. During the Talmudic period the doubts began to resonate in the minds of the Torah's most scholarly readers, including some scions of Rabbinic Judaism. But, despite some minor objections raised at that time, it would not be until the Middle Ages that any Jewish Bible commentators would raise the subject again.

There are many reasons why the rabbis of the Mishnaic period kept relatively silent about seeming problems with the Torah's text. First and foremost, they undoubtedly believed in Moshe's authorship under Divine tutelage. But they also lived, studied, taught, and wrote in a time of terrible crisis for the Jewish community in Judah, a period that featured severe repression by the Roman authorities, up to and including bans on circumcision and the public reading of the Torah on penalty of death. It was an era that culminated in a series of tragedies—the destruction of the Second Temple, the mass suicide at Masada, the crushing of the Bar Kokhba rebellion, and the martyrdom of Rabbi Akiva and nine other prominent rabbis. If you factor into this equation the alarming rise of Christianity (eventually with the support of the Roman authorities), you can forgive the rabbinic leadership if their instinctive reaction was to circle the wagons rather than to confront the ostensible flaws in the most sacred text of their faith. They were understandably more concerned with utilizing that text as the foundation stone on which they would erect a new intellectual edifice, Rabbinic Judaism.

EVOLUTION OF AN ALTERNATIVE THEORY

A parable, this one from Franz Kafka, that most Jewish of Jewish modernists:

> Leopards break into the temple and drink to the dregs what is in the sacrificial pitchers; this is repeated over and over again; finally it can be calculated in advance, and it becomes part of the ceremony.

For Rabbinic Judaism, something very similar may have happened regarding the alleged inconsistencies, anachronisms, and stutterings of the Torah text. Whatever qualms they had, they swallowed them. In time, their misgivings—if indeed there were any—were forgotten. (As we will see in the next chapter, the quirks of the text are a fertile subject for commentary.) And Mosaic authorship was accepted as a given by Christian theologians, most prominently Origen, the third-century scholar.

Surprisingly, one of the first authors to voice some concerns was a doyen of traditional Judaism, an upholder of the normative Jewish thought that today we would call Orthodox, Abraham Ibn Ezra. Ibn Ezra, who we will meet at greater length in the next chapter, is one of the most formidable of the medieval Bible commentators, a grammarian and philologist of great skill. When a well-known Jewish physician and author, Isaac Ibn Yashush, pointed out that in the list of Edomite kings given in *Bereishit* 36 there were several names that postdated Moshe, Ibn Ezra dismissed him as "Isaac the Blunderer," and said that the doctor's book ought to be burned.

But Ibn Ezra had his own doubts, and they can be discerned from a careful reading of some of the more ambiguous passages of his writings. He mentions passages referring to Moshe in the third person, describing places Moshe could not possibly have been, using language that clearly comes from an era after Moshe's death. Abraham Ibn Ezra will not openly state what is bothering him about those passages (although it should be fairly obvious), merely saying that the "prudent keep silent," and "if you understand, then you will recognize the truth." Or as some 1960s radicals used to say, "Those that know don't say, and those that say don't know." Still, those hints were enough to inflame Nahmanides, who denounced Ibn Ezra as "a talebearer who goes around with open rebuke and hidden love," prompting still other detractors to ask where Ibn Ezra's "hidden love" might be found.

Clearly, the great Judeo–Spanish scholar had trod on some sensitive toes. He wasn't the first and certainly wouldn't be the last to do so. The cost of defying the mainstream of religious thought was not as great for a Jewish writer as it would be for a Christian, but it is useful to keep in mind that Ibn Ezra was writing at a time when Christianity was still burning its heretics alive.

It should be noted that Judaism is a bit more lenient with its trouble-makers. The status of heretics in Jewish law is not clearly defined. While there are certain regulations scattered throughout the Talmud concerning the *minim*, the Aramaic word most resembling "heretic," these are mostly of an aggadic nature, and the law codes take little cognizance of them. The *Anshei Knesset Ha'Gedolah/Men of the Great Assembly* frequently exercised, from motives of self-defense, their power of excommunication against heretics, a power that rabbinic authorities continued to hold in reserve and use reluctantly even in the Diaspora. The *Shulkhan Arukh* defines *apikoros*, another term frequently translated as "heretic," as one who does not believe in the Divine origin of the Law and in prophecy. The laws concerning such an unbeliever are very strict. He may be killed directly, or his death may be caused indirectly. But I have not been able to find an example of such a death in Jewish history. Perhaps, as the rabbis say of the "rebellious son," it never happened. On the whole, even during the time when the Temple was standing, Judaism has been anything but monolithic, and dissent and schism, while not actively encouraged, were certainly tolerated to a high degree.

So Ibn Ezra merely found himself on the receiving end of some spirited name-calling. One of his successors, the Damascus-based scholar Bonfils, wrote in the fourteenth century that the disputed passages in the Torah were evidence that such verses were "written in the Torah later, and Moshe did not write it, rather one of the later prophets wrote it"; his book would be reprinted *without* this passage three and a half centuries later. Clearly this was dangerously contested territory. When a Flemish Catholic, Andreas van Maes, wrote (with two Jesuit scholars) that the Torah was primarily written by Moshe but expanded by later writers, his book was placed on the Index of Prohibited Books by the Vatican. When Isaac La Peyrère, a French Calvinist, wrote in the seventeenth century that Moshe was not the author of the Pentateuch, his book was banned and burned by the Catholic Church. The pope had him arrested, and he was told that to be released he would have to recant his views and become a Catholic.

But there was clearly a growing school of thought that challenged, to a greater or lesser degree, the idea of Mosaic authorship of the first five books of the Bible. Four years before La Peyrère's disastrous publication, Thomas Hobbes also challenged the concept, pointing, as those courageous few had done before, to such phrases as "in those days," as evidence of later authorship. And at roughly the same time, Benedict Spinoza, a Dutch Jew, would offer the most detailed challenge to the traditional view of the Torah's authorship.

Spinoza, whom Rabbi Bernard Bamberger has called "the first modern Jew," anticipates many trends that mark post-Enlightenment Jewish thought, not the least of which was his categorical rejection of Mosaic authorship of the Torah. He had already been excommunicated by the Amsterdam Jewish community in 1656, when he wrote a unified critical analysis of the Hebrew Bible, drawing together the many anachronisms, duplications, and contradictions presented by the text, eventually arriving at an emphatic conclusion, "[T]he Pentateuch was not written by Moses, but by someone who lived long after Moses." Spinoza believed the work to be the product of an overall guiding editorial hand, probably that of Ezra, a view that would prove prescient, as we will see. (He was also the first author to suggest that the line of books from *Bereishit* through *Melakhim* should be read as a single, continuous historical chronicle.) For his troubles, the already apostate Jew was also denounced by Protestant and Catholic authorities, his book placed on the Index, and his life threatened. But Spinoza (and Hobbes) had finally said aloud what before had been spoken only in whispers or hinted at by indirection.

Of course, if Moshe was not the sole author—or even the partial author—of the Torah, who was? It was to this question that scholars turned.

THE DOCUMENTARY HYPOTHESIS

To learn something about an author, first turn to the text.[1] That, in effect, was what an eighteenth-century French physician, Jean Astruc, did in his

"Conjectures on the Original Memoirs of Which It Appears that Moses Made Use in Composing the Book of Genesis." What Astruc discerned was that in *Sefer Bereishit*, the Name of God is frequently given as *Elohim*, but also as *YHVH* and, more infrequently, a composite of the two. Astruc deduced from this that more than one writer had been at work on this text. The idea of more than one authorial voice might explain the duplications, the repetitions, the contradictions found in the text. Astruc, whose intention was to defend Mosaic authorship from "freethinkers" of his time, deduced that it was from such various sources that Moshe learned of the events that preceded his birth when he sat down to write the Torah. Whether one accepted that particular interpretation or not, Astruc had opened the door to a new approach at least a crack (the slightness of that crack being the result of his research not extending beyond *Bereishit* and the first few chapters of *Shemot*, i.e., the events predating Moshe's birth).

Astruc's discovery triggered further delving into the books covering Moshe's life span. Gradually, scholars came to believe that the Five Books of Moses had been written by at least four people—none of whom was Moshe. The watershed came in the nineteenth century when several prominent German and Dutch Protestant Bible scholars identified the four putative authors and an editor, a process that culminated in the work of Julius Wellhausen. Wellhausen synthesized and organized the work of men like Astruc, Karl Heinrich Graf, and Wilhelm Vatke, adding considerable research of his own. His particular achievement was in tying the development of the four sources to the history of the Israelite religion and nation in the years following the conquest of Kina'an. The result was a highly detailed and sophisticated explanation of the writing of the Torah that came to be called the "documentary hypothesis," or source criticism. Wellhausen's paradigm has stood up under considerable scrutiny and, with significant modifications, is still accepted today by many if not most Bible scholars.

The key to unraveling the intricacies of the authorship question lay in the "doublets," the repetitions of certain stories. To give two examples, there seem to be two separate versions of the Creation in the Torah and three variations on the story in which one of the Patriarchs tries to pass off his wife as his sister, two of them involving King Avimelekh. By analyzing the variations between all the doublets, Wellhausen and his predecessors discerned different choices of language, different emphases and concerns that suggested the no-less-different personalities and agendas of the four authors. And, they reasoned, one brilliant editor, called the Redactor, eventually pulled the different versions together into a book that is, despite the repetitions and inconsistencies, remarkably coherent.

Who were these four authors and the editor who pulled their work together?

To understand the documentary hypothesis, one first has to know a little of the history of Israel in the aftermath of the conquest of Kina'an.[2]

HISTORY LESSONS

Our primary but not sole source for this information is the later books of the *Tanakh*, running from Yehoshua through *Melakhim Aleph*/I Chronicles, with *Ezra, Nekhemyah/Nehemiah,* and *Divrei Hayamim Aleph* and *Bet* added in.

Led by Yehoshua, *B'nei Yisrael* fulfill the prophecy and the Covenant by conquering Kina'an and establishing a nation there. At first, they are governed by the *shoftim*, men and women who combine the roles of military leader, chief justice, chief executive, and divinely guided prophet. Eventually, though, the people demand a king so that they can be like other nations and, reluctantly, the prophet Shmuel/Samuel grants their wish, anointing Shaul/Saul as king. This turns out not to have been a great choice. Shaul develops a pathological hatred toward David, and after his suicide on the battlefield, his surviving son ends up embroiled in a civil war with David, whose final victory puts him on the throne. David establishes Jerusalem as his capital city and the city consecrated to God as promised in the Torah. David's son Shelomo/Solomon builds the First Temple in 960 B.C.E.

Under ideal circumstances, this would be the end of the story, with the Temple serving as the seat of the priestly cult as outlined in the Torah and the people living happily ever after. Of course, because God gave humanity free will, a gift that empowers bad as well as good judgment, it is only the beginning of the Jewish people's struggles.

What happened next should come as no great surprise to anyone who has read the Pentateuch. That fractious, argumentative "stiff-necked" people who posed such a burden to Moshe began to divide themselves along many different lines. Those divisions, in turn, determined the points of view of the four putative authors of the Torah.

When Shelomo ascends the throne, Israel is at the peak of its power and size, a small empire in its own right. David has built that empire through military prowess, shedding the blood of his neighbors and compatriots. Of course, this is why the shepherd-boy-turned-king is not allowed to build the Temple, because of the blood that stains his hands. Instead, the task falls to his brilliant son. Shelomo, too, maintains the primacy of Israel in the region as well as its territorial integrity, but he uses an entirely different set of skills. Among other ploys, he will take on an enormous number of foreign wives and concubines, binding potential rivals to his cause through intermarriage. Although the short-term results are desirable, the long-term ramifications, both political and religious, will prove devastating.

Before the advent of the Israelites, Kina'an was populated by many peoples, worshipping many different gods, all of them pagan. In the book that bears his name, Yehoshua leads *B'nei Yisrael* in a war of conquest to drive the pagans from the land but, clearly, despite his apparent victory, pagans remained in *Eretz Yisrael,* and their counterexample was one that many Israelites found tempting. We find followers of Ba'al and Astarte competing for their attention throughout subsequent books of the *Tanakh.* Additionally, there was pagan pressure from outside the borders; witness David's triumph over the Philistine champion, Goliath. Where David made war against the neighboring pagans, Shelomo cut deals or made marriages.

Look at a map of the Middle East, modern or ancient. Israel is ideally situated as an entry ramp on the highway to regional domination, and in the ancient world, controlling the Mediterranean was tantamount to ruling the entire Western world. The Egyptians, Babylonians, Assyrians, Persians, Greeks, and Romans must have all looked at that same map and seen what twentieth-century German military planners saw in Belgium: not a nation but a gateway to be passed through en route to military success. And when Shelomo died, leaving his sons to squabble over the Davidic throne, the gateway was opened wide.

To understand the chaos that followed Shelomo's death, one must keep in mind that before his father unified Israel into a single kingdom it was divided into separate northern and southern groupings, the tribes of Yehudah and Binyamin in the south, the remaining ten tribes in the north. David united them with his military prowess and charisma, and held them together largely through the use of a professional army that included a sizeable number of foreign mercenaries. The *Mishkan* and the priesthood had previously centered on Shiloh in the north, but when David established Jerusalem as his capital, with the intention of erecting the Temple there, he had the *Mishkan* moved south. Shelomo would manage to keep the nation together as a single unit by the force of his personality, his diplomatic prowess, and the unstated but very real presence of his father's army. But his policies were more obviously discriminatory against the northern tribes than David's had been, and when his son, Rekhavam/ Rehoboam, ascended the throne upon Shelomo's death, the north broke away, naming the Ephraimite Yeravam/Jeroboam as its monarch.

Let's back up for a moment. When Shaul became the first Israelite monarch, he crushed the priesthood at Shiloh. Only one of the priests, Aviathar/Abiathar, escaped his murdering troops. David, in his wisdom, realized that in order to hold Israel together he would have to win the trust of the northern tribes. He established a dual priesthood, with Aviathar as the *Kohein Galol/High Priest* in the north and Zadok as High Priest in the south. As Richard Elliott Friedman observes, David's choice was as religiously astute as it was politically savvy, because Aviathar was a descendant of the Mosaic line, Zadok of the Aaronide. In one stroke, he had united north and south and the two great lines of the Israelite people.

Shelomo, in a rare example of a political misstep, removed Aviathar from office in order to assert the primacy of the Temple cult. He compounded that error by ceding northern lands to his Phoenician ally, Hiram, and by undercutting the tribal base of the nation's administrative structure, creating new districts in the north to oversee taxation. The northerners were hit with particularly heavy taxes. Rekhavam cemented the ill-feeling toward the royal family that resulted from these decisions by reaffirming his father's policies at a meeting in Shekhem early in his rule. The northern secession was virtually inevitable.

The division of the Davidic Kingdom into Israel, the northern kingdom, and Judah, the southern kingdom, would have disastrous consequences for the Jews. In the short term, it created a division not only in the political realm but also in the religious realm. At the time, of course, the distinction between the two was nonexistent, with the judges serving not only as jurists but as priests and prophets as well.

Israel was not nearly strong enough to sustain itself without help and additional protection from Judah's army. The Israelite throne was more unstable than post–World War II Italy. The nation lasted for two hundred years before it was conquered by the Assyrians in 722 B.C.E., its people dispersed throughout the Assyrian empire. Their disappearance into the Assyrian realm led to the myth of the "ten lost tribes of Israel."

And in a roundabout way, it also led to the writing of the Torah.

ENTER J AND E

With this historical background in hand, we can now identify two of the four principal authors of the Torah, as limned by the documentary hypothesis. The designation of these two authors—J and E—is based on one of the most discussed dichotomies in the Torah's text, the existence (particularly in *Bereishit*) of two different names for God, *Elohim* and *YHVH*. Obviously, E is the writer who refers to God as *Elohim;* J gets his or her name[3] from the (incorrect) vocalization of the Tetragrammaton as Yehovah, which is spelled Jehovah in German, the language of the scholars who first identified this author. Not coincidentally, J and E are the earliest of the authors of the Torah.

Who were these two writers and how do their contributions to the Torah reflect their very different politicoreligious affiliations?

It is generally believed that J and E were citizens of Judah and Israel, respectively. There is ample evidence to justify this belief in the texts themselves; as we are about to see, there is more to differentiate these two authors than just the name they give the Almighty.

Consider these facts: In the J version, Avraham lives in Khevron, David's capital before Jerusalem. Avraham is promised the land from "the river of Egypt" to the Euphrates, the actual boundaries of David's kingdom at its peak. There are two different stories of how the Patriarchs acquired Shekhem, the capital of the northern kingdom. In the J version, we have the well-known and brutal story of the massacre of the city's male population by Ya'akov's sons in revenge for the rape of Dinah (*Bereishit* 34). By contrast, the E story has Ya'akov purchasing the land from "the hand of the sons of Hamor, father of Shekhem" (*Bereishit* 33:19). When the Torah tells the story of the births of Ya'akov's sons, E describes the birth of the sons who will father the tribes of Israel (*Bereshit* 30:1–24), while J recounts the births of the forebears of the tribes of Judah (*Bereishit* 29:32–35).

In short, as Speaker of the House Tip O'Neill used to say, "All politics is local," and J and E are making very political decisions about how to retell their local history. Richard Elliott Friedman is blunt: "The J stories fit the cities and territory of Judah. The E stories fit the cities and territory of Israel."

But there is more to be gleaned from a close reading of these disparate texts. Perhaps the pivotal E text is the story of the sin of the Golden Calf. This story, familiar to almost anyone raised in the Western literary tradition, recounts the fears of the Israelites as they wait for Moshe to descend from Mount Sinai with the Word of God. As the forty days and nights draw to a close, those fears can no longer be contained, and Aharon, ever eager to make peace at any cost, urges them to collect the gold earrings and other jewelry of the women and create a molten statue of a calf to worship as a surrogate for (or avatar of) the invisible *Adonai* while they await Moshe's return. Of course, when Moshe sees what they have done he flies into an uncontrollable rage, smashing the tablets he has brought from God, rallying the Levites to punish this heresy, which they do with a significant amount of bloodshed. Yet Aharon isn't really punished. (And this sequence will be repeated when Aharon and Miriam take issue with Moshe over his "Cushite wife"; it is Miriam who is given leprosy and exiled temporarily from the camp, not Aharon.)

Why this story? Why this telling? Why a golden calf? Why is Aharon the instigator, yet not the one most severely punished? Why are the Levites the arm of Moshe's wrath? Why are the tablets smashed? The answer to these questions will bring us closer to the identity of E.

The choice of a golden calf is singular. When Yeravam established his kingship in the north, he created a new religious holiday, designed to set his nation apart from its former brothers' to the south. Its symbol, chosen in contradistinction to the golden cherubim that adorned the *Mishkan*, is golden calves. Hence, the golden calf may be seen as a foreshadowing of the exclusion of the priests of Shiloh by Shaul, a descendant of Aharon.

The story of the Golden Calf in *Shemot* emphasizes the heroism of Moshe, whose intervention with God makes the survival of the Israelites possible. It also places the Levites in a position of great trust, while making Aharon look particularly pusillanimous. Yehoshua, too, is singled out for glory.

Now the pieces begin to fall into place: the author is probably a descendant of Moshe, likely a Levite priest of the group whose immediate forebears were chased out of Shiloh. He is a northerner still, hence the heroism of Yehoshua, who was still seen as a tower of strength in the northern kingdom, and he lives with the reality that the Aaronide line still held the priesthood, so Aharon is depicted as weak but isn't punished by loss of position. And the smashing of the tablets? It's the final ingenious piece in the puzzle, a gesture by Moshe that means that the tablets in the Temple in Jerusalem aren't the originals, a story that simultaneously reminds readers of the period of the failure of Aharon and calls into question the legitimacy of the southern kingdom.

In short, it's as nicely plotted and neatly slotted as any mystery novel.

Add to that the emphasis in the E portions of *Shemot* on Moshe's youth and the growing intimacy of his relationship with God, and you have a strong case made from the internal evidence of the text itself. Of course, we don't know who E actually was but this looks like a fairly plausible profile.

And J?

As I have noted elsewhere in this chapter, some have speculated that J was a woman. In fact, the recounting of the story of Tamar in *Bereishit* 38 is unusually sensitive to her feelings and, quite frankly, allows her to triumph over Judah decisively. As Richard Elliott Friedman notes, the J stories are, uniquely among all four authors' works, concerned with women and their sufferings. Could J have been a woman, as Harold Bloom and David Rosenberg assert in *The Book of J?* It is possible, but one cannot say so with certainty. This much is clear from the internal evidence of the J text: the author was someone familiar with the workings of the court of the Judean Kings.[4]

Thus far the documentary hypothesis has offered us two authors of the Torah. To find the other two authors and the fifth individual who put all the pieces together, we must return to the history of the now shattered Israelite kingdoms.

HISTORY LESSONS CONTINUED

After 722 B.C.E. there was only one kingdom, Judah. Its rivalries with the northern kingdom had been removed in the worst way possible. Judah was more than bereft; it was crippled, a semimajor power reduced to a potential vassal state, a tollgate on the highway to world conquest. Judah would now be buffeted by the Assyrians, the Babylonians, the Egyptians, the Persians, the Greeks, and, finally, the Romans.

Of course, there were still internecine tensions, even without the existence of a second kingdom. Judah's sovereign, Khizkiyahu/Hezehiah, would institute a series of religious reforms aimed at centralizing worship around the Temple in Jerusalem and consolidating the power of the Temple priests. If you wanted to slaughter a sheep, you had to bring it to the Temple and the Levite priests. Khizkiyahu also would destroy a bronze snake reputedly made by Moshe himself, which had become a veritable worship object, with Judeans burning incense before it. Finally, Khizkiyahu defied the Assyrians both religiously and militarily, withstanding a siege of Jerusalem. Regrettably, on his death Khizkiyahu was succeeded by a son and grandson who were much less effective. Worship of other gods was reintroduced in Judah, and the "high places," the worship sites outside Jerusalem, were reestablished. Moreover, Assyria overran Judah repeatedly, possibly even imprisoning the Judean monarch. But when Yoshiyahu/Josiah, Khizkiyahu's great-grandson, ascended the throne, things would be very different indeed.

Yoshiyahu was only a child when he became the king upon the assassination of his father, Amon. We cannot know with certainty who ruled Judah while he was growing up (although under similar circumstances *Divrei Hayamim* reports that the High Priest served as regent), and we cannot know for sure who educated the boy king. But if we extrapolate back from the policies he enacted when he did come of age, it seems obvious that his teachers and advisers came from the same line of Temple priests that had prospered under Khizkiyahu. The evidence that leads to this conclusion is simple: Yoshiyahu reinstated Khizkiyahu's policies of centralized worship in the Temple under the supervision of the priests, and reasserted the sovereignty of Judah in the face of military threats from her more powerful neighbors.

In the eighteenth year of Yoshiyahu's reign, 622 B.C.E., something remarkable happened, an event that gave added impetus to his religious reforms. Khilkiyahu/Hilkiah, a priest of the Temple, reported to Yoshiyahu through the priestly scribe Shaphan the discovery of a "scroll of Torah" in the inner recesses of the Temple. After hearing it read aloud, Yoshiyahu let loose an agonized cry and tore his clothing, a traditional sign of mourning in the Ancient Near East. How far the Judeans had strayed from the path God had set for them!

What was in this scroll that so shook Yoshiyahu's royal sangfroid?

Bible scholars agree that the scroll contained the bulk of what we know as *Sefer Devarim*. But where had it materialized from, and who had written it?

ENTER D

To determine who wrote the "scroll of the Torah" that so moved Yoshiyahu, we need look no further than the Hebrew Bible itself for clues. By and large, the scroll is a code of law consisting of chapters 12–26 of *Devarim*, reflecting the back-and-forth struggle among the various priestly groups for the centralization of worship and the ongoing battle between the illicit forms of worship competing with the worship of *Yahweh* as sole god. The scroll comes down squarely on the side of the reforming kings, Khizkiyahu and Yoshiyahu, protecting the interests of the Levites but not those of the Aaronide priests or the rural Levites. At the same time, the scroll strongly recommends reining in the king. In other words, as Richard Elliott Friedman puts it, "It reflected the interests of the Shiloh priests at just about any time after the division of Israel and Judah."

Such content already offers strong hints as to the probable identity of the author, who is now called D. (In fact, there were probably two D authors, as certain anachronisms in the text suggest that the book was written in two separate periods of time.)[5] He was—and this time it was definitely a he—a member or descendant of the Shilonite priesthood.

Contemporary scholars have done stylistic and content analyses of the *Tanakh* and have found not only similiarities but an actual unity between *Sefer Devarim* and the historical books that follow: *Yehoshua, Shoftim, Shmuel,* and *Melakhim Aleph* and *Bet.* It is now generally believed that one author wrote a continuous narrative taking the Hebrews from the edge of the *Yardein/River Jordan* at the end of their time in the Wilderness through the rise and fall of two kingdoms, culminating in . . . the reign of Yoshiyahu. This is history told in terms of the Covenant between the Hebrews and *Adonai.* Kings are extolled or devalued on the basis of their faithfulness to the Covenant, as defined in *Devarim.* But the history written by D, what David Noel Freedman calls the Primary History (encompassing not only *Devarim* and the following books but the entirety of the Torah), rates Yoshiyahu alone as a wholly good king, comparing him favorably to Moshe and proclaiming that "none arose like him" in the entire history of Israel and Judah. There are over five hundred references to David in the Deuteronomic history; he builds a small empire and founds the dynasty—the Davidic throne—that is supposed to rule in the Promised Land forever, yet it is Yoshiyahu who is valorized even at the expense of his vastly more accomplished predecessor. This is nothing less than astounding. It is as if an American wrote a national history arguing that, say, Benjamin Harrison was the single greatest American president.

Who would put forth such a thesis? Obviously it had to be someone who was close to Yoshiyahu and his court, someone with a rooting interest against the pagan retentions in ancient Israelite society, someone with strong ties to the priests of Shiloh.

The trail that scholars followed led to a surprising and famous name.

The prophet Yirmiyahu.

What is the evidence for such a startling conclusion? First, there are striking linguistic parallels between the books of *Devarim* and *Yirmiyahu* (which was purportedly dictated by the prophet to his scribe Barukh). Yirmiyahu/Jeremiah is the only prophet to make reference to Shiloh and its priests. Most of all, though, he is the single strongest link between Yoshiyahu and his counselors and the Deuteronomistic history. Remember, it was the priest Khilkiyahu who "found" the "scroll of Torah," and his scribe Shaphan who brought it to Yoshiyahu. It was the sons of Khilkiyahu and Shaphan who delivered Yirmiyahu's letter to the Babylonian exiles, the sons of Shaphan who protected the prophet from his enemies when they threatened to stone him to death. It was the governor Gedalyah, grandson of Shaphan, who took Yirmiyahu under his personal protection. Finally, he introduces himself in the book that bears his name as "Yirmiyahu, son of Khilkiyahu, of the priests who were in Anatot." We cannot know if this is the same Khilkiyahu who found the scroll, but the people of Anatot were descendants of Aharon, and hostile to Yirmiyahu. There are more elements to this case, but it's now pretty obvious why many believe that Yirmiyahu was the D author.

If Yoshiyahu's reign was a golden era in the history of Judah and the Jews, it was to be a brief one. In writing his text, D had included warnings to the people in the books of *Devarim, Yehoshua,* and *Shoftim* that they would be punished by God for straying from divine commandments. Yet tragedy befell the good as well as the evil; Yoshiyahu was killed by an Egyptian arrow at the age of forty in 609 B.C.E. And worse still was yet to come.

The next blow was almost unimaginably catastrophic. Having made

Judah into a vassal state in 609 B.C.E., the newly powerful empire of Babylonia swept through Judah, in 587 B.C.E., destroyed the Temple, and seized most of the populace, exiling them to the invaders' homeland. A few Judeans escaped to Egypt.

The D author was faced with a particularly cruel dilemma. If Yoshiyahu was the pinnacle of God-fearing probity, why did he die so young? What could possibly explain the destruction of those two symbols of the Covenant, the Temple and the Israelites' residence in the Land? To explain these terrible events, D went back to his text and put the blame on Yoshiyahu's grandfather, Menasheh, who was such a dreadful ruler and bad influence that despite Yoshiyahu's reforms the people were punished in the most spectacular way possible—exile to Babylonia and Egypt. What could be a worse punishment than returning to the scene of the Jewish people's first enslavement? (Yet what could offer a brighter spark of hope than being sent back to the place where God first intervened on their behalf?)

EXILE, REMORSE, RETURN

We know very little about the period of the Babylonian exile. The books of the *Tanakh* don't offer much evidence, although *Eikhah* and *Tehillim* 137 provide eloquent witness to the traumatic effects of the destruction of the Temple and of Jerusalem. Archaeological evidence is—no pun intended—thin on the ground. However, we can make a few significant logical inferences from the sparse evidence available and from simple logic.

We are told repeatedly in the Torah that the Jews are to be "a people set apart." Surely exile is a graphic example of this, but consider also the nature of these exiled people: in a world of polytheists, they alone worship a single God, and this separates them from their new neighbors even more surely than differences in language, dress, and customs. At the same time, the Israelites had to be asking themselves what they had done to offend *Adonai* so badly that they were victimized by this terrible fate. Why did God allow this disaster to befall them? Or had the Eternal caused it? Had they really been behaving that badly, as the prophets had proclaimed? And what of the priests? What would their role be with no Temple to preside over, no sacrifices to be made? Like displaced workers too old to retrain for new jobs, they found themselves at a loss in defining their new role in the community.

This was the state of affairs among the Israelites in Babylonia. Things were only marginally better in Egypt, because not long after bands of displaced Israelites fled there (and erected a smaller version of the Temple at Elephantine, the town in which they landed), they found themselves once again facing the surging Babylonian forces, which now overran Egypt, too.

Very little in human history is as impermanent as an empire. Within fifty years, the Babylonians would fall to the rising tide of Persia. For some reason, the Persian emperor Cyrus showed the Israelites extraordinary mercy and allowed them to return home, urging them to rebuild their Temple. As we have seen in the opening of this book, Ezra would also reintroduce the Torah to the people at this time, but that is getting a bit ahead of the story.

There is one intriguing and mysterious sidelight to the rebuilding of the Temple. What happened to the ark? There is no mention of it in descriptions of the Second Temple in the *Tanakh* or in the texts unearthed by archaeologists since. Clearly the centerpiece of the First Temple had in some way vanished. Or had it never existed? Given the extraordinary detail lavished on its planning, construction, and consecration in the Torah, the latter theory is a bit hard to credit. But what is known about the Second Temple?

Many of the trappings of power and the Covenant that were to be found in the First Temple were now missing. Not only the ark, but also the *urim* and *tumim* and the cherubs were gone as well. We don't know the size of the new building, but we know it was built on the same site. There was a High Priest, a descendant of the Aaronide line rather than of Moshe. And all the other priests were descendants of Aharon as well, with the remaining Levites relegated to a secondary role. The Aaronide priests had won a complete victory in their power struggle with the descendants of Moshe, although it had taken the near destruction of the nation to bring that to pass.

When the Israelites returned home, they had new leaders, appointed by the Persian ruler. Whatever his intentions—today we might have called the Israelites puppets of Persian imperialism—Cyrus did them a huge favor, because Ezra and Nekhemyah were men of good judgment and actions, and it is they who restored the role of the Torah and completed the work of the reformers when they built the new Temple, finally centralizing worship in Jerusalem. Ezra brought to Jerusalem a "scroll of the Torah" that, as we have seen, he had read aloud before the Water Gate.

The book of the *Tanakh* that recounts that event makes it clear (from quotations found therein) that this scroll, unlike Yoshiyahu's, drew upon all
four source documents—J, E, D, and P—from which it may be inferred
that this was, indeed, the entire Torah. (Keep that fact in mind. It's going
to become important shortly.)

But where did that fourth author, designated P, come from, and when?

AND FINALLY P

What makes the identity of the fourth and final author of particular interest is the fact that the P document is equal in length to the other three
combined. P gives us one of the two versions of the Creation and the Flood,
the stories of Avraham and Ya'akov, and the Exodus from Egypt. His work
includes most of the law codes given in *Shemot*, *Vayikra*, and *B'midbar*. In
short, he wrote most of the Torah.

Julius Wellhausen, the brilliant nineteenth-century German scholar
who is, for all intents and purposes, the father of modern critical Bible
scholarship, believed that P was a postexilic author. Wellhausen believed
that, in the wake of the tragedy of the Babylonian conquest and exile, the
Jews would be understandably preoccupied with issues of guilt and sin—
why did God allow this to happen to us?—and that the introduction of
rituals like the "guilt offering" and the "sin offering" in the P document
reflected that concern. He also believed, incorrectly, that the prophets
never alluded directly to the P document, suggesting that it was written
after the prophetic period, which essentially ended with the return from
exile.

For Wellhausen, though, the key element in the placement of P in
the postexilic period was the *Mishkan*, so richly detailed in the Torah.
(Indeed, no other object in the entire book receives such lavish treatment.)
Given the dimensions of the *Mishkan* as reported in the Torah, Wellhausen reasoned, it must have been too large for a nomadic group to carry
in the desert. Expanding on the work of Karl Graf, one of his predecessors, Wellhausen in fact argued that the *Mishkan* never existed. It was,
rather, a polite legal fiction standing in for the eventually-to-be-built
Temple in Jerusalem. But by reporting at such length on a locus for centralized worship, P was assuming that worship was always centralized,
Wellhausen deduced. That assumption would only hold true for someone

writing after the return from Babylonia. Before that, you will recall, the primary battle in Israel and Judah was over precisely that issue.

But Wellhausen may have been wrong on all counts. Linguistic analyses made in the past thirty years have argued that the P document was written in a preexilic Biblical Hebrew. Both Yirmiyahu and Yekhezkel allude to P. Guilt and sin were important issues in Judean life long before the destruction of the First Temple, going back to the loss of the northern kingdom. And the supposed evidence of the *Mishkan* is based on a misunderstanding of the construction methods used and its role in the First Temple, a complicated issue that Richard Elliott Friedman unravels with an elegance that reminds me of the term engineers use for such wonderful solutions: technically sweet. I won't try to summarize Friedman's argument here but, briefly, he shows how the *Mishkan* was, in fact, placed *inside* the Temple itself. It is not only plausible that P was writing in the time of the First Temple but, given the mysterious disappearance of the ark, the cherubim, and other significant objects described in the Torah, it is probable.

Which brings us back to the original question: Who wrote the P document?

So far, we can say with some certainty that P was a male supporter or member of the Aaronide priesthood, a Judean, probably from Jerusalem. The P document displays an intimate knowledge of the priestly rituals, so he probably either witnessed or participated directly in the rituals. We can also, therefore, say that he may have written before the fall of the First Temple.

The most significant piece of evidence leading to his identity comes from scholarly work published in the mid-1960s that showed a close correspondence between the P text and the one that resulted from the combination of J and E. There is considerable importance to this fact. First, it establishes that P lived after the destruction of the northern kingdom in 722 B.C.E., since it was that event that drove E south. We already know that he wrote before 587 B.C.E., so we have narrowed the pool of suspects considerably.

Of what does the close correspondence between the P and JE documents consist? Herein lies the most important clue that P may be preexilic. P follows JE closely. JE places its emphasis on Moshe as prophet and leader, places the blame for the Golden Calf on Aharon, and says almost nothing about sacrifices. P, an Aaronide priest or fellow traveler, needed to counter the ideological position of JE, so he wrote an alternative to what was by then a well-known document (he couldn't just make it go away; he had to add to it), a version that made Aharon an equal to Moshe and featured lengthy descriptions of the priestly duties, chief among them receiving and presiding over sacrifices.

Even the doublets in *Bereishit* are designed to prepare the ground for the Aaronide priesthood. For example, in the two versions of the Flood story, Noakh takes seven (JE) or two (P) of each species of animal onto the ark. JE's version requires extra "clean" animals so that some are available for sacrifice, but P's version makes no such provision because no sacrifice could take place (in his worldview) until there was a priesthood in existence to perform the rites.

Indeed, P offers a radically different vision of the relationship between God and humanity. The priests are the direct intermediaries between the Almighty and mere humankind. There are no angels in the P text, no talking animals, no conversations between an anthropomorphic God and humans, a very different story than the one told in JE and almost joyously affirmed in D. And the result, not surprisingly, is a very different kind of literary text, too. It is devoid of anecdota, supporting cast, and wordplay. It has all the warmth of a leasing agreement. In its way, P is a business report offered on behalf of Aharon's Priests, Inc.

D actually refers directly to one story recounted in P, the episode of the spies, which is recounted word for word. So D must have had access to or knowledge of the P text. And Yirmiyahu, who we believe may have been D, quotes P in the book that bears his name, but he attacks the pro-Aharon P author at some length. So P predates D, which narrows still further the window of opportunity for the authorship of the fourth document. P probably wrote between 722 B.C.E., the destruction of the northern kingdom, and 609 B.C.E., the death of Yoshiyahu.

In that time period, only one Judean king shared P's major preoccupations, centralization of worship *and* the empowerment of the Aaronide priests. That ruler is King Khizkiyahu, who established the division between the priests and the Levites, mentioned only in the P document, and who destroyed the most prominent symbol of the Mushite priesthood, the bronze snake ostensibly mentioned in the Torah.

Frustratingly, although we can pinpoint him as an Aaronide priest in the court of Khizkiyahu, we cannot give a name to P. We can only imagine what he would say had he known that his text, so carefully crafted as a point-by-point rebuttal to the JE document(s), would be combined with them and with the D text as well, creating the book we now call the Torah.

THE REDACTOR

Someone went to a great deal of trouble to edit the four source documents—J, E, P, D—into a single text. If one looks at an annotated version of the Torah text with the source of passages clearly marked, it is immediately obvious that this was not merely a matter of appending four texts in sequence. This is an intricately woven tapestry of individual passages ranging in length from a few words to many pages. If we accept by now that the Torah was not created by Moshe, then we need to determine the identity of the editor, the "redactor" as Bible scholars refer to him. Why did he use all four sources so generously in creating this document, and who was he? The two questions are inextricably linked.

The identity of the redactor is not as obvious from the texts as those of the authors. He did much less original writing, so we cannot deduce his interests and ideology as easily. But, as in our previous investigations, some logical inferences can be made. Each of the five books of the Torah, as we have them today, begins with lengthy passages from the P document. The bulk of the Torah is, in fact, drawn from P, and the redactor uses the lists of generations, taken from P, as transitional devices throughout *Bereishit*. (Friedman concludes that the original material that the redactor did add is written in the style and point of view of P as well.) P is the armature on which the text as a whole is mounted. We are probably safe inferring that the redactor is an Aaronide priest supporter.

Think back to our discussion of the aftermath of the Babylonian exile, when the Persians urged the Hebrews to return to Judah under the leadership of the priest Ezra and the governor Nekhemyah. The priests were now facing the reality of a Jerusalem in which the First Temple was destroyed, the Tabernacle, the ark, and the cherubim vanished. Yet sacrifices had to be offered if the priests were to continue to have a theological-juridical function. A new Temple would have to be built, albeit without those important trappings of Divine power, and the people would have to be encouraged to return to God's ways. The surest way to do that was by offering them a holy text, a "torah of Moshe" that counseled sacrifices in the Temple once again, the observation of holy Festivals, the primacy of the priesthood. This text would have to include all the old, familiar stories, the long-known legal edicts, the folkways; hence the necessity of meticulously preserving as much of the four source texts as was possible in a new document.

The new document would give primacy to the Aaronide priesthood, now the theological and political government of the Second Temple period. There were no more kings; Judah would remain a vassal state under a succession of imperial rulers. All other priestly groups had been routed by events. When the Hebrews returned to Jerusalem, their priestly leader, the one who would read to them from the "torah of Moshe," a text that included elements of all four documents, a text that he alone possessed, was Ezra.

Ezra is the only person other than Moshe whom the *Tanakh* characterizes as a "lawgiver." Ezra, who came to Judah with the Torah of Moshe in his hand.

In short, Ezra, the redactor.

REACTIONS TO THE DOCUMENTARY HYPOTHESIS

This is a considerably simplified version of the documentary hypothesis. The reaction to this theory can be easily imagined. If Abraham Ibn Ezra, a great Torah scholar and pious man, could be denounced by his contemporaries for even hinting at more than one source for the text of the Torah, the reaction provoked by the systematic analysis of the book, claiming four authors and a separate editor, none of whom were on Mount Sinai with Moshe, was a veritable firestorm. (Matters were probably not helped by the reality that the original proponents of this view were almost all German Protestants.)

Committed to the idea of a single author, the traditionally observant have struggled for millennia with the paradoxes presented by the Torah text.

The most Orthodox authorities are emphatic in their rejection of historical criticism. They dismiss challenges to the idea that Torah was given by God at Sinai, that it is a unitary text with a single author, Moshe, and that in its current form it is identical to the text that God dictated to Moshe, not varying by so much as a single letter.

Writing from Spain at the end of the Middle Ages, Abravanel spoke forcefully for their viewpoint:

Our one consolation is that the Torah is with us in our exile, and if we agree with these scholars that the Torah has undergone a process of textual damage and confusion, we will have nothing left on which to rely. . . . The eighth pillar of faith, as laid out by the great master Maimonides in his Mishnah commentary, requires every believer to accept that the Torah we have today is the same as that given to Mosheh on Mount Sinai, with no changes whatsoever.

As Menachem Cohen observes, if a single incorrect letter invalidates a *sefer Torah*, "we cannot, according to [Abravanel], entertain the notion that any error whatsoever has crept into the received text."

Faced with a theory that posits not only an evolving text and scribal error but four human authors and a human editor, traditionalists like Rabbi J. H. Hertz can barely contain their ire. Hertz, then chief rabbi of the United Kingdom, wrote in 1937, "The so-called Analysis of Sources, with its series of non-existent authors and irresponsible 'Redactors,' is unsupported by any external evidence whatsoever. None of these imaginary sources has come down to us in its original form, or in any form for that matter."

It would be churlish to point out that the vast majority of the literature of the ancient world has been lost through the grinding mills of time, that we know little more about most ancient authors than their names and the titles of a few of their works. Let us concede that no one has produced an actual D or J or P or E document or notes of the Redactor.

The "argument from silence" is a notoriously unreliable one, and the traditionalists have to offer something better than that. Of course, one can always say—as Torah commentators frequently do—that the doublets and textual oddities are there to be interpreted. And they do frequently enrich our reading of the text. But once you accept the idea that everything in the Torah as we know it was placed there by God in order to give us more to chew on (as some "creationists" explain the fossil record), then there is nothing left to discuss. Everything is reduced to a choice between faith and unbelief.

I can't accept that. Nor do most scholars across the entire range of Jewish thought, including several Orthodox authorities. Rav Chaim Navon of Yeshivat Har Etzion, an Orthodox yeshiva in Israel, cites his colleague Rabbi Amnon Bazak, who has offered two arguments against ignoring the work of source criticism and its successor theories:

Firstly, even people who lack all fear of God . . . may have the capacity to propose meaningful interpretations of the Torah. God Himself testifies in the Torah: "For this is your wisdom and your understanding in the sight of the nations, who shall hear all these statutes, and say, Surely this great nation is a wise and understanding people" (*Devarim* 4:6). Rambam, in his introduction to chapter *Chelek*, objects to a certain position, arguing that it contradicts reason, and will therefore not bring the gentiles to recognize the greatness of the Torah, but rather to scorn it. Hence, that position cannot possibly be correct. . . . [H]ow are we to relate to the problems that [non-believers] raise? How are we to answer the questions that they ask? Rabbi Bazak argues that it is wrong to assume that a non-believer cannot suggest persuasive interpretations of the Torah; hence, he cannot be disregarded. He further argues that in any event, over and beyond the metaphysical questions, we must deal with the difficulties raised by the proponents of biblical criticism in and of themselves.

But where, one must ask, is the evidence?

A decade after Rabbi Hertz's impassioned rejection of the documentary hypothesis, someone found incontrovertible evidence of variant and evolving Torah texts. It surfaced, almost literally, from a cave in the desert near the Dead Sea in a village called Qumran.

THE DEAD SEA SCROLLS AND THE CASE FOR HIGHER CRITICISM

By now the story of the Dead Sea Scrolls is pretty well known. In 1947 a shepherd looking for a lost animal (and how biblical is that?) tossed a rock into a cave near Qumran, a complex of ruins about eight miles south of Jericho, and heard it hit something that sounded like pottery. He climbed down and found what was probably an ancient *genizah*, containing pots filled with ancient scrolls. The shepherd, who was probably named Mohammed edh-Dib, knew that antiquities hunters were buying such objects and he brought a sample to one dealer who may or may not have known the importance of what Mohammed found. Eventually, the entire area became an archaeological gold mine, with thousands of texts in various conditions found in eleven caves in the area. (For sheer volume, this discovery is nowhere near as massive as the Cairo *Genizah*. See "The Cairo *Genizah*," page 132.) The Qumran find may have been the property of a communal sect called the Essenes; there is some dispute over this, although most scholars accept that theory. The settlement probably dates between the second century B.C.E. and the first century C.E., certainly from before the fall of the Second Temple.

What is in these scrolls, and how do they bolster the case for the documentary hypothesis?

The scrolls are a cornucopia of texts, mostly in Hebrew or Aramaic, with a very few in the Greek of the era in which the Septuagint (an important Greek translation of the *Tanakh* dating back to the third century B.C.E.) was written. As Hershel Shanks puts it, "The various texts were bewildering—previously unknown psalms, Bible commentaries, calendrical texts, mystical texts, apocalyptic texts, liturgical texts, purity laws, Rabbinic-like expansions of biblical stories, and on and on."

Keep in mind, however, that these are Jewish texts, an archive of contemporary Jewish documents, the preponderance of which are Jewish religious writings. (If, as scholars say, the Dead Sea Scrolls give us new insights into the early years of Christianity, it is a Jewish insight, one that provides extensive proof of the Jewish roots of Jesus and his teachings. As Shanks writes, "The pre-Christian beatitudes found in the Dead Sea Scrolls are part of the Jewish heritage on which the beatitudes of the Gospels are built.")

The scrolls give us new insights into Jewish life and thought under the Romans before the beginnings of Christianity. More important for our purposes, they present a startling picture of the development of the Hebrew Bible, one markedly at odds with the concept of Mosaic authorship. We know that the final canonization of the *Tanakh* would not take place until the second century C.E. What was perhaps less clear before Qumran was that the process of creating a canonical text involved considerably more than just deciding which books to keep and which ones to discard. On the contrary, as the scrolls and fragments brought out of the caves immediately attested, there were a large number of variant texts in circulation, and someone had to make decisions regarding every single variation.

Shanks recounts a telling incident involving Frank Moore Cross Jr., who was at Qumran in the mid-1950s. He was gently, meticulously cleaning an illegible scrap of parchment. As he carefully removed nearly two thousand years of encrusted dirt, he began to recognize the fragment as a piece of the *Sefer Shmuel,* written in Hebrew, "but it was not the version of Samuel found in the standard text of the Hebrew Bible, the Masoretic Text (MT). It conformed instead to the Greek translation, known as the Septuagint, which meant that the Hebrew text used in the Greek translation was different from the standard *textus receptus*. . . . Cross describes the moment: 'I suddenly realized I had found something that to me and to other textual critics of the Hebrew Bible was earthshaking.' " Simply put, Cross was holding the Hebrew upon which the Septuagint had been based—and it wasn't the version of the Hebrew Bible everyone thought it was.

Suddenly, we are faced with the existence of many different versions of the supposedly unitary and infallible text. The scrolls include the oldest copies of biblical books discovered to date, some two hundred different biblical manuscripts, some dating back as far as the middle of the third century B.C.E. (About a quarter of the texts found in the caves were biblical, and every book except *Ester* is represented in the material.) Although they are as much as a thousand years older than the oldest extant Hebrew Bible, the scrolls confirm the overall accuracy of our modern texts.

We need to backtrack a moment and untangle this twisted skein of texts. We have come a long way from the Water Gate in Jerusalem. Essentially, there are three versions of the *Tanakh* in play when we study the Dead Sea Scrolls. The first is an early version of the Masoretic Text (MT), the Hebrew Bible that is the standard text we read today, compiled by a group of scribes in Tiberias in the tenth century C.E. (see "Men of Tradition," page 126). The second is a version of the Septuagint, the Greek translation commissioned in the third century B.C.E. by Ptolemy II from the Jews of Alexandria for the great library of that city. Finally, there is the Samaritan Pentateuch, the version of the Torah read by the break-away Samaritan sect, which may date as far back as Yoshiyahu, although the extant versions are post–Second Temple; this volume seems to follow the MT but has over six thousand variations.

Perhaps you now see the extraordinary nature of Cross's find. If the Septuagint, frequently consulted by Bible scholars when the MT's Hebrew is ancient and obscure, was derived from a different Hebrew version of the *Tanakh*, then what makes the Dead Sea Scrolls important to us is that they confirm the idea that the Torah was not a single, perfect text perfectly transmitted from generation to generation, without change or error.

The scrolls include at minimum three variant texts, prototypes of the Masoretic, Septuagint, and Samaritan Bibles. And they are precisely that: *prototypes*. The version of the MT that was in use at Qumran is significantly different from the one we have today.

Most important of all, study of the texts found at Qumran shows us that, as Menachem Cohen puts it, "the Qumran scribes did not have the notion of an 'ideal' text in the exact image of the current MT. . . . [T]here are no signs that the people of Qumran entertained the idea of one *single* version that was a fixed, sanctified text" (emphasis in the original).

Simply put, in the Qumran community many versions of the Torah and other books of the Hebrew Bible existed side by side and were accepted as the word of *Adonai*. No one text had a monopoly on holiness.

Why should the practice of one ostensibly small sect living in isolation at the edge of the Sea of Galilee concern us?

The members of the community of Qumran came from all over Judah. Although we are still unsure of exactly what the purpose of the settlement there might have been, the population was probably self-selecting and the inhabitants were drawn from all over the land. And the *genizah* or library or whatever it was in which the scrolls were kept contained a similarly representative collection of texts. So someone, somewhere in Second Temple–era Judah was using these variant texts for worship and/or study, which means that there was no definitive version of the Torah at that time. This directly contradicts the belief that a single, unitary text was handed down to Moshe at Sinai and passed on in the manner described in *Pirkei Avot*.

Obviously this doesn't confirm the documentary hypothesis, but it does add to doubts about Mosaic authorship. In fact, it was the Pharisees who began the process of discarding the multiplicity of texts, a process that the Dead Sea Scrolls help clarify incidentally. This process continued through the fall of the Second Temple in 70 C.E. and the disastrous Bar Kokhba revolt against the Romans in 135. The Masoretes came along about six centuries later, adding punctuation and vowel markings to the text, and the result became the template for every Hebrew Bible since.

MEN OF TRADITION

Whether or not God gave the Torah to Moshe at Sinai, that Torah was, like our own *sifrei Torah* today, a far cry from any book we would recognize and read. There was no division into books, chapters, or verses; no punctuation or paragraphing; no vowels, hence no indication of pronunciation; no cantillation marks. Moreover, as we note elsewhere in this chapter, there really wasn't a single agreed-upon version of the text. Someone had to sit down and create all of these utterly necessary accoutrements.

In reality, this was the work of centuries, with the process of standardization probably starting with Ezra and his colleagues. The bulk of the work would be done twelve hundred years later by a group of eighth-century scribes and scholars centered around two Torah academies in Tiberias, near the Sea of Galilee. The men who undertook the task were called the Men of *Masorah*, literally meaning "transmission" but understood to mean "tradition." For the most part working anonymously, they studied the texts carefully, arriving at a standardized version that is now known as the Masoretic Text (MT).

The earliest extant example of the MT is the Aleppo Codex, which dates from the 900s. For a long time the keepers of the codex, the heads of the synagogue at Aleppo, Syria, refused to allow modern scholars to examine it; in 1947 a mob of Syrians set fire to the synagogue as part of a protest against the United Nations resolution to partition Palestine/ Israel, and part of the codex was destroyed. The copy that modern scholars had been using, the Leningrad Codex, was written about a century later, probably based on the Aleppo document. As the oldest complete copy of the MT, the Leningrad manuscript is the base text for the *Biblia Hebraica*, the most famous and important critical edition of the *Tanakh*, still considered authoritative today, more than thirteen hundred years after the Masoretes completed their task.

ALTERNATIVES TO THE DOCUMENTARY HYPOTHESIS

One could say that the documentary hypothesis is a late-blooming flower of the Enlightenment (particularly given the early role of Hobbes and Spinoza in challenging Mosaic authorship), one more attempt to put God and man on an equal footing. But that would not address the question of whether it is an accurate explanation of the writing of the Torah.

Today, like the theory of evolution, the documentary hypothesis is accepted as proven and—more important—provable. Like evolution, it has received more than a century of fine-tuning and revision, but it still survives the main benchmark of scientific truth—that it is falsifiable by objective testing.[6] Like evolution, the most significant challenges to its position as the dominant paradigm in its field have come from those who are advancing another scientific theory that is as incompatible with the theory of Mosaic authorship as evolution is with a fundamentalist reading of the first chapters of *Bereishit*. And like evolution, it is due to new scientific evidence (some archaeological, some the result of more sophisticated linguistic methodologies) that shortcomings in source criticism have become a cause for further research. Today, the main controversies surrounding the question of who wrote the Torah and the rest of the Hebrew Bible center on the dating of the source materials—Preexilic? Monarchic? Postexilic?—and whether the original materials were transmitted orally or in some written form.

This latter question is of considerable import. Form criticism, the theory that has dislodged source criticism as the dominant paradigm in biblical studies, grew out of the work of one of the latter's staunchest proponents, when he became convinced of the oral beginnings of the texts. Hermann Gunkel (1862–1932) believed he could address the perception of holes in the theory by going back to the origins of the stories themselves and by breaking the text down into smaller units for analysis than the four source documents proposed by the documentary hypothesis. Gunkel's work led him to believe that the texts we read today had their roots in the collection of much older oral traditions of myth and legend. In his view, the source authors of *Bereishit*—J, E, and P—were, in fact, like folklorists anthologizing collectively held myths explaining the origins of the world and the phenomena in it. Of course, with its focus on Creation and the first generations of humanity, *Bereishit* lends itself particularly well to such an interpretation.

Gunkel thought he was offering a supplement to the documentary hypothesis. However, he was also undermining it. If J, E, and P were merely collecting orally transmitted legends, then their input into the content of the Torah was more limited than Wellhausen and his nineteenth-century followers believed. And the very anomaly that led to the documentary hypothesis—the doublets—had another, contradictory explanation. For example, there are three versions of the story of the ill-fated encounter of a Patriarch (Avraham in the first two versions, Yitzkhak in the last), his beautiful wife (Sarah in the first two versions, Rivkah in the third), and a royal host (Pharoah in the first version, Avimelekh in the last two). We attribute one to P and the other two to J. But if there are two versions given by J, why does he include both? They don't seem to contradict each other or enrich the narrative in the ways that we assume the source documents will. Does he include them because he feels constrained to do so by some other organizing principle, that is, because he's anthologizing the known versions of an oft-told tale? It's not a big hole in the documentary hypothesis, but it presents a problem.

Another problem arises with the transition between the Avraham stories and the Yosef stories. The former reads like a series of loosely connected tales, the latter like a tightly woven narrative. The former is a sort of metamyth, with Avraham the founding father of a nation, while the latter is a family drama that anticipates the creation of the novel with its psychological insights and structural clarity. Even the role of God is different in the two story-cycles, with the Eternal taking an active part in Avraham's story, commanding him, guiding him, debating with him; Yosef, although alluding to God's larger role in his story, has no real contact with the Divine. Yet the documentary hypothesis claims considerable overlapping between the authorship of these two sections of *Bereishit.*

If the documentary hypothesis doesn't offer satisfactory answers to these questions, form criticism is somewhat more helpful. The division of the text into smaller units—particularly in the early part of Genesis—makes somewhat more sense for the Avraham cycle with its collagelike juxtaposition of seemingly unrelated incidents, just as the repetitiveness of some passages of the Torah suggests the oral transmission methods of Greek epics (albeit quite a bit less systematically used).

There are other theories that address some of these questions directly. The renewed focus on dating the source materials of the Torah is designed to throw new light on the structural design and internal connections within the text. If we can say with greater certainty in what order the text(s) were combined and edited, we will have a clearer picture of the process by which the Torah was written and edited. To this end, we have seen the development of redaction criticism, an outgrowth of and corrective to form criticism, focusing on the way in which a text has been edited, discerning the stages in the development that led to the version we have today, and tradition criticism, also a by-product of form criticism, which studies how the traditions encountered in form criticism developed over time.

How have these developments affected the documentary hypothesis? I must admit that to a layperson, someone with little background in scientific Bible study, the newer paradigms do not seem to invalidate the basic approach of source criticism. Rather, they supplement and enrich it, providing a greater context for and richer understanding of the multiplicity of viewpoints apparently present in the Torah.

But if the Torah speaks in many voices, what of the Revelation at Sinai? The Torah is the foundation stone of all Jewish thought, a moral polestar that guides the followers of the Abrahamic religions. Alfred North Whitehead once said that all philosophy was nothing more than a series of footnotes to Plato. If one is willing to accept that diagnosis, why not live by Plato? The conception of Revelation at Sinai is, I believe, as David Weiss Halivni has said, the touchstone from which all Judaism proceeds. Without it there is no center to the Jewish faith. Can we reconcile the idea of a God-given Torah with the work of the "higher criticism"?

Obviously, for the most traditionalist Jewish thinkers the answer must be an emphatic no. Rabbi Tzvi Tau dismisses the "higher criticism" utterly:

> One who does not believe in the Divine origin and sublimity of the words, that they all flow from Divine truth that is infinite, absolute and eternal—one who lacks this faith will not understand the holy Scriptures whatsoever. All of his analyses, all of his investigations, all of his theories, and all of his "discoveries" fall into the category of nonsense. When all these ideas are missing, when humility and self-effacement are lacking, when these elements are absent, come the scholars—Jews or gentiles, it makes no difference—and search through the holy Scriptures. They raise objections, they erase, they distort, and they emend; they suggest theories, they demonstrate creativity, they present novel ideas—what is all this to us? How are we connected to them? We occupy ourselves in the truth of the Torah, we engage ourselves in the holiness of the Torah. One who lacks both the beginning and the end—there is no point in talking to him at all!

Obviously, Rabbi Amnon Bazak would disagree just as emphatically, even if his position is not entirely hospitable to the work of the various branches of critical theory. Many contemporary Orthodox and Conservative rabbis have offered no less thoughtful examinations of the "higher criticism" that willingly draw upon the insights they find useful without invalidating the idea of a God-given Torah.

For example, Rabbi Mordechai Breuer takes the position that one can accept the exegetical conclusions of modern research without embracing a theological corollary that rejects the sacredness of the Torah. He writes:

> That simple exegesis, which sees the Torah as one consecutive structure, without contradictions and uniform in style, has been irretrievably contradicted and rejected. The Torah's division into "sources" to which "were added" "interpretive comments" and "editorial supplements," is an irrefutable truth, which jumps out at the student, against his will, according to all linguistic standards and "the plain interpretations of Scripture that present themselves anew each day." All the forced harmonistic resolutions cannot stand up to the inner truth of the ingenious work of Wellhausen and his colleagues. . . . Come and see the glorious wreath of the Torah, go and ponder the glory and splendor of its pages: they go and slowly spread out, page by page, each in its unique channel—and you find before you living expressions of that Divine quality that crosses generations: the trait of the Tetragrammaton, the trait of the name of E-lokim, and the trait of the name of E-l Shad-dai—hidden traits that embrace all the worlds and bestow their bounty on high and below. So too the contradictions in the Torah are but imaginary contradictions regarding the ways of God's providence!
>
> Now, then, is it any wonder that the pages of the Torah clash, and the human intellect finds it difficult to reconcile the contradictions? Does not God's providence in the world—the visible expression of God's traits and holy names—does it not, as it were, clash with and contradict itself, God forbid, in the eyes of man and according to his human understanding? If the Holy One, blessed be He, embraces both justice and mercy, both lovingkindness and might, if He appears to Israel as an old man in a yeshiva and also as a young man at war, as merciful and gracious, and also as zealous and vindictive—how then can it be imagined that His Torah—all the letters of which constitute His holy names—will go forward in peace and calm, as a single continuum that settles in the heart of all? Were all the sages of the east and the west to assemble and seek a solution to the contradictions between the first two chapters of the book of Bereishit, they would not come up with even a broken shard.

Rabbi Breuer's reponse reaffirms the *mysterium tremendum* of the Holy One, the unknowability of God's will and being. In a certain sense, one might say that Breuer's viewpoint, surprisingly, accords harmoniously with that of Conservative and Reform rabbis who would argue that, whatever form the text of the Torah takes, its contents are divinely inspired.[7]

Regardless of which of those points of view one takes—and there is, of course, a world of difference between them—there remains at least one certainty that has guided the work of Jewish thought since the Torah was first read. To understand the words of the Torah, one must continually delve into them, read them, reread them, interpret and reinterpret them. If the Torah itself is the foundation stone of all Jewish thought, Torah commentary is the edifice that rests upon it. And it is to that edifice that we turn our attention next.

THE CAIRO *GENIZAH*

As noted in Chapter 1, one does not casually dispose of sacred texts. The repository for any writing bearing the name of God is the *genizah,* a storeroom that can be found wherever there are Jewish communities. Eventually the materials are given a ritual burial. It is possible that the caves in which the Dead Sea Scrolls were found in 1947 were just such storage places.

The *genizah* of the Ben Ezra Synagogue in Fostat, a suburb of Cairo, Egypt, is almost as famous as those caves. The synagogue had already been in existence for more than a thousand years in December 1896 when a young scholar named Solomon Schechter visited in the hope of obtaining some old manuscripts for Cambridge University. For some unknown reason, the materials in the Fostat *genizah* had never received burial, and what Schechter found was a veritable treasure trove, more than 210,000 texts and text fragments, secular and sacred, painting a remarkably complete portrait of Jewish life in the eastern Mediterranean in the medieval period. Thanks to the dry climate of Egypt, these materials were in remarkably good condition. Schechter (who would go on to achieve considerable fame in the United States, heading the Jewish Theological Seminary for decades) was able to secure 140,000 of them for Cambridge.

Stefan Reif, the current director of the Taylor-Schechter Genizah Research Unit at Cambridge, pinpoints the importance of this collection succinctly:

They represent the most important discovery of new material for every aspect of scientific Hebrew and Jewish studies in the Middle Ages. . . .

Among the subjects that have benefitted substantially are the emergence of Hebrew grammatical systems; the development of synagogal lectionaries and of translations and interpretations of the Hebrew Bible; and the literary history of such sectarian works as the Damascus Document and Ben Sira. Major impacts have also been made on the textual and exegetical study of Talmudic, Midrashic, liturgical and poetic literature, and on the evolution of Jewish religious law.

More than a century later, the scholars at the Genizah Research Unit, established in 1974, are still poring over the texts rescued from that storeroom in Fostat. Among the most exciting recent finds is a folio manuscript written by Maimonides. In addition to countless articles and books, the unit also produces a modest but entertaining newsletter, "Genizah Fragments," which appears in April and October every year. For more information on their work, go to http://www.lib.cam.ac.uk/Taylor-Schechter.

NOTES

1. There are many excellent books on the documentary hypothesis, but for this chapter I must express a particular debt to Richard Elliott Friedman's *Who Wrote the Bible?* which wears its considerable scholarship so lightly that the result reads like a thriller, and to a 1962 volume by Edward Zerin, *The Birth of the Torah*, which someone ought to bring back into print.

2. There is a distinction made in biblical study between the "higher" and "lower" criticisms. Lower criticism refers to so-called textual criticism, the intent of which is to determine the actual correct version of the Bible text. It is called lower because it is the foundation on which all other fields of inquiry concerning the text are based.

3. Some have claimed that J is a woman, most notably Harold Bloom and David Rosenberg in their best-selling *The Book of J*. It is virtually impossible to either prove or disprove this assertion, but J is definitely the only one of the Torah's authors who *could* be a woman.

4. In *The Hidden Book of the Bible*, Friedman goes one step further than Harold Bloom and David Rosenberg, reconstructing a book by J that incorporates many elements from the Primary History, extending well past the *Khumash*.

5. Or one of them. Frank Moore Cross believes that there were two D authors, one who was a contemporary of Yoshiyahu's and another who came later and beefed up the text to further the thesis of the first. It is highly possible that he is right, although as Richard Elliott Friedman notes, it is not impossible that a single author wrote the entire text since the span of years between Yoshiyahu's death in 609 B.C.E. and the Babylonian exile in 587 B.C.E. is well within a single life span. For the sake of clarity, I have chosen to treat D as a single author.

6. For some crucial examples, read *Empirical Models for Biblical Criticism*, ed. Jeffrey Tigay (Eugene, OR: Wipf & Stock Publishers, 2005).

7. For a brilliant and unusual response to this issue, I highly recommend *Revelation Restored: Divine Writ and Critical Responses*, by David Weiss Halivni (Boulder, CO: Westview Press, 1997). Halivni is one of the greatest living scholars of Talmud, and he proposes an elegant solution that reconciles the "higher criticism" and Revelation at Sinai using the events in the Wilderness as a jumping-off point.

4

THE REST IS COMMENTARY
Interpreting the Torah

Any jot or tittle may provide the occasion, just as any sound or image in the text may engage the inventive mind. The results follow their cause: the new "biblical" teachings are not abstract propositions, but forms of concrete discourse inspired by the shapes of Scripture.
—Michael Fishbane, *The Exegetical Imagination*

In *Pirkei Avot*, that wonderful, pungent collection of ethical sayings of the rabbis of the Mishnaic period, we are told regarding the Torah, "Turn it and turn it again, for everything is in it." Perhaps, but you may need help in finding what you seek. With that famous public reading in 444 B.C.E., there emerged a body of professional interpreters of the Torah. Right away, it became necessary for someone not only to translate this Hebrew document into Aramaic, the linguistic currency in which the ancient Jews dealt in that era, but also to explain much that was seemingly obscure, abstruse, or archaic to the ears of the average Jerusalem resident in 444 B.C.E.

And the explanations haven't stopped since.

Inevitably, one must ask, "Why all this commentary?"

First and most obviously, the Torah is a difficult text to understand. But the Torah is no mere literary artifact. On the most basic level, in interpreting the Torah, one is interpreting the entire world. For the traditional Jew, the Torah is the foundation stone upon which Creation itself rests, God's blueprint for the universe and, at the same time, humanity's operating manual. The Torah doesn't "lend itself" to multiple interpretations. Rather, it *demands* them, since the slightest mistake in interpretation could have ramifications more fraught than, say, producing a lousy staging of *Hamlet*. For the observant Jew in particular, the world itself may be said to hang in the balance.

But even the deeply religious may find the book as much a source of confusion as counsel. As we have seen in Chapter 3, whether one accepts the concept of Mosaic authorship (under God's hand) or the documentary hypothesis, the Torah is a complex, often contradictory text that frequently speaks with more than one voice. There is much that is unclear; there are many questions unanswered.

For example, we are told in the Torah that on the Sabbath we shall do no work. But what is the definition of work? The text is silent. Someone else has to fill in that all-important blank.

The trouble starts at the very beginning. Consider the commentary by Rashi, the greatest of the medieval Bible commentators, on the story of Creation. Noting that *Bereishit 2* begins with God's breath "hovering above the surface of the waters," he cautions, "You must question yourself . . . scripture not yet having revealed when the creation of the water took place." Perhaps, as Rashi explains it, the story of Creation is not told in chronological order. Or perhaps there is another explanation, but there needs to be *some* explanation, whether Moshe wrote the Torah at God's dictation or it was created by a series of authors and a redactor.

Even if we were to accept the laws of the Torah, to commit ourselves to all 613 *mitzvot*, there are still mysteries bred by the passage of time and the movement of history and science. What are we to do with the commandments that relate to the Temple, now that it is no longer standing? How do we apply the *mitzvot* to modern technologies? Can we drive on the Sabbath and Festivals? Turn on an electric light? What do the *mitzvot* say about gene-splicing research that uses porcine DNA to build a better tomato?

If you are a strictly observant Jew whose existence is guided by the Torah, these questions are not to be treated lightly. Even for a liberal Jew, they carry a certain intellectual weight, not merely as problem-solving exercises but as indications of how the rabbinic mind responds to sacred texts.

Faced with this panoply of problems—unclear texts, contradictory texts, "outdated" texts—the sages of the past responded by erecting a companion to the Torah. And that text quickly became a more massive edifice than the foundation on which it was based. But, regardless of their comparative size and heft, as Michael Fishbane observes, the new "biblical" teachings are not abstract propositions, but "forms of concrete discourse inspired by the shapes of Scripture."

ORAL AND WRITTEN TORAH REVISITED

You may recall from Chapter 1 that there are two Torahs, the Written and the Oral. The Written Torah is the *Khumash,* the Five Books of Moses given at Sinai. (For convenience, we will stipulate for the moment that Moshe received the Torah from God at Sinai.) This Torah was dictated by God to Moshe, and Moshe wrote it down for *B'nei Yisrael* and all mankind. But the story didn't end there. The Eternal also is said to have relayed to Moshe interpretations and explanations of the Torah's text, a second text as it were, that eventually became the Talmud. (In fact, as we noted in Chapter 3, there are those Torah scholars, the maximalists, who believe that all subsequent disquisitions on Torah by the sages were given at Sinai as well, up to and including today.)

One could argue in good faith that Moshe's final speech to the Israelites, which makes up the bulk of *Sefer Devarim,* is, in fact, the first example of interpreting the Torah, that Moshe is elaborating on and clarifying the laws handed down at Sinai. In fact, he does offer clarification—apparently in his own words—of passages from *Vayikra* and additional *mitzvot* as well.

The tradition of interpreting the Torah orally, which became Rabbinic Judaism and evolved into the manifold forms of Judaism that exist today, can be traced directly from that public reading of the Torah in 444 B.C.E. When Ezra read the Torah aloud to the Israelites assembled before the Water Gate in Jerusalem, the vast majority of his listeners spoke Aramaic. Consequently, they needed to have the Hebrew text both translated and explained, which the elders present did on the spot. Thus began two traditions of Torah commentary that continue to this day: midrash and translation of the Torah into the vernacular. (For a discussion of translation, see "Translating the Torah: Another Kind of Interpretation" on page 171.)

Midrash, a word that we have used frequently already, is derived from the three-letter Hebrew root *dalet-resh-shin* (d-r-sh), meaning variously "to investigate, to inquire, to study." A sermon explicating the Torah is a *derashah* (colloquially, a *derash*), which is pluralized as *derashot*. The person who gives such a talk is a *darshan* (male) or *darshanit* (female), pluralized as *darshanim* (or *darshaniyot*, if they are all women). The custom of hearing of *derashah* after a reading from the Torah is probably as old as the Torah itself; in *Devarim* 31 we find the description of such a ritual as part of the *hakhel* ceremony that was observed every seven years at Sukkot. However, the earliest documented example of someone explicating Torah in public orally is that famous reading in 444 B.C.E., the first of many such occasions.

Midrash—the process of interpreting sacred texts—may honestly be said to occur any time someone explicates or interprets Torah. The word is applied to the vast body of such literature that has accumulated over the history of the Jewish people or to a single example of such interpretative material. (The plural form is *midrashim*.) Although we still refer to this literature as Oral Torah, at some point the body of work had become so vast that it was impossible for any single person—or even a group of people—to memorize it all and, reluctantly, authorities permitted it to be copied down. Their reluctance was understandable; by recording the Oral Torah, they might be mistakenly perceived as according it the same status as the words God was supposed to have given Moshe at Sinai. (We will delve into the process of writing down the Oral Torah shortly.)

There are two types of midrash, and the difference between them goes to the heart of why midrash exists at all. *Halakhic midrash* exists to clarify and establish points of Jewish religious law, deriving practice from the *mitzvot* as enumerated in the Torah. *Aggadic midrash*, which has its roots in the preaching of the *darshanim*, grows out of a very different impulse, the desire to fill in the narrative gaps in Torah, to flesh out the stories of the Patriarchs and *B'nei Yisrael*, and to draw moral lessons from the text. *Halakhah* and *aggadah* are as different as night and day, yet they are both derived from the Torah's text, albeit frequently in unexpected ways, and each finds its chief expression in midrashim.[1]

SOME IMPORTANT MIDRASHIC TEXTS

Here is a brief list of key collections of midrashim, organized by chronology and type.* English translations of virtually all of these are available today.

Date	Exegetical	Homiletical	Narrative
Tannaitic	*Mekhilta* (H)		
	Sifra (H)		
	Sifrei (H)		
400–650 C.E.	*Bereishit Rabbah*	*Vayikra Rabbah*	
	Eikhah Rabbah	*Pesikta de'Rav Kahana*	
650–900	*Midrash Mishlei*	*Midrash Tankhuma*	*Pirkei de'Rebbe Eliezer*
	Kohelet Rabbah	*Devarim Rabbah*	*Tanna debe' Eliyahu*
900–1000	*Midrash Tehillim*		
	Shemot Rabbah		
	Rut Zuta		
	Eikhah Zuta		
1000–1200	*Midrash Tehillim* (by school of Rabbi Moshe Ha'Darshan)		*Sefer Ha'Yashar*

Late anthologies of midrash include: *Yalkut Shimoni; Midrash Ha'Gadol; Ein Y'aakov.*

*From "Midrash," by Barry W. Holtz, in *Back to the Sources: Reading the Classic Jewish Texts,* ed. Barry W. Holtz (New York: Simon & Schuster, 1984).
(H) Predominantly halakhic midrashim.

HALAKHAH VS. *AGGADAH*

Colloquially speaking, one might say that *halakhah* is the "bad cop" of Judaism, *aggadah,* the "good cop." The great Hebrew poet Hayim Nachman Bialik puts it more gracefully in a famous essay, "Law and Legend, or *Halakhah* and *Aggadah*":

> Halakhah wears an angry frown; Aggadah, a broad smile. The one is the embodiment of the Attribute of Justice, iron-handed, rigorous and severe; the other is the embodiment of the Quality of Mercy, essentially lenient and indulgent, as mild as a dove. The one promulgates coercive decrees and knows no compromise; the other presumes only to suggest and is sympathetically cognizant of man's shortcomings; she is shilly-shally and weak-willed. Halakhah represents the body, the actual deed; Aggadah represents the content, the fervent motive. Halakhah enjoins a dogged adherence and imposes upon us stern obligations; Aggadah, on the other hand, holds out the prospect of continual rejuvenescence, liberty and freedom.

In truth, this sort of comparison does a disservice to both halakhic and aggadic midrash, but particularly to the former. If the purpose of the Torah is, as Orthodox thinkers would tell us, to enumerate and confer "the yoke of the *Mitzvot*," those commandments given at Sinai (and after) that set the Jewish people apart from all other peoples, then the purpose of the halakhic midrash and the other postbiblical writings that focus on *halakhah* is to turn the steel skeleton of the *mitzvot* into a building in which an observant Jew can live every day, to iron out the inconsistencies, ambiguities, and contradictions in the Torah text and to allow it to be applied to the world even as the world has changed since the Revelation at Sinai. The word *halakhah* is derived from the Hebrew root *he-lamed-khof* (h-l-kh), "to walk or go," and *halakhah* is nothing less than the way a Jew is commanded to go through daily life, a legal code composed of Torah, a thousand years of commentary, and another thousand years of rabbinic responses to the ever-changing world (in short, more commentary).

Halakhah may be simply (perhaps oversimply) defined as Jewish religious law. Unsurprisingly, halakhic writings tend, as Bialik says, to "a dry prose, a stiff stereotypical style, a monotony of language, eloquent of the

Supremacy of Reason." Halakhic midrashim, the halakhic passages of the Talmud and the later halakhic writings that follow on their heels, are legal rulings with all the warmth and charm that implies.

But nothing could be more essential to understanding Judaism, in both Orthodox and non-Orthodox forms, than *halakhah*. It is not an exaggeration to say that the non-Orthodox streams of the Jewish religion are distinguished from their Orthodox predecessor by their attitude toward *halakhah,* which became the issue that drove all the divisions within modern Judaism.

With that in mind, let us examine the thread of *halakhah* as it runs from the *sefer Torah* to the contemporary rabbinate.

FOLLOWING THE THREAD OF *HALAKHAH*

That morning in Jerusalem when Ezra read the Torah to the assembled Judeans hungry for guidance from *Adonai* after the disasters of exile, his audience was eager to comply with the laws and precepts of the sacred scroll. Perhaps, as *B'nei Yisrael* said at Sinai, the Hebrews thought, "We will do and we will hear." Indeed, one might conceive of the public reading at the Water Gate as a reenactment of the Revelation at Sinai, much as every *Seder K'riat Ha'Torah* is a symbolic recapitulation of the Giving of the Law.

But, like the Israelites-to-be at Sinai, the Judeans of 444 B.C.E. were undoubtedly troubled by the opacity of the Torah text. For starters, they were no longer Hebrew speakers—they spoke Aramaic—and the text was in Hebrew (and a somewhat archaic Hebrew at that). Then there was (and is) the problem of a text that is rife with gaps and dislocations. In a delicious irony, Judah finally had the centralized worship that Yoshiyahu had craved, but the rules of that worship would remain problematic.

How can you live by a code of laws that you don't understand?

Consequently, elucidating the laws of the Torah—not just listing the 613 *mitzvot,* but explaining how they work—became a primary concern for the priests, the scribes, and the teachers who would eventually become the rabbis. Halakhic commentary on the Torah probably does not significantly predate its aggadic counterpart, but it is the legal materials that were the first to be codified, the first elements of the Oral Torah to be written down.

Tradition says that Ezra convened a body of scholars (120 or 85 in number, depending on the source) that would be known as the *Knesset Ha'Gedolah*. In a period that extended from roughly 539 to 332 B.C.E. (a stretch of time that predates Ezra, of course), these men offered oral rulings on the Torah and its precepts. Among their greatest tasks was the establishment of the canon of the Hebrew Bible. This version of the history of the period is the one favored by the sages of *Pirkei Avot*, tracing an unbroken line of authority from Moshe to their contemporaries. We do not actually know how much, if any of this, is historically accurate.

The Men of the Great Assembly were not only interpreters of Torah; each was a rarity in those days, a man who could read and write. Hence, they were also known as the *soferim/scribes*. These men had the daunting task of bringing order to the rapidly accumulating body of Oral Law. Imagine what it would be like to codify and organize all of the case law handed down in the United States since the ratification of the Constitution in 1787; now imagine how much greater that task would be if almost all the decisions had been made orally, and before you could organize them you had to record them. On a somewhat smaller scale, that was the task facing the *soferim*.

Their task would be complicated by a simple political fact: as the dance of empires across their land grew more fierce, the Jews lost ever-increasing amounts of autonomy and sovereignty. How do you hold a people together when they have no control over their political destiny? The Men of the Great Assembly had to construct a different set of ties to bind the Jews together: laws and precepts, rituals and festivals. The Jews were bound into a continuing nationhood by the leather straps of *tefillin*, the blue threads of their prayer shawls, and the holy language of Hebrew, now reserved exclusively for worship. This is the only kind of nationhood that can keep a scattered and landless people together in the Diaspora for nineteen hundred years, that can hold together a nation whose borders are conceptual and practical rather than geographic and political. No army can conquer it because it exists only in the minds of those who accept its laws.

MISHNAH

When Yehudah Ha'Nasi finished the redaction of the Mishnah, the first major collection of Oral Torah to be codified, the work of the Great

Assembly was, in some sense, complete. A learned body of Jewish leaders had assembled the extant rabbinic rulings interpreting the laws governing Judaism. At least in theory it should stand alone (although the Gemara, the other part of what we know as the Talmud, is a commentary on it).

When reading the Mishnah, it is useful to remember that these texts were originally transmitted orally and were designed to be memorized. Consequently, the language of the Mishnah is generally terse, compact, repetitive. Jacob Neusner characterizes it further as "small-minded, picayune, obvious, dull, routine—everything its age was not." But Neusner also explains that this seeming paradox was quite deliberate. The orderliness and routine of Mishnah represents an effort by Yehudah Ha'Nasi and his collaborators to resist the uncertainties of their age by reasserting verities of an older, more permanent vintage.

The Mishnah is organized in six *sedarim/orders*, which are then subdivided into between seven and twelve *masekhtot/tractates*, sixty-three in all. The tractates are then divided into *perakim/chapters* and, finally, into *mishnayot*, which may be as short as a single sentence. (The Gemara, not surprisingly, is organized along the same lines, although the tractates covered in the Babylonian and Palestinian Talmuds differ. For a fuller explanation of this and related matters, see *Essential Judaism.*)

Each of the six orders is named in a way that suggests one of its primary topics. The first order, *Zera'im/Seeds*, deals particularly with laws of agriculture. The second order, *Mo'ed/Appointed Seasons*, covers the laws governing the Festivals, the fast days, and the Sabbath. The third order, *Nashim/Women*, primarily is concerned with laws governing marriage, divorce, betrothal, and adultery (although this order also contains the tractates *Nedarim/Vows* and *Nazir*, which deals with the Nazirite vows of asceticism). The fourth order is *Nezikin/Damages*, which is largely concerned with what modern Anglo-American courts would call civil and criminal law, but also includes laws governing the treatment of idolators, and the most commonly read tractate of the Mishnah, *Avot*, a collection of ethical maxims. The fifth order, *Kodashim/Holy Things*, covers such Temple-related matters as sacrifices, ritual slaughter, and the priesthood. The sixth and final order is *Tohorot/Purities*, and the majority of the tractates within it deal with issues of ritual purity and impurity.

Several things are immediately apparent from a survey of the six orders of the Mishnah.

First, the structure of the book, despite some attempt at a systematic organization, is more than a bit haphazard. In part, the problem lies in

Yehudah Ha'Nasi's decision to incorporate large sections of material intact from earlier sources; earlier collections often grouped rulings by their authors rather than subjects. For instance, in the middle of Tractate *Rosh Hashanah*, we find a series of rulings from Yohanan ben Zakkai that have nothing to do with the festival of the New Year. However, the structure also reveals the associative techniques that were often typical of the rabbinic mind at work; if the order *Nashim* includes betrothal and marriage, wouldn't it make sense to include other laws governing vows as well? After all, each of these kinds of vows—betrothal and marriage, legal and financial—involved what was considered in ancient times to be a transfer of title to property. Thankfully, within each tractate only one subject is pursued.

Second, the prominence given to issues relating to the Temple—virtually the entirety of *Kodashim* and sections of all the other orders except *Nashim*—suggests that the Tanna'im, the rabbis of the period from the first century B.C.E. to roughly 200 C.E., were committed to preserving Jewish continuity in the face of disaster. Yes, the Temple had been destroyed more than a hundred years earlier, but they would carry on as if it were eternal. (Not every great Jewish thinker agreed with this focus on the long-defunct cultic rituals. Abraham Ibn Ezra, for one, decried scholars who devoted their time to the study of *halakhah* that had no practical relevance.)

Third, in its unusual focus on the quotidian—laws governing agriculture, criminal and civil law, and the nuts and bolts of religious observance—the Mishnah is an elegant reminder of one of the governing principles of Judaism as a belief system—that everything we do, no matter how mundane, has a spark of the holy within it. It follows then that everything one does should be done in a halakhically proper way. If we run through the areas of concern expressed in the tractates of the Mishnah, we can see how its worldview shaped Judaism.

At least in theory, the Mishnah parallels the legal aspects of the Torah, discussing the 613 *mitzvot*, filling in the holes, and interpreting the ambiguities. In practice, its commentary on scripture takes different forms. There are tractates that do little more than paraphrase scripture in order to clarify it—for example, the tractates in *Mo'ed* that deal with matters of ritual, particularly as it pertains to the observance of the Festivals in the Temple. Other tractates use as a point of departure facts stated in the Torah, and then head in directions that might have surprised, say, Moshe.

Neusner gives as an example Tractate *Parah*, which deals with the sacrifice of the red heifer. Because it occurs outside the Temple, the Torah would assume this sacrifice could not be conducted under circumstances of ritual purity, but the Mishnah actually not only assumes the opposite but demands circumstances of greater purity than could be found in the Temple, outlining the steps necessary to achieve such a state. Finally, there are tractates that deal with issues at best barely noted in the Torah. For example, the tractates governing marriage and divorce, *Ketubot* and *Gittin*, respectively, deal with issues that are covered in a few verses of Torah in passing; out of these few bricks, the rabbis erect a pair of multistory buildings.

Nearly 150 sages are mentioned by name in the Mishnah, ranging chronologically from Hillel and Shammai to Yehudah Ha'Nasi himself. Wherever a difference of opinion is found on a specific ruling, the Mishnah gives the minority view first, followed by the authoritative view, usually expressed as "R. Yehudah says . . ." or "but the sages declare . . ." Both sides (often, several sides) of an argument frequently are reported.

In order to understand how the Mishnah works, let us examine a passage from the opening of the first tractate, *Berakhot*.

From what time do we recite the evening *Sh'ma*? From the hour that the priests enter to eat their *terumah* [the regular offering given to them in the days of the Temple] until the end of the first watch. These are the words of Rabbi Eliezer. And the sages say: until midnight. Rabban Gamaliel says: until the beginning of sunrise. It happened once that his sons returned from a celebration and said to him: We have not yet recited the *Sh'ma*. He said to them: If sunrise has not yet begun, you are obligated to recite it. And not in respect to this alone did they so decide, but wherever the sages said "until midnight" the obligation to perform the *mitzvot* applies until the sun comes up. If this is so, why did the sages say "until midnight"? To keep a man from transgression.

In the Torah, we are obligated to recite the *Sh'ma* "when we lie down and when we rise up," that is, in the evening and the morning. We also know that the Jewish day begins with evening, as per *Bereishit* ("And the evening and the morning were the first day"). So the Mishnah begins its exegesis of the Oral Law with the first thing that a Jew would do upon beginning the ritual day (if not the workday)—reciting the evening *Sh'ma*.

This passage gives us three answers to the question "From what time do we recite the [evening] *Sh'ma?*" Rabbi Eliezer, a *tanna,* says that one recites the evening *Sh'ma* from the time that the priests enter their houses to eat the *terumah* until the end of the first watch. The first watch is when three small stars are visible in the night sky, a fact that the editors assumed the reader would know. In fact, in offering this answer to the question, Eliezer is merely restating an older practice dating to the days of the Temple.

The passage then offers a second answer, from the *tanna'im,* that one may recite the evening *Sh'ma* until midnight. This seems straightforward (particularly compared to Rabbi Eliezer's answer). But Rabban Gamaliel has a third answer, with a story to accompany it. Gamaliel, like Eliezer, is a second-generation *tanna,* the successor to Rabbi Yokhanan ben Zakkai as president of the Academy at Yavneh. In his story, Gamaliel shows how a certain leniency in a specific case—here toward his sons—allowed them to perform a *mitzvah* that Eliezer's more rigid version would have made them forgo.

But that brings us back to the final question asked in this passage: "Why did the sages say, 'until midnight'?" The answer now appears simple—so that a person does not run the risk of forgetting to say the evening *Sh'ma.* Yes, one may say it until sunrise, but the longer one postpones it, the greater the risk of not performing the *mitzvah.*

In this passage we find several important themes that will run throughout the Mishnah and subsequent works of Rabbinic Judaism. We see the relationship between holiness and time, the importance of the Temple cult, the tension between the rulings of the rabbis and the words of the Torah, the need to balance leniency and necessity, and the role of individual personalities in elaborating the Oral Law.

But the Mishnah is far from the final word on *halakhah.* At approximately the same time that Yehudah Ha'Nasi and his collaborators were compiling the Mishnah, an unknown group was putting together another collection of rulings and maxims of the *tanna'im,* called the *Tosefta* (from the Hebrew meaning "addition" or "supplement").

The *Tosefta* follows the structure of the Mishnah fairly closely, containing the same six orders and all but three of the same tractates (it omits Tractates *Tamid, Middot,* and *Kinnim*). The *Tosefta* includes a tractate not found in the Mishnah, *Avot de'Rabbi Natan,* which probably is meant to be a commentary on the Mishnaic tractate *Avot.* However, the *Tosefta* is four times as large as the Mishnah and, according to some scholars, less clearly written.

The materials on which the anonymous editor of the *Tosefta* drew are called *baraitot* (sing. *baraita*), from the Aramaic meaning "an external teaching." This term is used to designate any tannaitic statement not found in the Mishnah. It is also applied to writings from the next generation of sages, the *amora'im,* that were intended to elucidate the Mishnah. While some *baraitot* may include halakhic rulings not found in Mishnah, others openly contradict the Mishnah. The latter are introduced with the Aramaic *tanya/we have learned* or *tanu rabbanan/our rabbis taught.*

Neither the *Tosefta* nor other *baraitot* are considered authoritative for purposes of *halakhah.* Where they contradict Mishnah, the ruling of the latter is valid. However, they are useful tools, often elucidating matters on which the Mishnah is either unclear or silent. (Perhaps the closest equivalent in American jurisprudence is the function of a concurring opinion from a Supreme Court justice; the ruling is what matters but the opinion may elucidate that particular justice's thinking and may be invoked by someone deciding a future case. Another analogy may be made to the practice of studying the legislative history of a law, including debates in Congress, in an attempt to ascertain the intentions of the drafters.)

For purposes of comparison, here is the opening passage of Tractate *Berakhot* as it appears in the *Tosefta:*

> [From what time may the evening *Sh'ma* be recited?] From the moment when people go in to partake of their meal on the eve of the Sabbath. Thus says Rabbi Meir. But the sages say: From the moment the priests have the right to eat their *terumah.* The sign for this is the appearance of the stars. And although it cannot be proved, this is what is meant in *Nekhemyah* 4:15: "So we labored at the work, and half of them held the spears from the break of dawn till the stars came out."

LAYING DOWN THE LAW

Another oft-cited collection of *baraitot* is the *Midrash Halakhah.* In truth, this might be more accurately described as a collection of collections, focusing on the last four books of Torah, since that is where almost all the *mitzvot* are found. These midrashic collections can be divided essentially into two groups, those derived from the methods of Rabbi Ishmael and those derived from Rabbi Akiva, each of whom was expounding the method taught him by his master.

Ishmael, whose teacher was Rabbi Nehunya ben Hakaneh, concentrated on the simple meaning of a Bible verse—what we shall see shortly is known as the *peshat*—arguing that, as the Talmud says, "the Torah speaks in the language of man." Nekhunya ben Hakaneh studied the entire Torah utilizing the principle of *k'lal u'ferat*, that a general rule followed by one or more particulars is limited in scope to those particulars.

Akiva followed the teachings of his master, Nahum of Gamzu, who utilized the principle of *ribbui u'mi'ut*, whereby the extension of the scope or amplification of the Torah's text is modified by a term denoting limitation in scope. Akiva, unlike his colleague Ishmael, was famous for his belief that the interpretation of the Torah must include not only every word of the text but even the ornamentations upon the letters. He would find evidence for his interpretations not only in the plain meaning of the text but in the most minute differences in style, repetition of words, and seemingly superfluous letters.

In their highly useful text *Torah—The Oral Tradition*, Noah Aminoah and Yosef Nitzan offer a useful comparison of how the schools of Akiva and Ishmael interpret a seemingly simple injunction from *Shemot* 25:31: "And you shall make a candlestick of pure gold; of beaten work shall the candlestick be made." Akiva (or one of his followers) takes the first phrase, "And you shall make a candlestick" to be a *ribbui*, an extension permitting the use of any material for the candlestick, but reads "of pure gold" as a *mi'ut*, a limitation. He then interprets the second phrase—"of beaten work shall the candlestick be made"—as another *ribbui*. He invokes the principle that where a *ribbi* is followed by a *mi'ut* and then another *ribbui*, the result is *ribbui ha'kol*, a general extension. Consequently, Akiva would permit a candlestick of other materials, even wood. The limitation, he believes, applies only to a pottery candlestick, which would be impermissible.

By contrast, the school of Yishmael reads the text in a much more limiting fashion. "And you shall make a candlestick" is a *k'lal*, a general proposition, followed by a *perat*, "of pure gold," a particular. And "of beaten work shall the candlestick be made" is another *k'lal*. The principle invoked here states that where a *k'lal* is followed by a *perat* and then by another *k'lal*, only things similar to the particular are permissible. Since the particular here is a metal—gold—all the ritual vessels in question must be made of metal alone.

At approximately the same time that the Mishnah was being redacted, compilations of halakhic midrashim following these two schools were being compiled, one from each school for each of the final four books of the Torah. The school of Akiva was responsible for the *Mekhilta de'Rabbi Shimon bar Yokhai* (on *Shemot*), the *Sifra*, also known as *Torat Kohanim* (on *Vayikra*), *Sifrei Zuta* (on *B'midbar*), and the second part of *Sifrei Devarim* (on *Devarim*, from *parashat Re'eh* on). The compilations based on the school of Yishmael are the *Mekhilta de'Rabbi Yishmael*[2] (on *Shemot*), *Sifrei B'midbar*, and the first part of *Sifrei Devarim* (up to *Re'eih*). (There are also fragments on *Sefer Vayikra*.)

The existence of two competing schools of interpretation suggests that matters of *halakhah* did not become closed questions with the completion of the Mishnah and Gemara or the compilation of the books of halakhic midrashim. On the contrary, the piling up of rulings and disputations was just beginning.

THINKING IN CODE(S)

For starters, these debates and discussions gave birth to another literary subgenre of books enumerating the *mitzvot*, a growth industry in the Middle Ages. The numbering of 613 *mitzvot* is derived from midrashic statements of R. Simlai and R. Hamnuna, but it took several centuries before these statements were taken literally. As a result, there was much disagreement over how to count the *mitzvot*, and those who did the counting had to fit the laws into the schemes, yielding occasionally Procrustean solutions. How they were derived from the Torah, the biblical roots of *halakhah*, was a more contentious matter. The Karaites, a breakaway sect, challenged the right of the rabbis to interpret the Torah, rejecting the Talmud and all other postbiblical rabbinic texts. More than that, the Talmud, with its intricate tapestry of debates and decisions scattered over many volumes, was beyond the understanding of an ordinary Jew. How could one follow the *mitzvot* if the rules were so abstruse?

The rabbinic authorities responded with codes of law, the most notable of which is the *Halakhot Gedolot / Great Halakhah*, compiled by the eighth-century rabbi Shimon Kayyara. The heads of the North African rabbinic academies weighed in with their own books of law codes, the most famous of which is Rabbi Yitzkhak Alfasi's. Alfasi simplified matters for the Talmud-shy Jew, boiling down the pages of debate to their essence.

But the greatest of all the books enumerating and elucidating the *mitzvot* is undoubtedly the *Mishneh Torah* of Maimonides, published in 1180. Moses ben Maimon, to give him his proper Hebrew name, was a brilliant physician and philosopher. Rambam, as he is frequently called (an acronym for *R*abbi *M*oses *b*en *M*aimon), wrote this massive work at a time of great persecution of the Jews, who were caught between the hammer of the Crusaders and the anvil of the Almohade caliphate. It was a period, he argues in his introduction, in which the Torah, the Talmud, and the already-growing literature of halakhic commentary "are becoming difficult for many people to understand."

With that in mind, he created a vast but systematic work that divided the *mitzvot* into fourteen categories, with a book for each category. But even given Rambam's great wisdom and breadth of learning, some of the connections may seem obscure to a modern reader. For example, as Harry Gersh notes, Maimonides places *mitzvot* governing burial in the section of *Mishneh Torah* that deals with criminal law. The reason for this seemingly illogical choice is that burial is seldom discussed in the Torah, but one of the few citations occurs in a passage dealing with the disposal of the corpses of executed criminals. Similarly, he groups murder, incest, and desecrating the Sabbath because they are all capital crimes in Torah.

The *Mishneh Torah* is an astounding achievement for a single author, but like Maimonides' most famous work, *The Guide for the Perpelexed*, this masterpiece engendered controversy among rabbinic authorities. Some felt that he had simplified the Talmud to the extent that it would gradually be superseded by his work. Others objected to his use of the thought of Jesus and Mohammed, although his references to them are negative. Undoubtedly, his neo-Aristotelianism, the source of much of the distaste for *The Guide*, didn't sit too well with the rabbis, either. Regardless of the controversy, the *Mishneh Torah* was a milestone that continues to be read today. But its sheer bulk made it something less than a household item among Jewish families, so the production of codes of Jewish law continued.

It fell to a sixteenth-century rabbi, a victim of the Expulsion from Spain, to craft the book of Jewish law that would be the basis for the most widely read and consulted compendia up to the present day. Joseph Caro produced a large and comprehensive guide to Jewish law from Safed, Palestine, which he called the *Bet Yosef/House of Joseph*. But like its Maimonidean predecessor, it was too cumbersome for everyday use. Faced with that dilemma, he boiled its contents down to a single-volume guide to the larger work. This more manageable book he called the *Shulkhan Arukh*. Drawing on the works of Alfasi, Maimonides, and Rabbi Jacob ben Asher (known as the Tur for his law code, *Sefer Ha'Turim/the Book of Rows*), Caro stated his decisions flatly and authoritatively, eschewing the Talmud's invocation of competing viewpoints. Perhaps it was his categorical certainty (which he based on the majority decision of the three previous authors) that made his book so accessible to both Sephardic and Ashkenazic Jews. When Moses Isserles provided Ashkenazic alternatives in his commentary to Caro, the book's acceptance was significantly furthered. It certainly didn't hurt his cause that its publication coincided with the invention of movable type. Subsequent commentaries added to his guide, but for Orthodox Jews, Caro's table is the one at which they sit.

BY ANY OTHER NAME

Many of the most famous Torah scholars are best known by the acronyms of their titles and names or by the names of their most famous works. Here is a short alphabetical list of sobriquets you are likely to encounter in your reading and an identification of the men to whom they are attached.

Ba'al Ha'Turim—Rabbi Ya'akov ben Asher (c. 1270–c. 1343), German-born author of one of the great codes of Jewish law, *Arbah Turim/Four Rows*, and a Torah commentary that is based heavily on *gematria*.

Ba'al Shem Tov—Rabbi Israel ben Eliezer (c. 1700–1760), the Ukrainian founder of Hasidism, who was also know as the Besht (an acronym of Ba'al Shem Tov, which means "Master of the Good Name").

Beis Ha'Levi—Rabbi Yosef Dov Soloveitchik (1820–1892), first of the great *rashei yeshivot* of Brisk, Lithuania, and a great-grandfather of Rabbi Joseph Soloveitchik, the outstanding philosopher and teacher of Modern Orthodoxy. The *Beis Ha'Levi* was the title of his highly thoughtful Torah commentary, which covers both halakhic and aggadic subjects.

Khatam Sofer—Rabbi Moshe Sofer Schreiber (1762–1839), key opponent of the early Reform movement, German author of an important Torah commentary, *Torat Moshe*, and an important halakhic decisor.

Khofetz Khaim—Rabbi Yisrael Meir Ha'Kohen Kagan (1839–1933), one of the outstanding Lithuanian talmudists and a key figure in the *Mussar* (ethics) movement. The *Khofetz Khaim* was the title of his most famous work, a study of *lashon ha'ra/evil speech* (i.e., gossip and slander), but he also wrote commentaries on the Talmud, the Torah, and the prayer book.

Kli Yekar—Rabbi Shelomo Efraim of Luntchitz, Poland (1550–1619). Known as a great orator, his primary Torah commentary is, appropriately enough, a collection of his homilies whose title gave him his sobriquet.

Maharal—Rabbi Yehudah Loew (1525–1609), legendary rabbi of Prague whose sobriquet is an acronym for *Moreinu Ha'Rav Loew/Our teacher, Rabbi Loew*. Best known as a talmudist and mystic, he was the subject of many fabulous tales, most famously as the creator of the Golem.

Malbim—Rabbi Meir Leib ben Yekhiel Michael (1809–1879), Russian author of a massive and influential commentary on the *Tanakh*.

Netziv—Rabbi Naftali Tzvi Yehudah Berlin (1817–1893), one of the outstanding talmudists in the Mitnagdic tradition, head of the famous yeshiva in Volozhin, Lithuania.

Rabbenu Tam—Rabbi Ya'akov ben Moshe Tam (1100–1171), grandson of Rashi and younger brother of Rabbi Shmuel ben Meir (Rashbam). Leader of the *Tosafists* and one of the key figures in French Jewry in the medieval period.

Radak—Rabbi David Kimkhi (c. 1160–1235), the most famous of a renowned family of French rabbinical scholars, he authored one of the first authoritative Bible dictionaries and one of the key Torah commentaries.

Ralbag—Rabbi Levi ben Gerson (1288–1344), a.k.a. Gersonides. Important French medieval Bible commentator.

Rama—Rabbi Moses Isserles (1530–1572), author of *Ha'Mapeh/The Tablecloth*, a commentary on Caro's *Shulkhan Arukh*, which facilitated Ashkenazic acceptance of Caro's work.

Rambam—Rabbi Moshe ben Maimon (1135–1204), a.k.a. Maimonides. Spanish-born physician, philosopher, talmudist, and halakhic codifier par excellence.

Ramban—Rabbi Moshe ben Nakhman (1194–1279), a.k.a. Nahmanides. One of the great Torah and Talmud commentators, a chief figure among Spanish Jewry, and an important kabbalist.

Rashba—Rabbi Shelomo ben Aderet (1235–1310). The outstanding spiritual leader of Spanish Jewry of his era, he spent more than forty years as a rabbi in Barcelona. Author of a vast body of halakhic responsa, as well as commentaries on the Talmud and rabbinical legends.

Rashbam—Rabbi Shmuel ben Meir (c. 1080–after 1158), grandson of Rashi, older brother of Rabbenu Tam, and an important French Torah commentator whose work is based on *peshat*, drawing heavily on his extensive knowledge of Hebrew linguistics and the *targumim/ translations*.

Rashbatz—Rabbi Shimon ben Tzemakh Duran (1361–1444), outstanding North African halakhic authority and philosopher.

Rashi—Rabbi Shelomo Yitzkhaki (1040–1105). Perhaps the greatest interpreter of Torah, he is the author of what is certainly the single most used Torah commentary, which every student is trained to use. Also central for his Talmud commentary, his responsa, and other halakhic writings. Grandfather of Rabbenu Tam and Rashbam.

Rif—Rabbi Yitzkhak Alfasi (1013–1103), great North African codifier of *halakhah*.

S'fat Emet—Rabbi Yehudah Aryeh Leib Alter (1847–1905), the Second Gerer Rebbe, author of a brilliant but difficult Torah commentary, *S'fat Emet al Ha'Torah/The Language of Truth of the Torah*.

HALAKHAH IN CHANGING TIMES

The world does not stand still. Scientific advances and new technologies alter our daily lives. Political and social change have had a distinct (and frequently deleterious) impact on the Jewish world. For observant Jews old imperatives must be adapted to new realities. Rooted as it is in the quotidian, Jewish law had to be made to apply to the steam engine and medieval persecutions, to electricity and the *Sho'ah/Holocaust*, to genetic engineering and the newborn Jewish state in what had been biblical *Eretz Yisrael*. Even as the Talmud was being compiled, as Maimonides and Caro were drafting their great codes of Jewish law, rabbis were constantly being asked questions by their fellow Jews that required an immediate answer. This process of *she'elot/questions* and *teshuvot/answers* produced another vast body of halakhic literature called responsa.

Responsa probably predate the canonization of the *Tanakh*. In *Malakhi*

2:7, we are told, "[T]he priest's lips should keep knowledge and [the people] should seek the law at his mouth," and that is exactly what they did. At first, this process of seeking halakhic advice was probably conducted orally, and some of the early responsa undoubtedly found their way into the Mishnah. Just as the Oral Law eventually became a written adjunct to the Torah, responsa also became the result of a written process. An individual or a Jewish community would present a problem to a halakhic decisor in writing; he (and until very late in the twentieth century, it was always a male) would respond in writing. At first, written responses were terse, sometimes nothing more detailed than a curt "Permitted" or "Forbidden." Gradually, the answers became longer and more detailed. For example, the first prayer book was compiled as a response to a question about the liturgy.

The responsa multiplied in quantity as well. One 1959 reference book says that "about a thousand volumes" containing more than half a million separate responsa have appeared in print. I don't have a more recent estimate at hand, but I suspect that number has more than doubled in the past half century. Responsa literature makes for fascinating reading, even for those who have no investment in halakhic decisions. Reading a collection of *she'elot u'teshuvot/questions and answers* gives not only an insight into the workings of the halakhic mind and Rabbinic Judaism but also a detailed picture of Jewish life in a specific time and place. Gersh observes that it is only because we have a responsum of Rabbi Menachem-Mendel Krochman of Nikolsburg that we have an eyewitness account of the destruction of the Jewish community of Polni during the Chmielnicki massacres of 1648; a married woman whose husband was killed during the pogrom asked for a ruling from Krochman as to her marital status, given that there were no living witnesses to attest to her husband's death. In his reply, the rabbi included her entire description of the events at Polni, leaving us a firsthand account of the massacre there.

More than that, reading the responsa literature allows us to see how Jewish law evolves and adapts in response to change, much like case law in Anglo-American jurisprudence. To give a simple example, a traditionally observant Jew will not throw an electrical switch during Shabbat because the rabbis decided that the spark created by a completed circuit was the equivalent of lighting a fire, which is prohibited on the Sabbath. And just as case law is an ever-growing organism in Anglo-American jurisprudence, responsa continue to be written by contemporary rabbis from all the

streams of Judaism, addressing issues as diverse as intermarriage, homosexuality, genetic engineering, abortion, and euthanasia, as well as the
more traditional range of liturgical and ritual issues.

But on what basis do rabbis past, present, and future interpret the
Torah for purposes of *halakhah?* There is a set of basic principles that goes
all the way back to the *soferim,* rules of interpretation that have proven
remarkably durable.

THIRTEEN WAYS OF LOOKING AT THE TORAH

Hillel posited seven rules of interpretation of the Torah, rules that apply
primarily in halakhic interpretation. Hillel did not invent these rules—the
soferim had already been using them for many years—but he was the first
to catalog them as the basis for understanding the words of scripture.

Rabbi Ishmael, the great teacher of the generation before the Bar
Kokhba rebellion, developed these into thirteen rules. Eventually, Rabbi
Eliezer ben Yosei Ha'Gelili would expand these further to thirty-two, but
the thirteen *middot/measures* of Yishmael are so important a part of Jewish
tradition today that the Orthodox include them in the weekday morning
prayers. Here are Yishmael's thirteen *middot:*

1. *Kal va'khomer:* Inference from major to minor or minor to major; an
a fortiori inference. A simple rule of logic, often framed in terms of
leniency and strictness; that is, if a more lenient case contains a certain
stricter prohibition, then a stricter case must all the more; or if a strict case
contains a certain leniency, then a lenient case certainly will as well. One
of the most commonly offered examples is Moshe's argument to God:
"*B'nei Yisrael* have not listened to me, how then should Pharoah hear
me?" (*Shemot* 6:12).

Rabbi Meir Zvi Bergman, a contemporary Orthodox *rosh yeshiva* in
Israel, notes that the determination of whether a case falls into the categories of stringent or lenient are "a) logic; b) the laws of Torah that pertain
to the case." He offers examples of each, drawn from the Talmud. In the
first, drawn from Tractate *Bava Kama,* "If one is liable for the damages
caused by his animal when it did not intend any harm, then, certainly, he
should be liable for damages which the animal did intend to inflict." For
the latter category, he cites Tractate *Kiddushin:* "If a Jewish bondswoman,
who cannot be acquired by an act of cohabitation, can be bought with

money, then a wife, who may be acquired [for *kiddushin,* the first stage of marriage] through cohabitation, may certainly be acquired with money."

2. *Gezeirah shavah:* Drawing a conclusion by word analogy. An interpretative principle based in linguistics, *gezeirah shavah* holds that when two passages contain words that are similar or have identical connotations, the laws of the two passages are subject to the same regulations and applications. The contemporary scholar Rabbi Abraham Hirsch Rabinowitz offers the example of a famous debate between Hillel and *B'nei Bityra* on whether it is permissible to bring the paschal lamb for sacrificing on Shabbat. The question is settled by a *gezeirah shavah:* the passage covering the daily offering says it is to be brought *"be'mo'ado/in its due season,"* and this phrase recurs in the passage on the paschal lamb. Consequently, the rule governing the daily offering, which is not brought on the Sabbath, applies to the paschal lamb as well.

3. *Binyan Av:* In this interpretative principle, the meaning of a term is derived from one (*binyan av mi'katuv ekhad*) or two other texts (*binyan av mi'sheini ketuvim*) and applied to a wider range of cases. In short, a law that occurs in one passage of the Torah may be applied in other passages in which there is a structural similarity. Horowitz offers an example from Tractate *Yevamot:* "The school of R. Yishmael taught: Since the Torah mentions 'garments' in connection with several *mitzvot* without specifying their texture, and in one case the Torah specifies 'a woolen garment, or a linen garment,' wherever else 'garment' is mentioned it refers to a woolen or a linen garment."

4. *Klal u'ferat:* A generalization that is followed by a particular. One of the best-known examples of this principle is drawn from *Vayikra* 1:2, in which Jews are enjoined to bring an offering *"min ha'biheimah/of the beasts,"* a phrase that includes both wild and domestic animals, and *"min ha'bakar u'min ha'tzon/from the herd and from the flock,"* a phrase that suggests domestic animals only. The use of the more restrictive phrase after the generalization is taken to mean that wild animals are not to be brought for sacrifice.

5. *Perat u'klal:* A particular followed by a generalization (an inversion of the previous principle). In such a case, the particular is expanded by the more general term that follows it. When the Torah tells us that we must return lost articles to their rightful owners, it specifies "his ass . . . and his garment," then continues, "And you will do so with every lost thing of your brother's. . . ."

6. *Klal u'ferat u'klal:* A general law, limited by a specific principle, then referred to once again in general terms. In such cases, the law must be interpreted according to the limitation presented by the specific case. Conversely, there is the case of the *perat u'klal u'ferat,* a specification followed by a generalization followed by another specification. In such cases, the generalization is qualified by the specification.

7. *Klal she'hu tzarikh lifrat* or *perat she'hu tzarikh likhlal:* A general term that requires a specific term to clarify it, or a specific term that requires a generalization. Rashi explains that the difference between this principle and *klal u'ferat* is that in the latter the general rule is understood and the specific is included to limit its application, but in this case the specific is necessary because the general rule is unclear.

8. *Davar she'hayah bikhlal v'yatza min ha'klal li'lamed:* Something is included in a generalization, but was then singled out from the generalization in order to teach a specific lesson. Hence the exception that was offered is applied to the entire generalization (or else its inclusion would have been redundant). Attention is called to the specific instance because it teaches us something new.

9. *Davar she'hayah bikhlal v'yatza min ha'klal lit'on to'an akheir she'hu k'inyano:* A case in which something is included in a generalization but is then singled out from the generalization in order to discuss a provision similar to the general category. In such cases, the specific instance usually exists in order to be more lenient than the generalization would have been.

10. *Davar she'hayah bikhlal v'yatza min ha'klal lit'on to'an akheir she'lo ki'inyano:* A case in which something is included in a generalization but is singled out to discuss a provision not similar to the general category. In this case, the specific instance is brought up because it carries its own set of laws that are different from the ones discussed in the generalization.

11. *Davar she'hayah bikhlal v'yatza min ha'klal li'don ba'davar he'khadash:* A case in which something is included in a generalization but is singled out so that it will be treated as a new case. In such a passage, the principle of the generalization does not apply to this new case unless the Torah explicitly returns to the generalization.

12. *Davar ha'lamed me'inyano v'davar ha'lamed mi'sofo:* Interpretation of an obscure word or passage by inference from its context or from a subsequent statement in the passage.

13. *Shinei kituvim ha'makh'khishim zeh et zeh:* In a case in which two

verses contradict each other, the meaning can only be determined by using a third text that reconciles them.

Reading these thirteen principles of interpretation, it isn't hard to see how they would be used in making halakhic decisions in the past, present, and future. But interpreting *aggadah* would seem to present a rather different set of problems, and this baker's dozen of *middot* probably isn't as useful there, although it is applicable at times. Rather, the rabbis sought another network of associations to unravel the mysteries of biblical narrative.

FOUR GATES INTO THE PARADISE OF *AGGADAH*

We have already seen that the narrative offered by the Torah is often fragmentary, elliptical, or downright opaque. It is impossible to know whether the problems that reading the Torah presents are the result of materials missing, scribal or editorial mistakes, a simple lack of clarity, or even a deliberate literary ploy. What is certain is that there are times when the stories presented just aren't satisfying to us. The rabbis and other commentators have tried to fill in the gaps by providing us with thousands of commentaries and midrashim, a vast secondary literature of aggadic midrash designed for the express purpose of addressing the narrative content of Torah.

In the same way that the halakhic midrash is governed by a set of hermeneutic principles, *aggadah* also works within a set framework, albeit a looser one. As you can imagine, there are as many different Torah interpretations as there are Torah scholars. Because the commentators believed the Torah to be the Revealed Word of God, every single letter, even the ornamentations on the letters, was believed to have a meaning. But where *halakhah* is governed by thirteen (or thirty-two) interpretative guidelines, *aggadah* basically has four, borrowed from the fourfold sense used in Christian exegesis, which the medieval commentators recognized and practiced: *peshat*, the "plain sense" meaning of a passage; *derash*, the homiletical meaning (from which the word *midrash* is derived); *remez*, the allusive meaning; and *sod*, the hidden, mystical reading. Taken together, they add up to the acronym, *PaRDeS*. This is actually a word of Persian origin meaning an area surrounded by a fence, and it is used in the Talmud to mean an orchard or garden. (Taken into the Greek as *paradeisos*, the word also gave birth to the English word *paradise*.)

1. PESHAT

The most basic way of reading the Bible is for its "plain sense" meaning, the meaning that is inherent in the text as we have it before us. *Peshat* draws on the context of the passage, its grammar, philology, and historical content.[3]

For example, Edward L. Greenstein quotes Rashi and his grandson Rashbam to show the distinction between a homiletic and a plain-sense reading of the passage from *Bereishit* 49:7, in which Ya'akov says he "will divide" his sons Shimon and Levi and "scatter them in Israel." Rashi writes: "I shall separate this one from that one so that Levi will not be in the number of the tribes—and they are indeed dispersed among the tribes." He believes that Ya'akov is punishing them for having banded together to do evil in the wake of the rape of Dinah and has separated them "like a grade school teacher imposing discipline," as Greenstein puts it. By contrast, Rashbam sees the passage in its most literal historical context: "For Levi was dispersed among the twelve tribes, as it is written in *Yehoshua* (chapter 21)." In other words, this is the historical outcome of what befell the tribe of Levi. And that's all there is to it.

At the same time, *peshat* undertakes a literary endeavor, by placing a passage in the larger context of the passages surrounding it and understanding the rhetorical devices that may be operating there. Or it may draw on linguistic knowledge to interpret it, as Ibn Ezra often does.

Peshat readings are broad enough to encompass metaphoric and figurative language. Thus the passage in *Shemot* that says, "It shall be a sign upon your arm and a remembrance between your eyes," is understood by the Talmudic sages to refer to the wearing of the *tefillin* on the arm and head.

2. DERASH

Derash is a word derived from the verb *darash/to seek*. Used in the Bible, the verb means "to ask of a prophet," rather like the ancient Greeks consulting the oracle at Delphi. As an intepretative technique, *derash* uses homily and parable to inquire of the text its latent meaning, as opposed to its "plain" meaning. As we have already seen, such a homily or parable is called a midrash (pl. *midrashim*). The distinction between *derash* and *peshat* seems to date from the medieval period.

One of the most famous midrashim deals with the aftermath of the destruction of Pharoah and the Egyptian army in *Yam Suf*. The hosts of angels begin to sing as the last Egyptians disappear beneath the torrents and God rebukes them angrily, saying: "My children are dying and you sing!" This midrash underlines the delicate balance God walks through-out the *Tanakh* between stern judge and compassionate parent.

3. REMEZ

Remez is Hebrew for "hint," and as a method of Torah interpretation, it seeks the allegorical meaning through veiled allusions found in the text, focusing on the philosophical implications contained therein. The most obvious example of such a reading would be the statement by Talmudic sages that *Shir Ha'Shirim* is in reality about the relationship between the people Israel and *Adonai* rather than the highly erotic love song it first appears to be. The kabbalists who were responsible for the *Zohar* will find allegory in even the most straightforward of narratives.

4. SOD

There is a strong strain of mysticism in Judaism, best exemplified by Kabbalah (literally, "the tradition"), the mystical movement that arose in the twelfth century. Kabbalah would achieve its greatest flowering in Safed, in Palestine, in the sixteenth century, under the leadership of Isaac Luria, but mysticism in Judaism dates all the way back to the beginning of the common era.

Central to Jewish mysticism is the idea that truth cannot be expressed solely in words. Words can only denote that which is perceived by the intellect and the senses. Truth, on the contrary, is beyond human sensory perception and cognition; it cannot be expressed by mere human lan-guage. The Bible is written in human language, but it is Divinely inspired. Therefore, the mystics reason, the words must contain Divine truth, but not when read in the way that humans normally read them. In some way, these Divine words must symbolize truth beyond words. Reading for denotation and connotation will not uncover that truth. *Peshat* is dis-carded utterly.

Instead, the mystics read the Bible as a sort of code book, a dictionary of symbols to be deciphered by methods such as *gematria* and *notarikon*. As one mystical text puts it, "Many lights shine forth from each word and each letter."

Sod (literally, "mystery" or "secret"), the method of biblical interpreta-tion that searches for mystical significance, became the special province of the kabbalists who, more than other schools of Jewish mysticism, focused their attention largely on hermeneutics, the interpretation of texts (here, biblical texts).

Gematria is an interpretative system based on the fact that the letters of the Hebrew alphabet are also assigned numerical values. Applied to reading the Torah, it can be used to ferret out otherwise utterly unlikely readings. For example, the Hebrew word *yihyeh* is composed of two *yods*, each of which has a numerical value of 10, and two *heis*, each with a value of 5. In *B'midbar* 6:5, a passage delineating the ritual obligations of a Nazirite (one who has taken a particular vow of asceticism in the service of God), the phrase *kadosh yihyeh/he shall be holy* is thus interpreted as the reason that a Nazirite's vows last for thirty days [*yud* (10) + *he* (5) + *yud* (10) + *hei* (5) = 30].

Another method of interpretation designed to reveal hidden meanings is that of the *notarikon*, a word derived from the Latin *notarius* or "shorthand writer." There are two types of *notarikon*. In the first, a word is understood as an acronym for its real meaning. For example, the first word of the Ten Commandments, *anokhi/I*, is actually an abbreviation for *"Ana Nafshi Ketavit Yahavit/I Myself wrote and gave [them],"* so there can be no doubt that the Decalogue is the word of the Almighty. In the second type of *notarikon*, a word may be broken up into other words. For example, the name Re'uven becomes *re'u ven/see the son.*

As Gershom Scholem, the great historian of Jewish mysticism, wryly observes, "Explication at the level of *sod*, of course, had limitless possibilities, a classic illustration of which is Nathan Spira's *Megalleh Amukot* (1637), in which Moshe's prayer to God in *Devarim* 3:23ff is explained in 252 different ways."

As we shall see repeatedly in the pages that follow, Torah commentaries frequently make use of wordplay, punning, and deliberate misreadings, as well as *gematria* and *notarikon* in their search for hidden meanings in the sacred text. How can they get away with some of the more fanciful, even outlandish interpretations?

Aggadic midrash in its most extreme forms is the inevitable result of reading a text filled with gaps and dislocations, written in a language that, in its original presentation, has no vowel markings, no punctuation, no paragraphing. Under such circumstances, the Torah's text is almost infinitely malleable and, in the hands of the medieval commentators and the Hasidic masters, this already polysemous text becomes even more elastic, admitting a multitude of previously unimagined interpretations. When you factor into this process the unspoken knowledge that the Torah text contains scribal error (despite its putatively Divine origins) and the necessity for an interpreter to feel he is advancing our knowledge past the frontiers his predecessors have carved out, a certain hermeneutic extremism will occasionally rear its peculiar head.

Despite the temptation to move ever farther away from the most obvious reading of the Torah text, most of the great Torah commentators return repeatedly to the *peshat,* the plain meaning, as the starting point of their own writings. The Hebrew Bible is rich and complex enough to support a wide range of interpretations; why use a battering ram when the door isn't locked? And the ever-changing circumstances of our daily lives and sociopolitical milieu renew both our understanding of and need for the Torah in ways that should keep all but the most completely disengaged *darshan* busy.

Historically, aggadic interpretations of Torah have their roots in the work of the *darshan,* which is undoubtedly why such interpretations tend to be tied so strongly to *parashat ha'shavua.* The classical interpretations that grew out of the work of the *darshanim* are, then, the beginnings of Torah commentary, so it is to the *derash* that we must turn our attention.

THE VIEW FROM THE *BIMAH*

One could say that Moshe was the first *darshan.* After all, what is *Sefer Devarim* but a very long sermon explicating and expanding on the laws given at Sinai? And the elders who translated and verbally annotated the reading of the Torah in Jerusalem in 444 B.C.E. clearly fulfilled something of the same role. Subsequent *darshanim* have found themselves with a less patient listenership but less need to explain every single aspect of the entire text of the *Khumash* at a single sitting (a relief, no doubt, for both speaker and audience). As Hananel Mack notes, there is a definite link between the aggadic midrashim in such collections as *Midrash Rabbah* and the *sedarim* into which the Torah was divided for the three-year reading cycle that was in use in ancient Palestine. So it is safe to infer that these midrashim had their roots in the reading of the Torah in the synagogues of the time, not so different from what a modern rabbi does every Saturday morning. (Of course, there are collections of midrashim that are not tied to the weekly portion, for example *Pesikta de'Rav Kahana*, a medieval collection, but even this one consists largely of *derashot* for the special Sabbaths and Festival Days.)

The great collections of midrashim were written and compiled in the early medieval period, roughly between 400 and 1200 C.E. But these collections, such as *Midrash Rabbah*, a predominantly aggadic compilation that deals specifically with the Torah, drew their origins from the oral traditions of the sermon, the *derash*. The ancient *derashot* seldom have come down to us in their original form; the medieval collections of midrashim are, as Mack says, "the descendants of the descendants" of the originals.

The Torah's narrative style is laconic, to say the least. Even in a story as filled with psychological detail as the Yosef story is, there is little physical description and almost nothing of events away from the main narrative line. Here is where aggadic midrash comes to the fore, filling in the gaps and dislocations, attempting to reconcile contradictions within the text.

To draw upon a favorite example of mine, the story of Ya'akov and Eisav and the birthright, the Torah tells us that the Patriarchal line was destined to go through Ya'akov and that with Rivkah, his mother, Ya'akov arranged to deceive his father, Yitzkhak, into granting him the blessing usually reserved for the firstborn son. But the Torah doesn't tell us why Ya'akov was more suited to receive the blessing than his twin brother. There are extensive midrashim filling in the "backstory" that make it clear why, at the very least, the rabbis thought the Torah presented these events this way. Midrashim tell us of a pious and studious Ya'akov who sat and studied sacred texts while his brother hunted and cavorted in inappropriate ways. It is through midrash that we learn that Eisav's descendants become the nation of Edom, a sworn enemy of the Israelites, identified in later years with the many imperial powers that oppressed the Jewish people.

As Judith Plaskow has observed, the rabbis of the period obviously felt that by attributing to the Patriarchs the desire to found Torah academies and to study as they did, they were extending the authority of Rabbinic Judaism into the hallowed past. But, equally important, they were trying to understand their forebears in terms they could relate to, as men who lived by the same precepts as they did, whether this was logically supported by the text or not.

MIDRASHIM IN THREE KEYS

There are essentially three types of midrash: homiletical, exegetical, and narrative. The first two are keyed to specific verses within the Torah addressing passages that the rabbis deemed to be problematical in some way. As James Kugel has observed, the midrashic collections that we read from are so well edited that they give these verse-specific midrashim the misleading appearance of dealing with the entirety of a narrative sequence, a whole book or even the entirety of Torah. The editors, drawing from midrashic materials from a wide range of eras, have created systematic works where none really existed. However, there is no gainsaying that a reading of a wide range of classical midrash does give one a fairly good picture of the worldview of the rabbinic thinkers.

Homiletical midrashim have their origins, as the label implies, in the homilies, sermons delivered by rabbis before an assembled congregation in the ancient or medieval world. The most important collections of these midrashim date from 400 to 900 C.E. and include *Vayikra Rabbah* (which is mostly halakhic in nature, reflecting the focus of *Sefer Vayikra* on laws and precepts), *Pesikta deRav Kahana*, *Midrash Tankhuma*, and *Devarim Rabbah*.

Both homiletical and exegetical midrashim frequently draw on complex and subtle wordplay, puns, letter transpositions, and homophony; as might be expected, even in a great translation a lot of meaning gets lost. More than that, for a modern reader the obsessive wordplay seems an odd, not to say downright disrespectful, way to treat a sacred text. Reading these midrashim, it is important to recall two important facts: (1) the physical text of the Torah, having no punctuation or vowel markings, lends itself to precisely such a free play of sign and signifier, to suggestive associations that might otherwise never occur to someone whose first encounter with the Torah is in a modern, printed version, and, (2) the rabbis believed the text to be not merely sacred but the product of a Divine authorship whose every variation from the obvious reading was placed there to be deciphered. Looked at from that perspective, the Torah becomes a set of codes designed for the most adept cryptographer to work upon in order to find its meaning for the rest of us.

Barry Holtz offers an excellent piece of advice for the novice reader of midrash: when you read midrashim, keep the entire Torah passage in mind at all times, preferably close at hand. Read the passage in its entirety and its context, remembering that a midrash may only quote part of it, and not necessarily the part the rabbi is most interested in discussing.

Homiletical midrash poses the greatest problems for modern readers, particularly those with no Hebrew. Homiletical midrashim add to the readers' burden of wordplay a densely allusive literary structure. (In reality, only one of the many homiletical midrashim that we have today, found in the Babylonian Talmud in Tractate *Shabbat*, a *derash* from Rabbi Tankhuma bar Abba, is in its original, unaltered form.) The collections of homiletical midrashim have been edited and polished into a set of literary formulas that may baffle the casual reader. By comparison, exegetical midrashim are more verse-specific, pithy in their commentary on a single passage. Narrative midrashim are the easiest to comprehend. As the label suggests, they offer a sort of alternate version of the stories in the Torah, filling in the gaps in the story with legends from other sources. As Holtz notes, because a collection such as *Pirkei de Rebbe Eliezer* doesn't involve interpretation of preexisting texts but anthologizes other tales of biblical figures and legendary rabbis, some scholars are reluctant to call them midrashim at all.

How do midrashim work? Obviously, with so many different variant types, there is no single answer, but let's examine one exegetical midrash from a familiar passage of *Sefer Bereishit* to get a taste.

YOUR BROTHER'S BLOOD

After Kayin kills Hevel, God asks him what has become of his brother. The Eternal accuses Kayin, "The voice of your brother's blood is crying out to me from the earth" (*Bereishit* 4:10). In *Bereishit Rabbah* 22:9, Rabbi Shimon bar Yohai, one of the greatest of the second-century C.E. rabbis, analyzes this passage:

> It is difficult to say this thing and the mouth cannot plainly utter it. Think of two athletes wrestling before the king, and had the king wished, he could have separated them. But he did not so desire, and one overcame the other and killed him, he [the victim] crying out [before he died], "Let my cause be pleaded before the king?" Even so, THE VOICE OF THY BROTHER'S BLOOD IS CRYING AGAINST ME.
>
> (*The Soncino Midrash Rabbah*)

This is a pretty straightforward midrash. As Holtz notes in his discussion of this midrash, the opening formulation, "It is difficult to say this thing and the mouth cannot plainly utter it," is frequently used in rabbinic texts to signal a passage of particular interest, something challenging and difficult. Bar Yokhai uses the parable of the two wrestlers to suggest that the blood-guilt lies not on the hands of the one who killed, but rather on those of the one (or here, the One) who set them against each other. If the king "wished, he could have separated them" but he didn't. So, too, had God so desired, the brothers could have been separated without tragic consequences. Underlining this startling conclusion is the wordplay—invisible in translation but cleverly suggested by the translator in the repetition, in Aramaic, of the verse under discussion—on the Hebrew *eilai*, which can mean "to me," as in "your brother's blood is crying out to me," the more familiar translation, or "at me," as it is given at the end of the midrash, "Your brother's blood is crying out at me," in accusation of the Creator.

In one brief paragraph, you have several of the key elements of midrash: the parable used as analogy, the wordplay, and a strikingly original interpretation. If you were to continue reading in *Bereishit Rabbah*, you would find another key element of midrash; the next passage is a midrash by another rabbinic author, diametrically opposed to bar Yokhai's reading, placing the guilt for Hevel's death squarely on Kayin's shoulders once more, utilizing a similarly creative and insightful means to rebut and rebuke bar Yokhai. And that, too, is typical of midrash.

THE GOLDEN AGE OF BIBLE COMMENTARY

Midrash is a formidable underpinning upon which to build. Around the same time that the last of the classical midrashic collections was being finished, Jewish Bible commentary was entering what would be, arguably, its greatest period. Beginning with Sa'adia Gaon, the tenth-century philosopher and scholar, this might be called "the age of *peshat*," a period in which great commentators examined the Torah with a primary concern for the "plain meaning" of the text and a particular emphasis on philological issues. Not surprisingly, it is also the first age of great Torah translators, Sa'adia being a good example, and it would not be inappropriate to consider translation of the Torah as an especially refined form of commentary. (See "Translating the Torah: Another Kind of Interpretation," on page 171.)

Sa'adia's own major contribution to the Torah is his Arabic translation, *Targum Tafsir*. *Tafsir* is the Arabic word for "commentary," and Sa'-adia's translation includes rabbinic analysis of the text. His commentaries reflect the sense of danger that the Jews of Babylonia felt, surrounded as they were by a rapidly growing Islam. For Sa'adia, *peshat* meant eschewing recourse to the midrashic literature, returning to the Torah itself. A rationalist above all, like Maimonides after him, Sa'adia is utterly opposed to the anthropomorphizing of God. He is, for all intents and purposes, the father of Hebrew philology, and many of the key commentators who follow after him, Rashi and Ibn Ezra most prominently, owe him a significant debt for raising such linguistic issues.

Sa'adia's interpretation of the Torah rests on three foundations, as Dr. Aharon Gimani points out, "the plain sense of the scriptural verse, natural intelligence, and tradition *(ha'mekubbal)* in the sense of the transmitted traditions of the Sages." In that respect, he anticipates Rashi, Ibn Ezra, and the other rationalistic Torah scholars who would follow in his footsteps.

Although Sa'adia was based in the Middle East, it would be in Western Europe that his successors would come to the fore. In both Spain and northern France, several generations of exceptional Torah commentators would expand on his initial efforts and, ultimately, surpass his achievement.[4]

1. RASHI

Rashi—Rabbi Shelomo ben Yitzkhak to give him his full name—is a unique figure in Hebrew Bible commentary. He is the most popular and the most cited of all commentators on the Torah. His Torah commentary was popular enough to be the first printed Hebrew book. A copy of "*Khumash* with Rashi," an almost word-by-word explication of the text, can be found in the library of any observant Jew and is the starting point for anyone preparing a *derash*. In a sense, Rashi, who was born in Troyes, France, picks up the tradition from the great Talmudists; the year of his birth, 1040 C.E., is also the year that the academies in Babylon closed their doors. Appropriately, at the time of his death he was in the midst of writing a commentary on the Babylonian Talmud as detailed as his volumes on the Torah.

Like Sa'adia before him and Maimonides after him, Rashi is a rational-ist. Although he includes midrashim in his Torah commentary, his focus is primarily on *peshat,* and on conveying to the reader a clear, concise under-standing of what the text is saying. To do so, he concentrates on the indi-vidual verse or phrase, even the individual word. When he cites the Talmud, which he does frequently, he does so in the most straightforward way pos-sible. When he uses midrashic material, he generally relies on stories that are as close as possible to the plain meaning of the text. He is deliciously blunt about this issue; when he is explicating the story of the Expulsion from *Gan Eden,* he pauses to note, "There are many midrashic explana-tions. . . . I, however, am only concerned with the plain sense of Scripture and with such aggadot that explain the words of Scripture in a manner that fits with them." On the other hand, he will occasionally include a midrash chosen clearly for its literary (or, dare we say it, entertainment) value. And Rashi is not afraid to say, "I do not know the reason for this," when no explanation suggests itself.

Rashi's wide-ranging knowledge extends beyond the Jewish sacred texts. His writing displays firsthand experience of the everyday occupa-tions of his time. He is comfortable with the Onkelos (Aramaic) trans-lation of the *Tanakh* and displays a thorough command of Hebrew grammar. He frequently refers to Old French terms when explaining a passage from Torah. The inclusion of over three thousand of these *lo'azim,* as they are called in Hebrew, makes Rashi's commentary not only essential for Torah scholars but extremely helpful to philologists reconstructing the evolution of the French language.

2. ABRAHAM IBN EZRA

Born about a half century after Rashi, Abraham Ibn Ezra is the poster boy for polymaths. One of the last blossoms from the tree of Spanish Jewry, he wrote on grammar, philosophy, poetry, and the sciences. But his most lasting achievement is his Torah commentary, which not only reca-pitulates the previous work in the field written in Arabic but extends it in a graceful (and occasionally acerbic) Hebrew prose.

Unlike Rashi, whose commentary does not include an overview of the Torah or of his predecessors, Ibn Ezra opens with a pointed refutation of the methodology of many of the writers who came before him. He needles the *geonim* (particularly Sa'adia) for their longwindedness and for includ-ing secular material that he says has no bearing on the passages to which it is attached. He denounces the Karaites for rejecting all the rabbinic writings and assuming that they can understand the Torah without explication, and those who read the Torah as allegory. Finally, he excoriates the Christian scholars who attempt to interpret the Torah without understanding basic Hebrew grammar.

In contrast to these methods, he extols his own, which is "to explain every text according to the verse, the grammar, and the literal meaning." Although he is willing to take into account midrashim, he disapproves of those followers of Rashi who, he believed, took these inclusions to extremes.

He certainly departs from Rashi in tone. Where Rashi is modest, Ibn Ezra is almost arrogant. "God alone will I fear," he writes, "and I will not pretend (or show favor) with regard to the Torah." He can be snide and dismissive of those with whom he disagrees, but he is utterly fearless and totally independent. In that spirit, he is among the first Jewish authors to suggest that there are passages in the Torah that were not written by Moshe, drawing down the considerable wrath of Nahmanides. He is also one of the first to suggest that the last twenty-six chapters of the *sefer Yeshayahu* were written by a second author.

Rabbi Saul Leeman explains Ibn Ezra's methodology succinctly:

Abraham ibn Ezra . . . , a champion of *p'shat*, . . . is not unlike an archaeologist removing layer after layer of earth accumulated through the ages to arrive at the bedrock beneath. In like manner does ibn Ezra examine the scriptural text and remove all the accretions of *d'rash* (homiletical exposition) and exegesis that have accumulated throughout the generations to arrive at what the text meant when it was originally written. In this respect, ibn Ezra differs from all of the other commentators who permit much *d'rash* to seep into their interpretation.

3. THE KIMHI FAMILY

Ibn Ezra was forced to leave Spain, and during his lifetime he wandered throughout Europe. He was not the only exemplar of Spanish Jewry to find himself uprooted in the medieval period. Many great scholars were forced into exile, ending up in France or North Africa. Provence, in particular, became a prominent center of Jewish thought after the mid-twelfth century, with the result that Arabic, until then the prevalent language of Jewish scholars, was left behind. Consequently, many important works originally written in Arabic began to be translated into Hebrew (and Christian thinkers were becoming acquainted with these works when they were, in turn, retranslated into Latin).

Among the most important figures in this transition from Arabic were Joseph Kimhi, a contemporary of Ibn Ezra, and his sons Moses and David. Joseph was responsible for many translations from Arabic to Hebrew. Moses, known as the Remak, authored several volumes of Torah commentary that so closely resembled those of Ibn Ezra that some historians believe they may have been the work of the Spaniard.

But it is David, often called the Radak, who left the most distinct mark on the world of Torah commentary. He wrote a Hebrew grammar and dictionary that would be very influential, even in Christian circles, and his commentary on *Tanakh* is one of the most popular after Rashi's; his book on the *Tehillim* is considered particularly noteworthy. Frequently translated into Latin, his commentary even had an indirect but very significant influence on the King James version of the Bible.

Radak was a highly popular *darshan* during his lifetime, and his rather repetitious style suggests the oral origins of his written work. He frequently refers to Ibn Ezra and to his own father, but he draws on a wide range of sources, Talmudic, midrashic, philosophical, and poetic. Generally, his interpretations are in the mainstream of his time, but he was capable of heterodox statements, particularly in his writings on the Prophets.

4. NAHMANIDES

If Maimonides is the fountain of cool reason, Nahmanides is a geyser of fire. Solomon Schechter saw the duo as opposites, the rationality and logic of the Moses ben Maimon countered by the emotion and depth of feeling of Moses ben Nakhman. Certainly they were separated by their attitude to philosophy. Nahmanides accepts the Torah and the rabbinic writings as authoritative and puts no trust in philosophy. For him, religious truth has nothing to do with the human intellect.[5] It should come as no surprise, then, to learn that he was an early kabbalist as well as an important Torah commentator.

Nahmanides was born in 1195 in Gerona, Spain, and lived all but the last few years of his life in a now-Christian Spain. Like Maimonides, he was a highly successful physician and lived comfortably until, in 1263, he was challenged to a public disputation on the comparative merits of Christianity and Judaism by Pablo Cristiani, an apostate Jew. He handily bested his opponent, but such a public victory could only be disastrous for a Jewish scholar in a militantly Christian country and, despite the protection of King James of Aragon, he was forced to flee to Palestine, where he finished his commentary on the Torah and was instrumental in reviving the flagging Jewish community.

Nahmanides explicitly conceives his commentary on Torah as a response to Rashi and Ibn Ezra. For the former he has nothing but deference and respect, but he finds fault with Rashi's use of Old French, that is, non-Jewish, materials. On that score, he is less charitable. But for Ibn Ezra, Nahmanides shows little but disdain, even when he agrees with his countryman. Nahmanides can be as modest as Rashi, but when he comes up against Ibn Ezra, he is aggressive, even testy.

Unlike either of his predecessors, Nahmanides' approach to Torah is that of a pietist who is unconvinced by rational argument. He draws much more heavily than either of them on midrash and includes allegorical and mystical interpretations alongside *peshat*. Finally, where Rashi and Ibn Ezra are concerned primarily with verse-by-verse interpretation of the Torah, Nahmanides frequently draws attention to larger units of the text, commenting on their relationships, finding meaning in the juxtaposition of the chapters and the *parashiyot*.

With the new interest in Kabbalah and the willingness to engage in mystical interpretations of the Torah, to draw upon *remez* and *sod* freely, Nahmanides heralds another stream of thought in Jewish Bible interpretation. That is where we will turn our attention now.

TRANSLATING THE TORAH:
ANOTHER KIND OF INTERPRETATION

George Steiner has written, "However pedestrian or exalted, however, routine or re-creative, a translation is always a primary thrust of understanding." Appropriately, Steiner is himself a Jew—albeit a secular one—a polymath, polyglot Jew. In a sense, every Jew is a polyglot, an inheritor of multiple languages, no matter how assimilated. Kafka playfully reminded his fellow Jews that they "know more Yiddish" than they realized. He could as easily have said "more Hebrew." Still, the vast majority of us read the Torah first (if not only) in translation and, as Steiner says, translation is a form of interpretation and of commentary.

Translation is also an absolutely essential tool of Torah interpretation because, in some cases, it is the only clue we have to the intentions and meaning of the Hebrew original. It is not an accident that even Bible scholars as great as Rashi and Nahmanides have recourse to the various *targumim* to fill in the gaps in their understanding. Remember, too, that when the Torah was read in public by Ezra in 444 B.C.E. in Jerusalem, the listeners were mainly Aramaic speakers, so the text had to be translated for them by the elders as Ezra read. The idea of translating the Torah is an old one.

At first, the necessity of translation grew out of the linguistic changes that befell the Jews of ancient Judah. Aramaic in its various dialects displaced Hebrew as the language of everyday life. Then Aramaic was in turn driven out by Greek and then by Arabic. Hebrew remained the sacred (and literary) tongue, but like most American Jews today, the Jews of *Eretz Yisrael* had little contact with the language outside of the synagogue.

The rabbinic authorities were torn. They wanted people to understand the Torah, but they didn't want to encourage ignorance of Hebrew (and, by extension, the sacred text). And they didn't want to leave the Torah open to mistranslation, misunderstanding, and misbehavior. At first they permitted only one verse of the Torah (and three of the *Nevi'im*) to be read and translated at a time. Certain passages were not to be translated in public at all (*Bereishit* 35:22; *Shemot* 31:21–25; *B'midbar* 6:23–26; *Vayikra* 18:21). No copy of a translation was to be used in public services.

The dispersion of the Jews into the Diaspora changed all that radically. Now there were Jews who spoke and read only Greek, Jews in Palestine who were multilingual but whose language skills didn't encompass Hebrew. Worship practice became more flexible out of necessity, and translations became more commonplace.

The oldest version of the Torah translated by Jews is the Septuagint, a translation into the Greek dialect spoken by the Jews of Alexandria in the third century B.C.E. This translation was probably commissioned by the prosperous Jewish community there, and was supported by the king, probably Ptolemy II Philadelphus, who was sympathetic to the Jews. (The name, from the Greek word for "seventy," comes from the tradition that the king invited seventy-two Jewish scholars to create the translation.) The source text used was significantly different in some passages from the one that became the Masoretic standard and, for that reason, the Septuagint was rejected by large segments of the Jewish population throughout the world. However, where the New Testament quotes the Hebrew Bible, the quotations come from the Septuagint, and Philo's citations of Torah are also drawn from this version. The early Church Fathers accepted the Septuagint as the authoritative version of the Pentateuch for the new religion of Christianity.

After the destruction of the Second Temple, the rabbis, concerned about the emergence of Christianity, decided to commission a new, corrected Greek translation. They gave the assignment to a convert to Judaism, Aquila. Although only fragments of *Targum Aquila* exist, it is clearly a combination of a Greek translation and rabbinic interpretation of the text.

Aramaic translations of the *Tanakh* date back—no surprise here—to Ezra and Nekhemyah, but the best-known and most authoritative one is *Targum Onkelos*. Like Aquila, Onkelos was a convert to Judaism. His translation is so reliable, and provides so many additional insights into parts of the text whose age has rendered them unclear in meaning, that it is found in the *Mikra'ot Gedolot* (see "The Great Scriptures" on p. 182) alongside the Hebrew. Onkelos offers a straightforward translation but with small adjustments. Additionally, he occasionally offers a "clarification" of the original, most famously when he replaces the injunction "You shall not boil a kid in its mother's milk" with "You shall not eat meat with milk." There are several other Aramaic translations that exist only in fragmentary form, including *Targum Yonatan ben Uzziel* and *Targum Yerushalmi*.

As noted elsewhere in this chapter, Sa'adia Gaon authored the most important Arabic translation, *Targum Tafsir*, which includes considerable commentary as well. With the complete dispersion of the Jewish population around the world, this would become merely one in an ongoing series of translations. And with each new translation, controversies would arise over interpretations of the sacred text, appropriateness of accompanying commentaries, and the long-term effects on observance and worship of including vernacular language in services and/or holy books. The *Tanakh* and many of the key Torah commentaries were among the earliest Hebrew books selected for printing in the enthusiasm for books bred by the invention of movable type. Wherever there was a Jewish community, there would be a demand for Jewish books. In a posting to the H-JUDAIC list dated November 10, 2002, Leonard Greenspoon listed seventeen complete or partial Jewish translations of the Torah into English between 1785 and 1861.

Perhaps the most ambitious and influential modern translation of the *Tanakh* was the German version undertaken by Martin Buber and Franz Rosenzweig in the 1930s. As might be expected of a collaboration between two of the giants of twentieth-century Jewish thought (and of twentieth-century philosophy), this was no mere quick gloss. Rather, it was the product of extensive thought and reading by both men, leading to a radical new approach to the text.

The entire project was unprecedented in several ways. Most important, Buber and Rosenzweig sought to "make the German alien by means of the Hebrew," as Leora Batnitzky summarizes it. It was their stated belief that the role of the translator in such a work is not to smooth over the difficulties presented by the process of translation; rather, they envisioned their task as *creating* difficulties, expanding the distance between reader and text! They felt that the experience of reading the Bible in one's own tongue—a seemingly familiar text with a larger-than-life importance—should serve as a vivid reminder of the original in all its estrangement. Consequently, the Buber-Rosenzweig translation emphasizes re-creating the sound values and repetitions of the Hebrew as much as, if not more than, the literal meaning.

In a 1930 essay Buber writes:

The special obligation to create a new version of the Bible, which came alive in our time and led to our undertaking, resulted from the discovery that the passage of time had largely turned the Bible into a palimpsest. The original traits of the Bible, the original meaning and words, had been overlaid by a familiar abstraction, in origin partly theological and partly literary.

For the non-German reader who wishes to get a sense of what the Buber-Rosenzweig Hebrew Bible is like, a reading of Everett Fox's *The Five Books of Moses* is recommended. Fox has produced a translation of the Torah into English based on the principles that guided his German predecessors, creating an English text that has most of the repetitions, internal rhymes, echoes, and allusions of the original. At the same time, it is written in the same percussive, densely alliterative poetry of the Hebrew. The result is a formidable achievement, quite unlike any other Torah translation available in English today.

THE MYSTICAL STRAIN

Mysticism was not new to Jewish thought in the medieval period. Jewish mystical thought dates back to the second century C.E., the era in which the Mishnah was compiled, and possibly even earlier. Like the rest of Jewish thought to this point, the various schools of mysticism believe that the *Tanakh* is the source of all truth, the Revealed Word of God. So anyone who knows how to read the Bible can find the Truth. As we have already seen, there are many ways to read the Bible, to read it Jewishly, so obviously the mystics sought a new and different way.

Kabbalah, the dominant school of mysticism in Judaism, represented a clear and decisive break with all previous Jewish thought, even with previous versions of mysticism. As Arthur Green observes, the men who propagated Kabbalah were bound by the constraints of normative (that is, Rabbinic) Judaism; they were as "orthodox" in their practice as any Jews of the period. But the conception of God in Kabbalah is radically different from the unitary monotheistic Deity of all previous Judaism. Rather, the kabbalists envisioned the Supreme Being as a panoply of "potencies," to use Green's evocative word, and the relationship between them. As symbolized by the *sefirot*, the ten emanations of God, corresponding to the Ten Utterances with which God created the universe, the Holy One is a multifaceted entity. Which is not say that God is not a single Being—this is not the duality of Gnosticism. And yet, despite this epistemological break with all previous Jewish thought, the kabbalists relied on the Torah, both Written and Oral, to justify their beliefs, much as every other Jewish thinker had since the redaction of the Mishnah much as Trinitarian Christians had relied on the Hebrew Bible.

It should be fairly obvious, then, that the new way in which the kabbalists read Torah was a *really* new way.

The central text of all kabbalistic thought—not the first or last, but certainly the essential kabbalistic work—is the *Zohar*. As might be expected of such a momentous and esoteric book, even the origins of the *Zohar* were shrouded in mystery. Green puts it nicely: "Written in a lofty combination of Aramaic and Hebrew, the *Zohar* was first revealed to the world around the year 1300."

The circle of kabbalists centered in Castile disseminated it in fragments, orally and in writing, presenting it as an ancient text they had rediscovered. Its authorship would be attributed to the great sage Shimon bar Yohai. Bar Yohai is best remembered for the legend that during the Roman occupation of Palestine he took refuge with his son in a cave where the two lived for thirteen years, studying Torah and living on little more than air while the Roman soldiers sought to find and execute them. Bar Yohai was a brilliant scholar, reputed to have unusual powers, so he was the perfect author for a densely allusive mystical text.

Except that he didn't write the *Zohar*. The author probably was Moses de Leon, a protégé of Nahmanides. Why did de Leon pass off his own writing (or that of a circle of kabbalists with him at the center, as some recent scholars claim) as the work of a second-century sage? Undoubtedly, the simplest answer is the correct one: having a distinguished provenance for the book would give it an authority that de Leon himself lacked. It also gave him an imaginative freedom that he might not otherwise have had, and the book soars with that sense of liberation.

As already noted, *Sefer Ha'Zohar* is largely written in Aramaic, a ploy that de Leon used to establish its ostensible authenticity as an ancient text. However, the Aramaic he uses mixes Palestinian and Babylonian dialects and is full of anachronisms and awkward constructions that betray its medieval (and Latinate) origins. Moreover, as Gershom Scholem points out, many of its analyses of the Torah are simply too lengthy to be midrashim from the classical period, and owe their underlying structure to medieval Jewish philosophy.

Despite those linguistic and semantic peculiarities, at first glance the *Zohar* appears to be yet another collection of midrashim on the weekly Torah readings, organized around the notion of a traveling party of scholars, led by Shimon bar Yohai, making their way around Palestine, stopping periodically to discuss passages from holy texts. And that is, in fact, what the book consists of. But these midrashim are unlike any others written before. They are steeped in the vocabulary of Kabbalah and interpret Torah in ways that are completely unlike, say, *Midrash Rabbah*.

The purpose of these exegetical speculations is quite different, too. As

Michael Fishbane says, "Recovering theosophical truths in the teachings of Torah, the mystics ascend exegetically into God." The *Zohar* reads the Torah in a way that turns that sacred text into a complex set of codes and keys to a higher reality, daring to approach the Godhead itself. The Torah is seen not merely as sacred text, as law, myth, and narrative, as statement of love of *Adonai;* for bar Yokhai and his companions—and the readers who travel with them in the book's pages—the Torah is part of the very essence of God, and to read the Torah in their manner is to touch the wisdom and energy of the Eternal. Thus, Torah study becomes a form of elevated spirituality in itself, an intensification of the traditional importance of the study of sacred text in Jewish practice.

Arthur Green has a wonderful observation about the *Zohar* that helps to understand the linguistic and imagistic richness of the book. Because the second commandment prohibits the making of graven images, Jewish artists and thinkers could not express their love for and fascination with the Eternal in painting, sculpture, or stained glass, as their Christian counterparts could in this era. Instead, they were restricted to the use of the written word. As a result, as Green says, "the *Zohar* may be seen as the greatest work of medieval Jewish *iconography,* but one that exists only in the words on the written page, thence to be distilled in the imagination of its devoted students" (emphasis in original). What more appropriate vehicle for this monumental effort than exegesis of the Torah—the touchstone, the cornerstone of Judaism? (An aside: Following from Green's observation, it isn't hard to see why the first great Jewish artists were writers. Great Jewish painters and sculptors are pretty much a phenomenon of the twentieth century. But great Jewish writing can be traced in a line back to the Torah itself.)

The *Zohar* is the greatest achievement of Jewish mysticism, an enormous, beautiful work whose influence in traditional Judaism is surpassed only by that of the Torah and the Talmud. But it is not the end of the mystical tradition of interpreting the Torah. Rather, it is the beginning of an entire parallel mystical tradition of Torah interpretation that can be traced in the thought of both the Hasidim and their equally pious antagonists, the *Mitnagdim.* The Vilna Gaon, the brilliant eighteenth-century Lithuanian scholar who was a fierce nemesis of the Hasidim, was also a highly learned scholar of Kabbalah. Even a cursory reading of the *derashot* of the great Hasidic rebbes exposes one to a world of mystery.

Jewish history is downright Newtonian in its catalog of actions and reactions. Mysticism moved to the center of Jewish thought in the eighteenth century, just as the *Haskalah/Enlightenment* and the Emancipation were offering Jews an alternative to traditional observance, one thoroughly rooted in a new rationalism. Ironically, despite their enmity toward one another, the Hasidim and *Mitnagdim* were united in at least two beliefs: the centrality of mysticism to Jewish thought and a deep hatred of the nascent Reform movement and the Jewish Enlightenment. In Germany, a new figure would emerge who embodied everything they opposed.

TORAH + SCIENCE

Moses Mendelssohn is a pivotal figure in the history of Jewish Bible commentary and, more important, in the history of the Jewish people. The first significant figure in Jewish philosophy to come after Spinoza, he was faced with the aftermath of Spinoza's frontal attack on the Bible as received Divine Truth. Although he was an Orthodox Jew (at a time in Jewish history when that distinction first began to have meaning), he was also a figure of the Enlightenment, drawn to Spinoza's belief in Science, yet not quite ready to discard Revelation. He was a beneficiary of the improvements in Jewish life that came as a result of the Emancipation, and he was the first major Jewish figure to emerge from Germany since the early medieval period, albeit the first of a lengthy series that would encompass almost every major Jewish thinker of the modern era.

To see why Mendelssohn represents such a radical break in Jewish thought, we need to understand the historical conjunction that produced him.

During the Middle Ages and the Renaissance, the Jews of Western Europe were set apart by laws that forced them to wear distinctive outer clothing, hats, or yellow badges, and to live in walled enclaves called ghettos, under strict curfews that were enforced by the locking-in of the residents at night and on Sundays. They were barred from owning land and from many occupations. Condemned as the people who "killed Christ" and who denied Christ's divinity, they were the victims of expulsion from England, Spain, Portugal, Germany, and France, of suspicion everywhere. Nowhere were they citizens. At best they were non-Europeans, reluctantly and grudgingly accepted; at worst they were seen as avatars of the Antichrist.

There was one redeeming feature to this gruesome treatment. The Jewish community was forced to be self-reliant. At the beginning of the eighteenth century, there were 400,000 Jews in Western Europe. Segregated from non-Jewish society, kept in by the walls of the ghettos, they had complete autonomy within their own realm, with their own social service system, educational system, police, courts, leadership, and institutions.

This, briefly, was the state of Jewish affairs at the dawn of mercantilism, the socioeconomic force that would produce the Enlightenment in the West, pave the way for the birth of democratic societies from the painful gestation of revolution in America and France, and bring about the totally unanticipated Emancipation of the Jews in Western Europe. European society before the French Revolution was by and large organized around "corporate" bodies that received privileges in exchange for the payment of a fee—the medieval craftsmen's guilds, for example—and "estates" such as the Church, manors, universities, towns, and commercial and financial companies. In this system, many religious or ethnic groups were treated like estates, including the Jews. The rights of individuals were moot in this system; it was the rights of groups that were safeguarded.

The system was a mixed blessing. Hemmed in on all sides by restrictive laws, Jews could hold only those jobs permitted them by Christian rulers guided by a hostile Christian clergy. But the Jewish community was cohesive and had no problems with continuity. If a Jew had to wear a yellow badge or a conical hat, had to pay a tax to leave the ghetto by day and to reenter by night, that was the price—quite literally—of doing business in a Christian world.

Then the Enlightenment came along, spawning revolutions in philosophy and politics, and nothing was the same again. The Enlightenment led to the end of the corporate system, an anachronism ill-suited to a world in which capital and people moved quickly. The effect on the Jews was, in a word, Emancipation.

For the first time in their history, the Jews were now declared citizens of the nations that were their homes in the Diaspora. They had the same duties and rights as non-Jews. They were expected to become integrated into the society around them. The situation presented entirely new dilemmas, and in addressing them, both Jews and non-Jews were entering an unknown territory.

Emancipation meant that Jews were to be granted new rights *as indi-*

viduals. They no longer had to wear distinctive clothing. They were no longer confined to the ghettos. Gradually, in the few extant democracies of Western Europe, Jewish men were granted the franchise. Previously the Jews had had rights as a group, or as members of a group. These rights had helped to preserve the solidarity, the cohesiveness of the Jewish community under constant pressure from their non-Jewish neighbors. Those rights no longer existed.

In their place came an avalanche of problems stemming from one question: Could the Jews maintain their identity as Jews while becoming members of a civil society?

Mendelssohn, a lightning intellect encased in a stunted body, was a figure of such brilliance and so potent a champion of Jewish concerns that he quickly became the chief spokesman for Jews in this new world of individual rights. He soon established himself as a writer and literary critic; in 1763 he was awarded the first prize of the Prussian Royal Academy for his treatise, "On Evidence in the Metaphysical Sciences." That same year he received an even rarer honor, being granted the "right of residence" in Berlin by Frederick the Great. Although the Prussian ruler was notably liberal for this era, even toward his Jewish subjects, it was highly unusual for such a residency permit to be given.

But Mendelssohn was never allowed to forget who and what he was, or that all the success could be swept away with the stroke of a monarch's pen—that he was, as he himself ruefully noted, "a member of an oppressed race."

While he was defending the Jews to the Christian world, Mendelssohn was also seeking ways to integrate his coreligionists into an ostensibly welcoming non-Jewish world. In his major philosophical work, *Jerusalem* (1783), he argued that what distinguishes the Jew from the non-Jew is not a revelation of reason but a unique body of Mosaic law, a historical fact that is attested to by the 600,000 men, women, and children of the Hebrew people present at Sinai. Therefore, Jews can achieve fulfillment only by adhering to the laws of Moshe. The God of reason and the God of Sinai are unified in the observance of *halakhah.* It is the sheer *dailyness* of these observances that brings Jews closer to eternal truths. At the same time, Mendelssohn argues, in both this work and his later writings, that Diaspora Jews must integrate themselves into the cultures that host them.

To that end, he began the arduous task of translating the Pentateuch into German, at first only for his own children but eventually for publication. In order to make this new Torah more accessible to Hebrew and Yiddish readers, he wrote the German in Hebrew characters. And he enlisted a circle of his personal friends, mighty Judaic scholars all, to create a *biur/commentary* to accompany the translation. The Orthodox rabbis were appalled, convinced that this new book would lead Jewish youth away from the Torah and into the reading of secular—that is, German non-Jewish—texts, and they issued a ban against the work in 1779.

Needless to say, the proscription of the text didn't deter Mendelssohn or his colleagues, now known as the Biurists. In 1783, they completed publication of an entire *Tanakh*, called *Netivot Ha'Shalom/Paths of Peace*, which included a Hebrew introduction by Mendelssohn.

The doorway had been flung open, and all across Europe new colloquial translations of the Torah were being made according to the scientific principles espoused by the Biurists. For the first time in history, the principles of the "higher criticism" (see Chapter 3), originally espoused by Christian Bible scholars, were being adopted and adapted in Jewish Bible commentary. A major German-Jewish commentary by Ludwig Philippson would be published in 1827 that explicitly accepted the ideas of "scientific criticism." Although Jewish commentators had occasionally referred to non-Jewish sources—Sa'adia and Rashi both did this, to the dismay of other, more conservative commentators—Bible commentary had been almost exclusively a one-way street, with Christian authors drawing upon their Jewish contemporaries. Philippson and the Biurists sent the traffic spinning in the opposite direction.

The backlash that began with the 1779 ban on Mendelssohn's Torah translation and commentary would, inevitably, manifest itself in the pages of Jewish Torah commentary. With the Emancipation giving rise to a new version of Judaism—Reform—that rejected much of *halakhah* and questioned the Divine nature of sacred text, the emergence of a concomitant neo-Orthodox movement was hardly surprising.

Fittingly, the primary advocate of a revived Orthodoxy, forerunner of today's Modern Orthodox movement with its tolerant attitude toward secular learning and success, was another German Jew, Samson Raphael Hirsch. Hirsch himself was a brilliant student at the University of Bonn, where he became good friends with Abraham Geiger, who would become one of the key figures in Reform Judaism (no doubt to Hirsch's chagrin).

While Hirsch brought his secular learning to bear on larger philosophical questions, his position on the nature of Torah and the theophany at Sinai was unwavering:

> The whole question is simply this. Is the statement "And God spoke to Moses saying," with which all the laws of the Jewish Bible commence, true or not true? Do we really and truly believe that God the Omnipotent and Holy, spoke thus to Moses? Do we speak the truth when in front of our brethren we lay our hand on the scroll containing these words and say that God has given us this Torah and that His Torah, the Torah of truth and with it of eternal life, is planted in our midst? If this is to be more than lip service, mere rhetorical flourish, then we must keep and carry out this Torah without omission and without carping, in all circumstances and at all times.

As one might expect, Hirsch's Torah commentary reflects that ideological stance, drawing much more heavily on the classical sources than later ones. But Hirsch was not utterly inflexible in his response to the Emancipation. He prescribed a life of *Torah im derekh eretz/Torah with the way of the land*, that is, Torah combined with the necessity of earning a living, of living in a non-Jewish world. He would argue that it is possible to integrate the Jewish community into the modern world as long as the community remains loyal, first and foremost, to the precepts of Torah.

Nevertheless, the wall between Jews and non-Jews had been breached and then torn down. Except for the most utterly intransigent ultra-Orthodox communities, the reality of Jewish life in a non-Jewish world had to be faced. And even for the greatest minds produced by the Modern Orthodox world, Torah would now be read in a context of modernity.

THE GREAT SCRIPTURES

One of the most useful tools for studying the Torah is the *Mikra'ot Gedolot/Great Scriptures*, the so-called rabbinic Bible, whose pages include not only the text of the Torah and several other books of the *Tanakh* but also a wide range of classic commentaries. A typical modern edition will include the Masoretic notes to the text and the *Targum Onkelos*, as well as commentaries by Rashi, Ibn Ezra, Ramban, Rashbam, Radak, Sforno, and others.

The first published version was a source of no small controversy. Published in 1517–18 by the famous Venetian printer Daniel Bomberg, a Christian, the edition was compiled by an apostate Jew, Felix Pratensis. Bomberg applied to the Pope Leo X for an imprimatur before putting out the book, and the Jewish community was less than thrilled. Pratensis's version of the Masoretic notes received particularly harsh criticism, and in 1525 Bomberg published a new edition, edited by Jacob b. Hayyim of Tunis. This one met with general approval, so much so that it became the model for many subsequent versions of the book. (Jacob b. Hayyim converted to Christianity a few years after the publication of his monumental work.)

MODERNITY CONFRONTS SCRIPTURE

Whether by happenstance or by choice, the great Jewish thinkers of the twentieth century did not write Torah commentaries in the conventional sense of a line-by-line or even book-by-book interpretation, in the manner of Rashi, Nahmanides, and Hirsch. Although several of them were pulpit rabbis at some point in their careers—most notably Joseph Soloveitchik—and had written many *derashot,* the focus of their published work was on larger issues. Given the pervasive influence of existentialism in the works of Rosenzweig, Buber, Heschel, and Soloveitchik, they may have felt a need to speak to the big philosophical questions raised by a Christian counterpart like Kierkegaard. Maybe they just didn't feel they needed to add to the vast literature of Torah commentary already in existence, or perhaps they felt that the documentary hypothesis called for a different kind of commentary (although that is highly unlikely given their divergent attitudes on the subject of Revelation). For whatever reason, of this quartet only Soloveitchik left behind a substantial collection of *derashot* in English and, significantly, those were assembled by his students after his death. But, interestingly enough, all four of them spoke directly to the same issues that had motivated Rashi and the Talmudists. (Buber, for example, wrote a brilliant analysis of the last four books of Torah in the guise of a biographical work on Moshe, and Soloveitchik's classics, *Halakhic Man* and *The Halakhic Mind,* are unthinkable without the foundations laid in the Talmud.)

Nor should their choice to shift the ground of the debate to philosophy be understood as a denigration of those modern Torah commentators who chose to bind themselves to the weekly routine of *parashat ha'shavua*. Frankly, one of the fascinations of reading contemporary Torah commentators is seeing how they incorporate not only the classics but also the "higher criticism," and where and when they invoke less likely allusions both Jewish and non-Jewish. It would be hard to offer a single exemplar of the new, vibrant thinkers who are writing about Torah today, but Avivah Gottlieb Zornberg is certainly a good person with whom to start.

Dr. Zornberg's background bespeaks the breadth of her interests and influences. Scottish-born, she has a Ph.D. in English literature from Cambridge University. She is the daughter of an Orthodox rabbi and is herself a traditionally observant Jew. This combination of secular and religious backgrounds has made her uniquely well-suited to be the avatar of what can only be called, for lack of a better label, postmodern Torah commentary. Using the weekly Torah portion as the structure for her books on *Bereishit* and *Shemot*, she has written *derashot* that move nimbly between Freud and Rashi, Kafka and *Midrash Rabbah*. Her conception of midrash as "the repressed unconsciousness of the Torah," as the way that the text— through the rabbis—speaks that which cannot be said, and her comcomitant focus on the gaps and dislocations of the Torah as text are a short step away from Jacques Derrida and Emmanuel Levinas, the two great Jewish voices of postmodern thought.

Zornberg is important in one more way. She is a woman. As we will see in the next chapter, 51 percent of the Jewish people have long been silenced or, at the very least, muffled in their response to Torah by the constraints of the religion, possibly by the Torah itself. Given the historical circumstances, it seems both fitting and inevitable that when a new viewpoint on Torah emerged at the end of the twentieth century, its principal speaker would be a woman.

The process of making midrash, of writing commentary on Torah, is an unending one. In that respect, it reflects the nature of the Torah itself. *Sefer Devarim* ends not with the triumphant conquest of Kina'an by the Israelites but with the death of Moshe and *B'nei Yisrael* poised on the other side of the Yardein, about to enter the land they have been promised. In the synagogue, when we come to this final verse, we say *"Khazak, khazak v'nitkhazeik,"* and then we begin to read again, *"Bereishit bara Elohim/In the beginning God created . . ."* As the cycle of reading has no end, the process of understanding, too, is infinitely renewable. That is one of the beauties of the Torah.

Given its cyclical nature, one would think that the Torah is somehow outside of historical time. Yet, as we have seen, readings of the Torah change as contexts change. *Halakhah* has had to adapt itself to new realities. The influence of non-Jewish thought has made itself felt even to a pillar in the Modern Orthodox world such as Joseph Soloveitchik. Torah has always been part of a semipermeable membrane that surrounds the Jewish world. As we shall see in the next two chapters, the interaction between *klal Yisrael/the community of Israel* and the rest of the world has affected our reading of Torah even more profoundly in the past half century. The gates of the ark have been thrown open wider than ever.

A TIMELINE OF TALMUD SCHOLARS*

Dates (Approx.)	Group	Most Prominent Members
c. 350–200 B.C.E.	Men of the Great Assembly	Shimon Ha'Tzaddik
c. 200–1st cent. B.C.E.	The *Zugot/Pairs*	Yosei b. Yo'ezer, Yosei b. Yokhanan Yehoshua b. Perakhya, Mattai Yehudah b. Tabbai, Shimon b. Shetakh Shemayah, Avtalyon Hillel, Shammai

*The numbering of the generations of the sages is not an exact science. *The Enyclopedia of Judaism* has eight generations of *amora'im* in Babylonia; H. L. Strack has seven. Strack has five generations of *tanna'im*, but divides one of his generations into older and younger groups; Moses Mielziner numbers six generations of *tanna'im*, and only six generations of Babylonian *amora'im*. (I have followed the 1992 revised edition of Strack and Günter Stemberger, edited and translated by Markus Bockmuehl.)

1st cent. B.C.E.	*Tanna'im,* First Generation	School of Hillel School of Shammai Rabban Gamaliel the Elder Khananiah Shimon b. Gamaliel I Yokhanan b. Zakkai Eliezer b. Ya'akov the Elder Haninah b. Dosa
c. 90–130 C.E.	*Tanna'im,* Second Generation, Older Group	Rabban Gamaliel II Eliezer b. Hyrcanus Yehoshua b. Khananyah Yosei the Priest Eleazar b. Azariah
	Younger Group	Yishmael b. Elisha Akiva b. Yosef Tarfon Shimon b. Azzai (Ben Azzai) Shimon b. Zoma (Ben Zoma) Elisha b. Abuyah *(Akheir/the Other)*
c. 130–160 C.E.	*Tanna'im,* Third Generation	Students of Yishmael Students of Akiva: Meir Shimon bar Yokhai Yosei b. Halafta Yehudah b. Ilai Rabban Shimon b. Gamaliel II
2nd cent. C.E. (Redaction of Mishnah, *Tosefta*)	*Tanna'im,* Fourth Generation	Rabbi and his contemporaries: Yehudah Ha'Nasi (Rabbi) Shimon b. Yehuda

		Akhai b. Yoshiah
		Dosa
		Eleazar b. Shimon
		(Bar Yokhai)
		Yosei b. Meshulam
to 200 C.E.	*Tanna'im,*	Gamaliel III, son of
	Fifth Generation	Rabbi
		Hiyyah the Elder
		Bar Kaparah
		Rav Huna
c. 200–6th cent.	*Amora'im,*	
(redaction of	First Generation	
halakhic midrashim,	Palestine:	Haninah
c. 300 C.E.;		Yannai
aggadic midrashim,		Yehoshua b. Levi
Palestinian Talmud,	Babylonia:	Abba bar Abba
c. 400 C.E.;		Rav (Abba Arikha)
Babylonian Talmud,		Mar Shmuel
c. 427–650 C.E.)	*Amora'im,*	
	Second Generation	
	Palestine:	Yokhanan bar Napakha
		Shimon b. Lakish
		(Resh Lakish)
		Kahana II
		Simlai
	Babylonia:	Huna
		Yehudah b. Yekhezkel
	Amora'im,	
	Third Generation	
	Palestine:	Shmuel bar Nakhman
		Abbahu
		Zera I
	Babylonia:	Khisda
		Rabba bar Nakhmani
	Amora'im,	
	Fourth Generation	
	Palestine:	Haggai
		Hillel II

	Babylonia:	Abaye
		Rava
	Amora'im,	
	Fifth Generation	
	Palestine:	Pinkhas
		Yehudah IV
	Babylonia:	Papa bar Abba
		Huna b. Khanina
		Yehoshua
	Amora'im,	
	Sixth Generation	
	Babylonia:	Ravina I
		Huna bar Nosson
		Ashi
	Amora'im,	
	Seventh Generation	
	Babylonia:	Yemar (at Sura)
		Yosei
6th cent. C.E.	*Savora'im,*	Sama bar Yehudah
	Older Group	Akhai bar Rav Huna
		Rikhumai
		Shmuel bar R. Abbahu
	Savora'im,	Aina
	Younger Group	Simona
		Rabbai

NOTES

1. In reality, the line between two types of midrashim isn't quite so clear-cut; they are usually intermingled. As Hananel Mack aptly observes, "[T]he correct division is not into halakhic midrash and aggadic midrash, but into midrashim that are primarily halakhah and those that are primarily aggadah."

2. Actually, *Mekhilta de'Rabbi Yishmael,* which contains some of the oldest material in any of the midrash collections, is only about 40 percent halakhic in orientation. The majority of the text is aggadic.

3. It should be noted that when used in the Talmud, *peshat* means "the accepted interpretation as taught in the schools."

4. Or so it would appear. Actually, much of Sa'adia's Torah commentary outside the *Tafsir* has been lost, with only fragments remaining today.

5. Despite his disagreement with Maimonides' philosophical bent, Nahmanides fought hard against the anti-Maimonideans who wanted to ban and burn *The Guide for the Perplexed* and other of his works. In fact, Nahmanides tried to negotiate a settlement between the pro- and anti-Maimonideans, offering a detailed program that would have taken note of the differences between the Spanish and French Jewish communities and their attitudes toward the sciences. Unfortunately, the extremists on both sides managed to derail any such concord.

5

HEARING SILENCED VOICES:

Women and the Torah

Even where I dissent from biblical or rabbinic teaching, where I find it problematic, unjust or simply wrong, I still see it as part of a past that has shaped and formed me. As mine, it is a past for me to struggle with, not a past on which I am willing to turn my back.

—Judith Plaskow, *Standing Again at Sinai*

Up to this point we have examined many traditional ways of reading these sacred texts. The thirteen *middot* of the rabbis were designed to facilitate understanding through close reading and analysis of syntax and diction, line by line, even word by word. The four methods of exegesis presented larger ways of conceiving larger passages of Torah, verses, chapters, story arcs. What I want to propose here is quite a different method, what the French Marxist Louis Althusser called "a symptomatic reading," an interpretation based on what is missing from the text, from the structuring absences that shape a text by leaving certain things unspoken but assumed. I believe that the great unspoken absence that helps give the Torah its shape is that of a significant category of Jews who are largely (but not entirely) silenced by the text: women.

Consider this key moment in the Torah. God is instructing Moshe to prepare *B'nei Yisrael* to approach Sinai for the Revelation at the mountain. Moshe consecrates the people and they wash their clothes in preparation for the holiest moment in their history. And Moshe says to the people, "Be ready for three days. Don't come close to a woman" (*Shemot* 19:15). There is absolutely nothing in the Torah to suggest that women were not part of the nation, *ha'am/the people* who were present at Sinai. But Moshe instructs *B'nei Yisrael,* "Don't come close to a woman."

What unspoken assumptions are rattling around in that single sentence?

When we pray from a traditional siddur, we frequently invoke the God of our Fathers, Avraham, Yitzkhak, and Ya'akov. Only in the recently rewritten liturgies of the progressive movements of American Judaism do we also pray to the God of our Mothers, Sarah, Rivkah, Leah, and and Rakhel.[1] And when the literal *B'nei Yisrael,* that is, Ya'akov's children, become the heads of the tribes of Israel, there are twelve tribes, one for each son (and for Yosef's sons, Efraim and Menasheh), but no tribe for Ya'akov's daughter, Dinah.

There is no useful point served in gainsaying the obvious. The Torah, the entire *Tanakh,* and most of the Oral Torah are the product of patriarchy and speak with a male voice. The degree to which women's voices are suppressed in the classical Jewish texts is a matter for some debate, but there is no question that, while there are many women who take an active role in events in Torah, there is still a great silence. Classical midrash fills in some of that silence, but the Talmud frequently reinforces it, as might be expected of a male-authored text.

That is not to say that Jewish law is utterly biased against Jewish women. On the contrary, in many ways it is unusually progressive for its time in its treatment of women and their rights, and the rabbis offered many rulings that mitigated some of the cruelties, unintentional and otherwise, of *halakhah* and social custom.

But the voices of Jewish women are seldom heard in Jewish sacred texts because the texts themselves are written by men and reflect an androcentric viewpoint. How do we read those texts in the twenty-first century?

Of course, this raises an obvious question, one that I suspect will resonate for many Jewish women who have drifted away from the Jewish community: If these texts are so pernicious, why study them, let alone use them as a guide for living Jewishly?

I think that the quote from Judith Plaskow that opens this chapter speaks to that question directly. Rachel Adler, in the introduction to her book *Engendering Judaism,* addresses it from a theological standpoint:

> Mine is very much a text-bound theology . . . because . . . I believe that is where Jewish conversation takes place. As I understand it, theology's task is to allow the texts of the tradition and the lived experiences of religious commu-

nities to keep revealing themselves to one another so the sacred meanings of text and of experience can be renewed. In the course of this process, God becomes present in our midst.

A Jewish woman looking for a faith tradition not dominated by men will have as much luck inside Judaism as outside it. An engendered Judaism, to borrow Adler's phrase, will speak to and through the sacred texts to find a basis for a praxis of Judaism, a dialectical balance of theory and practice that one can live every day. Inevitably, that search will lead us back to the Torah as a starting point.

(AT LEAST) TWO KINDS OF READING

Let's return to Moshe's instructions to the (male) *B'nei Yisrael:* "Do not go near a woman." There are, of course, at least two ways to read this command. Moshe may be anticipating the strong connection in *halakhah* between female reproductive processes and impurity, the notion that a woman who is menstruating is somehow unclean and that the sex act, while highly valued, also contains within it some sort of polluting effect, something inherent in female sexuality. (It should be noted that seminal discharge in the absence of intercourse is also a pollutant.) However, at the same time Moshe may also be tacitly admitting that the male of the species is a weakling who is incapable of a bare minimum of self-control. (Indeed, male sexuality is also viewed with unease in some classical Jewish texts.)

One can exercise a similarly double reading of many of the texts before us. Theologian Phyllis Trible posits two kinds of feminist interpretation of sacred texts, a "hermeneutics of suspicion" and a "hermeneutics of grace."

The concept of a hermeneutics of suspicion actually comes from the French American philosopher Paul Ricoeur. He had something slightly different in mind from what Trible is proposing, but his initial conception is worth explaining briefly as a lead-in to Trible's related thinking. Ricoeur groups three important thinkers together as the pioneers of "the school of suspicion," Karl Marx, Friedrich Nietzsche, and Sigmund Freud. Each of them, he says, pursues a systematic reading of texts that regards their surface meanings with suspicion, readings that teach us to analyze our own conscious understanding and experience skeptically. (Not coincidentally, each is a scathing critic of organized religion.) For Ricoeur, this threesome is important because they explore the meanings behind or underneath a text; they seek the causal forces that explain the conscious phenomena by laying bare the true meaning of that phenomena. Such a heremeneutical stance treats the text as a kind of subconscious (echoing Avivah Zornberg's observation from Chapter 4). For Ricoeur this is a political as well as philosophical and ethical way of reading.

Trible's hermeneutics of suspicion has a similar but specifically feminist goal and is aimed at religious texts (as one might expect of a theologian). Simply put, a feminist hermeneutics of suspicion is concerned with reading sacred texts in a way that reveals and foregrounds misogynistic elements in them. By contrast, a hermeneutics of grace, or as many feminist religious thinkers call it, a "hermeneutics of desire"[2] has as its goal revealing texts that are supportive of women and of femaleness and reading less-well-known texts or giving a less familiar reading of those we know by heart to find a critique of patriarchy and a reaffirmation of the feminine in God.

There are two simple problems presented by this hermeneutical duet. First, the two hermeneutic "codes" may exist side by side or even within a single text. We've just seen an example of this in the possible understanding of Moshe's instruction, "Do not go near a woman."

This leads neatly into the other problem. Simply put, there is no single "right" reading of these texts. The Torah speaks in many voices (and when you factor in the vast range of midrashim, Talmud, responsa, and other commentary, you have a veritable cacophony); even within feminist hermeneutics, there must be room for a certain degree of pluralism. Alicia Suskin Ostriker is blunt: "As feminists we should find ourselves urging that the scriptural text is, on the contrary, *not* necessarily monolithic, *not* necessarily coherent, *not* necessarily unified, but riddled with gaps and contradictions and textual ambivalences allowing for plural readings of which *none can ever be definitive.* An insistent heterodoxy is, it seems to me, one of the great strengths of feminist thinking" (emphasis in original).

Ostriker offers a third way. What she posits is a third kind of reading, a "hermeneutics of indeterminacy," a postmodern acceptance of a text's resistance against a single fixed meaning. She explains, "What I mean is that we are aware . . . that an act of interpretation is occurring which may be immediately persuasive yet retains an irreducible element of the willful, the made thing, the playful poetic fiction: interpretation never collapses itself back into text, never makes what the philosophers call 'truth claims.' " A hermeneutics of indeterminacy recognizes the inherent limitations of its own reading of the text in the face of multiple meanings.

Of course, when reading a sacred text for religious purposes, it may be—at the very least—difficult to surrender one's right to claim that truthfulness is at work. But in the forests of Torah commentary there is an undeniable element of "indeterminacy" in almost any given reading, and more than that for many. As Reuven Kimelman says of the story of the Expulsion from *Gan Eden*, the "variety [of interpretations] is due to the fact that no single line of interpretation has accounted for all the data. . . . no single meaning of the story has exhausted all its features."

Feminist Jewish theologians and their non-Jewish counterparts are fully aware of these hiccups in the dual hermeneutics of suspicion and desire. Reality demands that we address sacred texts with what Dr. Zornberg calls "a dialectical hermeneutic," a method of reading that takes in suspicion and desire, acknowledges indeterminacy, and is fully aware of the interplay of all three. At the same time, such a dialectical hermeneutic would also recognize that in Judaism, more than in other Western faith traditions, there is also a dialectical relationship between text and practice, usually coming down on the side of the latter, as we shall see momentarily. Judaism is, as we have seen repeatedly, a religion based more on deed than creed, on ritual rather than profession of belief. (Or, to be more specific, profession of belief frequently takes place in the context of ritual, as in the public reading of the thirteen attributes of God as part of *Seder K'riat Ha'Torah* for the Festivals.)

That is why one of the central questions facing Jewish thinkers who wish to address the issues raised by Jewish feminists is the way that we speak of God in both scripture and liturgy.

A TORAH COMMENTARY FOR WOMEN:
TZE'NAH U'R'ENAH

The explosion of women's midrashim does not emerge from a vacuum. In the late Middle Ages, there were already precedents for this modern phenomenon, albeit somewhat more modest. There were women's prayer books called *tekhinot* and a remarkable Yiddish-language book colloquially known as "the *Khumash* for women," entitled *Tze'nah U'R'enah.*

Tze'nah U'R'enah, which was compiled by Rabbi Ya'akov Yitzkhak Ashkenazi sometime in the late sixteenth or early seventeeth century, is a series of commentaries on the weekly Torah portion. Written in Yiddish, the lingua franca of the European Jewish world of the time, the book was unusual in its strong focus on the role of women. As Dr. Julius Carlebach puts it, "Although it does not deviate in the slightest from the accepted halakhic definition of the female role, it manages to elevate it and to give it a significance which in other texts is at best only implicit. . . . [T]he social and economic roles of women receive continuous emphasis."

The book was a huge success and was widely read and studied by Jewish women for more than three centuries. The reaction within the male-dominated Jewish communal world was rather more mixed. On the one hand, the book sparked a growing interest in Jewish learning for women, supported by such leading rabbis as the Chafetz Chaim. But the early leaders of Reform were considerably less enthusiastic, frowning on the use of Yiddish, which they saw as a debased ghetto language that held back the tides of Jewish emancipation.

GOD HERSELF

So many versions, so many visions. The only improbable story is that God was originally male.

—Alicia Suskin Ostriker

It is an understandable lament of Jewish feminists that praying to a (textually) male God is a profoundly alienating experience. Judith Plaskow has written, "God's maleness is so deeply and firmly established as part of the Jewish conception of God that it is almost diffcult to document: It is simply part of the lenses through which God is seen." Until very recently, all the major streams of American Judaism used siddurim that were gender-specific, in which God was always identified by the universal male pronoun.[3]

One of the first prayer books to address this issue was *Siddur Nashim/*

Prayer Book of Women, created in the 1970s at Brown University by Naomi Janowitz and Margaret Moers Wenig. In their prayer book, Janowitz and Wenig addressed God as She, said "The Lord is my Mother," and offered new prayers appropriate to a feminine Deity. Rabbi Rebecca Alpert recalls a retreat for women rabbis and rabbinical students at which *Siddur Nashim* was the prayer book used:

> The experience of praying with Siddur Nashim that Shabbat transformed my relationship with God. For the first time, I understood what it meant to be made in God's image. To think of God as a woman like myself, to see Her as both powerful and nurturing, to see Her imaged with a woman's body, with a womb, with breasts—this was an experience of ultimate significance. Was this the relationship that men have had with God for all these millennia?

The movements frequently tinker with their prayer books for many reasons, not the least of which is the desire to keep the language of prayer "contemporary." But the Torah and the *Tanakh* are thought of as timeless texts that one shouldn't tamper with.

Let us put aside for a moment the fact that, as we have seen throughout this book, the "timeless" nature of the Torah is something less than a matter of fact and that translations and interpretations change in ways that reflect the times that produce them. In truth, reading the Torah through the lens of a feminist hermeneutic of desire, we can easily find many texts that support the idea that God is doubly gendered, both masculine and feminine in characteristics. Our male-gendered God-language is not merely a relic of a patriarchal reading of Torah; it is flat-out wrong.

The Torah makes this clear from the second mention of humanity, in *Bereishit* 1:27: *"V'yivra Elohim et ha'adam b'tzelmo; b'tzelem Elohim bara oto; zakhar u'nikeivah bara otam. / And God created the human in the image of God; God created it in God's image; God created them male and female."* The implication is clear and inescapable, "that the image of God is intrinsic in both man and woman, that, indeed, in the absence of either one—man or woman—there is no complete image," as Esther Shkop puts it. (Significantly, the name of the Creator used here is *Elohim,* a plural form that suggests the multiplicity, the many-faceted nature of the Eternal, a multiplicity that can and must contain both male and female.)

In Moshe's final speech to *B'nei Yisrael,* he refers to God as "the One who bore you," a specifically female image, and female God-imagery (particularly that of God as nurturing Mother) is rife in the prophetic texts. When Ya'akov, in the name of God, promises the Israelites a fertile land, he does so in the imagery of the feminine, offering "blessings of the breast and the womb" (*Bereishit* 49:25)

The most striking and familiar example of a feminine image of the Deity is the *Shekhinah/Divine Presence*. The *Shekhinah* is a guardian presence. According to some sources, She goes into exile with Israel when the Temple is destroyed. When two Jews sit together and exchange words of Torah, She hovers over them. The *Shekhinah* is a central concept of the Godhead in Kabbalah, with its fascination with sexuality as an integral part of God's Creation. As Rabbi Elyse Goldstein says, "Here are our ancient goddess symbols—moon, mother, water, earth—all embodied in our own authentically Jewish symbol." Goldstein cautions that the *Shekhinah* is the product of male projections of the Eternal, and is often anthropomorphized as "God's consort," a disempowering, patriarchal image, but it's a starting point.

So there is ample precedent for the depiction of God in Jewish thought as feminine.

It must be noted that, as Plaskow says, "Criticism of received images of God is not, of course, criticism of God. It is criticism of ways of speaking about a reality that, in its full reality, is finally unknowable." The language in which we speak of God is inadequate to the task of describing One-Who-Cannot-Be-Described. We can speak of God only in metaphors. We can only conceive of God in terms of our own limited grasp of the world. Jewish philosophers have repeatedly cautioned against anthropomorphizing the Eternal for precisely this reason. But as Maimonides reluctantly admits, a certain degree of anthropomorphizing is inevitable given the nature of the human mind. To worship a personal God, a Supreme Being who is thought of as nurturing and protective (or jealous and angry, for that matter), requires a certain anthropomorphic turn of thought. How can we cleave to something as abstract as the philosophers' notion of the Deity? The question that Jewish feminists raise, with considerable justice, is why the anthropomorphized God is always seen as male. As Rita M. Gross writes, "Though language about God cannot really tell us about God, because of the limitations of language and the nature of God, it can tell us a great deal about those who create and use the God-language."

How can we address the imbalance of genders in our God-language? First, regardless of how we address God in prayer or in sacred texts, we must tacitly acknowledge the sheer Otherness of God, that our relationship with the Eternal is shot through with this realization, and that our God-language is nothing less than an attempt to reconcile ourselves to that reality through a series of (ultimately) unsatisfying metaphors for God. To my mind, this is something of a take-it-or-leave-it proposition. The metaphors are useful, even beautiful, and they are a source of some comfort and joy, but God-language is not God described. We just don't have the tools for that job.

One can, following from that proposition, question the whole point of gendered God-language altogether. The newest version of the Reform movement's prayer book features gender-neutral language. I pray with this siddur on most Friday nights and it is adequate to the task. It is hard to develop a close personal relationship with an abstract concept. Perhaps, as Gross writes, "because expression and communication are inevitable, images and concepts of the Ultimate are also inevitable." The danger, as she says, is in not recognizing the limitations of expression and communication, and in literalizing and absolutizing our God-language.

That, of course, is what masculine God-language has always done. The way to counter that traditional force, obviously, is by offering a more pluralistic God-language, a God-language that proclaims the dual-gendered nature of the Eternal. If, as Gross says, "the concept of a personal Ultimate is at the living heart of the Jewish symbol system," then we need to proclaim that Ultimate as both male and female.

Hebrew, it must be recalled, is a gendered language. All Hebrew nouns have gender, and the verbs and adjectives attached to them in a sentence must agree in number and gender. That shouldn't present such an insurmountable problem for praying Jews. To speak of *Ha'Kedoshah b'rukhah Hee/the Holy One blessed be She* is not such a great leap from *Ha'Kadosh barukh Hu/the Holy One blessed be He*. And for an English-language siddur to refer to "God the Mother" rather than "God the Father" doesn't seem a particularly great leap, either.

There are those who will argue that God has no gender, so why should we be giving women "equal time"? Of course, God is genderless. So why are we so attached to the concept of "God the Father"? Clearly, this is one silence that must be shattered. The silence of the women in the Torah itself is another subject, one that is more ambiguous.

There are, of course, many important women in the Torah, more than twenty-five of them: Khavah/Eve, Noakh's wife, Sarah, Hagar, Lot's daughters and wife, Rivkah, Leah, Rakhel, Bilhah, Zilpah, Dinah, Tamar, Potiphar's wife, Shifra and Puah (the midwives to the Hebrew women), Yokheved, Miriam, Pharoah's daughter, Tipporah, the five daughters of Zelophekhad. Of course, many of those women are never named or never speak in the text.

Women are not depicted as unrelievedly evil or relentingly good in the Torah or elsewhere in Jewish sacred texts. Many of the women are drawn in considerable complexity; certainly the Matriarchs, Sarah, Rivkah, Rakhel, and Leah, are relatively well-rounded characters within the limitations of the book's psychological templates. Nor is the Torah relentlessly misogynistic in its handling of female characters. Women are frequently seen as powerful figures in their own right.

As Rabbi Goldstein says:

> The reality is that, in the Torah, women are complex, both subjects and objects. . . . The women of the Torah weave in and out of the frames of power and powerlessness. They act as both independent agents and as obedient dependents. They work within the patriarchal structure to change it for their own benefit, but they do not challenge the underlying structure of hierarchy and inequality for all women. They are fully human: they are curious, desirous, jealous, cooperative and co-opted.

THE MOTHER OF US ALL

To review the appearance of each woman in the Torah with recourse to midrash and classical commentary alone would require a book as long as this one. But to get a sense of how complicated the relationship between the Torah, the rabbis, women, and contemporary Jewish feminist thought is, we need only examine what can best be described as the foundational text for that relationship, the story of the Creation and the Expulsion from *Gan Eden*.

As we have already seen, *Bereishit* offers what may be read as two versions of the Creation of the first humans, in *Bereishit* 1:26–27, where "male and female God created them," and in the better-known version in *Bereishit* 2:18–23, in which God forms Khavah from Adam's rib or side. The rabbis were somewhat stymied by this double creation story, but picking up on the cue from *Bereishit* 2:23, where Adam says of his new companion, "*this* one is . . . flesh of my flesh" (emphasis added), mid-rashim were proposed in which the first version involved a different "first" woman, Lilith.

What happened to Lilith? Why was a second "first" woman created? A sizeable literature has grown up around Lilith. Myths depict her as an obstreperously independent woman who, having been created simultaneously with Adam, refused to accept a subordinate role. She even refused his demand to be on top during intercourse! When she finds that neither Adam nor God is in a mood to accept her equality, she flees *Gan Eden* (or is banished) to live alone.

From a purely narrative standpoint, Lilith is a delightfully inventive creation, filling in a seeming gap in the Torah text. She makes a single appearance in the *Tanakh*, in *Yeshayahu* 34:14, where she is seen resting among satyrs and hyenas in a wilderness. And there already was a rich folklore around a she-demon who collected the semen from men's nocturnal emissions to create demon children, and who threatened newborn infants.

If we accept the legends of Lilith, then clearly she is the first of the Written Torah's silenced women, not merely silenced but utterly expunged from the text for the sin of seeking equality with the other human of whom she was one half. Unlike the women who are left intact in the stories to follow, Lilith actually poses a significant threat and opposition to patriarchy (all the more reason, one suspects, to have her not only purged from the text but depicted as demonic wherever else she appears). The literature around Lilith is rich and various, and she has become a subject of much modern feminist midrash, even giving her name to the preeminent Jewish feminist periodical in the United States *Lilith*.[4]

Putting aside the creative narrative logic of the Lilith stories, we are left with the existing text. Which brings us to Khavah, often called "the mother of all the living," whose Hebrew name is the feminine form for *khai/life*. (Interestingly, she is not named until the Expulsion from the Garden; up to that point she is simply "the woman.")

The story of Adam and Khavah is probably the single best-known narrative in the entire Bible, perhaps in all of Western civilization. But there are many elements of it in Jewish thought that may not be as familiar to most of us; as read in that dialectic hermeneutic offered by contemporary Jewish feminists, they may be startlingly new.

As we have already seen, Khavah is either the second woman created by

God, or her creation from Adam's "rib" is an alternative version of how she was formed. Rashi points to the entire Creation story as an example of the Torah eschewing linear chronological order. Nahmanides offers a kabbalistic reading in which the "second" Creation is merely an elaboration of the first. The Lilith midrashim are designed to fill in the dissonance between the two stories. Rabbis, contemporary biblical scholars, and Jewish feminists are all divided on which is correct; obviously, for source criticism, the explanation devolves on the redaction of multiple documents. For our purposes, any of these explanations is probably acceptable.

Let's focus instead on a few details from the second version, which is the more familiar one. As Judith Antonelli notes, the Torah describes Khavah as having been fashioned from Adam's *tzela*. Antonelli writes that although this word is "frequently translated as 'rib,' [it] is more accurately rendered as 'side,' since this same word is used in Exodus 26:20 for the wooden beams forming the structure of the Tabernacle. To call such beams 'ribs' could only be a metaphor; clearly the term refers to the *side* of a structure (whether a human or a building)" (emphasis in original).

Why does this distinction matter? Saint Paul uses Khavah's creation from Adam's "rib" to argue for woman's subordinate status and her dependence on man. But if Khavah is not created from a mere appendage, a rib, but from Adam's side, it is harder to argue for a hierarchical relationship between them. "Side" bespeaks a degree of equality, even partnership. In a sense, Rabbi Eleazar makes the same point in Tractate *Yevamot*, elaborating on God's decision to make an *"ezer k'nedgo"* for Adam. *Ezer k'negdo* can be translated in a number of ways, including "helpmate," a frequently used rendering that, again, leaves Khavah as a subordinate. Eleazer puns on the literal meaning of *k'negdo/opposite*, drily observing that if Adam "is worthy [she will be] a help, if not worthy an opponent." Goldstein offers another interpretation of *ezer k'negdo*, returning to the story of the first Creation. She suggests that Adam's sadness—and both the Torah and the midrashim are very clear that he feels lonely when he sees all the animals with their partners—is for his previous androgynous state, that he yearns literally for his "other side," his female half.

Intriguingly, the pattern of the Creation, as Antonelli notes, runs "from lower to higher life-forms," with God creating plant life before animal life, fish, birds, mammals, and then humans. God creates man from the dust of the earth, from the mud, as she puts it, then creates Khavah from Adam, giving her a higher spiritual nature. *Bereishit Rabbah* says, "Whatever was created after its companion has power over it," and it is interesting to note that woman is the penultimate creation of God, followed only by the Sabbath.

The real sticking point for women's detractors, of course, comes when Khavah allegedly is seduced by the snake into eating fruit from the Tree of Knowledge of Good and Evil and, in turn, supposedly seduces Adam to joining in her sin. As before, there is more than one way to read this story.

For example, for some unknown reason very few commentators have remarked on the fact that God's warning to Adam about the "tree in the middle of the garden" is given before Khavah is created. It is very possible that her knowledge of the prohibition against eating of the tree's fruit is secondhand, passed along by Adam. (God doesn't speak directly to her until *Bereishit* 3:13 when the Eternal asks her, "What is this that you have done?") If so, it would certainly explain the discrepancies between God's warning to Adam and Khavah's recounting of that warning when asked by the serpent, suggesting that in order to impress upon her the solemnity of the prohibition (and his own importance in having been given it), Adam could have embellished it to include a ban on touching the fruit.

There are several telling details that somehow get left out of most conventional explications of this episode, omissions that seem designed for the express purpose of making Khavah the villain of the piece.

First, as Richard Elliott Friedman, Rabbi Lori Forman, and others have pointed out, in the actual text of *Bereishit*, Khavah turns directly to Adam after eating from the fruit and hands it to him. He has been there all along. If Khavah is "seduced" by the serpent's words, so is Adam. He never moves to stop her or to interrupt her dialogue with the serpent. Yet traditional commentators tend not to implicate him directly in the event.

Forman also notes that after Khavah hears the serpent's argument for eating the fruit, she pauses to consider its merits. "When the woman saw that the tree was good for eating and a delight to the eyes, and that the tree was desirable as a source of wisdom, she took of its fruit and ate, and she also gave some to her husband, who was with her, and he ate." Forman says:

> Eve looks at the fruit and comes to some very startling conclusions of her own. The fruit, she sees, is good for eating; it is edible and could satisfy hunger. It is pleasant to her visual sensibilities, satisfying her need for beautiful things. And Eve discerns that the fruit could make her wise, and increase

her intellectual abilities. The Torah, surprisingly, explains Eve's inner motives, quite out of character for the Torah. . . . Only after such contemplation does Eve actively reach for the fruit. It is not an impulsive act.

Khavah is neither seduced, nor a seductress.

Reuven Kimelman, in a densely and convincingly argued article, offers a genuinely inspired reading of Khavah's dialogue with the serpent. She is, he suggests, engaged in an interior debate with herself! I cannot do justice to his argument here, but he emphasizes several interesting points.

First, the serpent is called *nakhash*, a word for "snake" that has three "biblically attested images: a poisonous snake, a metaphor for venomous speech, and by homonymy divination and bewitchment." The narrative creates a nexus of all three images, offering us a venomously cunning creature whose untrustworthy speech bewitches Khavah by offering her a vision of the future. The snake is also described as *arum/shrewd*, which also happens to be a homophone for *erum/nude*, which is what Adam and Khavah find themselves to be in the next paragraph. (The English shrewd/nude rhyme is amusingly apt.) The third, and most interesting connection Kimelman offers is an intricate wordplay on Khavah's name. As he points out, if her name merely meant "life," as it is explained when she is named in *Bereishit* 3:20, it would be *Kayah*. But *Khavah* adds an allusion to the serpent: in Aramaic and related Semitic languages, the word for serpent is *khivya;* there does not appear to be a word *Khavah* in these languages, suggesting to Kimelman that *Khavah* is a neologism coined to combine *khaya* and *khivya*. And *Khavah* can also mean "speech," as it does in several places in *Iyov*. (The placement of her naming is arbitrary but suggestive; she has been "the woman" heretofore and could have been named *Khavah* at any time before the encounter with the serpent.)

Kimelman's reaction to this accumulation of wordplay is to suggest that the serpent may be understood as the animal instinct that is the *yetzer hara* that resides in all humans.

With the wiles of the serpent serving as a metaphor for the connivance of the evil impulse, it becomes explicable why this ancient symbol for primeval chaos is used to instigate the chaos in the individual soul that occurs upon usurping divine authority. The source of the opposition to divine structure . . . is not some primordial monster but the human arrogation of authority.

The standard objection against the interiorization of the serpent is that the serpent is actually cursed. That, however, occurs prior to its literary metamorphosis into the human drive for divinity. Until the woman is designated by the serpent-sounding *Havva*, the serpent is to be grasped in all its vivid animality. That is what gives it its punch. Only at the end, in a moment of self-revelation, does the reader realize she has been had.

As Kimelman notes, the role of the serpent in the story and in the curse is entirely a function of its interaction with Khavah. Dialogue—in fact any interaction at all—between Adam and the serpent is notably missing.

What does Khavah achieve by eating from the forbidden tree? We are told that God introduces human mortality into the world. Yet there are suggestions that Adam is mortal from the outset. Otherwise what sets him apart from God? We read that Adam and Khavah become aware of their nakedness and are ashamed. But ashamed before who? When they cover their nakedness and hide from God after eating the fruit, it is not from each other that they hide their nakedness; if there is shame here, it is shame at disobedience, not nudity.

I believe that what is introduced into the world by Khavah's bold action, whether it is right or wrong, is the *knowledge of the existence* of good and evil. And the other singular invention to emerge from the "sin" in *Gan Eden* is that mankind is impelled to create culture—to alter the natural in order to use it to human advantage. God gives Adam dominion over *Gan Eden* but other than the naming of the animals, Adam has no real duties. As the Torah tells us, there was no one to till the soil. Adam and Khavah are childlike, even childish in their behavior in *Gan Eden*. Only when they are expelled will they have to learn to feed themselves, fend for themselves, create for themselves. Only outside *Gan Eden* will they truly become partners with God in creation.[5] We were not meant to stay in *Gan Eden* in a state of perpetual infancy, and Khavah's disobedience, while palpable, was no sin. In fact, many commentators refer to the story of the Expulsion as "a maturation myth." Umberto Cassuto, the brilliant twentieth-century Jewish Italian Bible scholar, writes, "[B]efore they ate of the tree of knowledge, the man and his wife were like small children, who know nought of what exists around them. . . but man transgressed the prohibition, like a child who is under the suppression of his father and is constantly dependent on him; he wanted to learn by himself of the world around him, and to act independently on the basis of this knowledge."

Taken in that light, Khavah's transgression looks forward to the greatest moments of humanity in the Torah, to Avraham challenging God over the destruction of Sodom and Gomorrah ("Will the Judge of the world not act justly?"), and Moshe repeatedly calling God to account when the Eternal threatens to destroy *B'nei Yisrael*.

As even a superficial reading of contemporary Jewish feminist writings on the Torah will show, there are many counterreadings of the Torah's passages about the Matriarchs and the other great women of the Book that make it possible for us to see them in a well-rounded and frequently laudatory light. Without Rivkah's conspiratorial prowess, would Yitzkhak have given the birthright of the Covenant with *Adonai* to Ya'akov or to Eisav? Without the actions of the Hebrew midwives and the young Miriam, Moshe would not have survived to lead the Israelites out of Egypt. Not for nothing does God tell Avraham, "Listen to Sarah's voice and do as she tells you."

LAW OF THE FATHERS

As we have seen, narrative is only one part of the Torah. If the status of women is ambiguous in the stories we read, it is rather more obviously skewed against them when it comes to the law. By and large, in areas of women's sexuality—rape, marriage, adultery, and divorce—the Sinaitic laws are designed to protect male property rights, with the women treated as the property. The Torah makes the point in its choice of language: a man "gives" or "takes" a woman in marriage.

Judith Plaskow enumerates some of the ways in which the *mitzvot* given at Sinai hem in women's sexuality in the interest of patrilineality.

> The laws pertaining to women place them firmly under the control of first fathers, then husbands, so that men can have male heirs they know are theirs. . . . The *crime* of adultery is sleeping with another man's wife, and a man can bring his wife to trial even on suspicion of adultery, a right that is not reciprocal. Sleeping with a betrothed virgin constitutes adultery. A man who sleeps with a virgin who is not betrothed must simply marry her. A girl whose lack of virginity shames her father on her wedding night can be stoned to death for harlotry. . . . The subject of these laws is women, but the interest behind them is the purity of the male line. (emphasis in original)

In the same vein, the rapist of a married woman was put to death. The rapist of a virgin was ordered to pay a fine—to her father—and to marry her. Similarly, if a man seduced an unbetrothed virgin, he was required to pay the bride-price to her father. (*Sefer Devarim*, as Dr. Jonathan Ziskind observes, "regarded betrothal as an inchoate marriage to which the law on adultery was applied." I would add that the mere existence of bride-price is indicative of an intensely patriarchal society.)

Polygyny, having more than one wife, was permitted; polyandry, having more than one husband, was not. Jewish divorce law favors the husband as well. *Devarim* 24 gives the husband the right to divorce his wife by writing out a bill of divorce (*get*); she doesn't have the same right.

If this seems like a badly loaded deck, with men holding all the face cards and aces, that's because to some extent it is. In that respect, the Torah is not appreciably different from the laws of other cultures of the period.

Yet the Torah—and the rabbis of the Mishnah and Talmud—gave more rights to women than most of their contemporary counterparts elsewhere in the ancient world. A woman couldn't be sold into slavery to pay off her father's debts; a man could. As Blu Greenberg notes, "If she was 'sold,' it was to become the master's wife or his son's wife and she was treated accordingly." If a man divorced his wife, she was set free unencumbered by debt and could not be passed on to another man. In the case of the rape of a virgin cited above, the victim didn't *have* to marry her attacker; she could reject him. Adult women—and adulthood began at twelve or twelve and a half—had to consent to a marriage.

One of the most striking and famous examples of the Torah's ambivalence toward the rights of women occurs in *parashat Pinkhas*. Both scriptural and rabbinic law hold that a woman may not inherit her deceased husband's property (although the *ketubah* could and frequently did include provisions for either continued maintenance or a lump-sum payment to a surviving widow). But when Zelophekhad, of the tribe of Menasheh, dies in the Wilderness leaving five daughters and no male heir, the quintet (who are introduced by name, incidentally) goes before Moshe to protest the ruling that they may not inherit their father's portion of the Promised Land. They point out that he did not die as part of the rebellion of Korakh against Moshe and that his name will die out as they marry. The case proves sufficiently difficult that Moshe takes the highly unusual step of asking for guidance from God. The Eternal rules in favor of the daughters, and from then on where no male heirs survive, daughters inherit. (The ruling is somewhat hemmed in by addenda—primarily that the women must marry within their own tribe so that the land doesn't pass out of its control.)

There are many remarkable aspects to this story, none more surprising than the simple fact that it is recounted at all. As Greenberg asks, we don't have detailed explanations for the rationale behind all of the *mitzvot;* why this one?

I believe there is a tension in the Torah and in the rabbinic texts between the assumptions of a patriarchal system consonant with its historical period, a system created and defined by males, and the heightened concern for humanity manifested in the rules governing social justice that is sometimes far ahead of those contemporary systems. Frequently, when the *mitzvot* seem most jarringly pitched against women, a final clause or additional injunction will soften the blow.

This is not to deny that much—perhaps most—of *halakhah* derived from Sinai rests heavy on women's shoulders. But the ambivalence of the text is real and palpable. That ambivalence and the tensions it produces are, if anything, ratcheted up in the Talmud and subsequent rabbinic texts.

"SHELO ASANI ISHAH"

One of the key exhibits for the prosecution in any attack on Judaism as a sexist religion is the blessing said by traditionally observant Jewish men as part of the *Berakhkot Ha'Shakhar/Morning Blessings: "Barukh atah Adonai Eloheinu Melekh Ha'Olam shelo asani ishah./Blessed are You, Adonai our God, Ruler of the universe, for not having made me a woman."* Women thank God "for having made me according to His will."

What possible explanation can there be for such a blessing? The ArtScroll siddur, a fairly representative Orthodox prayer book, says that men "express gratitude that, unlike women, they were *not* freed from the obligation to perform time-related commandments. This follows the Talmudic dictum that an obligatory performance of a commandment is superior to a voluntary one, because it is human nature to resist obligations." The editor goes on to extol the virtues of women as the protectors of Jewish tradition and the Jewish home. Others have taken the blessing to be an expression of gratitude to God for having spared men the pains associated with reproduction—menses, child-birth, menopause.

This blessing is preceded by two others, almost as controversial, "for not making me a Gentile," and "for not making me a slave." Placed in this larger context, some scholars have said that the trio of *berakhot*, composed by Rabbi Meir in the second century C.E., are, in fact, a direct rebuke against Saint Paul, who wrote to the Galatians, "There is neither Jew nor Greek, there is neither bond nor free, there is neither male nor female: for ye are all one in Christ Jesus."

Is it still necessary to push Jewish particularism to this extent today? In a time of rising anti-Semitism in Europe, I am hesitant to say no. But there is no question that for many, probably most Jews of either gen-der, these blessings sit sourly on the tongue.* They have been rewritten in the Conservative, Reform, and Reconstructionist prayer books. The Conservative siddur, *Siddur Sim Shalom*, features representative reworkings: "*she'asani yisrael/who has made me a Jew*," "*she'asani ben [bat] khorin/who has made me free*" and "*she'asani b'tzalmo/who has made me in His image*."

It should also be noted that not every Orthodox rabbi was com-fortable with "*shelo asani ishah*." Rabbi Aharon Worms, a prominent *rosh yeshiva* and rav in Metz, France, a protégé of the outstanding nineteenth-century Torah scholar known as the Sha'agat Aryeh, wrote that saying the *berakhah* aloud in *shul* is a public insult of women and consequently impermissible. Regrettably, such enlightenment was and remains an exception in some Jewish circles.

---

*Why should the blessing "who has not made me a slave" be seen in such a negative light? I would argue that slavery is not a state anyone chooses willingly; it is imposed by humans more powerful and ruthless, hardly an act of God.

WOMEN IN THE RABBINIC LITERATURE

In a discussion of the nature of female sexuality as outlined in *Bereishit* 2 and 3, Rabbi Elyse Goldstein notes the comments of Rashi, Ibn Ezra, and Nahmanides, each of whom discourses learnedly on what women want and feel about their husbands. She wryly remarks,

> So, men busy explicating the female situation fill the commentary page, all from their personal, male points of view. Their views of women's "nature" totally color their biblical interpretations. We may imagine a woman's voice in the discussion, but we have to fill in the words she would say.

Obviously, as a man I cannot offer any better guess than Rashi, Ibn Ezra, or Nahmanides as to what the woman might say, but I suspect she would start by telling them, "What do *you* know about it?"

If women's voices are a muted whisper in the Torah, when we move on to the rabbinic texts that interpret the *Khumash*, they are almost completely stifled. The laws given at Sinai are the product of a genderless Deity, albeit filtered through a distinctly masculine sensibility (Moshe's or those of the various documentary authors). But the refined, defined, and codified laws of the Mishnah and the Gemara are the work of men, and no one but men. They are men who are frequently sympathetic to women's plight but men nevertheless. Even when they extend themselves to empathize with women—and that happens with greater frequency than you might expect—they can never take on a woman's subjectivity. The reality is even worse. As Dvora Weisberg notes, "[W]omen are almost invisible in rabbinic texts." She offers significant examples of their omission. There are only four references to women in the Mishnah tractate governing prayer, each of them a rule excluding women from types of prayer—not a big surprise. But there are "only a handful of references to women" in the tractates covering Shabbat and the preparation of food for the Festivals. The gendered nature of Hebrew results in some pretty spectacular imbalances, too. Because of the rabbis' use of the universal male, "the Gentile who takes in the laundry is the male, the person carrying a small child is male, and the individuals who deliver babies are male." (This will come as a great shock to Shifra and Puah, the Hebrew midwives.)

The most glaring and disturbing example of grammatical erasure of women from the Mishnah text that Weisberg finds is a passage in which it is said that when women die in childbirth it can sometimes be attributed to their negligence in lighting the Sabbath lamp. But when the Mishnah discusses the obligation to do so, it uses the masculine form of the verb, "they light," "they do not light," and "he who extinguishes the lamp."

Dr. Tamar Ross has said, "Irrespective of how we choose to interpret the metaphysical grounding of male hegemony in the Torah, there is no denying that a rigid view of gender and distinct gender roles became further entrenched with the development of the rabbinic tradition."

Thus, in the rabbinic law, only men may initiate marriage and divorce. A woman must consent to marriage and may petition a rabbinic court for divorce, but men are the active parties. Young girls may be given in marriage by their fathers without their consent and any woman may be divorced against her will, while a husband may refuse to grant a *get* despite the best efforts of the rabbis.

In a sense, women were disqualified from full entry into the Covenant by virtue of anatomical difference. *B'rit milah*, the ritual of circumcision that inscribes the Covenant into a male Jew's very flesh, is not available to women. Whatever the rationale behind circumcision, it is a rite of passage that until recently had no female equivalent. The rabbis were concerned enough with women's sexual enjoyment that they never for a moment considered female circumcision, a procedure whose primary—if not sole—purpose is to deprive women of sexual pleasure. (We'll come back to this issue momentarily.) But that concern, if it was what motivated the rabbis, still left women on the outside of the Covenant in some symbolic way.

By the same token, while one could argue that women are entrusted with three highly important *mitzvot—niddah/family purity*, *nerot/lighting candles* for Shabbat and the Festivals, and *hafrashat khallah/the baking of Shabbat bread and removing and burning a small portion of the dough* as a symbol of the dough-offering in the Temple—they are exempted from all time-bound commandments, not counted toward a minyan, not required to say *Kaddish* for a deceased parent, not encouraged to study Torah, and not permitted to serve as a witness in a rabbinic court. In short, they are excused and frequently even barred from two aspects of Jewish practice—prayer and Torah study—that are most central to Jewish life.

The rabbis concluded that "women are a unique class." Women are seen, in some fundamental way, as Other. They are as Other as—and even more inscrutable than—Gentiles. On some level, I suppose, that is an acknowledgment of precisely the lacuna mentioned earlier, the rabbis' inability to project themselves into a woman's consciousness. But it led to some pretty serious defects in rabbinic law as viewed from a modern perspective.

Weisberg writes, "rabbinic laws of marriage and divorce are enlightened compared to those of contemporary cultures." There are many examples of rabbinic authorities ruling to soften potential blows. Weisberg draws our attention to a significant change in rabbinic law in which Rabban Gamaliel ruled that a husband who had sent his wife a *get* was prohibited from convening a rabbinic court in another place to annul the *get*, which seems to have been a frequent practice. The purpose of this ploy was to entrap the woman in a situation in which she would be unaware that her marriage had not been ended; if she remarried, any children born subsequently would be illegitimate and she would be guilty of adultery.

Similarly, the rabbis repeatedly rewrote the financial particulars of the marriage contract to make better financial provisions for wives. Women were allowed to work outside the home and keep their earnings. In a famous *takanah/rabbinic ruling*, Rabbi Gershom held that a wife could not be divorced without her consent, and another *takanah* outlawed polygamy. Of course, as Weisberg notes, while it is admirable that the rabbis saw the necessity of protecting women from the arbitrary and capricious behavior of men, it is evidence of how severe the advantage that men enjoyed under the law was that such extra protections were needed at all.

One area in which the rabbis were ahead of their time was the issue of women's sexual pleasure. One of the few reasons for which a woman could demand a divorce from her husband was his failure to give her sexual pleasure. In fact, the law of *onah*, derived from *Shemot* 21:10, guarantees a wife the right to conjugal enjoyment. In the Talmud, the rabbis go into great detail, enumerating the frequency with which a husband must have sex with his wife to fulfill her needs (this is based on his profession: a traveling salesman isn't expected to be home as often as, say, a carpenter). Rape within marriage is utterly forbidden. And a woman's sexual enjoyment is separated from procreation; only men are enjoined to procreate.

Within the rabbinic literature, then, the attitude toward women is as conflicted as in Torah, if not more so. Women are given a fair degree of autonomy in the private sector. The sexes must be kept separate, yet marriage is encouraged and seen as a healthy outlet for sexual energies. Wives are to be honored and respected, and their property rights are protected to a surprising degree. The tension between a patriarchal (or more correctly, androcentric) worldview and the social justice concerns of *Vayikra* and other texts in the Jewish tradition continues to force male authorities into a difficult and not entirely successful balancing act.

Significantly, the rabbis exclude women from key moments in the life of the community, from prayer and from the study of sacred texts. While women have won gains in the less spiritually fraught areas of economic rights in all but the most intransigent rabbinic courts,[6] the *bet knesset* and *bet midrash*—the two focal centers of the Jewish communal world—have become a major battleground.

THE VOICE OF A WOMAN

One of the stumbling blocks on the path to an egalitarian Judaism that crosses all denominational lines is the prohibition of *kol ishah/a woman's voice,* which forbids a man to listen to a woman singing and is defined to include leading a prayer service. There are two places in the Talmud from which the ban is derived. The passages are somewhat cryptic—*Berakhot* 24a and *Kiddushin* 70a—but essentially they both state that "the voice of a woman is *ervah,*" usually translated as "erotic." The passage in *Berakhot* seems to be referring specifically to the ostensible distraction of hearing a woman sing while one is reciting the *K'riat Sh'ma,* the *Sh'ma* and its blessings, a time of maximum concentration. The passage in *Kiddushin* is more ambiguous and seems to suggest that hearing a woman singing is completely forbidden at any time. The idea, of course, is that a woman's singing voice will sexually arouse male listeners.

Authorities have debated this subject for almost two millennia. As Rabbi Gil Student explains after citing more than twenty commentators, "Some, such as Rosh, Rambam, and Tur, say that it does not apply to *kerias shema* (i.e., one can recite *kerias shema* while a woman sings) but does generally imply that a man is forbidden to hear a woman sing. Others, such as Rav Hai Gaon and Rav Yehudah Gaon say that it applies even to *kerias shema* . . . and probably also in general. . . . It is important to note that Rav Hai Gaon says that if one can ignore the woman's voice then it is permissible to recite *kerias shema* while she is singing." But Student also offers another authority, S'dei Chemed, who cites a book, *Divrei Cheifetz,* that says that "only listening to women singing erotic songs is forbidden."

Given the prominence of Miriam and the Hebrew women in the celebrations recounted in *Shemot* surrounding *Shirat Ha'Yam,* this entire debate is somewhat ironic. There are also passages in *Yeshayahu* (54:1) and *Zekharyah* (2:10) in which women sing in praise of God. And there are ample cases of prominent Orthodox rabbis, notably Samson Raphael Hirsch and Azriel Hildesheimer, who permitted women to sing Shabbat *z'mirot/table songs,* in the company of men who were not relatives.

Judith Hauptman, however, disputes the entire prohibition vigorously. She argues that the only time the phrase *kol ishah ervah* occurs in a halakhic context in the Talmud is in a passage in which it is used "to stop a man from reciting the nighttime Shema while hearing his wife's voice as they are preparing for bed." She bases her argument in part on the fact that the Talmud states (in *Megilah* 23a) that women are halakhically qualified to read from the Torah and would be permitted to do so "were it not for the dignity of the congregation." Moreover, she adds, numerous authorities hold that since a woman is obligated to hear the reading of *megillat Ester,* she can count toward a minyan for that reading and may read from the scroll. Finally, she concludes, halakhically women would be permitted to participate in Grace after meals with men, except for the supposed difference in status, which would be irrelevant if *kol ishah* applied.

THE BATTLE FOR WOMEN'S PRAYER AND STUDY

In the Reform, Reconstructionist, and Conservative movements, the right of women to be counted toward a *minyan,* to be called to the Torah, to serve as rabbis and cantors, is now fully acknowledged. Given their attitudes toward *halakhah,* these questions were not particularly divisive at the national or regional level within the Reform and Reconstructionist movements. What happened (and still occasionally happens) at the congregational level may be a different matter, but with both Hebrew Union College-Jewish Institute of Religion (the Reform rabbinical seminary) and the Reconstructionist Rabbinical College accepting more women students than men, the changes on the *bimah* are inevitable. Although the effects of such change were more painful in the Conservative movement, they, too, have accepted the idea of female rabbis and cantors, and all three movements have adopted egalitarian siddurim with apparent enthusiasm.

The Orthodox and ultra-Orthodox worlds are another story, and here the desire of women to become full participants in the spiritual life of the Jewish community has been a source of frequently bitter disputes. For the Modern Orthodox, who until now have prided themselves on their ability to coexist with the non-Jewish world while maintaining a halakhic Judaism, the divisions have been particularly distressing. Given their constant contact with outsiders, the Modern Orthodox community has been stirred by the same winds of feminism that already have drastically altered the liberal movements. For the ultra-Orthodox, whose communities are somewhat more hermetic, the drama has barely begun, but even they are beginning to confront the desire of Jewish women of all denominations to pray and learn like (if not alongside) Jewish men.

As noted earlier, even the most empathetic rabbi could not consider issues from a woman's point of view. That means that in order for women to be active participants in Jewish law and history, they must—as Zelophehad's daughters did—seize this role for themselves. The founding of the Jewish Orthodox Feminist Alliance in 1997, twenty-five years after the first woman rabbi was ordained by the Reform movement, represents a concerted effort by Modern Orthodox women to do precisely that. I should add that the Modern Orthodox movement is anything but monolithic; more than a few rabbis and scholars have been entirely sympathetic to the ambitions of Orthodox women and supportive of their efforts. But, by and large, institutional support has not been forthcoming.

In the realm of education, change has taken place. As Joel B. Wolowelsky, one of the more sympathetic Orthodox rabbis, has said, this is "the most Jewishly educated group of women in Jewish history," with women's programs in Talmud study now being offered at such high-profile institutions as Yeshiva University's Stern College for Women and a proliferation of women's yeshivot in the United States, Canada, and Israel.

But once you have a generation of women who can study the Torah and the Talmud, and who are well-versed in *halakhah*, they want to do something with that knowledge. As Wolowelsky writes, "[T]hey are exploring how this rich education should be reflected in their everyday religious life. They are committed to Jewish family values and know that their roles as mothers and wives can be reconciled with being a doctor, lawyer, or financial analyst."

When the real fighting began, the sticking points were predictable ones: women's *tefillah/prayer groups;* women's participation, along with men, in *minyanim;* and, somewhere down the road, women being ordained as Modern Orthodox rabbis. At the heart of the debate is the nature of *halakhah,* Jewish religious law: what it permits and prohibits, who makes it, and how it can be changed. It is also imperative that we understand the conceptual underpinnings to the rabbis' rulings because, as we will see in some cases, their thinking reflects an earlier era, and social change may occasionally have an impact on *halakhah.*

In fairness, it should also be noted that, despite its normative status, Rabbinic Judaism is not monolithic and never has been. And, as happens in Anglo-American law, today's minority decision may be tomorrow's majority ruling.

The questions on the table regarding issues of women's prayer represent a complex interlocking network of issues. Is prayer scripturally or rabbinically ordained? Are there certain time-bound *mitzvot* that women are obligated to perform? May women sit with men to recite the *Birkat Ha'mazon/the Grace After Meals?* Can they be counted toward the group of three necessary for the recitation of the introductory blessings to the *Birkat Ha'mazon?* May women serve as *shilkhot tzibur/prayer leaders* (literally, messengers of the community)?

How do these seemingly unrelated questions connect?

For starters, if prayer is rabbinically ordained (rather than a *mitzvah* from Sinai), then its originators, the rabbis, have the right to obligate whoever they see fit to perform it under whatever circumstances they assign. Why is the obligation to perform a *mitzvah* important? Because the general governing principle in the rabbinic writings is that one who is not obligated to perform an act cannot perform that act on behalf of others. Hence, because women are obligated to hear the reading of *megillat Ester* at Purim, a woman scribe may write a kosher scroll of Esther. Because a minor is not obligated to hear the blowing of the shofar at Rosh Hashanah, a minor may not blow the shofar on behalf of the congregation. So if a woman is obligated to offer certain prayers, she can, in turn, lead those prayers on behalf of the community. (But see the sidebar, "The Voice of a Woman," on page 212.)

The perfect example, for our purposes, and a pivotal case in the argument over women's role in prayer, is the *Amidah*, the "standing" prayer known also as the *Sh'moneh Esreih* and *Ha'tefillah/the Prayer*. It is one of the central prayers in Jewish liturgy. Our expectation would ordinarily be that because they are usually exempt from time-bound commandments, women would not be obligated to say *Ha'tefillah*. Interestingly enough, the Talmud holds the opposite. The Mishnah says that although women are exempt from reciting the *Sh'ma* and wearing *tefillin*, they are obligated to recite the *Amidah* and *Birkhat Ha'mazon*. What is the reasoning behind this exception?

The *Amidah* is a petitionary prayer. Many of the benedictions of which it is composed are pleas to God for health, for the well-being of the Jewish community, and so on. (In fact, on Shabbat we say only seven of the nineteen blessings included in the *Amidah;* it isn't appropriate to plead to God on the Sabbath.) The rabbis held that every human being had the right and the need to petition God. As Judith Hauptman explains, the rabbis believed that "since a woman serves as her own most effective advocate, she should recite *tefillah*." What's more, many rabbis are of the opinion that women are obligated to say the *Amidah* three times a day, just as men are. Hauptman adds, "Rashi and Tosafot hold that, since prayer is rabbinically ordained, its originators have the right to obligate women for whatever reason they see fit." Maimonides adds that prayer in its purest state is a commandment of the Torah that is not time-bound, so women are not exempt from praying; the addition of a fixed liturgy with set times and prayers was a convenience added by the rabbis of the Mishnah, with no distinction between the obligations of men and women.

The idea that women are exempt from praying *Ha'tefillah* is, in reality, a late addition by a seventeenth-century commentator on the *Shulkhan Arukh*, Abraham Gumbiner. But other Orthodox scholars—most prominently Meir Ha'kohen, known as the Chofetz Chaim—disagree, holding that women are obligated to say *Shakharit* and *Minkhah* each day and that, even though they are exempt from reciting the *Sh'ma* and its blessings, they still should verbally accept upon themselves the Yoke of Heaven (the actual content of the *Sh'ma*).

In theory, at least, this should mean that a woman can serve as a *shliakh tzibur* and lead a prayer service. Hauptman's answer is more complicated. If a woman is not obligated to pray, she may not pray on behalf of others.

But just because she *is* obligated to pray, the converse doesn't follow directly. There may be, and in fact are, other considerations.

Which brings us to *Birkat Ha'mazon*. The Mishnah rules that women are obligated to recite it. After all, everyone must eat and, it follows logically, everyone should thank God for the blessings of food and life. But the Mishnah also holds that while women are obligated to say the Grace, they may not be included in the leader's opening call to recite it, the *zimmun*. What is the missing ingredient that would allow women to join—or even lead—the *zimmun*? Hauptman notes that the Mishnah doesn't answer this question, but a *baraita* from the Babylonian Talmud casts light on the subject. The *baraita* says, "A woman may recite Grace for her husband . . . but a curse alight on any man who allows his wife to do so." Yet a man may say the Grace for another man.

Hauptman opines that the difference is that in addition to obligation one also needs social status to qualify as a prayer leader. Given the value placed in Rabbinic Judaism on the dignity of the community, this makes a certain sense. Elsewhere in the Talmud we are told that a prayer leader must possess a mature and dignified appearance. Minors, for example, are not supposed to lead prayer. In fact, a beard was generally considered one of the prerequisites for serving as prayer leader. This last requirement has long since been abrogated, and many Modern Orthodox men are clean-shaven. The Talmud also says that women who are qualified would be permitted to read Torah before the congregation except for the "dignity of the congregation." Hauptman notes that in the tannaitic period when the *baraita* was written, gender was a defining characteristic of social status. Clearly, it is the "disability" here.

But that is not the case today. Orthodox women have achieved elevated social status in the professions, have become doctors, lawyers, and corporate executives. Many have also become as learned in Talmud and in Torah as their husbands. So wherein lies the disability? It will be interesting to see if someone takes up the challenge of putting this question to a prominent *posek* and forces the issue.

We have strayed rather far from the fundamentals of Written Torah here. However, allow me to linger for a moment more.

Suppose we accept the maximalist position—that Moshe received not only the Written Torah and the Oral Torah at Sinai, but all the rabbinic commentaries and halakhic rulings ever to be made. Who is to say that God didn't whisper into Moshe's ear that eventually the rabbis would have to accept the ordination of women into the cantorate and into rabbinate as halakhic decisors and as great Torah scholars, and that women should eventually be permitted to be Torah readers and to be counted in a minyan? That is not, obviously, how I arrive at those positions myself or how contemporary Jewish feminists argue their points, but it seems to me that if you buy one part of the extreme position, you are stuck with all its logical corollaries. If God foresees and foreordains everything, then the Eternal One must have seen the rise of feminism in the Jewish world before even the women who were responsible for it did. Then what gives any Jewish male—no matter how exalted his *yikhes* or immense his learning—the right to assume otherwise?

The simple fact of the matter is that *halakhah* doesn't stand still, it evolves. If it didn't, there would be no need for the vast body of responsa literature. I readily concede that, as Orthodox feminist scholar Tamar Ross says, *halakhah* does not exist "to cater to certain spiritual needs or values which the Jewish tradition is said to embody," that religious law should not be subordinated to ideology or a political agenda. But as Ross also notes, the descriptive statements of the sages regarding the nature of Woman cannot be equated with "Absolute Truth, even when these have been expressed by great Jewish authorities." She invokes a formulation by Maimonides' son Abraham who, speaking for his father, says, "We are not obligated, in spite of the greatness of the wisdom of the Talmudic sages and the perfection of their understanding in Torah . . . to accept all that they say in matters of medicine or science or astronomy, and believe their statements as we believe them when they interpret the Torah."

The changing nature of the role of women in secular society means that social stratification based on gender is no longer necessarily valid. Halakhic opinions, while necessarily tied to sacred texts and historical precedent, "are not totally divorced from the concrete context in which they were formulated," as Ross puts it. I believe that the Jewish future will belong to those who find a way to remind the contemporary halakhic authorities that it was *Aseret Ha'Dibrot* and not the work of the rabbis that was etched in stone by the finger of the Ineffable.

Of course, the entire story of women in Torah is open-ended. While Dr. Tova Hartman and Dr. Elie Holzer are experimenting with new forms of Orthodox feminist worship, countless women writers are reclaiming the stories of Torah by writing new midrashim, reimagining the lives of Sarah, Rivkah, Rakhel, Leah, and the daughters of Zelophekhad. They are finding names for the unnamed and silenced women of Torah in ancient midrashim or creating new ones.

This, then, is the final act of courage: to refuse a reading of the Torah and other Jewish sacred texts that condemns women to subservient silence, yet to offer the hope that by wrestling with the dark messenger that is the patriarchal voice, Jewish women may win a blessing of their own. Jews have read and rewritten sacred texts since Moshe spoke to *B'nei Yisrael* at the edge of the Jordan, but never has there been more at stake.

In the last chapter of *Essential Judaism* I expressed my belief that "the most fruitful development in Jewish thought in the second half of the twentieth century is the rise of an explicitly feminist theology." Not only do I see no reason to retract that statement, I would go further today and say that the growing prominence of women in leadership roles in the Jewish religious world—the rabbinate and cantorate in Reform, Conservative, and Reconstructionist Jewry; halakhic decisors; and very, very active scholars in the Orthodox world—presages the greatest change in the Jewish religion since the advent of Rabbinic Judaism. In nonreligious terms, it should lead to a seismic shift that will nearly equal the impact of *Haskalah* and the Emancipation or the foundation of the State of Israel.

Consider these facts. The Reform movement ordained its first woman rabbi, Sally Preisand, in 1972, the Reconstructionists two years after. *Lilith*, a high-quality Jewish feminist magazine, began publication in 1976; on its cover was a picture of a woman wearing *tefillin* and a *tallit*. Nine years after that, the Conservative movement, amid considerable controversy and rancor, ordained its first woman rabbis.

While I was working on *Essential Judaism,* Blu Greenberg predicted the ordination of an Orthodox woman rabbi by the end of the twentieth century. While I was completely in accord with the idea, I thought she was being wildly optimistic; I couldn't know, as Greenberg did, that the groundwork was already laid for not one but two women to be ordained in 2000. And even if no Orthodox congregation would think of recognizing those young women as members of the rabbinate, in 1997 Nishmat/The Jerusalem Center for Advanced Jewish Study for Women began a program that trains Orthodox women as *yo'atzot halakhah/halakhic consultants* who are empowered to answer questions on *taharat ha'mish-pakhah/ the laws of family purity.* And they did so with the approval of numerous prominent Israeli rabbis. The Conference on Feminism and Orthodoxy that was held annually in New York beginning in 1997 became the Jewish Orthodox Feminist Alliance, and has been flexing its considerable intellectual muscle for more than five years.

In 1990 Judith Plaskow predicted that it would take a break as all-encompassing as the rise of Rabbinic Judaism to alter the balance that kept Jewish women all but silent for four millennia. The process is far from completed but change has begun, even in the Orthodox world. And we can say of *halakhah,* as Galileo did of the earth, *eppur si muove.* And still, it moves.

Feminist theologians and Bible scholars, both Jewish and non-Jewish, have forever altered the way that we read our sacred texts. They have reenvisioned God for us in profound and, I think, enriching ways. Such work is an essential part of maintaining a living Judaism that will continue to be meaningful to generations to come. As we shall see in the next chapter, they have laid the groundwork for a similarly fruitful approach to other aspects of the Torah as well.

WOMEN AND TORAH: INTERNET RESOURCES

Twenty-five years ago, the idea of Orthodox Jewish feminists would have seemed only slightly more absurd than the idea of the Internet taking over the planet. Today, both are a reality. If you wish to pursue the former, you may find it helpful to use the latter. I draw your attention to a few Web sites of continuing interest.

For starters, I recommend "A Step-by-Step Guide to Research on Jewish Women," compiled by Dina Ripsman Eylon, at http://www .utoronto.ca/wjudaism/all_sites/step_by_step.html and her "Internet Sources for the Study of Jewish Women" located at http://www .utoronto.ca/wjudaism/all_sites/internet_sources.html.

Bat Kol, a feminist House of Study in Israel, has a Web site at http://batkol.org/.

The International Directory of Women's Tefilla Groups is located at http://wtgdirectory.helping.org.il.

The Jewish Orthodox Feminist Alliance may be found at www. jofa.org.

Torah Study for Women Web site is located at http://www.torah-study-for-women.org/.

"Women in Judaism: A Multidisciplinary Journal" is filled with thought-provoking materials at http://www.utoronto.ca/wjudaism/.

NOTES

1. Of course, that ignores the fact that several of the Tribes of Israel were founded by the offspring of Ya'akov and his handmaidens, Bilhah and Zilpah.

2. I prefer the phrase "hermeneutics of desire" for two reasons and use it where applicable. First, a hermeneutics of grace seems to me inadvertently redolent of Christian theology (which given its origins in the work of Trible and other Protestant thinkers is understandable). I also find the replacement of "grace" with "desire" a nice way of directing our attention to an embodied Judaism, a Judaism reminiscent of early Hasidism that not only accepts but *celebrates* the physical joys of cleaving to the Eternal through ecstatic worship, eating, and sexuality.

3. This, of course, raises the question of why the "universal" pronoun should be male in the first place, given that men make up only 49 percent of the human race, but I leave that to the linguists to address.

4. It must be noted that Lilith's first extended appearance outside of orally transmitted folklore is in the post-Apocryphal *Alphabet of Ben Sira*, an eleventh-century text, definitely later than the classical midrashim. For a generous sampling of Jewish feminist writings on Lilith, see *Which Lilith? Feminist Writers Re-Create the World's First Woman*, ed. Enid Dane, Lilly Rivlin, and Henny Wenkart (Northvale, N.J.: Jason Aronson, 1998). You should also seek out a short film by Lynne Sachs, *A Biography of Lilith*, a witty avant-garde variant on the midrashim in which Lilith is a part-time go-go dancer working in New Jersey. The film is available on DVD with other films by Sachs, *A Collection of Films Exploring Women, Culture, Science and Myth*. http://www.microcinema.com/.

5. It is not a coincidence that *ednah/physical, erotic pleasure* has the same Hebrew root as Eden or that the Sabbath—that foretaste of the World to Come, a return to the pleasures of the Garden—is an exalted time for marital sex.

6. In the Orthodox world, despite progress on many economic issues, the plight of the *agunot* remains a thorny issue. And halakhic limitations are placed on women's reproductive rights as well, although even there the position of the rabbis is much more lenient than that of their fundamentalist Christian counterparts.

6

TROUBLING TEXTS

[T]he Pentateuch is a text that has, like some impregnable fortress, withstood the onslaughts of countless generations of commentators. It is an obscure, contradictory, sometimes shocking text, one that, albeit well and truly ours, has nevertheless also shown itself to be cruelly other. Century after century, it has had critics sweating blood and tears in the effort to re-appropriate it, to turn its words every which way in order to tease new, intelligible, acceptable meanings out of them. It has invited both ancient and modern thinkers to display the kind of hermeneutic daring which alone can save it.

—Esther Benbassa and Jean-Christophe Attias,
The Jew and the Other

When we read Homer, we may be shocked by the petty nature of the argument that sets Achilles to sulking in his tent, or appalled by the violence with which Odysseus and Telemachus dispatch the suitors. The moral code that condemns the sinners to the various circles of Hell in Dante's *Inferno* may puzzle, even outrage us. The depiction of Shylock in *The Merchant of Venice* has been giving sensitive directors fits for centuries, and the promiscuous use of a certain racial epithet frequently blinds contemporary readers to Mark Twain's vigorous denunciation of racism in *The Adventures of Huckleberry Finn*. In one way or another, texts from the past trouble us, but not so much that we can't find a way to read them creatively or with an understanding of the historical context that allows us to look past our own contemporary attitudes to discern what is great in them.

The Torah is older than most of these books, the creation of a civiliza-

tion far removed from our own in time and attitudes. Why are we surprised to find that there are many passages in it that challenge our contemporary sensibilities, that even offend us?

If you read the Torah merely as a literary classic, it isn't that hard to
reconcile yourself to these "troubling texts" in much the same way that
you adjust your mind-set to deal with discordant elements in Homer,
Dante, and Shakespeare. But my assumption in this book has been that
many of us read the Torah for other than literary reasons, especially if we
are engaged in a specifically Jewish reading of the book. Using the Torah
as an ethical yardstick and a guide to living a Jewish life necessitates a very
different relationship between reader and text. As we have already seen, a
Jewish understanding (or, more accurately, the many disparate Jewish
understandings) of the Torah calls for a different kind of reading experience, one that draws not only on the Torah itself but on two millennia of
midrash. Can we apply these tools to the texts that disturb us? Is there a
way to reconcile our sensitivities with the worldview of the Torah?

If you have read the previous chapter, you already know that my answer
to these questions is at least partially in the affirmative. Armed with the
tools of textual study that Jews have used for two millennia, one can read
these texts in intelligent and creative ways that do not defy the will of God
yet find new meanings in the gaps and dislocations that are an important
part of the Torah. Let's examine some general principles regarding "troubling texts"; then I want to put those principles into practice with two of
the more disturbing passages for contemporary readers: the *Akeidah* and
the passages in *Vayikra* that address male homosexuality.

TEXTS OF TERROR

A father is ordered to kill his son as proof of his loyalty to a superior. An
episode of *The Sopranos*?

A man uses a series of thinly disguised confidence games to fool his
father and to cheat his brother out of a sizeable inheritance. This week's
Law & Order twist?

An army is told to wipe out every single member of an opposing nation
without showing any sort of mercy. Headlines from the Balkans?

Of course, each of these plot lines is taken directly from the Torah, and
each of them gives modern readers pause and discomfort. Contemporary

biblical scholars occasionally call them "texts of terror," a backhanded tribute, no doubt, to their power to instill dread and even loathing in the reader.

The story of the *Akeidah,* of Ya'akov's relationship with Yitzkhak and Eisav, and of the command to blot out Amalek are merely three examples of incidents in the *Khumash* that many of us find disturbing. In each of these three cases, the source of our unease is pretty obvious. The *Akeidah,* with God's seeming demand for Avraham's blind obedience to the point of child murder, shakes our belief in faith itself. Ya'akov's manipulations raise problematic questions about what one may do to follow an ostensibly God-given destiny. The order to obliterate the Amalekites (and the many instances elsewhere in the Torah where the Israelites are told they will destroy the current occupants of Kina'an) appears to give credence to the claims of some that the Torah is a tract advocating genocidal violence.

But these are only the most obvious kinds of "troubling" texts. As we have seen in the previous chapter, there are many disturbing elements in the way that the Torah, the Mishnah, and the Gemara treat women. There are numerous passages governing the treatment of slaves that leave a modern reader with a bad taste, not the least of them the simple fact that the book seems to regard slavery as socially acceptable.

The level of violence perpetrated in the Torah—by man and by God— makes many of us shudder. The death penalty is freely prescribed for offenses that would barely raise an eyebrow in the modern world. After the sin of the Golden Calf, the Levites slaughter three thousand of the Israelites. God destroys Korakh and his followers and, with the Flood, wipes the human race from the face of the earth, except for Noakh and his family.

How are we to read and understand these texts? How are we to deal with a self-described "jealous God" who seemingly tolerates no deviation from the *mitzvot?* How are we to deal with those *mitzvot* that are either inexplicable or downright inimical to our twenty-first-century sensibilities?

First of all, we must recognize that feeling troubled by this text is not a reaction confined to our time. Even within the Torah itself, there are those who feel compelled to challenge God's sternest decrees. The most famous of these challenges comes from Avraham who, when God presented him with the decision to destroy Sodom and Gomorrah, rebukes the Creator: "Will not the Judge of all the earth deal justly?" Displaying even more audacity in his dealings with God, Moshe repeatedly argues, cajoles, bargains, and even threatens to resign.

Countless passages of Mishnah and Gemara essentially reverse or disarm halakhic strictures offered by the Torah. Despite the Torah's firm statement of the *lex talionis*—an eye for an eye—the rabbis interpreted the passage to refer to fiscal compensation for damages, and the restrictions they placed upon the death penalty rendered its use all but impossible.

Clearly the rabbis, too, found many passages of the Torah troubling. Perhaps the most famous example of a rabbinic reversal of a Torah decree is the case of the "rebellious son," who the Torah says emphatically shall be put to death. After extensive debate in the pages of the Talmud in which the rabbis redefine the passage in ever-narrowing ways, they finally declare that there is no such transgressor and that said punishment "has never happened," and they strongly imply that it never will.

So we are not alone in our disquiet. And that historical reality suggests an important truth to be kept in mind when one reads a troubling text. In Jewish thought and practice, the Written Torah is not the end of the discussion; it is merely the beginning of the debate. While Christian fundamentalists may argue for the inerrancy and literal truth of the Bible, that is not the position of even the most inflexibly ultra-Orthodox rabbi. Whatever the Written Torah says is always subject to the interpretation and rulings of Oral Torah, the law codes, and the rabbinic responsa, and it is always read and interpreted through the filter of midrash. As Judith Plaskow writes:

> [I]n the realm of Jewish religious expression, invention is permitted and even encouraged. Midrash is not a violation of historical canons but an enactment of commitment to the fruitfulness and relevance of biblical texts. It is partly through midrash that the inscription or document, potentially integrable into memory but still on the periphery, is transformed into narrative the religious ear can hear.

The first step in reading these troubling texts is to see them as part of a larger fabric of history and of Jewish sacred texts. I'm not suggesting that for every passage one reads in the Torah it is absolutely essential to trace the entire line of other interpretations through Jewish history, although that certainly would be interesting, educational, and fruitful (and frequently entertaining, as well). But when a text makes us pull up short, and when it catches in our throats, clearly some deep inner chord has been struck and we should see why it resounds so uneasily.

BRIDGING THE GAP

For a moment, let us put aside the problems of the troubling text and consider a more basic problem that afflicts our reading of any passage of the Torah. Quite simply, the distance in time between ourselves and the Torah is at least twenty-four hundred years.

Consider what that means in terms of our reading comprehension. Shakespeare's plays are about four hundred years old, Dante's *Divine Comedy* about seven hundred years old. Try reading either in an edition without footnotes and you'll find yourself frequently lost in a wood as impenetrable as the one in which *The Inferno* opens. Even with footnotes, we cannot hope to re-create the experience of reading these texts (or seeing them performed) that the authors' contemporaries had. Certainly we can read the footnotes and a stack of histories of medieval Florence and learn about Guido da Montefeltro, but his name will never strike us with the immediate resonance that it would a Florentine reader in, say, 1310.

And the Torah is more than three times as old—as distant from us—as Dante. To fully understand the Torah as given, we would need to fully understand the world into which it was thrust. As Barry Holtz says of *The Inferno*, "To read the poem, we need to bridge the gap to a world that viewed hell as a living reality, that saw nine circles of inferno populated by the souls of actual beings. This is a profound gap, and interpreters have struggled since the advent of modernity with ways of overcoming it." (And that is without taking into account a world in which the names of those actual beings would have been instantly recognizable.)

This is not an insurmountable gap, but it requires not only a huge amount of background reading but also an imaginative act of re-creation, a kind of reading that places the text in its own time. Reading the Torah this way calls upon our full attention to detail and overview, putting everything in context. We have seen examples of this kind of reading throughout this book.

For example, Yitzkhak's great achievement is reopening the wells his father dug; given the setting of the story in a desert society, that's a pretty important legacy. And given that setting, one can easily see why the emphasis on hospitality—a unifying cultural positive throughout the Middle East—is so great. Would either of these facts be as significant in a modern urban society, where one has recourse to hotels and motels, gas stations and fast-food restaurants? Obviously not.

But these are simple examples that don't call on a huge imaginative leap for us. The problems arise, I think, when we get into those thorny areas where we are distanced from the sociocultural context in such a way that the mind-set, the philosophy, and ethical assumptions of the text are drastically removed from our own. Our own societies are no longer built on tribalism, no longer revolve around customs like primogeniture or bride-price. Texts that involve and invoke xenophobic violence *should* fill us with horror. The advent of social structures based on individual rights and responsibilities dates back only as far as the Enlightenment, but it seems to us as if they have been here forever. When faced with a world in which such notions were utterly incomprehensible—and the world in which the Torah is set was such a world—we are as dumbfounded as Moshe would be if you handed him a cell phone.

As Holtz says, "The Bible has a symbol system and ideational framework that require explication and understanding. Its concepts of holiness, Covenant, divinity, prophecy, and law are all very different from those of our contemporary world."

This is a gap that is on some level unbridgeable. When we study these texts, we have to accept that reality, as surely as we must accept the reality that there are certain words in the Torah whose precise meaning we cannot reconstruct.

Perhaps that is where the most difficult texts arise, in those texts in which the Torah's philosophical view is so radically Other that we are shocked and upset by what we read. The acceptable level of violence in the Torah is far above what we ostensibly civilized moderns would tolerate. Or we see Ya'akov conniving for his blessing, marrying two women and fathering children by four.

This is the heart of the matter, the texts that set our teeth on edge.

There has been a great deal written on this subject in recent years, as the revival of interest in the study of sacred texts has combined (or collided) with the rise of feminism, queer theory, and other philosophies and hermeneutics of liberation. (I have already described the hermeneutics of suspicion, desire, and indeterminacy suggested by feminist theologians and scholars, a set of reading practices that I think are well designed for facing some of these texts.) How do we reconcile these dueling perspectives?

Aryeh Cohen, a professor at the University of Judaism, the Conservative movement's West Coast seminary, offers a three-step process for reading and responding to "troubling" texts. Appropriately, he draws his inspiration from three scenes in the Torah itself in which key figures face terrible situations.

The first of these scenes comes after Aharon's sons Nadav and Avihu have been killed by a fire from heaven during the dedication of the *Mishkan*. "Aaron's response is silence," Cohen says. "The silence, it seems, is his first acknowledgement that this too is 'a way of God.' Although this might be 'a way of God' that is problematic, it is still 'a way of God.' Aaron's silence lets the impact of the death and tragedy hang in the air, untainted by pieties or apologies."

Drawing on this example, Cohen calls for the reader, confronted with a deeply disturbing text, to respond first by allowing it "to wash over him or her as is, in all of its troubling aspects," without even invoking the explanation of historical distance. The simple fact of recognizing that one is troubled by the text would seem to be the outcome of this exercise.

In his next step, Cohen invokes Avraham's challenge to God before Sodom and Gomorrah. His equivalent is for the reader to ask if the troubling text "is living up to the ethical standards demanded by these texts." That is to say, is it consistent not only with the Torah's own ethics but with the rabbinic literature in general, "or is this text an aberration?"

Finally, Cohen reminds us of Moshe's argument with God in the wake of the catastrophe of the Golden Calf. Moshe challenges God, telling the Eternal to forgive the Israelites or "blot me . . . out of Your book in which You have written." With Moshe as a model, Cohen urges readers to decide "whether or not this text is Torah. Is this what one has in mind when reciting the blessing for studying Torah?" Faced with a passage that truly and deeply offends the reader's morality, Cohen tells us that the reader must decide "where the boundaries of Torah reside."

In theory, this model is not dissimilar from what the Reform movement and, to a lesser extent, the Reconstructionists have done—deciding which elements of *halakhah*, which *mitzvot* are binding upon us as modern Jews. It may come as a surprise, then, to hear me say that I find Professor Cohen's three-step program, well, troubling. Mordecai Kaplan, the founder of the Reconstructionist movement, said, "The past has a vote, not a veto," when describing the relationship of *halakhah* and the *mitzvot* to practice in his then-nascent movement. What is missing from Cohen's formulation, I think, is a sense that reading Torah doesn't occur in an ahistorical vacuum. Even if we don't grant the Jewish past a figurative veto, we must give it a voice. As Or Rose points out in a reply to Cohen, each of his biblical models acts alone, and each of his three steps is based on an individual's reaction to the text. What is the role of the religious community, of Jewish history, in this decision-making process? Throughout this book I have insisted on Torah as an evolutionary process and, while I find many aspects of Cohen's formulation satisfying—you certainly can't improve on his role models!—it is the sense of the individual reader as part of that historical process that I find is missing here.

Barry Holtz (who is, amusingly enough, a professor at the Conservative movement's *East* Coast seminary, the Jewish Theological Seminary of America) offers a five-point process of approaching these texts that is, I believe, somewhat more satisfactory. Like Cohen, he is writing from the perspective of someone teaching Jewish sacred texts.

Holtz's first reading strategy is, as he puts it, "more of an attitude than it is a way of working." He urges us to resist our initial impulse to leap to evaluative conclusions, to focus, in the rather tiresome Emersonian tradition of American individualism gone all solipsistic (my words, not his), on *our* reaction to the text. Not unlike Cohen, Holtz believes that our first reaction to reading a troubling text should be to step back and allow the text to speak for itself. He invokes a panoply of contemporary philosophers—Willard Quine, Ronald Dworkin, and Moshe Halbertal—to advise readers to extend to the text "the principle of charity," to try reading it in the most generous light. As Halbertal says, "The more canonical a text, the more generous its treatment."

Halbertal invokes Maimonides' example when confronting a text that we find inimical to our beliefs. Maimonides vows that if Scripture clearly was in conflict with what he knew to be scientifically true, he would read Scripture in harmony with scientific truth, a reading that would call for "maximal charity," as Halbertal puts it.

For a contemporary reader, such a strategy would call for a certain humility in the face of an ancient text, a level of respect that one would accord to a sage with whom one might disagree, but only with appropriate modesty. And reading a text as Maimonides suggests, "modifying perhaps the original intent of the text to make sense in a contemporary world," as

Holtz puts it, gives us some leeway in facing the most problematic passages in Torah.

Many of our problems were anticipated by the commentators of the past. The fabric of Jewish textuality is a rich weave that includes not only Written Torah but over two thousand years of commentary and metacommentary. Holtz's second reading strategy is to utilize this rich literature to see how our predecessors read the troubling texts before us. By reading the range of classical commentators, we are reminded that centuries before our time they asked many of the same questions, sought many of the same answers, that we face today.

Holtz's third approach is also an old one, but no less valid for that. The role of the teacher of Torah is to explain rather than to defend the text. In a study group, this is a role that everyone can and should take on. We have to accept that the religious message of the Torah is what it is. But we also must determine *why* that is the message and what it means for us.

At times, however, we find ourselves all but overwhelmed by what Holtz calls "the strangeness of the text." This, too, is something to which we must occasionally surrender. This fourth reading strategy calls on us not only to accept the Otherness of the Torah but to embrace it as part of how the text works. Holtz quotes the literary scholar Eugene Goodheart who, writing about teaching and learning "classics," says, "A classic does not necessarily convert us to its form of wisdom, but if it possesses the power implied by its status in the culture, it forces us to think about our resistance to it and to strengthen or overcome that resistance." In a sense, this is a reply to Cohen's entire agenda, a request that we not dismiss as "not Torah" those passages that we find baffling or disturbing, but that we struggle even harder with them.

However, Holtz acknowledges that there are times and texts that are just too strange, too troubling to allow us to assimilate their message in any meaningful way. For these texts, he asks that we attempt what the German philosopher Hans-Georg Gadamer calls "genetic understanding," that we seek the historical context out of which the text emerged and attempt to view it within that origin. Ironically, Holtz has brought us full circle, asking us to read the most intransigent texts in light of their history.

Needless to say, between Cohen and Holtz we have still only scratched the surface of possible reading strategies. (For example, one can reimagine a troubling text as allegory—the Amalek that we are enjoined to blot out may be understood as the *yetzer ha'ra/evil impulse* within us rather than an entire tribe of human beings.) To test some of these strategies, we must turn to one of the most famously troubling texts in Torah, a pivotal moment in the patriarchal story, Avraham's near sacrifice of Yitzkhak, and see what an accumulation of readings might produce.[1]

THE FINAL AND MOST TERRIBLE TEST

The story of the *Akeidah*, the binding of Yitzkhak, has been called by many commentators the most terrifying narrative passage in the entire Torah. Certainly, on first glance it presents an extraordinarily unpleasant moral situation in which Avraham is "tested" by God in the cruelest way imaginable, by being told to sacrifice his beloved son, Yitzkhak. Only when Yitzkhak is at the very brink of death does the Ineffable intervene through one of the angels to prevent tragedy, and Avraham is told that he has passed this final test of his faith.

The entire episode lasts only nineteen verses (*Bereishit* 22:1–19). Here it is in its entirety.

> And it came to pass after these things, that God tested Avraham, and said to him: "Avraham," and he said: "Here I am."
>
> And God said: "Take now thy son, your only son, who you love, and go to the land of Moriah; offer him there for a burnt-offering upon one of the mountains which I will show you."
>
> And Avraham rose early in the morning, and saddled his ass, and took two of his young men with him, and Yitzkhak his son; and he split the wood for the burnt-offering, and rose up, and went to the place of which God had told him.
>
> On the third day Avraham lifted up his eyes, and saw the place afar off.
>
> And Avraham said to his young men: "Abide here with the ass, and I and the lad will go yonder; and we will worship, and come back to you."
>
> And Avraham took the wood of the burnt-offering, and laid it upon Yitzkhak his son; and he took in his hand the fire and the knife; and they went both of them together.
>
> And Yitzkhak spoke unto Avraham his father, and said: "My father." And he said: "Here I am, my son." And [Yitzkhak] said: "Here is the fire and the wood; but where is the lamb for a burnt-offering?"
>
> And Avraham said: "God will provide the lamb for a burnt-offering, my son." So they went both of them together.
>
> And they came to the place of which God had told him; and Avraham built

the altar there, and laid the wood in order, and bound Yitzkhak his son, and laid him on the altar, upon the wood.

And Avraham stretched forth his hand, and took the knife to slay his son.

And the angel of *Elohim* called unto him out of heaven, and said: "Avraham, Avraham." And he said: "Here I am."

And he said: "Lay not your hand upon the lad, nor do anything to him; for now I know that you are a God-fearing man, seeing that you have not withheld your son, your only son, from Me."

And Avraham lifted up his eyes, and looked, and saw behind him a ram caught in the thicket by his horns. And Avraham went and took the ram, and offered him up for a burnt-offering instead of his son.

And Avraham called the name of that place *Adonai-yireh;* as it is said to this day, "on the mount where *Adonai* is seen."

And an angel of the Lord called to Avraham a second time out of heaven, and said: "By Myself have I sworn, *Adonai* says, because you have done this, and have not withheld your son, your only son, that in blessing I will bless you, and in multiplying I will multiply your seed as the stars of the heaven, and as the sand upon the seashore; and your seed shall possess the gate of his enemies; and in your seed shall all the nations of the earth be blessed; because you have hearkened to My voice."

So Avraham returned unto his young men, and they rose up and went together to Beer-sheba; and Avraham dwelt at Beer-sheba.

On a first reading, this is relatively straightforward but utterly appalling, a "text of terror" if there ever was one; an elderly man who has been vouchsafed a son in his late years is told by the same Eternal force that gave him the son to kill the boy. No explanation is given for this command, no resistance is forthcoming, and, until the very last moment, the outcome is in doubt. At the end of this "trial" the boy is saved and the father is lauded for—it seems—blind obedience to a vastly more powerful and apparently utterly capricious, even brutal deity. Given free will, who would pray to such a Deity?

In reading this text one is more aware than ever of how *withholding* the Torah is on the parchment. It gives us just the letters, with scant space between words, no vowels, no punctuation, no paragraphs. And those bare letters tell so little: We don't know what Avraham is thinking; we don't know what Yitzkhak is feeling; we don't know where Sarah is and what she has been told. Of course, we don't know what God is thinking either, but that is to be expected. The Incomprehensible does not, cannot share counsel with us.

Herein lies the terror of this text. We see a man we have grown to care for given a seemingly insane command—a command that contradicts what he has been promised. And he . . . goes . . . to carry it out . . . with no protest, no murmur of disagreement. We are excluded from his thought processes and, for three days, nothing is said, not even the most banal chitchat. As a result, when Avraham, Yitzkhak, and the boy-servants reach their apparent destination, every single word quietly spoken sounds to us like nearby gunfire, freighted with a lethal intensity. Is it too extravagant to ask who is being tested here—Avraham and Yitzkhak, or the reader?

Yitzkhak's role in this drama is much less discussed in commentary or midrash than Avraham's. Our mental picture of the *Akeidah* has an elderly man guiding a child through a wilderness of fear, and some critics have even twisted the story into a cautionary tale about abusive parenting. But the Torah seems quite explicit on this point: whatever his state of mind, he is too old not to be a willing, if passive, participant in this event. Regrettably and perhaps surprisingly, there is little midrash or commentary either classical or modern on Yitzkhak's role in and reactions to this event. The focus has always been on Avraham and God. So that is where our attention, too, must turn.

One could easily enough read the *Akeidah* as a test of Avraham's faith in and fear of God. There are ample midrashim and commentaries to support this interpretation. There is a Talmudic story, cited by Rashi among others, in which the Opponent Satan challenges God, asking what Avraham has done to merit such loving attention from the Almighty. He has never sacrificed so much as a single dove to You, Satan tells God, he just does everything for his son. And God sets this final test for Avraham as a way of refuting his mouthy underling. After all, what could be a greater show of loyalty than the willingness to sacrifice one's own son? A dove, even a full-grown bullock, looks pretty meager by comparison.

Other traditional commentators, Maimonides chief among them, argue that the *Akeidah* serves a very different purpose. God being omniscient, the Eternal needn't test the level of Avraham's devotion. God already knows how this test will come out. The real purpose of the trial, Maimonides argues, is not to know whether Avraham loves God but for the nations of the world to know of Avraham's extraordinary devotion. (This leads to some rabbinic hairsplitting when it is noted that only Avraham and Yitzkhak are present during the *Akeidah;* as Maimonides notes rather sniffily, it's in the Torah, so everyone who can read the story knows.)

Several commentators have remarked on the use of *nisah* in the first sentence of the story, a word that can mean both "test" and "flag," the implication being that God raises Avraham as a standard for the entire world to see and emulate.[2]

Nahmanides and Yosef Albo offer another, almost appalling justification for the *Akeidah*, arguing that the purpose of the trial is to improve the character of the subject, to train him to do good and open his eyes to his own spiritual potential. The *Zohar* offers a somewhat less unattractive variant on this theme. Using the ladder of the *sefirot*, the divine emanations of the Godhead, the mystics who wrote this medieval text argue that Avraham, "through discovering God and expressing love . . . had attained the rung of [*Khesed/Love*], but he was devoid of its complementary opposite: [*Din/Judgment*]." In order to achieve a balance between these two attributes and become a fully rounded human being, Avraham had to undergo this final test. (Irwin Kula offers a thought-provoking variation on this idea when he says that the *Akeidah*, coming as it does shortly after Avraham's challenge to God regarding Sodom and Gomorrah, reveals the complementary sides of the Covenant, man's autonomy from and submission to the Divine, inextricably linked in creative tension.)

These are all fascinating and even convincing analyses, but they do not erase our unease or make this text any less troubling. They do not address the seeming paradoxes of this episode. Why is Avraham who, only a few chapters before, was so willing to fight for the total strangers who lived in Sodom and Gomorrah, silent in the face of God's instruction that he sacrifice Yitzkhak as a burnt-offering? Why does he accept a command that is diametrically opposed to God's promise to him, that through Yitzkhak his seed will multiply and become a great nation? We know that child sacrifice, considered a pagan practice, is expressly forbidden, yet God seemingly demands it of Avraham.

What manner of Creator can ask such a thing? As Jay Ladin writes, "The horror of this story is not that God would demand child-sacrifice—clearly, God does not—but that God would put father and son through such a charade, looking on in approving silence through the carefully executed process the Torah details. . . . Then, adding insult to injury, God proclaims Isaac's last-minute reprieve a happy ending and Abraham's attempt at filicide an eternal source of blessing."

I find it highly suggestive, if of little comfort, that there is a considerable body of literature, mainly medieval, that invokes the *Akeidah* as a sort of precedent and template for the martyrdom of those Jews murdered by the Crusaders on their way to wreak havoc in the Holy Land. It also became a template for those Jews who killed their children rather than have them killed by Christians or converted. (Shalom Spiegel's superb *The Last Trial* is particularly eloquent on this literature.) The notion that these men, women, and children died *al kiddush Ha'Shem/in the sanctification of the Holy Name* and were therefore somehow going Avraham and Yitzkhak one better is profoundly disturbing; to make the logical extension and connect it to the *Sho'ah* is chilling. It proffers the idea that God desires nothing less than the blood of millions of martyrs as the proof of our love and awe.

How can we make this problem go away? In truth, we can't. Certain readings of the *Akeidah* are inescapably present in the text. As Ladin says, "Part of the hard-won spiritual knowledge embodied in Judaism is that we cannot get closer to God without facing this horror." Even if we don't accept the *Zohar*'s explanation that Avraham needed to acquire the faculty of judgment to balance his loving-kindness, we are stuck with the realization that those are two sides of the Eternal One, that God may be the loving Parent but is also *Dayan Emet/the True Judge*, as we say when someone dies. It's an uncomfortable balancing act for us but, given the real nature of the world, utterly necessary if we are to sustain belief in a Supreme Being. People suffer, often guiltlessly. As Rabbi Eliezer Berkovits says, "It is what is called in Hebrew *gezeirah*, an inscrutable divine decree."

Jewish tradition links the *Akeidah* with the blowing of the shofar on Rosh Hashanah, ostensibly because the ram's horn from which the shofar is fashioned was a tribute to the sacrifice that did take place on Mount Moriah. More important, though, is the association of Rosh Hashanah, the Ten Days of Repentance, and Yom Kippur with the concept of *teshuvah*, of returning to God through repentance. As the High Holy Day liturgy tells us, *"U'teshuvah, u'tefillah u'tzedekah m'avirin et ro'a ha'gezeirah/ But repentance, prayer, and charity temper judgment's severe decree."* So as inscrutable and cruel as the *gezeirah* may appear to us, it is within our ability to mitigate it.

Indeed, that is one of the messages of the *Akeidah* itself. As the rabbis point out, the first three times that God is named in this episode, the Holy One is called *Elohim*, the name that is associated with God's capacity for judgment, but when the second angelic voice speaks, reaffirming the Covenant, God is called by the Tetragrammaton, which is associated with

Divine Mercy. The implication for the rabbis is that Avraham's selfless devotion to God's commands, his *teshuvah/turning* to *Adonai*, secures the tale's satisfactory conclusion. (If so, then it is not a coincidence that Avraham must turn around to see the ram behind him.)

For Rashi, the *Akeidah* enunciates an important principle that is ostensibly new to the pagan world in which Avraham was raised: that animal sacrifice is an entirely acceptable substitute for human sacrifice. Drawing on midrash, the great French commentator argues that the seemingly unnecessary use of the phrase "instead of his son," in verse 13 occurs because "for every service of which [Avraham] did he would pray and say, 'May it be the Will [of God] that this be considered as if it were done to my son.' " Slaughtering the ram, Avraham would say, "I slaughter this ram instead of my son"; sprinkling the blood on the altar he would say, "I sprinkle this blood instead of my son's"; skinning the ram, he would say, "I skin this ram instead of my son"; and burning the offering until it was reduced to ash, he would say, "I reduce this offering to ash instead of my son." With such a lofty precedent, no one need ever again shed human blood for the glorification of God.

But despite all of the explanations offered above, the troubling nature of the *Akeidah* is not something we can either ignore or evade. There are in fact other readings of this text that are possible, and many of them offer some solace, "mitigating judgment's severe decree."

Even in the classical commentaries there is an accumulation of detail that underlines the rabbis' discomfort with this story. Rashi interprets God's initial words to Avraham, *"Kakh-na et-binkhah/Please take your son,"* as pleading in tone! He cites midrashim that suggest that Avraham, without explicitly refusing God's order, prolongs the dialogue with the Almighty in the hope of either reversing the command or, perhaps, conveying indirectly to God his dismay. Rashi also suggests that God takes the longest possible time to make it clear that Yitzkhak is the object of this lethal injunction because the Holy One is concerned that the shocking nature of the demand may drive Avraham into madness, an interpretation that suggests Rashi knows just how utterly dreadful the order is.

Even more extreme are the commentators, of whom there are several, who believe that Avraham either does not hear the first angel's command not to harm Yitzkhak or chooses to disbelieve it. There are numerous midrashim and commentaries in which Avraham actually *slays* his son, in some versions even burning his body to ashes. God then resurrects

Yitzkhak, who spends the next two years either recuperating in heaven or studying Torah. These midrashim are the product of one of the most peculiar details in the entire story, the fact that after the near death of Yitzkhak, Avraham seems to return to his servants alone: "So Avraham returned unto his young men, and they rose up and went together to Beer-sheba." (Ibn Ezra opts for a much simpler, philologically based explanation: that because Yitzkhak is in Avraham's custody it isn't necessary to state explicitly that the two of them returned; he dismisses these other interpretations as being clearly contrary to the Torah.)

In some ways, the narrative of the *Akeidah* is as mystifying as it is troubling. And it is in some of the inexplicable elements of the story that we can find alternate readings that dispel some of the bleakness of the traditional ones. To pick out some of the most obvious paradoxes:

- Why does Avraham, who protested the Divine decree of the destruction of Sodom and Gomorrah, not dissent when God asks him personally to commit an act of murder?
- Why does it take Avraham three days to fulfill God's orders? As Nahum M. Sarna points out, it does not take three days to ride from Be'ersheva to Jerusalem, the putative site of Mount Moriah.
- Why does Avraham cut wood for the offering at Be'ersheva? There is ample wood to be found along the way.

Let's consider three different readings of the story that address these questions, among others.

THREE WAYS OF LOOKING AT A NEAR TRAGEDY

For Lipmann Bodoff, the dilemma presented by the *Akeidah* in its traditional reading is straightforward. Bodoff, associate editor of *Judaism* in the 1990s, writes, "The message of the end of the Akedah is quite plainly that God does not want even his god-fearing adherents to go so far as to murder in God's name or even at God's command." The task that *Adonai* set for Avraham was unique, reserved only for this first Jew, "the first forefather of the Jewish people," as a demonstration of his fear of the Eternal. But Bodoff clearly is disturbed by the implications of the story: "Because Abraham is praised for being prepared to do what we may not do, and because God, the source of all morality, asked Abraham to do what no moral person before or since should ever contemplate, and expected Abraham to obey, the Akedah has remained one of the most difficult texts in Tanakh to understand, justify and transmit to new generations."

Like many modern readers of this story, Bodoff is unnerved by the idea that the Judge of the Universe would ask an obedient human servant to kill, and for no apparent reason. He is equally dismayed by the reciprocal concept that Avraham's fear of and devotion to God would be so great that he would carry out the order without so much as a clearing of the throat.

Bodoff's solution is to seek "a coded counter-message in the Akedah, running parallel to the traditional reading like a subterranean river of dissent." He bases his alternative reading on several of the paradoxes we enumerated before, aided by some creative use of rabbinic materials.

As a first principles, Bodoff offers the following:

- In matters of *halakhah,* the rabbis generally agree that a *bat kol/heavenly voice* carries no weight in decision-making.
- Murder is one of only three sins that a Jew is told to sacrifice his/her own life rather than perpetrate (the other two being idolatry and perverse sex acts like bestiality and incest).
- In determining the status of a false prophet, the main question is whether the alleged prophet has commanded a violation of Jewish law.
- "Worthy ends never justify anti-halakhic means except when the halakhah itself . . . gives the Sages (and prophets) the authority temporarily to set aside a law when special circumstances threaten the halakhah."

Above all this is the most basic biblical principle that, as creatures created *b'tzelem Elohim,* we should attempt to live in God's ways, showing compassion where the Holy One shows compassion.

Taking this seemingly disparate handful of principles as his starting point, Bodoff constructs a new midrash on the *Akeidah* in which the story is "a morality tale of Abraham's staunch defense of God's moral law against any temptation—even God's command—to violate it."

Avraham, Bodoff infers, is aware of the prohibition on murder. He may well know of the curse on Kayin, he certainly knows the seven Noahide laws. Given his reaction to God's proposed destruction of Sodom and

Gomorrah, this seems a safe inference. That last incident, only a few chapters before *Bereishit* 22, also provides Bodoff with one example (of many) of a prophet rejecting a Divine action that contradicts the received moral code. "A Jew is generally not required to obey what appear to be Divine commands to violate law," Bodoff says.

Why, then, doesn't Avraham protest God's command that he sacrifice Yitzkhak?

Bodoff finds an answer to that question in the text itself, albeit well concealed. He argues that the test that God inflicts on Avraham is not a trial of his fear of the Almighty, the traditional reading of the *Akeidah*. Rather, "God was testing Abraham to see if he would remain loyal to God's revealed moral law even if ordered to abandon it." The difference between Sodom and Gomorrah and the *Akeidah*, Bodoff points out, is that in the first instance, God is the (sole) agent of destruction; by contrast, in the latter event God is asking Avraham himself to commit murder. (Richard Elliott Friedman finds this distinction significant, too, as we shall see shortly.)

Avraham's response to an apparently immoral order from a superior, Bodoff argues, is to stall for time, neither agreeing out loud nor arguing against the order. Hence the long and tedious three-day journey from Be'ersheva to Mount Moriah, the slow and laborious assemblage of his retinue, equipping of animals, gathering and splitting of wood. This, Bodoff believes, is why Yitzkhak and Avraham *vayelkhu/walk* toward the mountain, it is the reason for the deliberately paced preparations for the sacrifice itself, with more attendant dialogue than we have heard throughout the previous three days of journeying.

At each step of the journey there seems to Bodoff to be an almost audible and deliberate pause as Avraham waits to hear a Divine voice telling him, "No, I don't really want you to go against everything I've sworn you to and promised to you." If there is a test being given here, it goes both ways, and God is waiting to hear Avraham reject the Divine command. Avraham never agrees to kill Yitzkhak, and he bides his time until finally God responds as Avraham had expected, by staying his hand and reiterating the Covenant.

How does Bodoff explain the second angel's restatement of the Covenant, "because you have not withheld your son"? This is, he believes, an angelic interpolation, a reminder that angels do not know the heart of human beings, unlike God. Their behavior is almost mechanical, an unquestioning obedience to Divine commandment, and they would assume that humans are the same.

What Bodoff proposes, then, is a radical reinterpretation of the final test:

> [T]he Almighty had a completely different test in mind—a test that would make sure that Abraham would not unquestioningly obey commands—even Heavenly commands—to commit immoral acts. In Jewish thought, man is not intended to be like the angels, but to exercise his free will to obey God's revealed moral law, indeed, all of God's revealed law, as interpreted by an educated, morally sensitized, pious, religious community. What God did not want, and does not want, is human beings who are prepared to commit acts which they know to be immoral just because a holy man has received a private communication from on high. The religion that Abraham and God agreed to at Moriah is the religion of a revealed God, a God who is revealed to all, and not privately, and Whose Law is similarly revealed . . . in a written text, publicly available for scrutiny, study and acceptance by all, and subject to subsequent interpretation and application—not on the basis of private, esoteric orders to a select few from Heaven, but the understanding of a religious community based on continuing study and piety.

Does this reading of the *Akeidah* satisfy our moral objections? I think so. Does it satisfy in the larger sense, that is, is it plausible and consistent with the text as given? I'm not sure. Admittedly, I have condensed Bodoff's article severely and, although it was not my intention, I may very well have done violence to its logic and flow. To do him full justice, you should seek out the original. There are moments when I think he is guilty of what a lawyer would call "bootstrapping," stringing a series of interlocking arguments together in such a way that you don't notice until much later that there is a severe flaw in the chain of reasoning and some barely concealed overreaching. But his is an undeniably creative and thoughtful contemporary midrash and certainly no more fanciful than some of the classical interpretations that bend proof texts into pretzels.

Richard Elliott Friedman takes as the model for his own interpretations of Torah the formidable figure of Rashi. Like Rashi, he is concerned first and foremost with the *peshat* of the text, and he brings a considerable knowledge of philology to the table. I think the other strength he brings to his commentary is an acute psychological insight into the Torah's characters, guided by a firm grasp of how the text shapes its narratives. He brings all those talents into play in his reading of the *Akeidah*.

Obedience, Friedman holds, is the key to Avraham's personality. When God tells him *"Lekh lekha/leave your land, your birthplace, your father's home,"* he does so without a thought. When he is commanded to circumcise himself, he does so. When God comes to him and again says *"Lekhlekha"* at the beginning of the *Akeidah,*[3] he complies without a word of dissent. His only response, Friedman notes, is "He got up early in the morning."

Yet this same Avraham fights with God over the fate of two cities in which he knows almost no one. What is the difference here? If he is fighting to protect Lot, that might be understandable, but Lot is his nephew while Yitzkhak is *his son.* "Even if it is his compassion for those morally challenged people of Sodom, still, there must also be compassion for his son," Friedman says. And Yitzkhak is, seemingly, a true innocent, while even Avraham concedes that the people of Sodom and Gomorrah are evil.

Friedman, like Bodoff, finds the difference in the fact that the always obedient Avraham is not being asked to take a role in the destruction of the cities of the plain. God informs him of the decision to destroy the cities, thereby opening the possibility of dialogue. But orders are orders. Additionally, Friedman says, it is precisely his closeness to Yitzkhak that makes it hard for Avraham to argue on his behalf; he can hardly be called an impartial observer, as he clearly was in the case of Sodom and Gomorrah. Besides, Avraham must remember that his argument on behalf of the two cities was made in vain, that God didn't find even ten righteous inhabitants and torched everything there, which God knew would happen. What would be the point of arguing again?

Instead, Friedman points out, it is precisely Avraham's obedience that saves Yitzkhak. Friedman is alive to the intensity of feeling that this story generates. He delineates brilliantly how the terseness of the dialogue between father and son on Mount Moriah feeds our anxieties, the twelve repetitions of "father" and "son" adding to the terrible nature of the test and the final repetition by the angel of "your son, your only one" bringing the story to a heart-wrenching climax in which the reward for obedience is clearly commensurate with the agony of the test.

Friedman, clearly, is reluctantly in accord with the conventional understanding of the *Akeidah.* Yet his focus on the painful nature of the episode, which he concludes by noting that father and son do not speak to each other again in the Torah (nor do Avraham and God), makes it equally clear that he is as unnerved and dismayed by the events on Mount Moriah as the rest of us. This is not a counterreading like Bodoff's, nor an intensification of the difficulties the text presents, as in the midrashim in which Yitzkhak actually dies. Rather, it is a modern reading that takes the Torah text for what it is and attempts to show us how, by its sheer art, it renders our pain and fear palpable. God's will is unknowable and we must, however reluctantly, accept that as a reality.

In the course of their various analyses of Jewish texts and history, several of the feminists cited in Chapter 5 arrive at a shared conclusion: there is an unspoken but real dialectical tension between the Jewish concern for social justice, stated openly and repeatedly in both Written and Oral Torah, and the ostensible means to that end, *halakhah.* Given that each of these is fundamental, even foundational, one might say that this tension is almost the very heart of Judaism. It certainly is, I believe, at the heart of the "troubles" we find in "troubling" texts. The third of our contemporary commentators, the Franco-Jewish philosopher Emmanuel Levinas, makes that dialectic the center of his response to the *Akeidah* and of his philosophical thought.

For Levinas, the basis of all philosophy is ethics. And all ethics is rooted in our relationship with the Other and the ethical obligation each human has toward the Other. For Levinas the key to ethics is the literally face-to-face encounter with the Other. By seeing the face of another we are forced to acknowledge our involvement with the Other. "I cannot disentangle myself from the society of the Other, even [if] I consider the Being of the existent [i.e., the free subject] he is."

It's not hard to see where this leads us in terms of the *Akeidah.* Levinas writes most explicitly about the binding of Yitzkhak in two essays addressed to Søren Kierkegaard's *Fear and Trembling,* itself a reimaging of the story that claims that Avraham's subjectivity "transcends ethics" to ascend to the religious. Levinas rejects that reading utterly. "[O]ne could think the opposite," he writes. "Abraham's attentiveness to the voice that led him back to the ethical order, in forbidding him to perform a human sacrifice, is the highest point in the drama. That he obeyed the first voice [asking him to sacrifice Yitzkhak] is astonishing: that he had sufficient distance with respect to that obedience to hear the second voice—that is the essential."

Seeing the face of the Other calls up in us the generous desire to do good for the Other. More than that, as Levinas writes in one of the most famous passages in his work, it involves a recognition of a shared humanity and a shared mortality; hence, to see the face of the Other is to be forcibly reminded of the edict, "Thou shall not kill." Much as the

I-Thou dialogue is at the center of Buber's philosophy, the face-to-face encounter is at the center of Levinas's thought. And, although the Torah doesn't state it explicitly, it is not hard to visualize the events of *Bereishit* 22:1–19 with an Avraham so transfixed by guilt that he cannot look his son in the face until the very moment when he raises his hand with the knife . . . and looks into his eyes. And in that moment, he recognizes and accepts the ethical responsibility that defines his humanity and his Jewishness, his inextricable link to another human being.

Thus Levinas rejects what he sees as Kierkegaard's "violence" and the violence of the story itself, and he sets for us an ethical standard that is wholly compatible with and utterly derived from the sacred texts of Judaism. The result is not that social justice trumps *halakhah*. Rather, the two must operate in tandem, with the ethical concern for the Other as the guiding principle. In a sense, Levinas has found the map of the borders of the Torah that Aryeh Cohen was seeking.

But what do we do when the very fabric of *halakhah* appears to reject the Other? What do we do when the law itself seems to be the bearer of unjustice? We have touched on this question in the previous chapter. Now we will confront it head-on in one of the most troubling texts facing twenty-first-century Jews, indeed, all twenty-first-century men and women of faith.

CAN A QUEER JEW GET JUSTICE FROM THE JUDGE OF THE WORLD?

The texts are seemingly straightforward and indisputable:

"And you shall not lie with a man like you would with a woman; it is an abomination" (*Vayikra* 18:22).

"And a man who will lie with a man like he would with a woman, the two of them have committed an abomination. They shall be put to death" (*Vayikra* 20:13).

But, as we should know by now, nothing in Torah is straightforward and indisputable, and when lives are at stake it is imperative that we get it right.

Of course, in matters of *halakhah,* as weighty as they may be, lives are almost never immediately at stake; the rabbis saw to that by making the death penalty almost impossible. (See my commentary on *parashat Emor,* page 432.) The rabbinic mind tended to err on the side of mercy wherever possible. The death penalty for two men involved in anal intercourse (which is the generally accepted reading of *"lo tishkav mishkevei ishah/not to lie with a man as with a woman"*) could be given only if there were two eyewitnesses to the act, and there is no recorded instance of the death penalty being meted out for a sexual crime.

But we are getting a bit ahead of ourselves.

Let's examine the sexual prohibition itself and the declaration that it is *to'evah/an abomination.*

Vayikra 18 appears at first to be an omnium-gatherum of loosely related laws governing sexual behavior—incest, bestiality, endogamous and exogamous marriage, male homosexuality—with verses 1–5 and 24–30 as similarly worded framing material bookending the statutes. Central to the chapter thematically is the idea that the Hebrews should set themselves apart from their pagan neighbors, particularly Egypt and Kina'an, by not replicating their behaviors. Incest, for example, was closely associated with the royal families of Egypt, and child sacrifice was considered a common Canaanite practice.

In a sense, then, these are laws about creating boundaries and borders between Israel and the non-Jewish world. As the anthropologist Mary Douglas has observed, "The body is a model which can stand for any bounded system. Its boundaries can represent any boundaries which are threatened or precarious." Setting up boundaries involving the body itself is an extension of creating boundaries around the tribe and the nation. (As Douglas also suggests, this is the reason for the religious concern with bodily effluences that cross boundaries—seminal discharges, menstrual blood, the fluids that are part of giving birth.) A closer examination of *Vayikra* 18 in that light reveals a more deliberate structuring than is apparent on a single reading. The laws governing sexual conduct stated in this chapter represent a series of outward ripples, from the individual body to the family to the tribe to the whole *Am Yisrael*. In each case, some kind of bordercrossing occurs that presents a threat to each in turn.[4]

It might seem obvious how sex between two men would fit into this model but, in fact, the relationship between this commandment and the others surrounding it is more complex than you might expect. Rabbi Steven Greenberg gives a more literal translation of *Vayikra* 18:22 that opens the door to some necessary questions: "And with a male you shall not lie the lyings of a woman: it is a *to'evah*."

As Greenberg notes, while there is no other example of "the lyings of a woman" in the *Tanakh*, the phrase *mishkav zahar/the lying of a male* occurs several times in *B'midbar*. In those appearances, the phrase seems to indicate "what a man experiences in intercourse with a woman, that is, the engulfment of the penis . . . penetrative intercourse."[6] Thus, the prohibition given in both *Vayikra* 18:22 and *Vayikra* 20:13 refers specifically to anal intercourse. This reading is consonant with the rulings of the rabbis in this matter. Only anal intercourse is explicitly prohibited; all other forms of sexual behavior between men are left undiscussed, and there is no prohibition against same-sex desire. (Although there was no prohibition against lesbianism in the Torah, the rabbis felt it necessary to offer a weak prohibition, calling it "mere indecency," a term of disapprobation without a punishment attached. Later rabbinic authorities would also disapprove of lesbianism as an example of "copying Gentile behavior.")

What about *to'evah*? There are several different translations, although they all have the same sense. The most recent version of the Jewish Publication Society's translation of the Torah has "an abhorrence" while the 1917 JPS, the King James, and the New American Standard Bible all have translated it as "an abomination." Richard Elliott Friedman translates the word as "it is an offensive thing." What all these and the numerous other variants have in common is the assumption that there is something inherently repellent in the act. The word occurs twenty-six times in the Torah, fifty-seven times in the *Nevi'im Rishonim/The Early Prophets*, once in *Tehillim*, and twenty-five times in *Mishlei*.

Vayikra calls many acts *to'evot* (the plural form of *to'evah*). Practicing idolatry is *to'evah*. So are bestiality and incest. Eating nonkosher food is *to'evah*. As you can see, *to'evot* are all over the proverbial map. (According to Yosef in *Bereishit*, in Egypt sheep and shepherds are considered *to'evah*.) What links these occurrences together is that they are used to describe actions that appear to be related to idolatrous behavior. Rabbi Gershon Caudill goes farther and infers that the actions in question involve "substituting the idolatrous behaviour of another religion's practice as a method of worshipping the Israelite concept of God," or in the case of the Egyptian antipathy toward sheep and sheepherders, substituting an Israelite behavior for an approved Egyptian one.

I have not included the instance from *Bereishit* as comic relief. As Richard Elliott Friedman notes, the fact that sheep were *to'evah* to Egyptians indicates that the term was understood as a relative one. Egyptians might have abhorred sheep, but Israelites worked with them all the time. What may be abhorrent to one may be a job to another.

This understanding of *to'evah* gives the injunctions in *Vayikra* 18:22 and *Vayikra* 20:13 a rather different meaning, particularly when placed in the context of the rest of chapter 18. The Torah finds nothing "abhorrent" in the fact that an Israelite man may have more than one wife and may even have sex simultaneously with both his wives. The laws governing levirate marriage look pretty offensive to us, but the Torah not only condones such unions, it orders them. What is it about anal sex between men that the Torah finds so much more appalling?

Several contemporary rabbis have argued that there is an association of male homosexuality with pagan cultic practices. These commentators refer to the existence of *kadeshim / temple prostitutes* as part of the worship practices of the Ancient Near East. In truth, we don't know what these functionaries actually did; however, given the context in which *to'evah* occurs, it is not a huge stretch to infer that it was the mixture of sex and worship that was problematic.

Rabbi Greenberg, who is probably best known as the first "out" gay Orthodox rabbi, offers another intriguing interpretation of the prohibition in *Vayikra*. Unlike other scholars who have argued against the reading of the text as a ban on homosexuality or on gay anal sex, his reading focuses on the first part of the sentence, *lo tishkav mishkevei ishah*.

The answer he derives is that the prohibition is not on anal sex per se but on taking a sexual partner forcibly, as an act of rape. Echoing the women's voices we heard in the previous chapter, Greenberg notes sadly that the biblical conception of rape is a far cry from our own. "There is simply no way to speak about the sexual penetration of women in intercourse as potentially humiliating and demeaning in cultures where women are beneath men in the hierarchy and where, by their station in society and in the creation itself, they are made to be mounted and penetrated," he writes. "In a male-dominated society sex cannot help but become part of this invisible violence."

Consequently, in a male-dominated society such as ancient Israel's, the category confusion created by a man using another man as he would a woman sexually ("like a woman's lyings") must have suggested a forcible rather than consensual sex act. Greenberg draws from this inference the conclusion that today we should read *Vayikra* 18:22 as a prohibition not against anal sex but against loveless, violent sex.

Greenberg's understanding of the text is, to say the least, a radical departure from any previous reading. But even if one doesn't entirely buy his argument, it is transparently obvious that the fundamentalist versions of *Vayikra* 18 don't meet the most basic standards of viability and that the use of the Bible to justify homophobia and worse is utterly inconsistent with the Jewish understanding of the Torah.

Even if one were to accept the traditional halakhic interpretations of *Vayikra*, keep in mind that although *Vayikra* 18:22 and *Vayikra* 20:13 clearly prohibit a specific sexual act (and *only* this act), there is no reference to homosexuality per se, because the idea of gayness as an identity didn't exist until the late nineteenth and early twentieth centuries. Homosexuality *as an identity* is a social construction that is not exclusively rooted in the sex act but, rather, in same-sex desire. This is a tricky distinction, but there is a difference between the prohibition in the Torah of specific acts and a nonexistent prohibition against a constructed identity that hinges only partly on such acts. That is to say, the Torah prohibits a specific act of homosexual sex, but not being gay. I believe one could go even further in making this distinction and argue that the only significant objection to gay marriage that can be drawn from the Torah is that such a marriage cannot produce children, the seeming purpose of marriage relationships in the Torah. But if you factor in modern reproductive technologies and the possibility of adoption in a world flooded with tragically unwanted children, then the principle of *piku'akh nefesh/saving a life*, would seem to me to argue powerfully in favor of extending the sanctification of marriage bonds to same-sex couples.[6]

As a Reform Jew, I don't accept the prima facie halakhic case against same-sex desire or same-sex acts. I'm not sure where Rabbi Greenberg's reading leads us or if it will resonate in the Modern Orthodox community. (Asher Lopatin, a Modern Orthodox rabbi, found Greenberg's book wanting in its use of Orthodox texts as evidence, but readily concedes that it opens new areas for discussion of this issue.) The divisions over the *halakhah* on this issue in the Conservative movement are deep and severe. By contrast, the Reform, Reconstructionist, and Renewal movements have gone ahead, ordaining openly gay and lesbian rabbis, celebrating Pride Shabbat services, and eagerly welcoming same-sex couples.

The situation facing the Conservative and Modern Orthodox streams of Judaism on these issues is a difficult one but not without precedent. As we have already seen in the previous chapter, the status of women in Jewish religious practice has moved forward, albeit with sometimes glacial slowness, in those communities. I believe the same change must take place regarding gay and lesbian Jews.

The issue is not just that the death penalty is off the table. (It never really was on it.) Today one can find even Orthodox rabbis—even some Hasidim—arguing that because none of us is without fault, because none of us keeps all the applicable *mitzvot,* it is unfair and inappropriate to exclude gay and lesbian Jews from the community. Rabbi Shmuel Boteach, a Hasidic rabbi, has written,

> [W]e speak today of *halakhah* as if it were a deity, an end in itself. Worse so, we are even seeing how the *halakhah* is being used to prevent Jews from coming closer to their Father in heaven. If we always followed the criteria that the purpose of *halakhah* is to establish a bond between God and man, then we would not make tragic mistakes that allow the *halakhah* to become a fence which isolates wayward Jews from the Creator. . . . Shouldn't the *halakhah* facilitate greater observance on the part of all Jews so that they can recite a blessing on God's eternal Law and enjoy divine communion? . . . To be sure homosexuality is strongly forbidden by the Torah. But why aren't homosexuals encouraged to keep the rest of the commandments? Why are they subtly ostracized from the community and from their God?

As I observed in Chapter 5, *halakhah* does not stand still. Until the nineteenth century, deaf-mutes were considered non compos mentis in Jewish law, unable to give testimony in a Jewish court, dispose of or inherit property, be counted in a minyan, marry, or divorce. (Their situation in civil society was every bit as dreadful.) That ruling was based on a complete misunderstanding of fact. Rabbi Simcha Bunem Sofer, a prominent Hungarian halakhist, was taken on a visit to the Vienna Institute for the Deaf and Dumb, where he was thunderstruck by the intelligence and achievements of the students. He was brought face-to-face with the error of *halakhah,* face-to-face, Emmanuel Levinas might point out, with the Other and his own ethical responsibilities. Needless to say, no contemporary halakhist would hold that the deaf are to be excluded from the ritual and communal life of the Jewish people. The Babylonian Talmud tells us emphatically, "The dignity of a person supersedes any prohibition" (*Shabbat* 81b).

Ultimately, it is imperative that we remember, as I said at the outset of this chapter, that many of the texts that trouble us troubled the rabbis, too, and continue to trouble Jewish thinkers. As Rav Aharon Lichtenstein points out, "The Gemara sharply criticizes Moshe's comments at the end of [*parashat Vayeira*]," and this is hardly an exceptional instance. The rabbis understood that the Patriarchs and Matriarchs, the prophets and the teachers were human and flawed. The rabbis even challenge God.

The sheer volume of midrash on the *Akeidah* testifies directly to how deeply the story has troubled Jewish readers and writers. But it also is a reminder of how many ways one can read the Torah. We can take some heart in the knowledge that in a text as plurivocal and polysemous as the Torah, the authority granted to a single reading of such texts is not absolute. With the help of the supporting texts that come after the Torah—the Mishnah and Gemara, midrashim, law codes, responsa, commentaries, contemporary *derashot*—we can seek out the interpretation that addresses what troubles us. We still may not like what we find, we still may be troubled, but at least we can decide if the text speaks to us in some way.

Why study these difficult texts at all? Barry Holtz has a blunt answer, to which I assent:

> Although there is, of course, a great deal of debate within the tradition about the purposes of Torah study, it is clear that Jewish texts are not to be studied simply for personal edification or entertainment, although there may also be that. The study of Jewish texts at its heart is viewed with the context of a religious obligation that often is aimed at leading the student toward certain kinds of behaviors (i.e., mitzvot) or, at the very least, at an involvement in a way of living within which study itself is a central element.
>
> Studying the Torah in its various guises is not simply a matter of learning the *whats* and *hows* of being Jewish. Studying is the essence of being a Jew. It defines who one is. Hence, Jewish learning is not only the instrumental gaining of skills, knowledge and competencies. It is the religious act par excellence. . . . [I]t is *being a Jew*, realizing one's Jewishness, in the very act of studying. (emphasis in original)

That is the way that Torah has always been read by the Jews, and it is an ongoing process, a work-always-in-progress. Shaul Magid suggests that all our sacred texts are in some fundamental way "troubled." Understanding these texts, he writes, is "inexorably born of the on-going, perpetual Jewish effort to read and re-read. Such an effort is 'troubled' from the beginning, for who can read these texts and not wonder how to live by them? For life we need ever new interpretations, and for new interpretations, we need new forms of life."

Anyone who chooses can be a part of that work. Of course, participation asks for study of the text, an endeavor that I have been steering you toward in the previous chapters. In the next chapter, I'd like to suggest some places and ways to begin.

NOTES

1. To see my own reading of this story from *parashat Vayeira*, see page 302.

2. Given how much of the Hebrew narrative revolves around movements of elevation and metaphors of height and ascension, this is a particularly elegant reading.

3. Note the echo of the threefold command of the first order, substituting "Take your son, your only one, whom you love" for "Leave your land, your birthplace, your father's house." (There is also the echo of "the land I will show you" and "the mountain I will show you.")

4. Jewish dietary laws appear also to be based around the idea of setting boundaries. Consider the issue of seafood. Eating fish without fins and scales is not permitted, nor are crustaceans or bivalves. Why? Because they live in the sea like more commonly found fish but seem to lack various components that would define them as belonging to the class "fish." Sharks have no scales; clams, mussels, and oysters have no fins, scales, or gills and are stationary; lobsters lack scales and fins and appear to walk like land creatures. In each case, there is a characteristic that puts them outside the category to which the rabbis thought they should belong.

5. I am greatly oversimplifying Rabbi Greenberg's analysis. For the full impact of his reading of this passage, I urge you to read his book, *Wrestling with God and Men*.

6. For a compelling statement on this issue in terms of *halakhah*, see "Gay and Lesbian Jews: An Innovative Jewish Legal Position," a responsa written by Rabbi Bradley S. Artson and published in *Jewish Spectator* (winter 1990). It may found at www.keshetjts.org/sources/index-modernTeshuvot.php. Many thanks to Rabbi Margaret Moers Wenig for recommending this article.

7

NOW GO AND STUDY . . .

How to Study Torah

The Bible [is] . . . a book that cannot die. . . . In fact, it is still at the very beginning of its career, the full meaning of its content having hardly touched the threshold of our minds; like an ocean at the bottom of which countless pearls lie, waiting to be discovered, its spirit is still to be unfolded. Though its words seem plain and its idiom translucent, unnoticed meanings, undreamed of intimations break forth constantly. More than two thousand years of reading and research have not succeeded in exploring its full meaning. Today it is as if it had never been touched, never been seen, as if we had not even begun to read it.
— Abraham Joshua Heschel, *God in Search of Man*

If you have read this far in *Essential Torah,* you are obviously interested enough in the subject to continue studying on your own. But where does one begin? As we have already seen, there is a huge library of commentary, of debate, even of different translations from which one can gain knowledge. But which ones should you read?

I put two simple questions to a wide range of scholars, rabbis, and writers in the hope that they could bring their own years of experience and breadth of knowledge to bear:

- How do you study Torah?
- What advice would you give to someone approaching the Torah for the first time?

Their answers appear at the end of this chapter.

I also wanted to hear from people for whom the experience of a first extended exposure to the Torah and its supporting texts was more recent, more or less self-taught Jewish investigators who had brought a great deal of reading and personal experience to bear in their own study of Torah. For that purpose I chose, logically enough, three members of the Torah study group with which I have met, on and off, for several years. Patricia Dorff, Connie Heymann, and Elizabeth Lorris Ritter are, like me, members of the *havurah* of Beth Am, The People's Temple, and of Hebrew Tabernacle, both Reform congregations in upper Manhattan. In one respect they are a little atypical, in that each is a professional by training: Trish is an editor at the Council on Foreign Relations, Connie a former attorney, Liz a former hospital administrator. So they are highly educated and pretty smart, too. But like me (a film critic and former sportswriter), Connie didn't continue her Jewish studies past her teen years, until she became involved with Beth Am, and Liz didn't become involved at all until she was an adult. Only Trish, who underwent extensive conversion classes several years ago, had been exposed to Jewish text study more recently. None of us was fluent in Hebrew.

So what happens when literate, engaged, and committed Jews embark on a program of Torah study?

"FIND YOURSELF A PARTNER"

The rabbis were pretty clear on one of the prerequisites to studying Torah, and all the experts I consulted agree: *kinei lekha khaver/find yourself a friend* with whom to study. As Rabbi Victor Appell notes, *Pirkei Avot* tells us that when two sit together speaking words of Torah, the *Shekhinah* hovers over them. I can tell you from firsthand experience that there are few intellectual experiences more satisfying than being in a room with friends exchanging insights from a sacred text.

Of course, there are those of a more solitary bent for whom such an exchange is an exercise in extended discomfort. And at some point in your Torah study, you will, inevitably, find yourself in a room alone with a pile of books. Connie had, in fact, spent a year studying on her own before our little *khevreh* was formed.

"You can only go so far on your own," she says, comparing her two very different study experiences. "I really think it's not something you can accomplish totally on your own. You won't get as far as you could by drawing on these other resources. It's really definitional that you have to 'talk' to Rashi or 'talk' to Nahmanides or *talk* to Liz."

In a sense, that is the key to Torah study. The very nature of Jewish study is to engage in a cross-generational dialogue with voices of the past. You are debating and discussing with a welter of viewpoints from the start. Adding live voices to that chorus is both inevitable and essential.

"One of the things I've found about the experience of studying together for a couple of years," Liz says, "is that if you make a stew by putting all of your ingredients in water and cooking it for a while, it'll be pretty good, but if you make it with boullion, it will be better, and if you make it with homemade stock, it'll be even better because there are all these added levels of richness that you brought from someplace else. That's what I feel like now when I read Torah. I've got—and I'm always going to have—all the stuff in my head that we came up with when we studied as a group."

I think Liz hits on another key component of studying in a group when she notes, "There are any number of things in the texts that I don't find troubling or problematic, so it doesn't even occur to me that someone else may want to examine that passage, and it isn't until I'm sitting in a room with someone else who has a different experience and background and education and they say, 'Well, I noticed this . . .' that you go digging into it and you say, 'Wow, not only is that really interesting but now that you mention it, I do have all these questions.' We've all gone back for each other countless times, and that's a big part of what studying in pairs or a group gets you."

It is precisely such a multiplicity of viewpoints that makes the study of the Torah "so layered," as Trish puts it. "If you study on your own, although you can get a lot out of it, you can miss the interactiveness that comes from hearing other perspectives."

She also raises a practical drawback to studying alone. It takes a person of unusual perseverance to sit down every week and read not only the Torah portion but a selection of commentary.

"Having a Torah class, a group of people with whom you study every week, forces you to fulfill this obligation," Trish says. "Not only do you make a commitment to yourself, you make a commitment to other people. You don't want to disappoint them. I don't have the discipline to sit down by myself every week to study, but I've found that if I'm with friends who are doing it I'll make the time and put in the effort."

To put it bluntly, drawing on my own experience, "real life" has a way of interfering when you are studying on your own. Work deadlines, social life, responsibilities to spouses, children, parents, and friends all come into play. For me, Torah study in a group is a way of repeating the "time out of time" experience of the Sabbath in the middle of the week. If Torah study is something I can "program" into my schedule with other people, I am unlikely to neglect it.

In fact, that is precisely how we came to study together in the first place. All three of my study partners have children in our congregation's Hebrew school. They could drop them off at the synagogue and run errands or go out for coffee but, as Connie says, "We wanted to do this."

So the four of us would meet in the synagogue library and study Torah while the children did the same in the classrooms.

Trish adds, "When I was growing up, many parents would make their children attend religious after-school programs but not do anything religious themselves. Personally, I think it's hypocritical to force your children to go to Hebrew school when you're not equally committed. I couldn't ask my son to learn Hebrew if I wasn't willing to learn it. I couldn't ask him to learn Torah if I wasn't willing to study Torah also."

"It was frustrating not knowing this stuff that your kids were studying," Connie says. "We all wanted to learn."

What qualities should one look for in study partners?

"A sense of humor," Trish says without hesitation, sparking laughter around the room. "A willingness to think, or at least to try."

"Tenacity," Connie adds. "Showing up is really important. Listening."

"Being open," Liz says.

Each of those is an important trait in a study partner. I would refine Liz's requirement of openness by adding that it is a virtue that should apply not only to one's relationship with the *khevreh*, but also to the text and commentaries as well. As we have seen over the course of this book, there are many passages in Torah that do not sit easily with our contemporary sensibilities. I firmly believe that good study partners read the texts with that hermeneutic dialectic that we discussed in Chapter 5: suspicion and desire, tempered by a recognition of indeterminacy, an understanding that the definitive interpretation may not be (indeed, probably is not) possible. Concommitant to that attitude toward the text is the realization that, because our reading may be open-ended, the process of study is unending.

When Simkhat Torah comes, we dance with the scrolls, then we start reading from the beginning all over again.

There is another, practical consideration in choosing study partners (assuming, of course, that you have the option of choosing in the first place): a group of people with varied backgrounds, life experiences, and intellectual training will make the stew, to borrow Liz's metaphor, that much more savory.

For example, my academic training is in literary and film criticism and my own personal interest for a long time has centered on narratology, the study of how stories are told; when I read the Torah, beyond what I glean from the commentators I have read, I tend to look at the text in terms of narrative structure. Connie, Liz, and Trish each have different educational backgrounds and life experiences, and they bring different insights to bear on their reading. They are women and mothers, which gives them a radically different experiential grid to fit onto the texts.

Unfortunately, one cannot always *choose* study partners. Unless you are lucky enough to have a friend or friends who are willing to embark on this journey with you, you may have to take potluck. Not surprisingly, the logical place to start looking for a home for Torah study is your local synagogue. Most congregations have an adult education program, and Torah study is a frequent component. Generally, they are delighted to have new participants.

The Internet has made it possible for even the most isolated would-be student of the Torah to find like-minded people. Given a choice between a class or study circle that meets in person and an online "discussion" somewhere in cyberspace, I would urge you to opt for the former. The leavening and pleasant presence of other human beings is one of the great side benefits of Torah study, and the give-and-take of an exchange of ideas with someone in the same room has more immediacy and spontaneity. (For more information regarding online resources, see "Torah on the Internet" on page 258.)

HEBREW AND ENGLISH

In an ideal world, we would all read the great works of world literature in their original languages. Without a doubt, a knowledge of Hebrew will greatly enrich your appreciation and understanding of the Torah and much of the classic literature around it. As Arthur Green writes, "[T]o do the Jewish spiritual life seriously, you really do have to know Hebrew. Our prayer traditions are highly verbal and tied to the intricacies of language, so that they just don't work in translation." But that does add another level of study to your agenda, and for the vast majority of us, a smattering of Hebrew is the best we can hope for. For many of us, that may even be enough.

"Of course we lost something in translation," Liz admits. "But it was a conscious decision on our part not to spend years studying Hebrew first. We would have lost more if we had waited until we could study it in the original."

Still, a certain very basic grounding in Hebrew is useful. At the very least, learn the alphabet and the vowel markings. (See "A Quick Introduction to the Hebrew Language" on page 7.)[1] The rich wordplay of the text is one of its many pleasures and an important part of the way it conveys meaning. Moreover, without at least a minimal understanding of the way the language works, a reader will get very little out of some key midrashic texts.

But given that you will be experiencing the Torah and other texts mainly in English translation, how should you choose a single translation of the Torah to read and study? Frankly, you shouldn't. No single translation read in isolation will give you a sufficient sense of the complexity of the text or its multiplicity of meanings. As Everett Fox, himself a distinguished translator of the Torah, and Arthur Waskow suggest elsewhere in this chapter, you should read more than one translation, either in succession or side by side.

The benefits of a comparative reading are numerous. Liz probably speaks for all four of our study group members when she says that the possible effects of comparing multiple versions of the text are several.

"One possibility is that you look at a passage of text in the most literal way and six translations have it exactly the same way, and that's how we know, 'that's exactly what it says.' Or in most texts it's given a little differently by this translation or by that one but the [discrepancy] is not a big deal. Then you have other passages that are translated *completely* differently from one to the next, or you have fairly similar passages in ArtScroll and [the Jewish Publication Society translation], for example, and then—boom—there's Fox with something totally different."

When the translators disagree radically, clearly something interesting is going on and a red flag should go up for you. That's when having access to supporting commentaries and certain reference books becomes a huge help.

Translation, Richard Elliott Friedman has written, is much more art than science. There is no such thing as a "literal" translation, because there are very few exact one-to-one correspondences in the vocabularies of different languages. And this is all the more so when you are moving from the (relative) precision and concision of biblical Hebrew to the vastly larger possibilities available in English.

So, to return to the previous question, what should you look for in your selection of translations? I would recommend a mix of traditionally observant (ArtScroll, Soncino, Metsudah), the modern "literal" (JPS, *Etz Hayim*, Plaut, Friedman), and the poetic (most notably Fox's *The Five Books of Moses* and Robert Alter's *The Five Books of Moses*). Starting with one from each of these columns will give you a fairly representative set of interpretations.

There are two other considerations.

First, there is the matter of commentary. For example, the Soncino commentary is the sole work of Rabbi J. H. Hertz, who was chief rabbi of Great Britain for many years; his own interpretations are strictly Orthodox, he disdains the documentary hypothesis, but he draws on a surprisingly wide range of outside commentators from the period in which this edition was prepared, even frequently quoting non-Jewish scholars. The many editions available from ArtScroll are no less Orthodox in their orientation (although more up-to-date in their language and choice of scholars), but they eschew non-Orthodox commentators. The Plaut Torah includes a massive amount of scholarly work covering a wide range of sources from Rashi to recent archaeology, from the Talmud to Plaut's own masterly commentaries. By contrast, Fox, Friedman, and any translated *Khumash* with Rashi will rely primarily on a single commentator, although even Rashi draws on other sources. There's nothing wrong with this—Fox and Friedman are formidable scholars, and Rashi is utterly indispensable—but you might want to balance them with a more multivocal book.

That brings me to the other consideration, which is, quite frankly, more practical. Most of these books are a hefty load by themselves. Pick up two or three of them at a time and you may have trouble getting to and from your study group without a truck.

One possible alternative, although it has no commentaries at all and the translation is a bit archaic for some tastes, is the Koren *Tanakh,* published in Jerusalem. This edition comes in three small volumes with a slipcase (or can be found as a single volume as *The Jerusalem Bible*). The Koren (or as we affectionately call it, "Tiny") contains the complete text of the Torah, both Hebrew and English, in a single book not much larger than the palm of your hand, weighing about four ounces. The principal drawback to this edition is that the print is as diminutive as the binding. ArtScroll publishes the complete *Khumash* with Rashi, in Hebrew and English, in a set of small paperbacks they call the Sapirstein edition, which is also very convenient in size.

Of course, if you and your partner meet at a local synagogue or are part of a study group there, you will undoubtedly find a wide array of translations and commentaries on hand.

TORAH ON THE INTERNET

Working on this book and its predecessor, I quickly became aware of the pervasiveness of the Internet as a study and research tool. It is safe to say that neither *Essential Judaism* nor *Essential Torah* would have been the same without the World Wide Web. To claim that access to the Internet is an essential of Torah study would be absurd; Jews managed to study and comment on the Torah for two millennia without computers, let alone modems and DSL lines. But there is no gainsaying what a powerful arrow it is to add to one's quiver.

Someone estimated recently that there are more than five hundred commentaries on the *parashath ha'shavuah* currently available by e-mail. Undoubtedly that number was increasing as the speaker was finishing the sentence. Trying to stay abreast of this flood of information is well nigh impossible. Consequently, what is on offer here is a sort of "greatest hits" package of commentaries that have proven useful in the writing of this book, and a few tips on places to look for more.

The first place to seek information on Torah on the Net is the aptly named Torahnet Web site, currently located at http://www.torahnet .org. Compiled and updated regularly by Eric Sholom Simon, this site lists and links to hundreds of Web sites and subscription lists dealing with Torah, Talmud, and other Jewish sacred texts. Simon is thorough and ecumenical; you'll find the entire gamut of Jewish belief represented here.

With that qualification in mind, let's go through some options by denomination. (Personally, I like Rabbi Irving Greenberg's joking self-definition: "I'm a post-denominational Jew; that means I don't care which stream of Judaism you belong to, as long as you're ashamed of it.")

Reform: "Torat Chayim" is a weekly commentary on the Torah portion with a generous archive of past years' essays, located at http://urj.org/torah/index.shtml. For a more family-oriented approach, including thought- and discussion-provoking questions, check out "Family Shabbat Table Talk" at http://urj.org/shabbat/. For a daily lesson, go to "Ten Minutes of Torah" at http://www.urj.org/torah/ten/. All of these are available by e-mail.

Reconstructionist: The Reconstructionist movement has an excellent and informative Web site with a weekly commentary on the Torah portion available both online and by e-mail. Their Web site is at http://www.jrf.org/index.html.

Renewal: The newest stream of American Judaism has its own Web site at http://www.jewishrenewal.org/, but you should also take a look at Rabbi Arthur Waskow's Web page for the Shalom Center if you're looking for commentaries: http://www.shalomctr.org/.

Conservative: The Jewish Theological Seminary offers an excellent commentary on *parashat ha'shavua* from its former chancellor, Dr. Ismar Schorsch, and other faculty and rabbis. These are archived at http://www.jtsa.edu/community/parashah/archives/ and at http://learn.jtsa.edu/topics/parashah/archive.shtml for previous years, and are available by e-mail.

Modern Orthodox: The Orthodox Union offers several dozen different teachers at http://www.ou.org/torah/default.htm. I am particularly fond of Rabbi Shlomo Riskin and anything from Yeshivat Har Etzion. YHE has its own extraordinarily extensive array of online classes, Torah commentaries, and other materials archived at their Web site, http://www.vbm-torah.org/, and available by e-mail. Project Genesis is another fabulous clearinghouse of Jewish teachings, with archives and current materials both available at http://www.torah.org/. Torah commentaries by Rav Joseph Soloveitchik are archived by

Shamash.org, about whom more below. Commentaries by Rabbi Abraham Kook can be found at http://www.orot.com/ and http://www .geocities.com/m_yericho/ravkook/. Another Web site with an excellent archive of writings by contemporary scholars (and lectures on video and audio as well) belongs to Edah, at http://www.edah.org/ index.cfm.

Hasidic/Mitnagdic: Aish HaTorah offers numerous online and e-mail Torah commentaries at http://www.aish.com/torahportion/. The Breslover Hasidim have a wonderful Web site with lots of Rebbe Nachman's writings available at http://www.breslov.com/. Chabad pioneered the use of the Internet to spread *Hasidut* and, as you might expect, their Web site is a treasure trove of Lubavitcher teachings, located at www.chabad.org. Another source of Hasidic commentaries online is http://www.nishmas.org/.

Unaffiliated: Shamash.org is a clearinghouse of Jewish information online, unaffiliated with any movement but including just about every type of Jewish organization you could imagine. The list of mailing lists it administers goes on forever and includes several dozen Torah-related lists from all over the world. To check out the mailing lists, go to http://shamash3.shamash.org/help/listoflists.shtml. For a searchable archive of their thousands of pages of *divrei Torah* go to http://www .shamash.org/tanach/dvar.shtml.

There are two excellent e-mail lists dedicated solely to the subject of Rashi's commentary on the *parashah* of the week, which I recommend heartily. Dr. Avigdor Bonchek, who has written a useful and thoughtful series of books *What's Bothering Rashi?* has an e-mail list of the same title, which can be found at http://www.shemayisrael.co.il/parsha/ bonchek/index.htm. Russell J. Hendel is the author of a weekly commentary, "Rashi Is Simple," which is available at shamash.org; it is also a highly intelligent and helpful guide to the greatest of the Torah commentators, albeit one geared more to those with some familiarity with Rashi's methodology.

Finally, there are the educational sites. First and foremost has to be the ORT's "Navigating the Bible" Web page, which offers not only commentary but sound bites of Torah cantillation, reproductions of each *parashah* as it appears in the scroll, and translations in three languages (English, Russian, Spanish): http://bible.ort.org/. Bar-Ilan University draws upon its distinguished faculty for a wide-ranging

weekly Torah commentary, which can be found archived at http://
www.biu.ac.il/JH/Parasha/eng/ and is also available by e-mail. Last
but by no means least, Machon-Mamre is a clearinghouse for texts and
information, located at http://www.mechon-mamre.org/index.htm.
At their Web site you can download many classic Jewish texts, including
the 1917 JPS translation of the Hebrew Bible and the works of Rambam and others in Hebrew.

CHOOSING COMMENTARIES

Of course that raises the obvious question of which commentaries to read.
Rashi is the logical starting point. With his focus on *peshat* and his profound common sense, he is the template for Torah commentary. At the
other end of the spectrum but no less impressive is Avivah Gottlieb Zornberg, who has authored excellent books on *Bereishit* and *Shemot*. Zornberg
is a contemporary academic who has absorbed the lessons of the great
Jewish existentialists—Buber, Rosenzweig, Heschel, and Soloveitchik—
and blends philosophical with theological and psychological insights, yet
manages always to return to the Torah itself. The range of her learning is
impressive and she writes extremely well.

It is actually another woman, Nehama Leibowitz, whose commentaries offer one of the best starting points for the beginning student. Her
method, steeped in the classical commentators, focuses first and foremost
on the psychology and motivations of the characters in a given *parashah*,
and the movement of plot and story. She poses thought-provoking questions on other commentators, such as Rashi and Nahmanides, to draw the
reader into the narrative at a highly sophisticated level, yet she manages to
do so for students with little or no Hebrew.

Another excellent source for the non-Hebrew reader is the three-
volume set, *A Torah Commentary for Our Times*, edited by Harvey Fields
and published by the Reform movement in the early 1990s. It offers a
week-by-week analysis of the *parashiyot* drawn from the great classical
commentators, the Hasidic masters, and contemporary scholars. Fields
focuses on a few issues central to each *parashah* and makes deft and illumi-
nating choices of commentary for those issues. He also offers excellent
introductory essays and a good glossary of commentators consulted.

I must admit that one of my longtime favorite study sources is a slightly more eccentric choice, the weekly Torah commentaries that Yeshayahu Leibowitz gave for the Israeli Defense Forces radio in the 1980s, which were compiled in book form and published as *Notes and Remarks on the Weekly Parashah* in 1990. Leibowitz, incidentally, Nehama's brother, was a brilliant scientist who was better known in Israel for his controversial views on human rights and the Israeli state. He was a staunchly Orthodox Jew and his views on the Torah and *mitzvot* are stern and uncompromising, which made his opposition to the Occupation of the West Bank and Gaza all the more interesting. His Torah commentaries do not dip into the political controversies he seemed to revel in, but they are unflinching and unexpected.

One experiment our group tried recently that seems to work well was to have each member responsible for the views of a single, key commentator. I bring Rashi to the table, Connie escorts Nahmanides, and so forth. It's one way of making sure that certain voices are always heard without adding to everyone's burden, and it guarantees that everyone will be involved even when personally not particularly inspired by the passage under discussion.

What makes a good commentary?

I have suggested some of the components in Chapter 4. Nehama Leibowitz identified four goals of Torah instruction in ascending order of importance; a teacher or commentator who can advance these goals is doing her job pretty well:

1. The accumulation of factual knowledge;
2. The development of independent learning skills;
3. The development of a love of Torah learning;
4. The observance of the *mitzvot*.

Given my personal commitment to a Reform Judaism that is firmly based in spirituality and in the ongoing Jewish tradition, I might amend the fourth to say "the understanding of the *mitzvot*, and a sense of attachment to Jewish thought and belief."

The real key to writing a good commentary is to achieve a series of balanced, functioning dialectics: synchronic vs. diachronic readings, detail vs. overview, theory vs. practice. Rabbi Matis Weinberg, in the introduction to one of his useful volumes of commentary, notes that "each *parasha[h]* is built around the interplay of themes complex enough to touch upon fundamental reality, yet simple enough to illuminate a single concept." You have to always keep before you the historical evolution (diachronic reading) and the conceptual underpinnings (synchronic). The tablets may have been etched in stone, but, as we know, Jewish thought and practice evolved nevertheless. How that evolution took place is an important part of understanding what God expects of us, an essential part of Torah commentary.

Richard Elliott Friedman writes, "What Rashi and the other commentators taught us to do was to look at a text critically. They were teaching us to do philology—the art of reading well, reading with care, and thinking about what the words of the text mean." I would add that reading the commentaries requires the same discipline.

The hardheaded among us may not want to be drawn into the web of midrash, with its occasionally far-fetched interpolations of legend (as we used to say in our Torah study, "and now Shabbat jumps out of the closet"), but it is important to know that midrash is there and that it has a certain function. Even fewer modern readers will probably be engaged by *gematria* or *notarikon,* but it is important to know that the rabbis were. I think it is highly useful to know that the rabbis could look upon the Torah as an occasion for wordplay, punning, and numerology, that they didn't shy away from the ludic element in their study. They found Torah to be not only inspiring and elevating but also fun.

That has certainly been our experience in several years of shared study, and I hope it will be yours as well.

BOOKS NO TORAH STUDENT SHOULD BE WITHOUT:
A PERSONAL LIST

1. At least two or three good translations of *Khumash,* if possible with the *haftarot* included, and preferably with Hebrew text on the same or facing page. The W. G. Plaut *Khumash* published by the Reform movement, the Soncino edition edited by Hertz, the Conservative movement's *Etz Hayim,* any of several editions published by ArtScroll are all highly recommended. I am particularly fond of Richard Elliott Friedman's *Commentary on the*

Torah. (Everett Fox's *The Five Books of Moses* is a superlative translation and a must, but it doesn't include the Hebrew text.)

2. Rashi. Even in translation, an absolute necessity.

3. Brown-Briggs-Driver, the Hebrew-English lexicon and concordance par excellence for *Tanakh.* Even if the only Hebrew you know is the alphabet, this volume will prove useful and suggestive. (It's also a bit pricey; there are smaller student lexicons on the market, not nearly as complete or helpful, so BBD is worth the expense.) There are also English-language concordances available.

4. A good Hebrew-English dictionary. My favorite is Reuben Alcalay's but it is a three-volume hardcover set and, consequently, is neither cheap nor portable. There are a number of paperback dictionaries available; I have gotten a lot of mileage out of the Langenscheidt Pocket Hebrew Dictionary. Make sure you're getting one for biblical Hebrew, not modern.

5. If you don't have any Hebrew, you ought to try to learn at least a bit. My own favorite textbook is *Ha'Yesod/The Fundamentals* (Feldheim Publishers). I have used *The First Hebrew Primer* (EKS Publications) when teaching beginning Hebrew and it is also helpful.

6. Even if you don't read a word of Hebrew, you will get a great deal out of Nehama Leibowitz. Because her focus is largely on narrative and psychology, and her work is geared specifically for study, with thought-provoking questions guaranteed to start a discussion, her books are the perfect starter kit. If you study *parashat ha'shavua* with Leibowitz by your side and aren't hooked after a couple of weeks, well, as they used to say in the 1960s, you got a hole in your soul.

ONE WEEK AT A TIME

It might seem self-evident, but the first time you read the Torah, you should read it all the way through, start to finish. As Richard Elliott Friedman writes, "The first portion of the Torah has a double role: It conveys its own story, and it sets the context of the entire Torah. . . . To read the

Torah at any level beyond 'Sunday school,' one must have a sense of the whole when one reads the parts."

I don't mean that you must read the entire *Khumash* by yourself before you can begin studying, although Connie Heymann did do that her first two times through the book. "The first time I just read it, not weekly, I just read it," she says. "The second time I didn't know what to bring to it. One of the smart people I know suggested that I pick a theme and read it for the theme. So the second time I read it for family relationships."

The real key is to read it through chronologically. Does that mean you should or must use the *parashiyot* as your structuring principle? Not necessarily, although for a Jewish reading with commentaries, it makes the most sense, since most *Khumashim* and almost all commentaries are organized that way, and if you use the schedule of readings in the synagogue as a guideline you will be reading them that way.

Of course, you don't have to be confined to the calendar of the readings in the synagogue. If you are fortunate enough to decide to begin studying in the fall, you probably can wait until Simkhat Torah passes and the Jewish world is reading *parashat Bereishit*. But if it's June, you can't wait to get started, and you have a partner or a group and they can't wait, either, by all means begin right away with *Bereishit*.

What I *don't* recommend is diving into the middle of the Torah, starting with some favorite story, and then trying to keep up with a study group that has read the earlier chapters. As Friedman says, "You can read the account of the binding of Isaac without being aware of the account of the creation or the account of the Covenant between God and Abraham, but you lose something. The something that you lose—depth—is one of the essential qualities of the Torah." So many of the qualities of the Torah that make study rewarding and the text inexhaustible are predicated on how the layers of meaning accumulate with each successive chapter—the wordplay, internal allusions, and echoes. Those are precisely the things one reads for and studies for. It would be a shame to lose them.

After you have been through the Torah once, it's up to you how to proceed for a second go-round. Our study group spent three years doing the weekly *parashah* and I think I can speak for all of us when I say that there was never a sense of diminishing returns in the last cycle of readings. But when we began again last fall, we decided to try something somewhat different; because we were less familiar with the *parashiyot* that are read in midsummer, we chose to focus on one of those to start, *B'ha'alotekha* (in *Sefer Vayikra*). We each read it on our own and then started examining specific sections of it. Eventually, we spent six months on this single Torah portion. So you can see that when I say the Torah and the supporting literature surrounding it are inexhaustible, I'm not kidding.

WHY STUDY TORAH?

I am completing this book shortly after Pesakh 5765. Only a few days ago, I sat with my wife and a dozen of our friends in our living room to celebrate the first seder, a joyous and occasionally raucous commemoration of the Deliverance from slavery in Egypt, an event that we evoke in our liturgy every single day. At one point in the evening I remarked to all present that for me the most satisfying part of having a seder was not the good food, good music, and good company, although I enjoyed all those; for me the single most important part of the seder is the knowledge that in Jewish homes and synagogues around the world, within that twenty-four–hour period, millions of other Jews—men and women and children I do not know and will never meet—were reading the same stories, saying the same *berakhot*, singing the same songs (albeit to dozens of other melodies). It is a moment in which I feel intensely connected to the Jewish past and the Jewish present, and intensely hopeful about the Jewish future.

Torah study makes me feel the same way.

When I sit down in the library at Hebrew Tabernacle with my study partners, I feel that I am sitting in a room with Rashi and Nahmanides, the Leibowitzes and the Schools of Hillel and Shammai, with all the sages and wise men and women who ever discoursed on Torah, with four thousand years of Jewish history, tragic and triumphant.

And with the *Shekhinah*.

Studying Torah, I feel connected to my heritage as a Jew and as a product of Western civilization, which rests in no small part on the cornerstone of the Torah.

It's worth it for that feeling alone.

But there are other satisfactions, too.

There is the satisfaction of having done serious intellectual work that is, of itself, pleasurable, and the knowledge that I can carry that work with me in my head for the rest of my life. As Connie Heymann puts it, "We own something we didn't have before we started. And every time we add to that."

There is the satisfaction of being part of a group of friends on a voyage together. Liz Ritter recalls the moment in her adult *bat mitzvah* ceremony when "there was a group *aliyah* for all of my study partners, a dozen people. That was pretty fabulous." And Trish Dorff adds, "It wasn't just reading it, it was being together as a group, celebrating the holidays, participating in synagogue, being involved in services. It was my first Jewish year."

I would never claim to speak for my *khevreh*—that's why I let them speak for themselves at this point in the book—but I find another benefit in Torah study, one that goes to the heart of why I wrote *Essential Judaism* and this book. In his introduction to Rabbi Elyse Goldstein's *ReVisions*, Rabbi Irving "Yitz" Greenberg writes about the healing potential of Torah study for a divided Jewish world:

> When learning Torah and applying its lessons to living is at the heart of the Jewish community, then the continuity crisis will be over and the Jewish renaissance will have begun. . . . [One must] inspire liberal Jews by showing them how much they can learn from tradition and how much they can contribute to it. [And one must] inspire traditional religious Jews by showing them how fascinating and full of unexpected twists and turns the process of learning Torah is.

The Torah is the one thing all Jews have in common, regardless of their attitude toward *halakhah*. Studying Torah is the one thing we can all do together. I believe the future of the Jewish people will hinge in some way on sharing the thrill of Torah study. And I hope you will be a part of that future.

NOTES

1. The National Jewish Outreach Program has been offering excellent introductory Hebrew classes across North America for many years at no charge. For more information, phone 1–800–44–Hebre(w) or go to http://www.njop.org/.

HOW I STUDY TORAH

I study Torah in a number of ways. I sit down with a *Chumash* and read through the entire portion. Right now, my favorite *Chumash* is *Etz Hayim*. I also subscribe to several e-mail lists from which I receive weekly *d'vrei Torah*. Among them are the Union for Reform Judaism's "10 Minutes of Torah" and Bradley Artson's postings from the University of Judaism Web site. Since I teach Torah a couple of times a week, I have a built-in incentive to make my study a regular habit.

For first-timers, I suggest they "do" Torah study on their own terms. Read the text, but also read a commentary that speaks to them. Begin with a good *Khumash* like *Etz Hayim* or Plaut. Then layer on commentary. If social action is their interest, sign up for the URJ weekly e-mail. If they want something that will help them relate Torah to their lives and to the world around them, perhaps they should read Artson's *The Bedside Torah*. If family dynamics resonate for them, see what Norman Cohen has written. For a feminist approach, perhaps *The Women's Torah Commentary*.

But of course, the best way to study Torah is with another. Find a weekly Torah study group to join. They are easier to find than most think. Synagogues run them all the time—during the day, at night, in the morning. They often meet in areas where people work. Most synagogues would be happy to have you become a part of their Torah study, even if you are not a member of the congregation. Or, start your own Torah study with a few interested friends. It is from *Pirkei Avot* that we learn that when two people sit down and words of Torah pass between them, the Divine Presence is there.

　　　　　　　—Rabbi Victor Appell, director of Small Congregations unit,
　　　　　　　　　　　　　　　　　　　　Union for Reform Judaism

HOW I STUDY TORAH

At this point in my life I'm not fluent in Hebrew (though I hope to become so within the next few years), so much of my Torah study happens in translation. I read different translations to get a sense for the different nuances (I'm a poet, so I'm especially fond of Everett Fox's *Khumash*). I also subscribe to a couple of different Torah commentary newsletters, so each week I get Torah-portion insights in my e-mail in-box; those give me a sense of some of the interesting questions associated with each week's Torah portion.

But lately I've been spending some time each week with my rabbi, slowly translating and discussing part of the week's Torah portion, and I'm finding that I really love this kind of slow and in-depth study. Even if we only study a paragraph or two, a handful of verses, I come away with a deeper understanding: of what the words mean, and also of what the Hebrew connotes, which is lost in translation. At this rate it will take me years, maybe decades, to work my way through the whole scroll, but that seems fine to me. Torah study is a lifelong endeavor, so it's okay to move slowly through it.

What advice would I give to someone approaching the Torah for the first time?

First of all, have fun. There's an old Eastern European tradition for a child's first day of *kheder/Hebrew school,* of taking a sheet of Hebrew letters and coating them with honey, so that the child might immediately associate Torah study with sweetness. Come to Torah study with a light heart and a sense of joy, because you're in for a treat.

Think of Torah as a lifelong companion whom you may be meeting for the first time now, but with whom you could easily spend years. The more you get to know Torah, the more you'll find there. Begin the process with that understanding—that the more you learn, the more learning will become available to you. Take it slow, don't rush, you've got a lifetime.

Remember that Torah can be read in an infinite number of ways. It's a collection of stories, it's sacred, it's profane, it's legalistic, it's narrative, it's poetry! On the surface the text might say one thing, but generations of rabbis might interpret it in different ways, and their interpretations won't always agree with one another. Let that point you toward an interpretive playfulness and a consciousness that there may be more than one "right" interpretation (or that your sense of what's the right interpretation may shift over time). This isn't a sign of the text's flaws—on the contrary, it's a sign of the text's richness.

Be prepared to love parts of it, and to wrestle with parts of it. Be prepared to be confused sometimes. Be prepared to bring yourself to the text, and over time don't be surprised if you find yourself changing in relation to the text. Come with an open heart and an open mind, and the first time you crack the book, toast yourself and say a *shehekheyanu*, because you're starting something wonderful.

—Rachel Barenblat,
poet and author of the blog *The Velveteen Rabbi*
(located at http://velveteenrabbi.blogs.com/blog)

HOW I STUDY TORAH

I go about my study keeping in mind two important considerations: First, our Torah is a sacred text that speaks of our biblical ancestors' search to discover G-d and to learn what G-d expected from them in their strivings to live a holy life. Second, that as one individual, one reader of Torah, whatever I am able to uncover, experience, understand from the words of a text is very subjective—dependent of course upon my own particular intellectual, spiritual, and emotional construct.

As a student of French literature and as an admirer of the writings of Robert Alter I have become over the years particularly sensitive to and interested in the literary aspects of Torah. The narratives in the book of Genesis are most appealing to me. I am also intrigued with the idea that the Torah has white spaces that invite us, the readers, to add new insight, to create a new layer of meaning.

Since English is my mother tongue, I begin my study by reading and rereading the New Jewish Version (the Jewish Publication Society translation) of *Tanakh*. Then, I read the passage in question in *Ivrit*, looking for the particularities of the Hebrew text, subtleties in expression, choice of words, and so on. An idea, a theme may emerge. Then, I would take a look at Rashi or other commentators—my favorite reference is Nehama Leibowitz's *(z'l) Studies of Torah*—and see whether the commentaries were also dealing with those same ideas or themes. Why, I might ask, did they write what they wrote on that verse? If they were alive today, how might they explain or elucidate that word or verse of Torah differently? Sometimes I imagine an exchange between

"Moses," a commentator of Torah, and myself, seeing where we might agree and where we might disagree.

There are many subjects that are found in a Torah passage: history, law, ritual, cultural data, depending upon my state of mind at the moment of reading the passage, I may gravitate toward one more than another. I had an Orthodox teacher in rabbinical school who told us that sometimes in *shul* he would find himself not only *davening* the text of the prayer book but also analyzing the grammar of the text! I also find great meaning and edification in just reading the biblical text in *Ivrit* and trying to figure out the *shorash/root* of a verb or understanding a particular grammatical point.

For a first-time learner of Torah: *kinei lekha khaver*—acquire a friend with whom to study; try to learn some Hebrew; get the linear text with Rashi commentary; try to understand that there is not only one right meaning of a verse of Torah, there may be several meanings.

—Rabbi Stephen Berkowitz,
associate rabbi of the Mouvement Juif Libéral de France in Paris

HOW I STUDY TORAH

I understand Hebrew and the commentaries. So I read a passage and absorb it and look at Rashi and look at the Ramban, who is a fascinating commentator. He is very wide ranging and, in my opinion, deals with *peshat* even more than Rashi does. I listen to the words and "see" if I "feel" there is any dissonance in the text. By that I mean, does anything have a strange ring to it? One must have a feel for the biblical text (and I can't say my "feel" is that accurate—but it's all I have) to get this sense. It is a sensitivity that comes with becoming familiar with the Bible. If I think something sounds strange or causes any other kind of question in my mind, I look to the *meforshim* [classical rabbinic commentators]. Depending on what kind of question, I look at certain *meforshim* for certain kinds of problems. (Malbim and Kesav Ve'ha'kabbalah for language. Ramban and Ibn Ezra for dificulties in understanding the meaning of the verse, etc.)

Your second question is easier for me to answer. Again the reader must read and reread the text and should absorb it and then ask questions—any and all questions that come to mind. In my book *Studying the Torah,* I devote the last chapter to the importance of learning to ask questions. Some questions will certainly be off base in the beginning, but eventually, as sensitivity is increased, the questions are more and more on target. I feel that asking questions is the key to understanding, and in the case of Torah it enables one to grasp and appreciate the depth and subtlety of the Torah.

—Dr. Avigdor Bonchek,
author of *Studying the Torah: A Guide to In-Depth Interpretation*
and the series *What's Bothering Rashi?*

HOW I STUDY TORAH

The advice I would give to someone studying Torah for the first time would be (a) to read a chapter/section/book straight through, first with one translation, then another; and (b) to use several (three or more) commentaries after that: Plaut, JPS, ArtScroll, mine, and so forth. That way, the breadth of what's both in the text and outside will become immediately apparent. As for how I study Torah, that's tougher to answer briefly, but I would say that I start with the big picture (again, either chapter, section, or book), paying careful attention in the Hebrew to repetitions, allusions, odd forms, odd expressions/words. My initial goal is to see if the text leaves clues.

—Everett Fox, translator and commentator,
The Five Books of Moses: Genesis, Exodus, Leviticus,
Numbers, and Deuteronomy

HOW I STUDY TORAH

I approach Torah first as a source of blessing for my life. I read the text as something that is happening inside me, right now. (I explain this better in the article "Torah as Blessing" [www.rabbishefagold.com]). Then I ask, what is the spiritual challenge that the Torah is giving me? How do I rise to that challenge? And what are the practices I can do that will help me to meet the challenge and thus receive the blessing of Torah?

This approach has sent me on an amazing journey that is both personal and universal. And I meet many others for whom this approach has meant that the door to Judaism is finally opening.

—Rabbi Shefa Gold, director of C-DEEP—
Center for Devotional, Energy and Ecstatic Practice,
and a leader in ALEPH: The Alliance for Jewish Renewal.
Her extensive writings on Torah can be found on her Web site.

HOW I STUDY TORAH

Your questions are deceptively simple, and I am not sure what to do with them. I am afraid that any answer I would compose would be equally deceptively simple. I know of no single one-line answer.

I guess my overall advice on studying is how I learned to study:

1. Don't be put off by people who know more than you do. Do what you can do. Finding meaning in Torah is a blend of you and Torah. I call it "Where life meets text." If you are not already an expert in text, you are in life.

2. Be serious. Do not settle for the recipes for study that others tell you to follow. Never say anything you do not believe. But how do you know what you believe until you say it, and what language do you use to practice the saying? You need a balance here. Use metaphor liberally, realizing that so-called religious language may mean nothing literally, but may be the only way to get at the deep issues you are after. And yet, never forget that the same language can hide ignorance by pretending to say something but really saying nothing. Other people with nothing to say will nod approval, making you think you are profound, not empty. So check to see that ordinary people nod with satisfaction. They

are better judges of what you say than the experts. You need to test what you say against life; ordinary people worry about life, "experts" may forget life for text. If you cannot address life from text, you are just addressing text from text and are becoming textually solipsistic.

Life and text are deep, so ordinary language will not suffice. Specialized language, however, may occlude. So avoid simplistic spiritual fluffiness that just clouds reality, but be willing to push a metaphor to arrive at insights that scientific prose will never capture. The test is whether you really and truly believe what you say; I mean *belief* here in a deep literary sense. Text is literature. Literature should address life in metaphoric ways that science does not.

3. Do not feel you have to know everything to say something. But do not think you can say just anything if you really know nothing.

—Rabbi Lawrence A. Hoffman,
Hebrew Union College–Jewish Institute of Religion,
author of *The Art of Public Prayer: Not for Clergy Only*
and numerous other books, and editor of the series,
My People's Prayerbook

HOW I STUDY TORAH

I study Torah in community with my *khavurah* or my feminist spirituality collective or my extended scholarly community. I would say to others, "Torah is not acquired except in fellowship." Find a workshop or a study group or a class or a congenial synagogue that has a Torah discussion.

—Judith Plaskow,
author of *Standing Again at Sinai:
Judaism from a Feminist Perspective*

HOW I STUDY TORAH

How do I study Torah? What advice do I have for someone studying Torah for the first time? As each of my efforts at Torah study seems like a new beginning, starting all over again, my answer to the two questions is the same. I like to think I follow the advice of the sages. But which sages?

An ancient sage, Joshua ben Perakhyah, said: "Provide yourself with a teacher; get yourself a companion; and judge all humans favorably" (*Pirkei Avot* 1:6, as quoted in *Daily Prayer Book*, translated by Philip Birnbaum [New York: Hebrew Publishing, 1977], p. 480; translation modified for gender equality). The logic of that recipe is impeccable and points to the multiple embeddings of Torah study—as indeed of all Jewish practice—in tradition, community, and social ethics. But a modern sage has different advice. The "recipe is to have no recipe," said Franz Rosenzweig, reflecting on the guidance many of us seek for deeper ground in Jewish learning (Rosenzweig, *On Jewish Learning*, ed. N. N. Glatzer [New York: Schocken, 1965], p. 66).

Rosenzweig's friend, Martin Buber, who also qualifies as a modern sage, applied this nonprescriptive prescription specifically to Torah study. The new and ever self-renewing student of Torah must, without preconceptions, "open himself up to this book [the Bible] and let its rays strike him where they will . . . and wait and see what will happen to him" (Buber, *The Writings of Martin Buber*, ed. Will Herberg [New York: New American Library, 1974], p. 242).

Where are tradition and community in this counsel? Their presence is muted, if discernible at all.

This is hardly the first time I find myself confronted with opposing Jewish opinions. But the opposition, in this case, is more apparent than real. Joshua ben Perakhyah was addressing Jews who could barely conceive their own identity apart from Jewish tradition and community; Rosenzweig and Buber had in mind Jews who had lost those moorings and who stood in need of recovering them. It is as though even after all else in the tradition has ceased to speak, the Torah can still be heard even by Jews with the deafest ears. The tradition may fracture, the community may self-divide, but the Torah remains whole and capable of imparting a sense of wholeness to the most fractured and self-divided of Jews.

For my part, though Jewish tradition calls to me over a great distance, I nonetheless hear enough of its voice to recognize and respond to the traditional divisions of Torah into weekly portions. Those divisions do not simply make convenient units of study. They provide a context for recovering a piece of lost community, since I know that, whenever I study a Torah portion during its appointed week, thousands of other Jews worldwide are doing the same. So far, I am with Joshua ben Perakhyah. But from here out, Buber and Rosenzweig become my teachers. It is possible to read a Torah portion diachronically, as a sequence of events, laws, or names. But it is also possible to read it synchronistically, as a chorus of simultaneously sounding words. (If prophets, like Isaiah, could see spoken words [*Yeshayahu* 2:1], perhaps we can hear written ones.) Each word has a voice and communicates an atmosphere of its own. As I read, some words sound out louder than others. It is as though the words modulate the volume of their voices to what they know their readers need to hear. (It is the privilege of self-contained wholeness to be so adaptable to fractured partiality in others.) The most resonant word of the portion breathes its atmosphere into the whole of the portion, inflecting it, indeed rewriting it, as though for my own eyes. In that way, an improbable harmony sounds between a moment in the cycle of the Torah readings and a moment in the murky sequence of progressions and regressions of my own life. For a brief while, Torah and I inhabit a shared space suspended over the courses of our otherwise separate narratives. I well remember how, at different points in the repeating cycle of Torah reading, certain words, by sounding out so efficaciously, have endeared their portions to me: the word *lasu'akh* (to meditate, *Bereishit* 24:63), in the portion *khayei Sarah,* describing Yitzkhak's act of attentive waiting in the field, before Rivkah appears; the word *nekhashim* (enchantments, *B'midbar* 24:1), in the portion *Balak,* describing the proscribed arts of divination practiced by Balaam; and the word *re'akha* (your friend, from *re'a/friend, Devarim* 13:7), and not merely your friend, but the one who is "as your own soul," in the portion whose name is almost a homonym of friend in Hebrew: *Re'ei/Behold!.* Each of those portions, having taken on the aspect of its inflecting word, shaped itself as though to my need, respectively, at different times of life, for proximity to the ideas of meditation, enchantment, friendship. If the Torah is, as the mystics and philosophers teach, infinite, then it can adapt its voice to an infinite variety of human needs. We need merely bring to it our need and then, as Buber says, wait and see what will happen to us.

—Dr. Ernest Rubinstein,
author of *An Episode of Jewish Romanticism:*
Franz Rosenzweig's The Star of Redemption

HOW I STUDY TORAH

I don't even know how to begin answering your question about how I study Torah. It is simply the most basic, all-encompassing activity of my daily life.

As to my advice to someone beginning, master the basics even if they seem less exciting than other material. You will never regret having started with the basics first.

—Rabbi Gil Student, president of Yashar Books,
author of the blog *Hirhurim* (at http://hirhurim.blogspot.com/)

HOW I STUDY TORAH

The first source of Torah should be our rabbinic tradition. We are blessed with two millennia of rabbinic commentaries and other writings that teach us how to live in God's world, interpersonal ethics, and ways of apprehending the sacred in our lives. We are equally blessed these days with an abundance of translations of these classical sources. In the end, however, learning Hebrew remains one of the keys to learning Torah.

I would also point out that Torah can be learned from almost everything around us—so we should read fiction, Christian and Muslim sources, view great art, and experience the wonders of God's natural creation. As it says in the midrash to *Mishlei:* if you don't open yourself to learning Torah from afar, you won't really learn the fullness of Torah.

Finally, I would say that the best—but perhaps hardest—way to learn Torah is to learn the very difficult skill of listening to others, especially those who differ with/from you. *Pirkei Avot* teaches that the sage is s/he who learns from every person. Or as *Vayikra Rabbah* tells it: the Torah is not "given as an inheritance" only to the rabbis, but to "the congregation of Jacob," that is to say: every Jew who desires to learn.

—Rabbi Burton Visotzky, Jewish Theological
Seminary of America, author of *Reading the Book:
Making the Bible a Timeless Text* and numerous other books

HOW I STUDY TORAH

Most weeks, I "weave" a Torah discussion at my *shul* (evoking thought from the *khevreh*, rather than starting with my *d'var Torah* and imposing it on them)—so my study is interwoven with my teaching.

Each week I read the *parashah* as a whole, and the *haftarah*, looking for a passage that I think may evoke deep exploration. When I choose it, I read it more carefully in Hebrew and in the Everett Fox translation into English, which I think is the closest rendition of the Hebrew. I often read the translation and notes in the Richard Elliot Friedman's *Commentary on the Torah* and the notes in *Etz Hayim,* the Conservative movement's *Khumash.* I also read the more detailed notes in the five-volume *Khumash* published by the Jewish Publication Society. Sometimes I also look at *Midrash Rabbah* on that passage, and sometimes I check to see whether Buber (in his amazing book, *Moses*) and Heschel have commented on it.

Then I ask myself what for me is the crucial question: What do I think was going on in the life of the person/s who wrote and edited this text? What problem, what question in life was *ootzing* him (almost certainly "him") as he turned to God to wrestle toward an answer? Was this text the result of a dialogue or debate with others in the Family

Israel? What may have been the other responses in the dialogue in which this text was one element? I don't ignore the "product"—the content on the page—but for me the process is deeper and wiser Torah than the product on the page. And then—I ask myself, what does this Godwrestling from the past teach me about my own Godwrestle today?

Then I may do either or both of the following: (a) Write a *d'var Torah*, an essay, for publication in our own Shalom Report or in the *Jerusalem Report* or *Tikkun* or various other (including some Christian) places; (b) lead the Shabbes morning Torah discussion by having the community, voice by voice, read aloud (a few verses at a time) the passage I've selected. If there are puzzled expressions over understanding what is happening in some passage—about its actual meaning, not about its meaningfulness—I may explain.

But mostly all I say is "What thoughts and feelings come to you?" and then encourage continuing dialogue. As I hear themes arise I make sure they are explored and that connections get made. That is why I call this "weaving" instead of "leading."

We have an hour. Sometimes close to the end I will toss in my own thoughts.

How the session begins and ends is important. I start with a version of the Torah study *berakhah* that uses the metaphor *"ru'akh ha'olam/ breath of the world,"* rather than king or lord, for God, and that breathes the *YHVH* as *Yahhh* rather than *Adonai*. The *berakhah* recognizes all life as intertwined breath and the words of *divrei Torah* as breathing shaped so as to aim toward wisdom.

And we end with a renewed version of *Kaddish d'Rabbanan/Kaddish for the Teachers* that focuses on *"shmei rabbah"/the "great name,"* the "great name," as that name that includes all the names of all the beings in the Universe. I ask people to begin envisioning that name and then to place in its pattern the names of our teachers, our students, ourselves.

My goal is to make the Torah study a spiritual exploration of our own lives—family, community, politics, and so on—in the light of the spiritual explorations of the members of Family Israel as they have explored before, including all the family disagreements.

As for beginners: If possible, find a partner. Read alone, the Torah seems to have only one voice—the one of your own that gets 51 percent of the vote in your mind. If you read with a partner, all the silenced voices in your own self are awakened by your partner. Two people equals a minyan of voices.

Then do what I've described, without all the background reading ahead of time. Use the Fox or Friedman translation, read, ask what feelings and thoughts arise, and talk about them.

—Rabbi Arthur Waskow, director, The Shalom Center (www.shalomctr.org) and author of *Godwrestling—Round 2*

8

EVERY WEEK, FIFTY-FOUR WEEKS
A YEAR: AN INTRODUCTION
TO THE *PARASHIYOT*

What follows is a set of commentaries on all fifty-four of the Torah portions. For each one I have included some basic statistical information, the breakdown by verses of the *aliyot* for that portion, and a paragraph or two on the *haftarah* associated with that portion. In addition, there is a brief introductory essay for each of the five books of the Torah.

But the heart of this part of *Essential Torah* is the commentaries themselves. As you know by now, the Torah is a multivocal text, densely textured with a complex interweaving of themes and a rich narrative structure, all of which is expressed in a fascinating mix of poetry and prose, punning, and other wordplay. The text is very nearly inexhaustible.

That is why there are literally thousands of books of commentary, now augmented by hundreds of e-mail lists and Web sites. And that's just the Jewish commentators!

A midrash says that when God spoke at Sinai, each of the six hundred thousand Jews present heard a different voice; to some extent, reading the Torah recapitulates that experience. Needless to say, what follows is anything but definitive. Rather, this is my own reading of these texts, based on several years of reading both the Torah and the literature surrounding it. I have tried wherever possible to cover what I take to be the major themes and events of the *parashah,* guided in no small part by two millennia of distinguished commentators who have preceded me on this journey.

SEFER BEREISHIT/THE BOOK OF GENESIS

First book of the Torah
12 *parashiyot*
50 chapters, 1,534 verses (longest book in the Torah)

If the Torah is first and foremost a compilation of the *mitzvot* commanded by God to the *B'nei Yisrael,* as Rabbinical Judaism would argue, why doesn't it begin with the Ten Commandments? Or, as R. Yitzkhak says, "The Torah should have begun with 'This month shall be [the first month].' " Let us leave aside, momentarily, the fact that God actually gives a few commandments before the Exodus from Mitzrayim/Egypt (the first coming when he tells Adam, "be fruitful and multiply"), which would be omitted if the Torah began with chapter 12 of *Shemot.* There are several excellent reasons why the Pentateuch has all five of its pieces.

Rashi offers an explanation based on the idea that the entire goal of Torah is to get the Israelites into *Eretz Yisrael,* as promised by God. For Rashi, the entire story of the Creation exists as a rebuke to those who would accuse the Jews of stealing Kina'an/Canaan from its previous occupants. He argues that knowing that God created the world ex nihilo allows us to respond to those detractors, "All the earth belongs to God. God created it and gave it to whoever the Eternal saw fit. It was God's will to give it to them and it was God's will to take it from them and give it to us."

Yet there is something infinitely more profound going on in *Bereishit* than merely establishing the validity of the Israelites' claim to *Eretz Yisrael.* Otherwise, it would be unnecessary to take us through the many, many generations in the genealogies that punctuate the storytelling in this book or, indeed, much of the storytelling itself. If ever there were clear evidence that the Torah is more than a compilation of edicts, proscriptions, and prescriptions, a book of laws, it is the very existence of *Sefer Bereishit.*

Think of *Bereishit* as a lengthy introduction, a sort of precredit sequence to the movie of *B'nei Yisrael* being delivered from bondage in Egypt, receiving the Law at Sinai, wandering in the desert, eventually reaching Kina'an. The purpose of the book, then, is twofold: to provide us with enough "backstory" to understand how these events came to pass and to give us a thematic underpinning for the issues of importance raised in the subsequent four books of the Torah. These two intentions are so closely related as to be almost inextricably linked.

From *Bereishit* we learn that all humanity has a common set of parents and, therefore, that no man or woman is somehow to be valued more than any other simply because of bloodlines. Rather, it is by their actions and their relationship to the Ineffable that they are to be judged. We are told that there is an instinctive gravitation in the human makeup toward evil, a *yetzer hara/evil impulse,* yet that impulse can be resisted and, in the case of a great man like Avraham, by and large overcome. So God has given people free will, although the exercise of that faculty is seldom easy.

By tracing the generations preceding Moshe and the bondage in Egypt, we see that God has had a troubled relationship with his human creations, a series of Covenants that men and women have abrogated, with the result being exile and/or destruction. Yet God has not abandoned humanity, although the Creator has narrowed the Covenant to focus on a single people, the Jews, on whom he has placed a terrible burden, "to be a light unto the nations." *Bereishit* gives us an inkling of how that came to pass.

Within the confines of *Bereishit* itself, this narrative expands and contracts, giving us the story of Creation, the Sin and Expulsion from the Garden, and the Murder of Hevel/Abel by his brother in a single *parashah,* but spends nearly four *parashiyot* on the story of Yosef and his brothers. The binding of Yitzkhak/Isaac, an event of a few moments' duration, takes as much space as the recounting of ten generations of the descendants of Noakh. Clearly the author(s) of the Torah had a sure sense of narrative drive, of how to use space and time to create suspense, to shift emphasis to the themes and ideas that really matter. So if the Torah spends about 26 percent of its verses (1,534 out of 5,845) in retelling the story of humanity before Egypt, it isn't an accident or a lapse in concentration.

PARASHAT BEREISHIT

1st Torah portion, 1st in *Bereishit*
Bereishit 1:1–6:8 (146 verses)
Haftarah: Yeshayahu 42:5–43:11 (Sephardic: *Yeshayahu* 42:5–21)

ALIYOT
First / Rishon:	1:1–2:3
Second / Sheini:	2:4–2:19
Third / Shlishi:	2:20–3:21
Fourth / Revi'i:	3:22–4:18
Fifth / Khamishi:	4:19–4:22
Sixth / Shishi:	4:23–5:24
Seventh / Shevi'i:	5:25–6:8
Maftir:	6:5–6:8

SYNOPSIS

God creates the universe from nothingness over six days, concluding with the creation of Shabbat:

Day One: Light
Day Two: the Canopy of heaven separating the waters above the earth and the waters under the earth
Day Three: Seas, Dry Land, Vegetation
Day Four: Sun, Moon, Stars
Day Five: Sea Creatures and Flying Creatures
Day Six: Land Creatures and Humans
Day Seven: God rests and, thereby, creates the Sabbath

Khavah/Eve is tempted by the serpent and eats from the Tree of Knowledge of Good and Evil, then gives the fruit to Adam, who eats, too. God expels them from *Gan Eden* and punishes the serpent as well. Kayin/Cain and Hevel/Abel, the sons of Adam and Khavah, quarrel and Kayin murders his brother. God condemns him to wander the earth but gives him a special mark so that no one will murder him. The final three *aliyot* list the ten generations from Adam through Noakh that lived during that time, as well as the breakdown of man's relationship with God. It is important to note that Noakh's generation was the first generation not to have personally known Adam.

COMMENTARY

The Torah is a masterpiece of narrative compression. When it chooses to, it can stretch out and tell a story in a leisurely fashion; the tale of Yosef and his brothers, for example, unfolds over four *parashiyot* and is filled with psychological insights depicted with utter clarity. But the first Torah portions of *Bereishit* are dense with incident, none more so than *parashat Bereishit*. In a mere 146 verses, we are given the Creation entire, the story of Adam, Khavah, and the Serpent, and the Expulsion from *Gan Eden;* the conflict between Kayin and Hevel; and the genealogy of their descendants unto Noakh. The central themes of the entire book—the omnipotence of God, the Convenant, family strife, exile, the general unreliability of humanity—are present in a highly charged form.

The best lens through which to examine how these themes play out is the actual creation of Adam and Khavah and the events leading up to the Expulsion from *Gan Eden*. Many of the classical commentaries on Torah have remarked on God's decision to create all humanity from a single couple, indeed from a single person. The ramifications of that choice are manifold:

- Because all humanity can claim a single parent, no one can say that his/her heritage is more distinguished than someone else's.
- Similarly, no one can say that his/her ethnic or national group is more favored by God than another.
- God created Adam with dust from "the four corners of the earth" so that no region could claim special benefits, but also, as Rashi puts it, "so that wherever man may die the earth will receive him for burial," and as another commentator says, people will be capable of adapting to conditions anywhere on earth.

Perhaps the most famous dictum derived from the uniqueness of mankind's lineage is found in the Mishnah, in Tractate *Sanhedrin,* in which it is written:

> Therefore man was created on his own, to teach you that whoever destroys one soul is regarded by the Torah as if he had destroyed a whole world and whoever saves one soul is regarded as if he had saved a whole world.

These are all splendid sentiments, but there are even more telling elements in how the Eternal creates Adam and Khavah.

Adam (and by extension, Khavah) is set apart from the other animals of the Creation by several important differences. This creation itself is different from that of the other creatures of the earth; of them God says *"totzheh ha'aretz/let the earth bring forth . . ."* as if they have arisen from the earth itself. The creatures of the sea are created by an utterance of God, much as the light was.

But we are told twice of the creation of Adam. Adam is the only animal of whom God says, *"Na'asei/Let us make . . . ,"* that is, the only creature for whom God has actively planned with deliberation. God says that man will be created "in Our image, after Our likeness," a statement that will have considerable consequences, as we will see momentarily. Adam and Khavah are the only creatures formed by God's own hands. When the creation of Adam is described a second time, in greater detail (*Bereishit* 2:6–7), the Creator "form[s] man from the dust of the earth" and blows "into his nostrils the soul of life, and man became a living being." Thus, Adam is unique among the original inhabitants of the earth in that he is compounded of both earthly and heavenly elements, the dust of the ground (from which he takes his name) and the breath of the Eternal. The animals, too, have souls but, as Rashi notes, the soul of a human is more active, having both intelligence and the ability to express itself; and as a corollary, humans are given free will, which, in concert with their intelligence, means that, unlike the other animals, they are not slaves to instinct.

Perhaps that is why God gives Adam dominion over the animals and plants of *Gan Eden*. God very explicitly gives him tasks to perform, the naming of the animals, tending the *Gan*. God "placed [Adam] in the Garden of Eden to work it and guard it" (*Bereishit* 2:15). Thus, Adam is made an active partner in Creation, and we see that Creation is an ongoing, never-ending process.

Rabbi Menachem Mendel Schneerson, the last Lubavitcher Rebbe, points out that the phrasing of the opening of *Bereishit* suggests a process not completed, "In the beginning of God's creating . . ." because humanity is here to continue the process, "helping God realize [the Eternal's] desire for a dwelling." He writes, "God created the material world but left to man the task of revealing the spiritual within it. The Zohar states that 'God looked into the Torah and created the world, Man looks into the Torah and maintains the world.' "

Obviously, the role of humanity as a partner in Creation is one of the reasons for the creation of humanity. Rabbi Mordechai Yosef of Isbitza offers a more sophisticated version of this explanation in his Torah commentary *Mei Ha'Shilo'akh / The Living Waters.* He writes:

> [F]rom the beginning God created all creation, and afterward, the creation understood and recognized that it was lacking, for it had no one to connect its vitality to the blessed God. By means of man, all the facets of this world may be connected to the blessed God, for man raises everything up. . . .

If the first chapter of *Bereishit* is about the Creation, then the second chapter and the rest of the entire book is about relationships, as Rabbi James Prosnit has noted. Martin Buber wrote, "In the beginning was relation. Not just God who longed to be, but God who longed to be with." There is a midrash that says that God created man because the Eternal was lonely.

(Or perhaps as an old Jewish saying has it, "God loves stories" and without humanity there wouldn't be any stories or anyone to tell them.)

If God gets lonely, how much more so poor Adam, a mere human and the first one, at that? There are numerous midrashim that elaborate on this theme, but the Torah itself is explicit enough: "And *Adonai Elohim* said, 'It is not good for man to be alone. I shall make him *ezer k'negdo,*' " which has usually been translated as "helpmate," but that term is too heavily weighted toward the notion of the woman as subordinate. As Judith Antonelli notes, elsewhere in the Bible God is described as an *ezer* to Israel. *Ezer* does indeed mean "help(er)," *k'negdo* means "opposite" or "against," and as Rashi wryly puts it, "If he is worthy of her, she will be a helpmate. If he is not worthy, she will be against him, to fight him." Nahmanides adds that she should stand opposite him so that they may either come together or separate as the relationship merits.

As before, the creation of Khavah is described twice, the first time in a way that has provoked some extraordinary commentary. In *Bereishit* 1:27, the text reads, "male and female [God] created them." In *Bereishit Rabbah* Rabbi Yirmiyahu b. Elazar says that when he was first created, Adam was a hermaphrodite, dual-gendered; Nahmanides elaborates, writing that when Adam named the animals, s/he was still in that state. It is at this point, remember, that God gives humanity dominion over the earth.

When read this way it becomes apparent that the "second" creation of

Adam and Khavah, the one more familiar to us, is another stage of the first, with God dividing the genders into separate, independent entities. (Thus, Khavah, like Adam, is the direct product of God's hands, unlike the other creatures.) It is also significant that the word for the body part from which God creates Khavah is the *tzela/side* rather than the rib; the word will turn up again in Torah as a description of the beams that make up the structure of the *Mishkan.*

Khavah is thus the penultimate product of Creation, followed only by the Sabbath. In *Bereishit Rabbah* it is said, "Whatever was created after its companion has power over it." That hardly sounds like an affirmation of the inferiority of woman. Elsewhere in rabbinic writings it is said that man is incomplete without a woman by him but, as Antonelli points out, there is no comparable statement made about women.

Let's backtrack for a moment to the creation of Adam and Khavah one last time. After each of the other major stages of the Creation has been completed, God steps back, examines the finished product, and pronounces it good, *"ki tov."* But there is one notable exception. As Rabbi Yissocher Frand writes:

> . . . There is no "ki tov" for the creation of Adam.
> The insect gets a "ki tov." The elephant gets a "ki tov." Every creature gets a "ki tov." But Man himself, formed in God's Own Image, the top of the pyramid, does not merit a "ki tov."

There are two related reasons for this singular omission. The first is that the human being is not a finished product, unlike the other creations. Even after God addresses Adam's most conspicuous lack by giving him a mate, something all the other animals have, humanity is still a work in progress. (Hence their role in the ongoing drama of Creation itself.)

Alone among the animals, humans have the capacities for cognitive growth, for learning and change. The medieval commentator Rabbi Yosef Albo says that when an insect or an apple tree is created it is possible to say "it is good," because each has reached a sort of perfection or completion. Other than actually bearing its fruit, the apple tree has reached its full potential merely by its existence. Men and women, however, are another story altogether. They are born with untapped potential and we cannot judge whether they are/were good or not until they have lived out their days.

That untapped potential is the key to the other reason why Adam and Khavah don't inspire God to say *"ki tov"*; Unlike the rest of the animal world, they have free will and are not slaves to their instincts, genetic imprinting, or pure appetite. Men and women can and must choose between good and evil. As God warns Kayin, "Is it not so that if you improve, you will be forgiven? If you do not improve, sin crouches at the door, longing for you, but you can rule over it." This, too, is an untapped potential that can be judged good or bad only when all the evidence is in.

What, then, of the Tree of Knowledge of Good and Evil, that tree that stands in the center of *Gan Eden,* whose fruit is forbidden to Adam and Khavah? Can we judge the propriety of our actions without that knowledge, without being able to distinguish the light from the dark? Remember that humans are the only creatures created *b'tzelem Elohim,* and that carries a certain responsibility with it—to try to live up to that high standard, to live as God would live, *imitatio dei.* Surely for that reason alone, humanity was entitled to a certain degree of knowledge of good and evil.

Perhaps, as Rabbi Aron Tendler suggests, we were never really meant to live in *Gan Eden* for eternity. Tendler has some interesting things to say about the eating of the fruit from that forbidden tree.

The fact that Khava[h] "then gave Adam to eat of the forbidden fruit" revealed the social desire of humans to share with one another both the good and the bad. Although independently created, "it is not good for the human to dwell alone." We crave being with each other and sharing with each other. Khava wished to share her experience with her helpmate and Adam wanted to follow Khava's lead and be accepted by her. However, Hashem's intent was for each of us to share with each other the joy and discovery of [the Eternal's] reality and goodness as manifest within the limitless boundaries of nature, not to seek out new avenues for self-expression and sharing. If we had simply "worked and safekept the garden" we would have been content and happy. . . .

It was never intended for us to live in Gan Eden. It was intended that we make our world into a Gan Eden. In spite of the sweat of our brow and the pain of child-rearing, we acknowledge and praise our dependency upon [the Eternal's] benevolence and love. Man might be destined to sin and fail, but he is equally capable of Teshuvah and success. The serpents of the real world are both within us and outside of us. . . . Selfishness, self centeredness and ego are "the most cunning of all [Hashem's] creations," and it is our mission to channel passion into devotion and desire into service.

It is only then that we will have fulfilled the promise of being created *b'tzelem Elohim.* And as we will see in succeeding *parashiyot,* it is by their ability to rise above selfish concerns that men and women will be measured in the Torah.

ADDITIONAL NOTES
- For the traditionally observant Jew, time and history begin with *Bereishit;* the year 1 marks the creation of humankind, and the Torah portion covers one and a half millennia, through the birth of Noakh's three sons in 1556, hence the Jewish calendar's numbering system for years.
- Although she is never mentioned in the Torah, Adam may have had a wife *before* Khavah, a woman known as Lilith. The idea that this woman existed first probably derives from the seeming paradox of the two descriptions of the creation of Adam and his companion. There is little commentary about her until the ninth century C.E., when her story is told in a midrashic compilation called *The Alphabet of Ben Sira.* According to Ben Sira, Lilith was formed from the earth like Adam and, with that basis for equality, she disputed with Adam on many things, not the least her refusal to occupy the "female submissive" position during sex. Finally, she uttered the Forbidden Name of God and flew off, ending up on the shores of the *Yam Suf.* Since she never ate from the forbidden fruit in *Gan Eden,* she is immortal. Subsequent texts, particularly the *Zohar,* ascribe to her all manner of evil behavior, including stealing newborn babies and begetting a race of demon children using seed secured from men's nocturnal emissions, which she causes with her considerable powers of seduction.

  For contemporary feminist Jewish thinkers, however, Lilith is an exemplar of the independent woman who will not be ruled by a man. As our taste for demons and spirits has waned, our appreciation for Lilith as a symbolic figure has increased.
- Khavah is the first human being to use the name YHWH for God. (Bereishit 4.)
- Speaking of forbidden fruit, just what *did* Khavah and Adam eat that got them into so much trouble? Although Christian texts seem pretty comfortable with the idea of the apple, the Torah itself is silent on the topic. Commentators suggest the fig—which is why the fig tree was willing to allow Adam to wear its leaves—as well as the pomegranate (a

popular Mideast symbolic fruit, usually connoting fertility), and even a sheaf of wheat.

HAFTARAH

The *haftarah* for *parashat Bereishit* opens with a quick recapitulation of the Creation: "So said the Eternal, *Adonai,* who creates the heavens and spreads out the earth and what grows on it, and gives a soul to the people upon it and a spirit to those who walk on it." With this as the obvious link to the *parashah* (and the use of the present tense as affirmation that Creation is an ongoing event), the prophetic reading continues with Yeshayahu/ Isaiah recalling the ways in which Israel, in a parallel to Adam and Khavah, has faltered, then reminds the Israelites of God's promise to redeem them and renew the Covenant.

PARASHAT NOAKH

2nd Torah portion, 2nd in *Bereishit*
Bereishit 6:9–11:32 (153 verses)
Haftarah: Yeshayahu 54:1–55:5 (Sephardic: *Yeshayahu* 54:1–10)

ALIYOT
First / Rishon: 6:9–6:22
Second / Sheini: 7:1–7:16
Third / Shlishi: 7:17–8:14
Fourth / Revi'i: 8:15–9:7
Fifth / Khamishi: 9:8–9:17
Sixth / Shishi: 9:18–10:32
Seventh / Shevi'i: 11:1–11:32
Maftir: 11:29–11:32

SYNOPSIS

Disgusted with the corruption of humanity, God decides to cause a flood that will destroy the world, sparing only Noakh's family and the animals that Noakh gathers together on the ark. Life starts over again after the Flood. God uses a rainbow to make a symbol of the Covenant with mankind (through Noakh), promising that God will never again destroy the world by water. Noakh plants a vineyard, makes wine, and drinks himself into a stupor. His son Ham uncovers his nakedness while Noakh sleeps and is cursed for the transgression. Ten generations pass. Speaking the same language, the people start to build a city and the Tower of Babel. God scatters the people and "confounds their language, having them speak in many different tongues." The *parashah* concludes by listing the ten generations from Noakh to Avram.

COMMENTARY

Noakh, the Torah says, was a *tzadik / righteous man* "in his generation," a man who "walked with God." This description, which sounds highly complimentary, engenders considerable argument among commentators, with a lengthy passage of Talmud devoted to a debate among the rabbis about just what it means to be a man who walked *with* God, as opposed to

Avraham, who "walked before God" (as we will see in the next *parashah*). Indeed many of the Talmudic sages were unimpressed by the characterization of Noakh as righteous "in his generation." After all, this was, as Rabbi Mordechai Kamenetzky calls it, "a generation of spiritual chaos," a generation so decadent that God brought the Flood rather than let them continue on earth.

What was so terrible about his generation that God had to wipe the slate clean? Was Noakh great? Was he as great as Avraham? And where does the story of the Tower of Babel come into all this?

In fact, these issues are of a piece.

The Torah says that the generation of the Flood was violent and corrupt. At the end of *parashat Bereishit*, in a cunning reversal of the Creation, it is written that "God saw that great was humankind's evildoing" (*Bereishit* 6:3). Midrash tells us that their greatest sin was robbery, an idea that is troubling to contemporary readers. God wiped out nearly all that God created because of crimes against property?

Nahmanides is one commentator who has no problem with that idea. Thievery is one crime that everyone in the prediluvian world *knew* was wrong without a prophet coming to warn them against wrongdoing. Moreover, he adds, it is a crime against both humans and God. One might even argue that it is precisely because it is a crime against property that robbery is such a profound indicator of the baseness of the generation upon whom the Flood was visited. Dov Ber, the Maggid of Mezeritch, one of the great early Hasidic rebbes, taught that it was their great sin to put material matters before spiritual ones, reading the passage "the earth was corrupt before *Adonai*" as a statement that people placed the earth—quotidian concerns—before God. (It is also apposite to remember that God did not kill Kayin for the murder of Hevel but condemned him to wander. Obviously, the Creator's priorities are a bit different from ours.)

Noakh is cut from a different cloth than his contemporaries. That much is immediately clear from the text. But the rabbis of the Talmud are not terribly impressed. Rabbi Yohanan actually intimates that had Noakh lived in a generation less completely rotten than the one before the Flood, he might not be considered anything special. He was okay, but he was no Avraham! (What can you expect from a man whose name means "easy, pleasurable" in Hebrew?)

The *Zohar*, the central book of Jewish mysticism, agrees, suggesting that while Noakh saved his own family and household, he did nothing to save the rest of humanity. Certainly we don't have a story of Noakh comparable to the argument between God and Avraham about the destruction of Sodom and Gomorrah. Indeed, Noakh never engages in *dialogue* with God, but Avraham does, which may suggest what the Torah thinks of their comparative merit. Noakh "walks with God," just as a small child holds his parent's hand, unable to cross the street alone; Avraham "walks before God," an independent and self-reliant adult, not an equal of the Almighty, of course, but willing and able to challenge the Final Authority when his moral code demands it.

Some commentators even downplay Noakh's faith in God. *Me'am Loez* takes a seemingly unnecessary phrase in the Torah as evidence of this. The text states that Noakh and his family came into the ark "before the waters of the flood." Rabbi Ya'akov Culi seizes upon this phrase as redundant; if not for the flood, why else would they enter the ark at all? His answer is that Noakh did not enter the ark until the waters were up to his knees, that his faith in God's promise wasn't strong enough by itself to drive him shipboard. Noakh, Culi says, was too trusting of God's mercy, believing that the promise of the Flood was just so much saber-rattling to scare the unbelievers.

The ambiguous nature of Noakh's righteousness is brought to the fore once again when the earth has dried and the ark has emptied out. In a sense, Noakh's family is humanity reborn, as alone in the world created out of chaos as Adam and Khavah, the people from whose loins all who come after will spring. They must reinvent the world for themselves and future generations. As Rabbi Matis Weinberg notes, the Talmud suggests that all of this Torah portion is a Creation narrative. In Tractate *Avodah Zarah*, it is written: "The first two thousand years, until Avraham and the people he influenced in Haran, were years of *tohu*," the word the Torah uses to describe the chaos out of which God creates the world.

And Noakh's first instincts are certainly sound ones. He sacrifices to God, engendering the promise that no future flood will destroy humanity. He invents animal husbandry and seems to be establishing a new harmony between people and the earth. He plants . . . a vineyard.

Big mistake, that. Should have been wheat, barley, rice, some staple on which the human diet depends. But Noakh plants a vineyard, grows grapes, makes wine, and gets falling-down drunk. As the Torah says, "He profaned himself." It's that human thirst for physical, material pleasure hard at work all over again, the tendency toward self-indulgence.

As we will see repeatedly in the following Torah portions, Avraham is not perfect, far from it. But he keeps his eye on the larger issues, so much so that one might argue that his failings grow out of a certain overzealousness—fathering Yishmael to ensure that there will be off-spring to enjoy God's promise of increase, expelling Yishmael and Hagar from his house when Sarah says that the older boy is picking on his half brother, readying to sacrifice Yitzkhak at Mount Moriah.

By contrast, the first antediluvian generation is guilty of a sin of materialism, the construction of the Tower of Babel. Rashi notes that there are no building stones in Babylon, where the Tower is supposedly being built. Hence the builders' joyous cry, "Let us make bricks," which leads directly in the narrative to the decision to build the Tower itself. Like Noakh, the inhabitants of a cleansed, almost new world have created a new industry, so to speak, and immediately put it to an inappropriate use. There is a famous midrash on the building of the Tower that underlines a parallel to the generation of the Flood. In *Pirkei de'Rebbe Eliezer*, it is written that during the building "if a person were to fall and die, no one would notice him, but if even a single brick were to fall, they would sit and cry, 'Woe unto us, for when will another brick be brought up in its stead?' " Once again, it's profits and property before people.

Yet God does not destroy the builders of the Tower. In an interesting analogy to the Expulsion from Eden, and the curse of Kayin, who is condemned to wander the earth, God scatters humanity across the globe and "confounds their language." There are two reasons for the Eternal's decision. First, God makes good on the promise not to bring another flood and destroy all that lives upon the earth. Second, as Rashi observes, the generation of the Tower were living in harmony with one another, working in concert on a project in which all shared, a distinct contrast to the men and women whose violence and lawlessness were a stench in God's nostrils.

Still, God has offered a Covenant to all of humanity twice and each time the result has been failure. Now a new Covenant will be proclaimed, but this time it will apply to a select group, a chosen people, as it were. But that requires a man of greater stature than Noakh, a man who slips into the narrative almost unnoticed at the end of this week's *parashah*, Avram.

ADDITIONAL NOTES
- The cubit is the smallest measure of distance in the Torah, probably equivalent to 18 inches. So, given the dimensions God dictates to

Noakh, the ark is roughly 450 by 75 by 75 feet, which is a substantial craft. (One midrash says it took 120 years for Noakh to build it.)

- One question that plagues the more literal-minded among us: Does God destroy the fish? Rashi says that the fish are not destroyed because they are not implicated in the sins of humanity. After all, unlike the birds and other wildlife, they don't live "upon" the earth. However, there are midrashim that characterize the flood waters as "boiling," so the fish may not have gotten off so easily after all.

- In the Covenant the Creator offers after the floodwaters go down, God permits Noakh to eat meat (which was not allowed to Adam). However, he must not eat blood, nor eat the flesh of a living creature. Here we find the roots of one aspect of *kashrut*. This is also the basis on which the so-called Noahide laws are erected, created by analogy from the sins of the prediluvian generation and Noakh's own missteps.

HAFTARAH

Although he disappears from the Torah after his death, Noakh is invoked several times by the prophets, most notably Yekhezkel and in this week's *haftarah*, from *Yeshayahu* 54:1–55:5. Yeshayahu speaks to Israel as a barren woman "who bore no child." In urging faith and patience, he specifically recalls the Covenant with Noakh as a sign of God's forgiveness. "For this to Me is like those [waters] of Noakh:/As I swore that [the waters of] Noakh/would never again flood the earth,/So I swore I will not/Be angry with you or rebuke you" (*Yeshayahu* 54:9) And in a clever allusion two verses later, God calls Israel "storm-tossed."

PARASHAT LEKH LEKHA

3nd Torah portion, 3rd in *Bereishit*
Bereishit 12:1–17:27 (126 verses)
Haftarah: Yeshayahu 40:27–41:16

ALIYOT

First / Rishon:	12:1–12:13
Second / Sheini:	12:14–13:4
Third / Shlishi:	13:5–13:18
Fourth / Revi'i:	14:1–14:20
Fifth / Khamishi:	14:21–15:6
Sixth / Shishi:	15:7–17:6
Seventh / Shevi'i:	17:7–17:27
Maftir:	17:24–17:27

SYNOPSIS

God speaks to Avram and tells him to "leave the land of your fathers" and promises to make him the father of a great nation. Avram, Sarai, and Lot go to Kina'an. Famine takes them to Egypt, where Avram identifies Sarai as his sister in order to save his life. Avram and Lot separate. A war breaks out between two groups of local kings; Lot is taken captive in the ensuing action, and Avram rescues him. Sarai is barren, but urges Avram to conceive with her handmaiden, Hagar. With Hagar he has a son, Yishmael (who will be the father of the Arab nation). God establishes a Covenant with Avram. The sign of this Covenant is circumcision of male babies on the eighth day after birth. (Avram and Yishmael are circumcised at their respective ages of ninety and thirteen; hence the Muslim practice of circumcision at thirteen.)

COMMENTARY

Is exile the natural state of mankind? Of Jews? Blaise Pascal famously said that it was man's greatest curse that he was unable to sit quietly in a room, and journalist and novelist Bruce Chatwin picked up this statement and ran with it, developing a theory of human evolution based on the idea of mankind as essentially nomadic.

Certainly in the Torah, exile is a central element in both human and Jewish existence. Adam and Khavah are expelled from *Gan Eden,* Kayin is condemned to wander the earth, Noakh and his family are literally set adrift on a raging sea, the builders of the Tower of Babel are scattered across the globe.

When we meet Avram at the end of *parashat Noakh,* he is already living the life of one uprooted by circumstance, taken by his father Terakh to Haran, far from the family's apparent Chaldean roots. But God singles him out for a mission and sends him wandering even farther afield. Oral tradition says that Avraham undergoes ten tests from God. This is the first one.

Many commentators have remarked on the peculiar command that *Adonai* gives to Avram, virtually the opening words of the *parashah:* *"Lekh lekha mei-artzikha u-mim'olad'tikha o-m'beit avikha el ha-aretz asher er'ehkha. / Go forth from your land, from your birthplace, and from your father's home to the land that I will show you."*

There are two anomalies in this opening command that have drawn the attention of commentators over the millennia.

First, consider the unusual order of God's instructions to Avram: "from your land, from your birthplace, and from your father's home . . ." They go in stages from the general to the particular, from the peripheral to the innermost core of the personality, and from the easy to the gut-wrenchingly difficult. Clearly, God does not intend this to be a merely physical and geographical journey, but one that will challenge Avram's very identity.

The second anomaly speaks directly to the kind of journey God is prescribing. *"Lekh lekha,"* the opening words of God's commandment that give this *parashah* its name, literally means "Go for yourself." As Rashi says, "Go for your own benefit, for your own good." You must grow from this journey, you must explore who and what you are, and, it is implied, change.

All of this calls for a supreme leap of faith, even given the promise of fathering a great people, and *Adonai* isn't going to make it easier by telling Avram his destination: "[Go] to the land that I will show you."

When I think you're ready.

Because God doesn't tell Avram that the land to which he is eventually going is Kina'an, the land to which his father had intended to take him at the end of the previous *parashah.* But Avram cannot go to Kina'an with

Terakh, his father. His father is not merely a worshipper of idols; he is a maker of idols. (We do not know this from the Torah but from midrash and oral tradition.) God will only inform Avram of his destination later, when the transformations that the Eternal One has sought have taken place, when Avram becomes Avraham, a circumcized adherent of and proselytizer for ethical monotheism.

Then the exile can end, at least momentarily.

In the meantime, Avram will continue to wander. He has his nephew Lot as a splendid warning of what happens if you aren't careful where you finally choose to settle down. In this Torah portion and the next, Lot's unwise choice of dwelling place—the city of Sodom—will lead to disaster for him and a lot of extra work for his uncle.

None of this explanation answers one larger question that has bothered commentators since the Torah was written: Why Avram?

Nahmanides states the question quite thoroughly:

> Now this parasha did not explain things at all, for why should God command Avraham to leave his land and why would God bestow upon him such great-ness, the likes of which there never was, without stating beforehand that Avraham was a worshipper of God or "blameless and righteous" [like Noakh], or why not state that the command to leave his homeland was to bring him closer to God? The way of Scripture is to write, "Draw near to me and I will do good for you," as was said to David and Solomon and as the Torah says in general, "If you follow My laws . . . I will grant your rains" (*Lev.* 25:3–4). And Isaac was promised [good] "for the sake of My servant Avraham" (*Gen.* 26:24) but this makes no sense if [all Avraham did was to leave the land.]

The only thing we know about Avram is that he and his father and nephew had come to Haran on their way to Kina'an.

There is a considerable body of midrashim created to fill in the blanks on Avram's youth and to answer this question. These tales show Avram as one who recognized the existence of but one God as early as his third year, a boy who argued with his father over the propriety of making idols and who, finally, was cast into a furnace by Chaldean idolators, only to emerge unscathed (like Danyel in one of the last books of the Hebrew Bible). Nahmanides even offers an explanation for the omission of these stories from the Torah: "The Torah did not want to enlarge on the opinions of idolaters and to state explicitly the differences between Abraham and the Chaldeans in matters of faith." Why give free publicity to the other side?

(In truth, Nahmanides' observation is not without some basis in fact; the Torah generally doesn't give space to the arguments of idolators and pagans.)

To my mind, this is one of those cases in which the backstory filled in by midrash has the distinct feeling of *post hoc ergo propter hoc* special pleading. I prefer the explanation offered by Dr. Ephraim Yitzkhaki, a professor in the Department of Talmud at Bar-Ilan University:

> Abraham's destiny was to propagate the name of God in the world. In order to be suited for this mission Abraham had to be prepared to make a total break with his past: his country, his homeland, even his father's house. He would now have to wander from place to place. He had to accept being different from others, even being persecuted for his beliefs. Therefore "Go forth," *lekh lekha*, is Abraham's first trial, a most difficult (though not the most difficult) task. The Torah sees no purpose in telling about Abraham's past or youth because Abraham's assignment and his being chosen did not depend upon his past activities but rather upon the future—his ability to stand up to the challenge of going forth in the world.

In the next *parashah*, God will challenge Avraham one final time, in almost exactly the same language used in the opening of this *parashah*. But the nature of challenge will shift from a break with Avraham's past to a dangerous gamble with his—and the Jewish people's—future.

ADDITIONAL NOTES

- This portion essentially marks the beginning of the Narrative of the Patriarchs—Avraham, Yitzkhak/Isaac, and Ya'akov/Jacob, and the sons of Ya'akov, who will found the Twelve Tribes of Israel. In that respect, the first two *parashiyot* may be seen as having the same structural and thematic purpose in relation to this narrative as the entire book of *Bereishit* does to the four following books of Torah.
- Both Avram and Sarai undergo a change of name; throughout the Torah we will see that naming is an act with real power, from Adam's being asked to name the animals (making him a full partner in the Creation), through the naming of the many altars to *Adonai* erected by Avraham and subsequent leaders of the Israelites, and, perhaps most important, the renaming of Ya'akov as Yisrael. However, Sarah is the only woman who is renamed in the Torah.
- Circumcision is the first quid pro quo asked of Avraham by God after his name change. It marks him—in the most direct and profound

way—as a different man, different from the Avram he once was, different from the nonbelievers who are uncircumcised. Unlike circumcision in other cultures, where it is part of a rite of passage associated with puberty and, eventually, marriage and reproduction, circumcision among Jewish males carries a different symbolic weight. Coming on the eighth day after birth, it is inevitably linked back to the Creation. Thus, circumcision in Judaism is not a sign of membership in a tribe or the future acquisition of a bride (although both are strongly implied in the language of God's Covenant with Avraham), but represents a lifelong promise between God and all Jews.

HAFTARAH

At the outset of *parashat Lekh Lekha*, Avram is sent into exile with a mission to proselytize for God. In the *haftarah* to this Torah portion, Yeshayahu urges Israel to remain steadfast in its devotion to *Adonai* even during its own exile. The imagery invoked to encourage the Israelites is an echo of God's promises to Avram.

PARASHAT VAYEIRA

4th Torah portion, 4th in *Bereishit*
Bereishit 18:1–22:24 (147 verses)
Haftarah:Melakhim Bet 4:1–37 (Sephardic: *Melakhim Bet* 4:1–23)

ALIYOT

First / Rishon:	18:1–18:14
Second / Sheini:	18:15–18:33
Third / Shlishi:	19:1–19:20
Fourth / Revi'i:	19:21–21:4
Fifth / Khamishi:	21:5–21:21
Sixth / Shishi:	21:22–21:34
Seventh / Shevi'i:	22:1–22:24
Maftir:	22:20–22:24

SYNOPSIS

Avraham welcomes three visitors, who announce that Sarah will soon have a son. Avraham argues with God about the destruction of Sodom and Gomorrah. Lot's home is attacked by the people of Sodom. Lot and his two daughters escape as the cities are being destroyed. Lot's wife is turned into a pillar of salt. Lot impregnates his daughters, and they bear children who become the founders of the nations Moab and Ammon. Avimelekh, king of Gerar, takes Sarah as his wife after Avraham claims that she is his sister. Yitzkhak is born, circumcised, and weaned. Hagar and her son, Yishmael, are sent away; an angel saves their lives. God tests Avraham, instructing him to sacrifice Yitzkhak on Mount Moriah. At the last moment, God sends a ram for Avraham to sacrifice in his son's stead.

COMMENTARY

At the beginning of *parashat Vayeira* Avraham, who is about one hundred years old, is still recuperating from his circumcision, no doubt in considerable discomfort. Three mysterious strangers appear and no sooner has he seen them than he leaps to his feet to offer the hospitality of his home. Such hospitality is at the center of this *parashah*.

What makes the conferring of hospitality on strangers so important in the cultures of the Ancient Near East (and not just in Judaism)? Consider the nature of travel in this region, particularly two and three millennia ago. The land is unforgiving, a mixture of rocks and desert sand, parched and harsh. One can travel for days without encountering a human settlement, without finding water or food. With resources scarce on the road itself, travelers must be able to rely on the few inhabitants of the region for food, water, and lodging in order to survive. The political and personal economy of the area requires it of everyone. Consequently, the principle of hospitality to the wayfarer—regardless of circumstances—is utterly essential.

Not surprisingly, this principle, called *hakhnasat orkhim/hospitality*, is a central one in Jewish thought; welcoming strangers is greater, says the Talmud, than welcoming the *Shekhinah* herself. But even so, Avraham's eagerness to greet his three guests is seemingly beyond the call of duty. Consider the way in which the Torah depicts his actions: "He *lifted* his eyes and *saw*, and there were three men standing near him. He *saw* [them] and he *ran* from the opening of his tent to *greet* them and he *bowed* down to the earth." As Harvey Fields observes, this flurry of activity is conveyed in a staccato flurry of active verbs.

Avraham has been sitting in the midday sun at the door of his tent, and that description in the opening verse of the Torah portion moved the Gerer Rebbe to say that the reason Avraham always kept an open door was so that he could invite people to partake of his hospitality and learn of the true nature of God. "He sat by the door to greet personally the passerby and [to] teach that one should be free from pride, aloofness, and envy, for that would be the path to spiritual perfection."

(By contrast, when Lot welcomes two of these same strangers—and by then we know that they are *malakhim*, messengers of God—it is at night and he takes them inside, almost furtively, hiding them from his neighbors in Sodom. The fault lies not entirely with Lot, although he lives in Sodom by his own choice; the great sin of the people of Sodom is that they not only do not observe the rules of hospitality but actively oppose them. Rabbinic commentators have said that to welcome a stranger was actually a crime in Sodom. Yekhezkel/Ezekiel charges the Sodomites with ignoring the needs of the poor (Yehezkel 16), and the Talmud calls them mean, inhospitable, uncharitable, and unjust. The desire of the Sodomites to smite the visitors when they discover Lot is protecting them bespeaks a cruel xenophobia and this, not their sexual practices, is the reason God brings down the rain of fire upon the cities of the plain. As *Shofrim* 19 makes clear, the crime here is gang rape.)

At last, we have some inkling of why God chose Avraham to father the Jewish people, to bring the message of ethical monotheism to the world. In *Bereishit* 18:19, the Eternal One says, "I have singled out [Avraham] because he will command his children and household after him to keep the ways of *Adonai,* doing what is just and right. . . ." Simply put, Avraham will pass it along to those who come after him, has passed it along to those he has encountered. The chain of continuity will be generational—passed from Avraham to Yitzkhak to Ya'akov to *B'nei Yisrael*—but it will also spread outward. Avraham and Sarah are traditionally depicted as keeping two doors open, with Avraham talking to the men, Sarah to the women, about *Adonai.* (Where else would he have gotten the 318 men who helped him rescue Lot during the War of the Kings in the previous *parashah*? They couldn't have all been mercenaries.)

But there is no gainsaying that Avraham's primary responsibility is to father Yitzkhak and through Yitzkhak become founder of a great, monotheistic nation. God has made that abundantly and explicitly clear to Avraham in the previous *parashah,* telling him that "only he that will come from within your body will be your heir" (*Bereishit* 15:4) and "I will establish my Covenant with Yitzkhak" (Bereishit 17:21). Thus, Avraham knows—has been told specifically—that Yitzkhak is the carrier of the line, the next bearer of the Covenant with God.

What, then, are we to make of the most crucial event of this *parashah,* one of the signal events in Jewish lore and the last and most difficult of the ten tests to which Avraham is subjected, the *Akeidah*? (For a detailed discussion on the wealth of commentary on the *Akeidah,* see Chapter 6.)

The *Akeidah* is a difficult, troubling text. It seems the cruelest possible test of Avraham's faith in God, cruel not only to Avraham but to Sarah and Yitzkhak as well. There are many who believe that the juxtaposition of the *Akeidah* at the end of *Vayeira* and the death of Sarah at the opening of *Khayei Sarah,* the next *parashah,* implicates the stress of knowing her only son's life is in danger in Sarah's own demise. What sort of brutal Supreme Being could ask for a human sacrifice? Isn't this the sort of bestial blood-spilling worship that *Adonai* was supposedly telling mankind to grow beyond?

In fact, Judaism is frequently distinguished from other faiths elsewhere in the Torah precisely by its refusal to engage in human sacrifice and—

to be blunt—God doesn't allow Yitzkhak to be killed. Let's examine the sequence of events more closely.

When God speaks to Avraham about the *Akeidah*, two things leap out at us immediately. First, God says, *"Kakh na et binkhah/Take your son. . . ."* As Rashi points out, the use of *kakh na* suggests a request rather than an order, "please take your son," so to speak. Rashi says that God is pleading with Avraham, "Withstand this test, that the first ones not be said to have been false tests."

After that, God says, *"Lekh lekha el eretz Ha'Moriah . . ."* and we've already seen this sentence construction before. "Go *for yourself* to the land of Moriah. . . ." Is God telling him that one more time, Avraham is to endure a test that will contribute to his personal betterment? I think not. After reading many dozens of commentaries on the *Akeidah*, I would like to suggest a different reading of this seminal event. The *Akeidah* will benefit Avraham, but not in the same way that leaving his home did.

In some ways the most important fact to keep in mind when discussing the *Akeidah* is one that goes against the common understanding of the event. At the time of the *Akeidah* Yitzkhak is thirty-seven years old. He is not, as is commonly supposed, a child. He is an adult, albeit one who has been left largely undefined by the text. Indeed, one of the complaints often voiced about the narrative of the Patriarchs is that Yitzkhak is pretty much a passive character, ill-defined and undescribed. It's not that we don't know what he looks like—almost none of the characters in the Torah have their appearances described—but we have no idea what makes him tick. As we will see in the next two *parashiyot*, Yitzkhak seems more acted upon than active. His father's servant chooses a wife for the young man. He is the seeming victim of the machinations of Rivkah, his wife, and Ya'akov, his younger son. (There is one singular exception and I will come back to it momentarily to make my larger point.)

What do we have on Mount Moriah, then? A man of over 120 years and his 37-year-old son, preparing for what seems to be the sacrifice of the latter to a God whose demands surpass all human understanding. They have left their servant and pack animal behind them and climbed the last yards together. Before he is bound and placed upon the makeshift altar, Yitzkhak asks the obvious question: "Here are the fire and wood, but where is the lamb for the burnt offering?" There is no other human being around, seemingly no animal. Yitzkhak *has to* know what his father is thinking. Yet, apparently, he doesn't resist this very elderly man who binds him and places him atop the wood and raises his knife.

Surely he could overpower his father, yet he makes no attempt. Why not?

Because Yitzkhak is not the passive participant in the process, not a victim at all, but the active element in the test. Because at some point in the journey from home to Moriah, the *Akeidah* ceases to be a test of Avraham's faith for Avraham's benefit, but a demonstration of Avraham's faith and God's final mercy for the benefit of Yitzkhak. Avraham benefits in a direct way: he knows that Yitzkhak, who was not born during the other tests and has not heard the voice of God himself, has seen his father's faith and God's intervention, and he knows that Yitzkhak will be a fit carrier of the tradition and the Covenant.

And Yitzkhak has willingly held still—literally—for this dangerous test. Instead of thinking of Yitzkhak as a guinea pig, think of him as a test pilot trying out a possibly lethal new experience for the benefit of all humanity. God, essentially, congratulates Avraham for withstanding this test after it is over, but the praise belongs at least as much to Yitzkhak. Just as Adam became God's partner in Creation once he took on the job of naming the creatures, Yitzkhak has become his father's partner by making possible the completion of the *Akeidah*.

That is essentially the role that Yitzkhak takes on when he performs the one "active" task he is allotted in the narrative, the reopening of the wells once dug by his father. As I have already noted, the function of this act is one of great significance for our understanding of the Patriarchs, and particularly of Avraham and Yitzkhak.

What is the work of Avraham that Yitzkhak completes? The most important manifestations of Avraham's work in which his son is involved are two acts of complete selflessness, the *Akeidah* and the digging of the wells. And therein lies the key to Avraham's greatness.

It's not that he is perfect. He is far from that. None of the Patriarchs is perfect; they are human and their failings are many and amply detailed in the Torah. Avraham's conduct toward Hagar and Yishmael is deplorable (as is Sarah's). His attempts at passing Sarah off as his sister bring disaster on Avimelekh, whose only sin is fulfilling the requirements of hospitality to guests. Avraham is a flawed man, but he is a great one. He is great because he is selfless in his devotion to God, his willingness to take great risks for other people—his nephew, the strangers who approach his tent, even the putative righteous of the cities on the plain. He is even willing to argue with God if he believes the Almighty is wrong. He risks everything in a process of human growth that is truly impressive to behold. *"Lekh lekha / go for yourself"* is a command that he fulfills by going in selflessness, without selfishness. In the end he inverts the order of the first command to leave, building for himself and the future a family, a tribe, and a nation.

ADDITIONAL NOTES

- *Bikur kholim* is an important tenet of Jewish belief and it has its roots in the opening sentence of this *parashah*, when God comes to Avraham after the circumcision, which the classical commentators take as the first instance of this good deed.

HAFTARAH

The relationship between this *parashah* and *haftarah* that accompanies it is more transparent than many of the pairings we will consider elsewhere. The *haftarah*, from *Melakhim Bet /* II Kings, tells of the Shunamite woman who was barren until the prophet Elisha visits her and tells her she will have a child (as Sarah and Avraham were visited by the mysterious guests). Later her son will narrowly escape death, just as Yitzkhak survives the *Akeidah*.

PARASHAT KHAYEI SARAH

5th Torah portion, 5th in *Bereishit*
Bereishit 23:1–25:18 (105 verses)
Haftarah: Melakhim Aleph 1:1–31

ALIYOT
First / Rishon:	23:1–23:16
Second / Sheini:	23:17–24:9
Third / Shlishi:	24:10–24:26
Fourth / Revi'i:	24:27–24:52
Fifth / Khamishi:	24:53–24:67
Sixth / Shishi:	25:1–25:11
Seventh / Shevi'i:	25:12–25:18
Maftir:	25:16–25:18

SYNOPSIS

Sarah dies at the age of 127. Avraham purchases the cave of Makhpelah in order to bury his wife Sarah. Avraham sends his servant to find a bride for Yitzkhak. Rivkah/Rebecca shows her kindness (and fitness to be Yitzkhak's wife) by giving the servant water and offering to draw water for the servant's camels at the well. The servant meets Rivkah's family, including her brother Lavan/Laban, and then takes Rivkah to Yitzkhak, who marries her. Avraham takes another wife, named Keturah. At the age of 175, Avraham dies, and Yitzkhak and Yishmael bury him in the cave of Makhpelah.

COMMENTARY

At the end of his short story "Eve's Diary," Mark Twain pictures Adam standing beside Eve's grave, where the grieving First Man says, "Wheresoever she was, *there* was Eden." How we wish the Torah had given us such a scene, how much we regret its absence. Khavah, the "mother of all the living," richly deserves such a eulogy. We don't even know when and at what age Khavah dies.

Although she isn't the only female character of whose death we will read in the Torah, Sarah is the only one who is honored by the text revealing the extent of her life span. Sarah dies at the outset of this Torah portion, the only one to bear the name of a woman (and given that only 7 percent of the names in the Hebrew Bible belong to women, that's quite a compliment). And we know how much her death means to her widower husband, Avraham. Avraham, whose sangfroid isn't dented at having to leave his home, at risking the life of his cherished son (and at risking his entire future at the same time)—this same Avraham breaks down and weeps on the death of his beloved wife, Sarah.

And yet, there is a clue, just the faintest hint, of his enormous self-control, even under these circumstances. There is an anomaly in the Torah itself that gives us the clue: the word *ve'livkotah/and he wept* is spelled with a small *kof.* Remember, there are no upper- and lower-case letters in Hebrew, but the *kof* is in a smaller type size than the word in whose middle it appears. Perhaps, as some commentators have suggested, Avraham's weeping is as restrained as that letter is undersized.

Or not—the verb that precedes it, *lispod/to mourn,* is said by some to connote the loud wailing that accompanied mourning in the region at that time. It doesn't matter. For the first time in the Torah, a husband mourns his wife visibly and audibly.

Recall, too, that Avraham has just returned from a sorry task; one set of midrashim say that he has just buried his father, Terakh, but as Rashi points out, this Torah portion begins with Sarah's death immediately after the near tragedy at Mount Moriah, the *Akeidah.* There is one tradition that says the shock of hearing what had happened there is what kills Sarah, who at 127 might have been expected to live somewhat longer. (After all, Avraham will die at 175.)

Even without the enormous stress under which Avraham must face his wife's death, it is an event that clearly shakes him to his core. Although he has apparently been a highly successful businessman—remember the rapid growth of his flocks in *Lekh Lekha*—it is only when he must bury his wife that Avraham buys himself land for the first time. Significantly, that land, a burial field, is in Kina'an, the land that has been promised to him by God. And he is insistent on buying the land rather than accepting it as a gift, so that his title to a little piece of Kina'an is beyond dispute. And then he sends his servant (probably Eliezer, whom we met earlier) to find a bride for Yitzkhak.

Even though the *Akeidah* is the last of the ten tests God has devised for him, Avraham is not unmindful of what remains: aging and death. He has, at last, begun to plan for the future beyond his own life span, putting his house in order for what is inevitably to come.

By doing so, he is confirming a pattern that runs throughout *Sefer Bereishit*, the close narrative linkage of death and burial, marriage and new life. When Hevel dies, Enokh is born to Kayin and his wife, then Shet is born to Adam and Khavah. When Sarah dies, a bride is found for Yitzkhak. Yitzkhak's death is closely followed in the narrative by the betrothals of his sons and so on. Perhaps it is not a coincidence that, as Rabbi Matis Weinberg notes, Rivkah's name is an anagram for *Kevurah,* the Hebrew word for burial. Or that key episodes of *Bereishit* are punctuated by lists of genealogies. It's all about family; it's all about keeping the line going, passing on the Covenant. Not coincidentally, many of the Patriarchs and Matriarchs will be buried in the cave of Makhpelah in Khevron.

And not coincidentally, Khevron's name comes from the same root— *khof-vav-resh*—as the word for friend, *khaver,* a root found in many words that have to do with bonding and deeply felt personal ties. The family connections in this *parashah* go very deep.

Consider a famous midrash that says that Keturah, Avraham's wife of his old age (with whom he has six more children), is, in fact, Hagar. As I said previously, Avraham and Sarah treat Hagar deplorably. Yet clearly Avraham feels some guilt, some attachment to both the handmaid and the son she bears him. Even putting the midrash about Keturah to one side momentarily, we must keep in mind two important facts that emerge in *parashat Khayei Sarah.* First, Yitzkhak is now living in Be'er-Lekhai-Ro'i, where Hagar was informed by an angel of Yishmael's imminent birth. Second, and even more telling, when Avraham dies and the time comes to bury him alongside Sarah, the Torah tells us "and Yitzkhak and Yishmael, his sons, buried him in the cave of Makhpelah."

Thus the story of Avraham and Sarah closes with a powerful image of reconciliation. It is as if Yitzkhak has been waiting for his half brother at the place where the older man's birth was foreseen, waiting for him so that the two men can join together one last time and bury the man who fathered them both.

ADDITIONAL NOTES

- Lavan and his mother tell Eliezer that they must ask Rivkah personally if she will go with him to Yitzkhak, thereby establishing the principle in *halakhah* that a woman may not be given in marriage unless she consents.

- When Rivkah and Eliezer come upon Yitzkhak in the fields, he is "supplicating" as evening approaches. The Talmud and midrash pick up on this detail, explaining that it was thus that Yitzkhak was the first to observe the *Minkhah* service. Similarly, the creation of the *Shakharit* service is ascribed to Avraham (*Bereishit* 19:27) and the *Ma'ariv/Evening* service is credited to Ya'akov (*Bereishit* 28:11), so by the middle of *Bereishit,* the foundation for Jewish worship has been put into place symbolically. (In reality, the pattern of prayer services corresponds to the pattern of sacrifice in the Temple in Jerusalem.)
- The story of Eliezer's finding and bringing back Rivkah is sixty-seven verses long, generally considered the longest self-contained narrative unit in the Torah.

HAFTARAH

The *haftarah* for this *parashah* tells of the last days of King David. Like Avraham, he is an elderly man who needs to establish a clear line of succession. Unlike Avraham, who still has a strong spark of sexual energy left to him, David is not intimate with Avishag the Shumanite woman who is found to minister to him. And unlike Avraham, whose passing of the Covenant to Yitzkhak is foreordained, David faces a power struggle between his sons *Shelomo/Solomon* and Adoniyah.

PARASHAT TOLEDOT

6th Torah portion, 6th in *Bereishit*
Bereishit 25:19–28:9 (106 verses)
Haftarah: Malakhi 1:1–2:7

ALIYOT

First/Rishon:	25:19–26:5
Second/Sheini:	26: 6–26:12
Third/Shlishi:	26:13–26:22
Fourth/Revi'i:	26:23–26:29
Fifth/Khamishi:	26:30–27:27
Sixth/Shishi:	27:28–28:4
Seventh/Shevi'i:	28:5–28:9
Maftir:	28:7–28:9

SYNOPSIS

After a difficult labor, Rivkah has twins, Eisav/Esau and Ya'akov. They grow up to be very different men. Yitzkhak's favorite, Eisav, is a hunter and man of the fields, but Ya'akov, favored by Rivkah, is bookish and quiet (in the Rabbinic tradition). Eisav sells Ya'akov his birthright in exchange for some lentil stew. King Avimelekh is led to think that Rivkah is Yitzkhak's sister and later finds out that she is really his wife. Later, Yitzkhak—now elderly and nearly blind—plans to bless Eisav, his firstborn. Rivkah and Ya'akov deceive Yitzkhak so that Ya'akov receives the blessing. Eisav threatens to kill Ya'akov, who then flees to Haran.

COMMENTARY

The Torah is not in the habit of delivering moral judgments on its protagonists or their behavior. As Nehama Leibowitz has written, "[A]s a rule, Holy Writ allows the events it describes and the actions of its characters to speak for themselves." Not to split hairs with a great scholar, there are often well-hidden clues to the attitude of the text to those actions, but you have to know where to look.

The deception Ya'akov and Rivkah practice on Yitzkhak may well be the classic example of reading between the biblical lines. To most modern readers, Ya'akov's behavior in these instances is disturbing at the least, morally questionable if not downright repugnant at worst.

There are two separate issues worth looking at here. First, how does Ya'akov view his own behavior? Second, how does the Torah view it and, by extension, what moral teaching does the text offer us as readers?

In fact, there are commentators who find buried in the text evidence of Ya'akov's own reluctance to participate in the fraud his mother has devised. Rabbi Jacob Zvi Mecklenberg, the nineteenth-century author whose *Ha'Ketav Ve'Ha'Kabbalah/The Written and the Oral Traditions* is an important analysis of Torah, finds a telling indication in the text's use of a single word in *Bereishit* 27:12.

Rabbi Mecklenberg notes that the Torah often uses the word *pen/lest* when the speaker does not wish an event to come to pass. He offers as one example the passage from *Bereishit* 3:22, in which God expresses his concern that Adam not eat from the Tree of Life "lest he put forth his hand and take also from the Tree of Life and eat and live forever." In *Bereishit* 41:4, as Mecklenberg points out, Ya'akov would have used this word and sentence construction had he not wanted Yitzkhak to find him out, but that's not what he says to his mother. Instead, Ya'akov uses the word *oolai/perhaps*, "perhaps my father will feel me," a word that is usually used when the speaker wants an event to take place.

Mecklenberg offers another piece of evidence on behalf of Ya'akov's conscience. When Avraham greeted the guests at his tent door at the outset of *parashat Vayeira*, he did so with great alacrity, expressed quite distinctly in the text: "He ran to meet them," and he urged Sarah to "quickly make ready three measures of flour." When Eliezer meets Rivkah at the well, we place great stock in the fact that she "hastened and let down her pitcher . . . and hastened and emptied her pitcher into the trough." But when Ya'akov brings the meat for his mother to prepare the stew for Yitzkhak, Mecklenberg writes, " 'He went and took and brought.' This indicates that he did not apply himself with any enthusiasm but reluctantly carried out his mother's behest."

What of the Torah's attitude toward Ya'akov?

Judge for yourself. Here is one of the Patriarchs, one of the Chosen of God, yet his life is one long string of miseries after he receives his father's blessing, the blessing that confirms him as the next in line to receive the Covenant. He is forced to flee for his life, as his own brother prepares to murder him. He works for seven years for his uncle, only to be cheated of the bride he was promised, then must work for another seven years to get the woman he wanted all along. His favored wife is barren for most of their marriage, then dies giving birth to her only child. Ya'akov isn't even able to bury her alongside his antecedents. The night before he meets his brother once more he wrestles with a mysterious figure who dislocates his hip and leaves him with a permanent limp. His favorite son is sold into slavery, vanishing without a trace from his life for twenty years. He finally dies in exile in a foreign country.

As Ya'akov tells Pharoah in one of the last *parashiyot* of *Bereishit*, his years have "been few and hard." Clearly, he is being punished for *something*.

What is he being punished for? Simply put, he is clearly the chosen son, chosen not by his mother, Rivkah, but by God to be the bearer of the Covenant. If there was any doubt, consider *Adonai*'s explanation when she asks why she is suffering so much: "Two nations are in your womb . . . and the elder shall serve the younger." The decision has already been made; for Rivkah and Ya'akov to force the issue is presumptuous in the extreme. It isn't even necessary for him to "buy" the birthright from Eisav, although this incident is proof of how ill-suited Eisav is for the role of Patriarch.

(The constant overturning of the established order of things, with older sons being supplanted by younger throughout the Torah, suggests one more way in which Judaism was a radical departure from the norms of the Ancient Near East. Moreover, each of the men thus defeated—Kayin, Yishmael, Eisav—is a hunter-gatherer, a man of "action." Obviously, Judaism posits a very different set of values.)

Yitzkhak cannot be entirely unaware of these issues, despite how much he favors Eisav. First, the Torah explicitly states that Eisav's marrying a Hittite woman pains *both* Rivkah and Yitzkhak. Midrash shows him teaching Ya'akov about the One God and the Covenant; Eisav can't be bothered with "book learning." Can he possibly be fooled by a ruse as ludicrously obvious as the one perpetrated by his wife and younger son?

Many commentators don't think so. W. G. Plaut notes that a single word from the real Eisav, *"Hineni/Here I am,"* is sufficient for his nearly blind father to recognize him, yet he exchanges many more words with Ya'akov without tumbling to the deception. Rashi drily observes that when Ya'akov, speaking as "Eisav," tells his father that God helped him to find a deer quickly to make the venison dish, the father "thought to himself, 'It is unusual for Eisav to mention God's Name.' " I would add, further, that a great hunter like Eisav would be loath to give credit for a quick kill—a sign of his singular prowess—to anyone else, even God, particularly before his father.

Perhaps Yitzkhak is once more the reluctant accomplice in a test of God, just as he was in the *Akeidah*. It is certainly worthy of note that Yitzkhak never reprimands Ya'akov or Rivkah even after their trick has been revealed to him. As Plaut says, Yitzkhak is the weak son of a strong father, of elderly doting parents, someone who never leaves Kina'an, unlike his father and mother, unlike his sons, grandchildren, and great-grandchildren. In our discussion of the *Akeidah*, I have argued that he is not a passive character, but he clearly is one who probably believes "to get along, go along" (particularly if God is the one with whom you want to get along). Significantly, he doesn't add anything to the tradition or the Covenant, while both Avraham and Ya'akov do, nor does he have his name changed, unlike his father and his son.

But he is important as the bearer of the tradition, the one who reopens the wells that Avraham dug, who revives their names—names that glorify God—and keeps their memory alive. If I may be permitted a slightly irreverent analogy, Yitzkhak is like a talented artist who works in an established tradition; he's not an innovator, a Charlie Parker or a D. W. Griffith, if you will, but without the men and women who carry on the tradition, the work of those geniuses would wither and die.

Still, it will fall to Ya'akov, tormented though he is, to father the sons who will found the Twelve Tribes, whose descendants will finally enter *Eretz Yisrael* and bring the Covenant to its realization. And for that to happen, he must leave the land first, as his father never did, leave it in order to return to it, only to leave it again in order to return one last time for burial.

ADDITIONAL NOTES

- If much of *Toledot* seems familiar, perhaps that's because, as Rashi points out, there are thirteen echoes of previous incidents from *Bereishit* in this portion: a barren wife; battling siblings; parental favoritism; the offering of game (Kayin and Hevel); Avimelekh being deceived about a wife/sister; fight over water rights; fear of intermarriage; a famine; directions from God; Yitzkhak becoming wealthy; digging of wells; a younger son supplanting his older brother; sending away for a wife from afar. Well, we all know there are only seven plots in literature (or twenty-five or thirty-nine or whatever number suits your fancy); the important thing is that all of these elements are found in a different configuration herein.

HAFTARAH

The prophetic passage associated with *parashat Toledot* opens with a consideration of God's love of the *Am Yisrael* compared with the Eternal's choice of Ya'akov over Eisav. It goes on to detail God's punishment of Eisav as progenitor of Edom, sworn historical enemy of Israel, then exhorts the Israelites to live up to the Covenant so that they may deserve their Chosen status.

PARASHAT VAYEITZEI

7th Torah portion, 7th in *Bereishit*
Bereishit 28:10–32:3 (148 verses)
Haftarah: Hosheya 12:13–14:10 (Sephardic: *Hosheya* 11:17–12:12)

ALIYOT

First / Rishon:	28:10–28:22
Second / Sheini:	29:1–29:17
Third / Shlishi:	29:18–30:13
Fourth / Revi'i:	30:14–30:27
Fifth / Khamishi:	30:28–31:16
Sixth / Shishi:	31:17–31:42
Seventh / Shevi'i:	31:43–32:3
Maftir:	32:1–32:3

SYNOPSIS

On the road to Haran, Ya'akov has a dream of angels going up and down a ladder at the top of which God stands. God blesses him in the dream. Ya'akov awakens, realizing the profound nature of this vision, and names the place Bet-El. Ya'akov works for his uncle, Lavan, seven years in order to marry Rakhel/Rachel, Lavan's younger daughter, but Lavan tricks Ya'akov into marrying Leah, her older sister. Ya'akov marries Rakhel but only after having to commit himself to seven more years of working for Lavan. Leah, Rakhel, and their maidservants, Bilhah and Zilpah, give birth to eleven sons and one daughter. Finally, God opens Rakhel's womb and she gives birth to Yosef. Ya'akov and his family leave Lavan's household with great wealth.

COMMENTARY

When he leaves his family home, Ya'akov has nothing but a staff and the clothes on his back. He has been stripped of everything but the birthright and his father's blessing, both of them obtained by questionable means. With his brother's threats ringing in his ears, he has been reduced to a primal state, as surely as Adam and Khavah on their expulsion from *Gan Eden*.

In such a state, he is a perfect receptacle for a vision of God. In *Panim Yafot,* an eighteenth-century commentary, it is written:

> When can man experience God's nearness? Only when he is suffused by "I don't know," when he himself knows that he does not know and does not pretend to have wisdom and insight.

Ya'akov has achieved this state the hard way; not only his material belongings but also his moral certainties and his family supports have been taken away. For all that his father may have taught him about God and the Covenant, he has experienced little of real life until now. The time is ripe.

As we have noted elsewhere, classical commentators have ascribed to Ya'akov the creation of the *Ma'ariv/Evening* service on the strength of this Torah portion. Their reasoning, which is a bit odd, ties directly into the incident of Ya'akov's dream, offering some sense of Ya'akov's troubled state of mind and how that contributes to this extraordinary moment, an event that Nahum Sarna has called the turning point in his entire life.

The second verse of this *parashah* begins, *"Va'yifga ba'makom va'yelen sham ki va ha'shemesh./He reached the place and spent the night there, because the sun had gone down."*

This seems pretty straightforward and it's hard to imagine how the rabbis derived from this the notion that Ya'akov created the evening prayers. Their interpretation pivots on a passage from Yirmiyahu in which the same verb, *fei-gimel-ayin,* appears in a very different context: *"V'al tifga bi/Do not entreat me."* You or I might read that *tifga* as "do not reach out to me" but for the sages of the Talmud, it was clearly a reference to prayer as a form of entreaty, supplication. As S. David Sperling points out, the rabbis also used ha'Mahom as a name for God; therefore one could read "va'yifga ba'makom . . . ki va shemesh" as "he entreated God because the sun had set. Rabbi Sperling explains that this is the reason the rabbis credit Ya'akov with "inventing" Ma'ariv.

But it is the second half of the sentence that Rashi finds particularly revealing, *"ki va ha'shemesh/because the sun went down."* Shouldn't it say "and the sun went down and he spent the night there"? Rashi asks. He replies that "the sun set suddenly for him, not at its appointed time so that he should stay *there* overnight."

Is this not, after all, a perfect metaphor for what has transpired in

Ya'akov's life so far? He has gone suddenly from being a comfortable son of a wealthy landowner and farmer to sleeping in the middle of the desert with a rock for a pillow and no discernible prospects. The sun of his prosperity has set unexpectedly, due as much to his own and his mother's machinations as anything else; but he is now on the road literally and figuratively to a new life, a new understanding of his place in a larger scheme of existence.

Understandably, when Ya'akov awakens from his dream, he is stirred but also frightened. He now understands that he has reached a place of "I don't know," a place for which nothing in his previous life could have prepared him. "God was in this place and I did not know it," he exclaims with a mixture of awe and terror—"va'yira/he was afraid"—shaking as his father shook when he realized he had given the blessing to the "wrong" son.

At this point, Ya'akov offers a vow to *Adonai*, the first vow in the Torah. The vow itself presents a problem that many commentators have grappled with. It appears that Ya'akov's vow is that he will take *Adonai* as his God "if *Elohim* will be with me and guard me on this path I am traveling and gives me bread to eat and clothes to wear and [allows me to] return to my father's house in peace." On its face, this is a pretty smarmy quid pro quo: "Okay, God, forgetting that you vouchsafed me a vision of Heaven, I've got a deal for you—you cover my back and I'll worship you." As Abravanel harshly writes, "His grandfather Avraham did not act this way, but was tried many times and withstood temptation."

Rashi argues that "And *Adonai* shall be my God" means that God's "Name shall be upon me from beginning to end, that God may not find anyone unfit among my descendants." Moreover, he believes, it is the building of an altar at Bet-El and tithing to God, the second half of the vow, that are dependent on his surviving his journey, not his adhering to the God of his grandfather and father.

Maybe so, but there is still something unseemly about the barely concealed horse-trading going on here, particularly after God has told Ya'akov in his dream that God will "guard you wherever you go and . . . bring you back to this land." In *Bereishit Rabbah* Rabbi Aibu is sufficiently troubled by this passage to suggest that the entire narrative order is wrong, that Ya'akov's vow *must* have come before the vision or else why would he have said, "If God will be with me"?

There are two other possible explanations, though. First, as Nehama

Leibowitz writes, God does not offer an unconditional promise to even the righteous. One must continue to live a righteous life to merit God's protection. Even the righteous stand on the brink of judgment at all times, depending on their behavior. As Nahmanides says, the "if" is not conditional on God's adhering to the bargain; "the reason for the condition, the 'if' qualification, was lest sin should intervene."

But there is another possible explanation, one offered by W. G. Plaut, that takes us back to the very heart of Ya'akov's situation. Plaut writes:

> . . . Jacob at Bethel is not yet the man of faith who wrestles with the angel. He is only at the beginning of his quest. This is his first experience with trial. Understandably in his anxiety he cries that he will do anything if only someone will help. Jacob, to be sure, does not deliver a "proper" prayer. He prays realistically, from the heart. His vow is his human response to the convenant that God has offered him. It is the expression of his experience, not of his philosophy, and in similar ways men have always prayed and promised when in moments of crisis God appears as the only help.

It is perhaps revealing that it will be at Bet-El, the scene of this first vow, that God will change Ya'akov's name to Yisrael, at last divesting him of the errors of his past and of the identification of his old name with sharp practices and double-dealing. (We'll look at that name change more closely in the discussion of the next *parashah*.) He is no longer the man who lay his head on a stone and dreamed of a Guardian and Rock, a God who would protect him. After countless trials and many years, he has become a man who has such a God protecting him and, more important, a man who has faith in and reverence for that God.

ADDITIONAL NOTES

- This *parashah* is unique in the Torah in one important respect. It is the only *parashah* written with no paragraph breaks whatsoever. The S'fat Emet, Rabbi Yehudah Aryeh Leib of Ger, suggests that the reason for this oddity is that Ya'akov never took his thoughts off *Eretz Yisrael*, his home, during his entire journey. Rivkah tells Ya'akov at the end of *Toledot* that he should stay with his uncle Lavan "a few days" and, the Gerer Rebbe says, those decades felt like only a few days to him because he never lost sight of his love for *Eretz Yisrael* and his family. Whether one accepts that explanation or not, the lack of paragraphing does give the *parashah* a certain breakneck feeling.

HAFTARAH

The *haftarah* associated with this Torah portion, drawn from the prophet Hosheya/Hosea, opens by recounting Ya'akov's flight to Aram, then continues its narrative by recalling Ephraim's flirtations with idolatry. Ultimately, it promises redemption to those who return to God and reject idols. Not coincidentally, the final eight verses of the *haftarah* are also the prophetic reading for *Shabbat Shuvah/the Sabbath of Returning,* the Sabbath that falls between Rosh Hashanah and Yom Kippur.

PARASHAT VAYISHLAKH

8th Torah portion, 8th in *Bereishit*
Bereishit 32:4–36:43 (154 verses)
Haftarah: Hosheya 11:7–12:12 (Sephardic: *Ovadyah* 1:1–21)

ALIYOT

First / Rishon:	32:4–32:13
Second / Sheini:	32:14–32:30
Third / Shlishi:	32:31–33:5
Fourth / Revi'i:	33:6–33:20
Fifth / Khamishi:	34:1–35:11
Sixth / Shishi:	35:12–36:19
Seventh / Shevi'i:	36:20–36:43
Maftir:	36:40–36:43

SYNOPSIS

Ya'akov prepares to meet Eisav. He sends his entire retinue across the River Yabok, then waits alone. There he wrestles with a "man," who changes Ya'akov's name to Yisrael. Ya'akov and Eisav meet and part peacefully, each going his separate way. Dinah is raped by Shekhem, the son of Hamor the Hivite, who was chief of the country. Ya'akov's sons Shimon and Levi take revenge by murdering all the males of the city of Shekhem, and Ya'akov's other sons join them in plundering the city. Rakhel dies giving birth to Binyamin and is buried in Ephrah, which is present-day Bethlehem. Yitzkhak dies and is buried in Khevron. Ya'akov's and Eisav's progeny are listed.

COMMENTARY

It is night at the River Yabok, the darkest and most disturbing night Ya'akov has known in the twenty years since he slept with only a stone for a pillow at the place he named Bet-El. Tonight, he is even more alone than he was then, even though he has two wives, two concubines, a dozen children, and great riches. He has sent everyone on ahead of him, for tonight he must wrestle with his conscience, his deepest fears, his worst vision of himself, a terrible preparation for the next day, when he will cross the

Yabok and face the brother he wronged two decades before, a brother who comes with a retinue of four hundred armed men.

But is it his conscience with which Ya'akov wrestles? Or a "man" or "angel" who appears to him and with whom he grapples until dawn?

As is so often the case with Torah, it depends on who is doing the reading. This is one of the most stirring moments in *Bereishit,* and it has produced a considerable amount of argument. *Bereishit Rabbah* suggests that the "man" is Satan, working as an emissary from Eisav. Maimonides characterizes the incident as a "prophetic vision" given to Ya'akov, but Nahmanides counters by asking how a prophetic vision could leave Ya'akov with a severely dislocated hip and a limp. Gersonides believes there may be a natural explanation for the entire event, that it could be a dream reflecting Ya'akov's terrible inner conflicts, and Abravanel nods in agreement, suggesting that the limp and the pains could be real but psychosomatically induced, a physical manifestation of that mental torment. Rashbam sees the injury as a Divine punishment for the way that Ya'akov deceived his brother and father.

Benno Jacob presents one of the most ingenious responses. A few verses earlier, Ya'akov has pleaded with God to prevent his brother from killing him. Yet that plea seemingly meets with no response. Then night falls, and the mysterious being appears and wrestles with Ya'akov, injuring him just before dawn breaks. That morning, when Ya'akov approaches his brother, what does Eisav see before him? A limping, battered cripple surrounded by women and children. He takes pity on Ya'akov and the two are reconciled.

Rabbi B. S. Jacobson offers another explanation. Rashi, he notes, says that Ya'akov made three kinds of preparation for meeting his brother; he prayed, he plied his adversary with gifts, and he readied his camp for combat. But we are left to wonder about another, more personal kind of preparation. Rabbi Jacobson surmises this was the time that Ya'akov finally reviewed the events of the past twenty years, for the first time considering the effects his behavior had on those around him. In short, as I said at the outset, he wrestled with his conscience. Yeshayahu Leibowitz depicts him struggling with his own sense of guilt and the knowledge that he cannot wholeheartedly fight against Eisav because his brother was indeed wronged. At the end of his wrestling with the stranger, who may be a dark emissary of his brother, he asks for a blessing, a fitting conclusion to the struggle that has gone on within his breast and an apt reversal of his and his brother's roles.

On another level, as some have written, the dark stranger with whom Ya'akov wrestles is *yetzer ha'ra* that resides within all men and women. Ya'akov has had this fight before but tonight he battles the dark side of his own personality to a standstill, and that truly merits a blessing—and the promise of a new name. (He is not renamed here, for reasons we will come to momentarily, but he is informed that his name will be changed.)

The old Ya'akov bore a name that, with its echo of the heel he had grabbed in the womb, was redolent of his conflict with Eisav. It is also a name that has associations with crookedness, unfair practices, and questionable behavior. (It will continue to carry those resonances. See *Hosheya* 12:4 and *Yirmiyahu/Jeremiah* 9:3.) In the incident at the river, all those negative connotations reverberate as the text puns on his name—*Ya'akov, Yabok, ya'avek/wrestled*. But when his name is changed, all those associations will be obliterated, to be replaced by a name—Yisrael—that proclaims him "one who has striven with God and man."

But before he can be given that new name, he must make his peace with Eisav. What does Eisav see when the two meet on the plains that morning? The clever, guileful Ya'akov of their youth is gone. He has been replaced by a man who is bruised and limping and dirty from a night of struggle, a man who prostrates himself on the ground seven times before his older brother. He sees a man who is, as Yeshayahu Leibowitz says, not obsequious but self-accusing, a man who knows that he wronged Eisav before. In a telling turn of phrase that Leibowitz calls a Freudian slip, Ya'akov tells Eisav, "Take my *blessing* that I have brought you" rather than "my gift." It is a powerful sort of closure for both brothers, one that ends with the best possible resolution: tears, forgiveness, reconciliation, although with a realization that they must go their separate ways, reuniting only for their father's funeral at the end of the *parashah*.

Poor Ya'akov. If only his troubles ended here, with the new certainty that his brother is no longer filled with the desire to kill him! Instead, in an episode that seems clearly calculated to show us that although he has finally foresworn tricky dealings, he hasn't been able to pass the wisdom gained by painful experience on to his sons.

The rape of Dinah would be a terrible tragedy under any circumstances, but how much more agonizing to Ya'akov that his sons Shimon and Levi avenged her *bi'mirmah/with guile*, as the text says, echoing Yitzkhak's accusation after the ruse secures Ya'akov the blessing, "Your brother came *with guile* and took your blessing." Ya'akov must feel as if he is trapped by his own past, by his very name, as if his sons have learned nothing. His rebuke to them, "You have muddied what was clear," that is, his reputation, indicates how painfully self-conscious he has become about his past transgressions. He will curse them again on his deathbed in even more explicit terms, a reminder that he chose reconciliation with Eisav rather than renewed conflict. Just as King David will be unable to build the Temple in Jerusalem because as a warrior he has shed too much blood (even though it may have been justified by events), Yisrael strips Shimon and Levi of their share of *Eretz Yisrael* for the massacre they perpetrated at Shekhem.

This Ya'akov has become a very different man. He has become Yisrael. Whoever he wrestled with that night at the Yabok, he emerged from that trial utterly transformed, someone who is, at last, a worthy bearer of the Covenant.

ADDITIONAL NOTES

- There is an unusal marking—dots over each letter—above the word *va'yishakayhu/and [Eisav] he kissed,* as it appears in the pointed version of the Torah. Some commentators suggest that this means that Eisav's kissing of his brother was insincere, but Rabbi Shimon bar Yokhai said it is a sign of how deeply felt the emotion of the moment was, that Eisav's compassion for his brother broke through any other feelings he may have had. The reasoning at work here is intriguing; the placement of a dot over a letter usually means that the letter is "erased," that is, nullified and therefore the placement of dots over all the letters of this word would mean that its meaning was reversed. Shimon bar Yokhai argues that knowing of Eisav's hatred for his brother, we might expect the kiss to be insincere, but since the dots modify the meaning of the word, they bespeak the degree to which his buried feelings of love for Ya'akov emerged in this intense moment.
- We will find ourselves at the River Yabok again in *B'midbar* 21:24; it is here that the Israelites will begin their campaign for the conquest of *Eretz Yisrael.*
- Although God changes Ya'akov's name to Yisrael toward the end of this portion, he will frequently continue to be referred to by his old name. In fact, Benno Jacob counts forty-five uses of Ya'akov and only thirty-four of Yisrael in reference to the Patriarch in the remainder of *Bereishit.* The aptly named Jacob finds a thematic distinction at work here, with

the uses of Ya'akov coming in the context of material or familial concerns, those of Yisrael in a spiritual context.

• *Vayishlakh* is the longest Torah portion in *Bereishit*, with 154 verses, the fourth-longest portion in the Torah.

HAFTARAH

This is one of those infrequent occasions on which the Ashkenazic and Sephardic *haftarot* are from completely different books. The Ashkenazic reading is taken from *Hosheya* and focuses on issues of reconciliation and change, as befits the accompaniment to the *parashah* in which Ya'akov makes peace with his brother. As Rabbi Howard Cohen has observed, the entire reading features "a strong sense of the potential harm and destruction that could be unleashed out of vengeful anger" unless Eisav and Yisrael make peace with each other. At the same time, the *haftarah* can be read as a caution against violent revenge such as when the sons of Yisrael take on Shekhem.

Intriguingly, the Sephardic reading takes an opposite point of view. Although it uses the reconciliation of Eisav and Yisrael as its starting point, it denounces the Edomites, the descendants of Eisav for their treatment of *B'nei Yisrael* at the time of the destruction of the First Temple, and Ovadyah calls for revenge against the sons of Eisav.

PARASHAT VAYEISHEV

9th Torah portion, 9th in *Bereishit*
Bereishit 37:1–40:23 (112 verses)
Haftarah: Amos 2:6–3:8

ALIYOT

First / Rishon:	37:1–37:11
Second / Sheini:	37:12–37:22
Third / Shlishi:	37:23–37:36
Fourth / Revi'i:	38:1–38:30
Fifth / Khamishi:	39:1–39:6
Sixth / Shishi:	39:7–39:23
Seventh / Shevi'i:	40:1–40:23
Maftir:	40:20–40:23

SYNOPSIS

Ya'akov shows he favors his son Yosef, whom the other brothers resent. Yosef has dreams of grandeur, which he shares rather too eagerly with his brothers and father. After Yosef's brothers have gone to tend the flocks in Shekhem, Ya'akov sends Yosef to report on them. After discussing what to do about him, the brothers decide against murdering Yosef but instead sell him into slavery. After he is shown Yosef's coat of many colors, which had been dipped in the blood of a kid, Ya'akov is led to believe that Yosef has been killed by a beast. Yosef is transported to Egypt. Tamar successively marries two of Yehudah's sons, each of whom dies. Yehudah does not permit her levirate marriage to his youngest son. She deceives Yehudah into impregnating her. God is with Yosef in Egypt until the wife of his master, Potiphar, accuses him of attempted rape, whereupon Yosef is imprisoned. In prison he is known for his integrity and trusted by the warden. He meets Pharoah's cupbearer and baker, both of whom are out of favor and under arrest, and successfully interprets their dreams.

COMMENTARY

Vayeishev introduces the story of Yosef and his brothers, one of the best-known and most detailed stories told in the Torah. Taking place over four Torah portions, this is the most detailed narrative episode in *Bereishit* and one of the most fully developed story lines in the Pentateuch. Not surprisingly, it is also one of the most acutely observed, filled with psychological detail of the sort not usually found in the Hebrew Bible.

To the extent that the remainder of *Bereishit* is Yosef's story, it is the story of his coming to maturity, his emotional and psychological growth, from snotty adolescent to self-assured adult. (At least, that is one of the traditional descriptions of his development; as we will see shortly, there are other ways of reading his journey.)

At seventeen, Yosef is still rather immature, a *na'ar/youth*, the Torah calls him. His brothers, all born in a six-year period in Paddan-Aram, are rather older than he and have been working for their father as shepherds, a hard job that is about as intellectually satisfying as being a file clerk. Yosef, the kid brother in every sense, is—as his mother was—clearly Ya'akov's favorite recipient of a special garment, the *k'tonet pasim* (which has been translated as everything from "coat of many colors" and "ornamented tunic" to "shirt with long sleeves"). And he's a tattletale, rushing home with news of his brothers' bad behavior.

Now the little brat comes to his brothers to tell them a dream about sheaves of wheat bowing down to him, a dream in which he clearly has bested all his elders. To make matters worse, he then tells his father of a similar dream in which he is clearly even ascendant over his parents. The Talmud says, "A person dreams at night that which he thinks about during the day."

Is it any wonder his brothers can't decide whether to kill him or merely sell him into slavery?*

Yosef's behavior, annoying though it is, admits of a couple of other possible readings. Yael Tzohar, a member of the Bible Department at Bar-Ilan University, believes that the seesawing fortunes of this young man are the result of his "naïveté and trust in people."

---

*Rabbi Joseph B. Soloveitchik offers a fascinating explanation for the brothers' extreme dismay at the telling of Yosef's first dream. Ha'Rav Soloveitchik notes that the brothers are shepherds, men who represent a traditional way of life and are resistant to change. They watch the flocks, use the milk and cheese for food, the skins and wool for clothes and possibly even for shelter. Their lives are contemplative (one might say downright dull, I think), and allow them time for meditation on God and Torah. Yosef, by contrast, sees a larger destiny looming, one that calls for a shift to agriculture—the sheaves—and technology. This is a more labor-intensive version of the world, and one fraught with change, a prospect that undoubtedly terrifies his older siblings.

Tzohar writes that Yosef just doesn't understand that his brothers are jealous of him, that they don't share his fascination with his dreams. He doesn't "get" that his father disapproves of the dream in which he is subordinated to his second-youngest son. Yosef can't conceive of someone lying about him as an act of revenge, as Potiphar's wife (called Zelikhah/Zeuleika in one midrash) does, or of the cupbearer forgetting his generosity in prison when restored to the throne room.

Tzohar may well be right. Yosef is certainly eager to please, a veritable puppy dog. When he is sent to Shekhem (an unlucky town for this family, to say the least) in search of his brothers, he doesn't give up after failing to find them. He asks a stranger (some midrashim say another angel) to direct him to where they are encamped. Rashi says of the encounter that follows, "He [Yosef] came with praise, rejoicing." Similarly, when he rejects the advances of Zelikhah, he explains to her that he can't betray her husband, not the answer she is seeking, and when he sees the cupbearer and baker in prison, he earnestly asks, "Why are you so downcast today?" And he actually listens to their answer.

Maybe this Yosef is not the spoiled brat he is usually taken for. Molly Rubenstein, a friend of the author, offers a shrewd insight into Yosef, an insight available to her as a teenager herself that most of us might miss. The Torah calls Yosef *ben liz'kunav/son of [Ya'akov's] aging years*. But the Talmud, she notes, understands the root *zayin-kof-nun* to apply to "one who acquires wisdom." Thus, she writes, "Joseph is the son of his father's wisdom; his father was his teacher." (Rashi states this even more radically, saying that "everything that happened to Ya'akov will happen to Yosef.")

Here Yosef has a relationship with his brothers that closely resembles Ya'akov's relationship with his own brother, Eisav. He's younger but much smarter, somewhat sheltered, and not as concerned with "manly" pursuits. And like his father before him, he has become alienated from his siblings by his father's actions.

Thus every act that we read as the product of arrogance is really a response to his emotional isolation, his overeagerness to make an impression on a world in which everyone in the family seems to be older, tougher, and not interested in him. Perhaps, as Rubenstein says, the prospect of being alone with his big brothers, no father watching over them, is actually thrilling to him. Perhaps, as she speculates, he is looking for love, for a companion, a soul mate. Indeed, it probably wouldn't be far from the mark to say that Yosef spends his entire life engaged in that search.

Tamar, too, is looking for love in all the wrong places, as the old song goes, when she stands at the crossroads disguised as a harlot so that she may solicit her father-in-law, Yehudah/Judah. The placement of this episode, which comes immediately after the sale of Yosef to a passing caravan, is superficially a mystery to the reader. Seen purely from the standpoint of narrative structure, it is nothing more than an attempt to extend the suspense surrounding Yosef's predicament, a cliff-hanger. But there are strong thematic links as well, not the least of them being Yehudah's central role in the selling of Yosef to the Midianites and eager participation in the deception the brothers employ against Ya'akov.

In fact, *Bereishit Rabbah* draws a couple of rather snide comparisons: "The Torah laughs at men. The Holy One said to Yehuda[h], 'You deceived your father with a kid of goats [when the brothers splashed its blood on Yosef's tunic]? Tamar will deceive you with a kid of goats.' " And when Tamar confronts Yehudah with his signet ring, cord of office, and staff, she says, "Examine these: whose are they," a deliberate echo of the brothers' request to Ya'akov, "Examine this: is it your son's tunic or not."

In fact, Tamar bests her father-in-law because he is unable to control his sexual urges. As Yehudah finally admits, "She is more righteous than I am." How appropriate then, that we immediately return to Yosef, now in Potiphar's house, where he is maturing in the hard school of slavery. This Yosef has begun to learn what it means to be a man of integrity, to be a *tzadik/righteous one,* as the Sages call him; he spurns the advances of his master's wife when the risk in doing so is probably greater than the rewards for giving in. As Nahum Sarna writes, "He is a slave and . . . sexual promiscuity was a perennial feature of all slave societies. Moreover, an ambitious person might well have considered that the importuning woman had presented him with a rare opportunity to advance his personal and selfish interest." Instead he rejects her and lands in prison for twelve years for his troubles.

Clearly this Yosef is no longer the self-regarding, brash figure of the opening of the story. He does the right thing for the right reasons. And he is utterly consistent in proclaiming that his abilities all come from God. It's a pretty paradox, this: in the story of Yosef, from which Divine intervention and miraculous rescue are conspicuously absent (after all, he spends an additional two years in prison before the cupbearer remembers him), we have the first protagonist in the Torah who attributes all his successes to the will of the Eternal One.

ADDITIONAL NOTES

• Levirate marriage—the marriage of a childless widow to the brother of her late husband, as in the case of Tamar—is a custom that, while common in the Ancient Near East, is probably baffling to most modern readers. Of course, it has its roots in the frequency of infant mortality in the premodern world and the need to continue the family line, two phenomena that haven't nearly the power today that they did even a century ago, although it may be found even today in tribal societies. At any rate, it was apparently a practice that predated Yehudah's dalliance with Tamar by centuries. Although it was and is permitted in the Torah, levirate marriage, *yibum* in Hebrew, was severely limited in Jewish law, applying only to the brother's wife and even then under highly circumscribed circumstances. Moreover, as Judith Antonelli points out, there was a way to avoid such a marriage, *halitzah,* a ritual that released the widow from the obligation to marry the dead man's brother. (For more information, see my *Essential Judaism* or Antonelli's *In the Image of God.*)

HAFTARAH

The connection between *parashat Vayeishev* and its accompanying prophetic reading from the *Sefer Amos* is slightly more oblique than most. Except for a passage that angrily proclaims, "Father and son go to the same girl and thereby profane My holy name," clearly an allusion to Yehudah and Tamar, there doesn't appear to be a specific reference to the story of Yosef and his brothers. But in his denunciation of the exploitation of the poor by his contemporaries and their relentless avarice, Amos clearly offers a parallel to the chilling decision by the brothers to sell their sibling into slavery.

PARASHAT MIKETZ

10th Torah portion, 10th in *Bereishit*
Bereishit 41:1–44:17 (146 verses)
Haftarah: Melakhim Aleph 3:15–4:1

ALIYOT
First / Rishon:	41:1–41:14
Second / Sheini:	41:15–41:38
Third / Shlishi:	41:39–41:52
Fourth / Revi'i:	41:53–42:18
Fifth / Khamishi:	42:19–43:15
Sixth / Shishi:	43:16–43:29
Seventh / Shevi'i:	43:30–44:17
Maftir:	44:14–44:17

SYNOPSIS

After languishing in prison for a dozen years, Yosef finally gets his opportunity. He successfully interprets Pharoah's two dreams and predicts seven years of prosperity followed by seven years of famine. Pharoah places Yosef in charge of food collection and distribution. Yosef marries Asenat, and they have two sons, Menasheh and Efraim/Ephraim. When Yosef's brothers come to Egypt to buy food during the famine, Yosef accuses them of spying. He holds Shimon hostage while the rest of the brothers return to Kina'an to retrieve Binyamin/Benjamin for him. The brothers return to Egypt with Binyamin and for more food. Yosef continues the test, this time falsely accusing Binyamin of stealing and declaring that Binyamin must remain his slave.

COMMENTARY

What is the source of Yosef's greatness, that he should be the one who follows Avraham, Yitzkhak, and Ya'akov as the bearer of God's Covenant? The key lies in two qualities that drive the narrative of *parashat Miketz* (and in part the ending of the previous portion as well), both of which can be seen in his skill as an interpreter of dreams.

The first, Rabbi Shlomo Riskin says, is that Yosef is "a powerful and careful listener." Thus, Riskin observes, he is able to hear the similar dreams of the cupbearer and the baker, yet discern subtle differences between their dreams and infer the very different fates that Pharoah has chosen for them.

Yosef's interpretation of Pharoah's dreams provides some outstanding examples of his listening skills at work. Dr. Masha Turner writes that it is by working out a clue provided by Pharoah himself that Yosef offers one of his most important insights into the dream of the cows.

> Pharoah describes his dream to Joseph, adding, "Looking at the [scrawny] cows, you could not possibly know that anything had been consumed by them" (Gen. 41:21). Joseph uses this comment as an important element in his interpretation: "Observing the effect of the famine when it comes, you could not possibly know that years of plenty had been experienced in the land previously" (Gen. 41:31).

There is a grammatical anomaly in Pharoah's description of the first dream that has not escaped other commentators. Pharoah says he is "standing by the river," but the Hebrew preposition used is *al/on*, that he was standing *on* the river. Think for a moment of the enormous importance of the Nile to Egypt. Without this vast river the country would be just so much more of the Sahara Desert. Not surprisingly, in ancient Egypt, the Nile was considered a deity. Yet in his dream, Pharoah finds himself standing atop this godlike entity. For Pharoah, as Yeshayahu Leibowitz writes, the river is the means to an end; for all his faith in Egypt's gods, he sees himself bestriding them, using them. And remember, too, that it is out of the Nile that the cows emerge in the dream that follows this description.

I point this out because it brings our attention to an important larger message to be gleaned from the repeated reference to dreams in *Bereishit*, particularly in the Yosef cycle. Dreams play a considerable, often pivotal role in *Bereishit*. The dreamers are many, both pagan and Hebrew. God comes to Avimelekh and Lavan in dreams to warn them not to harm the Eternal's chosen ones, Avraham and Ya'akov, respectively. *Adonai* appears to Avraham and Ya'akov in dreams to elaborate on the Covenant. But in the Yosef cycle, God does not appear in the dreams, and their meanings are somewhat more cryptic, and there are six dreams recounted in detail.

Yet, as Yeshayahu Leibowitz observes, no one dreams in the remaining four books of the Pentateuch!

It is as if God need not take the long way home to speak to the Hebrews when they are either in or on their way to *Eretz Yisrael*. Dreams do not play a part in the Hebrew Bible again until the *Sefer Danyel*, a book about Jews in exile in Babylon. Then, as with Yosef, it is a Jew who is a good listener, Danyel himself, who is called upon to interpret the dreams of a pagan monarch.

The pattern is obvious: a Jew in exile interprets dreams for a foreign king. (It is also worth noting that Avraham and Ya'akov have their dreams while on the road.) The historical basis is sound. Both Egypt and Babylon were cultures in which oneiromancy—telling the future from dreams—was a widely accepted practice. It is telling that Yosef doesn't offer an interpretation of his own dreams (although their meaning is transparent, as the outrage they provoke testifies).

But there is another point to be taken here, and it brings me back to the question of the source of Yosef's greatness. When Yosef offers to "read" the dreams of the cupbearer, baker, and Pharoah, he immediately disavows special skills—his ability to discern the meaning of their dreams comes from God. Elsewhere I have pointed to this statement as an indicator of his newly won maturity. But it also bespeaks another quality of Yosef's, one that is equally important in keeping him—and his family—intact, a quality that will enable the Jews as a people to survive four centuries of bondage in Egypt.

Although he is entirely comfortable in Egyptian society, dressing like an Egyptian, speaking the language fluently, Yosef maintains his Hebrew identity throughout his long time in exile. He recognizes his brothers even though they do not recognize him. He gives his sons Hebrew names; midrash says that the reason the Jews survived slavery in Egypt is that they kept their names. (There is even a strong midrashic tradition that says his wife Asenat is not an Egyptian either but the daughter of Dinah.) In short, he remains a Hebrew.

Most of all, he firmly believes, as he tells his brothers when he finally reveals himself, that his exile in Egypt had a larger purpose, to preserve the family that will become the Twelve Tribes of Israel. The strength of his sense of Hebrew identity and the willpower to maintain it, to raise his sons with it despite being in an entirely Egyptian society, that is the quality that makes him a fitting recipient of the Covenant.

ADDITIONAL NOTES

• In an observant Jewish home, part of the Friday night rituals for welcoming the Sabbath are the blessing of the children. At that time, Jewish boys are exhorted to be "like Efraim and Menasheh," Yosef's two sons. (Girls are told to be like the Matriarchs, whose merit is obvious to us.) Yet from the text of this *parashah* it is unclear what makes these two so important other than their parentage. The sages taught that despite having been raised as virtually the only Jewish children in Egypt, Efraim and Menasheh were loyal to the teachings of their father's faith, something a Jewish boy should strive to emulate.

HAFTARAH

Both *parashat Miketz* and its *haftarah* pivot on the dreams of great royal personages, dreams that will have a powerful effect on the nations they rule. However, where Pharoah needs Yosef to interpret his dreams, Shelomo/Solomon understands his as the logical extension of the promises of the Covenant so often vouchsafed to his ancestors in the same form. He is then faced with the famous dilemma of the two women who both claim the same infant; like Yosef counseling Pharoah, Shelomo exercises great wisdom in finding a solution that is both just and workable.

PARASHAT VAYIGASH

11th Torah portion, 11th in *Bereishit*
Bereishit 44:18–47:27 (106 verses)
Haftarah: Yekhezkel 37:15–28

ALIYOT

First / Rishon:	44:18–44:30
Second / Sheini:	44:31–45:7
Third / Shlishi:	45:8–45:18
Fourth / Revi'i:	45:19–45:27
Fifth / Khamishi:	45:28–46:27
Sixth / Shishi:	46:28–47:10
Seventh / Shevi'i:	47:11–47:27
Maftir:	47:25–47:27

SYNOPSIS

Yehudah pleads with Yosef to free Binyamin and offers himself as a replacement. Yosef reveals himself to his brothers and forgives them for selling him into slavery. Although the famine still rages, Pharoah invites Yosef's family to "live off the fat of the land." Ya'akov learns that Yosef is still alive and, with God's blessing, goes to Egypt. Pharoah permits Yosef's family to settle in Goshen. Pharoah then meets with Ya'akov. With the famine increasing, Yosef designs a plan for the Egyptians to trade their livestock and land for food. The Israelites thrive in Egypt.

COMMENTARY

It is late at night in Kina'an. Ya'akov is preparing for what will be the last journey of his lifetime, to join his long-lost son Yosef in Egypt. The next time he travels it will be as a corpse for burial back in Kina'an.

Unlike his grandfather Avraham, Ya'akov is not one of those people who travels easily, which is unfortunate because his life has been a restless and circuitous journey, from Kina'an to Haran, Haran back to Kina'an, and now Kina'an to Egypt. He has been forced into exile out of fear of his brother's wrath, returned home to reclaim the birthright he had taken possession of by means fair or foul, been forced once more into exile by famine and the desire to see Yosef before he dies.

And he is tormented once again by the uneasy night that precedes a long and dangerous journey.

Adonai appears to Ya'akov *b'marot ha'lailah/in night visions* and says to the last patriarch:

> I am God—the God of your father. Have no fear of descending to Egypt, for I shall establish you as a great nation there. I shall descend with you to Egypt, and I shall also surely bring you up; and Yosef shall place his hand on your eyes.

And Ya'akov arises—he wakes up from his night vision—and he departs from his home one last time.

Of course, this is not the first time God has reminded Ya'akov of the promise of the Covenant with Avraham. It seems like Ya'akov needs constant reassurance, like the child who constantly asks, "You do love me, don't you?" At some point, you begin to fight the urge to say, "Yes, I love you dammit, now shut up!"

In fact, *Adonai* repeats some version of the Covenant to Ya'akov only three times, each time at night, in a vision or a dream. The first time is during the first night on the road to Haran, at Bet-El, when Ya'akov lies down, his head uneasily pillowed on a stone. God speaks to him of the greatness that awaits his family in generations, ages to come.

The second time occurs when Ya'akov has returned from Paddan-Aram, having built the altar at Bet-El. God appears to Ya'akov and changes his name to Yisrael, and repeats in even more exalted terms the Convenant—"a nation and a congregation shall issue from your loins." Shortly thereafter, Rakhel will give birth to Binyamin and die.

And now, on the verge of a final emotionally wrenching reunion, Ya'akov is visited one last time by God, who reminds him he is watched over, that nothing will happen to him as long as the Eternal One guards him. As Nahum Sarna points out, the tenor of this visit is somewhat different from the previous ones, "transforming the descent into Egypt from a family visit into an event of national significance, which has its preordained place in God's scheme of things." Indeed, as W. G. Plaut points out, this turning point in the history of the Hebrews, the transfer of an entire people to Egypt, is the culmination of a running theme of rescue and deliverance, moved from the personal sphere (Lot being the most obvious example) to the historical/political.

But why does God keep appearing to Ya'akov? Why is it necessary?

Even in the terrifying night before he meets his brother, Eisav, for the first time in some twenty years, Ya'akov is confronted by a Divine messenger, the strange man with whom he wrestles beside the River Yabok.

Look at these four events. In a terrible lifetime—so terrible that elsewhere in this Torah portion Ya'akov tells Pharoah, "Few and bad have been the years of my life"—God has appeared to him just before some of the most terrible moments: when he is forced to abandon his parents and home, when he is about to face his brother's wrath and possibly a violent death, just before he loses his beloved wife, and now, on the verge of a final journey, as the light of his eyes is growing dimmer.

A parable:

A mother and father have three children. One is smart, self-reliant, capable. Another is quiet, unassuming, but dedicated to study. The third is sickly of body and mind. Which child will get the most attention from his parents? Of course, the one whose need is greatest, the one who is least able to do for himself.

Of the three Patriarchs Ya'akov fits that description best, whether by circumstance or character. And God, like a good parent, comes to Ya'akov at night when a frightened child cries out in terror of the darkness. The darkness is the uncertain future, the tormented past, the pain of remembering one's own failings—and Ya'akov has plenty to remember—and one's losses—and he has plenty of those, too.

And in the darkness, he is given something to cling to, an anchor whose sureness is incontrovertible—the One called *Tzur Yisrael*—truly the Mountain of Israel.

ADDITIONAL NOTES

- Yehudah's speech to Yosef is the longest oration reported verbatim in *Bereishit*, the entirety of chapter 44.

- In October 1960, Pope John XXIII (born Giuseppe Roncalli) met with a group of 130 Jewish leaders from around the world. He opened his remarks, "I am your brother Joseph."

- Although anti-Semites often refer to Yosef's manipulation of the famine to disenfranchise on behalf of Pharoah as an example of Jewish perfidy, the 20 percent rental payment to the throne was actually considerably less onerous than that demanded by other contemporary monarchs. Indeed, it only doubles the regular tax, which was 10 percent. Plaut notes that in Syria, Jews were required to pay one-third of their seed and half of their fruit to the Crown. (The situation also anticipates the use of Jewish bureaucrats as tax collectors in places like Poland to deflect hatred for the ruling class onto the Jews for policies that those middlemen had no say in.)

HAFTARAH

The prophet Yekhezkel/Ezekiel is a master of vivid allegory. In the *haftarah* to this portion, he invokes the reunification of the sons of Ya'akov (as depicted in the opening section of *parashat Vayigash*) as a symbol of the reunion of the divided kingdoms of Israel.

PARASHAT VAYEKHI

12th Torah portion, 12th and last in *Bereishit*
Bereishit 47:28–50:26 (85 verses)
Haftarah: Melakhim Aleph 2:1–12

ALIYOT
First / Rishon:	47:28–48:9
Second / Sheini:	48:10–48:16
Third / Shlishi:	48:17–48:22
Fourth / Revi'i:	49:1–49:18
Fifth / Khamishi:	49:19–49:26
Sixth / Shishi:	49:27–50:20
Seventh / Shevi'i:	50:21–50:26
Maftir:	50:23–50:26

SYNOPSIS

Ya'akov blesses his grandchildren Efraim and Menasheh, reversing his hands at the last moment to give the greater blessing to the younger son. Ya'akov's twelve sons gather around his deathbed, and each receives an evaluation and a prediction of his future. Yosef mourns his father's death and has Ya'akov embalmed. Ya'akov is buried in Khevron in the cave of the field of the Makhpelah in the land of Kina'an. Yosef assures his concerned brothers that he has forgiven them and promises to care for them and their families. Just before he dies, Yosef tells his brothers that God will return them to the Land that God promised to the patriarchs. *B'nei Yisrael* promise Yosef that they will take his bones with them when they leave Egypt.

COMMENTARY

The story of Yosef is all but over. The Patriarchal epic is drawing to a close, but there is still some unfinished business and it serves as a logical lead-in to the main story of the Torah, the exile and redemption of the Israelites, the giving of the Torah, and the fulfillment of God's promise of the "land flowing with milk and honey." But somewhere at the end of that long road, someone will have to rule *Eretz Yisrael*.

What remains to be done, then, is to assign the tasks that are incumbent on an autonomous nation, including choosing a ruler. The heart of this *parashah* consists of the blessings and curses that Ya'akov bestows on his sons, a lengthy passage that is often cryptic and sometimes downright baffling. But Abravanel offers an explanation of this extraordinary flourish of rhetoric that makes some sense of a difficult text. There are four reasons that Ya'akov calls together his sons, Abravanel says: (a) to bestow blessings on them; (b) to rebuke those who have transgressed; (c) to foretell the future of the family and, by extension, the tribes of Israel; and (d) to bequeath to the sons (and the tribes that will spring from their loins) specific parts of *Eretz Yisrael*.

Given the degree to which this speech is about the future rather than the present or past, it should be no surprise that, as Abravanel reads it, Ya'akov's larger purpose is to avert future quarrels over the kingship of Israel by explaining to the twelve sons which of their virtues and deficiencies leaves them ill- or well-suited for the throne. Only one can rule, and Ya'akov's final act—other than securing Yosef's promise that he will be reunited with Avraham, Sarah, Yitzkhak, and Rivkah in the cave of Makhpelah—is to decide whose line will have that distinction.

It is worth noting at the outset that the only two sons to whom Ya'akov speaks directly are Yehudah and Yosef. The rest are described in the third person, often in most unflattering terms. But Yosef, the favorite, and Yehudah, who is chosen to rule, are set apart rhetorically by direct address.

What does Ya'akov see as the failings of the sons who are not fit to rule? Re'uven is "superior in rank and . . . power" and as the firstborn should by rights be the chosen one—but by now we know that being the firstborn counts for nothing in this new God-driven world. For all his possibilities, Re'uven is as "unstable as water," and therefore unfit to rule. Shimon and Levi are rebuked even more stingingly than before for the massacre at Shekhem, told that they are brothers in violence; not only will they not rule but, unlike their other brothers, they are to be denied a portion of *Eretz Yisrael* (and, indeed, the Levites will be forbidden from owning land as part of their dedication to the priestly caste).

It would seem at first glance that Yehudah's dalliance with Tamar might have disqualifed him from the kingship, but in some ways it is his finest moment. After all, he publicly acknowledged his sin and took responsibility for it in a way that few of the characters in *Bereishit* do. *Bereishit*

Rabbah says that "because you did confess, your brothers shall praise you in this world and the world to come." One senses that it is the respect that he has merited from his brothers that gives Yehudah the right to be father of kings.

Conversely, although their hatred of Yosef is perhaps unfair, it is precisely that hatred that leaves the favorite son unfit for monarchy. Yosef's blessing is the longest of the twelve sons', indicative of his enormous importance vis-à-vis the Covenant and of his continuing role as Ya'akov's favorite but, significantly, his brothers "made him bitter and quarreled with him." As much as Ya'akov loves Yosef, he cannot help but know that a king without the love or, at the least, the support of his people has no chance of ruling successfully or well.

The remainder of the sons are clearly totally incapable of ruling a nation. Indeed, it seems at times as if Ya'akov feels they are incapable of ruling themselves. Zevulun will be a successful merchant, but a merchant cannot be a king in a warrior's world; Yisakhar is too passive and easygoing—"he saw that rest is good;" Dan will be a good judge (a nice pun on his name—the Hebrew for "he will judge" is *yadin*) but that requires a different set of qualities from ruling; Gad is too reckless, exposing himself to capture by his enemies; Ashur is a farmer, not a leader; Naftali is a born diplomat, shrewd and smooth-tongued, but he is a courtier by temperament, a follower; Binyamin is too impetuous, as one might expect of the youngest son.

Clearly, if one accepts Ya'akov's judgments and analyses of his sons, Yehudah is the best-suited to be king. But a family of seventy is not a nation. There remains one important task to be done, and Ya'akov implies what that is when he calls the sons together.

The Torah uses words sparingly. The sages say that there are no superfluous words in a Holy text. So why does Ya'akov gather his sons using the verbs *hei'asfu* and *hikavtzu*, which are nearly identical in meaning, both essentially saying "gather around" or "get yourselves together."

Rabbi Ya'akov Kaminetsky writes that, although each of the brothers received an individualized blessing (except for Shimon and Levi, who were yoked together in shared infamy), it was imperative that they realize that they could only function successfully as a unit, community, in order to prevail over the forces arrayed against them.

As Rabbi Lawrence Littlestone writes, "Although each had his own destiny and purpose, they were part of a much larger project. Judah would be destined for kingship, Levi for priesthood, Zebulun for the world of commerce and so on. Only when it was recognized that they were more than mere individuals—partners in a large unit called *Klal Yisrael* [the Community of Israel]—would they reach their full, joint potential."

Until now, the Torah has told the story of this one family, through several generations, the Chosen Ones of God. Now, they must begin the hard work of forging a nation from these beginnings.

The prologue is over. Now the story of *Am Yisrael*—the central story of the Torah—can begin.

KHAZAK, KHAZAK, V'NITK KHAZEIK.

ADDITIONAL NOTES

- This is the only *parashah* that begins in the middle of a paragraph in the *sefer Torah*.
- The blessing that Ya'akov bestows in *Bereishit* 48:16 is recited every night by observant Jews as part of the "bedtime" *Sh'ma*.
- Ya'akov and Yosef are the only two Hebrews in the Torah who are embalmed. Although embalming is counter to Jewish practice, in their cases exigent circumstances intervened; in order to bury them in *Eretz Yisrael*, it would be necessary to transport their remains a great distance and, in Yosef's case, centuries after his death.

HAFTARAH

Just as *parashat Vayekhi* encompasses the last will and testament of Ya'akov, the *haftarah* that accompanies it includes the final will of David. And like Ya'akov, he is primarily concerned that his son, in this case Shelomo, follow the Torah and ensure the future of the Jewish people. Both the Torah portion and the *haftarah* close with the death of a great leader, Yosef and David, respectively.

SEFER SHEMOT/THE BOOK OF EXODUS

Second book of the Torah
11 *parashiyot*
40 chapters, 1,210 verses

With *Sefer Shemot* the Torah begins the story that will occupy the remainder of its pages, that of the creation of a unified nation of Israelites and, more important, their unification as a nation living under God's *mitzvot*. Although there is no gainsaying the importance of the first book of the Torah, it is here that the special relationship between God and Israel comes to fruition and achieves a degree of realization only hinted at in *Bereishit*. As we will see in *parashat Yitro*, God will finally ask for something very specific in return for Divine protection, guidance, and redemption.

What has God given the Israelites? In the first four *parashiyot*, the Creator liberates them from slavery in Egypt and destroys Pharoah and the Egyptian army. After that, the Almighty restates the Covenant made with the Patriarchs but in much more detail, with more specificity. What God asks in return is adherence to the *mitzvot*, usually translated as "commandments." The remainder of *Shemot* consists largely of a statement of some of the *mitzvot* and the story of the building of the *Mishkan* in which the Tablets of the Law are carried.

This last theme, which occupies all or part of four Torah portions, baffles many contemporary readers. Why are we buried under the details of this construction project? The answer is contained in the process of its realization. Before Sinai, the Israelites are a rabble who will dedicate themselves to God little more than a mob. It is imperative that they be welded into a nation, that a project bring them together in a positive way (unlike the flight from Egypt, which can be ascribed to the survival instinct pure and simple). With its lengthy lists of donations and assigned labors, the recounting of the building of the *Mishkan* shows us a community in formation, a group of people who find themselves systematically dedicated to a shared goal of greater import than their own survival.

At the same time, it is a project that will further another theme of the remainder of the Torah, a theme that emerges only after the story of the Patriarchs is complete—the differentiation and separation of the Hebrews from their pagan neighbors. Although there is a clear distinction made in *Bereishit* between those who believe in *Adonai* and those who worship many gods (and/or idols), they coexist more or less peacefully.* With the story of the Exodus from Egypt, that distinction breaks into open hostility and that conflict will be a significant theme throughout the remainder of the Torah. As we will see later, many of the laws given at Sinai exist primarily to set the Israelites apart from those who do not accept *Adonai*. And the *Mishkan* is a highly visible signifier of that separation, a vivid reminder that this is a people who worship a God, who follow the teachings and laws of a Deity who is not the god(s) of their neighbors.

---

*There are many midrashim about Avraham in particular that focus on his conflict with idolators, but there is nothing of this sort in *Sefer Bereishit*.

PARASHAT SHEMOT

13th Torah portion, 1st in *Shemot*
Shemot 1:1–6:1 (124 verses)
Haftarah: Yeshayahu 27:6–28:13; 29:22–23 (Sephardic: *Yirmiyahu*
   1:1–2:3)

ALIYOT

First / Rishon:	1:1–1:17
Second / Sheini:	1:18–2:10
Third / Shlishi:	2:11–2:25
Fourth / Revi'i:	3:1–3:15
Fifth / Khamishi:	3:16–4:17
Sixth / Shishi:	4:18–4:31
Seventh / Shevi'i:	5:1–6:1
Maftir:	5:22–6:1

SYNOPSIS

The new king of Egypt makes slaves of the Hebrews and orders their
male children to be drowned in the Nile River. A Levite woman places her
son, Moshe / Moses, in a basket on the Nile, where he is found by the
daughter of Pharoah and raised in Pharoah's house. Moshe kills an Egyptian taskmaster who was abusing a Hebrew slave. Discovering that his act
was seen, he flees to Midian. Moshe marries Tzipporah, daughter of Yitro,
a priest of Midian. They have sons named Gershom and Eliezer
(although the latter is not introduced by name until chapter 18). God
appears to Moshe from a burning bush and commissions him to free
the Israelites from Egypt. Moshe and Aharon / Aaron request permission
from Pharoah for the Israelites to celebrate a festival in the wilderness.
Pharoah refuses and makes life even harder for the Israelites.

COMMENTARY

The second book of the Torah begins with the letter *vav*, the Hebrew
prefix meaning "and."

"And these are the names . . ."

Of course in a *sefer Torah* there is little indication of a new story beginning, just a few lines left blank. The physically continuous and contiguous placement of the text is an inescapable reminder that this is all one grand story, one that we will repeat many more times. (One more excellent reason, by the way, for reading the Torah from scrolls: their roundness reminds us of the cyclical nature of the reading as ritual.)

By beginning this new phase of the Torah in medias res—"And these are the names"—the interconnectedness of this story to what has gone before is obvious, despite the passage of some four centuries of historical time. (It is worth noting that the next two books, *Vayikra* and *B'midbar*, also begin "And." *Devarim*, the final book of the Torah, does not, but it begins with a very clear echo of the closing line of the previous book.)

As we have seen throughout *Bereishit*, the Torah places great stock in the giving of names to persons, places, and things. So the fact that the primary story in this book—the Exile and Redemption of *B'nei Yisrael* and the Giving of the Law—is called *Shemot* and begins with a genealogy may not come as a surprise. If nothing else, we are by now familiar with the structural arc of death-burial-genealogy that recurs several times in the previous book. Names, not surprisingly, play a pivotal role in *Sefer Shemot* and *parashat Shemot*.

As we have already seen repeatedly, both names and the act of naming have great power. A name carries within it something of the essence—from the Latin *esse/to be*—the core being of the person, place, animal, or thing named. Significantly, even the names by which God is known are linked to the essential nature of the Eternal (in both senses of the word *essential*). The revealed name of God—*yud-he-vav-he, Yahweh*—contains within it the verb root for "to be," *he-yud-he*. We'll return to this point momentarily.

Within this Torah portion the use of names is singularly odd. On the one hand, the opening genealogy repeats the names of the Patriarchal line, albeit in the order in which they appeared in *Bereishit* 35:23. As Rabbi Matis Weinberg writes, "We need to see the distinctive individuality of the founding generation, people we know by *name*, within the teeming mass of unidentified men and women who form the exploding population of the nascent nation of Yisrael."

Yet, while we are told at length about the exploding population of the Israelites, the demographic phenomenon that leaves Pharoah feeling so threatened, we are not told the names of any of the Israelites until the naming of Moshe. (There are two notable exceptions that we will consider in a moment.) And Moshe is given his name by an (unnamed) Egyptian princess. One could argue, undoubtedly with considerable justice, that this merely is indicative of the folkloric nature of the story and its transmission. However, considering the importance of names throughout *Bereishit* and the title of this book, it does seem peculiar.

The exceptions, of course, are the heroic midwives Shifrah and Puah. There is considerable argument among classical commentators as to who these women are. When the text calls them "Hebrew midwives," does it mean that they are midwives of Hebrew extraction or midwives to the Hebrews? Depends on whose interpretation you're reading. There is a considerable body of midrashic writing that identifies them as Yoheved, the mother of Moshe and Aharon, and Miriam, their sister and a prophetess in her own right. The simple fact that they are identified by name—whether those are their names or their pseudonyms—makes them stand out in this context as sharply as their heroism.

Then there is the question of the naming of Moshe. According to biblical folk etymology, his name is derived from the Hebrew verb meaning "to draw out or from." That he is so named by an Egyptian princess may be seen as ironic or as testimony to her compassion for the oppressed Israelites. In proper Hebrew, she should have named him *Mashui/I have drawn him out,* but Sforno says she named him Moshe—the future tense—because he will draw the Hebrew people out of bondage in Egypt.

As Richard Elliott Friedman points out, people tend to misremember the order of this story: the princess does not name him when she pulls him from the Nile but, rather, when he is grown. What did they call him while he was growing up in the palace? His parents must have given him a Hebrew name before setting him adrift in the basket on the Nile (although he certainly couldn't have been identified by that name while in Pharoah's palace), but we are never told that name. In *Vayikra Rabbah* we are told that "the Children of Israel were redeemed from Egypt because they would not change their names" to Egyptian ones. Yet we are pointedly not told his previous name.

Professor Elazar Tuito offers an interesting explanation:

. . . As the Torah generally ascribes great importance to the names given to people and to the meaning of the names, we should understand that the Bible's disregard of any previous names of Moses and the names of all the other people involved in the saga intends to lay great emphasis on the symbolism of the name "Moses" and the significance of the act of naming itself. This baby had previous Hebrew names (cf. *Yalkut Shimoni*, Exodus 166); his parents and sister had names, of course; but all these names belong to the past, to the period of exile. The Bible wishes to make us sense the future and the approaching redemption; this is accomplished by calling the person destined to liberate the Israelites by a name which symbolizes the future liberation and redemption: Moses is the man destined to draw his people out of slavery and exile, just as he was drawn out from the water and saved.

Finally there is the extraordinary moment when Moshe, speaking to God manifested through the burning bush, asks the Almighty what name he should give when the Israelites ask who has sent him. God replies, "*Eyeh Asher Eyeh.*" As noted before, the name by which God is identified, *yud-he-vav-he / YHVH*, very likely is related to the verb meaning "to be," but here the Holy One makes the relationship much more specific—*Eyeh Asher Eyeh* translates roughly as "I am what I am." Or "I am what I will be." Or "I will be what I am." Or "I will be what I will be." Given the way in which tense is expressed with this Hebrew verb, any and all of these may be correct.

As Yeshayahu Leibowitz rightly asks, what difference does tense make to a God in whose "eyes a thousand years are but a moment"? Simply put, God is pure essence, pure being, timeless and infinite. "I am what I am" or "I am what I will be" or "I will be what I am" or "I will be what I will be"—it simply doesn't matter. God precedes Creation and exists after everything else is gone; the kabbalists called the Holy One *Ein Sof—the One who is Without End*. God is nowhere else in the entire Torah called *Eyeh Asher Eyeh*—it seems to be a secret shared with Moshe alone, much as Moshe is the only human to glimpse even the Supernal Presence—but none of the names by which the Deity is called is more fitting. No further explanation is given, none would do. As many Torah scholars have noted, the Patriarchs had only glimpses of God's true essence; it is Moshe to whom it will be revealed in full—to the extent that any human could comprehend it—and Moshe who will make it manifest to *B'nei Yisrael* and, through the Torah, the world.

ADDITIONAL NOTES

- An interesting and telling linguistic detail from this Torah portion: the word *teivah*, used for the basket in which Moshe is cast adrift on the

Nile, is used in only one other place in the Torah. It is the word used to designate the ship on which Noakh, his family, and the creatures he has saved wait out the Flood. Thus, in each case, the *teivah* is the vehicle—literally—through which the Covenant between God and a segment of humanity is preserved in the face of possible annihilation.

HAFTARAH

Both the Ashkenazic *haftarah*, drawn from *Sefer Yishayahu*, and its Sephardic counterpart from *Sefer Yirmiyahu*, tell of the eventual redemption of the house of Ya'akov after lengthy trials. As such, they relate rather obviously to the *parashah*, in which the process of redemption from bondage has begun.

PARASHAT VAYEIRA

14th Torah portion, 2nd in *Shemot*
Shemot 6:2–9:35 (121 verses)
Haftarah: Yekhezkel 28:25–29:21

ALIYOT

First / Rishon:	6:2–6:13
Second / Sheini:	6:14–6:28
Third / Shlishi:	6:29–7:7
Fourth / Revi'i:	7–8:6
Fifth / Khamishi:	8:7–8:18
Sixth / Shishi:	8:19–9:16
Seventh / Shevi'i:	9:17–9:35
Maftir:	9:33–9:35

SYNOPSIS

Despite God's message that they will be redeemed from slavery, the Israelites' spirits remain crushed. God instructs Moshe and Aharon to deliver the Israelites from the land of Egypt. The genealogy of Re'uven, Shimon, Levi, and their descendants is recorded. Moshe and Aharon perform a miracle with a snake and relate to Pharoah God's message to let the Israelites leave Egypt. God brings down the first seven plagues on Egypt: blood, frogs, lice, insects, animal disease, boils, and hail. After each episode, Pharoah reneges on his offer to let the Israelites leave Egypt to worship God.

COMMENTARY

The ten plagues are the most sustained manifestion of Divine wrath since the Flood, way back in *parashat Noakh*, an awesome display of the power of the Creator. What are we to make of this display of God's rage? Pharoah's role in this symphony of destruction is pivotal, but we will discuss it in the context of *parashat Bo*. For now let's look at the plagues themselves (which are completed in the following Torah portion, *Bo*).

One could offer a series of logical explanations for the ten plagues. In fact, contemporary scholar Greta Hort did so in the late 1950s in a

German academic journal. Briefly, Hort's theory, as reported by Nahum Sarna, is that the Nile basin was the recipient of a heavy runoff from more intense rains than usual in the African Highlands that feed it, with the result that the river overflowed its banks with devastating results, in the process discharging unusual concentrations of red sediment, giving the river the appearance of blood. This turn of events unbalanced the ecosystem of the Nile basin temporarily, causing an overabundance of microscopic organisms and bacteria, killing the fish. The dead fish, in turn, drove the frogs inland, where they would have died from bacteria passed from the fish. The third plague could be explained as an intensification of the seasonal attacks of mosquitoes, amplified by the Nile's flooding. Hort identifies the fourth plague as a particularly nasty blood-sucking fly endemic to the region. The death of the cattle would be caused by their pasturing where the bacteria that killed the fish and frogs were present as the waters of the Nile receded.

And so on, through the first nine plagues. The tenth plague, the death of the Egyptian firstborn, could, one supposes, be explained as an exaggerated report of a generalized outbreak of some deadly virus, but Hort apparently chose not to seek a "rational" explanation for this final plague, accepting the idea that such a devastation could only be Divine intervention.

This is all very logical, but rather unsatisfying (and probably unconvincing, even if you've read a great deal of current literature on the domino effects engendered by more recent ecological misbehavior by mankind). Indeed, to many, such explanations are pointless. The plagues are not historical events but, as Sarna calls them, theological ones.

Interestingly, the Torah does not call them miracles, as we noted in Chapter 2. The Hebrew word for miracles, *nes* (pl., *nessim*), is not used here. The plagues are called *ot u'mofet/signs and wonders*, and they are depicted by the Talmudic sages as having been hardwired into the system by God *before* Creation.

But if these are "signs," what do they signify? For whose amazement are the "wonders" intended?

There are really two answers to these interlocking questions. The obvious answer to both is the Egyptians, those polytheists who deify the Nile, the sun, and Pharoah. God is pretty explicit about this, saying that the Almighty will "smite their gods" and that God knows "that the king of Egypt will only let you go because of greater might." Thus several of the plagues are aimed directly at (or emanate from) the deities of Egypt. The Nile turns to blood and vomits up frogs (who are minor demigods in Egyptian lore), the sun is blotted out, and the Egyptian magicians are utterly confounded, throwing in the towel after the first three plagues. Two of the plagues—wild beasts and hail—take place after Pharoah is specifically warned during his morning tour of inspection at the Nile.

This is the same Pharoah who taunted Moshe before the first plague, demanding to know "who is the God of the Hebrews" that he should heed such threats and entreaties. By the time the final, most devastating plague has befallen Egypt, Pharoah knows only too well who this God is and will even ask a blessing for himself. And, of course, Pharoah, who is himself considered a god in Egypt, is utterly vanquished by the final series of events, trapped by his own arrogance and his pagan beliefs.

This marks the introduction of a new theme that will run through the remainder of the Torah, the ongoing battle between ethical monotheism and polytheism. As we will see repeatedly in the second half of *Shemot* and throughout the rest of the Torah, the Israelites will be enjoined to set themselves apart from the non-Jews around them and never to follow their practices. In fact, one could argue with some justice that most of the *mitzvot* given at Sinai are designed specifically to create a distinction between the Israelites and their neighbors.

The plagues also serve as a subtle reminder to Pharoah and the Egyptians of their forgotten and ignored debt to Yosef. Recall, if you will, that at the outset of *Shemot* the current ruler of Egypt is described as a "king who knew not Yosef." Yet were it not for Yosef, Pharoah would have no realm over which to rule, perhaps no forebears to have given him birth.

Richard Elliott Friedman points out an intricate and highly suggestive series of internal echoes in this Torah portion and the next that hearken back to the Yosef cycle. The most striking of these occurs in the narrative's description of the dead frogs, which are "piling up" all over Egypt. The verb used, *v'yitzb'ru / and they piled up*, only occurs in two other places in the Torah, both of them in *Bereishit* 41, where they refer to Yosef's "piling up" of grain against the expected famine.

There are several other allusions of this sort scattered throughout the recounting of the plagues. In *Shemot* 8:22, Moshe says to Pharoah, "*Lo nakhon / It's not right*," echoing Yosef to Pharoah in *Bereishit* 41:32. Yosef describes the famine as "heavy," a word that is also used to describe the cattle disease and the hailstorm. Moshe also uses the phrase "offensive to the Egyptians" in *Shemot* 8:22, again echoing Yosef (*Bereishit* 43:32). Finally, as Friedman points out, Moshe warns Pharoah not "to continue" to toy with the Israelites; the Hebrew word for "continue" used here is *"yosep."* Remember that in the Hebrew alphabet the letters *f* and *p* are interchangeable—especially in the Torah text, which has no markings to distinguish between them. Even if this Pharoah "continues" to forget Yosef after he reluctantly liberates the Israelites, there is no question that this is payback for one of the original *B'nei Yisrael.*

But there is another kind of pedagogy operating here as well. The Egyptians aren't the only audience to this spectacular power struggle. Although they are not as intimately involved in the back-and-forth between Pharoah, Moshe and Aharon, and God, the Israelites have even more at stake. Yet they have already displayed an unbecoming level of skepticism. Although God has told Moshe what to tell them, his human messenger knows their audience better than one might guess. The Hebrews are, indeed, quite unconvinced by Moshe's proclamations of God's sensitivity to their plight, and every setback seems to breed renewed timidity in them. God states the basic premise explicitly in *parashat Bo,* "I have hardened Pharoah's heart . . . in order that you may recount to the ears of your son and your son's son that which I have wrought in Egypt and the signs which I have placed there, and you shall know that I am *Adonai.*"

Perhaps that is why the text tells us quite pointedly that several of the plagues visited upon the Egyptians do not befall the Israelites, as a "sign" of God's awareness of their suffering, and of their previous faithfulness. This sequence will reach its climax in the following Torah portion with the Passover, in which the Hebrews, by explicitly acknowledging their identities—not merely acknowledging but publicly proclaiming them by daubing blood on their lintels—and their separateness, thereby ward off the visitation of the final plague.

As Roberta Louis Goodman observes, the final plague is as much a test of the Hebrews as of the Egyptians; while they were protected from the earlier plagues by God, in this case, they must take positive action, a sign of their faith. If they keep faith with God by following the directions they have been given, they will survive. If not their own firstborn will die as surely as those of the Egyptians.

Finally, it is this separateness from the polytheists, commanded by God, that is tacitly stated in the restatement of the Covenant that occurs in *Shemot* 6:6–7, the fourfold promise that we recite every year at the seder that begins Pesakh, "I will bring you out, I will deliver you, I will redeem you, I will take you to me as a people."

ADDITIONAL NOTES

- In one of the more peculiar narrative strategies occurring in the Torah, the story stops abruptly for a genealogy of Moshe's family early in this Torah portion. We learn a couple of interesting facts about the family—the names of Moshe's parents, for example. In one of the more suggestive items to emerge here, we find out that Amram, Moshe's father, is also the nephew of Yokheved, Moshe's mother. As we will see later in the Torah, this kind of marital relationship will be prohibited after Sinai. Why, one may ask, does the Torah make a point of telling us that the greatest prophet of the Jewish people is the product of a forbidden relationship? Hizkuni writes that knowing of this flaw in Moshe means that "he would not lord it over the people."

- The placement of the genealogy of Moshe's family occurs immediately after he tells God once again of his uncertainty of speech. The phrase used is *aral sifatayim/uncircumcised lips*, suggesting a blockage of sorts (echoed by the reference elsewhere in both the Torah in the prophetic writings, to "circumcizing" the hearts of the unfeeling *B'nei Yisrael*). Then, after the genealogy, Moshe repeats the statement; now that we know how pedigreed his line is, the repetition underlines his modesty, the trait for which he will be lauded at the end of the Torah.

HAFTARAH

The *haftarah* associated with this Torah portion is filled with explicit references to the destruction of the Egyptians. Yekhezkel has a vision of God, who tells him, "Turn against Pharoah, king of Egypt, and prophesy against him," as Moshe once did. The Eternal then proceeds to enumerate a new series of destructions that will befall Egypt for its mistreatment of the Israelites.

PARASHAT BO

15th Torah portion, 3rd in *Shemot*
Shemot 10:1–13:16 (106 verses)
Haftarah: Yirmiyahu 46:13–28

ALIYOT

First / Rishon:	10:1–10:11
Second / Sheini:	10:12–10:23
Third / Shlishi:	10:24–11:3
Fourth / Revi'i:	11:4–12:20
Fifth / Khamishi:	12:21–12:28
Sixth / Shishi:	12:29–12:51
Seventh / Shevi'i:	13:1–13:16
Maftir:	13:14–13:16

SYNOPSIS

God sends the plagues of locusts and darkness upon Egypt and forewarns Moshe about the final plague, the death of every Egyptian firstborn. Pharoah still does not let the Israelites leave Egypt. God commands Moshe and Aharon regarding the Passover festival. God enacts the final plague, striking down all the firstborn in the land of Egypt except those of the House of Israel. Pharoah now allows the Israelites to leave. Speaking to Moshe and Aharon, God repeats the commandments about Passover.

COMMENTARY

At the outset of this Torah portion, we are presented with a perplexing problem. God speaks to Moshe, saying, "Go to Pharoah, for I have hardened his heart and the hearts of his servants, so that I will be able to display these signs in their midst." We already know that a major purpose of the ten plagues is to impress upon the Egyptians the omnipotence of *Adonai*. Yet there seems to us to be something manifestly unfair about God making Pharoah stubborn, then punishing him and all his people for that stubbornness.

The tension between free will and determinism is a theme that runs throughout biblical literature, and it is nowhere more adroitly foregrounded than in the story of the plagues. What do the commentators tell us about Pharoah's hardened heart?

Clearly the great sages were troubled by this development. After all, Judaism is a faith tradition that is sustained in no small part by its belief in free will (admittedly with strong strains of predestination running parallel to that belief). In *Shemot Rabbah* Rabbi Yokhanan protests against midrashim approving of the hardening by God of Pharoah's heart. "This provides a pretext for the heretics to say that God did not allow Pharoah to repent." But Shimon ben Lakish replies brusquely, "The mouths of heretics be closed! If it concerns the scorners [God] scorns them."

Shimon then offers an argument that is based on an important thread developed in *parashat Vayeira*. He notes that on several occasions it is Pharoah who hardens his own heart after the spectacle of the earlier plagues. "When [God] warns one on three occasions and he does not turn from his ways, [the Eternal] closes the door of repentance on him in order to punish him for his sin. Such was the case with wicked Pharoah." In fact, as Shimon notes, God gave Pharoah *five* chances to repent and let the Hebrews go out of Egypt, to no avail. For that reason, he argues, God told Pharoah, "You have stiffened your neck and hardened your heart, I will double your defilement." And, as we have seen in this *parashah*, Pharoah continues to haggle over the terms of the Hebrews' release from bondage through the ninth plague! (It is intriguing to note that in the dialogue between Pharoah and his courtiers that takes place at the outset of the *parashah*, they clearly blame their monarch for the troubles that have befallen the Egyptian people.)

For Ovadiah Sforno, the issue isn't whether Pharoah lets the Israelites go free but that he do so "for the right reasons." God, Sforno argues, doesn't want the Egyptians to liberate their Hebrew slaves merely out of fear of continued plagues; consequently the Holy One hardened Pharoah's heart so he would endure the plagues themselves, only freeing the slaves when he had finally come to understand the awesome power of the real God. (Sforno also echoes our discussion of the previous Torah portion, observing that the "signs and wonders" are intended as much for the Hebrews as for the Egyptians.)

Menachem ben Yashar of Bar-Ilan University expands on this idea convincingly, arguing that it is only after the plague is removed that Pharoah's heart is hardened once again; therefore, "Once the pressure is removed free will and choice are restored to Pharoah." He continues: "He can choose to submit . . . and recognize [the Eternal's] sovereignty, or continue stubbornly to deny it." So what really happens is that God allows Pharoah to *choose* to renege on his agreements, to harden his own heart. Thus, ben Yashar argues, "Pharoah's hardening of his own heart, and [the Holy One's] hardening of it indirectly are . . . one and the same."

Of course, one can always read the "hardening of Pharoah's heart" as a metaphor and sidestep the entire issue of free will. Or we can put this question into another context, relating it to another compelling theme of the Torah, *teshuvah*.

As important as free will is to Jewish thought, the concept of *teshuvah* is even more significant. *Teshuvah* is usually translated as "repentance" but actually carries a more complex set of associations, including "turning" or "returning" to God. Clearly, Pharoah is the "scorner" par excellence, who considers himself and is considered by his people to be a god; one might call him a king of unbelievers in more than one sense. Yet even he is finally vanquished by the might of God's signs and wonders, so much so that he even asks Moshe, *"U'veirakhtem gam oti/And bring a blessing upon me, too."*

Both Maimonides and Rashi argue that *teshuvah* is the key element in this part of the story, accepting the midrashic version in which God limits Pharoah's free will in order to punish him for his failure to repent before. Abravanel finds serious fault with this argument, pointing to the famous passage from *Sefer Yekhezkel* that states that "it is not the death of sinners that God desires but that they should repent."

Surely Pharoah's request for a "blessing for me, too," constitutes a real act of *teshuvah*?

One must answer in the negative. Finally, as we will see in the next Torah portion, Pharoah is unable to alter his own nature, and that is the key to the dilemma posed at the outset of this discussion, or so some commentators argue. Moshe Greenberg writes:

> Events unfold under the providence of God, yet their unfolding is always according to the motives of the human actors through whom God's will is done without their realizing it. . . . Pharoah conducted himself throughout conformably with his own motives and his own godless view of his status. God made it so, but Pharoah had only to be himself to do God's will.

One is reminded of the rueful "Chinese proverb" from Orson Welles's *The Lady from Shanghai:* "He who follows his own nature will end by retaining that nature."

There is, I think, another clue in this *parashah* contained in one of those frustrating digressions from the main narrative line.

In the midst of the drama of the night of the first Passover, we are given a lengthy disquisition on the laws to govern the holiday that will commemorate this event. In the course of this "sidebar" God tells the Hebrews that this event inaugurates a new calendar year, indeed a new calendar, for them. As usual, we find ourselves asking, "What is this passage doing here?" Of course, it anticipates the great Giving of the Law that will take place once the Israelites are out of bondage and into the Wilderness, but there is a symbolism of more immediate impact.

A slave people does not control its own time. A free people does. A new calendar marks that change in the most concrete way possible. In a sense, then, time begins with the liberation from Egyptian bondage. A free people controls its own time and its own destiny, and once freed the Israelites will go out into the Wilderness and agree to accept "the yoke of the *mitzvot*," as Yeshayahu Leibowitz calls it. They go out, then, for the greater glory of the Eternal One—Moshe has not lied to Pharoah about that. And when Pharoah follows them it is for the basest and cruelest of reasons.

Ultimately, we realize, Pharoah was never a free man inasmuch as he has never accepted a basic limitation on his powers, the fact of his own mortality. He is not a god, he is not eternal, he is only a man. One may say that, in that context, the issue of free will versus determinism is a false one for Pharoah and for all of us. Everything on earth dies and our mortality must always place a limitation on our freedom.

ADDITIONAL NOTES

- The first use of the word *torah* in the Torah occurs in this *parashah* at *Shemot* 12:49.

- Many modern readers are troubled by one of the final acts of the liberation drama, the stripping of Egypt of its gold by the departing slaves. We will see later in *Sefer Shemot* that God, as usual, has a specific reason for providing the fleeing Hebrews with this vast wealth, but there is another, more modern "spin" on the issue as well. We live in an era in which many activists argue that the descendants of men and women who lived as slaves are entitled to reparations for the generations of damage done to their forebears by the cruelty of their bondage. Clearly on some level, the Torah believes that there is a sort of collective national guilt operating in Egypt, and this wholesale payback represents a sort of economic justice.

- The *mitzvah* of the Paschal Lamb, which is given in this *parashah*, is usually considered the first "official" commandment of the 613 contained in the Torah (although "be fruitful and multiply" is often described as the first commandment given by God in the book). The lengthy passages enumerating the laws governing Pesakh are something of a prelude to the Giving of the Law on Sinai and after. Two other important *mitzvot* are, at the very least, implied in this Torah portion, the wearing of *tefillin* (*Shemot* 13:9) and the sacred status of the firstborn (*Shemot* 13:11–14).

HAFTARAH

Yirmiyahu/Jeremiah, from whose prophecies this *haftarah* is taken, was one of those Israelites who survived the Babylonian exile living in Egypt. In this *haftarah*, he preaches powerfully against the Egyptians, who he predicts will be punished by God as they were in the days of Moshe: "Fair Egypt will be shamed. . . . Be not dismayed, O Israel,/I will deliver you from far away,/Your folk from their land of captivity."

PARASHAT BESHALAKH

16th Torah portion, 4th in *Shemot*
Shemot 13:17–17:16 (116 verses)
Haftarah: Shoftim 4:4–5:31 (Sephardic: *Shoftim* 5:1–31)

ALIYOT

First / Rishon:	13:17–14:8
Second / Sheini:	14:9–14:14
Third / Shlishi:	14:15–14:25
Fourth / Revi'i:	14:26–15:26
Fifth / Khamishi:	15:27–16:10
Sixth / Shishi:	16:11–16:36
Seventh / Shevi'i:	17:1–17:16
Maftir:	17:14–17:16

SYNOPSIS

B'nei Yisrael escape across the *Yam Suf* from Pharoah and his army, who drown when the sea closes upon them. Moshe and the Israelites sing a song praising *Adonai*. In the wilderness, God provides the grumbling Israelites with quail and manna. God instructs the Israelites to gather and prepare on the sixth day food needed for Shabbat. The people complain about the lack of water. Moshe hits a rock with his rod and brings forth water. Israel defeats Amalek, Israel's eternal enemy. God vows to blot out the memory of Amalek from the world.

COMMENTARY

The center of this week's *parashah* is *Shirat Ha'Yam. Adonai* has parted the Red Sea and allowed the Hebrews to cross "as on dry land," then closed the sea on the crack cavalry troops of the Egyptian army, the elite of their office corps and their ruler, the would-be god, Pharoah. If you think back to the story of Yosef, you may recall that Pharoah's predecessor by some four hundred years dreamed that he walked upon the Nile. Now his successor is at the bottom of the *Yam Suf.*

So Moshe and *B'nei Yisrael* sing a song in praise of *Adonai,* "who has overthrown horse and rider" and utterly destroyed the Egyptians.

Then Miriam, whose name we learn for the first time and who is called a prophetess, leads the Israelite women in a spirited song and dance.

And they all lived happily after.

For about a day.

Now the Hebrews commence what will be forty years of wandering in the wilderness. And forty years of grumbling, complaining, and muttering dissension. In swift succession we are shown three separate incidents of complaining and possible insurrection, and there will be more to come.

How is it possible that the Hebrews, who were singing God's praises so ardently in the *Shirat Ha'Yam,* turned so quickly into the doubting, kvetching masses who could accuse Moshe with "You have brought us to this desert to starve this entire congregation to death" and could ask at Rephidim, "Is the Lord in our midst or not?"

In fact, this *parashah* seems broken-backed, broken in its exact middle. Yeshayahu Leibowitz notes that this Torah portion divides neatly in half—116 verses, 58 of them about the events at *Yam Suf,* the other 58 about the aftermath in the Wilderness. One-half triumph and ecstasy, one-half whining and despair. Why?

In the text of his wonderful *Sans Soleil* the French filmmaker Chris Marker says that the morning after the triumph of the anticolonial revolution in Guinea-Bissau, Amilcar Cabral must have looked around him and "as the head of every successful revolution probably said, 'Now comes the hard part.' "

After you've experienced the miraculous, the business of daily living seems boring, tedious, a grind. A revolution is a tremendous rush; running a government on a daily basis is a drag. What a letdown, a collective emotional hangover.

We're out of slavery, the Egyptians are dead. Now comes the hard part. As Cabral and his contemporaries discovered after ridding themselves of the Europeans who had been living off their backs for a century, when you've been doubled over under the weight of chains, you don't stand up straight quite so quickly.

Don't forget that the Israelites have lived in bondage for four hundred years. Even in biblical terms, that's at least five generations. They have known nothing but slavery from infancy to death. They have never experienced the thrill of freedom or—even more important—the responsibilities that accompany it. They have not, let us assume, ever had to buy something in a store, transport themselves to someplace on their own, cultivate their own fields.

In short, they are like children who are out alone for the first time in their lives.

But there is something else going on here, something about faith.

What happens after the triumph at *Yam Suf* is not a question of a people with a short memory asking "What have you done for me lately?" The way that the subsequent events play out suggests that something else more complex is happening here, something a lot less contemptible than ingratitude.

There's a wonderful midrash on the miracle of Hanukah that seems apposite. The great miracle of Hanukah was not that the supply of consecrated oil lasted for eight days; for God that's not a great feat. The great miracle is that every night the priests would look at their supply of oil and say, "Well, that's enough oil to last for one day. Let's light the lamps and say the blessings anyway." The miracle is that the priests had enough faith in God to do what was right and assume that God would provide.

Consider a comparable midrash on the parting of *Yam Suf.* It is said that when the Israelites found themselves with the Egyptian army at their backs, facing *Yam Suf,* they hesitated fearfully and no exhortation from Moshe would push them onward. Then Nakhshon ben Aminadav plunged into the waters and moved steadily forward until, with the water touching his very nostrils, the sea parted. A test of faith that only he passed, but that act of faith by Nakhshon was enough.

Consider the behavior of the Israelites in the Wilderness afterward. Moshe says, "God is going to send you manna every day." What happens when the manna comes? Some people decide to hoard manna because they fear that there won't be any the next day. The manna turns rotten and wormy. But there is manna the next day. Nobody starves. And when they are told that a double portion will fall the day before the Sabbath, that they are to observe a day of rest on the seventh day, there are still some obstinate Hebrews who go out looking for manna on Saturday. (By the way, this is the true first Sabbath experienced by humanity in the Torah, and the first time that the day is observed by humans.)

Clearly these people lack faith. Perhaps after four hundred years of slavery and of God seemingly not hearing their cries, it is understandable.

But they've seen God's handiwork on a grand scale already. What do they want?

As Leibowitz says, faith is not something that comes from outside forces. The flashy show of burning bushes, plagues, parting and closing seas, all those cosmic parlor tricks are impressive. But they are external to the people who have witnessed them. Remember, even Moshe, who clearly wants desperately to believe, resists God's initial command and needs to be convinced that he can fulfill the task *Adonai* sets for him.

Dr. Ismar Schorsch writes, "Miracles may alter the course of nature, but they leave human nature essentially unaltered. The Torah is wary of sudden conversions. A nation of slaves is not refashioned in an instant by a display of divine power."

Faith is not the product of externals; it has to be planted like a seed and nurtured within your heart. It will grow slowly, not in the fires of the miraculous, but in the sun and rain of daily life. And faith has as one of its components doubt. Doubt is not the same as fear or lack of trust, which is what the Hebrews have before they enter *Yam Suf.* Doubt is the probing that makes it possible to sustain a thoughtful but not unquestioning attitude to the Holy.

Recall the opening of *parashat Beshalakh*. God chooses the route for the Israelites and leads them "roundabout." Crossing the Sinai Peninsula to Kina'an even on foot is a matter of weeks, not years. Yet it is not an accident—it is by Divine will—that these people will wander for forty years, long enough for the generation of slaves to die of natural causes. Only their children will enter the land of Kina'an—men and women who do not have the slave mentality, the slave mind-set, the slave consciousness. Men and women who have survived forty years in the Wilderness during which time they have had to make their own way and their own mistakes.

And their own faith.

ADDITIONAL NOTES

- The Sabbath on which this *parashah* is read is called *Shabbat Shirah/ the Sabbath of Song*. When *Shirat Ha'Yam* is chanted, the entire congregation stands, as if they were present when the liberation from slavery took place.
- *Shemot* 15:11 in *Shirat Ha'Yam* is a passage that is sung daily in the liturgy as *Mi khamokha*.

HAFTARAH

The *haftarah* for this week is an obvious parallel to *parashat Beshalakh*. It tells the story of the defeat by the Israelites of Sisera and his army and of Devorah's song of triumph at their defeat.

PARASHAT YITRO

17th Torah portion, 5th in *Shemot*
Shemot 18:1–20:23 (75 verses)
Haftarah: Yeshayahu 6:1–7:6; 9:5–6 (Sephardic: *Yeshayahu* 6:1–13)

ALIYOT

First / Rishon:	18:1–18:12
Second / Sheini:	18:13–18:23
Third / Shlishi:	18:24–18:27
Fourth / Revi'i:	19:1–19:6
Fifth / Khamishi:	19:7–19:19
Sixth / Shishi:	19:20–20:14
Seventh / Shevi'i:	20:15–20:23
Maftir:	20:19–20:23

SYNOPSIS

Yitro/Jethro brings his daughter Tzipporah and her two sons, Gershom and Eliezer, to his son-in-law Moshe. Moshe follows Yitro's advice and appoints judges to help him lead the people. *B'nei Yisrael* camp in front of Mount Sinai. Upon hearing the Covenant, the Israelites respond, "All that God has spoken we will do." After three days of preparation, the Israelites encounter God at Mount Sinai. God gives the Ten Commandments aloud directly to the people. Frightened, *B'nei Yisrael* ask Moshe to serve as an intermediary between God and them. Moshe tells the people not to be afraid.

COMMENTARY

With this *parashah*, we have reached the pivotal moment in the entire Torah, the Revelation at Sinai, the moment in which God's Presence is made manifest to the Israelites. With *Matan Torah/the Giving of the Torah* at Sinai, the Covenant is sealed; as we will see momentarily, the very language of the Ten Commandments corresponds to that of a treaty document of the Ancient Near East.

More than that, as Nahum Sarna observes, this awesome event marks the first time that "God's redemptive acts on Israel's behalf require a reciprocal response on the part of Israel." Israel is no longer to be a passive group of slaves/ex-slaves, buffeted by the waves of history and the will of the Eternal. They must weld themselves into a community and act in accordance with the agreement forged in flame and thunder at the base of Mount Sinai.

We have discussed some of the ramifications of that process in Chapters 2 and 4, and will come back to the specifics repeatedly as we pass through *Sefer Shemot* and the subsequent books of the Torah. For the moment, let's look more closely at the heart of this Torah portion, what is called in Hebrew *Aseret Ha'Devarim/Ten Utterances (or Words or Things)*. Note that its Hebrew name is *not* the Ten Commandments; in fact, some Torah scholars would argue that there are nine commandments (and David Noel Freedman has even used that phrase as the title of a book) or eleven.

This position pivots on two interesting facts. First, as just noted, *devarim* does not mean "commandments." Interestingly enough, the phrase *Aseret Ha'Devarim* never occurs in the Hebrew Bible outside the four books covering the Exodus from Egypt and the wanderings in the Wilderness. And as carefully as the Tablets on which the Ten are inscribed may be treated, they never appear outside those four books until one final mention in *Melakhim Aleph*, when Shelomo places them in the ark of the Temple in Jerusalem.

Clearly these Ten Utterances, while incredibly significant, carry a different weight for Jews than for the other Abrahamic faith traditions.

Rabbi Jacob Chinitz offers an interesting take on what the significance of the Ten Words might be. He refers to some earlier passages in this *parashah*, noting that, when Yitro counsels Moshe to appoint judges and to delegate some of his authority, it is understood that Moshe has been making decisions that must have some basis in preexisting laws. When discussing the judicial process, Yitro tells his son-in-law to teach the Israelites *"khok/statute," "torah/teaching,"* and *"derekh/way."* Elsewhere, we find references to *mitzvot, mishpat/judgment,* and several similar terms. Yet, Chinitz says, only the Ten are called *devarim*. He concludes, "The Ten are principles, and more general in nature than the specific commandments."

Thus, he argues, *Aseret Ha'Devarim* are general principles that should govern human conduct. In this, he echoes Umberto Cassuto, who sees the Ten as the prologue to the complete code of the *mitzvot*, which will be enumerated at great length over much of the remainder of the Torah.

There is a second fact that lends weight to the notion that there are only nine *mitzvot* explicitly stated in the *Aseret Ha'Devarim*. The language with which the Ten opens—"I am *Adonai* Your God, who brought you out of the land of Egypt, from the house of bondage"—is highly reminiscent of the structure of treaties and similar documents common to the Ancient Near East. As Richard Elliott Friedman explains, "Introductory statements such as this one are common and fundamental to these documents: stating the name of the one who is dictating the terms and stating the history of what this one has done for the recipient of these terms." Friedman believes that if one counts the opening of the Ten as a "commandment," you have eleven.

Still, it is not hard to accept the compelling argument, offered by Rashi, Nahmanides, and countless others since them, that without this initial statement of God's powerful actions in history the rest are superfluous, if not downright meaningless. As Dr. Ismar Schorsch says, paraphrasing Nahmanides, "This is the first of the commandments, the sacred soil in which the others are planted."

Does it matter if there are Nine Commandments or Ten? For the traditionally observant Jew, the answer is probably no, because ultimately it is the grand total of 613 *mitzvot* given at Sinai that really matters. For non-Jews, the answer is undoubtedly quite different, but that is not relevant here. The status of the Ten Principles—to adopt Chinitz's phrase—in Judaism is a little ambiguous.

Dr. Schorsch notes:

> At one time, when the Second Temple still stood, the recitation of the Ten Commandments, along with the three paragraphs of the *Shema*, was part of the daily liturgy. The Palestinian Talmud reports, however, that once the Temple was destroyed, the Rabbis did not transfer the reciting of the Ten Commandments into the synagogue liturgy. The reason given is that people should not be misled into thinking that only the Decalogue was revealed at Sinai. And to this day there is no trace of the Ten Commandments in the text of our daily prayers.

As *mitzvot*, this handful is at once both the root of the other 603, yet not privileged over them. We stand when they are read on *Shabbat Yitro*, but the symbolism—we are all present at Sinai to receive the Revelation of God's Presence—doesn't obscure the fact that they are the prelude to many more pages of commandments that will follow these.

Is the Revelation at Sinai history?

One must reply with a qualified "yes," adding, with Dr. Schorsch, "It is history as theological preamble." Whether or not *Matan Torah* at Sinai has the status of a historical fact, like the assassination of Abraham Lincoln or Caesar crossing the Rubicon, the force of the story of what happened at Sinai has resonated for three millennia.

The Revelation at Sinai represents a "turning point in the world's spiritual history," as Rabbi Menachem Schneerson calls it. Not only do these "Ten Commandments" become the foundation stone for much that is basic in the morality of Western civilization but, as Schneerson observes, they do something more. With *Matan Torah,* he writes, the spiritual and physical realms, once separated by Divine decree (as restated in *Tehillim* 115:16, "The heavens are the heavens of God, and the earth God gave to humanity"), are once more unified by God's descent to the material world at Sinai. This fusing of the spiritual and material, as we will see in much of what remains of the Torah, is at the heart of Jewish practice and belief.

ADDITIONAL NOTES

- This is where we finally learn the names of the sons of Moshe and Tzipporah, who are called Gershom and Eliezer. Eliezer's name presents an interesting conundrum, being translated as meaning "God rescued me from Pharoah." Is this a prophecy or an anachronism?
- When Yitro leaves the Israelite encampment, he returns to Midian. Rashi, for one, says he does so in order to convert his family to Judaism.
- Sa'adia Gaon says that "all the *mitzvot*" are included in *Aseret Ha' Devarim*. He is not speaking metaphorically but esoterically: the Ten contain exactly 620 Hebrew letters, one for each of the 613 *mitzvot* given at Sinai plus the seven prescribed later by the rabbis.

HAFTARAH

The *haftarah* to *parashat Yitro* parallels the communal revelation at Sinai with a more personal revelation experienced by the prophet Yeshayahu. Where God comes down to the people in the Torah portion,

Yeshayahu is brought up to the Throne of the Almighty. His "unclean lips" are purified by a seraph holding a red-hot coal to them (perhaps an echo of the "uncircumcised lips" of Moshe), and he is sent back to earth to prophesy against the excesses of the Davidic line, much as Moshe is sent to Pharoah as the vehicle by which the Israelites will be liberated from Egypt.

PARASHAT MISHPATIM

18th Torah portion, 6th in *Shemot*
Shemot 21:1–24:18 (118 verses)
Haftarah: Yirmiyahu 34:8–22; 33:25–26

ALIYOT

First / Rishon:	21:1–21:19
Second / Sheini:	21:20–22:3
Third / Shlishi:	22:4–22:26
Fourth / Revi'i:	22:27–23:5
Fifth / Khamishi:	23:6–23:19
Sixth / Shishi:	23:20–23:25
Seventh / Shevi'i:	23:26–24:18
Maftir:	24:15–24:18

SYNOPSIS

Interpersonal laws ranging from the treatment of slaves to the exhibition of kindness to strangers are listed. Cultic laws follow, including the commandment to observe the Sabbatical Year, a repetition of the Sabbath injunction, the first mention of the Three Pilgrimage Festivals, rules of sacrificial offerings, and the prohibition against boiling a kid in its mother's milk. The people assent to the Covenant. Moshe, Aharon, Nadav, Avihu, and seventy elders of Israel ascend the mountain and see God. Moshe goes on alone and spends forty days on the mountain.

COMMENTARY

Parashat Mishpatim offers a welter of civil and criminal legislation, assembled in what seems to be an almost random order. As Rabbi Matis Weinberg observes, from this point on, there will be considerably less narrative in the Torah and a new emphasis on laws and law-giving. Even the word *mishpatim,* derived from the same root—*shin-fei-tav*—as *shoftim / judges,* means "rules, judgments, or ordinances." We have discussed the principles behind the *mitzvot* elsewhere (see Chapters 2 and 4), but there is a famous and suggestive oddity in this *parashah* worth pondering at some length.

When Moshe first repeats the new round of *mitzvot* to *B'nei Yisrael*, they respond, "All that *Adonai* has commanded we will do (*na'aseh*)" (*Shemot* 24:3). Moments later, after he has read to them the record of the Covenant, they fervently respond, "All that *Adonai* has spoken we will do and we will hear (*na'aseh v'nishma*)" (*Shemot* 24:7).

"We will do" and *then* "we will hear"? This ordering of promises seems so illogical that many translators render it as "will do and obey." The *Mikra'ot Gedolot* notes that the *targumim* (Aramaic translations of the *Tanakh*) give it as "we will do and we will accept." But the verb *nishma* clearly means "we will hear." Remember the most famous watchword of the Jewish faith, *Sh'ma Yisrael / Hear O Israel.*

Of course, one can follow Richard Elliott Friedman, who points out that in Hebrew and English, "hear" can be used to mean "obey," as in "Listen to your mother!" or "Do you hear me, young man?" The latter is seldom if ever an audiological inquiry.

The rabbis of the Talmud have no hesitation in interpreting this seeming anomaly. The Israelites are so eager to comply, they argue, that anything God asks they will do and only ask questions later.

The Beis Halevi compares the two promises, do and hear, to the two categories of the *mitzvah* of Torah study. One studies Torah in order to know how to fulfill the other commandments, a practical necessity. But you also study Torah for its own sake. Hence, he argues, "we will do" includes Torah study as a prerequisite to the fulfilling of the other *mitzvot*, and "we will hear" refers to *Torah v'lishma / Torah for its own sake* (a neat pun, I would add, on *v'nishma*).

Cantor Jordan Franzel points to Rashi's distinction between two categories of *mitzvot*, the *mishpatim* and the *khukim*. The *mishpatim* are that category of commandments that relate to the quotidian world of human relations. They follow an obvious human logic—don't steal, don't bear false witness, don't kill. By contrast, the *khukim* are not easily explicable by human logic. Mostly pertaining to ritual observance, they include such seemingly arbitrary *mitzvot* as the laws governing *kashrut*, circumcision, and the Festivals. We do them because God so commanded. What Franzel suggests—and it's almost counterintuitive—is that we do the *mishpatim* without having to think about them; we understand them so they are almost automatic. But the *khukim* don't come so easily and therefore it's not just a matter of *"na'aseh,"* but of listening to the voice of God that we carry in our hearts to tell us that we should attach a *mezuzah* to our doorpost, fast on Yom Kippur, say the *Amidah* at appointed times.

Menachem Mendl, the Kotzker Rebbe, had a similar but simpler explanation. Why, he asked, do otherwise brilliant people misuse their wisdom? He contrasts their follies with the Israelites who "possess special instruments that elevate their perceptual capacity . . . and these are their instruments: the performance of the *mitzvot*." The Kotzker recalls the reply of *B'nei Yisrael* at Sinai and says, "Through the power of the *mitzvot* we perform, we are able to understand." In a sense, he reverses Cantor Franzel's explanation; he argues that it is by performing the *mitzvot* that we draw nearer to God and to an understanding of the Eternal.

ADDITIONAL NOTES

- There are fifty-three different *mitzvot* given in this *parashah.*
- At *Shemot* 22:30 the Israelites are instructed that they may not eat the flesh of an animal "torn [by] beasts." Herein lie the roots of one of the principles of *kashrut*, the Jewish dietary laws. Meat can only be eaten if it comes from an animal slaughtered according to the specific (rabbinic) prescriptions for ritual killing, rules that were designed to cause a minimum of suffering to the animal. The Hebrew word translated as "torn [by] beasts," *t'refah*, evolved into the Yiddish (and now English) word *treif,* meaning nonkosher.
- The passage at *Shemot* 23:19 in which the Hebrews are instructed, "You shall not boil a kid in its mother's milk," will be repeated almost verbatim at *Shemot* 3:26 and *Devarim* 14:21. This proscription is the basis of the separation of dairy and meat dishes in Jewish dietary laws, although the enormous thicket of law governing *kashrut* is rabbinic in origin.
- The laws governing the treatment and liberation of Hebrew slaves are extended in *Vayikra* 25:2, in which is stated that in the Jubilee year, all slaves must be freed.
- The forty days and nights that Moshe spends on Mount Sinai can be read as a metaphorical rebirth that echoes the cleansing of the world after the Flood, caused by forty days and nights of rain.

HAFTARAH

The *haftarah* for this Torah portion comes from *Sefer Yirmiyahu* and refers at some length and with a good deal of specificity to the laws governing *eved ivri / a Hebrew slave*. *Yirmiyahu* refers to the laws that liberate people held in bondage and tells of an egregious violation of those laws by the ruling class of Israel, which brings disastrous consequences upon them.

PARASHAT TERUMAH

19th Torah portion, 7th in *Shemot*
Shemot 25:1–27:19 (96 verses)
Haftarah: Melakhim Aleph 5:26–6:13

ALIYOT

First / Rishon:	25:1–25:16
Second / Sheini:	25:17–25:30
Third / Shlishi:	25:31–26:14
Fourth / Revi'i:	26:15–26:30
Fifth / Khamishi:	26:31–26:37
Sixth / Shishi:	27:1–27:8
Seventh / Shevi'i:	27:9–27:19
Maftir:	27:17–27:19

SYNOPSIS

God asks *B'nei Yisrael* to donate gifts *(t'rumah)* for the building of the Tabernacle so that God may "dwell among them." Instructions for the construction of the ark, table, and menorah are provided. Detailed directions are given on how to build the *Mishkan*.

COMMENTARY

In *Pesikta de'Rav Kahana* there is a midrash on *parashat Terumah* that brings together several issues that are confusing or troubling about this first of several *parashiyot* on the building of the *Mishkan*. It reads:

> Three things that Moshe heard from the Almighty startled him and made him apprehensive. When God said to him, "And let them make Me a sanctuary [*Shemot* 25:8]," Moshe said to the Holy One, blessed be HaShem, "Lord of the Universe, all the Heavens cannot contain You, yet You say to make You a sanctuary?"

Rabbi Shimon Golan of Bar-Ilan University responds, "For this reason the generally accepted exegetical view is that the Tabernacle and its furnishings were not commanded to satisfy a need of God, as it were, but to fulfill specific needs of human beings. One could add that more than ordinary 'human' needs are at issue; the furnishings also hint at sublime and esoteric things."

We'll return to that latter observation shortly. But what of Rabbi Golan's remark that the building of the *Mishkan* was designed "to fulfill specific needs of human beings"?

A parable.

There is a king, a wise and compassionate ruler under whose leadership the nation has prospered. The people are happy, their farms and businesses are successful, their children well fed, well clothed, well educated. The king's birthday comes and the people want to express their gratitude. What can they possibly buy or make for the king? He wants for nothing. His every need is met. Yet he does not turn them away when they come to ask him what he wants as a gift. He knows that the importance of the gesture is not that he receives a present but that his people have the satisfaction, the pleasure of having given him one.

There is a phrase that occurs early in *parashat Terumah* that reveals that God's motivation is the same. When *Adonai* begins his instructions to Moshe on the building of the ark and its furnishings, Moshe is told that donations for its construction should come "from every person whose heart so moves him" (*Shemot* 25:2).

"Whose heart so moves him."

In Jewish sacred texts, the heart is not only the seat of the emotions but the cockpit of free will. Nekhemyah/Nehemiah speaks of God "finding [Avraham's] heart true before You." Avraham's virtue is that he acted righteously from the heart, from his own free will. The rabbis called the worship service "the service of heart."

So God does not command that everyone contribute to the building of the *Mishkan*, only those "whose heart so moves him." Like the king in our parable, God knows that this gift does more for the giver than for the one who receives it, that it is a small but deeply felt token of the gratitude the people feel for a just and compassionate Ruler.

Why are the instructions so detailed? Yeshayahu Leibowitz notes that the construction of the *Mishkan* occupies somewhere between 250 and 300 verses over four *parashiyot;* by comparison the entire Creation takes up only 34 verses, including God's Shabbat rest, in one Torah portion. This looks like a severe misallocation of resources.

There are several reasons for this imbalance. First, it is a reflection of the comparative knowledge of the authors. Whoever wrote the Torah—and we'll stipulate for the moment that it was not Divinely authored—knew a lot more about the building of an ark, holy or otherwise, than about the creation of the world. As Wittgenstein says, "About that which we cannot speak we must remain silent." So God's Creation occurs in thirty-four verses with very little detail. But the Priestly author, or whichever of the several authors to whom the Pentateuch is attributed, knew how to make a tenon-joint construction, knew how to fasten rods through rings to make a carrier for a large burden, knew what the menorah in the Temple looked like, and so on. So he could expatiate in mind-numbing detail.

Leibowitz offers another, even more compelling argument.

The Creation *is*.

It just is.

It is inalterable, beyond the power of man to change. It is not a product of human activity and it is ultimately indifferent to man's fate. The *Mishkan*, by contrast, is the product of man's hand, shaped to the greater glory of the Divine Creator. Therefore, it needs to be described in greater detail.

There is a third explanation, one on which we touched earlier. The many components of the *Mishkan* are redolent of a complex symbolic language, a system of esoteric signs that has kept Jewish mystics busy for roughly two thousand years. This is a subject worthy of an entire book—indeed it occupies two hundred very difficult pages of the *Zohar*.

I'll merely offer one fairly simple example, a relatively straightforward one.

It is clear from the description of the ark given in *Terumah* that some of the poles for carrying portions of the ark are removable. However, the poles for carrying the Tablets are clearly designed to be permanent. Why?

The Torah—symbolized by the Tablets in a classic synecdoche—must accompany the Jewish people everywhere—in exile or in the Temple in Jerusalem. It is not an accident that God gave the Torah at Sinai, in the midst of the desert, rather than in Kina'an, where the people were to put down roots. The desert is a no-man's-land, a place to pass through; but the Torah and its precepts must accompany the Jews even *Ba'Midbar/in this barren Wilderness*. So the poles must be permanent because unlike the other accoutrements, the Law is always with us.

There is one other aspect of the instructions given in *Terumah* and in *Tetzaveh*, the next *parashah*, worth mentioning here. We now have the answer to a small but troubling question from the story of the Passover itself. Why did God instruct the Israelites to strip Egypt of its wealth before they departed for the Wilderness? We have considered the issue of reparations for four hundred years of slavery earlier, and there is a certain satisfying symmetry to that—particularly taken in the context of the socioeconomic strictures of the *mitzvot* about not withholding a laborer's wages and so on. But what are the Hebrews going to do with hundreds of pounds of gold and silver and jewels that they're shlepping in circles in the deserts around Sinai?

God, of course, can take the long view, a much longer view than that of which humans are capable. The Holy One knew that the point would come when the Jews would want to express their gratitude for the signs and wonders of the *Pesakh*, the victory over the Egyptians, the release from bondage, the great Revelation at Sinai. In appreciaton of such gifts one would not want to give a paltry present in return.

As the Maggid of Mezeritch says, "God chose silver and gold and the like to build . . . [the] *Mishkan* because God actually loves silver and gold—impossible! Rather these things are valuable in the perspective of human beings, and when a person contributes to God something beloved, it is as if one gives love to God."

What God asks for in *parashat Terumah* is a rich and detailed physical object, one that will call upon all the wealth the Jews have at their disposal. How sad the Israelites would be were they unable to honor God in an appropriate manner! It is a mark of God's compassion and omniscience that this eventuality has been provided for.

It's like the parent who gives a child an allowance. When the parent's birthday approaches the child wants to buy a gift that expresses love—but that takes money. Perhaps the child asks for an increase in his or her allowance or an advance. The parent must know that the money will end up going toward the gift. But one doesn't feel that the parent is merely buying a present for herself through the vehicle of the child, even if the child asks the parent what she wants for her birthday. This is a freely given exchange based on love and gratitude.

So, too with the *Mishkan*. Does God, Who is greater than the heavens themselves, *need* the *Mishkan*? Of course not. Hence Moshe's surprise.

What this is finally about is a process, a way of expressing love and interdependence. Otherwise, the passages on the building of the *Mishkan* would belong in *Popular Mechanics* and not in a sacred book.

ADDITIONAL NOTES

- More verses are devoted to the ark proper than to any of the other items described in this *parashah*, thirteen in all. By comparison, the table and its implements receive eight; the lamp stand and its implements, ten; the copper altar, eight; the altar of gold, six.
- All of the dimensions of the ark involve fractions.
- Unsurprisingly, many of the ritual objects described in the Torah, especially in this portion, are found in scaled-down versions in contemporary synagogues. Most notable among these are the seven-branched menorah (not to be confused with the *hanukiyah*, which has eight branches) and the *aron ha'kodesh* which finds its modern equivalent in the identically named ark that contains the *sifrei Torah*. The menorah has become so ubiquitous a symbol of Judaism that it was chosen for the seal of the State of Israel.

HAFTARAH

The *haftarah* for *parashat Terumah*, which recounts the conscription of thirty thousand men for the construction of the Temple in Jerusalem, contains clear links to the *parashah*. First, like Moshe asking for donations of goods for the building of the *Mishkan*, Shelomo will require a huge labor force of Israelites. And that labor will be used to create a magnificent and (ostensibly) final and permanent home for the Tabernacle and the Tablets from Sinai.

PARASHAT TETZAVEH

20th Torah portion, 8th in *Shemot*
Shemot 27:20–30:10 (101 verses)
Haftarah: Yekhezkel 43:10–27

ALIYOT

First / Rishon:	27:20–28:12
Second / Sheini:	28:13–28:30
Third / Shlishi:	28:31–28:43
Fourth / Revi'i:	29:1–29:18
Fifth / Khamishi:	29:19–29:37
Sixth / Shishi:	29:38–29:46
Seventh / Shevi'i:	30:1–30:10
Maftir:	30:8–30:10

SYNOPSIS

B'nei Yisrael are commanded to bring pure olive oil for the *ner tamid* above the sanctuary. Aharon and his sons, Nadav, Avihu, Eleazar, and Itamar, are chosen to serve God as priests. God instructs Moshe to make special clothes for the priests; the *urim* and *tumim* are to be inserted into the breastplate they will wear. Aharon and his sons are ordained in a seven-day ceremony. Aharon is commanded to burn incense on an altar made of acacia wood every morning and evening.

COMMENTARY

What are the *urim* and *tumim?*

Consult almost any translation of the Hebrew Bible and you will remain disappointingly unenlightened. The best guess anyone will hazard, using logical inferences drawn from the four passages in the *Tanakh* in which these mysterious objects appear, is that they were a device by which the High Priest was able to communicate with, to discern the will of God. Hertz, in the Soncino *Khumash,* writes:

The Ineffable Name of God was inscribed on some (unknown) material and placed in the fold of the breastplate. By means of it the Divine will was revealed in clear terms (like the 'light') and its promises were verified ('made perfect'). Hence the name Urim and Tumim, meaning 'lights' and 'perfection.'

Ibn Ezra suggests that they were made of silver and gold, and writes at some length comparing them to the tools of the astrologers, but Nahmanides dismisses him harshly, "[W]hat he said is of no import." By contrast, his own explanation involves the letters inscribed on the priest's breastplate, which he claims would light up to answer the priest's inquiries. Frankly this electronic Ouija board is even less satisfying than Ibn Ezra's guess.

The fact is, simply, no one knows.

Rashi says that by the time of the Second Temple, the High Priest no longer wore the *urim* and *tumim* in his breastplate, which suggests that like the *Mishkan* itself they were a casualty of the destruction of the First Temple and the Babylonian exile. We'll never know.

But it doesn't matter.

What is significant is not the mechanics of the *urim* and *tumim* or their composition but the fact that they were an integral part of the High Priest's garb and—even more important—his duties. With that knowledge, we can address two more important questions that have troubled readers of *parashat Tetzaveh*.

Why is so much space allotted to the description of the priestly garments?

Why is this the only Torah portion in the final four books of the *Khumash* in which the name of Moshe doesn't appear?

There are, of course, eminently logical, downright hardheaded answers to both questions. At least part of the Torah was either written or edited by a member of the Judean priesthood. Of course, he would be fascinated and gratified by all this material that glorified his predecessors and, by implication, him. The division of the text into *parashiyot* is a relatively arbitrary one and a late phenomenon; Moshe's name appears in the verse immediately after the end of this *parashah*, so it's just happenstance.

Perhaps. But let's return to the *urim* and *tumim* again. They may not reveal the Divine will to us, but they do suggest richer answers to these other questions.

The High Priest does not consult the *urim* and *tumim* for his own sake. He does it as the representative of *B'nei Yisrael*. You only need look at him

in his priestly garments to see that. Where are the *urim* and *tumim?* Tucked
into the folds of his robe behind the breastplate. What is inscribed on the
breastplate? The names of the Twelve Tribes, literally, the sons of Israel,
formerly called Ya'akov. The detail in which these garments are described
suggests the importance of every element of their design, a design that
clearly defines the role of the priests vis-à-vis the community and the
Eternal.

That is, of course, one of the functions of a uniform, which is, after all,
what these formal robes are. Rabbi Yehudah Henkin observes that a uniform has two roles, one for those who see it and another for those who
wear it. A uniform invests the wearer with authority, identifying him as
someone in a specific role, identifying him to others and instructing them
in how to interact with him. ("There's a policeman. Ask him for directions.") At the same time, it identifies him in his own conciousness and
guides his behavior. ("Don't bring dishonor on the uniform, soldier.")

The phrase used to describe the priestly garments is a telling one:
l'khavod ul'tiferet. This is the only time in the Torah that these two adjectives are yoked together. *L'khavod* is derived from a root meaning "heavy,
burdensome, honored." *Tiferet* means "beauty." These are seemingly
opposed qualities, but the Torah says that they both must be present in the
robes and adornments, which should be solemn but graceful, ceremonial
but pleasing.

And that is a quality that we try to find in all the *mitzvot.* It is not
enough merely to meet the barest obligations the commandments place
upon us. We are repeatedly enjoined in rabbinic texts to beautify the
mitzvot and to do them with joy. How appropriate, then, that the High
Priest himself should be clothed in a way that brings out this difficult but
rewarding dialectic.

At the same time, as uniforms do, it sets him apart from the rest of the
people. This is what Moshe, too, is doing for the priests. By following
God's instructions in this matter, he is establishing a hierarchical system,
surely the mark of a nation in formation. Yet the priesthood is assuredly
not an aristocracy. As we will see later, the *kohanim* are not permitted to
own land, the primary source of economic power in the ancient world.
Nor is succession guaranteed by a mere accident of birth, as Aharon's sons
Nadav and Avihu will find out shortly, to their great pain.

It is important to remember that the High Priest was specifically forbidden to officiate without donning his robes. Out of uniform he's just

another Hebrew. The Talmud says that the *kohanim* are only apart from the community when they wear the robes of office.

At that moment, a *kohein* is transformed, no longer a member of the community but an instrument of it, a bridge between *B'nei Yisrael* and the Divine Will, bearing the *urim* and *tumim* under his breastplate. Yet he is not that far apart from the community, as it is written in *Shemot* 29:29: "Aharon must carry all the names of all *B'nei Yisrael* on the breastplate on his heart when he comes into the Sanctuary, to be forever remembered by God." Significantly, both the names of the tribes and the *urim* and *tumim* are next to his heart, the biblical seat of wisdom and judgment.

The placement in the narrative of the description of the priestly garments, immediately following the *parashah* in which the *Mishkan*'s component parts are described, then followed by *parashat Ki Tisa* with its powerful narrative events—Moshe's climb up Sinai, the incident of the Golden Calf, the smashing of the Tablets, Moshe's pleading for the people—suggests that we are to consider the priest's uniform, even the priests themselves, as an integral part of the *Mishkan* as a whole. The midrashic collection *Pesikta de'Rav Kahana* says that the *Shekhinah*, the feminine manifestation of the Divine that accompanies the Hebrews on earth, could not occupy the *Mishkan* until Aharon entered as *kohein*. It was necessary for him to be there to light the menorah. As Matis Weinberg says, Aharon "provides consciousness to the Mishkan." Thus the priests—as Israel's representatives, her embodiment, as it were—are as much a part of the *Mishkan* as all the poles and rings and candelabrum. They are the human component without which Creation is never complete, the second and utterly necessary half of the dialogue that is the Covenant.

Moshe is not a part of that process, which is why his name doesn't appear in this *parashah*. His absence may, in fact, be completely arbitrary, but it is neither trivial nor meaningless. Although neither he nor we know it yet, he is destined not to be permitted to enter Kina'an. Therefore it is imperative that someone be empowered to speak to God after Moshe is gone. That someone, brightly garbed, with the names of his fellow Hebrews upon his heart and the means of communicating God's will beneath his tunic, is the High Priest.

ADDITIONAL NOTES

- The light that is not allowed to go out, described at the beginning of *parashat Tetzaveh*, is the basis for the *ner tamid* that is found at the front of modern synagogues, usually above the *aron ha'kodesh*.

HAFTARAH

The *parashah* ends with an elaborate description of the incense altar. The *haftarah* picks up from this element, with Yekhezkel describing a restored Temple in which incense is offered to God. The Creator will return to that newly rebuilt Temple and dwell therein, much as was promised in the culminating moment of *Shemot* 24.

PARASHAT KI TISA

21st Torah portion, 9th in *Shemot*
Shemot 30:11–34:35 (139 verses)
Haftarah: Melakhim Aleph 18:1–39 (Sephardic: *Melakhim Aleph*
18:20–39)

ALIYOT

First / Rishon:	30:11–31:17
Second / Sheini:	31:18–33:11
Third / Shlishi:3	33:12–33:16
Fourth / Revi'i:	33:17–33:23
Fifth / Khamishi:	34:1–34:9
Sixth / Shishi:	34:10–34:26
Seventh / Shevi'i:	34:27–34:35
Maftir:	34:33–34:35

SYNOPSIS

Moshe takes a census of the Israelites and collects a half shekel from each person. God tells Moshe to construct a water basin and to prepare anointing oil and incense for the ordination of the priests. Beztalel and Aholi'av, skilled artisans, are assigned to make objects for the priests and the Mishkan. The Israelites are instructed to keep the Shabbat as a sign of the Convenant. God gives Moshe the two tablets of the Pact. The Israelites ask Aharon to build them a Golden Calf. Moshe implores God not to destroy the people and then breaks the two tablets of the Pact on which the Ten Commandments are written when he sees the idol. God punishes the Israelites by means of a plague. Moshe goes up the mountain with a blank set of tablets for another forty days so that God will again inscribe the Ten Commandments. Other laws, including the edict to observe the Pilgrimage Festivals, are also revealed. Moshe comes down from the mountain with a radiant face.

COMMENTARY

That the Israelites sinned greatly in the incident of the Golden Calf no one doubts. If only as an example of impatience and ingratitude, their behavior is egregious. The exact nature of their sin has been the subject of considerable debate among the rabbis and Torah scholars. Some hold that the making of the statue was an example of idolatry, others that it represented not God but the absent leadership of Moshe. Rashi harshly notes that the Israelites committed their transgression while still at the foot of Sinai where, six weeks earlier, they had promised, "We will do and we will hear," to God. Rashi cites a remark by Ulla in the Talmud: "It is a miserable bride who prostitutes herself under the very wedding canopy."

Given the skittishness, the seeming inconstancy of these people—which under the circumstances is not entirely surprising—the great shock, I think, is not that they sinned (again). Rather, the truly breathtaking events in *parashat Ki Tisa* take place after the fiasco of the Golden Calf and concern the reaction of Moshe when he descends the mountain and sees the product of their folly. As well we know, this prophet of God, having come down from a forty-day sojourn with the Almighty, the tablets of the Law in his hands, hurls those tablets to the ground, shattering them irreparably. Then, after he has "sorted out" the transgressors (to use a pungent piece of British slang), he goes back up the mountain to speak with God.

Given Moshe's well-earned reputation for having a quick temper, the shattering of the *lukhot/tablets* might have been predicted. But the sequence of events is more complicated than our casual recollection suggests, and the same may be said of the reason for the shattering of the tablets.

First, it should be remembered that Moshe has already been told by God that "your people" have committed the grievous transgression of the *Eigel Zahav,* and has said he will destroy them and give Moshe a new nation over which he may rule. Moshe's response is telling. He rejects the characterization of the Hebrews as "his" people and reminds the Eternal that they are "Your people," then pleads with God not to destroy them. Mustering considerable arguments, he actually stays the hand of the Almighty.

It is only after this exchange that Moshe descends the mountain and smashes the *lukhot* and, with backing from the Levites, wreaks terrible punishment on the three thousand who were actively worshipping the statue. Then he ascends the mountain once more and asks God to forgive him or to "erase me from the book You have written." God, like an indulgent but nettled parent, tells Moshe that "I will decide" who to erase or not erase, then tells him to lead *B'nei Yisrael* to their appointed destination.

Considered in this context, the smashing of the tablets takes on a very different coloration. There is a midrash that states quite explicitly that Moshe shatters the tablets as a consciously chosen, calculated act, not as a rash outburst of anger. Why? The Gerer Rebbe says that Moshe chose to destroy the tablets "to bind his soul to his people" who have already sinned. *Shemot Rabbah* states the case succinctly: "When [Moshe] realized that there was no future hope for Israel, he linked his own fate with theirs and broke the tablets so that God would have to save [the Hebrews] in order to forgive him."

Moshe has already indirectly felt the rough side of God's tongue and knows that the fate of the entire nation hangs on his decision. He also knows that the Almighty is prepared to leave him in charge of whatever people end up going to Kina'an. The only way he can secure the future of the Israelites is by forcing God to consider him as one of them, a sinner.

What we see in this Torah portion is nothing less than Moshe "at the summit of his leadership, in his relation to his people as well as to God, in his function as intermediator," as Rabbi B. S. Jacobson puts it. Moshe confronts God, he argues with God, and he does so in terms more audacious than any of the previous heroic figures of the Torah.

As the *Zohar* notes, Noakh never raises an objection to God's decision to wipe away the entire population of the earth; Avraham, for all his courage, bases his bargaining with God on the idea that he can find two handfuls of righteous people in Sodom and Gomorrah. But Moshe argues on behalf of a group of the most blatant sinners and challenges God in no uncertain terms: "My people? *Your* people!" "What will the Egyptians says about You if You destroy the Israelites here in the desert? How is that going to look?" These are the arguments of a strong man, not a timid one.

Playing his trump cards—the smashing of the tablets, the offer to have his name wiped from the Book (like Amalek!)—is an act of monumental courage, a gamble of his own life and name and future on behalf of a people whose loyalty to him and to God is still at issue. More than that, Moshe will continue to debate and bargain with God throughout the remainder of the *parashah*, even asking that he be allowed to see God face-to-face: "Show me your glory." This is a far different Moshe from the young man who slew the taskmaster, who doubted his own ability to speak on behalf of the Israelites in bondage. Indeed, the maturing of Moshe is one of the most satisfying and, dare I say, moving developments in *Sefer Shemot*. We have seen this seemingly simple and truly humble man grow in stature in a truly extraordinary manner.

All that remains is the most bizarre transformation, perhaps the only one possible after he has reached this stage of his development. When he descends from the mountain one final time, having seen the back of God as the Eternal One passes him, Moshe's face is flooded with some preternatural radiance, so bright, so strange that he must wear a veil for the rest of his life to protect the Israelites from the sight of his glowing countenance. In short, his encounter with God has left him both disfigured and transfigured, elevated out of the commonplace in a way that forever sets him apart from *B'nei Yisrael*.

And yet, wasn't he always set apart? Raised in the palace like a member of Egyptian royalty, he married into the family of a Midianite priest. When no other Hebrew would stand up against oppression, he struck down the taskmaster. He alone has spoken with God, and done so repeatedly. Now his separateness is made manifest in a way that affirms his gift of prophecy—the greatest such gift in all Jewish history, the rabbis tell us.

Prophecy, like leadership, is a poisoned chalice, a gift that keeps on taking, and one senses that Moshe has already paid a terrible price in isolation and alienation from his people. But the worst price will be exacted later.

For now, let us leave him as he is at the end of the *parashah*, bathed in the glow of his encounter with the Awesome.

ADDITIONAL NOTES

- With 139 verses, *Ki Tisa* is the longest *parashah* in *Sefer Shemot*, the tenth longest in the Torah.
- Although it goes against every depiction of the *lukhot* we have ever encountered, the Torah states quite clearly in *Shemot* 32:16 that they had the words of God engraved on both sides. Wonder how a couple of thousand years of artists missed that one?
- The census taken at the outset of this *parashah*—the first of many we will see in the remainder of the Torah—was usually associated in the Ancient Near East with the assembly of an army (and we will see it in that context shortly). Consequently, one way of understanding the rather odd "ransom" of the half shekel is to read it as a form of absolution *avant le lettre* for a body of soldiers who are nothing less than

killers-in-waiting. War may be a necessary evil for *B'nei Yisrael*, but it is still an evil.

- The juxtaposition in this *parashah* of the laws of Shabbat with the appointment of Betzalel and Aholi'av as master craftsmen in charge of the construction of the *Mishkan* is undoubtedly what caused the rabbis of the Mishnaic period to use the thirty-nine forms of labor expended on the *Mishkan* as the guidelines for the types of labor forbidden on the Sabbath.

- One passage in the discussion of the Sabbath will be immediately familiar to anyone who attends Shabbat services. *Shemot* 31:16–17 is sung at both *Ma'ariv* and *Shakharit* services as *Veshamru*.

HAFTARAH

Much as Moshe confronts *B'nei Yisrael* after the sin of the Golden Calf, so does Eliyahu confront those who would proselytize for idol worship in this *haftarah*. (There is even a recurrence of the symbolism of the young bull in his test of the powers of *Adonai* against those of the "prophets" of Baal.)

PARASHAT VAYAK'HEIL

22nd Torah portion, 10th in *Shemot*
Shemot 35:1–38:20(122 verses)
Haftarah: *Melakhim Aleph* 7:40–50 (Sephardic: *Melakhim Aleph*
   7:13–26)

ALIYOT*

First / Rishon:	35:1–35:20
Second / Sheini:	35:21–35:29
Third / Shlishi:	35:30–36:7
Fourth / Revi'i:	36:8–36:19
Fifth / Khamishi:	36:20–37:16
Sixth / Shishi:	37:17–37:29
Seventh / Shevi'i:	38:1–38:20
Maftir:	38:18–38:20

SYNOPSIS

Moshe teaches the rules of Shabbat. Moshe then repeats the words that God commanded him (beginning in *Shemot* 25) concerning the materials needed for the *Mishkan* and its furnishings; Betzalel of the tribe of Yehudah and Aholi'av of the tribe of Dan are mentioned specifically by name to be the artisans and creators of all the furnishings and artwork. Moshe then tells Betzalel and Aholi'av all of God's instructions (although he changes the order of the items). Betzalel and Aholi'av make all the items asked for.

COMMENTARY

Sefer Shemot is primarily the story of Moshe's relationship with God, his growth as a human being, and how that changes and is changed by his position vis-à-vis the Israelites as a collective entity. Consequently, there are few subsidiary characters who don't have some direct impact in those areas. Pharoah, Aharon, Tzipporah, Yitro—they all exist in *Shemot* largely, if

*See Additional Notes on page 391 for the *aliyot* when *Vayak'heil* and *Pekudei* are read together.

not exclusively, as yardsticks against which Moshe measures himself (and we measure him), or as people who help him in his personal growth.

It is only at the very end of *Shemot* that we are introduced to an important secondary character who doesn't seem to serve one of those functions.

What are we to make, then, of Betzalel?

Betzalel is introduced by God to Moshe in *Shemot* 31:1–2 (in *Ki Tisa*) in precisely the same terms that Moshe will use to introduce him to *B'nei Yisrael* in *parashat Vayak'heil*. He is a master craftsman whose skills extend to many fields and that, as Nahmanides remarks, is impressive in and of itself:

> Since the Israelites were crushed by their hard labor with mortar and bricks in Egypt, and they never learned the craft of silver, gold, or precious stones, it was a miracle that anyone was skilled in working with silver and gold, and that anyone could skillfully cut precious stones, [be a] weaver or embroider. Even among the disciples of the wise, a master of all crafts is rarely found. Moreover, it was a phenomenal event for a person to possess, in addition to his craftsmanship, wisdom, insight, understanding of the secrets of the *Mishkan* and all its fixtures, including the reasons they were ordered and what they symbolized.

How does God introduce Betzalel?

"I have called Betzalel . . . by name and I have imbued him with *ru'akh Elohim/the spirit of God*, with *khokhmah/wisdom, tevunah/insight, da'at/knowledge,* and all manner of craftsmanship. . . ." And Moshe essentially repeats this passage verbatim. This passage, taken together with his name, tell us key facts about him.

Betzalel means "in the shadow of God" and *Or Ha'Khayim* says of his work on the *Mishkan* that he has made a shade for God, that is to say, a resting place for the *Shekhinah* as a manifestation of the Eternal. More than that, though, Betzalel echoes *"b'tzelem Elohim,"* the description of the Creation of humanity. This resonance cannot be fortuitous; Betzalel's work of creation is a Divinely inspired ("I have called Betzalel") effort at *imitatio dei*, the imitation of God, a small *c* counterpart to the Creation itself.

The text repeatedly draws parallels both explicit and implicit between the building of the *Mishkan* and the Creation of the world. As we have already seen, there is a recurring juxtaposition of the laws of Shabbat and the instructions for and construction of the *Mishkan*. God has instilled in Betzalel *"ru'akh Elohim,"* a phrase we first encountered at the very beginning of the Torah (*Bereishit* 1:2): "And *ru'akh Elohim* was on the face of the waters." The language that is used to describe the completion of the *Mishkan* in *parashat Pekudei* is a deliberate parallel of the language used to describe the completion of the Creation. Finally, and perhaps most significant of all, are the three attributes that God has instilled in Betzalel, *khokhmah, tevunah,* and *da'at.* In *Mishlei* 3:19–20 these are the three qualities that are attributed to God in the act of Creation.

Thus, creativity is seen as both a counterpart to the Divine and a product of a "calling" of God-inspiration and—given that the blueprint for the *Mishkan* is repeated several times in the course of the text—guidance. God does not limit the inspiration of the Eternal to prophets or leaders. It can find expression in art and craft. Remember the words describing the priestly robes: "for glory and beauty." The aesthetic is an integral part of the spiritual, and beauty is an element necessary to spiritual fulfillment.

Finally, though, Betzalel's achievement, while great, is not comparable to that of the Creator. He makes the *Mishkan* from a plan, with the help of thousands of Israelites, from materials donated by the entire community. As we have insisted throughout, it is a collective effort. (In fact, the classical commentators all state that the reason for the second presentation of Betzalel by Moshe is that the community must assent in his appointment as the chief craftsman.)

By comparison, what distinguishes the "Jewish" God from other deities of the time and region, and the Jewish cosmology from that of other pre-Abrahamic peoples is that God makes the world from *tohu v'vohu* and that is something that no mere mortal artisan can do, no matter how skilled or imbued with a Godly inspiration.

ADDITIONAL NOTES
- Usually paired with *parashat Pekudei*.
  When they are paired the *aliyot* are as follows:

First / Rishon: 35:1–35:20
Second / Sheini: 35:21–37:16

Third/Shlishi:	37:17–37:29
Fourth/Revi'i:	38:1–39:1
Fifth/Khamishi:	39:2–39:21
Sixth/Shishi:	39:22–39:43
Seventh/Shevi'i:	40:1–40:38
Maftir:	40:34–40:38

- There is a grammatical anomaly at *Shemot* 35:22 that has become a source of much imaginative interpretation. The Torah describes the "men and women coming together" to donate for the building of the *Mishkan*. This passage would stand out anyway since it is one of the rare occasions in *Sefer Shemot* in which the role of the women is given equal prominence to that of their male counterparts. But the Hebrew is rather odd, saying that the men came *"al ha'nashim/upon the women."* Rashi takes this to mean that the women were there first, so eager to be a part of this sacred event that they preceded their laggard husbands in their fervor. This interpretation ties in nicely with a running theme of the incident of the Golden Calf, that it was the men who wanted to create this statue and that they did so despite the express disapproval of the women. There is a strong midrashic tradition that the men were unable to persuade the women to give their earrings and bracelets for the creation of the Golden Calf and therefore had to contribute their own.

- The trio of *khokhmah, tevunah,* and *da'at* resonates so powerfully in Jewish lore that it became the basis of the name given to the Lubavitch Hasidim, Chabad—<u>Ch</u>ochmah, <u>B</u>inah (a grammatical variant on *tevunah*), <u>Da</u>'at.

- What, you are probably wondering, about Betzalel's colleague Aholi'av? It is evident from the comparative involvement of each in the text itself that Aholi'av is a somewhat subordinate figure, but the rabbis find it interesting that he comes from the tribe of Dan, one of the lesser tribes of Israel. From this, they believe, we are to understand that no one's ability to contribute to the community is to be discounted regardless of one's humble origins.

HAFTARAH

The parallel between *parashat Vayak'heil* and its *haftarah* is quite obvious. Where the *parashah* focuses on the building of the *Mishkan*, its prophetic counterpart recounts the building of the Temple by Shelomo, with Khiram/Hiram serving as the master-builder counterpart of Betzalel and Aholi'av.

PARASHAT PEKUDEI

23rd Torah portion, 11th and last in *Shemot*
Shemot 38:21–40:38 (92 verses)
Haftarah: Melakhim Aleph 7:51–8:21 (Sephardic: *Melakim Aleph*
    7:40–50)

ALIYOT*

First / Rishon:	38:21–39:1
Second / Sheini:	39:2–39:21
Third / Shlishi:	39:22–39:32
Fourth / Revi'i:	39:33–39:43
Fifth / Khamishi:	40:1–40:16
Sixth / Shishi:	40:17–40:27
Seventh / Shevi'i:	40:28–40:38
Maftir:	40:34–40:38

SYNOPSIS

A statistical summary of the materials used for the Tabernacle and an account of producing the priestly vestments are recorded. Moshe blesses the Israelites for the work they did. Upon God's instruction, Moshe sets up the *Mishkan* and the priests are anointed and consecrated. A description is given of a cloud that covers the *Mishkan* by day and a fire that burns by night, indicating God's Presence therein. The portion and *Sefer Shemot* ends with the Glory of God filling the Tabernacle.

COMMENTARY

With the completion of *parashat Pekudei*, we reach another milestone in the annual cycle of Torah readings, the end of the book of *Shemot*. We have read two-fifths of the Torah, we begin the middle book of the *Khumash* next week. And if I say that the Jews are in the heart of their journey, I could be referring to Moses and *B'nei Yisrael* wandering in the Wilderness or to contemporary Jews working their way through Torah.

*See Additional Notes on page 397 for *parashat Vayak'heil* for *aliyot* when this portion is read with *Vayak'heil.*

Taken together, as they frequently are, *Vayak'heil* and *Pekudei* present some interesting problems. They seem to be little more than a repetition of *Terumah* and *Tetzaveh*, the two portions that precede the high drama of *Ki Tisa*. Like those two earlier passages, these seem merely to be enumerations of the materials and procedures for building the *Mishkan*. I find this bracketing of the incident of the Golden Calf quite satisfying from the point of view of narrative structure.

Two portions on the building of the *Mishkan*, the disastrous sin of the Golden Calf, two portions on the building of the *Mishkan*, end of book.

Neat.

But it's more than simply graceful.

There are, as we have noted elsewhere, commentators who believe that the story of the Hebrews in the Wilderness is not told in strictly linear chronology, that the incident of the Golden Calf takes place before the instructions for the building of the *Mishkan* and that what we read in *Ki Tisa* is a flashback of sorts. If one accepts that interpretation, it makes the relationship between these five *parashiyot* much less problematical for the reader.

But even if it isn't correct, that structural device upon which I have remarked still has a deeper purpose. Remember that in *Terumah* Moshe is told that donations for the construction of the *Mishkan* should come "from every person whose heart is moved" (*Shemot* 25:2). That instruction is repeated in both the two portions before and the two portions after the Golden Calf. And in these *parashiyot* we are told that the people were so eager to contribute that there was a surplus of materials for the construction of the *Mishkan* and a surplus of labor, that the job got done ahead of schedule and under budget, so to speak. And finally Moshe tells the Hebrews, "That's enough. Stop bringing already!"

What has happened here? Think back to the bracketing structure of this final movement of *Shemot*—the bookending of the sin of the Golden Calf by the work of the *Mishkan*. Yes, the people have sinned grievously, so much so that God contemplates their destruction and has to be talked out of it by Moshe. Blood is spilled within the community of the Hebrews and much guilt is incurred.

Then the Hebrews come together as a community—as a community, mind you—to work collectively to build the *Mishkan*. And the work of the actual building of the *Mishkan* is something that explicitly calls upon an entire community, each utilizing the skills she and he have at their disposal for the greater glorification of the Eternal.

But not only for the glorification of the Eternal. Also in gratitude of the wonders God has performed for the Israelites and in repentance for the collective sin of building and worshipping the Golden Calf.

And here's one more way in which the bracketing structure is significant. From instructions on how to honor God, we move to a futile effort in which nearly the entire community is involved in honoring something else, not God but a pagan idea of godlike power. Although a tiny percentage of the Hebrews are directly implicated in the sin of the Golden Calf— 3,000 out of some 600,000—most of the community is complicitous because of its grumbling and its failure to stop that dangerous splinter group. Consequently, only by the act of the entire community can that sin be expiated. Collective sin, collective atonement.

So the act of building the *Mishkan* is a collective act of *teshuvah*, of repentance and of turning back to the Creator.

That also explains one of the oddities of the last two *parashiyot* that has troubled commentators both classical and contemporary, the sheer repetitiveness of the description of the building process. We were told in copious detail of the plans for the building of the *Mishkan* before the incident of the Golden Calf. Now much of that detail is repeated virtually verbatim as the construction actually occurs. It is as if the "narrator" feels obliged to show us that the Israelites conformed to the original plans, to tell us that despite the hideous lapse committed shortly before, they are committed to the Covenant as it was enunciated at Sinai.

Finally, the building of the *Mishkan* renders honor to the Creation by reenacting it. In fact, *Shemot* 39:43 echoes *Bereishit* 2:1: when the Creation is completed, God pronounces it good "and blessed the seventh day"; when the building of the *Mishkan* is completed, "Moses saw the entire work and lo! they had done it. . . . So Moses blessed them."

As the work of building the *Mishkan* is a communal effort, it also builds a community. In *Shemot* 36:13 it says, "It came to pass that the Tabernacle was one [whole]." And so, too, are the Hebrews. At least for the moment.

There is one oddity in these two *parashiyot* that can be best understood if we consider this thematic development. As we have noted before, at the beginning of *Vayak'heil* there are three verses concerning the observance of the Sabbath. These appear to come out of nowhere and they break up the seeming flow of the narrative. What are these doing here? Why is Moshe reminding us yet again of the Sabbath?

The one thing that initially set the Jews apart from other peoples is the Sabbath, an observance of sanctified time rather than sanctified space or a sanctified object. At the outset of the work of building, Moshe calls the Jews together to reaffirm that concept of sanctified time, time set apart from the dailiness of work, a reminder of what makes them a people apart just as they are about to engage in a work that unites them as a community in the service of God. The echoes of the Creation that we will see shortly are echoes of the Creation of Shabbat. It is not an accident that when the rabbis sought to define what forms of work were forbidden on the Sabbath they used the building of the *Mishkan* as their guide.

The people Israel and the Sabbath and the Creation and the service of God are as intimately, as integrally intertwined as the cords that were woven to hold the High Priest's ephod.

KHAZAK, KHAZAK, V'NITKHAZEIK.

ADDITIONAL NOTES

- Frequently paired with *parashat Vayak'heil.*
- The building of the *Mishkan,* as outlined in the last two *parashiyot* of *Sefer Shemot,* takes approximately four months. It is now nine months since the Israelites arrived at the base of Mount Sinai.
- An interesting and suggestive detail in the building of the *Mishkan:* the bronze of the women's mirrors is used in the creation of the altar and incense stands. Samson Raphael Hirsch says that the inclusion of this detail bespeaks the importance of the sensual as a component of the spiritual. There is a midrash that says that Moshe didn't want to use the mirrors because they were indicative of vanity but God told him that they were more important as a reminder that the women— who donated them—sustained and kept alive the Hebrews throughout the difficult years of slavery in Egypt.
- *Shemot* ends with Moshe silent. We last hear him speak in direct address in the final verse of chapter 39. Thus, as Richard Elliott Friedman notes, *Sefer Shemot* ends as it began, with its focus on the Israelites and their relationship with the Almighty. In between, aptly enough, Moshe serves as a mediator in that relationship.

HAFTARAH

As in its immediate predecessor, *parashat Pekudei* is paralleled by a *haf-tarah* that recounts the comparable stage in the building of the Temple by Shelomo. Like the *parashah*, it shows readers the completion of a God-inspired and -ordained construction project. Now the *Mishkan*, so laboriously constructed in the Wilderness, will have a permanent home in Jerusalem.

SEFER VAYIKRA/THE BOOK OF LEVITICUS

Third book of the Torah
10 *parashiyot*
27 chapters, 859 verses, the shortest book of the Torah

As Richard Elliott Friedman notes, *Sefer Vayikra* comes as something of a surprise after the tumult of *Bereishit* and *Shemot*. Those books were filled with incident, miracles, and action, with narrative spilling over itself. By contrast *Vayikra* has almost no narrative at all, little poetry to speak of, no movement in space, and little passage of time. The entire book takes place at the foot of Mount Sinai as God imparts the *mitzvot* to Moshe and *B'nei Yisrael*. In short, this is a book filled with the words of God, not the acts of God.

As Friedman says, the laws are given as part of the flow of narrative, dictated by Moshe. The situation grows organically out of the flow of the story, with the Divine presence made manifest in the Tent of Meeting, as reported at the end of *Sefer Shemot*.

The logic here is impeccable. *Sefer Bereishit* traced the roots of a people. *Sefer Shemot* showed them being welded into a nation, first through the shared experience and history of slavery and liberation, then by a shared project and labor, building the *Mishkan*. We can take it as given that this is now a budding nation, but what kind of a nation will it be? That is what *Vayikra* is meant to address, and the answer is quite explicitly given in the course of this book. They are to be a nation consecrated to *Adonai*, who says, "You shall be holy because I, *Adonai*, your God, am holy." (Not surprisingly, the first elements of a hierarchical society are the *kohanim* and *levi'im*, castes dedicated to performing the rituals outlined here.)

The process of making this nation a holy one begins with the rituals of sacrifice. From this point on, all worship is centralized. The only place where one can bring and make sacrifices to God is the altar at the entrance to the Tent of Meeting. That will remain the case, at least theoretically, until the destruction of the Second Temple in 70 c.e. (which housed the same altar). For now, one can only atone for sins through sacrifice, but that must of necessity change after the Second Temple is razed. At that point, much of the ritual detailed here becomes moot and, unless and until the Third Temple is erected and the Messiah comes, must so remain.

Yet we study these laws, which occupy much of the first part of *Sefer Vayikra,* to some purpose. Perhaps, as Bernard Bamberger says, the purpose is historical, to trace the path that took our ancestors through the Wilderness to Kina'an and from "a nation of priests" to a scattered people worshipping in a very different way. At the very least, reading these laws can give us some insight into the mind-set that informed ancient Judaism. In that respect, it is useful to note that the book falls into two halves, the first a disquisition on the separation between the pure and impure in all aspects of daily and ritual life, the second a code ordaining "holiness."

As we will quickly see, there is much to be learned from *Vayikra* that has a practical use for us in our daily lives. It is here that we will find the most basic moral precepts that have ostensibly governed behavior in Western civilization for three millennia, as well as specifically Jewish phenomena like the dietary laws and rituals of the Festivals. In short, whatever *Vayikra* lacks in narrative drive and length, it more than makes up for in pith. You could say that *Sefer Vayikra is* essential Torah.

PARASHAT VAYIKRA

24th Torah portion, 1st in *Vayikra*
Vayikra 1:1–5:26 (111 verses)
Haftarah: Yeshayahu 43:21–44:23

ALIYOT

First / Rishon:	1:1–1:13
Second / Sheini:	1:14–2:6
Third / Shlishi:	2:7–2:16
Fourth / Revi'i:	3:1–3:17
Fifth / Khamishi:	4:1–4:26
Sixth / Shishi:	4:27–5:10
Seventh / Shevi'i:	5:11–5:26
Maftir:	5:24–5:26

SYNOPSIS

God instructs Moshe on the five different kinds of sacrifices that are to be offered in the sanctuary:

- The *olah* or "burnt offering" is a voluntary sacrifice that had a high degree of sanctity and is regarded as the "standard" offering. The entire animal, except for its hide, is burned on the altar.
- The *minkhah* or "meal offering" is a sacrifice made of flour, oil, salt, and frankincense that is partly burned on the altar and partly given to the priests to eat.
- The *zevakh sh'lamim* or "sacrifice of well-being" is a voluntary animal offering from one's herd, sometimes brought to fulfill a vow.
- The *khatat* or "sin offering" is an obligatory sacrifice offered to expiate unintentional sins. This offering differs from the others in the special treatment of the blood of the animal.
- The *asham* or "penalty offering" is an obligatory sacrifice of a ram that is required chiefly of one who has misappropriated property.

COMMENTARY

The Random House Dictionary of the English Language says:

Sacrifice: 1. The offering of animal, plant or human life or of some material possession to a deity, as in propitiation or homage. 2. Something that is so offered. 3. The surrender or destruction of something prized or desirable for the sake of something considered as having a higher or more pressing claim. 4. The thing so surrendered or devoted.

The word is derived from the Latin *sacer,* meaning "holy," the same Latin root that is found in a word like *sacerdotal,* meaning "priestly."

But that's not quite what *parashat Vayikra* says.

The Hebrew word used to describe all the offerings detailed in this Torah portion is *korban,* and it has a very different meaning, "that which is brought near." Literally, of course, it is the offering that is brought near to God but, as Abravanel says, "It likewise implies that the offering, if brought in the right spirit, is the medium whereby man attains to closer nearness to the Divine."

But—and this is an important question—what constitutes "the right spirit"?

Much of this Torah portion and the next are dedicated to answering a related question: What constitutes the right procedure? Judaism is very much a religion of the commonplace and the methodical, of daily occurrences and ordered procedures. Indeed, much of the book of *Vayikra* consists of the laws governing the correct procedures for doing things like making offerings to God.

The answer to Abravanel's thornier question can be found in *parashat Vayikra,* too. That answer actually suggests that the Jewish understanding of *korban* and the Latin-derived English word *sacrifice* are closer kin than one might suspect.

Consider the instructions regarding the burnt offering, the first one described in *Vayikra.* In *Vayikra* 1:3, it states that the animal brought as an offering shall be "of the herd or flock" and "it shall be a male without blemish."

"Without blemish." That instruction is repeated in the description of subsequent offerings. It is repeated in nine different cases. And the animals sacrificed are always taken from the herd or flock. These are never wild animals, never animals that have been rejected as having some flaw. They are the best.

And in several cases males are specifically called for. This isn't some patriarchal sexist prescription; for a farmer, a male will be more valuable, able to breed almost at will, unlike females who must be in heat and who can only bear once or twice a year, and stronger, able to pull a plow or an oxcart and therefore capable of multiplying the value of farmland.

When a meal offering or an offering of flour is called for, the text is equally specific. It must be the finest flour and oil. The offering should include salt, a commodity of great value in a society in which refrigeration is unknown. As Rabbi J. H. Hertz notes, these "are not natural products, but are obtained as the result of toil."

In other words, what is called for in making an offering to God is that you give up something of value: a steer or ram from your flock; birds that take time and skill to capture; the best flour you have to offer, with salt.

This would seem to be completely congruent with our dictionary definition 3: "The surrender or destruction of something prized or desirable for the sake of something considered as having a higher or more pressing claim." And the linkage of sacrifice with the holy is inescapable.

But there is an important caveat.

In *Vayikra* 5:7, in the discussion of the sin offering, the Torah states, "And if he is not able to bring a lamb, then he shall bring his trespass that he committed two turtle-doves, or two young pigeons, unto *Adonai*." And a few sentences later, in verse 11, it continues, "But if his means suffice not for two turtle-doves or two young pigeons, then he shall bring his offering for that wherein he hath sinned, the tenth part of an ephah of fine flour. . . ."

God does not expect us to impoverish ourselves in order to draw near to the Divine Presence.

The laws governing the sacrifices are incredibly detailed, entailing a series of difficult choices for the one bringing an offering to *Adonai*. As my frequent *khevruta/study partner* Connie Heymann writes:

Consider the web of decisions needed to be made in contemplation of a *korban*. What relationship with God am I attempting to achieve? Am I thanking God (and for what), asking for God's attention, atoning for a sin, consecrating my work? If I am a sinner, what was the sin? [Was it] intentional or unintentional? Is further action, restitution, or punishment needed? What are my economic circumstances—what offering can I afford? What type of offering is appropriate? Am I making this sacrifice as an individual or communally? This is a multifaceted, multidimensional diagnostic.

Obviously the complexity of the laws governing the sacrifices reflects the even greater complexity of our relationship with God. In a sense, then, the answer to the question of "right spirit" is embodied in the specific circumstances of the sacrifice.

And yet . . .

When the Temple fell, the sacrifices ordained in *Vayikra* could no longer be brought to Jerusalem for the *kohanim*. The rabbis, in their great wisdom, looked upon a battered and beaten Jewish people, the feet of the Roman Empire's finest soldiers on their necks, and decided that the appropriate substitute for the offerings of cattle, sheep, birds, and fine flour would be the words of prayer that we speak even today.

And therein lies the answer to the question, What constitutes "the right spirit" in which to draw near to God? The rabbis called prayer the service of the heart, and it should come from the heart, from the innermost part of ourselves. Like the offerings made in the *Mishkan* and the offerings made at the Temple in Jerusalem, it should be a gift to God, given out of a sense of love, of free will, or given as an act of *teshuvah*, of repentance and returning, turning to God. And it should be the best of ourselves that we can bring.

ADDITIONAL NOTES

- In the Torah scroll, the first word of this *parashah*, *"vayikra/and [God] called"* ends with a small letter *aleph;* there is a midrash that explains this oddity by saying that God welcomes any sacrifice, no matter how small or seemingly insignificant.

- In *Vayikra* 2:13 we are told to sprinkle salt on every grain offering. Today, that ritual is recalled in the custom of eating salt with one's bread when making *motzi*, the blessing for bread that is part of every meal of an observant Jew.

- *Minkhah*, the meal offering, would eventually give its name to the afternoon service, which replaces it in the calendar of daily observances.

- Why is a bird offered in sacrifice first divested of its crop? The other animals offered are domesticated and their diets are presumably regulated by their owners. But birds go where they please and eat whatever comes their way. So we are addressing a question of ritual purity by removing a part of their digestive system. (Incidentally, in the stricture that a bird sacrificed not be cut into pieces, unlike the other animal sacrifices, the ritual regulations echo Avraham and the "Covenant of the Pieces.")

HAFTARAH

In the *haftarah* to this *parashah*, Yeshayahu contrasts the idol worshipper with Ya'akov, showing that Ya'akov's devotion to *Adonai* helped give *B'nei Yisrael* the opportunity of serving God in the Temple, God's own "home" on earth. Like the Torah portion, the *haftarah* is very much concerned with how one establishes the proper attitude to service of the Almighty. Yeshayahu prophesied in the aftermath of the destruction of the First Temple and he urges the Jews in exile in Babylonia to bring "offerings of the heart," that is, prayer, as a substitute for the sacrifices delineated in the *parashah*.

PARASHAT TZAV

25th Torah portion, 2nd in *Vayikra*
Vayikra 6:1–8:36 (97 verses)
Haftarah: Yirmiyahu 7:21–8:3; 9:22–23

ALIYOT

First/Rishon:	6:1–6:11
Second/Sheini:	6:12–7:10
Third/Shlishi:	7:11–7:38
Fourth/Revi'i:	8:1–8:13
Fifth/Khamishi:	8:14–8:21
Sixth/Shishi:	8:22–8:29
Seventh/Shevi'i:	8:30–8:36
Maftir:	8:33–8:36

SYNOPSIS

The five sacrifices that the priests are to perform are described. Limitations on the consumption of meat are delineated. Moshe consecrates Aharon and his sons as priests, and the preparations of the *Mishkan* as a holy place are given.

COMMENTARY

The opening verses of *parashat Tzav* are recited in many congregations around the world as part of the daily morning service. The subject matter—the complexities of the *olah*—is one that would seem to have no practical purpose, other than the injunction to engage in the study of sacred texts. The *mizbe'akh/altar* in the *Mishkan* no longer exists. With the Temple destroyed, the laws governing animal sacrifice are suspended. The fire on the altar has been extinguished for almost two thousand years.

Or has it?

The S'fat Emet says that the line from *Tzav* stating that the fire on the altar is not to go out is "a prohibition, but also a promise." If one takes the fire as a metaphor, the nature of that promise may be better understood.

Rabbi Mordechai Katz notes that there were really two inextinguishable fires in the *Mishkan*, the *ner tamid,* described at the beginning of *parashat Tetzaveh,* and the *eish tamid/perpetual fire,* the burnt offering described in the opening of this *parashah.* "The former was a flickering light which burned continuously on the Menorah, while the latter was a fire of powerful warmth that blazed without a stop on the [*mizbe'akh*]." Katz likens the flames to the attitude a Jew should have to the Torah, that one must pursue Torah with the unrelenting intensity of the *eish tamid,* yet maintain the modesty of the smaller, but no less constant *ner tamid.* And this combination of modesty and enthusiasm must be maintained with consistency or the "flame" of Torah will go out in our life.

The S'fat Emet reminds readers of another aspect of that constancy and consistency. Every morning the priests would bring new wood for the fire, just as we pray in the morning service that God renews our lives each day. With this ritual of beginning anew every day we experience a process of renewal and redemption, and the fire of the *eish tamid* is symbolic of that process. The fire of Torah, he continues, is like the fire on the altar, both giving light and threatening to burn us: in the Torah, Rabbi Alter reminds us, there are 248 positive *mitzvot,* performed out of love, and 365 negative *mitzvot,* obeyed "from fear of heaven." Thus, we engage in prayer, the replacement for the fire offerings, as a way of renewing our souls each day, and as a way of acknowledging the awesome (and fearful) power of *Adonai.*

Rabbi Schneerson offers a slightly different take on the fire on the *mizbe'akh.* For him, the fire is also a metaphor for the way one lives the Jewish tradition. "It is not a private possesion to be cherished subconsciously. It must show in the face a person sets toward the world." Thus one must speak words of Torah "with fire," so that they penetrate to the very core of your being. Torah study must not become dull rote, but should be done with a constant enthusiasm, a fire that never goes out, if you will. After all, didn't the Jewish mystics say that the Torah was written with black fire on white fire?

There is another telling detail in this *parashah* that reinforces our understanding of the *eish tamid* as a symbol. Each day the priest is enjoined to remove the ashes of the previous day from the altar. In *Vayikra* 6:3–4 he is instructed to dress in his linen tunic and pants, to lift up and place the ashes beside the altar, to change into other clothes, and then to "take the ashes to an undefiled place outside the camp."

This is a dirty and probably unpleasant job. But it must be done by a *kohein.* There is a Jewish saying from the Palestinian Talmud that speaks directly to this legal requirement: *Ein gedulah b'falatin shel melekh/In the king's palace no rank is recognized.* In other words, no one should approach the Almighty, the true Sovereign, with a superior attitude. In the eyes of God, all are alike, children of Adam, created *b'tzelem Elohim.* (At the same time, notice that the priest removes his priestly garments before taking the ashes away; as the Talmud says, "The clothes worn to cook a stew for one's master are not worn to pour wine for him." Proprieties must be observed in the public sphere.)

What intrigues me about this tidbit is the implication that, although he has an exalted relationship with *Adonai* (remember the *urim* and *tumim*), the priest is still just an ordinary guy, especially when he's out of his robes of office. And even though his role is exalted, he is not the only one responsible for maintaining a relationship with God. In the Temple in Jerusalem, there was a system of twenty-four watches kept over the two permanent flames; for this all-important job, not only *kohanim* and *levi'im* were selected. Jews from all walks of life and levels of education and income participated in the watch. Josephus reports that there was an annual day on which all Jews from across Israel and Judea would bring wood to be burned on the altar of the Second Temple.

Remember, too, that while being a priest or a Levite was predicated on membership in a specific tribe, it was not strictly hereditary. As Yeshayahu Leibowitz notes, "The Torah given to any Jew is not handed down by inheritance. Each generation must study it on its own, and does not inherit it from its fathers." The only men who come into the high priest-hood directly by heredity are the sons of Aharon (hence the instruction to Moshe in *Vayikra* 8:2, "take Aharon and his sons with him. . . ."). As we will see in the next *parashah*, the result of this line of succession is nothing less than disastrous and tragic.

The fact is that although the nation that God, through Moshe, is build-ing has a hierarchical system, it is surprisingly nonhierarchical in some important ways, hardly a democracy but, as we will see many times in the remainder of the Torah, not a rigid ladder of class and privilege either. Instead it is the sort of society in which the consecrated priest of God has to take out the rubbish (so to speak) and starts the process in his uniform of office.

All this can be gleaned from reading the first few verses of *parashat Tzav.* Perhaps there is a message even in the most abstruse and seemingly irrelevant passage of Torah. In that sense, it is the Torah itself that is the fire that never goes out.

ADDITIONAL NOTES

- The middle verse of the Torah, *Vayikra* 8:8, occurs in this *parashah*.
- The sin offering is made in the same place as other offerings. The reason for this is quite simple and says a great deal about Jewish ethical concerns. Being made at the same location as other offerings means that it is impossible to distinguish a sin offering from those others, with the result that those who bring a sin offering are not shamed by the community having knowledge of their identity.
- Moshe's washing of Aharon as part of the consecration rite anticipates the function of the *mikveh* in the Diaspora. In fact, *Sifra* states that Aharon was completely immersed in water, as one is at a *mikveh*.

HAFTARAH

Yirmiyahu begins the *haftarah* to this *parashah* by referring to the system of sacrifices enumerated in *parashat Tzav*, enunciating their true meaning. In denouncing the corruption of Israel, he echoes the ear, hand, and foot symbolism of the anointing of the priests: "[T]hey did not listen, nor inclined their ear, but walked in their own counsels." He then excoriates *Am Yisrael* for their faithlessness toward *Adonai* (in contradistinction to the implied obeisance of the consecration ritual).

PARASHAT SHEMINI

26th Torah portion, 3rd in *Vayikra*
Vayikra 9:1–11:47 (91 verses)
Haftarah: Shmuel Bet 6:1–7:17 (Sephardic: *Shmuel Bet* 6:1–19)

ALIYOT

First / Rishon:	9:1–9:16
Second / Sheini:	9:17–9:23
Third / Shlishi:	9:24–10:11
Fourth / Revi'i:	10:12–10:15
Fifth / Khamishi:	10:16–10:20
Sixth / Shishi:	11:1–11:32
Seventh / Shevi'i:	11:33–11:47
Maftir:	11:45–11:47

SYNOPSIS

Aharon and his sons follow Moshe's instructions and offer sacrifices so that God will forgive the people. Two of Aharon's sons, Nadav and Avihu, offer "alien fire" to God. God punishes these two priests by killing them immediately. God forbids Moshe, Aharon, and his surviving sons from mourning but commands the rest of the people to do so. Priests are told not to drink alcohol before entering the sacred *Mishkan* and are further instructed about making sacrifices. Laws are given to distinguish between pure and impure animals, birds, fish, and insects.

COMMENTARY

What does it mean to be a priest of Israel? What does the job actually entail? Reading *parashat Tzav* and *parashat Shemini*, one gets a sense of both the complexity and the gravity of the task. This weighty load of responsibilities is nowhere more apparent than in chapter 10 of *Vayikra*, when we see the completion of the consecration of the *Mishkan*.

In the final section of *parashat Tzav*, we shift back into narrative for one of only two occasions in *Sefer Vayikra*, the lengthy, solemn ceremony in which Moshe consecrates his brother and nephews as priests of *B'nei Yisrael*. As Everett Fox says, this rite derives much of its power on the

printed page from its insistent, rhythmic "alternation of verb and garment," as Moshe clothes Aharon in the robes of his new office. Then
Aharon and his sons sit down at the threshold of the *Mishkan* to wait for
seven days, and we, too, are left waiting for the week between *Shabbatot*.

There is a hushed, expectant air to this wait.

Something is about to happen, something awesome and, finally, terrible. When the next *parashah* begins (virtually) with the word *shemini/
eighth*, the waiting is over. At first, everything goes according to plan, with
a fire from heaven coming forth to engulf and consume the offering on the
altar. *B'nei Yisrael* are stunned by the spectacle and fall on their faces
in awe.

Then Nadav and Avihu enter "each with his firepan," burning incense
and offering *"eish zarah/strange (or unfitting) fire."* Again fire comes from
heaven—described in almost the exact same words—but this time, it is
the two eldest sons of Aharon who are consumed. (Or, to be more accurate, killed. Their bodies are left intact, making it necessary for their
cousins, who are not *kohanim* and, therefore, not forbidden to have contact with the dead, to remove their remains.)

What just happened here? Why are these two young men killed under
the watching eyes of their father, brothers, uncle, and the assembled
nation of Israel?

The death of Nadav and Avihu is one of the most difficult and troubling passages in the Torah, mysterious and shocking, not the least for its
startling suddenness. *Vayikra Rabbah* offers a dozen different explanations proffered for God's killing of the two young priests, and most commentators reluctantly admit that even these are not satisfying.

Among the many explanations that have piled up over the years:

- Nadav and Avihu were drunk when they made their terrible mistake.
  This explanation, favored by Rashi, among others, is derived from the
  fact that immediately following the events of the consecration, God
  relays to Aharon the injunction, "Do not drink wine or intoxicating
  drink when you enter the sanctuary and you will not die." This sounds
  like an ex post facto response to the events of the morning. (Significantly, it is the first time that God has spoken directly to Aharon alone
  since sending him to meet Moshe early in *Sefer Shemot*.)
- The two sons of Aharon were, by virtue of their positions as eldest offspring of the High Priest-to-be, so arrogant that they remained unmar-

ried, disdaining all the women of the Israelite camps as being beneath them. (And being unmarried, they were also childless.)

- In their arrogance, they dared to give halakhic rulings in front of Moshe.
- They dreamed of the day they would supplant their father and uncle, muttering, "When will these two old men die?"
- They didn't believe that God would ignite the offering and brought their firepans in order to do it themselves. Rashbam, who supports this hypothesis, suggests that the fire that consumed the burnt offering was the same fire that killed them.
- They entered the Holy of Holies without being commanded to do so.
- They entered the Holy of Holies without washing their hands and feet.
- Their death was actually a punishment of Aharon for the incident of the Golden Calf.
- They didn't consult each other, but acted impulsively, swept up in the spirit of the moment of the consecration, too foolish to think about the results of their actions.
- Conversely, they weren't being punished at all. They had achieved such an exalted level of enlightenment that God took them to the Throne on the spot.

None of these explanations is sufficient in itself. Taken together, they may be suggestive. Certainly there are some threads that run through most of them that we can weave together. With the exception of the non-punishment school (a small minority in the commentaries I have read), there seems to be agreement that Nadav and Avihu acted improperly, bringing "strange fire" that they were not commanded to bring, breaching the complicated rules with which they were presented at the outset. Whether this breach was the product of arrogance or excessive zeal is open to debate.

My own inclination is to return to the actual text of the Torah to look for the answer. There are some clues embedded there that skilled commentators have pried out for our examination. Consider, for example, an odd notation remarked upon by Samson Raphael Hirsch, a series of points that occur over the identification of Nadav and Avihu as "the sons of Aharon." Hirsch suggests that this is meant as a reminder that these two young men were only individual members of *B'nei Yisrael* and, acting as such, had failed to seek advice from their elders, that they were "not at one with the Nation."

Rav Chanoch Waxman finds an even more telling motif in the *parashah.* Throughout chapter 9 he finds the recurrence of two important roots, *kof-resh-vav,* meaning "to come close/approach/offer," and *tzadi-vav-he,* "to command." *Adonai* commands, Aharon approaches the altar, God commanded that the offering be made, and so on. In describing the ritual to come and its actual occurrence, Waxman notes, the term *command* appears five times, *approach/offer* eight times. Then Nadav and Avihu appear at the beginning of chapter 10, "and they offered [*va'yakrivu*] before *Adonai* a strange fire which [God] had NOT commanded [*tzivah*] them." Waxman finds their error here, in their failure to recognize that there is a connection between approaching God and obeying the Almighty's commandments, that "[o]nly by virtue of the fulfillment of the exact command can one achieve 'closeness' with God."

Many commentators argue here that there are times when it is not appropriate to improvise. One does not juggle live hand grenades. One does not invent new rituals under the very eyes of the Creator. (Coming on the very first day of the actual use of the *Mishkan,* this bespeaks particularly atrocious judgment.)

More than that, it shows a failure of understanding, a failure to realize that as priests, Nadav and Avihu are supposed to represent *Am Yisrael,* not themselves. They are literally *shlikheit tzibur/messengers of the community.* Not to stretch a point, but when they appear before God with their ill-fated offering, the text describes them each carrying "HIS firepan" (emphasis added). They are atomized individuals, not engaged in representing a community. They have severely abrogated their responsibilities on many levels.

Whatever their other failings, Nadav and Avihu suffer from lack of control over their emotions. Whether the cause is arrogance or excessive zeal for God, they allow their fervor to overwhelm the teachings they have received and have lost any sense of self-restraint. Is their punishment excessive? One does not run wildly through a minefield and expect that there will be no consequences. It's a comfortless answer, but that seems to be what the text is saying.

Perhaps we must accept the notion that there isn't an entirely satisfactory answer to the question of why Nadav and Avihu are killed. The Khatam Sofer remarks that when Moshe sees God's back on Mount Sinai, it is indicative of the reality of our relationship with God, that we only perceive the Eternal One's actions when they are in the past. We cannot understand God in the present tense, let alone the future. And that means, ultimately, that we can only guess at God's motives in the past as well. All we can do is try to regulate our own behavior so that it is appropriate to the gravity of the moment, all the more so when we stand on holy ground. And that is something Nadav and Avihu failed to do.

ADDITIONAL NOTES

- The middle words of the Torah, *darosh daresh,* occur in this *parashah,* in *Vayikra* 10:16.
- In the word meaning "belly," which occurs in *Vayikra* 11:42, the *vav* is written larger than usual. This is the middle letter of the entire Torah.
- Another possible lesson to be gleaned from the story of Nadav and Avihu has to do with crossing the line between the pure and the impure. One can infer that lesson by noting that the remainder of the *parashah* is a detailed accounting of the laws of *kashrut,* which are predicated on precisely such a division.

HAFTARAH

The *haftarah* to *parashat Shemini* presents us with another great celebration and consecration, David's establishment of the capital at Jerusalem and the arrival of the ark at its proper resting place in the City of Peace. But, as in the *parashah,* the rejoicing is marred by a breach that is punished instantaneously by death, when Uzzah touches the ark to steady its progress and is struck down (perhaps, as some commentators have suggested, crushed by the oxen of the cart bearing it).

PARASHAT TAZRIA

27th Torah portion, 4th in *Vayikra*
Vayikra 12:1–13:59 (67 verses)
Haftarah: Melakhim Bet 4:42–5:19

ALIYOT*

First / Rishon:	12:1–13:5
Second / Sheini:	13:6–13:17
Third / Shlishi:	13:18–13:23
Fourth / Revi'i:	13:24–13:28
Fifth / Khamishi:	13:29–13:39
Sixth / Shishi:	13:40–13:54
Seventh / Shevi'i:	13:55–13:59
Maftir:	13:57–13:59

SYNOPSIS

God describes the rituals of purification for a woman after childbirth. God sets forth the methods for diagnosing and treating a variety of skin diseases, including *tzara'at* (a skin disease usually translated—inaccurately— as "leprosy"), as well as those for purifying clothing.

COMMENTARY

There is a ceiling that limits human aspirations. Death, which comes to us all, writes an end to our dreams and plans, whether we are Nadav and Avihu or Moshe and Aharon. This fact is at the heart of the sequence of *parashiyot* that deals with the issues of ritual purity (*toharat*) and impurity (*tumah*) that are the primary topic of *Shemini, Tazria,* and *Metzora*. In an obvious way, the litany of skin diseases, inflammations, discharges, and other not terribly appealing bodily behaviors, bundled together as *nega'im tazria / the affliction of tazria* (commonly but inaccurately translated as "leprosy"**) are cheerless reminders that eventually we will all die and

---

*See Additional Notes on page 417 for the *aliyot* when *Tazria* and *Metzora* are read together.
**Hansen's disease, the illness that is known today as leprosy, was not identified until considerably later in Western history than the biblical period, and is a very different condition from

that our bodies will decay, returning to the earth out of which God formed Adam.

Yet *parashat Tazria* begins with the seeming opposite, a woman giving birth. It's not that hard to see the connection. The pessimist will say that a person is born only to die. The realist, looking at it in a less jaundiced way, will not say that only God is *"b'li reishit, b'li takhlit/without beginning, without end,"* as we sing in *"Adon Olam."* Seen in that light, one can even understand the anomaly by which a woman who gives birth to a daughter underwent a purification period twice as long as one who had a son. This stricture is not a comment on the comparative worth of male and female children but a tacit acknowledgment that it is the female child who has the potential to carry on the cycle of birth and death through childbearing.

Even so, there is something bewildering to the modern reader about this lengthy and, frankly, tedious discussion of corpses, menstruation, skin disease, mildew and dry rot in the walls of the home. Samson Raphael Hirsch, that pillar of German nineteenth-century Orthodoxy, links the discussion to the classic mind/body problem of philosophy, albeit in an indirect way. Presaging the existentialists, Hirsch writes that "contact with dead bodies . . . awaken[s] the idea of the human lack of freedom" by reminding us in a terrifyingly immediate way of our own mortality, of the "conditions which are capable of endangering the consciousness of moral freedom . . . as they prevent living Man from succumbing to physical necessity."

Consider the range of topics covered in these three *parashiyot:* clean and unclean food, birth, menstruation, disposal of the dead, skin afflictions, circumcision. In each case, we are dealing with the brute biological facts of life, the often messy necessities of our biological nature. In each case, we are presented with *mitzvot* designed to impose some order on the chaos of biology. We divide potential foodstuffs into the permitted and prohibited, the people with whom we come in contact into pure and (temporarily) impure. We are presented with ways to consecrate the impure and, in circumcision, a way in which, Hirsch says, we assert our "mastery over, and moral consecration of, the sensual body."

In short, these laws represent nothing less than a means of sacralizing the daily world in which we live, of acknowledging our connection to the

---

that described in the Torah, which seems to contain elements of eczema, gonorrhea, and psoriasis.

Eternal in even the most ordinary aspects of life, of elevating even "the biological foulness of human existence," to use Yeshayahu Leibowitz's evocative phrase. (Remember that Judaism even has a prayer to be uttered after going to the bathroom.)

By doing so, Judaism offers its own take on the mind/body problem. As Leibowitz observes, one must worship God not merely with the mind but with a unity of mind and body. By imposing a spiritual dimension on quotidian concerns like meals and medical concerns like *tazria*, we are doing just that.

ADDITIONAL NOTES

- When *Tazria* and *Metzora* are read together, the *aliyot* are as follows:

First / Rishon:	12:1–13:23
Second / Sheini:	13:24–13:39
Third / Shlishi:	13:40–13:54
Fourth / Revi'i:	13:55–14:20
Fifth / Khamishi:	14:21–14:32
Sixth / Shishi:	14:33–15:15
Seventh / Shevi'i:	15:16–15:33
Maftir:	15:31–15:33

- With the destruction of the Second Temple in 70 C.E., nearly all of the *mitzvot* governing ritual purity were suspended. The only exceptions are *niddah* (laws governing menstruation) and *tevilah* (laws governing immersion in the *mikveh*), which are actually as much about sexuality as ritual purity. In the case of a woman who has recently given birth, she may be called to *bentsch gomel*, that is, to thank God for delivering her from a life-threatening situation, a sort of liturgical substitute for the thanks offerings of the Temple (another link between birth and death and, until the mid-twentieth century, still a real danger).
- *Tohorot* is the order of Mishnah that deals with the issues of ritual purity. It is the largest of the six orders of Mishnah, suggesting that the rabbis of the period felt that these were still problems worth discussing in detail even if there were no Temple in Jerusalem.
- Maimonides points to the command to circumcise male children given in this *parashah* as the reason for observing that rite. He rejects the explanation based on God's instruction to Avraham, as well as medical

explanations, asserting the primacy of the Sinai experience in Jewish law.

HAFTARAH

Not surprisingly, the *haftarah* for *parashat Tazria* deals with an account of someone suffering from a skin disease, in this case King Na'aman, who offers anything to the prophet Elisha if he can devise a cure. Elisha tells him that God alone can cure him but that he must bathe seven times in the Yardein. Na'aman reluctantly does so and is cured, but when he offers gifts to Elisha, the prophet rejects them, reminding him that it was God who effected the cure.

PARASHAT METZORA

28th Torah portion, 5th in *Vayikra*
Vayikra 14:1–15:33 (90 verses)
Haftarah: Melakhim Bet 7:3–20

ALIYOT*

First / Rishon:	14:1–14:12
Second / Sheini:	14:13–14:20
Third / Shlishi:	14:21–14:32
Fourth / Revi'i:	14:33–14:53
Fifth / Khamishi:	14:54–15:15
Sixth / Shishi:	15:16–15:28
Seventh / Shevi'i:	15:29–15:33
Maftir:	15:31–15:33

SYNOPSIS

Priestly rituals to cure *tzara'at* when it afflicts humans are described. Rituals to rid dwelling places of *tzara'at* are presented. The *parashah* discusses male impurities resulting from a penile discharge or seminal emission. The *parashah* concludes with accounts of female impurities caused by a discharge of blood.

COMMENTARY

> A lie will go round the world while truth is pulling its boots on.
> —Charles Haddon Spurgeon (1834–1892)

In Tractate *Sanhedrin* of the Talmud, the rabbis state emphatically, "The house affected by the plague never existed and is not destined to exist. [The case] was stated for the purpose of edification." If so, we must ask, what is going on here? What are we supposed to learn from the incredibly complicated explanation of *tzara'at* in the walls of a house? And does this apply, by extension, to the no less complicated and thor-

*See Additional Notes for *Tazria* on page 417 for the *aliyot* when *Tazria* and *Metzora* are read together.

oughly mysterious rituals and rules surrounding *tzara'at* in a human being?

Even a cursory reading of the classical commentaries will alert you to the fact that a lot of what is happening in this *parashah* was just as baffling to the sages eight hundred years ago as it is to us (which should come as a relief). Their first instinct is to look for a cause of *tzara'at*, hoping to work backward to find a way to apply these rules and rituals in some discernibly practical fashion.

As so often happens in such cases, the rabbis fell back on the peculiarities of the written Hebrew language. Once again the lack of vowel markings enables them to find multiple meanings in a word; this time the word is *metzora/one afflicted with tzara'at*. In its place they read *motzi ra/one who brings forth evil*, while some of them also suggest that *metzora* is an acronym for *motzi shem ra/one who brings forth an evil name*. But they all agree, following that line of reasoning, that *tzara'at* is a punishment for engaging in *lashon ha'ra* (literally "an evil tongue"), that is, gossip and slander.

To understand how they justify this interpretation from the text itself, we must fast-forward to the middle of *Sefer B'midbar*. In chapter 12, Miriam denounces her younger brother Moshe for marrying a Cushite woman and monopolizing the right to prophesy. She is punished with a horrible case of *tzara'at*. Rashi makes an additional connection between "bad" speech and bad skin: when Moshe demurs before the Burning Bush, telling God that the Israelites will not listen to him, one of the signs that *Adonai* gives him is to turn his hand white and scaly, which Rashi infers is a punishment for his disrespect for the Hebrews. Elsewhere in the *Tanakh* there are numerous cases in which slanderous talk results in *tzara'at*. For Maimonides, the relationship was incontrovertible: "*Tzara'at* is not a natural phenomenon but rather a sign and wonder for the people of Israel to warn them against *lashon ha'ra*."

In fact, *lashon ha'ra* is a deplorable form of conduct, one that the Chofetz Chaim, author of the definitive text on the subject, says violates no fewer than thirty-one *mitzvot*. In the small, self-contained communities where the Jews lived between the liberation from Egypt and the Emancipation in Europe, the sin of malicious talebearing could have particularly devastating effects. Whether in the traveling caravans of the Wilderness, the urban ghettos of Western Europe, or the shtetls of rural Poland, Ukraine, and Russia, gossip had the power to destroy a community as great then as in the era of the Internet and satellite TV hookups. The sages were well aware of the danger it presented to the unity of the Jewish people in those cloistered worlds. As Samson Raphael Hirsch notes, the laws governing *tzara'at* are really as much about social misbehavior as ritual impurity. To be reintegrated into society, he observes, "requires the complete surrender of egoism . . . on [*metzora's*] reentry from the unsocial animal attitude to life of the social human one."

Rashi finds a satisfying metaphor for this process in a tool of the purification ritual itself, the bundle of cedarwood and hyssop tied with a scarlet thread that accompanies the bird offering. For him, the cedar is a tall, imposing tree, signifying the haughtiness of the gossip; hyssop is a low, humble bush, standing for the way that the transgressor must humble himself to be reunited with the community; and the red thread symbolizes a kind of worm (Rashi here is punning on the Hebrew, *tola'at*, which means both "thread" and "worm") that despite its seeming unimportance can fell even a mighty cedar by dint of slow, repeated efforts.

Now we can see the dry rot of the home affected by *tzara'at* as something other than a literal phenomenon that the rabbis themselves place little credence in. Rather, it is the damage done metaphorically to the *shalom bayit/peace of the house* by those who spread slander, a life-denying, community-destroying practice that, as it is written, threatens the very existence of three: the one who repeats the tale, the one who listens, and the one who is the subject.

ADDITIONAL NOTES

- Because the *parashah* opens by referring to the "day of cleansing," a phrase not used elsewhere in this context, the rabbis inferred that this purification ritual could not be performed at night.
- A log, the fluid measure used in several places in this *parashah* and the previous one, is thought to be the approximate equivalent of a half liter.
- While *tzara'at* is not leprosy (see footnote to commentary on *parashat Tazria*, page 415), at least one of the sets of symptoms described in this *parashah* corresponds to an all-too-common contemporary illness, gonorrhea. According to Professor Yeshayahu Nitzan, the description in chapter 15 of a man "who has a running issue out of his flesh" fits the etiology of that sexually transmitted disease.

HAFTARAH

The fate of an embattled Jewish community hangs on the actions of four *metzora'im* in the *haftarah* to this *parashah*. The inhabitants of the city are being starved out by an Aramean siege. When the exiled "lepers" go to the Aramean camp in search of food, they discover that the Arameans have fled for unknown reasons. They notify the Jews that the siege has lifted and the community survives. The implications of this story are clear enough: that even the *metzora* can serve a valuable role for the community and eventually be reintegrated.

PARASHAT AKHAREI MOT

29th Torah portion, 6th in *Vayikra*
VAYIKRA 16:1–18:30 (80 verses)
Haftarah: Yekhezkel 22:1–19 (Sephardic: *Yekhezkel* 22:1–16)

ALIYOT*

First / Rishon:	16:1–16:17
Second / Sheini:	16:18–16:24
Third / Shlishi:	16:25–16:34
Fourth / Revi'i:	17:1–17:7
Fifth / Khamishi:	17:8–18:5
Sixth / Shishi:	18:6–18:21
Seventh / Shevi'i:	18:22–18:30
Maftir:	18:28–18:30

SYNOPSIS

The duties that the High Priest must perform on Yom Kippur are delineated and the ceremony of the scapegoat is outlined. Moshe instructs Aharon about the Yom Kippur laws for fasting and atonement. Warnings are issued against the offering of sacrifices outside the Sanctuary and about the consumption of blood. Moshe condemns the sexual practices of some neighboring peoples. Certain forms of sexual relations are prohibited.

COMMENTARY

If there is one day on the Jewish ritual calendar that brings all but the most alienated Jews to a synagogue, it is Yom Kippur, the Day of Atonement. Yom Kippur is usually (and accurately) described as the holiest day of the Jewish religious year, called in this Torah portion *Shabbat Shabbaton / the Sabbath of Sabbaths.* Yet the description of the observance of this solemn occasion is seemingly perfunctory, shorn of the gravitas and mystery that custom has invested it with over the nearly two millennia since the rabbis began to codify Jewish law.

*See Additional Notes on page 425 for the *aliyot* when *Akharei Mot* and *Kedoshim* are read together.

For starters, as Menahem ben Yashar points out, the sections of the Torah that deal with the holidays usually begin with the date on which the festival is observed. ("In the first month, on the fourteenth day of the month, there shall be a passover offering to *Adonai*" [*Vayikra* 23:5].) In fact, there is a later reference to Yom Kippur, in *Vayikra* 23:27, that says, "Mark this, the tenth day of the seventh month is the Day of Atonement."

But in chapter 16 the solemn rites by which the *Kohein Gadol/High Priest* marks *Yom Ha'Kippurim* are outlined as an aftermath (and perhaps a response) to the deaths of Nadav and Avihu. The larger communal implications of the holy day are only introduced—with the traditional formula—at the end of the chapter.

There is, I believe, a fairly simple explanation for this departure, one that grows out of the unique nature of Yom Kippur and the place this passage occupies in *Sefer Vayikra*.

With *parashat Akharei Mot*, we have reached the midpoint of the Torah and the midpoint of *Sefer Vayikra*. Appropriately enough, this *parashah* is a fulcrum, a pivot point at which we move from a discussion of the priesthood and issues of ritual purity (often called the Priestly Code or Purity Code) to a discussion of how all of *B'nei Yisrael* are to live in harmony with *Adonai* in the Covenant (called the Holiness Code). In a sense, as Rabbi David Zvi Hoffman notes, *Sefer Vayikra* is structured as a response to God's injunction to the Hebrews at Sinai: "You shall be to me a kingdom of priests and a holy nation." *Vayikra*, then, is an operating manual for fulfilling that pledge, outlining the job of the priests and explaining how individuals and communities can be holy.

This duality is reflected in the use of the word *kippur* and its cognate forms. The word describes purging of ritual uncleanliness, but also the canceling of guilt for moral obligations. As Rabbi Abraham Walfish observes, we can see the transition happen in consecutive uses of the *khof-pei-resh* root in chapter 16:

> Thus he shall purge [*ve'khiper*] the Shrine of the uncleanness and transgression of the Israelites, whatever their sins. (*Vayikra* 16:16)
> For on this day atonement shall be made for you to cleanse you [*yekhaper*] of all your sins. . . . (*Vayikra* 16:30)

The rituals to be performed by the High Priest are a combination of the two, the cleansing of the *Mishkan*, not merely in the wake of the disastrous events of the day but also as an annual rite, and the purging of the sins of the community through the rather cryptic ritual of the two goats.

(There is a school of thought that says that the actions performed by Aharon at the outset of this Torah portion are specific to the aftermath of his sons' deaths rather than an annual event. The failure of the text to invoke the formula for Festivals lends some credence to that point of view. But the ritual of the "scapegoat" seems to be intended as a repeated event in the ritual calendar.)

Yom Kippur marks the transition between—or more properly, the unification of—ritual purity and collective and individual confession/atonement. To be holy, we must be cleansed of our sins. We must perform *teshuvah*, not merely "repentance" but literally and figuratively, a (re)turning to God. In the days of the *Mishkan* and the Temple, the *Kohein Gadol* could serve as our representative to further that process, but in the world post–70 C.E., we must make our own peace with those against whom we have sinned, make our own turning to God. Only then can we reach a state implied by the English word *atonement:* to be *at one* with the Creator.

The Torah is also very clear on a related point. With the shift from the Purity Code to the Holiness Code, we move from ritual into ethics, and much of what follows is about how we live with other humans. In *Vayikra* 18:5 we read, "When a human shall do [the *mitzvot*] he will live through them." Thus, the laws and precepts of Torah are not only a way to be at one with God but also to be at one with our neighbors, a path to life. And, as we will see in the next *parashah*, that path must take us into healthy relations with all other human beings, pagan or Jew.

ADDITIONAL NOTES

- When *Akharei Mot* and *Kedoshim* are read together, the *aliyot* are as follows:

First / Rishon:	16:1–16:24
Second / Sheini:	16:25–17:7
Third / Shlishi:	17:8–18:21
Fourth / Revi'i:	18:22–19:14
Fifth / Khamishi:	19:15–19:32
Sixth / Shishi:	19:33–20:7
Seventh / Shevi'i:	20:8–20:27
Maftir:	20:25–20:27

- The term *scapegoat*, so evocative of the ritual described at the beginning of this Torah portion, was coined by William Tyndale, the first great English translator of the Bible.

HAFTARAH

The greater part of this *parashah* is a catalog of forbidden sexual relationships. It is to the this section that the *haftarah*, drawn from *Sefer Yekhezkel*, refers for much of its length. Yekhezkel castigates *Am Yisrael* for their many violations and profanations of the Sabbath and other *mitzvot*, but gives particular attention to the sexual depravity of the Hebrews before predicting their downfall.

PARASHAT KEDOSHIM

30th Torah portion, 7th in *Vayikra*
Vayikra 19:1–20:27(64 verses)
Haftarah: Amos 9:7–15 (Sephardic: *Yekhezkel* 20:2–20)

ALIYOT*

First / Rishon:	19:1–19:14
Second / Sheini:	19:15–19:22
Third / Shlishi:	19:23–19:32
Fourth / Revi'i:	19:33–19:37
Fifth / Khamishi:	20:1–20:7
Sixth / Shishi:	20:8–20:22
Seventh / Shevi'i:	20:23–20:27
Maftir:	20:25–20:27

SYNOPSIS

God issues a variety of commandments, instructing the Israelites on how to be a holy people, following the Divine example ("I am holy, therefore you shall be holy"). Various sex offenses are discussed and punishments for them are presented. Many ethical and social commandments are given here as well.

COMMENTARY

"Be holy because I am holy."

"Love your neighbor as yourself."

Parashat Kedoshim contains some of the most famous and familiar *mitzvot* in all of Torah, commandments that we know by rote—which is not the same thing as "by heart."

Yet in these all-too-familiar, all-too-easily recited words are a series of the most profound, most difficult, and most abstruse commandments. Only their familiarity disguises the demanding nature of what is being required of us. This *parashah*, we are told in *Sifra*, contains the essence of

---

*See Additional Notes for *Akharei Mot* on page 425 for the *aliyot* when *Akharei Mot* and *Kedoshim* are read together.

the entire Torah. As Bernard Bamberger observes, *Kedoshim* exacts a higher morality than "Be good in order to be happy." Rather, it urges us to be holy "for God is holy." We have been told since the very first *parashah* that we are created *b'tzelem Elohim* and, as Martin Buber writes, "The fact that it has been revealed to us that we are made in [God's] image gives us the incentive to unfold the image and in doing so to imitate God."

But what does it mean to be holy? What can we, mere humans and mortal, do to imitate God?

Of course, the *mitzvot* given in this Torah portion and elsewhere provide the most direct and obvious answer. Follow My commandments, God tells us, and you will be Holy like Me. Why else would the phrase "*Ani Adonai / I am Adonai*" occur sixteen times in chapter 19 alone, usually after a series of edicts?

Although, as we have established before, *Aseret Dibrot,* are not privileged in any way over the other 603, they certainly provide a clear set of guidelines and a starting point. At least, that is how I interpret the fact that they are repeated in the Holiness Code, here in chapter 19.

There are small but significant differences between the two occurrences of the Decalogue. The first, "I am *Adonai,*" becomes "I am *Adonai* your God." We are enjoined not to make molten gods, not to swear falsely by God's name, to keep (rather than remember) the Sabbath, to fear (rather than respect) our parents. The parallels become less exact as we shift to the second half, but as Rabbi B. S. Jacobson notes, there are definite correspondences:

First appearance of Decalogue	*Equivalent in Holiness Code*
You shall not murder.	You shall not stand idly by the blood of your neighbor.
You shall not commit adultery.	You shall be holy.
You shall not steal.	You shall not steal.
You shall not bear false witness.	You shall not go about as a talebearer.
You shall not covet.	Love your neighbor as yourself.

The *mitzvot* given here are a wide-ranging lot, and if there is a logic to their order it has escaped two millennia of commentators.

But that is precisely the logic.

The *mitzvot* of the Holiness Code are given randomly by design. No commandment is privileged over any other, there is no prioritization, no compartmentalization. (Yehuda Henkin notes that this portion contains more seemingly unrelated commandments than any other in the Torah.) The result, as Everett Fox notes, is that the Holiness Code reads holiness into all the aspects of daily life, as surely as the Priestly Code does so for ritual life. There is seemingly no aspect of our life into which the *mitzvot* do not extend, just as there is no area of Creation in which God is not present. Consequently, if we are to be holy, we must acknowledge and welcome the spiritual element into even our most ordinary and material concerns (just as, conversely, the Priestly Code projects the role of the priests into the messiest realities of keeping the *Mishkan* running).

The emphasis of the Holiness Code on ethical concerns and interpersonal relations is another measure of how important such affairs are in *imitatio dei*. Recall, if you will, what we said about the Creation, that all humanity descended from one couple (and after the Flood, from one family); the care lavished on rules of interhuman conduct is merely a confirmation of what the Torah has already told us, that we are all of one family, one line of blood. In *Vayikra* 19:34 we are told that the "stranger who dwells among you shall be as one born to you and you will love him as yourself." To twist the Roman playwright Terence a little, no one who is human is alien to me.

As Richard Elliott Friedman notes, the commandment "*v'ahavta l're'akha kamokha / and you shall love your neighbor as yourself*" is inherently unusual in *Sefer Vayikra*. Virtually all the other *mitzvot* here are about separation, distinction, difference. We are taught to distinguish between foods that are permissible and forbidden, between sacrifices that are acceptable and unacceptable. We are enjoined not to mix seed, not to interbreed animals of different species, even to eschew clothing of mixed fabrics. Yet this commandment—love your neighbor as yourself—is predicated on refusing difference. As Friedman writes, "[I]t stands out as anomalous. . . . In relations with one's fellow human beings one is commanded instead to *equate* them—to oneself and, by necessary implication, to one another" (emphasis in original).

But who are these neighbors? Friedman points out that the word *re'ah* may be translated variously as "neighbor," "companion," or "fellow," and means "a member of one's own group, a peer." Sometimes it may mean something as narrow as "fellow Israelite" or as broad as "fellow human." But the remainder of the chapter includes specific injunctions to love the alien as well as oneself.

I would go further. Those who read this commandment narrowly to suggest that only fellow Jews are worthy of such treatment are defying a basic principle of the Torah, the unity of all humanity derived from a single set of original parents, the negation of difference among people.

There is support for this position in the text itself. Jacobson sees verses 17 and 18 as a self-contained unit commanding altruistic love with five explicit *mitzvot:*

- You shall not hate your brother in your heart;
- You shall surely rebuke your neighbor;
- You shall not take vengeance;
- You shall not bear a grudge;
- You shall love your neighbor as yourself.

Yet, as Samson Raphael Hirsch notes, these call not for personal emotion but for personal feeling, the care and practice of works of love, "to participate in the welfare and woe of others."

How can we be like God?

We have already been made partners in the Creation. We must continue in that role by restoring balance in an imperfect world, by *tikkun olam* through acts of justice and loving-kindness. As Rabbi Menachem Mendel Schneerson said, "One can invest daily life with holiness by living in a way that reflects the teachings of God, the actions of mercy and compassion." In that way we are truly living *imitatio dei,* as beings created in the image of God.

ADDITIONAL NOTES
- In Tractate *Sanhedrin* of the Talmud, criminal courts are instructed to select the most lenient mode of punishment, particularly in capital cases, in accordance with the commandment to "love your neighbor as yourself."
- The *parashah* opens with Moshe being told to instruct "the whole congregation." The Khatam Sofer explains, "This does not mean the hermit's holiness of isolation and seclusion as a way of seeking the holy way. On the contrary, what is spoken of is the holiness of the commu-

nity, a holiness that springs precisely from being within a community, a congregation, mingling with other human beings."

HAFTARAH

Amos, from whose prophecies this *haftarah* is taken, is the prophet of social action par excellence, a speaker for justice and compassion first and foremost. The opening of the *haftarah* echoes the dialectic of individual and community found in the Torah portion, while the bulk prophesies the destruction of those who do not live up to the ideals of the *mitzvot*.

PARASHAT EMOR

31st Torah portion, 8th in *Vayikra*
Vayikra 21:1–24:33 (124 verses)
Haftarah: Yekhezkel 44:15–31

ALIYOT

First / Rishon:	21:1–21:15
Second / Sheini:	21:16–22:16
Third / Shlishi:	22:17–22:33
Fourth / Revi'i:	23:1–23:22
Fifth / Khamishi:	23:23–23:32
Sixth / Shishi:	23:33–23:44
Seventh / Shevi'i:	24:1–24:23
Maftir:	24:21–24:23

SYNOPSIS

Laws regulating the lives and sacrifices of the priests are presented. The set times of the Jewish calendar are named and described: the Sabbath, Rosh Hashanah, Yom Kippur, and the Pilgrimage Festivals of Pesakh, Shavuot, and Sukkot. God commands the Israelites to bring clear olive oil for lighting the sanctuary menorah. The ingredients and placement of the displayed loaves of sanctuary bread are explained. Laws prohibiting profanity, murder, and the maiming of others are outlined.

COMMENTARY

Much of *parashat Emor* seems to be a restatement or refinement of the rules governing the priesthood, or an outline of the biblical-era Festivals (Pesakh, Rosh Hashanah, Yom Kippur, Sukkot, and Shemini Atzeret chief among them). There is, however, one famous passage that has provoked so much comment—much of it negative and some of it bordering on anti-Semitic—that I feel obliged to focus on it here. It is in this *parashah* that we find the formula "an eye for an eye." (Actually, it is a restatement of a theme given a more detailed discussion in *Shemot* 21, but the phrase is hammered home here.)

The passage in which the principle of "an eye for an eye" (known in legal language as the *lex talionis*) occurs is one of the most controversial in the Bible. Jesus explicitly denies its validity. Others have pointed to it as an example of the vengeful nature of justice in the Hebrew Bible. Many liberal Jews are uncomfortable with the message it sends.

But does it send that message?

When Judaism's detractors use this passage as an example of the bloodthirsty nature of the "Hebrew God," they apparently ignore the fact that this formula applies only to human rather than Divine justice. One might say with equal merit that the God of Texas and Florida, two American states that apply the death penalty with alarming eagerness, is more vengeful than the God of Rhode Island, which does not have the death penalty on its books.

In discussing this passage, the Talmud specifically states that it is monetary compensation that is to be sought for an injury inflicted, rather than a comparable wound. Perhaps this interpretation is merely after-the-fact amelioration. It is hard to know for sure. This much is certain. The very earliest postbiblical sources we have are quite explicit in reading this passage as metaphorical, requiring monetary compensation for an injury rather than physical retaliation. As for the death penalty itself, we will return to that subject momentarily.

At least one recent commentator, Dr. Avigdor Bonchek, offers another perspective, one that views this passage of Torah in a startlingly new light. Dr. Bonchek (who is both a rabbi and a clinical psychologist) notes that in a contiguous passage discussing a man who is injured in a quarrel, the law demands a cash payment for "the loss of his time" until he is fully healed (*Shemot* 21:18–19). But in the passage in which the "eye for an eye" statement first occurs, *Shemot* 21:22–25, the reference is clearly to an accidentally incurred injury: "And if men strive and hurt a woman with child so that she have a miscarriage . . ."

This juxtaposition, he notes, would be odd enough—the accidental injury leading to a more severe penalty than the deliberate one. But if one refers to the Hebrew, a very different meaning becomes apparent. The passage reads, "But if there be harm then you shall give soul for soul, eye for eye, tooth for tooth, hand for hand, burn for burn, wound for wound, bruise for bruise." First, Bonchek notes, the logical wording would be "take soul for soul," and so on, but the Hebrew clearly says "give." This diction suggests compensation. What seals the case for him, though, is the use of the Hebrew word *takhat*; this word appears many times in the

Torah, he explains, "always with the meaning 'in place of' or 'on account of,' and never 'as identical substitution for.'" Consequently, he reasons, the meaning of the passage is that recompense must be *given in place of* the injured organ.

Seen in this light, it would appear that the ancient Israelite understanding of the *lex talionis* is considerably less savage than its counterpart in other Near Eastern societies of the time. This is not to suggest that Jewish law in these circumstance was somehow morally superior to that of its contemporaries. However, it is important to understand the drive toward a justice that could be applied meaningfully to real-world situations. One additional point worth noting: the insistence in *parashat Emor* on equal treatment for "stranger" and member of the community calls for a single standard of justice for all, and that is most definitely unusual.

But what about the issue of capital punishment? There is no escaping the horrific incident of the blasphemer who is stoned to death outside the camp at the end of this *parashah*. This shocking incident is made all the more disturbing by two facts. First, after fifteen chapters of legal materials, we are suddenly plunged back into the narrative, albeit briefly. Second, as Richard Elliott Friedman points out, when the elders "lay their hands on the head" of the alleged blasphemer, they are repeating the gesture that precedes a sacrifice given as a sin offering, an eerie parallel indeed.

That said, it must be noted that the sages of the Mishnaic period were very uncomfortable with the idea of capital punishment. In *Pirkei Avot* it is said that a court that put a man to death once every seven years should be considered excessively bloodthirsty; one of the sages quoted in *Pirkei Avot*, Rav Eleazar ben Azariah, went further, saying a bloodthirsty court was one that issued a death decree once every *seventy* years. Rabbis Akiba and Tarfon responded that had they been on a court with the power to issue the death penalty, no one would have been put to death.

The Oral Law makes it very difficult, virtually impossible, to execute someone for murder. In order for the death penalty to apply, two witnesses must have seen the perpetrator about to commit the crime and warned him of the potential penalty. The perpetrator must then acknowledge that he is aware of the illegality of his act and its consequences. The witnesses must see the actual murder; circumstantial evidence is not admissible in such cases. A capital case could only be heard by a panel of twenty-three judges, but such a panel could only be convened when the Temple was standing. Even then, although a majority of one for acquittal would mean the defendant was found not guilty, a majority of two was needed to convict. Finally, in a case in which the judges voted unanimously for conviction, there still could be no execution; in the legal system of the time, the judges served as both prosecuting and defending attorneys, so if a unanimous decision came down from the court it was considered as if the defendant had not been provided with counsel. As a result, the death penalty was never used, although lengthy prison sentences were often given when guilt could be established. (It is interesting to note that the State of Israel does not have the death penalty in murder cases. The only criminal ever executed in Israel was Adolf Eichmann; the state does reserve the right to use the death penalty in cases of crimes against humanity.) This issue will come up again in *Sefer Devarim* and we will examine it further then.

ADDITIONAL NOTES

- One could trace most of the Hebrew ritual calendar from this Torah portion. Among the Festivals ordered by *Adonai* here we find Pesakh, the "holiday of first fruits" (presumably Tu B'Shevat), Rosh Hashanah, Yom Kippur, Sukkot, and Shemini Atzeret. Intriguingly, the only one that is given a historical justification is Sukkot. We also find here instructions regarding the Counting of the *Omer*.

- However, in the Torah's calendar, Rosh Hashanah begins the seventh month of the year and the first holiday observed is Passover. The ritual calendar we use is of later origin.

HAFTARAH

The prophet Yekhezkel outlines the duties of the descendants of Zadok, the generation of priests-to-be who will minister in the New Temple of the New Jerusalem when the Babylonian captivity is over.

PARASHAT BEHAR

32nd Torah portion, 9th in *Vayikra*
Vayikra 25:1–26:2 (57 verses)
Haftarah: Yirmiyahu 32:6–27

ALIYOT*

First / Rishon:	25:1–25:13
Second / Sheini:	25:14–25:18
Third / Shlishi:	25:19–25:24
Fourth / Revi'i:	25:25–25:28
Fifth / Khamishi:	25:29–25:38
Sixth / Shishi:	25:39–25:46
Seventh / Shevi'i:	25:47–26:2
Maftir:	25:55–26:2

SYNOPSIS

God instructs Moshe to tell the Israelites that in every seventh year, the land shall observe a Sabbath of complete rest: fields should not be sown and vines should not be pruned. In addition, after forty-nine years (seven times seven), a *Yovel/Jubilee* year is to be celebrated when all the land that had been sold during that time should be returned to its original owners and slaves are to be freed.

COMMENTARY

Earlier we observed that one purpose of the commandments given at Sinai was to help shape the kind of nation that the Israelites were to become when they received the land promised them by God. The answer, as we have seen, is a nation of priests and a nation that dedicates itself to following the ways of God, of being holy. In *parashat Kedoshim* God instructed the Hebrews in many aspects of social conduct that contributed to the act of *imitatio dei*, of being holy like God. In *parashat Emor*, the Israelites are given a complex cycle of observances of holy days for the

*See Additional Notes on page 439 for the *aliyot* when *Behar* and *Bekhukotai* are read together.

purpose of sanctifying time. In *parashat Behar*, God completes the equation by linking holy time and holy space in a series of *mitzvot* that have, finally, a major social impact.

Although there remains one final *parashah* in *Sefer Vayikra*, the *mitzvot* given in this portion are essentially the last laws handed down in this book. Fittingly they are statutes governing the use of the land on which the new nation is to be erected, a series of ordinances that look forward to the near future, but also to a somewhat more remote one. The focus of the *parashah* is evident from the opening, in which *Adonai* tells *B'nei Yisrael*, "when you enter into the land that I assign you . . . "

Clearly, this is a special place, *Eretz Yisrael*, not merely a place of great abundance ("flowing with milk and honey") but of great holiness. Judaism in general does not place much stock in the notion of sacred place. Mount Sinai itself is not as important as what happened there, nor are the many altars erected by the Patriarchs the scenes of modern pilgrimages. There really is no Jewish equivalent of Lourdes or San Juan de Compostela. (Although the *Kotel/Western Wall* has assumed something like that role since the destruction of the Second Temple.) But *Israel* and the *Miskhan* are the notable exceptions. Consequently, the laws governing agriculture in the Land have a special resonance. Indeed, the only place in which the ordinances calling for a "Sabbath for the land" and the fifty-year Jubilee observance are applied is *Eretz Yisrael*.

God ordains that the land itself is to have a Sabbath, a year of rest every seventh year, in which no planting is to be done. Called the *shemitah*, from the root meaning "to let [something] drop," the year is also marked by remission of debts. Farmers are permitted to gather the yield of the seventh year—after all, the natural cycles go on even when cultivation is suspended—for the common good, with not only the landowner to partake of the results but the whole community. The result of this ordinance, as W. G. Plaut notes, is that the "landowner and the landless pauper are to be on an equal footing" for the length of the *shemitah*. (Incidentally, this represents a clarification and extension of *Shemot* 23:11.)

But this is to be more than a year of no labor. As Maimonides notes, this cannot be merely an exercise in responsible agriculture; one can achieve a more effective result with crop rotation or by letting land lie fallow in alternate years. As Shabbat is a day dedicated to God, so the *shemitah* is a year of holiness. Interestingly enough, in this context as in several others, the text personifies the land of Kiaa'an; where before it was said that the land would "vomit out" sinners, here the land requires a rest. Much as one rests one's animals on the Sabbath, the land itself demands to be dedicated periodically to the Eternal.

But *Behar* goes further.

It prescribes a Jubilee year, a *Yovel,* to occur every fifty years in which the land will, again, lie fallow; landed property will revert to the original owners (going back to the parceling out of *Eretz Yisrael* to the Twelve Tribes in the Torah) and all Hebrew slaves are to be liberated. The land does not belong to humanity. It is God's. As the Creator tells the Israelites, "The land is Mine; you are but strangers residing with Me." You cannot sell this land in perpetuity, you can only sell, in effect, the crops raised in the years leading up to the next Jubilee. Moreover, the Israelites ultimately serve only one master, God; hence the guarantee of periodic manumission of slaves. It is useful to recall that slavery in this context is the result not of conquest or abduction, as in the case of the African slave trade, but of a falling into dire poverty, a process that begins with selling one's land and ends in indentured servitude; the *Yovel* guarantees that one cannot remain a "servant" forever, except in serving God. (Significantly, the words for *servant* and *slave* in Hebrew come from the same root, and both have a wider range of meanings and associations than their English equivalents.)

The upshot of these two observances, the *shemitah* and the *Yovel,* is that every seven years the slate of debt is wiped clean, and every fifty years a family, no matter how impoverished, improvident, or imprudent, is given back the lands it has lost. The result is nothing less than a periodic redistribution of wealth (particularly so in an agrarian world in which land is the most basic form of riches). As Richard Elliott Friedman says, "The nation as a whole can never degenerate into a two-tiered system of the very rich and the very poor." This is a brilliant example of what Heinrich Heine calls "the moralization of property," and it grows out of the specifically sacred nature of this place.

At the same time, the *shemitah* and the *Yovel* represent the epitome of sacred time, a central concept in Judaism. Indeed, they are the culmination of a cycle of sevens, as Rabbi J. H. Hertz notes. Shabbat is, of course, the seventh day; Shavuot occurs on the seventh week (after Pesakh), commemorating the Giving of the Torah; Tishri, the month in which Rosh Hashanah, Yom Kippur, Sukkot, and the medieval festival of Simkhat Torah all occur, is the seventh month; *shemitah* occurs every seven years; and *Yovel* marks the completion of seven cycles of seven years, coming after the seventh *shemitah*, that is, in the fiftieth year. (Not coincidentally, I suspect, the description of the *shemitah* occurs in the first seven verses of the *parashah*.) All these observances are about the sacralization of time; the neatness of the cycle of sevens merely underlines that fact. Taken in tandem with their confirmation of the sacredness of *Eretz Yisrael*, the *shemitah* and *Yovel* represent a unique unification of sacred time and sacred space. (Remember, too, that this portion ends with a reaffirmation of the sanctity of the *Mikdash*, an acknowledgment, as it were, of the other example of sacred space to be found in the Torah.)

They also point to the kind of nation that God expects the Israelites to become. There is an insistence on social justice implicit in this Torah portion that goes beyond the tribal. Yes, only Hebrew slaves are covered by the *Yovel*, and the land laws imposed here are geared mainly to the Israelites. But text, which emphasizes the transient nature of even the Hebrew presence in the Land—you are but *strangers* who reside with Me—and the inalienable nature of the Land itself, that it can only be held in trust for God, held for fifty years at most before it reverts to its previous owners, suggests a more universal application of these principles. As Maimonides puts it, these ordinances are meant to instill "sympathy toward others and to promote the well-being of all."

ADDITIONAL NOTES

- When *Behar* and *Bekhukotai* are read together, the *aliyot* are as follows:

First / Rishon:	25:1–25:18
Second / Sheini:	25:19–25:28
Third / Shlishi:	25:29–25:38
Fourth / Revi'i:	25:39–26:9
Fifth / Khamishi:	26:10–26:46
Sixth / Shishi:	27:1–27:15
Seventh / Shevi'i:	27:16–27:34
Maftir:	27:32–27:34

- One verse from this *parashah* is particularly well known to many Americans. *Vayikra* 25:10, "Proclaim liberty throughout the land unto all the inhabitants thereof," is inscribed on the Liberty Bell.
- The Reform movement's guidelines for rabbinical contracts call for a sabbatical for a rabbi every seventh year. (Of course, no rabbi would use that year to "lie fallow.")

- There is a postbiblical text called the book of Jubilees, a Hebrew volume dating from some time in the Second Commonwealth, which recounts history from the Creation to the Revelation at Sinai in forty-nine-year increments. Oddly enough, it doesn't mention the *mitzvah* of the Jubilee Year.
- The Jewish National Fund's not-for-profit acquisitions of land in Israel, begun in the early days of the Zionist movement, were directly inspired by this Torah portion.
- A group of international activists chose this text as the basis for their political activities in the area of Third World debt. For an interesting contemporary attempt to apply the concept of the Jubilee year, take a look at www.jubileeusa.org and www.jubilee2000uk.org.

HAFTARAH

The prophet Yirmiyahu, although imprisoned for his vocal dissent foretelling the destruction of Jerusalem and the Babylonian captivity, manages to redeem a piece of land, keeping it in his family. Building upon the significance of this act (with its obvious echoes of the Jubilee Year), he predicts the eventual redemption of the Jews and their return from captivity to *Eretz Yisrael*.

PARASHAT BEKHUKOTAI

33rd Torah portion, 10th and last in *Vayikra*
Vayikra 26:3–27:34 (78 verses)
Haftarah: Yirmiyahu 16:19–17:14

ALIYOT*

First / Rishon:	26:3–26:5
Second / Sheini:	26:6–26:9
Third / Shlishi:	26:10–26:46
Fourth / Revi'i:	27:1–27:15
Fifth / Khamishi:	27:16–27:21
Sixth / Shishi:	27:22–27:28
Seventh / Shevi'i:	27:29–27:34
Maftir:	27:32–27:34

SYNOPSIS

God promises blessings to B'nei Yisrael if they follow the law and warns about the curses that will befall the people if they do not observe the *mitzvot*. Gifts made to the Sanctuary, whether by conditional vows or by unconditional acts of pious gratitude, are discussed.

COMMENTARY

The litany of blessings and curses that is the heart of *parashat Bekhukotai* is troubling to some commentators. For many these passages confirm the worst characterizations of the "Old Testament God" as vengeful, stern, and unforgiving. For others there is the simple incongruity of their presence at the end of *Sefer Vayikra*. Let's deal with the latter problem first.

In fact, as Rabbi Jacob Milgrom points out, a series of blessings and curses is frequently found at the end of legal documents from this period and region. The Code of Hammurabi ends with a passage not dissimilar to the bulk of chapter 26 and, in such documents, the curses invariably outnumber the blessings, which is the case here as well. (Nahmanides takes

---

*For *aliyot* when *Behar* and *Bekhukotai* are read together, see Additional Notes for *parashat Behar* on page 439.

issue with this measurement, however, arguing that "the blessings are stated as generalizations whereas the curses are stated in detail in order to frighten the hearers.")

The passage from the Code of Hammurabi reads in part:

> If that man has heeded my words, which I have inscribed on my monument, has not made light of my commandments . . . may Shamash enlarge that man's empire like mine . . . and may he lead his people in justice. If that man has not heeded my words which I have inscribed on my monument . . . may the great god Anu, father of the gods, deprive that man, . . . break his scepter, curse his destiny. . . .

There is a significant difference between the blessings and curses on offer in the Code of Hammurabi and those invoked in the Torah portion. As Milgrom notes, the nonbiblical curses are, in fact, prayers to the gods urging them to act against those who abrogate the contract. By comparison, the blessings and curses enumerated in the Torah are stated simply as the outcome of behavior: *if you do X, God will do Y, but if you do Z, God will do A.*

This goes to the heart of the ethical part of ethical monotheism. Behaviors have consequences. It's not just that there is one God; there is one God who punishes immorality and rewards goodness.

What is at stake here is not the power of God; that is inalienable, indisputable, infrangible. Rather, this is about the power of the word when spoken in God's name. We have seen this power in practice already repeatedly. Blessings, curses, vows, and oaths are all binding beyond any other human compact when the name of God is invoked. (We shall see this principle at work again in the discussion of oaths in *Sefer B'midbar.*) In a sense, that is why the blessings and curses are here, as the validation of that principle. Perhaps this is what Rabbi Menachem Mendel Schneerson meant when he said that *Behar* is about personal strength and fortitude (to withstand the demands of the *shemitah* and *Yovel* years) but *Bekhukotai* is about self-transcendence. By linking our vows to God we are asking ourselves to surpass our mere humanity.

Yeshayahu Leibowitz cuts to the heart of the matter by asking how long we can live on the merits of our ancestors. Yes, God remembers the Covenant, as promised, but the Jews must do their part for the Covenant to be fulfilled. Redemption itself depends on their fulfillment of the pact, not on what the Patriarchs and Matriarchs may have done in the past. They—and we—must make the God of Avraham, Yitzkhak, and Ya'akov their God, our God as well.

Redemption is a theme that runs through these last two *parashiyot*. As Milgrom notes, we are told in succession about the redemption of the Israelite slave, the redemption of the land, and, finally, of the possibility of redemption from exile "if [the Hebrews] demonstrate contrition for [their] sinful part." (The final section of *Bekhukotai* with its return to the mundane concerns of the *Mishkan* actually may be seen as a continuation of this theme, albeit in the most quotidian of manners.)

None of this mitigates the seemingly forbidding nature of the *tokhekhah/rebuke*, as the curses of this *parashah* are frequently called. We need to consider the implicit threat herein more carefully.

I find the use of the word *tokhekhah* in this context quite revealing. Recall the admonishment that God offers in *Kedoshim:* "You shall surely rebuke your neighbor. . . . You shall not stand idly by the blood of your neighbor." The word *rebuke* used there is derived from the same root as *tokhekhah*. God expects us to correct a neighbor who sins; it is an integral part of the Holiness Code, a corollary of the command to love that neighbor. We cannot stand by as he puts himself at risk through error or foolishness. How much more imperative then for the Creator to rebuke us, creations of the Eternal in God's own image, when we do the same. We have already been given the Divine promise that God will never blot out life on earth again, but there must be some consequences to our actions or free will is a farce.

At the bare minimum one can read the curses as a prophecy of the social and ecological consequences of unbridled greed, self-regard, and thoughtless exploitation of the Creation for selfish ends. Many contemporary Jewish thinkers, writing in a "green" vein, have interpreted these passages as expressing explicitly environmentalist concerns in line with the thrust of the *shemitah* and *Yovel*.

For all the sternness of the warnings, as Rabbi Bernard Bamberger writes, the Torah still offers us a "glimmering of hope" for even those who would ignore its precepts. The possibility of redemption is always inherent in the concept of *teshuvah*, of turning back to God. As Harvey Fields says, "[W]e may suffer the consequences of our choices but we are never completely doomed by them."

In a larger sense, the pattern of the *mitzvot* is so all-encompassing, so pervasive in our daily life that the mere fact of our existence—fraught with setbacks, disappointments, and the inevitability of death—is an interlocking series of causes and effects, so densely layered as to be almost unintelligible to us, beyond our understanding. The Talmudic sage Yannai said, "It is not in our power fully to explain either the well-being of the wicked or the suffering of the righteous," a disquieting thought that is repeated in many forms throughout the Rabbinic literature. Rabbi Robert Gordis expands on this by noting that we "are too close to the pattern of existence, too deeply involved in it, to be able to achieve the perspective that is God's alone."

Perhaps this is not a comforting notion. It is unsatisfying to say we simply don't know or understand the larger picture, especially if we are contemplating our own lived experience. To let it go at that, on the other hand, is an evasion of our responsibility as thinking beings, an insult to the One who gave us the power to reason. The negative consequences of violating the commandments governing our relationship with other humans, with the earth, and with other creatures should be self-evident. Perhaps Richard Elliott Friedman is right when he suggests that this *parashah* not be read as a promise of reward and punishment but, instead, as the logical outcome of having a society whose fabric is so weak, a community whose links are so attenuated, that events can topple it with a catastrophic force that goes beyond individual strife to a general societal breakdown, as in Sodom and Gomorrah, destroyed because they refused the most basic hospitality to guests.

Nor are we utterly bereft of a moral compass, of guidelines for our behavior. That, after all, is what the *mitzvot* are for.

KHAZAK, KHAZAK, V'NITKHAZEIK.

ADDITIONAL NOTES

- It is customary in most synagogues to read the *tokhekhah* in a low voice in order to avoid upsetting or embarrassing the congregants.
- Notice the specifically agrarian nature of the blessings and curses, a reflection of the concerns of the society the Hebrews were erecting.
- This *parashah* has a particularly poignant resonance for Yemenite Jews. They consider the passage from *Vayikra* 26:41, "*veheiveiti otam be'eretz oyvehem o az yikana levavan he'arel/when I have removed them into the*

land of their enemies then at last shall their obdurate hear humble itself" to be a direct reminder of one of the most tragic moments in their history. They consider the final letters of the last four words of this passage— *m, o, z, a*—as a mnemonic for Moza, a desolate town on the coastal plain of *Yamsuf*, to which they were expelled in 1679 and 1680 by the Muslim rulers of Yemen, a reaction against the rise of the false messiah Shabbetai Tzvi.

- There is a parallel catalog of blessings and curses in *Devarim* 28–30.

HAFTARAH

Like the Torah portion to which it is linked, this *haftarah* is filled with the threat of punishment, conveyed by God to the Israelites through the prophet Yirmiyahu. In chapter 17 of the book that bears his name, Yirmiyahu alludes to the future sins of the descendants of the original Twelve Tribes and warns them that God will "make you a slave to your enemies in a land you have never known."

SEFER B'MIDBAR/THE BOOK OF NUMBERS

Fourth book of the Torah
10 *parashiyot*
36 chapters, 1,288 verses
Sefer B'midbar contains the three longest *parashiyot* in the Torah:
  Naso (176 verses), *Pinkhas* (168 verses), and *B'midbar* (159 verses).

With *Sefer B'midbar* we return to the story of the journey of *B'nei Yisrael* toward Kina'an. Where *Vayikra* was predominately a catalog of laws with a (very) few narrative elements included, *B'midbar* is a narrative that incorporates a few more laws. It is certainly rich in plot elements: the rebellion of Korakh and his followers, Pinkhas's brutal vengeance of the man who lies with a Moabite woman; the running war with the Moabites, including the surprisingly funny incident of Balaam and his talking donkey; and a spate of grumblings from discontented Hebrews followed by testy replies from an increasingly impatient Moshe.

What ties these narrative elements together and even infiltrates its way into the *mitzvot* found in *B'midbar* is a new concern with the Hebrews as a nation. Rabbi Yonatan Grossman draws an interesting set of distinctions among *Shemot, Vayikra,* and *B'midbar.* Grossman writes:

In general, we might say that the book of Shemot describes the manifestation of God's presence, making God the protagonist of the account. In fact, the book concludes that "the cloud covered the Tent of Meeting and Hashem's glory filled the Mishkan" (40:34). The book of Vayikra related the story of the Mishkan's sanctification, and stresses the service of the Kohanim. Thus, the text relates that the Kohanim had the most important role to play during the days of dedication, and Hashem's presence descended on the eighth day to the exterior ALTAR, the focal point of the Kohanim's service. . . . [T]the book of Bamidbar now adds the wider national aspect. . . .

Of course, as we have seen amply illustrated in the previous two books, the entire process of the Exodus, the Revelation at Sinai, and the wanderings in the Wilderness from which this book takes its name is a necessary part of *B'nei Yisrael* becoming the adult nation of Hebrews that will conquer Kina'an, a nation consecrated to *Adonai*. But what happens in this book—the passing away of the generation of slaves with their slave mentality and attitudes and their replacement by a generation raised in freedom, occurring over a thirty-nine-year-long period—is an essential part of creating that nation.

Finally, this book contains the three longest *parashiyot* in the Torah and, in chapter 7 with its 89 verses, the longest chapter in the book as well. I like to think that these statistical happenstances are not coincidental but, rather, a recognition that building a nation is among the most difficult and time-consuming of human endeavors.

PARASHAT B'MIDBAR

34th Torah portion, 1st in *B'midbar*
B'midbar 1:1–4:20 (159 verses)
Haftarah: Hosheya 2:1–22

ALIYOT

First / Rishon:	1:1–1:19
Second / Sheini:	1:20–1:54
Third / Shlishi:	2:1–2:34
Fourth / Revi'i:	3:1–3:13
Fifth / Khamishi:	3:14–3:39
Sixth / Shishi:	3:40–3:51
Seventh / Shevi'i:	4:1–4:20
Maftir:	4:17–4:20

SYNOPSIS

God commands Moshe to take a census of all the Israelite males over the age of twenty. The duties of the Levites, who are not included in the census, are detailed. Each tribe is assigned specific places in the camp around the Tabernacle. The sons of Levi are counted and their responsibilities are set forth. A census of the firstborn males is taken and a special redemption tax is levied on them.

COMMENTARY

With *Sefer B'midbar* we begin a new phase in the life *of B'nei Yisrael.* The events of the previous two books of Torah took place over a fairly compact period of time. For example, from *Matan Torah* at Sinai to the opening of this new book, only a month has elapsed. Little more than a year has passed since the Exodus from Egypt. But *B'midbar* will take place over thirty-nine years. In that time, almost all of the generation that lived in slavery will die off, leaving a new generation of leaders to emerge from their offspring. That generation will conquer Kina'an, fulfilling the promise of redemption and homeland.

B'midbar, then, presents us with the story of a people in transition, a passage that must be completed before they can achieve a long-desired goal. Now this wandering rabble of former slaves must shape itself into a nation, complete with the means to defend itself against hostile neighbors. Consequently, it is at this point that God orders a new census, organizing the Hebrews on a war footing.

The English name of this book, Numbers, suggests that it is centered on this census and others that will follow, and there certainly are an abundance of numbers and counting. But the Hebrew title, *B'midbar/In the Wilderness*, suggests other issues, ones that are more pressing and of greater import in the long run. In fact, the rabbis who assembled the great collection *Midrash Rabbah* opened their consideration of this Torah portion by asking a question that might have seemed more apposite earlier in their discussion of Torah: Why does God choose to give the Israelites the Torah in the midst of the Wilderness (or desert, as it is often rendered)?

The fact that this book is entitled *B'midbar* suggests how important this choice is. Consider the names of the books so far. *Bereishit* is not merely the beginning of all Creation and the beginning of our story, but also the story of the beginning of the Jewish people and of the lines of descent that will bring us to Moshe, Aharon, and Miriam, the story of the Exodus from Egypt, and the Revelation at Sinai. We have already discussed the importance of naming in *Sefer Shemot* and it would be hard to imagine a more apt name for the book containing much of the *mitzvot* than *Vayikra/And God Called*. So clearly the name of this book has not been chosen casually.

Besides, much of the action of the last three and a half books of the Torah takes place in the Wilderness of Sinai. The Israelites have been in this wilderness since they left Egypt and will remain there until the opening of *Sefer Yehoshua*. Even now, as *Sefer B'midbar* opens, they stand at the threshold of the land God has promised them, yet they will falter repeatedly in the Wilderness, as we will see.

This wandering in the Wilderness has both a literal and metaphoric quality. On the one hand, the life *bamidbar* is surprisingly well ordered. God provides manna to eat and water to drink. The Israelites have had little contact with Gentiles so far. The miraculous—the manna, the pillars of cloud and fire—is a daily occurrence and they are, obviously, as close to the Divine Presence as humans have ever been allowed to get in a group. Except for the fairly constant grumbling, this is a bit like being back in *Gan Eden*.

Or in childhood.

Therein lies the problem. The Israelites are becoming infantilized by the desert experience. They have not had to fend for themselves much. The desert is perilous and the conditions are hard, but up till now the troubles have been relatively few. This is a people only a year and a half out of slavery; they have no inkling of how to provide for themselves in a nonurban setting. This is the Hebrews' first encounter with nature in the raw since they were wandering shepherds in the time of Ya'akov and his sons, but they are becoming as utterly dependent on a higher power as they were when slaves in Egypt. If the point was to teach them self-reliance, a desert in which their needs are met by God may not be the best place to instill the lesson.

Yet this is where God chose to make manifest the Divine, to reveal the Torah in a show of fire, smoke, and thunder.

Why here?

There are many commentaries on this question, ranging from the practical to the metaphysical.

The practical commentaries tend to focus on the elements I have already mentioned, as well as the physical suffering engendered on the journey and the testing and hardening of this people as they slowly are prepared for the battles for Kina'an that will come as soon as they cross the Yardein/Jordan into the Land. As we see in this *parashah*, they will organize themselves into an armed camp, prepared for war for the first time in the Torah. It's all part of the process of becoming a nation, independent and ready to defend itself, a sort of mass boot camp.

But there are other ways of reading the Wilderness experience. The philosopher Philo says that the desert is a place that is devoid of the temptations and corruptions of Egypt and its cities, that one can only receive Torah in a place that is far from vice. The Noam Elimelekh, a Hasidic sage, says that Torah was given in the desert so that we will maintain a state of humility, much as God chose a lowly mountain, Sinai, rather than a taller, more majestic peak, as the location for the Revelation. In Tractate *Nedarim*, the Talmud says that the Torah was given in the Wilderness as a reminder that we must be like the desert itself, open on all sides, open to learning. Similarly, others say that one must be as free as the desert to receive Torah.

Finally, *midbar* belongs to no one. No one can say, "My nation is so great that God gave Torah to the world on our soil." And no one can say,

"Well, God gave Torah to the world in the land of the Midianites, so it can't possibly apply to me."

On the contrary, the Torah and its teachings are for all humanity.

ADDITIONAL NOTES

* With 159 verses, this is the third-longest *parashah* in the Torah.
* For those of you who are fascinated by numbers, here is a quick breakdown of the results of the census by tribe, in descending order of size: Yehudah—74,600; Dan—62,700; Shimon—59,300; Zevulun—57,400; Yisakhar—54,400; Naftali—53,400; Re'uven—46,500; Gad—45,650; Asher—41,500; Efraim—40,500; Binyamin—35,400; Menasheh—32,200. In addition, the Levites number 22,300, divided among the Gershonites (7,500), Kohatites (8,600), and Merari (6,200).

HAFTARAH

The connection between *parashat B'midbar* and the *haftarah*, taken from the *Sefer Hosheya*, is the prophet's reference to going to the Wilderness and to Israel's youth "when she came up from the land of Mitzrayim." (Hosheya 2:17)

PARASHAT NASO

35th Torah portion, 2nd in *B'midbar*
B'midbar 4:21–7:89 (176 verses)
Haftarah:Shoftim 13:2–25

ALIYOT

First / Rishon:	4:21–4:37
Second / Sheini:	4:38–4:49
Third / Shlishi:	5:1–5:10
Fourth / Revi'i:	5:11–6:27
Fifth / Khamishi:	7:1–7:41
Sixth / Shishi:	7:42–7:71
Seventh / Shevi'i:	7:72–7:89
Maftir:	7:87–7:89

SYNOPSIS

A census of the Gershonites, Merarites, and Koathites between the ages of thirty and fifty is conducted and their duties in the *Mishkan* are detailed. God speaks to Moshe concerning ritually unclean people, repentant individuals, and possible cases of adultery. The last case involves the rite of the *Sotah*, a form of trial by ordeal imposed on a woman suspected of adultery. The obligations of a Nazirite vow are explained. They include abstaining from alcohol and not cutting one's hair. God tells Moshe how to teach Aharon and his sons the Priestly Blessing. Moshe consecrates the Sanctuary, and the tribal chieftains bring offerings. Moshe then speaks with God inside the Tent of Meeting.

COMMENTARY

Rabbi Yonatan Grossman, as we have noted previously, has an interesting observation about the progression that takes place in the middle three books of the Torah. Grossman points out that there is a movement from a focus on God as the primary actor in *Sefer Shemot*, to the role of the *kohanim* in *Sefer Vayikra*, to the placement of the entire nation of Israelites at the center of concern in *Sefer B'midbar*. What, he asks, is the distinguishing characteristic that ties all three books together? In this *parashah*, the answer becomes obvious: the *Mishkan*.

Grossman writes:

[Shemot] concludes . . . "the cloud covered the Tent of Meeting and Hashem's glory filled the Mishkan" (40:34). The book of Vayikra related the story of the Mishkan's sanctification, and stresses the service of the Kohanim. . . . Our section in the book of Bemidbar now adds the wider national aspect, relating the story of the offerings of the Princes of the tribes of Israel. These individuals represent the people, as the verse states: "The Princes of Israel came near, the heads of their clans; They were the Princes of the tribes, the ones who oversaw the census" (Bemidbar 7:2). This verse provides three descriptions of the Princes (the heads of their clans/the Princes of the tribes/the overseers of the census), all of which stress their communal role and relate to their capacity as representatives of the people.

Of course, the completion of the Mishkan is related in this book for another reason, and this is in fact the main one for its inclusion. The book of Bemidbar describes the journey to the land of Israel, after the people take leave of Mount Sinai. This journey is very much a function of the Mishkan, since it is the movement of this building which determines the moment that the people are to break camp. . . .

All this demonstrates that part of the function of the Mishkan was to signal the beginning of journeying and camping. This is the context for the appearance of the Mishkan in Bemidbar, and by relating the account of the Princes' sacrifices, here the story of the Mishkan is completed.

The story of the *Mishkan*, as completed in *parashat Naso*, becomes an all-pervading theme, despite the seemingly variegated and disparate elements of this longest of Torah portions. Consider the primary elements in *Naso:*

- The sending away of the ritually unfit from the camp;
- The guilt offering associated with theft;
- The ritual of the "bitter waters" as a trial by ordeal for a woman suspected of adultery;
- The vows and responsibilities of the Nazirite;
- The dedication of the *Mishkan*.

(I have omitted the Priestly Benediction, one of the most familiar passages in Torah and a most important one in this *parashah*, but I will return to it shortly.)

On one obvious level, the sending away of the ritually unfit is another example of the division between pure and impure that was the principle concern of the first part of *Vayikra*. But it is the presence of the *Mishkan* in the encampment, a "holy of holies," that must be safeguarded by the exclusion of the impure. The same is true of the guilt offering in a case of theft, which—like all offerings—can only be made at the *Mishkan*. The ritual of the *Sotah* takes as one of its central components dust from the floor of the *Mishkan*. The would-be Nazirite must present himself at the *Mishkan*. Finally, all the tribal leaders make their offerings for the dedication of the *Mishkan*.

Each of these elements of the *parashah* depends on its relationship to the *Mishkan*, but there is a progression at work here, too. The separation of the *tema'im/ritually impure* is a measure taken for the benefit of the entire community. The guilt offering of the thief is meant to expiate for a sin that is committed against *Adonai*, but also against a fellow congregant and, by extension, the community. The rite of the *Sotah* is a protection against the breakup of the family unit, while the Nazirite vows are about the relationship between individual and God. Then the bringing of the gifts completes the circle by placing the *Mishkan* once more at the center of the entire nation.

What makes the *Mishkan* so significant, so central to our story, not only here but throughout the middle section of the Torah? Quite simply, it is the physical manifestation of, a reminder and correlative to the Revelation at Sinai and all that accompanied that extraordinary, theophany. The Word of God was revealed at Sinai and the *Mishkan* is literally the bearer of that word, both sets of tablets, one of which was engraved by the very finger of the Eternal.

The importance of words is at the heart of *parashat Naso*. We have discussed at some length the importance of the word, both spoken and written, particularly when the Name of God is invoked—blessings, curses, naming are all weighty examples that run throughout the Torah. That theme recurs here in several forms. Obviously, the Nazirite is bound by an oath to God. One of the components of the "bitter waters" to be drunk in the rite of the *Sotah* are the words that the High Priest has dissolved in them (perhaps the only example in Jewish ritual and law of a permissible erasure of the Name of God). The Priestly Benediction consists of words uttered by the *kohanim* on behalf of God, as instructed by God through Moshe. Even the repetition, seemingly endless to us, of the twelve days of gifts given by the tribal leaders—identical in substance and, except for a couple of minor changes of order, in wording—are about words; why include the same material twelve times except to validate the reality of each tribe's contribution?

There is one grammatical oddity in the recounting of the Priestly Benediction that I think reveals something significant underlying all these elements of the Torah portion. As Rashi points out, the use of the phrase *"amor lahem/speak to them"* is slightly unconventional, an infinitive version of the verb (although not the actual infinitive, grammatically speaking). He compares it to the injunctions to remember and keep the Sabbath (*zakhor* and *shamor*) in the Decalogue. These are not traditional imperative forms, he says. Instead, they are without tense, timeless versions of the verbs. Why? Because God is always with us, omnipresent and outside of time.

Indeed, when God manifests the Divine Presence at Sinai it is in the form of sound foremost. One might say with some justice that God reveals the Eternal as words, that the words of God (or Word of God) are the signifier of the Divine (an idea that Christian theology will expand on).

The priests are to *"amor lahem,"* just as we are to *"shamor v'zakhor"* Shabbat. These obligations are perpetual, not bound by time, just as the word of God is not bound by time.

ADDITIONAL NOTES

- At 176 verses, *parashat Naso* is the longest Torah portion.
- One of the most satisfying explanations of the repetitions of the gifts is that each of the tribes saw its gift as a reflection of its own concerns. Thus to Yehudah, the tribe of sovereigns-to-be, the gifts reflected the aspect of their role as leaders; to Yisakhar, a tribe of scholars, they pertained to Torah study, and so on. Hence although the gifts brought were identical, their meaning was different for each tribe.
- Moshe had to make a difficult choice in this gift-giving process: Which tribe was to go first? He chose Yehudah, not, it is generally believed, for its "leadership" role but as a way of doing honor to Nakhshon ben Aminadav, the one Israelite who fearlessly plunged into the waters of *Yam Suf,* his faith in God's promise to protect these people utterly unshaken.

HAFTARAH

With the Torah portion in which the duties of the Nazirite are outlined, what could be a more logical fit than the story of the birth of the most famous Nazirite of them all, *Shimshon / Samson*? Interestingly enough, he is dedicated to God as a Nazirite by his parents rather than by his own oath, and it appears from the full version of the story that his vows are open-ended, which is inconsistent with *toratha'Nazir*.

PARASHAT B'HA'ALOTEKHA

36th Torah portion, 3rd in *B'midbar*
B'midbar 8:1–12:16 (136 verses)
Haftarah: Zekharyah 2:14–4:7

ALIYOT

First / Rishon:	8:1–8:14
Second / Sheini:	8:15–8:26
Third / Shlishi:	9:1–9:14
Fourth / Revi'i:	9:15–10:10
Fifth / Khamishi:	10:11–10:34
Sixth / Shishi:	10:35–11:29
Seventh / Shevi'i:	11:30–12:16
Maftir:	12:14–12:16

SYNOPSIS

God speaks to Moshe, describing the menorah for the Tent of Meeting. The Levites are appointed to serve as assistants under Aharon and his sons. Those who are unable to celebrate Passover during the first month are given a time in the second month to observe a *Pesakh Sheini / second Passover.* A cloud by day and fire by night show God's Presence over the *Mishkan.* When the cloud lifts from the *Mishkan,* the people leave Sinai, setting out on their journey, tribe by tribe. The Israelites complain about the lack of meat, and Moshe becomes frustrated. God tells him to appoint a council of elders. God provides the people with meat and then strikes them with a very severe plague. Miriam and Aharon talk about the "Cushite woman" whom Moshe has married. In addition, they complain Moshe is special because God speaks through him. Miriam is struck with *tzara'at,* and Moshe begs God to heal her. After her recovery, the people resume their journey.

COMMENTARY

Rabbi Joseph Soloveitchik, the towering giant of Modern Orthodox thought, described *parashat B'ha'alotekha* as one of the most difficult to understand. The problem, he explained in one of his many lectures, was not that the *mitzvot* presented herein are obscure but that the portion contains so many seemingly unrelated topics, ranging from the lighting of the seven-branched lampstand, the menorah, to the falling out among Moshe, Aharon, and Miriam and its devastating results for Miriam. Indeed, although it is rather shorter than the formidable *Naso*, this *parashah* seems to be even more of an omnium-gatherum than its immediate predecessor. However, there are several narrative elements that occur here that are intertwined, as much by their foretaste of troubles to come as by themselves.

There is a marked shift in the tone of the narrative that occurs as the people set out once more on their journey. As Rav Soloveitchik observed, the first half of this *parashah*, which concludes the preparations for the resumption of the trek through the Wilderness, is optimistic, filled with the expectations of a people feeling renewed by a long sojourn after a difficult journey; the lampstand and the trumpets, the *Pesakh Sheini*, the first lurching movements of the ark, all these bespeak a dynamism and a rush of energy that is breathtaking to behold.

Then everything goes sour. The people begin to grumble for no apparent reason, Moshe feels oppressed by his leadership role, his sister and brother jump down his throat because of his marital situation and their own insecurities about their roles, Miriam is afflicted with *tzara'at*, and Moshe goes into a deep funk. Worse will follow almost immediately after Miriam is cured and the march begins again.

The change is immediately apparent from the language used in the text. The word *ra/evil* doesn't occur once in the first ten chapters of *B'midbar*. In the story of Moshe's parting from his father-in-law, the word *tov/good* occurs in some form four times in five verses. But the first part of chapter 11 utilizes the word *ra* four times in reference to the behavior of the grumbling Hebrews and the reaction of their suddenly sullen leader. We move from the orderliness of the march, with its rhythmic listing of tribes and leaders, to the chaos of a camp seething with dissension.

How can we explain this abrupt shift, particularly if one considers, as Rav Yair Kahn notes, that the Israelites seem to be a mere eleven days' march from Kina'an, from the arrival in the land promised to them by God (and as Soloveitchik hints, the coming of the Messianic Age)?

The answer, I believe, lies within the narrative itself.

The Israelites have been encamped at Sinai for a year. Although conditions are undoubtedly less than ideal, they have become settled, accustomed to their surroundings. Now they are being told to pull up their tents and start moving again, with the added burden of sacred objects and *mitzvot,* neither of which they had to deal with before. Whatever uncertainties they may have felt in the past now rise to the surface in the form of complaining. They have not yet shed the slave mentality of Egypt; they are not yet ready for the responsibilities that come with freedom. As Richard Elliott Friedman observes, the first time we are told of the people's grumbling, at the outset of chapter 11, no reason is given; it's just generalized peevishness.

Consider the incident of *kivrot ha'ta'avah,* the "craving" for meat. As the S'fat Emet points out, their desire is described in the text as "*hitavu ta'avah,*" literally, or "they craved a craving." Like cranky children on a too-long car trip, they are looking for an excuse to burst out in a tantrum. And Moshe's reaction, to complain to God that his burden is too much to bear, is that of a frustrated, stressed-out parent. From here on, the Israelites and their leaders become one huge dysfunctional family, split into factions, riven by constant grumbling and suffering from leadership that is alternately too stern and too lax, stretched to its emotional limit. The eleven-day journey becomes a thirty-nine-year forced march in circles and the Sinai Peninsula is transformed from an easy route to Paradise to a Kafkaesque labyrinth of bad feelings and bad faith.

The incident of Miriam and Aharon confronting Moshe and its aftermath is a telling indication of what is happening here. This is a complicated and confusing story, particularly as recounted in the Torah itself. The many commentaries don't exactly clarify matters either, but this much seems clear. Miriam is upset at Moshe for his neglect of Tzipporah, seemingly in favor of a second wife, a Cushite (i.e., Sudanese). Her concern is apparently triggered by the incident of the two "freelance" prophets, Eldad and Medad; according to one midrash she hears Tzipporah lament the troubles that the gift of prophecy will wreak on their wives who will now be estranged from the duo as she is from Moshe. Miriam and Aharon—and no one is clear on who the instigator is—confront Moshe but, instead of calling him to account for his treatment of Tzipporah, they lash out at him for the exclusivity of his rule in the camp: "Hasn't God spoken through us as well?"

Regardless of the rights or wrongs of their quarrel with Moshe about his familial responsibilities, Miriam and Aharon have made a terrible mistake in confusing the realms of sacred and ordinary, violating the most fundamental principles of the *mitzvot* that were the subject of so much of the previous book by invoking questions of prophecy in a marital quarrel.

And what happens next is that God intervenes by punishing Miriam. She asked for God to get involved and he has; talk about answered prayers! Her punishment, an infection of *tzara'at*, is usually offered by rabbinic authorities as proof of the connection between this skin disease and *lashon hara* (although Richard Elliott Friedman has an ingenious second explanation in which Miriam is punished for the racism of denouncing the Cushite wife by having all the pigmentation removed from her own infected skin).* Moshe's reaction to this event is surprisingly but typically selfless; he prays ardently for his sister's recovery.

Equally significant is the reaction of *B'nei Yisrael;* they wait a full seven days for Miriam's recovery before resuming their journey. Is this a sign of respect for the prophetess? A recognition, as midrash has it, of her wait by the Nile when her baby brother sat in his basket in the river? Or an act of solidarity with one of the disgruntled? I have yet to see a commentary that suggests this last interpretation but given what will transpire in the next Torah portion and the subsequent events of *Sefer B'midbar*, this gesture on Miriam's behalf by the Hebrews could just as easily be an act of covert resistance to Moshe's leadership and God as a tribute to her stalwart behavior.

Regardless of the motivation of the Israelites, like Charles Foster Kane "they're gonna need more than one lesson and they're gonna get more than one lesson." Although the origins of this breakdown of social order are obscure, this is only the beginning of a dangerous spiral.

ADDITIONAL NOTES
- Moshe's prayer on behalf of his sister is usually described as the shortest prayer in the Torah: "God, please heal her."
- The passage occurring at *B'midbar* 10:35–36, *"Va'yehi binsoa Aharon . . ."* is part of the Torah service, intoned by the *hazan* as the ark is opened to reveal the scrolls. (See Chapter 1.)
- Although many of the classical commentators say emphatically that the events recounted in the Torah are not in chronological order, the expla-

---

*Why isn't Aharon punished as well? One might ask why he isn't punished for his part in the incident of the Golden Calf. When Aharon is finally given his sentence—and it is a harsh one—in *parashat Khukat*, we will address those questions.

nation of the *Pesakh Sheini* is one of the clear cases in which the story definitely and deliberately involves a flashback. That it is a flashback to the aftermath of the Exodus, coming just before the people begin to grumble about going back to Egypt, is a significant detail.

HAFTARAH

At the center of the *haftarah* linked with *parashat B'ha'alotekha* is the prophet Zekharyah's vision of a golden lampstand identical with the menorah described in the *parashah*. Besides that rather obvious connection, the *haftarah* is also about the rebuilding of the Temple, so the thematic link is even stronger than the more explicit visual one.

PARASHAT SHELAKH

37th Torah portion, 4th in *B'midbar*
B'midbar 13:1–15:41 (119 verses)
Haftarah: Yehoshua 2:1–24

ALIYOT

First / Rishon:	13:1–13:20
Second / Sheini:	13:21–14:7
Third / Shlishi:	14:8–14:25
Fourth / Revi'i:	14:26–15:7
Fifth / Khamishi:	15:8–15:16
Sixth / Shishi:	15:17–15:26
Seventh / Shevi'i:	15:27–15:41
Maftir:	15:37–15:41

SYNOPSIS

Moshe sends twelve spies to *Eretz Yisrael* to report on the inhabitants and the country. Despite the positive report of Yehoshua and Kalev, the people are frightened. God threatens to wipe out *B'nei Yisrael* but relents when Moshe intercedes on their behalf. To punish the people, God announces that all those who left Egypt will not enter *Eretz Yisrael* except for Yehoshua and Kalev. Moshe instructs the Israelites regarding setting aside khallah, the observance of the Sabbath, how to treat strangers, and the laws of *tzitzit*.

COMMENTARY

Freedom is a very frightening thing for someone who has never experienced it. It takes more strength of character to adjust to making one's own life than all but the most determined can muster. Perhaps you remember the case of Jack Henry Abbott, a state-raised con, as they call them, who wrote a startling memoir of his life behind bars; when his case was championed by Jerzy Kosinski, Norman Mailer, and other literary figures, Abbott was paroled, but within months he had stabbed a waiter to death in a Greenwich Village restaurant and was back in prison for good. Anyone who had read Abbott's book could have seen that coming. A man who had lived all but a handful of his years—as a child and adult—inside the cocoon of state institutions, he was totally unequipped for life outside the walls.

Perhaps we should have expected the same of the generation of Hebrews who emerged from the four-hundred-year ordeal of Egyptian bondage. There are hints in this week's *parashah* that God has no illusions about what these people will be able to withstand, that the Almighty knows that they aren't ready for war, for governing themselves, for just being ordinary freedmen and -women.

In fact, the signs were there long before, if we had thought to read them. Remember that God sends the Israelites on a roundabout trajectory toward Kina'an in order to keep them out of the path of the Philistines. The Eternal provides them with the pillar of smoke and the pillar of fire, with manna, even with meat when they brazenly demand it, with water either from Miriam's traveling well or through Moshe's actions. In short, like children they are protected from all possible contact with harm and given their basic needs. They run from the Egyptians and are saved through no action of their own and circumvent the Philistines; the one time they skirmish with a neighboring tribe, it is the Amalekites who attack them from behind.

According to midrash, the Israelites want to be told that Kina'an really is a land of milk and honey and that conquering it will be a cakewalk, with God providing all the necessary muscle. The people in the encampment ask Moshe for an undercover reconnaissance group to scout the land that God has promised them. That, the rabbis tell us, is why this week's *parashah* opens with that by now familiar formation, "*Shelakh lekha / Send out for yourself*" a team of spies. God is not giving Moshe an order, Nahmanides says; God is giving him permission. Go ahead, send the spies for yourself.

Nahmanides believes that Moshe was pleased with the people's request. He writes, "Scripture does not [allow man] to rely on a miracle in any of its affairs," but that is precisely what the Hebrews have done so far and Moshe, he infers, thinks their request marks a new interest in taking an active role in what befalls them. Consequently, he assembles a team to scout out the land.

"To scout" is precisely what *latur* means, the infinitive form of the verb he uses to charge the dozen men he has chosen, one from each tribe (except Levi, but they will not be landowners when the Hebrews get to

Kina'an, so it is entirely appropriate that they aren't represented). The men he chooses are "leaders" from each tribe, not the banner-bearers but men of similarly exalted stature, and we learn of their names and tribal associations in detail.

Therein, several commentators argue, lies the problem. Compare these men with the spies who seek out Rahav the harlot in the *haftarah*. In *Shelakh*, a dozen men are sent, a large delegation for a secret mission, to say the least; by contrast, Yehoshua sends only two men. In the *parashah* we learn their names and tribes; in the *haftarah* we never are told their identities, only their mission. One has the impression, particularly from the choice of language describing the travels of the tribal leaders in Kina'an, that they conducted themselves more like a trade delegation than a cabal, while stealth would seem to be the principal virtue of the pair sent by Yehoshua (who clearly learned what *not* to do from his experience here). Interestingly, although traditional commentators refer to the sin of these elders as *kheit ha'miraglim/the sin of the spies*, they are never called spies in the Torah text, and their mission seems at least as much economic espionage as military. (The commentator's wording is based on Yehoshma 14:7.)

All of this seems somewhat beside the point but, in reality, it does suggest some of the shortcomings of their behavior. If they were sent on a military mission, then their decision to report to the assembled people is a disastrous breach of security. If not, then the message they bring is too heavily—and deliberately, it would seem—weighted toward the negative and, as might be expected, causes a near panic among the Israelites.

What do they report? At the outset, they tell the truth: they describe the natural wonders of this extraordinarily fertile land, they show off the enormous bunches of grapes and other fruit they acquired on their travels. Even their description of the fortified cities and large warriors of Kina'an are essentially the unembroidered truth. But once Kalev expresses his confident belief that the land is theirs for the taking, the spin doctors go to work with a series of grim tales of a land "that devours its inhabitants."

To most commentators, the most telling statement of *ha'miraglim* comes when they say that "in our own eyes we looked like grasshoppers, and that must be how we looked to them as well." Menachem Mendl, the Kotzker Rebbe, says that the latter statement is a perfectly reasonable one but the first one gives them away. "What possible difference could it make for you [to know] how you appear in the eyes of others," he asks sternly. To the Kotzker, with his obsessive search for truth, to have such a petty concern bespeaks a self-absorption that is entirely at odds with the nature of their task.

It also betrays their true interest. Like so many men with a whiff of power, they are perfectly happy with the status quo. Yes, the Wilderness is a pretty inhospitable place, but God provides for their every need, as we noted before. Why risk change, especially if it means the possibility of war and other terrible dangers?

Within both classical and contemporary commentaries one can find many variations on this reading of *kheit ha'miraglim*. Rabbi Morris Adler says their sin is the abuse of their position and power; they used their influence to stir up fears that otherwise might have been tamed by the evidence of the abundance awaiting the Israelites in Kina'an. The great second-century mystic Shimon bar Yokhai offers a similar point of view; he believes that the ten who offered the negative report on the land had always intended to do so.

One needn't be convinced by the suspicions of these two gentlemen to accept that the failure of the "spies" and the panicked reaction of the people who believed them is rooted in a lack of faith in God, despite all the evidence of their own experience of the Creator's bounty and protection. That lack of faith is the product, I think, of the mentality of the slave, of men and women who have become inured to pain and disappointment on a daily basis and who, more important, have not learned how to live with the blessing and burden of freedom. Unlike Jack Henry Abbott, they haven't killed another person, only their own dreams. And just as the State of New York placed Abbott back in prison for the remainder of his life, God immures the generation who grew up in Egyptian bondage in the prison of the Wilderness, a vastly more open-ended but no less final sentence.

ADDITIONAL NOTES
- The image of the bunch of grapes so large that it is carried by two men on staves is such a compelling one that it is part of the coat of arms of the State of Israel.
- At the outset of the spy mission, Moshe changes his young charge's name from Hosheya (from the imperative form of "save") to Yehoshua (YHWH is a noble). (However, he has already been called by this name in *parashat Ki Tisa*.)

- The Talmud says that the night of weeping described herein (*Bamidbar* 14:1) is Tisha B'Av; like an irritated parent, God hears the cries of the frightened Hebrews and vows that someday they'll really have something to cry about on this night. Tisha B'Av, of course, is the most somber day on the Jewish calendar, the commemoration of the destruction of the First and Second Temples.

HAFTARAH

The story of Rahav, the harlot who sheltered the two Israelite spies, is taken from *Sefer Yehoshua*. For more details, see "Commentary" on page 464.

PARASHAT KORAKH

38th Torah portion, 5th in *B'midbar*
B'midbar 16:1–18:32 (95 verses)
Haftarah: Shmuel Aleph 11:14–12:22

ALIYOT

First / Rishon:	16:1–16:13
Second / Sheini:	16:14–16:19
Third / Shlishi:	16:20–17:8
Fourth / Revi'i:	17:9–17:15
Fifth / Khamishi:	17:16–17:24
Sixth / Shishi:	17:25–18:20
Seventh / Shevi'i:	18:21–18:32
Maftir:	18:30–18:32

SYNOPSIS

Korakh and his followers, Datan and Aviram, lead a rebellion against the leadership of Moshe and Aharon. God punishes all these rebels by burying them and their families alive. Once again, God brings a plague on the people. The chief of each tribe deposits his staff inside the Tent of Meeting. Aharon's staff brings forth sprouts, produces blossoms, and bears almonds. The *kohanim* and *levi'im* are established and assigned the responsibility of managing the donations to the Sanctuary. All of the first-born offerings shall go to the priests and all the tithes are designated for the Levites in return for the services they perform.

COMMENTARY

> Shimon and Levi are brothers; swords are their instruments of cruelty.
> Let my soul not enter their counsel; let my honor not be attached to
> their assembly, for they killed a man in their anger. . . .
> —Ya'akov on his deathbed (*Bereishit* 49:5–6)

Any dispute that is conducted for the sake of heaven is destined to last, and one that is not for the sake of heaven will not last. Which dispute was for the sake of heaven? The dispute between [the schools of] Hillel

and Shammai. Which was not for the sake of heaven? The dispute of
Korakh and his band.

—Pirkei Avot 5:20

In this Torah portion Moshe faces the gravest challenge to his leadership that will occur in the entire Torah. Previously the Israelites have
complained about biological or physical challenges—lack of food or water,
no meat, the hardness of desert life, fear of enemy armies. As Rabbi Joseph
Soloveitchik points out, "These were not political disagreements or ideological controversies. . . . Even the golden calf was not precipitated by
idolatrous ideas that corrupted the people . . . [but] by the feeling of terror
similar to that felt by the sheep that is lost in the wilderness."

One could say that Moshe's authority has never been challenged. The
people might grumble about his effectiveness as a leader but they have
never questioned his suitability or right to lead them.

Korakh is after something very different.

At first glance, his opposition to Moshe seems to be highly ideological,
the product of a powerful populist, democratic inclination. Rabbi Shlomo
Riskin, in fact, reduces the battle to "the classic confrontation between
the democratic rebellion of [Korakh] and the divine authority of Moses."
Orthodox commentators frequently identify Korakh with the revisionist
impulses of the non-Orthodox streams of modern Judaism, arguing that
one cannot pick and choose the *mitzvot* one will follow. This thread proceeds from Korakh's challenge to Moshe: "The entire community is holy
and God is among them; why do you raise yourself above the community
of God?"

As is so frequently the case, the actual text is a bit cryptic. It is generally
believed that the story of Korakh's rebellion was compounded of two different stories of revolt, which would explain the rather odd inclusion of
Datan and Aviram, who seem to be emanating from another narrative
altogether. We actually know very little about these men from the Torah
itself. So we must fall back on the extensive midrashic literature to fill in
the gaps. (Of course, the midrashim surrounding this story, while rich in
detail, are frequently contradictory.)

For example, one commentator says that Datan and Aviram were the
two Hebrews who informed on Moshe after he killed the Egyptian over-
seer, the two who taunted Moshe and Aharon in Egypt in *parashat Shemot*, the ones who gathered manna on Shabbat. In contrast, *B'midbar*

Rabbah posits that their part in the rebellion was the result of their proximity to Korakh's band, citing the proverb "Woe to the wicked and woe to their neighbor!" We do know that they are of the tribe of Re'uven, and the Reuvenites had some cause for resentment, since their status as sons of the firstborn son was overridden.

We know a bit more about Korakh from the text. He is the first cousin of Moshe, Aharon, and Miriam. He is a Levite and a Kohatite, the *primus inter pares* of the Levites. Like Datan and Aviram, he has a historical justification for a grudge; his uncle was appointed leader of the family over his father.

Again, we have recourse to midrash. There is a story that says that Korakh was a man of incredible wealth, one who consorted with Pharoah during the Egyptian bondage. He is seen mocking and deriding Moshe and Aharon repeatedly, both in Egypt and in the desert. The most telling of these stories involves him confronting Moshe over fine points of *halakhah* from the newly minted commandments and mocking the prophet (and by extension the laws from Sinai).

But is he a populist? Does he represent a truly democratic rebellion against an authority imposed upon the Hebrews—quite literally—from above? The clues to be found in the text suggest otherwise.

First, unlike the grumbling of the Hebrews, the rebellion of Korakh involves a very limited number of men, 250 leaders of the tribes. From the outset, this looks rather more like a coup d'état than a popular revolution. The timing of the uprising is certainly "convenient," occurring after *kheit ha'miraglim*, and the condemnation of the generation of Egypt to die in the Wilderness. This revolt catches Moshe at his lowest ebb, both in power and trust and in emotional energy. Recall, too, that this trough comes on the heels of what should have been a moment of great triumph, with Moshe convinced that the Israelites were less than two weeks away from entering Kina'an. That doesn't feel like an accident.

Most of all, what is it that Korakh demands? The position of High Priest. For a would-be populist, he seems awfully eager to advance his own standing in the community.

Perhaps the best clues to Korakh's nature are to be found in an odd bit of wording at the outset of the *parashah*. In the very first sentence of the Torah portion, we are told, "Korakh . . . took, and got up in front of Moshe." Took what? Took himself and his followers, took them to one side, took them apart from the community. Rashi cites the midrash of Rav

Tankhuma: "He took himself to one side to dissociate himself from the congregation, to contest the [appointment of Aharon]" as High Priest.

Moshe's response to this challenge is extraordinarily measured. He is prepared to step back and allow God to sort out the mess, using the bringing of incense as the litmus test. Yet he is utterly frank with Korakh and his followers, warning them that the losers will pay the ultimate penalty and scheduling the test for the following morning, giving them ample time to reconsider. Surely, having witnessed the deaths of Nadav and Avihu the rebels must know what will happen to them, yet they persist. This is an act, I think, bordering on madness, although some commentators ascribe it to a fear of loss of face, others to the heatedness of an argument that clouds judgment.

Of course, as we know, the inevitable happens and the rebellion is crushed by God; the firepans, like the *tzitzit*, are to serve as a reminder of the compact between the Eternal and the Hebrews, and, in a wonderful piece of irony, Moshe and Aharon use incense to stave off a plague that threatens the encampment.

Yet it is hard not to read this story and feel a certain unease. After all, isn't there a grain of truth in Korakh's claim that the entire community is holy?

Yeshayahu Leibowitz takes a stern line, but one that I find quite compelling. He links the rebellion to the preceding passage, the commandment of the *tzitzit*. Leibowitz notes that the commandment concludes by explaining "that you may remember and do all My *mitzvot* and be holy unto your God." This sentence is followed almost immediately by the introduction of Korakh. Leibowitz writes that "[t]he difference between the holiness mentioned in the verse on the *tzitzit* and that in regard to [Korakh] is the difference between faith in God and idolatry." We are enjoined to "be holy," by God; we are not told that we *are* holy. Holiness is not a sinecure, it is a state toward which one strives. Like trust, it is earned by deeds and behavior, not merely claimed.

It is proverbial that a Torah portion is never named for a wicked person (although we will run up against this problem again with Balak). There are five *parashiyot* that are named for individuals—*Khayei Sarah, Yitro, Korakh, Balak,* and *Pinkhas*. The first two cases are pretty obvious ones, but the latter three are troubling to varying degrees, and to draw the conclusion that Korakh is not without goodness from this slender thread may seem extreme, but there are other readings of his character possible. (Of course, his descendants are allowed to serve in the Temple and are, in fact, credited as the authors of several of the Psalms.)

Rabbi Menachem Mendel Schneerson offers a compassionate and not unsympathetic reading of Korakh's personality that suggests one possible reason for the eponymy of this *parashah*. First, he argues, there is at least a grain of truth in Korakh's contention; each Jew has an internal spark of holiness. Korakh's desire was for this spark to flourish, his followers were seeking a heightened spirituality in which all would participate, and Korakh's zeal in claiming the priesthood is a not altogether bad thing either, a failure of excessive religiosity, if you will. Yet Korakh, Schneerson argues, never realized the fatal error he had made, that his uprising was divisive rather than unifying, his actions dangerous to the well-being of the entire community rather than life-enhancing. And for that, Schneerson says, he was punished.

ADDITIONAL NOTES

- Korakh's rebellion may not have lasted long, but his name has come down in Jewish lore as a terrific negative symbol. Among Ladino-speaking Jews, to "become like Korakh" is to suddenly acquire great but unfounded wealth. Similarly, they also may use the phrase "to shower Korakh's curses on [someone's] head." S. David Sperling points out that Yiddish speakers use the phrase "as rich as Korakh," which he believes is based on "rich as Croesus."
- Korakh stretches Moshe's patience to the breaking point. Although Moshe is described as angry in several passages of Torah, it is only in this *parashah* that he "becomes very angry," *vayikhar le'Moshe m'od*.

HAFTARAH

The connection between *parashat Korakh* and its corresponding *haftarah* is one of the more oblique ones. Shmuel/Samuel has reluctantly anointed Shaul/Saul as the first king of Israel; he exhorts the assemblage to follow the precepts of God and reminds them that everyone, even Shaul, is subject to the Divine will and laws. How does this relate to the story of Korakh? First, Shmuel is a descendant of Korakh. Second, although he is descended from the leader of the most notorious rebellion in the Torah, he urges the people to follow the Torah, reminding them that their greatness is dependent not on social, political, or economic factors but on their relationship with *Adonai*, a far cry from his forebear's dangerous preachings in the Wilderness.

PARASHAT KHUKAT

39th Torah portion, 6th in *B'midbar*
B'midbar 19:1–22:1 (87 verses)
Haftarah:Shoftim 11:1–33

ALIYOT*

First/Rishon:	19:1–19:17
Second/Sheini:	19:18–20:6
Third/Shlishi:	20:7–20:13
Fourth/Revi'i:	20:14–20:21
Fifth/Khamishi:	20:22–21:9
Sixth/Shishi:	21:10–21:20
Seventh/Shevi'i:	21:21–22:1
Maftir:	21:34–22:1

SYNOPSIS

The laws of the red heifer to purify a person who has had contact with a corpse are given. The people arrive at the wilderness of Zin. Miriam dies and is buried there. The people complain that they have no water. Although God tells him merely to speak to a rock and bring forth water, an angry Moshe strikes it to get water for them. God tells Moshe and Aharon that as punishment they will not live to enter *Eretz Yisrael*. The king of Edom refuses to let *B'nei Yisrael* pass through his land. After passing the priestly garments on to his son Eleazer, Aharon dies. After they are punished for complaining about the lack of bread and water, the Israelites repent and are victorious in battle against the Amorites and the people of Bashan, whose lands they capture.

COMMENTARY

With this *parashah* the crisis of leadership that has been building throughout *Sefer B'midbar* comes to a tragic, perhaps inevitable end. Miriam and Aharon die, and Moshe is told by God that he will not be the one who leads the Israelites into the new land promised to them.

*See Additional Notes on page 475 for the *aliyot* when *Khukat* and *Balak* are read together.

(Significantly, he is not punished by death for the sins he commits in this Torah portion; he will, in fact, live to be 120. Rather, he is punished by exile, by not being permitted to enter Kina'an with the rest of the Hebrews. Like Adam and Khavah, he must remain forever outside.) Almost from the very moment of Moshe's condemnation, the strife within the Israelite camp will become of secondary importance to threats from outside and the remainder of the principal narrative focuses on these external dangers.

Intriguingly, the source of the final collapse of the old slave-era leadership will be the always fraught issue of water. What could be more precious to a desert people than water? In the Wilderness, water is life itself, as Avraham knew when he dug his wells, as Yitzkhak knew when he reestablished those wells, as Hagar knew when the angel showed her the miraculous stream from the rock that enabled her and Yishmael to survive their private ordeal in the desert, as Moshe knew when he heard the cries of the Israelites once more after his sister died.

The narrative connection between Miriam's death and the incident at Merivah where Moshe brings forth water from the rock while disobeying God's orders is not casual. It is causal. Or so the midrash goes.

The story is that Miriam was the keeper of a well that traveled along with the Israelites in the Wilderness, that as long as she was alive the well brought forth water and sustained them. This is merely the last in a chain of water-related miracles associated with Miriam. After all, it is Miriam who is intimately connected to the trip of the infant Moshe down the Nile to Pharoah's daughter and Miriam who takes timbrel in hand to lead the Hebrews in song after *Yam Suf* inundates Pharoah's army. Tractate *Ta'anit* of the Talmud makes the casual connection causal: "When Miriam died, the well was removed, as it says, 'And Miriam died there.' And immediately after, 'And there was no water for the congregation.' "

Moshe restores the flow of water when he strikes the rock, yet he is punished gravely—most gravely—for that act. It is the final and, as we will see momentarily, necessary generational shift in the leadership of the Hebrews. When this *parashah* is completed, Moshe will be the only one of the three great leaders of the people still left alive, and he will begin grooming Yehoshua to succeed him when the Israelites enter Kina'an.

But what is the great sin that Moshe commits when he strikes the rock? The people are desperately in need of water; surely he has acted in their interests.

As you may expect, this is a question that has troubled commentators, provoking a considerable body of exegesis and midrash. Certain themes run through the literature consistently and taken as a group they suggest not so much a single sin as series of interlocking failures of leadership, problems of temperament that have hovered beneath the surface throughout the story of Moshe, a bubbling pot that finally boils over at Merivah.

We have already seen several times how Moshe's patience is tested by this "stiff-necked" people. Although he has repeatedly defended them against the wrath of the Almighty, there has clearly been a cost to his always shaky grip on his temper. Confronted once again by their complaints, coming on the heels of the death of his beloved sister (so beloved, recall, that when she is stricken for traducing him, he prays fervently for her recovery), he rebukes them harshly: "Hear now, you rebels!" To Maimonides, this utterance is not merely inappropriate—these people's lives are, after all, at stake when there is no water—but bespeaks Moshe's final inability to control his rage. Maimonides argues that the striking of the rock—not once but twice—is indicative of the same. (Don't forget, we are talking about a man who has already slain an Egyptian in cold blood, albeit with provocation.)

But there is also the matter of the actual miracle of the water and the rock. As Rashi sternly points out, Moshe disobeys God's instructions. He is told to speak to the rock to bring forth water, yet he strikes it with his staff twice. More anger.

Yet Nahmanides finds these explanations wanting. He notes that Moshe gets angry on other occasions and isn't punished for it (although it should be added that there are interpreters who believe that Moshe's punishment was already foreordained, a sentence for his killing of the taskmaster). Moreover, Nahmanides observes, it is God who tells Moshe to bring along the staff. And the verse that follows explicitly says that it is for a lack of faith that Moshe is punished.

Nahmanides finds the source of Moshe's sin in his statement before bringing forth the water, "Shall we bring forth water from this rock?" We? What do you mean "we," Moshe? Who's "we"? Isn't it God who is doing the heavy lifting here?

The staff has been associated throughout the three books of Torah that deal with the narrative of the liberation from Egypt and laborious progress toward Kina'an with the powers of leadership. Why else would so much weight be placed on the miracle of Aharon's staff blossoming? I believe that Moshe is instructed to take his staff for its symbolic significance, emblematic of office. That he uses that emblem to disobey God and, whether by a slip of the tongue fueled by his ire or in a deliberate and foolish act of hubris, claims credit for the miracle itself are severe transgressions of a similar nature. If you factor into this equation the unnecessary rebuke he directs toward the Israelites, then it is hard not to see Moshe as a man who has exhausted his capacity for leadership, a man who is no longer able to lead a nation into an arduous war of conquest against superior numbers.

God may not have made his decision before this moment, but it is not a hard decision to comprehend. Moshe is not the man to lead the Israelites into Kina'an. Nor can he accompany them. Were he to do so, to paraphrase a line from John Ford's classic film *She Wore a Yellow Ribbon*, every time Yehoshua gave an order, the Israelites would look at Moshe to see what he thought. Whether one sees it as divine punishment for a terrible breach of conduct or the sad but inevitable passing of the staff of power, it is hard not to accept God's decision as the right one.

ADDITIONAL NOTES

• When this *parashah* is read with *Balak* the *aliyot* are as follows:

First / Rishon:	19:1–20:6
Second / Sheini:	20:7–20:21
Third / Shlishi:	20:22–21:20
Fourth / Revi'i:	21:21–22:12
Fifth / Khamishi:	22:13–22:38
Sixth / Shishi:	22:39–23:26
Seventh / Shevi'i:	23:27–25:9
Maftir:	25:7–25:9

• When Eleazar receives the command regarding the red heifer in *B'midbar* 19:3, it marks the first time that Aharon's eldest surviving son is given a direct command by God, a sign that the torch of priestly leadership is about to be passed to the next generation.

• The incident of the snake attacks on the Israelites is the second example of an affliction occurring in *B'midbar*, following close on the heels of Miriam's "leprosy," that is anticipated in the dialogue between Moshe and God at the Burning Bush.

• When the Israelites sing in joy at the springing forth of water at *B'midbar* 21:17, it marks the first time they have sung as a community since *Yam Suf*.

- There are two significant echoes of dark moments in the Patriarchal narrative that occur at this juncture in the Torah, the hostility of the Edomites, descendants of Eisav, and the running battle with the Moabites, descended from the incestuous union of Lot and his daughter.

HAFTARAH

The haftarah for *parashat Khukat* tells the story of *Yiftakh/Jephthah*, a great warrior and judge of Israel, and his rash promise to God, which put his daughter in jeopardy of being sacrificed. While one might be tempted to draw a parallel between his poor judgment and the wrath of Moshe, the more obvious connection between the two readings is the series of messages that the judge sends to the king of the Ammonites, recalling the sequence of events in which the Edomites and Israelites narrowly avoided conflict over territory.

PARASHAT BALAK

40th Torah portion, 7th in *B'midbar*
B'midbar 22:2–25:9 (104 verses)
Haftarah: Mikhah 5:6–6:8

ALIYOT*

First / Rishon:	22:2–22:12
Second / Sheini:	22:13–22:20
Third / Shlishi:	22:21–22:38
Fourth / Revi'i:	22:39–23:12
Fifth / Khamishi:	23:13–23:26
Sixth / Shishi:	23:27–24:13
Seventh / Shevi'i:	24:14–25:9
Maftir:	25:7–25:9

SYNOPSIS

Balak, the king of Moab, persuades the prophet Balaam to curse the Israelites so that he can defeat them and drive them out of the region. Balaam tries unsuccessfully to carry out this mission three times and finally blesses *B'nei Yisrael* instead, prophesying that Israel's enemies will be defeated. God punishes the Israelites with a plague for consorting with the Moabite women and their god. The plague is stayed after Pinkhas kills an Israelite man and his Midianite woman.

COMMENTARY

From one of the most tragic moments in the entire Torah—Moshe being told that he will not be permitted to enter the land promised to the Israelites—to a story with elements of pure farce—Balaam and his poor put-upon talking donkey. If this isn't the most improbable turn of events and shifts of tone in all of the Torah—in all of the Hebrew Bible!—someone should point out a more outrageous juxtaposition.

Of course, even the story of Balaam's failure to put a curse on the

*See Additional Notes to *Khukat* on page 475 for the *aliyot* when *Khukat* and *Balak* are read together.

Israelites is at its heart deadly serious. And the story of Balak and his Moabite warriors conspiring against the Hebrews with the help of a (somewhat inept) sorcerer points to a shift in theme that occupies much of the rest of *Sefer B'midbar* as our attention, heretofore focused on the internal problems in the Israelite camp, is once more drawn to an exterior threat. The story that occupies us here is primarily about worshippers of Baal-Peor who are arrayed against the Israelites, and much of what follows will be about the need for the Israelites to eschew the temptations of the worship of a Moabite deity. As we will see at the end of the *parashah*, the failure to do so has grave consequences for them (which we will discuss in our reading of *parashat Pinkhas*).

The early commentators, certainly up through the medieval period, consider Balaam to be an unredeemably evil figure. As several Talmudic commentators note, for all intents and purposes he is running a very clever con game on Balak, offering to place a curse upon the Hebrews for pay, forcing Balak and his increasingly beleaguered followers to build twenty-one different altars and offer sacrifices of twenty-one rams and twenty-one bulls on three different mountaintops, all the while knowing that he cannot utter the curses Balak has hired him to deliver. In commentaries as diverse as Tractate *Sanhedrin,* in which Rabbi Yohanan says that God must force the blessings out of his mouth "with a hook," and Abraham Ibn Ezra's characterization of the pagan prophet as a scheming liar, Balaam is painted in varying shades of black.

Certainly subsequent events seem to bear out that analysis. Balaam will be among those put to the sword by the Hebrews later in *B'midbar* (31:8) when they win their final victory over the Midianites.

Yet some modern commentators find this vilification hard to swallow. Everett Fox likens Balaam's "acknowledgement of God's power and Israel's glory" to those of Yitro, Rahav, and the Queen of Sheba, "wise or inspired pagan[s]." And it should be noted that God appears directly to Balaam to give him instructions at the outset of his mission. As Richard Elliott Friedman observes, this incident is something of a throwback to *Bereishit,* in which the connection between God and all humanity is made explicit, and in which God appears to many non-Jews, including Noakh, Adam, and Khavah.

Friedman finds echoes of *Bereishit* at several points in this Torah portion, and they are telling ones. Balaam says, "Those who bless you, he is blessed. Those who curse you, he is cursed," just as God tells Avraham,

"And I'll bless those who bless you, and those who curse you I'll curse."
The incident with Balaam's donkey begins very much like the *Akeidah*,
with a man on an ass, two servants, and an encounter with an angel; once
again, a man with a specific and deadly set of directions is thwarted by the
will of God. Moreover, as Friedman adds, as a result of Avraham's obedience at Mount Moriah, God blesses him yet again and promises to make
him numerous, while the incident of the donkey is caused as a result of the
fertility of the Israelites and ends with Balaam uttering another blessing
upon the Hebrews.

But there is an even more surprising link with Balaam that runs
through even the classical commentaries, a connection to *Sefer Iyov Job*.
As Pinchas Peli points out, in Tractate *Bava Batra*, the Talmud states,
"Moshe set down in writing his own book, the Book of Balaam and the
Book of Job."

The notion that Moshe wrote down not only the Torah but also these
two others is quite shocking; what possible link could there be between
this sorcerer and the sadly put-upon Iyov? Both men are non-Jews and
that, Peli suggests, makes their stories inherently interesting in the context of the *Tanakh* for what they tell us about the laws handed down at
Sinai from the perspective of an outsider.

Iyov suffered perhaps more than any other figure in the *Tanakh* and the
story of his suffering, taken in tandem with the stories of the Creation, the
Patriarchs, the Revelation at Sinai, and the Laws given there, says something profound to us about the necessity to keep in mind the suffering
individual when we interpret the *mitzvot*. As Peli elegantly puts it, "When
religious laws become divorced from the human situation they cease to be
an expression of the will of God who cares." That is why Moshe's constant pleading on behalf of the Hebrews, bespeaking his own rather tor-
tured sense of compassion even when he is on the receiving end of their
complaints, is such a powerful measure of his greatness as a leader and a
human being; he seldom loses sight of the humanity of his followers, of
the sufferings they are undergoing, even when they behave badly.

Yet, Peli concludes, by the same token it took the curse-turned-into-
blessings of Balaam to remind the beleaguered Moshe of the greatness of
his own people. How lovely are their tents, indeed! And it took Balaam, a
Gentile soothsayer, to recognize the greater power of a people beloved by
God in the face of the seemingly superior military might of the Moabites
and to communicate that message to a resisting Balak.

ADDITIONAL NOTES

- There is one other, rather more abstruse link between the story of Balaam and *Sefer Iyov*. In *B'midbar* 22:32 a word, *yarat*, occurs whose meaning is obscure today. The passage in question refers to God's wrath at Balaam, apparently for being too quick to go along with Balak's ministers. This is the only appearance of the word in the Torah. The only other time the word is found in the entire Hebrew Bible is in *Iyov* 16:11.
- This Torah portion bears the name of a distinctly evil individual, the king of the Moabites who tries to destroy the Hebrews. How do the rabbis reconcile this seeming contradiction? As the Moabite king, Balak is also a forebear of Rut and, therefore, of David and the Davidic line.
- Perhaps the most famous line from this *parashah*, spoken by Balaam, is used to open morning services: "How lovely are your tents, O Jacob, your dwelling places, O Israel."

HAFTARAH

The *haftarah* for this *parashah* is drawn from the prophecies of Mikhah, a witness to the destruction of the Northern Kingdom of ancient Israel who warned the people of Judah that a similar fate would befall them if they did not put aside their sinfulness. In the course of his prophetic writings herein he recalls the plotting of Balak against the Israelites in the Wilderness and the failure of Balak and Balaam to bring those plots to fruition.

PARASHAT PINKHAS

41st Torah portion, 8th in *B'midbar*
B'midbar 25:10–30:1 (168 verses)
Haftarah: Melakhim Aleph 18:46–19:21

ALIYOT

First / Rishon:	25:10–26:4
Second / Sheini:	26:5–26:51
Third / Shlishi:	26:52–27:5
Fourth / Revi'i:	27:6–27:23
Fifth / Khamishi:	28:1–28:15
Sixth / Shishi:	28:16–29:11
Seventh / Shevi'i:	29:12–30:1
Maftir:	29:35–30:1

SYNOPSIS

Pinkhas is rewarded for killing the Israelite and the Midianite woman who cursed God. Israel fights a war against the Midianites. A second census is taken. The daughters of Zelophekhad force a change in the laws of property inheritance that allows them to inherit their late father's share of Kina'an. Yehoshua is chosen to be successor to Moshe. The sacrificial ritual for all Festival occasions is described in detail.

COMMENTARY

The time has come for Moshe to choose his successor as leader of the Israelites. He and we know that he will not be allowed to enter Kina'an and the people will need a firm leader who can handle himself with violence if necessary. The chosen one is Yehoshua.

Why not Pinkhas? Doesn't it seem a bit odd that Pinkhas, who has been rewarded for an act of violence at the outset of the Torah portion, who seems to be a true zealot for *Adonai,* isn't considered as the next leader of the Hebrews? What does the choice of someone else tells us about God's desires and about the nature of leadership for this people God has selected?

The incident at the end of the previous *parashah* in which Pinkhas kills Zimri and Kozbi, the Hebrew and Midianite couple who have sex in what may well be the Tent of Meeting (we'll come back to this all-important detail in a moment), is one that has provoked some of the most painful self-examination in all of Torah commentary. Commentators are divided on whether Pinkhas's act of violence was acceptable or not, on whether his zealotry is a good or bad trait, and on whether this act is what disqualifies him from consideration as Moshe's successor. There is even a spirited debate on the exact meaning of the *Berit Shalom/Covenant of Peace* that God gives him at the outset of this Torah portion.

For the modern reader, the entire sequence of events is deeply troubling. If we accept the word of commentators who approve of his act, then we must also accept their view that an Israelite who had sex with a non-Jew was to be executed. Needless to say, this goes against everything that contemporary readers believe, particularly in a pluralistic society like the United States.

Indeed, I am appalled that Rabbi Menachem Mendel Schneerson, the last Lubavitcher Rebbe, could agree with the passage in Tractate *Sanhedrin* that states that when a Jew and a non-Jew cohabit, "the zealous have [the right to] strike him." (Schneerson notes that this is not an obligation, merely a right. Halakhically, one is obligated to give a warning and can only perform the execution while the act being punished is actually taking place. Moreover, while the punishment may be justified, one cannot instruct another to inflict it.)

In the context in which the events herein occur, however, the question isn't quite so clear-cut as it would be if it were, say, New York City—or Jersualem—in the year 2006. First, the relations in question take place between a Hebrew and an idol worshipper; many of the laws propagated in the Mosaic books of the Torah address directly the urgent need for the Jews to eschew foreign worship and its practices, to separate themselves from the polytheists who surrounded them in the ancient world. Additionally, the Israelites are in a state of war with the Midianites; that was the whole point of the incident with Balaam, you will no doubt recall. This woman is one of many sent by Balak to seduce the Hebrew men, to undermine the fabric of their society in wartime.

Richard Elliott Friedman argues another extenuating circumstance, that the crime of the couple is a ritual one. He believes that their sex act takes place not in just any tent but in front of the *Mishkan,* a space that non-Levites are not even permitted to enter. The desecration here is about as serious as one can imagine, if his interpretation is correct, and it's not the sex that's the problem. His reading of the passage at the end of *Balak* explains one of the seeming contradictions in the opening of *Pinkhas* that troubled the classical commentators: How can Pinkhas take matters into his own hands without consulting Moshe? The answer follows from Friedman's position. A ritual crime is instantly punishable, with no trial and no question of motives, because such a violation is indefensible; if the issue were an ethical one, he says, there would be a trial and inquiry.

One may also offer an argument of justification, as it is called in Anglo-American jurisprudence, that by killing the couple, Pinkhas averts a plague that would follow the violation of a holy place (as in the aftermath of the rebellion of Korakh and his followers).

Even those who are most completely at ease with Pinkhas's behavior, Rabbi Schneerson among them, readily acknowledge that zeal is not a character trait that is admired in Jewish thought. Schneerson notes that the tradition links Pinkhas with the prophet Eliyahu/Elijah (in some sources even saying that they are one and the same man, although their life spans are separated by several centuries), who killed the priests of Baal and Asherah. What sets the zealousness of Pinkhas and Eliyahu apart is that theirs is a zealousness for God and for the well-being of the Israelites, not for themselves. Yet God teaches Eliyahu that his zeal must be tempered with love and, as Schneerson observes, the prophet's return will herald the coming of universal peace and the Messiah.

Despite all these arguments in defense (or expiation) of Pinkhas's act, it still makes us as modern readers uneasy, if not outraged altogether. For what it's worth, we are not alone in our dismay. We have ample company among the great sages of Judaism.

Consider the statement of Rav, the head of the yeshiva at Sura, one of the great sources of Talmudic wisdom. He condemns Pinkhas unequivocally. He says that when Pinkhas challenges Moshe by reminding him that he taught that God has said that a Jew who has sex with a non-Jew may be put to death by zealots, Moshe replies, "Let God who gave the advice execute the advice."

Another scholar of this period, Rabbi Judah bar Pazzi, argues that had God not intervened in the outset of this Torah portion, the Jews would have ostracized him for his failure to consult Moshe (yes, Rav uses a different midrashic reading from bar Pazzi), and only God's approbation of Pinkhas's act keeps him among the people, the implication being that while the end result might have been acceptable, Pinkhas's failure to go through channels was not.

More recently, prominent nineteenth-century Hasidic rabbis have expressed similar misgivings. Naftali Zvi Yehudah Berlin, known as Ha'-Emek Davar after his most famous book, has a deep distrust of Pinkhas's motivations and believes that even Pinkhas himself is troubled by the violence with which he acted. That, he says, is why God's gift to Pinkhas is a Covenant of Peace, that it is with this Covenant that he will be able to restore peace to his own soul; it's not a reward for his act, it's a cure for its aftermath. As the S'fat Emet notes, Pinkhas can only continue as a priest after God permits it with a special Covenant of priesthood; otherwise, by shedding blood he would have disqualified himself from the priesthood, much as King David is not permitted to build the Temple because of his history as a warrior. And Yehuda Eiger notes that *parashat Pinkhas* is both preceded and followed by double portions—*Khukat/Balak* and *Matot/Ma'asei*—and infers from that happenstance that fanatics must live alone, in isolation from society. He concludes, "Woe to a generation when the fanatics are joined together!"

Finally there is the question of the succession to leadership. The Kotzker Rebbe says that Moshe didn't want Pinkhas as his successor precisely because of his anger and zeal, and Moshe knows something about the dangers of uncontrolled anger. Significantly, it will be Yehoshua to whom the reins of leadership are handed at the end of the Torah portion that bears the name of Pinkhas.

ADDITIONAL NOTES
- With 168 verses, this is the second-longest *parashah* in the Torah.
- For a discussion of the incident of Zelophekhad's daughters, see Chapter 5, "Hearing Silenced Voices: Women and the Torah."

HAFTARAH

As noted above, Pinkhas and Eliyahu are frequently equated in the rabbinic literature. It is only fitting, then, that the *haftarah* to this Torah portion should be the story of Eliyahu's flight after he kills the false prophets of Baal. Significantly, much as Pinkhas is not named as Moshe's successor, Eliyahu will not be anointed as a prophet; rather, Elisha will take his place.

PARASHAT MATOT

42nd Torah portion, 9th in *B'midbar*
B'midbar 30:2–32:42 (112 verses)
Haftarah: Yirmiyahu 1:1–2:3

ALIYOT*

First / Rishon:	30:2–30:17
Second / Sheini:	31:1–31:12
Third / Shlishi:	31:13–31:24
Fourth / Revi'i:	31:25–31:41
Fifth / Khamishi:	31:42–31:54
Sixth / Shishi:	32:1-32:19
Seventh / Shevi'i:	32:20–32:42
Maftir:	32:39–32:42

SYNOPSIS

Moshe explains to the Israelites the laws concerning vows made by men and women. Israel successfully wages war against the Midianites. The laws regarding the spoils of war are outlined. The tribes of Re'uven and Gad request permission to stay on the east bank of the Yardein; at first Moshe rebukes them but they promise to serve as shock troops for the conquest of Kina'an and he relents.

COMMENTARY

Through most of the second half of the Torah, we have watched with dismay as a generational split has underlined Moshe's fading leadership abilities. Clearly it is the younger generation of Israelites—Nadav and Avihu, Kalev and Yehoshua, Korakh and his followers, Pinkhas—who have increasingly taken the initiative, for better or worse, as Moshe has gradually lost control of situations. As he faces one final-seeming rebellion, with the tribes of Re'uven and Gad seeking to remain outside *Eretz Yisrael,* the better to raise their by now huge herds of livestock, we cannot help but fear the worst. And for a moment it looks as if Moshe's severely

*For aliyot when *parashat Matot* is read with *Ma'asei,* see Additional Notes on page 489.

frayed patience will finally snap. Yet the end result of this dispute is a surprisingly amicable negotiated settlement.

Let's briefly review what actually happens at the end of this *parashah*. The war with Midian has been successfully concluded, the booty distributed. The tribes of Re'uven and Gad (later to be joined by half of the tribe of Menasheh) come to Moshe asking that they be permitted to settle the lands of Jazer and Gilead on the east side of the Yardein, prime grazing land for their by now huge herds of livestock, as they explain to him. Moshe responds with rage, accusing them of abandoning their brother Israelites, invoking the sin of the spies as a bleak precedent. They demur, pledging that they will act as shock troops leading the way in the wars to come while accepting no portion of Kina'an. His anger appeased by their generous offer, Moshe accepts, cautioning them against breaking their oath (an appropriate warning in a Torah portion that opens with a lengthy discussion of oaths to God).

At least superficially the incident looks like an embarrassing replay of the strife at Merivah, with a group of Israelites making a not unreasonable request (water, good grazing land) and being met with a strident, almost shrill rebuke from Moshe, their leader. It was at Merivah, remember, that Moshe overreacted so badly that God decided he would not be allowed to enter *Eretz Yisrael*.

Yet the rabbinical commentators are divided in their interpretation of this dispute and the older interpretations actually tend to favor Moshe, which suggests that the incident may not be as clear-cut as it appears on first glance. What is different here, and how does it affect the outcome?

First, the rabbis believe that the dissident tribesmen are motivated in no small part by selfishness (unlike the desperately parched Israelites at Merivah). The clue, they argue, can be found in the ordering of priorities expressed in their request to Moshe: "We will build here sheepfolds for our flocks and towns for our children." In *B'midbar Rabbah* the sages argue that this request reveals their true concern—we need to protect our investments and, oh yes, also our families, too. In that respect, some commentators say, their dissent resembles more closely that of Korakh than the Israelites at Merivah, hardly a suitable role model.

But there is a second element of this schism that harks back to more destructive internecine fights in the Israelite camp. What the Reuvenites, Gadites, and dissident Menashites are calling for is nothing less than a division of the Hebrew people, a withdrawal of their tribes from a God-imposed mission. Moshe makes it clear by his response that the analogy he sees is not to Merivah but to the *miraglim/spies*, another incident in which internal dissension (and a lack of faith in *Adonai*) threatens to divide the people and divert them from their God-directed mission. Yitzchak Etshalom, a contemporary Orthodox rabbi, writes, "Since the saving grace of the people throughout the desert was their unity and sense of common destiny and mutual responsibility, the 'abandonment' of the B'nei Yisrael by these two tribes was a dire threat indeed."

But not all of the sages who have written on *parashat Matot* are as comfortable with Moshe's reponse as those who point to the alleged selfishness and divisiveness of the breakaway tribes. Nahmanides, although sympathetic to Moshe's anger, believes that the great leader has misunderstood his followers this time. He says that the tribal leaders have come to Moshe with a request, not a demand, and that Moshe has misread their reticence as cowardice in the face of an impending war of conquest.

And Abravanel continues this line of reasoning, suggesting that the awkwardness with which their request was worded—put to Moshe as a negative, "do not move us across the Yardein"—is the reason for the misunderstanding and the match to the fuse of Moshe's anger. Isaac Arama, a contemporary of Abravanel's, goes even further, arguing that Moshe owes them an apology for his hasty assumption that the Gadites and Reuvenites are trying to duck out of their responsibilities to the Hebrews as a nation. Arama says that what Moshe reads as fear is nothing more than a confusion among the tribal leaders trying to express their conflicting motives.

There is an anomaly in the text itself that suggests the complexities of this exchange. In the middle of the Gadite-Reuvenite petition to Moshe, immediately after *B'midbar* 32:4, there is a paragraph break, which is then followed by the rest of their request. Abravanel believes that this strangely placed pause is indicative of the hesitancy with which they approach Moshe, that the dissident tribesmen themselves realize that what they are asking is fraught with problems, perhaps even wrong. And Moshe's reply—"Shall your brothers go to war while you sit here?"—is as harsh as any he gives in the entire Torah.

What sets this incident apart from the terribly wrenching events surrounding the deaths of Nadav and Avihu, the betrayal by the spies, the rebellion of Korakh and his followers, and Moshe's disastrous outburst at Merivah is that both sides continue to talk to each other, with the result that clarity and an agreement are finally reached. The process is laborious by Torah standards, as the pause in the middle of the original petition suggests, but the end result is the preservation of the unity of the Hebrews, with the two and a half tribes guaranteeing their presence at the head of battle.

Ultimately what is important here is not whether Moshe or the Gadites and Reuvenites were right. What is important, I believe, is that both sides in this dispute managed to make themselves understood—admittedly with difficulty—with the result that no irreparable harm was done to the Israelites. Moshe reasserts his leadership role one last time, securing the participation of all twelve tribes in the battles to come and holding the nation together. Gad and Re'uven maintain their rights while upholding their responsibilities as Hebrews. The nation is preserved and its God-ordained mission reaffirmed.

And that is what really matters.

ADDITIONAL NOTES

- When *parashat Matot* is read with *parashat Ma'asei*, the *aliyot* are as follows:

First / Rishon:	30:2–31:12
Second / Sheini:	31:13–31:54
Third / Shlishi:	32:1–32:19
Fourth / Revi'i:	32:20–33:49
Fifth / Khamishi:	33:50–34:15
Sixth / Shishi:	34:16–35:8
Seventh / Shevi'i:	35:9–36:13
Maftir:	36:11–36:13

- The passage in chapter 31 outlining the cleasing of the spoils by fire is the basis for the rules by which one "kashers" (renders kosher, ritually pure) utensils, as delineated in the Talmud and subsequent halakhic commentaries.
- Although it is strongly implied that all the Midianites are wiped out in this *parashah*, that is clearly not the case, because they turn up again in *Yehoshua* 6–8.

HAFTARAH

This is the first of three *haftarot* of rebuke that precede Tisha B'Av. As the opening section of the Torah portion concerns the making of vows to God, so Yirmiyahu warns Israel that her failure to fulfill the words of God will lead to the nation's destruction.

PARASHAT MASS'EI

43rd Torah portion, 10th and last in *B'midbar*
B'midbar 33:1–36:13 (132 verses)
Haftarah: Yirmiyahu 2:4–28, 3:4 (Sephardic: *Yirmiyahu* 2:4–28,
   4:1–2)

ALIYOT*

First / Rishon:	33:1–33:10
Second / Sheini:	33:11–33:49
Third / Shlishi:	33:50–34:15
Fourth / Revi'i:	34:16–34:29
Fifth / Khamishi:	35:1–35:8
Sixth / Shishi:	35:9–35:34
Seventh / Shevi'i:	36:1–36:13
Maftir:	36:11–36:13

SYNOPSIS

The itinerary of the Israelites through the Wilderness from Egypt to Yardein is recounted. Moshe tells *B'nei Yisrael* to remove the current inhabitants of the land that God will give them and to destroy their gods. The boundaries of *Eretz Yisrael* are defined, along with those of the Levitical cities and the cities of refuge. God makes a precise distinction between murder and manslaughter. The laws of inheritance that apply to Israelite women are explained.

COMMENTARY

The Israelites have come a long way since slavery, but humanity has come even farther since leaving *Gan Eden*, and at the center of this *parashah* is a vivid reminder of hard-won progress in human behavior. The heart of *parashat Mass'ei* is a lengthy discussion of the *arei miklat/ cities of refuge*, set aside for one who has committed involuntary manslaughter. The nineteenth-century Italian Torah scholar S. D. Luz-

---

*For aliyot when *parashat Mass'ei* is read with *Matot*, see Additional Notes to *parashat Matot* on page 489.

zatto makes an interesting observation about the principles governing the cities of refuge that casts this passage into an intriguing light. In early generations, at times when no central government with judicial function and authority had yet been established, blood feud was a sacred obligation in every family. The closer the family relationship to the slain person, the greater the duty to avenge his death. The Torah established judicial function and authority, judges and instruments of law execution; herewith the law was taken out of the hands of arbitrary individuals and vested in the community as such. If now a murder had been committed, it was possible to calm the avenger of blood by promising him: leave the matter to the judges. They will handle it correctly.

Of course, this progress begins with the Noahide laws, all the way back in the second *parashah* of *Bereishit*, but we can see the development of institutions of human justice throughout the middle three books of the Torah, as the "social" *mitzvot* teach people to behave in a more humane way toward the stranger, the widow and orphan, the Other.

The establishment of the cities of refuge represents a striking example of this principle at work in juridical matters. The simple fact that the law will distinguish between one who commits deliberate murder and another who takes a life inadvertently is an enormous step forward. The cities of refuge, which seem to bear a dual function, are the logical next step; they provide a haven for the man-slayer, thereby removing the temptation of others to engage in blood feud; they provide a means for the expiation of guilt and reintegration into the community of one who has taken a life.

Luzzatto believes that while the law courts will stay the hand of the family of a murder victim, these are not sufficient to defuse the anger of someone who has lost a relative through accident and, therefore, has no such recourse. Perhaps that premise is debatable, but *arei miklat* certainly provide the means for an enforced "cooling-off period," which seems a sensible way to break the never-ending, spiraling cycle of blood vengeance.

But the primary purpose of the cities of refuge is redemptive and recuperative. The word *miklat* carries connotations of absorption and retention, suggesting that these havens were designed to allow the man-slayer to be reintegrated into the community. It is also suggestive that the cities of refuge and the cities assigned to the Levites are discussed together; as Samson Raphael Hirsch notes, one of the roles of the *kohanim* and *levi'im* is to seek expiation for the inadvertent sinner.

The postbiblical texts that deal with this issue make it abundantly clear that the inhabitants of *arei miklat* have a responsibility to look after not only the material but also the spiritual needs of the refugee. Maimonides writes that it is permissible (and one gathers even expected) that the man-slayer's teacher go into exile with him to enable him to continue his studies of Torah. After all, if the purpose of the cities of refuge is to allow the man-slayer to live, Rambam argues, it should be considered that a life without Torah is no proper life at all.*

It is significant, in this context, that it is upon the death of the High Priest that the man-slayer is released from his exile and permitted to return home. Only death can compensate for life; the death of the High Priest is symbolic recompense for the death of the victim of involuntary manslaughter. Moreover, the death of the High Priest traditionally was associated with the expiation of sins. Finally, as Maimonides suggests, if the aggrieved family sees that even the most important and powerful among the Israelites eventually dies, perhaps they can learn to accept the death of their loved one as part of the cycle of life.

What is missing from this discussion is any notion of the cities of refuge as part of punishment for a crime (albeit inadvertently committed). As B. S. Jacobson points out, incarceration, the loss of personal liberty, is almost never invoked in the post-Sinai passages of the Torah. The Hebrews have been enslaved for four centuries. God does not need to threaten them with a return to bondage, not even as a justifiable punishment for wrongdoing.

KHAZAK, KHAZAK, V'NITKHAZEIK.

ADDITIONAL NOTES

- In the recounting of the journeys of the Israelites that begins this *parashah*, forty-two place-names are given. There are some contradictions in the order of the journey between this passage and *B'midbar* 21.
- Rephidim, mentioned in *B'midbar* 33:14, is also the site of the battle with the Amalekites (described in *Shemot* 17:8). There is a modern city

---

*There are two practical elements involved in the establishment of the cities of refuge. There will be six of them, placed throughout the areas under Hebrew jurisdiction so that they are easily reachable by a refugee. This, however, presupposes the existence of an Israelite state.

called Rephidim, located in the Sinai Peninsula near the Suez Canal, but there is a consensus that this is not the same place.

- The description of the borders of the Promised Land given here in *B'midbar* 34:1–12 is the most detailed of the three passages describing these boundaries. Interestingly, it describes an area somewhat smaller than those delineated elsewhere. The Talmud says that for purposes of *halakhah* governing practices specific to *Eretz Yisrael* these are the boundaries that apply.

- The two-thousand–cubit measure used in *B'midbar* 35:5 to define the common ground in the Levitical cities was adopted by the rabbis as the basis for the limit on walking permitted on the Sabbath.

HAFTARAH

The *haftarah* that accompanies *parashat Mass'ei* is the second of the two "sermons of rebuke" drawn from the prophet Yirmiyahu. Yirmiyahu tells the Israelites that God says they "have defiled My land," an echo of the stark passage from the *parashah* in which we are told that "blood pollutes the land." And *Yirmiyahu* 2:6 offers something of a miniature recapitulation of the Exodus and wanderings in the Wilderness, another echo of the Torah portion. Significantly, the *haftarah* ends not with Yirmiyahu's scathing denunciation of the Israelites' misbehavior, but with verses added in recognition of the stricture against ending a reading on a note of doom and gloom.

SEFER DEVARIM/THE BOOK OF DEUTERONOMY

Fifth and final book of the Torah
11 *parashiyot*
34 chapters, 956 verses

On its face, *Sefer Devarim* would seem to be an unnecessary repetition of what has gone before in the three books that immediately precede it. There is little narrative left, other than the death of Moshe. His farewell speech, which takes up most of the book, seems at first to be little more than a restatement of the laws given at Sinai and in the Wilderness.

Yet there is more to it than that. First, it represents the completion of Moshe's long, strange, and improbable journey from a basket in the Nile to the edge of the Yardein, from being a castaway child of slaves to the leader of a nation-in-birth. The mere fact that he can make a speech that, by one commentator's estimate, lasts eleven days is remarkable enough, given his protestations at the Burning Bush that he is too slow of tongue to lead. But more than that, this speech represents his ethical will, his instructions to and wishes for the Israelites as they enjoy the fruits of a hard-won nationhood and sovereignty. He does not merely repeat the teachings from Sinai and after, he elaborates on them in significant ways, a vehicle through which God refines and distills the *mitzvot*.

In a structural paradox that is typical of the way the Torah works as narrative, we have gone from a book—*B'midbar*—that covers 38 years in twenty-six chapters, to one that covers less than two weeks in thirty-four chapters yet recapitulates 440 years of slavery, redemption, revelation, and generational transition in that same period of time. As Rabbi Yair Kahn has written, "*Sefer Devarim*, as it is written, flows from the tragic events of *Sefer B'midbar*." Because the generation that "knew Egypt" (as the new Pharoah of *Shemot* did not know Yosef) died in the Wilderness, Moshe must teach once again the lessons of the yoke of the slavery and the yoke of the *mitzvot*. The Israelites of the previous generation died *ba'midbar* but their legacy to the next generation must not be extinguished. *Devarim*, with its message of faith in and to God and its structure of a teaching handed down *l'dor va'dor/from generation to generation*, may well be the central text of all Judaism.

PARASHAT DEVARIM

44th Torah portion, 1st in *Devarim*
Devarim 1:1–3:22 (105 verses)
Haftarah: Yeshayahu 1:1–27

ALIYOT

First / Rishon:	1:1–1:11
Second / Sheini:	1:12–1:21
Third / Shlishi:	1:22–1:38
Fourth / Revi'i:	1:39–2:1
Fifth / Khamishi:	2:2–2:30
Sixth / Shishi:	2:31–3:14
Seventh / Shevi'i:	3:15–3:22
Maftir:	3:20–3:22

SYNOPSIS

Moshe begins his final words of instruction to *B'nei Yisrael*, focusing first on recounting their physical journey, downplaying some of the more negative aspects of that trek. Moshe reviews the people's reactions to the negative reports of the spies and the appointment of Yehoshua to succeed him. Moshe recounts that all of the Israelite leaders who left Egypt died, as God had intended, and the people continued their wanderings and defeated their enemies. Moshe reiterates that *Eretz Yisrael* was allocated to the Israelite tribes. God informs Moshe that he will not be allowed to enter the Promised Land.

COMMENTARY

With *parashat Devarim*, we begin the final book of the Torah, the final movement that fulfills the promise that God made to Avraham all the way back in *Bereishit* 12:1. *B'nei Yisrael* have become a mighty nation, more numerous than the stars. They are perched on the edge of the land that will be theirs, Kina'an. What more remains to be done?

Moshe calls *B'nei Yisrael* together one last time, on the banks of the River Yardein, knowing that he will not speak to them again, that they will cross that river into *Eretz Yisrael*, leaving him behind for the first and only time in forty years. These are the last instructions Moshe will give them before they depart on the final, most momentous leg of a journey that has been not merely spatial—a hard trek through the deserts and barren places, mountains and wadis, through hostile tribes and hostile nature—but also a journey through time. After all, God decreed that the generation that left Egypt would not live to see Kina'an, and left them to wander in the Wilderness for thirty-eight years. (In that sense, by the way, these really are the *children* of Israel.)

Even more important, this has been a *spiritual* journey. Indeed, Moshe's final oration should serve as a powerful reminder of that fact. Within this *parashah* there are two interesting passages that in contrasting ways underline that aspect of the past forty years.

In chapter 2, Moshe recounts the story of hostile lands through which *B'nei Yisrael* have passed—the Edomites, descendants of Eisav, and the Moabites, whose king sent Balaam to curse the Israelites without success. Of the Moabites, Moshe recalls, "And *Adonai* said to me: 'Be not at enmity with Moab, neither contend with them in battle; for I will not give unto thee of their land for a possession, because I have given Ar unto the children of Lot for a possession' " (*Devarim* 2:9). And there is a similar passage regarding Edom.

What is this? God has gone to two of Israel's sworn enemies—Moab, which had sent the harlots of Midian to disrupt the Israelite camp only weeks ago, and Edom, traditionally identified with such enemies of the Jews as Babylon and Rome—and God has given them land, land that is explicitly forbidden to the Israelites. And the passage goes further and makes it clear that the Edomites and Moabites have gained that land by driving out or destroying its previous occupants, just as God has promised to do for the Israelites in Kina'an.

At first glance, it appears that God is being as profligate with tribal lands as a big winner at a casino is with tips. What about the Israelites' status as Chosen People?

The answer to this seeming paradox is lodged in the heart of this final book of Torah and can be discerned from the opening passages of *Devarim* (although anyone who has enough Greek to decipher the roots of the word *Deuteronomy* can figure it out even more quickly).

Devarim opens, *"Ehleh ha'devarim asher diber Moshe el kol Yisrael bi'ever Ha'Yardein/These are the words that Moshe spoke to all Israel at the Jordan."* There's something a bit unusual about this opening sentence—not something grammatical or arcane, nothing to do with *gematria, remez,* or *sod*. It's nothing hidden—it's right there for anyone to see.

These are the words that *Moshe* spoke. By himself, for himself. Yes, in the third verse it will add that he spoke according to what *Adonai* had given him as commandments and, indeed, nearly the entire text of *Sefer Devarim* will consist of his speech recounting the commandments that were given in the Wilderness. But this is one of the few passages in Torah in which Moshe speaks on his own initiative, without prompting from God, to convey a spiritual message to *B'nei Yisrael*.

How does Moshe begin his spiritual message, his ethical will, as it were? He begins by recounting the lengthy journey, some of the many hazards that befell the Israelites on the way to the banks of the Jordan. But he doesn't recount many of the bad moments, the moments of self-doubt, of loss of faith, of dissension within the tribes and faltering will. He doesn't enumerate the many times that the Israelites wished they were back in Egypt.

We have moved past all that. In the course of this journey, these four decades, *B'nei Yisrael* have moved past these dark moments, have grown spiritually. They don't need to be reminded that they have stumbled. What does Moshe remind them of—and how does it answer the question about God's giving of land to other tribes?

The word *Deuteronomy* comes from the Greek words meaning "second" and "statute," and it refers to Moshe's lengthy restatement of the *mitzvot* that were given at Sinai and after. For the remainder of Torah is nothing less than a summation and repetition of the "laws and precepts."

This is what sets the Israelites apart from the Edomites, the Moabites, the Canaanites who they will soon put to flight or the sword. Nations rise and fall, they defeat their enemies and are in turn defeated by them. That's human history in all its brutal glory or disgrace. Israel is not exempt from its workings, as a casual perusal of the blood-soaked pages of Jewish history will tell you. And if God chooses to give land to the Edomites or the Moabites, so be it.

But the Covenant that God made with Avraham, with Yitzkhak, with Ya'akov, the Covenant that is restated throughout Torah, is at the heart of this book, is of a different sort. Yes, we will be given the land of Kina'an, this "land flowing with milk and honey," and we are made a great people up to a point. In fact, unlike the Moabites and Edomites the Israelites are never stronger than their neighbors; they defeat them because God goes before them. And the Covenant that makes that possible carries with it a significant price tag.

It's those laws, those 613 *mitzvot*.

What sets *Am Yisrael* apart from Moab or Edom or Kina'an is the decision to accept the yoke of the *mitzvot*. In discussing the previous two *parashiyot*, *Matot-Ma'asei*, Yeshayahu Leibowitz observes that the land of Kina'an is not inherently holy, and now that we know that God has bestowed other lands on other peoples, we can see that. What makes Kina'an holy, Leibowitz reminds us, is that God dwells there in the midst of *B'nei Yisrael*. And God dwells there because we accept the responsibility, the burden, the honor, and the pleasure of observing the *mitzvot*.

Or as God says, "You will be holy because I, *Adonai*, am holy."

That's the bargain.

And now, as the nature of the journey changes, it falls to Moshe—the man who once called himself slow of tongue—to speak for himself, to remind *B'nei Yisrael* of what they have achieved in spiritual growth and of what is expected of them once they have crossed the Yardein. God gives the *mitzvot*, but it falls to Moshe to remind them, person to person, so to speak, of their duty. Indeed, what he is reminding them of is nothing less than the reason they are crossing the Yardein—to fulfill the Covenant.

ADDITIONAL NOTES

- Two telling details occur early in this *parashah*, in *Devarim* 1:5. The verb used to describe Moshe's recounting of the story is *ho'il*, which has the connotation of eagerness, gladness. Hence Moshe is eager to expound the story and the laws. What does he expound? "*Et Ha'Torah*."

- In *Devarim* 1:16, judges are enjoined to "hear out" the participants in a law case. From this passage the Talmud derives the principle that a judge shall not take testimony from a party to an action until both parties are present.

- Although it is no longer observed, the fifteenth of Av, traditionally considered the day the Israelites were given permission to enter Kina'an, was once a day of great rejoicing. As part of the observance, young unmarried women dressed in white like brides and danced with the eligible men, inviting them to choose a future spouse. It was also the time of a wood offering, when firewood for the altars was brought to Jerusalem.

HAFTARAH

The opening of the *Sefer Yeshayahu* echoes Moshe's words of reproof from the *parashah*. Yet, like those words, it also contains a grain of hope in redemption. As the prophet says at the end of this passage, "Zion shall be saved in the judgment;/Her repentant ones in the retribution." This *haftarah* is always read on the Sabbath before Tisha B'Av, which is therefore known as *Shabbat Khazon*, after the opening word of the reading.

PARASHAT VA'ETKHANAN

45th Torah portion, 2nd in *Devarim*
Devarim 3:23–7:11 (122 verses)
Haftarah: Yeshayahu 40:1–26

ALIYOT

First / Rishon:	3:23–4:4
Second / Sheini:	4:5–4:40
Third / Shlishi:	4:41–4:49
Fourth / Revi'i:	5:1–5:18
Fifth / Khamishi:	5:19–6:3
Sixth / Shishi:	6:4–6:25
Seventh / Shevi'i:	7:1–7:11
Maftir:	7:9–7:11

SYNOPSIS

Moshe pleads with God to let him enter *Eretz Yisrael* with the people, but God once more refuses his request. Moshe orders *B'nei Yisrael* to pay attention and follow the laws given by God in order to be worthy of the land they are about to receive. Specific areas of the land are set aside to serve as cities of refuge. The Covenant at Sinai, here called Horeb, and the Ten Commandments are recalled. Once again, the people are exhorted to heed God's commandments. Moshe speaks the words of the *Sh'ma*, the credo of Judaism, and commands Israel to show their love for *Adonai* and keep God's laws and ordinances. Moshe warns the people not to commit idolatry by worshipping the gods of the nations they will conquer in Israel.

COMMENTARY

At the heart of *parashat Va'etkhanan* one finds the most familiar sentences in all of Hebrew liturgy.

Sh'ma Yisrael, Adonai Eloheinu, Adonai ekhad.
Hear, oh Israel, *Adonai* our God is One.

This affirmation of the Unity of the Eternal is both the starting point and the heart of Jewish belief. There is but one God; the Creator is a Unity, indivisible, ineffable, indefinable.

It's one of those precepts that you take on faith—literally—or not at all. And so much else proceeds from the acceptance of that sentence. Four thousand years of Jewish history and everything that entails. Two thousand years of Christian history, fourteen hundred years of Islamic history. And so on. One might say, with justification, that a sizeable chunk of Western civilization is born from that simple sentence.

If we are even moderately observant Jews, we read that sentence several times a day, seven days a week. It is probably the first prayer we ever learned. For some of us it will be the last words we utter. That is the Jewish tradition, and it was passed on to us by our parents and our teachers.

Such a passing on of ideas and rituals is what the next words of the Torah portion call for, as we undoubtedly know, and I want to talk a bit about that injunction momentarily. But for most or even all of us, these words are worn thin by overuse, their meaning obscured in the repetition.

Before we are told to pass these teachings on—*"v'shinantam l'vanekha"*— we are told to love God. Indeed, colloquially we call this part of the prayer the *V'ahavta / You shall love.*

How are we to love God? *B'khol l'vavekha, u'v'khol nafshekha, u'v'khol m'odekha.* In the translations that we are most familiar with, this phrase is given as "with all your heart, with all your soul, with all your might." On a base level that's an adequate translation, but it loses a lot of nuance and, in one case, is something of an unintentional distortion. *L'vavekha* does, indeed, mean "your heart." But in the Torah, the heart is traditionally understood not as the seat of the emotions, as we take it to be in Anglo-American literary tradition. Rather, the heart is considered the home of the intellect. Moshe is instructing us that the act of loving God begins in the intellect, in the active mind.

That looks counterintuitive on paper, but think about it for a moment. Think of someone you love. Try to explain to yourself why you love that person. Ultimately, you are reduced to a series of intellectual propositions that underpin an inexplicable emotional leap of faith.

Ironically, it is *nafshekha,* "your soul," that Jewish tradition holds to be the place of the emotions, but in Jewish thought these two powers— intellect and intuition, thought and feeling—are inextricably linked, like the Miltonic apple with its inseparable halves of good and evil.

Finally, there is the one real misunderstanding, the translation of *m'odekha* as "your might." Your might, in the sense of physical strength, might be better rendered in Hebrew as *gevuratekha*, to suggest one viable option. But *m'odekha* has its root in the word *m'od*—which might be read as "much" or "very." *Tov m'od/very good.* So when we are told *"V'ahavta Adonai . . . v'khol m'odekha,"* it might be more apt to say, "You shall love God with all your quantity" or as the ArtScroll Siddur has it, "all your resources," that is your material wealth, but also the intangibles like time and energy that come under that heading.

We are told in three places in Torah to love a specific being—love the stranger, love your neighbor, love God. How can you order someone to love another? For the Jew, the answer lies in the place of honor given to the performance of the *mitzvot*, in the paramount significance of ritual and repetition. It's not so much that one can achieve love as an emotional state—remember the *V'ahavta* tells us to love God first *"al l'vavekha,"* with the intellect. Remember, too, that the next instruction is that these words should be *"al l'vavekha,"* upon your heart—ingrained in your intellect, as it were. And the inclusion of *v'kol m'odekha* in this instruction suggests that the author of the Torah understood that achieving something like love is the result of a process and of the investment of resources.

The nature of that process is revealed in the following sentences, those in which we are told to teach these words to our children, to recite them, bind them upon our arms, place them on our doorposts, and so on.

The key phrase here is *"v'shinantam l'vanekha."* That has always been translated for us as "teach them to your children." But the verb chosen is not the one we would usually use for teaching; *v'shinantam* takes its root from the same verb that means "to sharpen," as by rubbing on a whetstone, a process of repetition. This is not so much teaching as instilling by repeating, by honing, making more incisive, sharper. Everett Fox gives the verb as "inculcate." Instill, ingrain, as I had it before, these all capture somewhat more accurately the intentions of this passage.

There is a distinct shift in emphasis in *Devarim* from the three previous books that deal with Moshe, the Exodus from Egypt, and its aftermath. Up to this point in the Torah, this story has been about God delivering the Hebrews from the yoke of slavery in exchange for their assuming the yoke of the *mitzvot*, the final piece of the Covenental puzzle that leads them to Kina'an. But once in Kina'an, the Jews have a responsibility to continue to live up to their part of the bargain. And for that to happen, it is imperative that they pass on what they have learned in the Wilderness, the *mitzvot.* As Professor Arnold Eisen writes, the previous three books of Torah were about the observance of the *mitzvot,* the how if not the why. But *Sefer Devarim* is about the transmission of the *mitzvot* by *B'nei Yisrael,* and that can only be accomplished if they are passed along.

"*V'shinantam l'vanekha,*" "instill them in your children" and, as Rashi interprets this phrase, in your students. Teach them Torah, teach them to love God. Tell them what God did for you when you were delivered by the hand of the Almighty from Egypt.

(I think it is not a coincidence that we are instructed to place these words *al mezuzot* upon our doorposts, just as we were told to daub our lintels with blood so that the messenger of Death would pass over the houses of the Israelites when he struck down the Egyptian firstborn. The first thing that you see when you enter the house of an observant Jew is the *mezuzah* on the door frame, just as the messenger of Death first saw the blood of the paschal sacrifice on the door frames of the Israelites in Egypt. Both signs announce, "Here is someone who is set apart, separated by the Covenant from other peoples.")

How can we instill these words, these values, these ethical and moral precepts in our children, our students, our contemporaries, and ourselves? We can live our lives in a way that illustrates and instills the values of Torah. We can try to be a living manifestation of the injunction to love our neighbors, the strangers in our midst, to love our God. Then we will be fulfilling this most basic commandment of the Jewish faith.

ADDITIONAL NOTES
- Moshe's words, "I call heaven and earth" as witnesses (*Devarim* 4:26) are actually a formulaic statement typical of Ancient Near Eastern legal documents, particularly treaties.
- We recite *Devarim* 4:39 as part of the *Aleinu* in contemporary liturgy.
- This *parashah* contains the second version of the Ten Commandments. As is the case when the first version is read in *parashat Yitro,* the congregation will stand for the reading of this passage, as if they, too, were present at Sinai.
- One of the principal arguments in favor of the idea that God gave humanity free will is derived from the passage in *Devarim* 5:26 in which Moshe says that God hopes Israel will revere the Almighty and follow the *mitzvot.* The obvious implication is that we have the choice to do neither.

HAFTARAH

Another passage from *Sefer Yeshayahu*, but very different from the one read with *parashat Devarim*, this *haftarah* is the first of a series of "sermons of consolation" that are read in the weeks following Tisha B'Av. In this portion, Yeshayahu invokes "the Presence of *Adonai*," much as the *Sh'ma* does in the *parashah*.

PARASHAT EIKEV

46th Torah portion, 3rd in *Devarim*
Devarim 7:12–11:25 (111 verses)
Haftarah: Yeshayahu 49:14–51:3

ALIYOT

First / Rishon:	7:12–8:10
Second / Sheini:	8:11–9:3
Third / Shlishi:	9:4–9:29
Fourth / Revi'i:	10:1–10:11
Fifth / Khamishi:	10:12–11:9
Sixth / Shishi:	11:10–11:21
Seventh / Shevi'i:	11:22–11:25
Maftir:	11:22–11:25

SYNOPSIS

Moshe tells the Israelites that if they follow God's laws, the nations who now dwell across the Yardein will not harm them. He reminds them of the virtues of keeping God's commandments. He also tells them that they will dispossess those who now live in the Land only because they are idolatrous, not because the Israelites are uncommonly virtuous. Moshe then reviews all of the trespasses of the Israelites against God (by way of illustration of their less attractive traits). Moshe says that *Eretz Yisrael* will overflow with milk and honey if the people obey God's commandments and teach them to their children.

COMMENTARY

Many people, including not a few Jews, are uncomfortable with the idea of the Jews as God's "Chosen People." For contemporary adults, the concept smacks of a triumphalism and a particularism that makes us ill at ease with its echoes of ugly racial politics. Small wonder that the Reconstructionist movement eliminated all references to chosenness from its siddurim.

Such a response, while understandable and even laudable, is based on a misreading of the message of the Torah. As outlined there, chosenness has a very different meaning. The significance of God's Covenant with the Jews is at the heart of *parashat Eikev;* the picture that Moshe paints of the nature of the Covenant in this Torah portion is a far cry from the idea that *B'nei Yisrael* have been singled out for God's approbation like some nation of spoiled favorite children. Indeed it looks rather more like a burden, the yoke of the *mitzvot,* as Yeshayahu Leibowitz repeatedly calls it throughout his commentaries on the weekly *parashiyot.*

Eikev opens with Moshe's insistence once more on a universe in which acceptance of the *mitzvot* is rewarded and breaches are punished. One might say with tongue only slightly in cheek that this is where the ethical is put in "ethical monotheism," the then-radical concept that there is but one Supreme Being and that a person's choice of behavior has consequences, that one receives good or ill based on a Divine (or divinely inspired) morality.

Consider two famous midrashim relating the story of God choosing the Jews.

In one, God shops the Torah around to other nations. One group asks, "What's in it?" and God replies, "Thou shalt not steal." "Well, that's how we make our living. Not interested." Another people ask what the Torah contains and God tells them, "Thou shalt not kill." "We're a nation of warriors; we can't do that, sorry." Finally, God asks the Hebrews and they agree to accept the Torah.

Another midrash says that God lifted Mount Sinai into the air, suspended it over the heads of the Israelites, and told them that if they did not accept the Torah, he would drop the mountain on them.

Clearly on some level the rabbis felt a certain ambivalence about the concept of Chosenness. But the real nature of God's choice, the real nature of the responsibilities that choice confers upon the Israelites, is clearly delineated by Moshe in this *parashah.*

The Hebrews were not chosen for their righteousness, he says emphatically, "but because of the evil of those nations God pushes them away from before you, and in order to fulfill the word that God swore to your forefathers, to Avraham, Yitzkhak, and Ya'akov." The Israelites are only being given *Eretz Yisrael* because of the merit of their ancestors and the vileness of their neighbors.

The structure of the passage in which this statement occurs underlines how totally God and Moshe mean it. The point is made three times, in consecutive verses, that the Israelites are not being rewarded for their behavior but, rather, that the other nations are being punished for theirs. Moshe puts a (metaphorical) exclamation point to it by sternly warning them, "Remember, do not forget!"

Israel is being given a chance to put aside its rebelliousness—which Moshe goes on to recount in detail—and to serve as a model for other nations by following the *mitzvot* and earning the land on their merits. As Rabbi Baruch Sienna says, following Richard Elliott Friedman, "The Bible itself endorses a very conditional, action-oriented idea of 'chosenness.' . . . This conditional idea of 'the chosen people' says simply that the Jews have been chosen for Torah and *mitzvot* and, if they rise to the challenge, there will be blessings for all humanity."

In fact, as Rabbi Yaakov Menken notes, the Torah is generally quite critical of the Jews. "When something good happens to the Jewish people, it is because of the merit of our forefathers," he writes. "It is only misfortune for which we are held responsible."

The words that Moshe speaks in his final address to the Israelites are a caution against complacency. Yes, "you are a Holy Nation to *Adonai* your God," but you are a stiff-necked people who must "circumcise your hearts," to be worthy of the gift God is bestowing.

In a sense, the entirety of Moshe's final speech is a way of preparing the Hebrews for the task of self-government, for coming into *Eretz Yisrael*, claiming it for themselves, and running on their own, without the daily interventions of God that sustained them in the Wilderness. What will happen to them when the obviously miraculous is no longer a daily occurrence? Will they become arrogant and self-satisfied? Moshe is desperately trying to jar them out of that kind of thinking before they even cross the Yarden.

He urges them, "What does *Adonai* your God demand of you, but to fear the Eternal One, to walk in all God's ways, and to love God and to serve *Adonai* your God with all your heart and with all your soul, to keep for your own good all the *mitzvot* of *Adonai* and the statutes of the Almighty which I command you this day?"

This makes an interesting complement to the words of the prophet Mikhah in the *haftarah* to *parashat Balak*: "It has been told to you O man what is good and what *Adonai* requires of you: only to do justly, and to love mercy, and to walk humbly with your God." How can we, mere mortals with very limited abilities and a finite life span, possibly "walk in the ways of God"? By remembering that we were created *b'tzelem Elohim*, and emulating those Divine attributes that are available to us by being merciful and just, yet remaining humble, recalling that we can only *imitate* God.

At the same time, we must be grateful to God for the bounty of life itself. Not surprisingly, the rabbis took Moshe's injunction to the Hebrews to bless God after they have eaten their fill as the inspiration for *Birkat Ha'Mazon/the Grace After Meals* (which includes the pertinent passage from this *parashah*).

Think again of those two midrashim.

The Jews were not chosen for their superiority but for their willingness to accept God's laws.

Or the Jews were Chosen because they dared not refuse.

Either way, the worldview these two stories propound is one in which being Chosen is a responsibility and a burden. Judaism teaches that "Chosenness" does not mean that non-Jews cannot experience a profound relationship with the Eternal. (Unlike the teachings of fundamentalist Christians sects, it doesn't mean that only the Chosen are "saved.") Properly understood, it does not dehumanize non-Jews. And if the Jews are Chosen, it is a status that is available to anyone who agrees to accept the requirements that accompany Jewishness.

As Rabbi Arthur Hertzberg writes, "God says, I chose you not because you are more numerous or more powerful, and not because you are morally, spiritually, or intellectually superior. You are not. I chose you out of my unknowable will."

ADDITIONAL NOTES

- There is an interesting echo of two of the Ten Commandments in one of Moshe's warnings to the Israelites in this *parashah*. At *Devarim* 7:25, he warns them of "the graven images of their gods . . . thou shall not covet the silver or gold that is on them."
- In *Devarim* 8:3 we find one of the most famous phrases from the Torah in common use in English, "Man does not live by bread alone."
- Several verses, beginning at *Devarim* 11:13, are recited daily by observant Jews as part of the *V'ahavta*.

HAFTARAH

Drawn once again from the prophet Yeshayahu, this is the second of the "sermons of consolation," read in the weeks following Tisha B'Av. The prophet counsels Iisrael that God will not forget them at their lowest ebb but will redeem them once more, scattering their enemies before them, as promised in the *parashah* as well.

PARASHAT RE'EH

47th Torah portion, 4th in *Devarim*
Devarim 11:26–16:17 (126 verses)
Haftarah: Isaiah 54:11–55:5

ALIYOT

First / Rishon:	11:26–12:10
Second / Sheini:	12:11–12:28
Third / Shlishi:	12:29–13:19
Fourth / Revi'i:	14:1–14:21
Fifth / Khamishi:	14:22–14:29
Sixth / Shishi:	15:1–15:18
Seventh / Shevi'i:	15:19–16:17
Maftir:	16:13–16:17

SYNOPSIS

God places both blessing and curse before the Israelites. They are taught that blessing will come through the observance of God's laws. Moshe's third discourse includes laws about worship in a central place; injunctions against idolatry and self-mutilation; dietary rules; and laws about tithes, debt remission, the release and treatment of Hebrew slaves and firstlings. Moshe reviews the correct sacrifices to be offered during the Pilgrim Festivals, Pesakh, Sukkot, and Shavot.

COMMENTARY

Although it can be utterly straightforward, the Torah is a frequently elliptical, often frustrating text. *Parashat Re'eh* contains one of the most famous examples of a seeming gap in the text, in 12:21 when Moshe instructs B'nei Yisrael that they "may slaughter any of the cattle or sheep that *Adonai* gives you in the manner in which I have instructed you." The passage is wonderfully clear except for a small detail: although the rituals of sacrifice are explained in copious detail elsewhere, there are no instructions on how to slaughter sacrificial animals. Although one assumes that Moshe did in fact elucidate these slaughtering methods at some time in the forty years in the Wilderness, we are left in the dark.

This is a classic "How did they get from here to there?" moment. As Moshe's remarks imply, the rules governing kosher slaughtering (which is, after all, what we are talking about) are complex and rigorous. But where did they come from if not the Torah?

Of course, the answer, as we have seen elsewhere, is that the rabbis of the Talmudic period devised the rules, based on their own understanding of the tenets of belief outlined in the Torah.

Moshe is quite clear that we are not to eat the blood of an animal; this injunction occurs both in *Vayikra* and here. We are not to eat the severed limb of a living animal, nor to "boil a kid in its mother's milk." We are commanded not to take the young from the nest when the mother bird is present.

Putting these commandments together, the rabbis discerned an underlying theme: although it is permissible to use animals for food, it is not permitted to make them suffer unnecessarily, either physically or emotionally.

Applying that reasoning to the job of the kosher slaughterer (the *shokhet*), the rabbis came up with a series of rules and rituals designed to meet that challenge. Thus, the *shokhet* must have steady hands. His knives must be examined regularly and tested for sharpness; any dent or nick in the blade and the knife is discarded. The animal is killed with a swift horizontal cut across the throat that severs the trachea, esophagus, and the vagus nerve. In theory this is very quick and painless death, and toward that end, subsequent halakhic authorities elaborated on the regulations governing the work of the *shokhet* as part of that ongoing, ever-outward spiral of halakhic logic that has the Torah at its center.

(Not all Jewish commentators are satisfied with this system, though. Rabbi Avraham Kook, the brilliant twentieth-century thinker, was a vegetarian and argued that the eating of meat was nothing more than a compromise between the ideal spiritual state to which we should aspire and our baser physical needs. Kook noted that in *Bereishit* Adam and Khavah are not told they may slaughter animals for meat; this is permitted only after the Flood. Morever, he contends, in the Wilderness, the people are sustained by manna, until their complaints become more than Moshe can bear and God brings down quail "until it comes out of their nostrils." Kook believes that even the laws governing kosher slaughtering are cruel and shameful, that they exist precisely to shame human beings into resisting their appetite for meat.)

Why does Moshe insist on the rules for slaughtering? Why do the rabbis erect this complex edifice of regulations governing the *shokhet*, not to mention the many other dietary laws? One can see the logic by which not boiling a kid in its mother's milk gradually becomes a prohibition on mixing meat and dairy, perhaps even understand how that prohibition can lead one to own four sets of dishes (everyday meat and dairy, Pesakh meat and dairy that haven't been contact with *khametz*). The lengthy list of prohibited foods, detailed in Vayikra 11, speaks for itself; no shellfish, no pork, no "winged swarming things," and so on. But to what end? To what purpose?

The answer, I believe, can be derived from recalling the context of this *parashah*. As we have already noted, the Hebrews are now on the edge of the Yardein ready to cross over into Kina'an and claim the land that God has set out for them. Moshe's instructions in Devarim are being given to a people who are about to become their own rulers for the first time, responsible for their own behavior in a way they haven't been since before Egypt. In short, these are rules for self-government—government of oneself.

How did the Hebrews survive in the Wilderness? They ate manna, a daily miracle provided directly by God.

But when they find that they must—and can—provide for themselves on a daily basis, will they forget that however well they manage on their own, they are still ultimately being sheltered, clothed, and fed by the Creator? Will they begin to think, "Hey I raised this cow, fed it, nurtured it until it was ready for slaughter and I paid the butcher who killed and carved it up. I'm doing for myself now"?

Eating is one thing we all must do in order to live. If we invest all the stages of acquiring and ingesting food with an aura of the spiritual, if we instill food gathering and meals with elements of ritual, we are unlikely to forget Who, finally, is really feeding us.

ADDITIONAL NOTES

- For a more detailed discussion of *kashrut*, I rather immodestly recommend my own *Essential Judaism*, particularly for the Orthodox Union's guide to kosher food, one of the appendices (also available online at www.ou.org.)
- This *parashah* begins with one of those fascinating grammatical anomalies: *Re'eh / See*, the opening of the portion, is singular, but in the rest of the sentence, Moshe addresses the Hebrews in the plural. The Kotzker

Rebbe explained this oddity by saying that although the Torah was given to all the Jews, not everyone understands it equally. Bachya Ibn Pakuda had another explanation, saying that although the *mitzvot* are placed before all of us, we must "see" ourselves and decide individually whether to follow them.

• The opening of this *parashah* also represents a powerful argument in favor of the idea that God has given humanity free will: "I have set before you life and death. Choose life, that you may live."

HAFTARAH

The haftarah to *Parashah Re'eh* is the third of the "sermons of consolation." In it Yeshayahu expands on the opening warning of the *parashah*, that God has placed before humanity the choice between blessing and curse. Knowing that the Hebrews have already felt the pain of the curse, he offers them a promise of blessings to come, "for the sake of *Adonai* the Eternal, the Holy One of Israel who has glorified you."

PARASHAT SHOFTIM

48th Torah portion, 5th in *Devarim*
Devarim 16:18–21:9 (97 verses)
Haftarah: Yeshayahu 51:12–52:12

ALIYOT

First / Rishon:	16:18–17:13
Second / Sheini:	17:14–17:20
Third / Shlishi:	18:1–18:5
Fourth / Revi'i:	18:6–18:13
Fifth / Khamishi:	18:14–19:13
Sixth / Shishi:	19:14–20:9
Seventh / Shevi'i:	20:10–21:9
Maftir:	21:7–21:9

SYNOPSIS

Moshe details the most important characteristics of a judge: the ability to remain objective and the strength to refuse bribery. Nothing must deter him from rendering objective judgments, nor from carrying out his additional mission to write his own *sefer Torah* and carry it with him at all times. Moshe again addresses the place of the tribe of Levi, reemphasizing the attention due to them from *B'nei Yisrael.* Only God's justice can be trusted to take into account all variables and possibilities. Moshe instructs the people on the difference between true and false prophets and warns against all forms of necromancy. He reviews the laws governing manslaughter and murder, the conduct of warfare, and the ritual of the red heifer.

COMMENTARY

At the heart of *parashat Shoftim* is one of the most famous passages in the entire Hebrew Bible: "*Tzedek, tzedek tirdof. / Justice, justice you shall pursue.*" A great deal has been written about the repetition of the first word in this sentence. On the most obvious level, in a language whose orthography makes no provision for capitalization or punctuation, the repetition of a word of phrase is one of the few ways available to convey emphasis.

Over the centuries, commentators have offered other explanations. The Hasidic master Rav Bunim says that to achieve righteousness (another translation of *tzedek*) we must do battle using righteous means, acting justly to pursue justice. Moshe Leib Lechner echoes him, saying, "The Torah demands that righteousness and truth must be based on righteousness."

Others shift the focus from the necessity of acting justly in the quest for justice to the idea that one must act with care as well. The third-century B.C.E. sage Shimon ben Lakish says that the repetition of *tzedek* is designed to make us proceed with caution when we probe for the truth, to seek out and expose deception, to arrive at a carefully considered verdict, not to judge in haste. Maimonides expands on this theme, urging judges to act in consultation with one another, rather than relying on their individual perceptions.

The Gerer Rebbe, the S'fat Emet, offers another compelling reading of this passage, concentrating not on the famous repetition but on the verb that follows. He writes:

> "Justice, justice you shall pursue," is a formula said in no other case, because this is the foundation of everything. That is why it says "pursue." We can never really come to truth in the fullest sense in this lying world. We have to keep pursuing justice, knowing that we have not yet attained it.

Justice is a continuing theme in the Torah and *Tanakh*, indeed throughout Jewish sacred texts. Justice is one of the pillars on which the world rests, say the sages of the *Pirkei Avot*. The prophet Mikhah says that the Eternal requires of humanity that we "act justly, love mercy and walk humbly with God." The Psalmist says that righteousness and justice are the foundations of God's throne. But what does it mean to pursue justice?

In fact, the answer to that question is at the heart of this *parashah* with its lengthy disquisition on judicial behavior; one could argue convincingly that it is at the heart of all the *mitzvot* that deal with interpersonal behavior. A significant clue may be found in the first *pasuk* of *Shoftim*, "*Shoftim v'shotrim titein lekha b'khol she'arekha asher* Adonai *Elohekha notein lakh.* . . . / *You shall appoint judges and officers unto yourself at all your gates that* Adonai *your God is giving you.* . . .*"

There's that word again: *lekha*, for yourself. Needless to say, commentators have found its presence here highly suggestive. Moshe Feinstein says that this injunction *titein lekha* should be understood to mean that one must appoint himself as a judge of proper conduct, hence all should study and master Torah. The S'fat Emet goes even further, saying that this opening verse is not only a commandment but "also a promise to the Jew, saying, 'You will be able to make yourself into your own judge and officer.' " As such, it affirms the sovereignty of the Hebrews over themselves as a nation, a far cry from their status in Egypt a mere forty years earlier, and an appropriate instruction for a people about to create their own country.

At the same time, it testifies to the need to govern oneself as an individual, because *lekha* is the singular form. With political autonomy and sovereignty comes the responsibility to act justly and properly as a person as well as a citizen. As Ibn Ezra notes, the commandments given in *Devarim* 16:19 and after relating to the conduct of judges are phrased in the singular, "as though they were an exhortation to each judge individually."

Or to each Jew.

As Rabbi Menachem Mendel Schneerson observes, reading the opening verse again, the commandment uses the singular form of "your gates," suggesting that in the search for justice, "the efforts are incumbent on every individual." Moreover, he says, one can interpret the "gates" as a metaphor for our own sensory organs, through which the world enters our perception; we must guard our own conduct in order to act justly.

Go back to that famous phrase and finish it: "*Tzedek, tzedek tirdof l'ma'an tikh'yeh v'yarashta et ha'aretz asher Adonai Elohekha notein lakh/Justice, justice you shall pursue in order that you may live and occupy the land that Adonai your God is giving you.*" What is at stake is nothing less than our very existence and our ability to cross over the Yardein and into the Promised Land.

One interesting question follows inevitably from the opening lines of this *parashah*: *Who* appoints judges and officers? The answer, implicit in the remainder of the *parashah*, is that the people do, exercising their newly found autonomy. And the rules governing judgment are designed to keep those judges and officers fair and true.

Yet human justice must inevitably be flawed, as humanity is flawed. As the S'fat Emet says, the best we can do is pursue justice. As we say in a blessing that is spoken by mourners as they tear their garments, "Blessed are you *Adonai*, our God, Ruler of the universe, the True Judge."

ADDITIONAL NOTES

- There is an interesting discrepancy in the roll call of nations to be conquered in Kina'an given in this *parashah* at *Devarim* 20:17. Here, the list includes six nations, but in *Devarim* 7:1–3 there are seven. Ibn Ezra notes that the nation omitted, the Girgashites, were the smallest and relatively insignificant.

- When the Hebrews are instructed to be *tamim/wholehearted* with God in *Devarim* 18:13, the word used, which is derived from the root meaning "complete," echoes the characterization of the recipients of the first two Covenants, Noakh and Avraham. As Richard Elliott Friedman notes, from this point on, all the Hebrews are recipients of the third Covenant and must emulate these two great men in order to keep their part in it.

HAFTARAH

The fourth of Yeshayahu's "sermons of consolation," this *haftarah* tells of God's restoration of Israel to an honored place and the bringing down of her oppressors. The description of Israel's unjust treatment at the hands of the Assyrians, who "have robbed them, giving nothing in return," echoes the concern for justice that is at the heart of the *parashah*.

PARASHAT KI TETZEI

49th Torah portion, 6th in *Devarim*
Devarim 21:10–25:19 (110 verses)
Haftarah: Yeshayahu 54:1–10

ALIYOT
First / Rishon:	21:10–21:21
Second / Sheini:	21:22–22:7
Third / Shlishi:	22:8–23:7
Fourth / Revi'i:	23:8–23:24
Fifth / Khamishi:	23:25–24:4
Sixth / Shishi:	24:5–24:13
Seventh / Shevi'i:	24:14–25:19
Maftir:	25:17–25:19

SYNOPSIS

Moshe reviews a wide variety of laws regarding family, animals, and property. Various civil and criminal laws are delineated, including those regarding sexual relationships, interaction with non-Israelites, loans, vows, and divorce. Laws of commerce pertaining to loans, fair wages, and proper weights and measures are given. The *parashah* concludes with the commandment to remember for all time the most heinous act committed against the Israelites—Amalek's killing of the old, weak, and infirm after the Israelites left Egypt.

COMMENTARY

In this week's Torah portion, we are enjoined to build a parapet upon the roof of a house, lest we incur bloodguilt if someone falls off the roof. This seems a simple and humanely based commandment, one designed to save the unwary, the unwise, or the clumsy from incurring death inadvertently, through carelessness or foolishness.

Indeed, we are constantly pointed to the compassionate nature of so many of the *mitzvot*. Consider some of the strictures in *parashat Ki Tetzei*. Do not withhold the wages of a laborer. Do not yoke an ox and an ass together at the same plow.

Or this passage: If, along the road, you chance upon a bird's nest, in any tree or on the ground, with fledglings or eggs and the mother sitting over the fledglings or on the eggs, do not take the mother together with her young. Let the mother go, and take only the young. . . . (*Devarim* 22:6–7).

Ki Tetzei contains seventy-two *mitzvot,* the most of any Torah portion, and many of them appear to contemporary readers as models of humane and progressive behavior, injunctions that we contemporary Jews have no qualms about fulfilling, even applauding.

In contrast, there is the *mitzvah* regarding the wayward and rebellious son. This passage occurs in *Devarim* 21:18–21:

If a man has a wayward and defiant son, who does not heed his father or mother and does not obey them even after they discipline him, his father and mother shall take hold of him and bring him out to the elders of his town at the public place of his community. They shall say to the elders of his town, "This son of ours is disloyal and defiant; he does not heed us. He is a glutton and a drunkard." Thereupon the men of his town shall stone him to death. Thus you will sweep out evil from your midst: all Israel will hear and be afraid.

I'm sure they will be afraid. Very afraid.

Nor is this an exceptional text: there are thirty-six different crimes for which the Torah authorizes the death penalty, most of them as hard for us to conceive of as capital crimes as being "a wayward and defiant son." This is, after all, the Torah portion in which we are instructed to stone to death adulterers.

What happened to all that compassion?

The answer to that question lies in the way that the rabbis of the Talmudic period read this text and others.

The story of the wayward and rebellious son presents an immediate problem. Of what exactly is he guilty? His parents say, "This son of ours is disloyal and defiant; he does not heed us. He is a glutton and a drunkard."

Those are not admirable traits, but they are hardly the stuff of capital crimes. Indeed, there is nothing elsewhere in the Torah to suggest that not heeding one's parents, overeating, and drunkenness should be punished by death.

His real crime, the rabbis say in the Talmud, is what he might do. He is, they write, "sentenced because of his future." A son who doesn't heed his parents, is a drunken slob, will probably come to no good end. The rabbis, in fact, say that he will "become an armed robber."

But there is no place else in the Torah—or in subsequent Jewish texts—in which a person is condemned to death or other punishment because of what he *might* do in the future. (And clearly it is given only to *Adonai* to know what is in the future anyway!)

What do the rabbis finally say of the wayward son?

"The case of the rebellious son never happened and will never happen."

In other words, they acknowledge that it is not given to man to foresee the future, only to the Creator, and that one cannot make human law on the basis of maybes.

But the rabbis go even further in this instance. In interpreting the case of the "wayward son" they note that the parents say, "He will not heed our *voice*." Note that "voice" is in the singular. The rabbis ruled that if the mother and father do not have the same voice, two voices with an identical sound, the rule governing the wayward son does not apply. And what, you may ask, are the odds on that?

You see, the rabbis acknowledged that God could give laws at Sinai and after that called for death by execution. The Eternal One is perfect and all-knowing. But humans are neither. And laws, once given by God, are administered by humans. So the rabbis made it very hard—many would say impossible—to carry out the death penalty in any of the thirty-six instances in which it is prescribed.

For the death penalty to be carried out the following must happen:

- No fewer than two eyewitnesses must have testified to the events that took place, and they must have actually seen the crime committed;
- They must testify that the perpetrator was warned that his act was in fact criminal and that it carried the death penalty as its punishment; and
- The perpetrator must tell them that he is fully aware of the punishment but intends to carry out his criminal act regardless.

And there are further restrictions that apply in capital cases. The accused was not allowed to incriminate him- or herself in testimony. Capital cases could only be heard by a special panel of twenty-three judges, but such a panel could only be convened when the Temple was standing in Jerusalem. A majority with a margin of at least two votes was required to convict but only a margin of one was necessary to acquit. Finally, because the judicial system of the time combined the roles of both prosecutor and defense attorney in the judges, if a unanimous decision were reached to convict a man of a capital offense, the case was thrown out because it proved that the accused had not had adequate defense counsel. (And as the previous Torah portion clearly states, the accuser and the presiding judges must strike the first blows if a guilty verdict and death sentence were returned, a provision that would surely give many pause.)

Yes, the Torah is stern in its call for the death of certain sinners. But, as we pray on Yom Kippur, it is not the death of sinners that *Adonai* seeks, it is that they should repent and mend their ways. Knowing that, the rabbis followed the instructions of one of the compassionate *mitzvot*—they built a parapet around the Torah, that the Jewish people would incur no blood-guilt.

ADDITIONAL NOTES

- The prohibition against disinheriting the firstborn son whose mother is an "unloved wife" certainly makes interesting reading when placed alongside the several breaches of primogeniture found in the Patriarchal stories. Perhaps this passage should be seen as a reaction against the chaotic family lives of our forefathers and foremothers.

- There are several excellent examples in this *parashah* of the principle known as *tza'ar ba'alei khayim*, which may be roughly rendered as "concern for all living things," and which manifests itself here as kindness to animals. The most obvious ones are the injunction to help a neighbor to raise his ox or ass that has fallen, which is not only about cooperation with other people (even enemies, as is strongly implied here) but about compassion for an animal in trouble. Likewise, the prohibition against plowing with an ox and ass yoked together, while of a piece with other *mitzvot* concerning the unnecessary mixing of species (like the *sha'atnez* test), is also designed to prevent cruelty to animals of unequal strength.

HAFTARAH

The fifth of the "sermons of consolation," this prophecy from Yeshayahu could be said to follow logically from the hopeful note that ends the *parashah* with its message of compassion for the poor, orphaned, widowed, and strangers in the midst of the community. Yeshayahu uses the metaphors of the barren wife and the widow to remind the Jews that God will not forsake them, that the Eternal's love of Israel will not falter despite their downcast state.

PARASHAT KI TAVO

50th Torah portion, 7th in *Devarim*
Devarim 26:1–29:8 (121 verses)
Haftarah: Yeshayahu 60:1–22

ALIYOT

First/Rishon:	26:1–26:11
Second/Sheini:	26:12–26:15
Third/Shlishi:	26:16–26:19
Fourth/Revi'i:	27:1–27:10
Fifth/Khamishi:	27:11–28:6
Sixth/Shishi:	28:7–28:69
Seventh/Shevi'i:	29:1–29:8
Maftir:	29:6–29:8

SYNOPSIS

The Israelites are instructed to express their gratitude to God for their bountiful harvests and freedom from slavery by tithing 10 percent of their crops for the Levite, the stranger, the orphan, and the widow. The people are told to display on large stones God's commandments for all to see. The Levites are to proclaim curses upon those who violate God's commandments. The Israelites are told that if they obey God's *mitzvot* faithfully, they will receive every blessing imaginable. They are also told that if they do not fulfill their *b'rit/covenant* with God, many curses will descend upon them. Moshe reminds the Israelites of the miracles they witnessed in the Wilderness and commands them to observe the terms of the Covenant so that they may succeed in all that they undertake.

COMMENTARY

What are we to make of the litany of blessings and curses that occurs at the end of this Torah portion? As readers in the (supposedly) enlightened twenty-first century, how do we react to a lengthy passage of Torah that reduces observation of the *mitzvot* to such a crude matter of reward and punishment with the punishments in particular stated horrifically? Are we back in the realm of the midrashic God who is said to have suspended

Mount Sinai over the heads of the Hebrews as a way of convincing them to accept the *mitzvot*—on pain of certain destruction?

Of course, one can argue, as my *khevruta* Elizabeth Lorris Ritter does, that the blessings and curses are to be understood metaphorically, but given the detail and intensity with which they are stated, that explanation feels, at the very least, insufficient.

Allow me to propose another way of getting to the heart of this thorny matter. Rather than reading the blessings and curses directly, perhaps we can better understand the Jewish attitude(s) to the workings of God in history by reversing the procedure, by looking at how the sages and their modern descendants have responded to catastrophe. Many commentators reading this *parashah* have ruefully observed that all the curses uttered herein did, in fact, befall the Jews, most notably in the biblical period with the fall of Jerusalem and the destruction of the Temple, the Babylonian exile, the fall of the Second Temple, the utter erasure of Jewish (political) sovereignty, and the Diaspora. When you factor in the many cataclysms that have claimed Jewish lives—pogroms across a millennium of European life, the Expulsion from Spain, and, finally and most horrifically, the *Sho'ah*—it is hard to argue with Abba Eban, who wrote, "Some things in Jewish history are too terrible to be believed, nothing in Jewish history is too terrible to have happened."

We are faced, then, with a cosmic disconnect. On the one hand, God's active role in human history seems to be an essential part of the Covenant with Israel. Otherwise, why promise the land, why give out blessings and curses? If God does not take an active part in history, rewarding the good and punishing the evil, then these promises, blessings, and curses are empty, meaningless.

Yet if God is a Divine Actor upon humanity, how can we explain the punishment of the good and rewards to the evil? How can we possibly countenance the four thousand blood-soaked years of Jewish history? What did God choose the Jews for, to be a cosmic punching bag? When ultra-Orthodox Jews say that we are being punished for failing to observe the *mitzvot*, how can they justify the extermination of an entire generation of Torah scholars in the death camps? If God is setting the bar so high that even the most pious cannot help but fail, isn't there something wrong?

We are now moving into a very specific aspect of theological thinking known as theodicy, the branch of theology that defends God's goodness and justice in the face of the existence of evil. It is a question that has plagued theologians of all faith traditions since monotheism was born. In a sense, biblical and Rabbinic Judaism sidestepped the question neatly by not formulating a theology, a description of God, per se. As Rabbi David Hartman writes in his book *A Living Covenant,* the God of the *Tanakh* is not a one-dimensional God and the theology of Hebrew scripture is not a systematic theology. There are many facets to the God of the Torah, as implied by the many Names God bears.

What one does get from the Torah, though, is what Hartman calls "biblical optimism," a firm belief in an ethical monotheism in which good behavior is rewarded and evil is punished. This viewpoint sees God as the primary mover in human history; in Talmudic and biblical times alike, Hartman writes, "Jews perceived every aspect of reality in their world as expressive of the personal will of God." On the positive side, that meant that they expected God to keep the promises of the Convenant and eventually to reward them for keeping the *mitzvot.* But it also meant a converse proposition that might be more difficult to accept, that when things went wrong, the Jews were being punished for they knew not what.

For the traditionally observant Jew of the past, this presented no major problem. *Pirkei Avot* cautions that one cannot know the Divine Will, that it is not given to us to know why someone suffers, someone else prospers. For many the *Sho'ah* shattered that certainty, but there were and are some who say that the murder of six million Jews by the Nazis was merely a more extreme version of previous atrocities, and they note that eleven million Jews survived.

There is another way of viewing this paradox that can be found in the Talmud and other texts of the same period, that the rewards are based on our actions in *Olam Ha'Zeh/This World,* but will be bestowed in *Olam Ha'Ba.* Thus, if we strive to fill our lives with *mitzvot,* we are assured of the blessings of eternity. Of course, this presupposes a belief in the doctrine of the resurrection of the dead when the Messianic Age arrives.

Taken this way, the list of blessings and curses—to return to our original subject—takes on a pedagogical aspect for Rashi, a way of teaching the value of the *mitzvot.*

Now we seem to be back where we started, with a quid pro quo arrangement that cannot help but make many contemporary readers uncomfortable. Rabbi Hartman suggests a balanced view of the *mitzvot* that I think addresses some of this discomfort. Concerning the Jewish response to suffering he writes:

By utilizing tragedy and suffering as a catalyst for active moral renewal, the Judaic tradition prevents political powerlessness from creating feelings of personal impotence. If events in the larger world are unpredictable, if the nation is subject to the violence and whims of foreign rulers, the rabbinic mind does not fall victim to despair, disillusionment, and escapism, but rather focuses on the personal and the communal as the framework to contain its activist dignity. The call to repentance—"If a man sees that painful sufferings visit him, let him examine his conduct"—should not, therefore, be seen as a metaphysical justification of evil. Rather, it is advice that encourages the Jew to sustain and give meaning to the covenantal relationship despite the mystery of suffering.

The covenantal spirit of Sinai is crushed when a person feels paralyzed to act. It is broadened and deepened, however, when it is discovered that suffering can energize us to strive actively for moral renewal. The shift of focus from the might of the Roman legions to the moral quality of the community's behavior as the cause of exile does not reflect a naïve, self-centered moralism that explains everything in terms of one's own feelings, thoughts, and actions. Rather, it gives expression to a covenantal activism that strives to salvage some degree of human dignity and responsibility in an unpredictable, chaotic world.

The difficult task before us, then, is to invest the *mitzvot* with a meaning that has a moral force yet which does not put all the weight of world events back on God, that allows us to both succeed and fail. Inevitably, we will fail, because as the rabbis themselves readily acknowledged, even when the Temple stood in Jerusalem, no one could possibly keep all 613 *mitzvot*. By striving to keep those that we can, we reach toward the Covenant with a yearning born of the love of God as much as the fear of God. And when we fail, well, as Hartman notes, "Nor need [our] failures to live up to that responsibility create in [us] a fear of rejection by God, since the gates of repentance, as the rabbis say, are always open."

ADDITIONAL NOTES
- The first fruits offered as outlined in the first part of *Ki Tavo* are the seven species cited earlier in *Devarim* 8:8—wheat, barley, figs, vines, pomegranates, olives, and date honey.
- The prayer spoken at the offering of the first fruits is one of the few prayers in the Torah that is written out (as distinct from a spontaneous utterance).

- *B'nei Yisrael* are instructed not to use iron implements in making the Tablets of Instruction because metals are also used in making weapons of war. This injunction is echoed in the prohibition against iron tools placed upon Torah scribes today. (See Chapter 1.)
- The Deuteronomic code ends with this Torah portion. What remains in the last four *parashiyot* is Moshe's final speech of farewell.
- The curses that constitute the text of *Devarim* 28 are read in the synagogue by a volunteer whose *aliyah* is announced not with his Hebrew name but as "he who wishes." The curses must be read without interruption in a low voice.

HAFTARAH

The *haftarah* to *Ki Tavo* is the sixth "sermon of consolation" offered by Yeshayahu. Here, the prophet holds out the promise of Divine Redemption for Israel, with God dispelling the darkness of despair, returning "gold for brass" and peace to the cities.

PARASHAT NITZAVIM

51st Torah portion, 8th in *Devarim*
Devarim 29:9–30:20 (40 verses)
Haftarah: Yeshayahu 61:10–63:9

ALIYOT*

First / Rishon:	29:9–29:11
Second / Sheini:	29:12–29:14
Third / Shlishi:	29:15–29:28
Fourth / Revi'i:	30:1–30:6
Fifth / Khamishi:	30:7–30:10
Sixth / Shishi:	30:11–30:14
Seventh / Shevi'i:	30:15–3:20
Maftir:	30:15–30:20

SYNOPSIS

Moshe tells the assembled people that God's Covenant speaks to them and to all of the generations who will follow. God warns the Israelites that they will be punished if they act idolatrously, the way the inhabitants of the other nations do. Moshe reassures the people that God will not forsake them and that they can attain blessings by following God's commandments.

COMMENTARY

As the Torah draws to a close, as Moshe's life and mission draw to an end, the intertwined issues of posterity and continuity take on ever greater significance. In *parashat Vayeilekh* Moshe will announce his successor, the man who is to lead *B'nei Yisrael* on the next leg of their divinely ordained journey and quest. But first, and perhaps more important, Moshe presents them with a summation that demands they focus beyond the immediate issues of succession, leadership, and conquest. What is at stake in this *parashah* is nothing less than the future of all humanity.

One of the most satisfying aspects of reading the Torah in its entirety is

---

*For aliyot when *Nitzavim* is read with *Vayeilekh*, see Additional Notes below on page 533.

the gradual recognition one gains of the intricate literary structures at work in the text, a labyrinth of symmetries, echoes, and allusions that adds immeasurably to the book's resonance and emotional impact, as well as amplifying its power as a sacred text. The final four *parashiyot*, Moshe's farewell speech to his people, contain majestic examples of the way that formal invention can augment the content of the text.

In a manner both fitting and satisfying, Moshe's farewell speech echoes many other passages of the Torah. Of course, the image of the Hebrews "standing before *Adonai*" echoes Sinai, but there is another, more subtle, allusion to *Bereishit* in the sentence that immediately precedes the opening of this *parashah*. As Richard Elliott Friedman notes, the word *haskil/understanding* occurs in that sentence and in the description of the ability that humans acquired by eating from the forbidden tree in the middle of *Gan Eden*, but nowhere else in Torah. What is the context in which Moshe uses it? Understanding is the Godlike power of negotiating the world that *B'nei Yisrael* will acquire by observing and doing "the words of this Covenant."

There are many other echoes of earlier passages contained in Moshe's final speech and scattered throughout the last *parashiyot* of the Torah; many contemporary commentators (most notably and skillfully, Friedman) have tracked them and placed them in their larger context. It isn't necessary to enumerate them here. But they do point to an important reality and, ultimately, suggest something enormously powerful about the intended audience for Moshe's final speech, which is not limited to the Hebrews hearing him that day.

In the Torah's end is its beginning. On Simkhat Torah we read the end of *Devarim* and the opening of *Bereishit*. The cycle continues. We are told that at the giving of the Torah at Sinai, Moshe read to *B'nei Yisrael* from its sacred text; the sages say that he read to them *Bereishit* and *Shemot* up to the point in time at which they had arrived. Rabbi Joseph Soloveitchik says, "The Sinaitic Covenant was built on the exodus that was in turn built on the Covenant with the patriarchs. . . . Hashem mentions that He will recall the original Covenant with Jacob, Isaac and Abraham. In other words, the entire Sinaitic Covenant is based on, and is the continuation of, the Covenant of the forefathers and transfers from generation to generation." And the cycle continues down to us and our children and our children's children and . . .

These are the real recipients of Moshe's address, the generations to come. There is a hint of this in the emphasis he places on the intergenerational nature of the Covenant earlier in *Devarim*, for example, in the declaration he makes regarding the ritual of firstfruits, "for the one who is not here with us today." It is underlined by his use of the phrase "your heart's seed" (*Devarim* 30:6), meaning "your offspring." It is repeated in his injunction that the Hebrews "love God and walk in *Adonai*'s ways, that you and your seed may live *and multiply*" (emphasis added). And it is made explicit and emphatic in his final injunction, "Choose life so that you and your seed may live."

The Covenant is not just between God and those present at Sinai or at Mount Horeb. As Soloveitchik makes clear, it goes back generations and forward generations.

The Covenant is not merely between God and those anointed to the priesthood or of the tribe of Levi. Moshe underlines this fact at the outset of this *parashah:* "You stand here this day, all of you, before *Adonai*—your chiefs, your tribes, your elders, your officers, all the men of Israel, your children, your women, your strangers that are among you, from the woodcutter to the drawer of water . . . to have you enter into the Covenant of *Adonai* your God."

The Covenant is not between God and an intellectual elite. Moshe makes this explicit, too: "It is not hidden from you, nor is it far away. It is not in heaven that you should say, 'who can go up and bring it to us . . . ?' "

This Covenant, as Ha'Rav Soloveitchik says,

> was not only given to the generation that stood before Moses prior to his death. Rather . . . [it] was and is given to each and every individual generation. We are not bound to this Covenant through lineage, or through the patriarchs. It is our own responsibility.

Everyone, cautions Rabbi Barukh of Medzibozh, should share in the labor.

To choose life for oneself and for one's children is to forge a bond that stretches from generation to generation, *l'dor va'dor,* just what we pray for every single day. It is a legacy as tangible as any that a Jewish parent can pass on, as real as money or land or property, and infinitely more powerful.

ADDITIONAL NOTES

- When *parashat Nitzavim* is read with *parashat Vayeilekh*, the *aliyot* are
  as follows:

First / Rishon:	29:9–29:28
Second / Sheini:	30:1–30:6
Third / Shlishi:	30:7–30:14
Fourth / Revi'i:	30:15–31:6
Fifth / Khamishi:	31:7–31:13
Sixth / Shishi:	31:14–31:19
Seventh / Shevi'i:	31:20–31:30
Maftir:	31:28–31:30

- With only forty verses, this is the second-shortest Torah portion.
  Appropriately enough, it is frequently paired with *Vayeilekh*, which is
  the shortest.
- *Nitzavim* and *Vayeilekh* are almost always read together. The one
  exception is when there are two Sabbaths between Rosh Hashanah and
  Sukkot, of which neither is a holy day.
- In the passage from *Devarim* 29:27 that reads "*vayashilikhem / and cast
  them,*" the *lamed* is traditionally written as a large letter in *sefer Torah*.
  This is one occasion, however, where the explanation for this practice
  is apparently lost.

HAFTARAH

The seventh sermon of consolation is read before Rosh Hashanah; like
the *parashah* it accompanies, it urges the Hebrews to choose life and
promises deliverance by the hand of God.

PARASHAT VAYEILEKH

52rd Torah portion, 9th in *Devarim*
Devarim 31:1–30 (30 verses)
Haftarah: Yeshayahu 55:6–56:8

ALIYOT*

First / Rishon:	31:1–31:3
Second / Sheini:	31:4–31:6
Third / Shlishi:	31:7–31:9
Fourth / Revi'i:	31:10–31:13
Fifth / Khamishi:	31:14–31:19
Sixth / Shishi:	31:20–31:24
Seventh / Shevi'i:	31:25–31:30
Maftir:	31:28–31:30

SYNOPSIS

Moshe prepares the people for his death and announces that Yehoshua will succeed him. Moshe instructs the priests and the elders regarding the importance of reading the Torah. God informs Moshe that upon his death, the people will commit idolatry and "many evils and troubles shall befall them." God tells Moshe to teach the people a poem that will "be My witness."

COMMENTARY

> Moshe received the Torah from Sinai and transmitted it to Yehoshua;
> Yehoshua to the Elders; the Elders to the Prophets; and the Prophets
> transmitted it to the Men of the Great Assembly.
> —*Pirkei Avot* 1:1

We have known for some time that Moshe would not be leading the Israelites into Kina'an, since *parashat Pinkhas*, in fact. Moshe has known it since then; the Israelites have known it, too. It was then, recall, that

---

*For *aliyot* when *Vayeilekh* is read with *Nitzavim*, see Additional Notes for *parashat Nitzavim* on page 533.

Moshe struck the rock at Merivah to bring forth water and, by his impulsive and angry act, incurred the wrath of God. Wisely, he asked *Adonai* to appoint a successor then and there "so that *Adonai*'s people will not be like sheep without a shepherd," and *Adonai* chose Yehoshua, an appointment that Moshe confirmed before all the people.

Now the end is drawing nigh and Moshe will actually hand over power to the younger man. What do we know of this son of Nun, this Yehoshua?

We know that he is an Ephraimite, that he has been Moshe's personal attendant, the one who accompanied him on his ascent of Sinai. He has been the guardian of the Tent, a weighty task indeed, and a military commander who fought well against Amalek. This last experience undoubtedly recommended him to God and Moshe, as both know that the Israelites will soon find themselves in repeated hard combat.

But the most prominent role Yehoshua has taken on in public is the one that tells us the most important things about him: he and Kalev were the only two who spoke up for God when the spies reported back from Kina'an. It was Yehoshua, you will recall, who said it would be possible for the Israelites to conquer the Land despite the apparent threat of the Canaanites and other pagan tribes who occupy it.

Commentators on Torah have long puzzled over the choice of Yehoshua to succeed Moshe. Why not Moshe's sons Eliezer and Gershom? There are many midrashim that paint Moshe's offspring as idlers, disrespectful of their father, and less than fervent in their faith; by contrast, the midrashim say, Yehoshua is a faithful attendant and a man who believes profoundly in God. As we have seen since *Bereishit*, the mere accidents of biology that make one man a firstborn son or a son at all are not the events that should govern the conduct of those who are committed to *Adonai;* just because they are Moshe's sons doesn't make them any more qualified to lead the Israelites than Eisav's emerging first from the womb fitted him to carry on the Convenant.

Why not Pinkhas, Aharon's son, who it seemed was being groomed for the job until he killed Zimri and Kozbi? Certainly that was the act of a decisive man, a man of action. But, as we saw in our discussion of the *parashah* that bears his name, Pinkhas has the same failing for which Moshe was condemned by God—he is impulsive and easily angered. He consulted no one before taking his violent action, and that is not the mark of a leader.

Nor is merely being a man capable of violence the indicator of courage.

Here, too, Yehoshua is the better model for leadership than Pinkhas. In the incident of the spies, he and Kalev, although outnumbered by their comrades in giving the report to Moshe and the people, refuse to take the easy way out. In the face of overwhelming opposition, they stand fast for God and assert their position forcefully (but not violently). Yehoshua is described as "a man in whom there is spirit," which Rashi interprets as "a man who knows how to stand up against the spirit of each one of them." What better recommendation could there be for a leader than someone who listens to others, as Yehoshua does, but then acts on his conscience despite holding an unpopular position?

(Interestingly, Yehoshua and Kalev are also unique transitional figures in this narrative. They alone experience both the Exodus from Egypt and the conquest of Kina'an.)

Significantly, Moshe hands the reins of power to Yehoshua "before all the people," that is, publicly. Before the assembled Israelites he tells the younger man, "You will get [the Land] for them as a legacy." Power passes while Moshe still lives "before the eyes of all Israel," so that there can be no doubt that Yehoshua is the one that their beloved (if frequently embattled) leader has personally chosen and, by implication, is the handpicked choice of *Adonai*. And to cement that fact for all, in an echo of God's promise to Ya'akov, Moshe tells Yehoshua, "God will be with you. [God] won't let you down and won't leave you."

Perhaps it is not an accident that with this *parashah* and the one that precedes it, almost always read together, the Israelites have moved from *nitzavim/we stand* to *vayeilekh/he went*, from a final meeting of the tribes under Moshe back into motion, if only metaphorically.

ADDITIONAL NOTES

• With only thirty verses, this is the shortest *parashah* in the Torah.

• "Moshe wrote down this teaching," we are told in this *parashah*. But was what he wrote the entire Torah, as the sages taught, or just parts of *Sefer Devarim*? Of course, the traditionally observant, using this passage as their justification, believe that Moshe wrote the entire Torah (except perhaps the final passages that occur after his death), taking dictation from God at Sinai. However, it is telling that when the Israelites are enjoined to read "this teaching" every seven years, at Sukkot, what the leaders (usually the monarch) read was only *Devarim* up to 6:9, followed by 11:13–21, finishing with 14:22 to the end of chapter 28. Of course, if that is *torat Moshe* it raises all those questions about who wrote the Torah that we discussed in Chapter 3.

- The rabbis took God's injunction to Moshe, "Write this song for them," to be the final *mitzvah* given in the Torah, that one should write a Torah scroll.

HAFTARAH

This *parashah* and its *haftarah* are often read on *Shabbat Shuvah*, the Sabbath occurring between Rosh Hashanah and Yom Kippur. Understandably, the principal theme of this observance is repentance and returning to God, and the *haftarah* strikes that note from its opening words: "*Shuvah, Yisrael / Return, Israel!*"

PARASHAT HA'AZINU

53rd Torah portion, 10th in *Devarim*
Devarim 32:1–52 (52 verses)
Haftarah: Shmuel Bet 22:1–51

ALIYOT

First / Rishon:	31:1–31:6
Second / Sheini:	32:7–32:12
Third / Shlishi:	32:13–32:18
Fourth / Revi'i:	32:19–32:28
Fifth / Khamishi:	32:29–32:39
Sixth / Shishi:	32:40–32:43
Seventh / Shevi'i:	32:44–32:52
Maftir:	32:48–32:52

SYNOPSIS

Moshe sings his last song, a love poem to God and a chastisement of the people, who are not worthy of *Adonai*. The poem recounts the blessings that God has bestowed on the Israelites, the wicked deeds they have committed, and the punishments that God then inflicted upon them. God tells Moshe to begin his ascent of Mount Nebo, from where he will see *Eretz Yisrael* from a distance but will not be allowed to enter it.

COMMENTARY

There are times when reading the Torah that we become so caught up in the complexities of its content, the far-reaching implications of its message, that we forget that it is also a great work of literature, one of the greatest produced in the Western world. Perhaps because my own training was in literature and the arts, because I only came to the Torah as a Jew later in my life, the literary qualities of this book are always hovering at my ear, whispering to me as insistently as the *mitzvot* and the Covenant do.

Parashat Ha'azinu is a wonderful example of the brilliant architecture of the Torah as a literary work. As this vast text draws to a close, its author(s) allude once more to the book's very opening. Moshe's final song is filled with echoes of *Bereishit*, utilized to extraordinary effect (particularly for those who read Hebrew).

A few examples leap off the page. When Moshe likens his words to rain on plants, he uses the word *desheh* (often translated as "grass"), a word that hasn't appeared anywhere else in the Torah except in *Bereishit* 1, where God makes vegetal life spring forth by a Divine utterance. Shortly after, Moshe uses the word *tohu/chaos*, another reference back to the very beginning of the Creation, when God creates the earth out of *tohu v'vohu/chaos and nothingness*. Similarly, when Moshe likens God to an eagle hovering over the nest, the verb root, *resh-khaf-fei*, is one that hasn't appeared since it was used to describe the spirit or breath of the Creator hovering over the waters. An even more explicit reference occurs when Moshe invokes the division of the peoples of the world into nations, an allusion to the aftermath of the Tower of Babel. And is the persistent use of fire imagery a subtle warning that God's promise of the rainbow does not preclude the partial destruction of humanity, as in the fiery doom of the cities on the plain, Sodom and Gomorrah, also invoked herein?

At the same time, Moshe's song contains echoes of *Shirat Ha'Yam*, which marked his first triumph as leader of the Israelites, and echoes of his recapitulation of Israelite history that opened *Sefer Devarim*. And the phrase that God uses to tell Moshe of his impending death—he will be "gathered to [his] people"—is the same one used to recount the deaths of Avraham and Ya'akov, the bookends of the Patriarchal Covenant.

But these literary devices are not merely ornamentation. Rather, they are an integral part of the message and intent of Moshe's farewell song, of the Torah itself. There is a clue contained in the opening of the *parashah*, when Moshe invokes both the sky/heaven and the earth as witnesses to the speech that follows: "Give ear, heaven, that I may speak and let the earth hear what my mouth utters." Of course, as many contemporary commentators quickly note, this trope is standard language in contracts and treaties in the Ancient Near East, "as heaven and earth are my witnesses," and so on. Yet as written here this standardized language takes on greater force and, as several Hasidic and Mitnagdic commentators noted, they anticipate a similar but inverted statement by the prophet Yeshayahu, who opens the book of his prophecies, "Hear O heavens and give ear O earth,"

The Vilna Gaon and several of the Hasidic masters have written extensively on this parallel, but I find the explanation given by Rabbi Menachem Mendel Schneerson the simplest and most direct. He notes that it is one of the fundamental principles of Jewish thought that "we must relate to both heaven and earth." We pray to God but we act on earth. Judaism is a unique combination of the spiritual and the material, with the *mitzvot* and their seemingly endless skein of dos and don'ts rooted in such mundane realities as food, dress, agriculture, and horticulture—the very earth itself—serving as a way of reaching up to the spiritual. As the S'fat Emet says, "The greatest heights and the greatest depths depend on each other."

Heaven and earth, spiritual and material worlds.

At the same time, it is both appropriate and imperative that Moshe alludes to the past, for it is nothing more or less than the prelude to the immediate future, the conquest of Kina'an and the establishment of the ancient nation of Israel, the fulfillment of God's first promises to the Patriarchs. The Khatam Sofer points to God's statement, "See, then, that I, I am the One. There is no other God beside me," as proceeding directly from the Eternal's answer when Moshe asked at the Burning Bush for the Name and was told, "I am what I will be." That was before, this is now and the future. As the Khatam Sofer writes, "[I]n the singing of Moshe's farewell song . . . a future redemption is mentioned, for the Holy One says 'Now that time when "I, I am the One" has arrived. Then I spoke in the language of the future, "I will be," and now that the time has arrived, I speak in the language of the present, "I, I am the One." ' "

Finally, though, *Ha'azinu* is about closing the circle, about those echoes of the beginning of the Torah, of the beginning the Creation, about the unending cycle of Torah. As the S'fat Emet says, "Torah is . . . a commentary or interpretation of Creation itself." We live every day with the aftermath of the Creation, regardless of our faith. Torah can be a useful guide, a gloss, so to speak, on Creation itself.

ADDITIONAL NOTES

- In *Devarim* 32:44, Moshe refers to Hosheya, the name that Yehoshua used to be known by. Why does he do this? Sifre says that "it is to show us [Yehoshua's] modesty," that although he is about to become the leader of the Israelites, he is still as he was when he was a youth in the Wilderness.

HAFTARAH

As the dying Moshe offers a farewell song to God, David offers a song of thanksgiving to God who has saved him from his enemies. And as Moshe tries one last time to impress upon the Israelites the necessity of faith in *Adonai* and acceptance of the *mitzvot*, David expresses his gratitude to and faith in Divine intervention and mercy.

PARASHAT V'ZOT HA'BERAKHAH

54rd and last Torah portion, 11th and last in *Devarim*
Devarim 33:1–34:12 (41 verses)
Haftarah: Yehoshua 1:1–18 (Sephardic: *Yehoshua* 1:1–9)

ALIYOT*

First / Rishon:	33:1–33:7
Second / Sheini:	33:8–33:12
Third / Shlishi:	33:13–33:17
Fourth / Revi'i:	33:18–33:21
Fifth / Khamishi:	33:22–33:26
Sixth / Shishi:	33:27–34:12
Seventh / Shevi'i:	*Bereishit* 1:1–2:3
Maftir:	*B'midbar* 29:35–30:1

SYNOPSIS

Moshe is now ready to take his leave of *B'nei Yisrael*. He offers a final blessing to them, citing each tribe (except Shimon), and reminds them that the Torah is their heritage. He ascends Mount Nebo, from whose peak he is permitted by God to see the Promised Land. He dies there and is buried somewhere in Moab. The location of his final resting place is kept a secret. After a thirty-day period of mourning, Yehoshua assumes the leadership of the Israelites. The Torah concludes with an encomium to Moshe, "whom *Adonai* singled out, face-to-face."

COMMENTARY

Conclusions, the rabbis tell us, are enormously important. In Tractate *Berakhot*, we are told that "they summarize the content of all preceding concepts," Rabbi Menachem Mendel Schneerson explains. Further along in that same book, the sages emphasize the importance of concluding a text "with words of praise and comfort."

How does the Torah end?

Of course, since this *parashah* is only read on Simkhat Torah and is fol-

*See Additional Notes on page 544 for an explanation of the *aliyot*.

lowed almost immediately by a reading of the beginning of *Sefer Bereishit*, one could truthfully say that the Torah doesn't end at all, merely loops back to the beginning, a notion to which we will return shortly.

One might note that the Torah ends with an inversion of the Patriarchal narrative beginning; God tells Moshe, "You will not enter the land," as he first commanded Avram, "Go from your home." The irony of those paired commands is unmistakable. Avram/Avraham will become uprooted as the first part of God's promise to give his successors *Eretz Yisrael.* Yet his direct descendant, Moshe, will be denied entry into that very land, and the final fulfillment of the Covenant with Avraham will not take place in the Torah at all. (Of course, when we read the *haftarah* for this *parashah*, the opening of *Sefer Yehoshua*, the process of conquering the land begins.)

One might say that the Torah ends as the Patriarchal narrative ended, with the last father—Ya'akov, Moshe—bestowing a paternal blessing on the twelve tribes: *"V'zot ha'berakhah/This is the blessing. . . ."* A great deal of ink has been spilled in comparing these two blessings. We will merely content ourselves with noting that while Ya'akov is frequently scathing in his criticism of his sons, Moshe, who has already sternly rebuked the Israelites in his previous "song," leaves them on a gentler note, as if to send them on their destined journey of blood, fire, and iron with a sense of their own worth and a brimming confidence for the battles ahead. Although Moshe struggles against God's decree of his death, the subject of a huge number of midrashim, Moshe dies resigned and seemingly tranquil, unlike Ya'akov who seems embittered by his torments right up to the end.

How does the Torah end?

God takes Moshe up Mount Nebo so that he may, at the last, see the Promised Land. What *Adonai* has granted Moshe is a unique vision, ranging geographically from far to near, of the entire Land. Sifre says that what Moshe saw, though, was not merely a geophysical entity; the Eternal showed Moshe a vision of Israel in both prosperity and adversity, a glimpse of the future of the land and of his people. In a sense, although the Torah does not show us the Convenant fulfilled, God does show this sight to Moshe.

That is entirely fitting. After all, at the outset of this *parashah*, Moshe is called *"ish ha-elohim/the man of God,"* a title that is used nowhere else in the entire Torah. As Pinchas Peli has written, the emphasis here is on "man." For all the greatness he is rightly credited with in the closing verses of the Torah, Moshe is only a mortal being and must die.

And this is how the Torah ends. Moshe dies "*al pi Adonai/by the mouth of Adonai much as Adam was given life.*" Rashi and subsequent commentators have interpreted that phrase literally, saying that God took Moshe's life gently, with *mitat neshikah/Divine Kiss*. Who buries Moshe? The text is somewhat unclear but one of the most moving and, to my mind, satisfying midrashim says that the Creator buried Moshe.

The Torah tells us one thing that is absolutely incontrovertible: no one knows where Moshe's final resting place is located. A midrash says that those who live in the valley (of Mount Nebo) say he is buried on the mountain. Those who live on the mountain say he is buried in the valley.

Why is this so? We know, ostensibly, where the Patriarchs and Matriarchs are buried. Why not Moshe? There are many explanations given but the answer, I think, is simple. Moshe, in his greatness, so praised in the closing verses of the Torah, needs no burial ground, no single location that could become a source of almost idolatrous gatherings. Rather, his absence becomes a kind of omnipresence—we can't see his grave, but we are always aware of his lingering influence and turn back to God as he would have wished. The Apter Rebbe asked why Moshe was described as "the servant of God" even after his death. This, I believe, is the answer to that question, that as he did repeatedly in his lifetime, Moshe in his death asks us once more to give all the thanks, the credit, and the praise to the Holy One.

How does the Torah end?

With its beginning.

With God.

KHAZAK, KHAZAK, V'NIT KHAZEIK.

ADDITIONAL NOTES

- *Parashat V'Zot Ha'Berakhah* is read only on Simkhat Torah, and the pattern of *aliyot* differs from what happens on the Sabbath. The Torah service begins with five (or six) *aliyot* from this *parashah* but the *aliyot* will be repeated over and over until every male in a traditionally observant congregation or every member over age thirteen in a progressive congregation has had an *aliyah*. One *aliyah* is reserved for the congregation's children. The final reading from *Sefer Devarim* is done by *khatan Ha'Torah*, usually a scholar; this is considered a particularly great honor. When everyone has had an *aliyah*, the *khatan Bereishit* will read the final *aliyah*, which is the opening of *Bereishit*, commencing the cycle of Torah readings from the beginning once again. The *maftir* is drawn from the passage in *parashat Pinkhas* that outlines the ritual calendar of the Festivals.

- After Moshe's death, the Israelites observed a thirty-day period of mourning, as they did for Aharon. This practice is carried on today in the form of the *shiloshim*, the extended thirty-day period that includes *shivah*, the seven days immediately after the death of a family member.

HAFTARAH

Just as the reading of the Torah itself is cyclical, ensuring that the day's Torah portion will not end with the sadness of the death of Moshe, the *haftarah* that accompanies the final *parashah* also picks up the story immediately, this time with the opening verses of *Sefer Yehoshua*, in which the Israelites cross over into Kina'an and begin the arduous task of conquering the Land. Fittingly, the new book begins with God telling Yehoshua that Moshe has died.

APPENDIX 1

Torah and History

I had originally planned to include an entire chapter on the subject of the relationship between the Torah and historical fact. Once I began to research the chapter, I felt as though I had stepped through an open door expecting to enter an elevator and had, instead, begun falling in an empty, endless shaft. The literature appraising the "historical truth" of scripture is vast and wildly contradictory. To evaluate it requires some expertise in archaeology and related sciences and in the history of the Ancient Near East. These are not insurmountable obstacles, but as I embarked on my initial reading for the chapter, a series of nasty scandals erupted in the world of biblical archaeology as several seemingly important finds were revealed to be, in fact, elaborate and cunning forgeries.

I felt myself unable and unwilling to sort through the morass of claims and counterclaims, piled atop a precarious stack of books and journal articles in a discipline with which I have little familiarity. Discretion is the better part of valor, as the saying goes, and I have chosen to reduce what was to have been a full chapter on Torah and history to some brief notes suggesting areas worth further research for those who are particularly concerned with the subject.

The most obvious question, which fascinates everyone, can be simply stated: Is the Torah, is the *Tanakh* an accurate recounting of history?

Unfortunately, one cannot offer an equally simple answer. Within biblical archaeology there are at least two schools of thought: the traditionalists, who believe that there are some finds that confirm our belief in the Hebrew Bible, and the minimalists, who think that very little in the ostensibly historical passages of the *Tanakh* are true. Of course, there is a spectrum of opinion between those two positions.

It is hard to establish with any certainty the truth-claims of texts that purport to recount events that took place before the Age of Judges, probably 1200–1000 B.C.E. Evidence from before then is scarce on the ground, partly because the possible forebears of the Israelites were nomadic peoples who would not have left much behind in the way of material culture, partly because of the passage of time.

Ze'ev Herzog, an archaeologist at Tel Aviv University and one of the most outspoken of the minimalists in Israel, told a reporter for *Haaretz*, "This is what archaeologists have learned from the excavations in the Land of Israel: the Israelites were never in Egypt, did not wander in the desert, did not conquer the land in a military campaign and did not pass it on to the 12 tribes of Israel." To some extent his statement reflects a consensus among archaeologists and historians of the period over the last two decades.

At this point in time, scholars in the field are agreed that the Bible's historical passages are not literally accurate descriptions of historical events. The further back in time one goes, the less extrabiblical evidence there is to either confirm or contradict the *Tanakh*. There is no external evidence to confirm the story of the Exodus or the Patriarchs and Matriarchs.

Of course, that blade cuts both ways. As Mordechai Cogan, a historian from Hebrew University, insists, "It is . . . possible to write history from the Bible, it contains primary sources. The lack of evidence in the ground is not sufficient to negate evidence in writing, and archaeologists need to be reminded of that morning, afternoon and night."

Amihai Mazar, an archaeologist from Hebrew University, echoes Cogan. "[T]here's general concurrence that when it comes to the proto-history of the Israelites, archaeology can say very little. . . . If we take a general look at the cultures of the Middle East in that time [rather than just the archaeology of Israel], we get a broad and very interesting background against which it is possible to understand the sources of the biblical stories."

One can, of course, read the Torah and succeeding texts as part of the ensemble of folklore of the contemporary Ancient Near East. In that context, there are distinctive features that set it apart from its neighbors, not the least of them the idea of a single God who preexists Creation; in almost any other "primitive" culture you can name there is a myth of theogony, the creation of God(s) that leads up to the creation of the earth and humanity.

Taken purely as folklore, the Torah certainly fits certain paradigms. Almost all ancient civilizations for which we have recorded folklore and cosmologies have a flood story. Why should that be the case? Because almost all ancient civilizations had floods, a fact that doesn't testify to the truth-value of the flood story itself but, rather, to the reality that civilization in the ancient world could not exist without easy access to water, that rivers overflow their banks, and tides can be unpredictable.

Read as source material, as Cogan suggests, the Torah shows some affinities with other legal and historical documents of the region and period as well.

But the author(s) of the Torah didn't think they were writing history per se. As Charles David Isbell, director of the Jewish Studies program at Louisiana State University, observes, if they had been, they wouldn't have deliberately omitted so much information. In *Sifrei Malakhim/1 and 2 Kings*, there are frequently passages in which the reader is referred explicitly to other texts, such as "the Book of the Chronicles of the Kings of Judah" and "the Book of the Chronicles of the Kings of Israel," for more information on events not recounted. Someone writing a history wouldn't do that; they would simply give the data themselves. Likewise, Isbell writes, the author(s) of *Sefer Shemot* consciously omit such basic information as the name of the Pharoah, the location of *Yam Suf*, and Mount Sinai. This is not the mark of historical writing.

If one does not approach the Torah looking for a history of ancient Israel and its neighbors, there are no grounds for disappointment. What history book would purport to describe God's active role in historical events in the first place? The Bible is not a history book; it is a book of moral instruction, folklore and myth, poetry and philosophy. Did the events recounted in the Torah actually happen? Symbolically, yes. Really? Who cares. To paraphrase Richard Elliott Friedman, the important thing isn't who wrote the Bible, but who reads it, how, and why.

APPENDIX 2

A Timeline of Major Torah-Related Events

c. 1850–1700 B.C.E.	Avraham and Sarah, Yitzkhak and Yishmael; Origin of traditions of the "Abrahamic Covenant," Traditions of Ya'akov/Yisrael and the Twelve Patriarchs
c. 1300–1200 B.C.E.	Mosaic period (Israel); Exodus from Egypt, Torah given at Sinai, entry into Kina'an (1250–1200?)
c. 1200–1000 B.C.E.	Judges rule in Israel
c. 1000–587 B.C.E.	Monarchical period in Israel; Shaul (c. 1030–1010); David, making Jerusalem his capital (c. 1010–970); Shelomo, and building of the First Temple (c. 970–931)
c. 931 B.C.E.	Secession of Northern Kingdom (Israel) from Southern Kingdom (Judah)
c. 750–720s	Amos, Hoshea, and Yeshayahu prophesy
722–720	Assyrians invade and conquer Israel; Northern Kingdom destroyed (Ten Lost Tribes)
640 B.C.E.	Reign of Josiah begins; prophecies of Zephaniah
c. 626 B.C.E.	Yirmiyahu is called to prophesy
612 B.C.E.	Nineveh is destroyed by Babylonians and Medes
597 B.C.E.	Yekhezkel taken in captivity to Babylonia
586 B.C.E.	Destruction of the First Temple
568–538 B.C.E.	Babylonian Exile
c. 550 B.C.E.	"Second Yeshayahu" prophesies
520–515 B.C.E.	Second Temple built
539 B.C.E.	Babylonian empire falls to Persians
c. 520 B.C.E.	Prophecies of Haggai, Zekharyah

c. 450–400 B.C.E.	Ezra returns to Judah with the "Torah of Moshe," with Nekhemyah begins reform of Judaism in the spirit of the Torah; Torah begins to gain recognition as Scripture
c. 400 B.C.E.	Beginnings of group prayer as a Jewish phenomenon
c. 350–200 B.C.E.	Men of the Great Assembly
third century B.C.E.	Rise of the Sadducees
	Septuagint, Greek translation of Hebrew Bible
c. 200 B.C.E.	*Nevi'im* recognized by some as Scripture; weekly readings of *haftarot* become the norm
c. 200–first century B.C.E.	The *Zugot / Pairs*
165–163 B.C.E.	Maccabees fight against Syrian rulers of Palestine (events commemorated by Hanukah)
first century B.C.E.	*Tanna'im,* First Generation
c. 20 B.C.E.	Philo Judaeus born
c. 50 C.E.	Philo dies
c. 50–125 C.E.	Christian Testament writings
66 C.E.	Beginning of Jewish rebellion against Roman rule
70 C.E.	Second Temple destroyed on the ninth of Av
c. 90–130 C.E.	*Tanna'im,* Second Generation
c. 90–150 C.E.	*Ketuvim* discussed and accepted as sacred scripture; canonization of Hebrew Bible is essentially complete
first century C.E.	Prayer service begins to evolve toward its present structure
c. 130–160 C.E.	*Tanna'im,* Third Generation
second century C.E.	Onkelos authors Aramaic translation and commentary on Torah; Peshitta, the Syriac Bible, written; *Tanna'im,* Fourth Generation; Redaction of Mishnah, Tosefta
c. 200–sixth century	*Amora'im*
219 C.E.	Academy at Sura founded
c. 220 C.E.	Judah Ha'Nasi (Judah the Prince, a.k.a. Rabbi) dies
259 C.E.	Academy at Pumbedita founded
third century C.E.	Rabbi Simlai states that there are 613 commandments given by God in the Torah
c. 300 C.E.	Redaction of halakhic midrashim

358 C.E.	Rabbi Hillel II introduces permanent fixed ritual calendar
c. 400 C.E.	Redaction of aggadic midrashim, Palestinian Talmud
404 C.E.	Jerome completes Vulgate, the Latin translation of the Bible
c. 427–650 C.E.	Redaction of Babylonian Talmud
sixth century	*Savora'im*
seventh century	*Targum Yonatan*
	Targum Yerushalmi (or Pseudo-Yonatan)
ninth and tenth centuries	*Targum al-Tafsir,* Arabic translation of Torah by Sa'adia Gaon; Masoretic text, with vowel markings and cantillation, becomes the accepted version of Hebrew Bible
1040–1105	Rashi (Rabbi Shelomo Yitzkhaki)
1075	Judah Ha'Levi born in Spain
c. 1092	Abraham Ibn Ezra born
1138	Moses ben Maimon, called Maimonides, born in Spain
1140	Abraham Ibn Ezra begins writing his Torah commentary in Rome
c. 1141	Judah Ha'Levi dies
c. 1160	Radak (Rabbi David Kimhi) born
1165	Maimonides publishes *Mishneh Torah,* a monumental compendium of Jewish law
1167	Abraham Ibn Ezra dies
late twelfth century	Ashkenazic Hasidim, early kabbalists in Spain
1180	Maimonides named court physician to Saladin
1194–1270	Nahmanides (Rabbi Moses ben Nahman)
1204	Maimonides dies
1230	Some rabbinic authorities argue for a ban on Maimonides' *Guide for the Perplexed*
1235	David Kimhi dies
c. 1270	Ba'al Ha'Turim born
late thirteenth century	Rise of kabbalistic circles in Gerona and Barcelona
fourteenth century	John Wycliffe's translation of the Bible, including both Hebrew and Christian scriptures and Apocrypha, first complete English translation

1290s	De Leon writes *Sefer Ha'Zohar*
c. 1343	Ba'al Ha'Turim dies
c. 1400	First known examples of *bar mitzvah* ceremony
1437	Isaac Abravanel born
1475	First Hebrew book—Rashi's commentaries on Torah—printed in Reggio, Italy
1492	Jews expelled from Spain
1497	Jews expelled from Portugal
1508	Isaac Abravanel dies
1517–1518	Bomberg publishes first printed edition of *Mikra'ot Gedolot*
1530s	Joseph Caro publishes the *Shulkhan Arukh*, definitive code of Jewish law
1531	William Tyndale's translation of Bible from Hebrew and Greek into English, first translation to be printed
1534	Isaac Luria (the Ari) born
1560s	Joseph Caro writes *Shulkan Arukh*
1611	King James Version of Bible published
1632	Baruch Spinoza born in Amsterdam
1656	Spinoza is excommunicated
1670	Spinoza writes *Tractatus Theologico-Politicus*
1677	Spinoza dies
1700	Israel Ba'al Shem Tov, founder of Hasidism, born
1760	The Ba'al Shem Tov dies
1808	Samson Raphael Hirsch born
1809	Malbim born
1810	Israel Jacobson opens his synagogue (beginnings of Reform), introduces confirmation ceremony
1820	Yosef Dov Soloveitchik (*Beis Ha'Levi*) born
1839	The Chofetz Chaim born
1842	Society of Friends of Reform founded in Frankfurt
1854	Isaac Leeser publishes new translation of *Tanakh*
1865	Birth of Abraham Yitzkhak Kook
1874	Samson Raphael Hirsch dies
1875	Union of American Hebrew Congregations (Reform) established; Hebrew Union College (Reform) opens in Cincinnati
1878	Martin Buber is born in Vienna

1879	Malbim dies
1885	Pittsburgh Platform (Reform) rejects *halakhah* as binding upon contemporary Jews
1886	Jewish Theological Seminary (JTS; Conservative) founded
	Franz Rosenzweig is born in Germany
1892	Yosef Dov Soloveitchik dies
1898	Founding of Orthodox Union in the United States
1902	Solomon Schechter becomes head of the Jewish Theological Seminary
1903	Buber stumbles across the tales of Rabbi Nakhman of Breslov; Yeshayahu Leibowitz is born in Latvia; Joseph Dov Soloveitchik is born in Belarus
1905	Nehama Leibowitz is born in Latvia
1907	Abraham Joshua Heschel is born in Lithuania
1917	First JPS *Tanakh* translation, *The Holy Scriptures*, published
1922	Mordecai Kaplan opens his synagogue, the Society for the Advancement of Judaism; his daughter, Judith Kaplan, is first girl to undergo *bat mitzvah* ceremony
1923	Martin Buber's *I and Thou* is published
1925	First sections of Buber-Rosenzweig translation of Torah are published
1929	Rosenzweig dies after long struggle with amytrophic lateral sclerosis
1932	Soloveitchik immigrates to the United States, settling in Boston
1933	The Khofetz Khaim dies
1937	Buber appoints Abraham Joshua Heschel head of the *Lehrhaus* and immigrates to Palestine
1941	Soloveitchik appointed to faculty at Yeshiva University's rabbinical seminary; by the time of his retirement in 1985, he will have ordained over two thousand rabbis
1945	Heschel appointed to faculty of the Jewish Theological Seminary
1956	Nehama Leibowitz awarded Israel Prize in Education
1962	JPS translation of the Torah published

1965   Martin Buber dies
1967   Reconstructionist Rabbinical College opens in
                Philadelphia
1972   Abraham Joshua Heschel dies; Reform movement
                ordains its first woman rabbi
1974   Reconstructionist movement ordains its first woman
                rabbis
1979   Arthur Waskow founds *Menorah*, which will become
                official publication of Jewish Renewal movement
1984   Conservative movement ordains its first woman
                rabbis
1985   JPS publishes completed translation of *Tanakh*
1993   Joseph Soloveitchik dies
1994   Yeshayahu Leibowitz dies
1995   *The Five Books of Moses*, new translation of Torah by
                Everett Fox, is published
1997   Nehama Leibowitz dies; Jewish Orthodox Feminist
                Alliance founded in New York
2003   Conservative movement publishes its new *Khumash*,
                Etz Hayim, distinguished by its extensive
                commentary

GLOSSARY OF TORAH COMMENTATORS

The following is a list identifying many of the authors who are cited in the commentaries on the *parashiyot* that form the second half of this book. (Needless to say, for living authors, herein designated as "contemporary," identifications are as of the time of the writing of this glossary.)

ABRAHAM IBN EZRA: Twelfth-century Spanish Torah commentator, known for his great erudition in matters of science and linguistics, with the latter a particularly important part of his writings on Torah.

ABRAVANEL, ISAAC: Fifteenth-century Sephardic scholar and statesman who began his life and career in Spain but after the Expulsion in 1492 went to Italy, where he died in 1508.

ADLER, MORRIS (1906–1966): Twentieth-century Conservative rabbi based in Detroit. Was murdered during a service by a mentally ill congregant.

AIBU, RABBI: In fact, there are five scholars of this name cited in the Talmud; this one is probably of the amoraic period.

AKEIDAT YITZKHAK: Commentary on the Torah by Isaac ben Moses Arama.

ALBO, YOSEF: Fourteenth-to-fifteenth-century Spanish Torah commentator and philosopher.

THE ALPHABET OF BEN SIRA: Ninth-century compilation of midrashim.

ALSHIKH, MOSHE BEN KHAIM: Sixteenth-century Palestinian commentator, based in Safed. (Sometimes given as "Alshekh" or "Alshich.")

ALTER, YEHUDAH ARYEH LEIB (1847–1905): The Gerer Rebbe, also known as the S'fat Emet, author of a brilliant but difficult Torah commentary, *S'fat Emet al Ha'Torah/The Language of Truth of the Torah,* which gave him his sobriquet.

ANTONELLI, JUDITH: Contemporary American author and Orthodox feminist.

ARAMA, ISAAC BEN MOSES: Fifteenth-century Spanish rabbi and author of *Akeidat Yitzkhak.*

ASHKENAZI, ELIEZER BEN ELIYAHU: Sixteenth-century European rabbi and author of *Ma'aseh Ha'Shem.*

ASHKENAZI, SHIMON: Twelfth-century European rabbi and author of midrash collection *Yalkut Shimoni.*

ASHKENAZI OF YANOF, JACOB BEN YITZKHAK: Thirteenth-century rabbi who authored important Yiddish Torah commentary for women, *Tze'enah U'R'enah.*

AVOT: See *Pirkei Avot.*

BA'AL HA'TURIM, YA'AKOV: Fourteenth-century commentator on Jewish law, born in Germany but fled persecution and did his main work in Spain. Best known for his *Arba'ah Turim/Four Rows,* an important precursor to Joseph Caro's *Shulkhan*

Arukh. His volumes of Torah commentary, called *Ba'al Ha'Turim*, rely heavily on *gematria.*

THE BA'AL SHEM TOV (1698–1760): The founder of Hasidism, an itinerant preacher, then rabbi in eighteenth-century Eastern Europe. Also called "the Besht."

BAKHYA BEN ASHER: Fourteenth-century Spanish Torah commentator, ethicist, and kabbalist.

BAMBERGER, BERNARD: Prominent twentieth-century Reform rabbi and Torah scholar, worked with Plaut (see below) on the movement's *Khumash.*

BARUKH BEN JEHIEL (1757–1810): Important early Hasidic leader, grandson of the Ba'al Shem Tov, he was most closely identified with his congregation at Medzibozh.

BEIS HALEVI: See Yosef Dov Soloveitchik.

BEN YASHAR, MENACHEM: Faculty member, Department of Bible, Bar-Ilan University.

BERLIN, NAPHTALI ZVI YEHUDAH (1817–1893): Nineteenth-century rabbi, head of famous yeshiva at Volozhin. Author of *Ha'Emek Davar*, a collection of his commentaries on the weekly Torah portion, he is often referred to by the title of this book.

BICK, EZRA: Rabbi and faculty member at Yeshiva Har Etzion, Israel, and director of their Virtual Beit Midrash Project.

BONCHEK, AVIGDOR: Contemporary Bible scholar based in Israel and author of series of books, *What's Bothering Rashi?*

BUBER, MARTIN (1878–1965): Twentieth-century German Jewish philosopher and one of the key figures in religious existentialism.

BUNIM, RAV (1767–1827): One of the early Hasidic masters, identified most closely with his congregation at Pshis'cha.

CASPI, JOSEPH BEN ABBA MARI: Philosopher and commentator who lived in medieval France in the late thirteenth–early-fourteenth centuries.

CASSUTO, UMBERTO: Outstanding Italian Bible scholar of the twentieth century.

CHINITZ, JACOB: Orthodox rabbi, currently leading a congregation in Montreal.

COHEN, HOWARD: Contemporary American rabbi, affiliated with the Reconstructionist movement.

CULI, YA'AKOV: Eighteenth-century rabbi and author/compiler of the most famous Sephardic Torah commentary, *Me'am Loez.*

DOV BER, THE MAGGID (PREACHER) OF MEZERITCH (1704?–1770): Inheritor of the mantle of Hasidic leadership after the death of the Ba'al Shem Tov, his pupils included almost every major figure in the next generation of Hasidic rebbes.

EIGER, YEHUDA LEIB (1816–1888): Prominent Hasidic rabbi from Poland.

EISEN, ARNOLD: Professor in Jewish Culture and Religion at Stanford University. Expert in the modern transformations of Jewish religious belief and practice and author of numerous books.

ELEAZAR BEN AZARIAH: Important first-to-second-century Palestinian *tanna.* Cited more than 150 times in the Babylonian Talmud.

FEINSTEIN, MOSHE (1895–1986): Twentieth-century Russian-born Orthodox rabbi, considered one of the great halakhic authorities of his time.

FIELDS, HARVEY: Contemporary American Reform rabbi and author of an excellent three-volume set of commentaries on *parashat ha'shavua* titled *A Torah Commentary for Our Times.*

FOX, EVERETT: Professor of Judaic and Biblical Studies at Clark University and author of highly acclaimed translation of Torah, *The Five Books of Moses* (1995).

FRAND, YISSOCHER: Contemporary Orthodox rabbi.

FRANZEL, JORDAN: Reform cantor based in New York City.

FREEDMAN, DAVID NOEL: Professor of Hebrew Bible at the University of California at San Diego and editor of the Anchor Bible series.

FRIEDMAN, RICHARD ELLIOTT: Professor of Hebrew and Comparative Literature at the University of California at San Diego and author of *Commentary on the Torah* and *Who Wrote the Bible?*

GERER REBBE: See Yehudah Aryeh Leib Alter.

GERSONIDES, A.K.A. RABBI LEVI BEN GERSON (1288–1344): Important medieval Bible commentator.

GOODMAN, ROBERTA LOUIS: Contemporary Jewish American educator, currently based in Cleveland.

GREENBERG, MOSHE: Professor of Bible at Hebrew University, winner of the Israel Prize for Bible, and author and editor of countless books of Torah commentary.

GROSSMAN, YONATAN: Rabbi and faculty member at Yeshiva Har Etzion, Israel.

HA'EMEK DAVAR: See Naphtali Zvi Yehudah Berlin.

HARTMAN, DAVID: American-born contemporary rabbi, now based in Israel where he heads the Shalom Hartman Institute. Modern Orthodox, a student of Joseph Soloveitchik, an eloquent defender of pluralism in the Jewish community.

HENKIN, YEHUDA: Contemporary Orthodox rabbi and author of many books of Torah commentary.

HERTZ, J. H. (1872–1946): Twentieth-century British rabbi, chief rabbi of Great Britain, best known in the United States for his translation and commentary for the Soncino *Khumash*.

HERTZBERG, ARTHUR: Contemporary Conservative rabbi, prominent Jewish activist, and author.

HIRSCH, SAMSON RAPHAEL (1808–1888): Nineteenth-century German rabbi, the father of Neo-Orthodoxy, and one of the central figures of Modern Orthodox Judaism.

HIZKUNI: Torah commentary by Khizkiyahu ben Manoakh, thirteenth-century French scholar.

HOFFMAN, DAVID ZVI (1843–1921): A leading German rabbi who wrote outstanding commentaries on *Vayikra* and *Devarim*.

HORT, GRETA (1903–1967): Twentieth-century Danish scholar, a polymath and pioneer in women's education whose interests included the Hebrew Bible.

IBN EZRA, ABRAHAM: Twelfth-century Spanish rabbi. One of the key figures in medieval Torah commentary, his work is included in *Mikra'ot Gedolot*.

JACOB, BENNO: Nineteenth-to-twentieth-century rabbi and Bible scholar.

JACOBSON, B. S.: Twentieth-century Israeli rabbi and author of *Meditations on the Torah*.

JEREMIAH BEN ELAZAR: Third-century Palestinian *amora*, a prominent expert on *aggadah*.

JOSEPHUS, FLAVIUS: First-century general and historian. Originally an Israelite general, he switched sides in the war against Rome. His history, *The Jewish War*, and his other books offer an apparently reliable picture of Jewish life at the time.

KAHN, YAIR: Rabbi and faculty member at Yeshiva Har Etzion, Israel.

KAMENETZKY, MORDECHAI: Contemporary Orthodox rabbi and *rosh yeshiva*.

KAMINETSKY, YA'AKOV (1891–1986): Twentieth-century Orthodox rabbi, author of the commentary *Iyunim Ba'Mikra*. Prominent *rosh yeshiva* who was important part of the revival of post–World War II Orthodoxy in the United States.

KATZ, MORDECHAI: Contemporary Orthodox rabbi and prolific author of books on Judaism and Torah.

KHATAM SOFER: See Moshe Sofer Schreiber.

KIMKHI, DAVID (c. 1160–1235): The most famous of a renowned family of rabbinical scholars, he compiled one of the first authoritative Bible dictionaries and wrote one of the key sets of Torah commentary included in the *Mikra'ot Gedolot*.

THE KOTZKER REBBE: See Menachem Mendl Morgenstern of Kotzk.

LEIBOWITZ, NEHAMA (1907–1997): Twentieth-century Israeli Bible scholar and author of outstanding series of books on the weekly portion. Sister of Yeshayahu Leibowitz.

LEIBOWITZ, YESHAYAHU (1903–1994): Twentieth-century Israeli scientist, philosopher, political commentator, and author of a series of commentaries on the weekly portion for broadcast on IDF radio. Brother of Nehama Leibowitz.

LITTLESTONE, LAWRENCE: Contemporary Orthodox rabbi based in London.

LUZZATTO, SAMUEL DAVID: Nineteenth-century Italian scholar, professor at the Padua Rabbinical College, and author of a Torah commentary that focuses on ethical issues.

THE MAGGID OF MEZERITCH: See Dov Ber.

MAIMONIDES: See Moshe ben Maimon.

MALBIM: See Meir Lev ben Yekhiel Michael.

ME'AM LOEZ: See Ya'akov Culi.

MECKLENBERG, JACOB ZVI: Rabbi and author of *Ha'Ketav Ve'Ha'Kabbalah/The Written and the Oral Tradition*, an important nineteenth-century book of Torah commentary.

MEI HA'SHILO'AKH: See Mordekhai Yosef of Isbitza.

MEIR LEV BEN YEKHIEL MICHAEL (1809–1879): Author of a massive and influential commentary on *Tanakh*.

MENKEN, YA'AKOV: Contemporary Orthodox rabbi, very active on the Internet, currently based in Baltimore.

MILGROM, JACOB: Rabbi and professor emeritus of Bible at the University of California at Berkeley and author of several volumes of the Anchor Bible Commentary, now living in Jerusalem. Particularly expert on *Sefer Vayikra*.

MORDEKHAI YOSEF OF ISBITZA: Nineteenth-century Hasidic rabbi and author of Torah commentary *Mei Ha'Shilo'akh*, by which name he is frequently referred to.

MORGENSTERN, MENACHEM MENDL OF KOTZK: Popularly known as the Kotzker Rebbe, a leading figure in nineteenth-century Hasidism. A mysterious figure who secluded himself from human contact for much of the last twenty years of his life, considered by many a precursor of Jewish existentialist thought.

MOSHE BEN MAIMON, A.K.A. MAIMONIDES (1135–1204): Physician, philosopher, Talmudist, and halakhic codifier par excellence.

MOSHE BEN NAHMAN, A.K.A. NAHMANIDES (1194–1279): One of the great Torah and Talmud commentators, a chief figure among Spanish Jewry and an important kabbalist.

NAHMANIDES: See Moshe ben Nahman.

PANIM YAFOT: Sixteenth-century commentary, written by Reb Pinkhas Halevi Horowitz.

PELI, PINCHAS (d. 1989): Contemporary Israeli Orthodox rabbi and author.

PHILO JUDAEUS: First-century Jewish philosopher.

PIRKEI AVOT: Tractate of the Mishnah Avot, with an additional chapter; focuses on sayings, primarily ethical, of rabbis.

PLAUT, W. GUNTHER: Contemporary Canadian Reform rabbi and author; editor of the *Khumash* used in most Reform synagogues today.

PROSNIT, JAMES: Contemporary Reform rabbi and spiritual leader of B'nai Israel in Connecticut.

RADAK: See David Kimhi.

RALBAG: See Gersonides.

RAMBAM: See Moshe ben Maimon.

RAMBAN: See Moshe ben Nakhman.

RASHBAM: See Shmuel ben Meir.

RASHI: Rabbi Shlomo Yitzkhaki (1040–1105): Perhaps the greatest interpreter of Torah; author of what is certainly the single most used Torah commentary, the fundamental commentary text that every student of Torah is trained to use. Also central for his Talmud commentary, his responsa, and other halakhic writings. Grandfather of Rabbenu Tam and Rashbam.

RAV: Second-to-third-century Babylonian *amora*, also known as Abba Arikha and Abba bar Aibu. Founder of the Talmudic academy at Sura; one of the most important halakhists in the Babylonian Talmud.

RISKIN, SHLOMO: Contemporary Modern Orthodox rabbi, formerly in New York, now in Israel.

SARNA, NAHUM (1923–2005): Distinguished Bible scholar and author of JPS Torah Commentary on *Bereishit* and numerous other books.

SCHNEERSON, MENACHEM MENDEL: Twentieth-century Hasidic rabbi, the last Lubavitcher Rebbe (to date).

SCHORSCH, ISMAR: Contemporary Conservative rabbi and scholar and president of Jewish Theological Seminary.

SCHREIBER, MOSHE SOFER, A.K.A. KHATAM SOFER (1762–1839): Key opponent of the early Reform movement and author of an important Torah commentary, *Torat Moshe*, and important halakhic decisor.

S'FAT EMET: See Yehudah Aryeh Leib Alter.

SFORNO, OVADIAH: Sixteenth-century Italian rabbi, distinguished Talmudist, and Torah commentator whose work is included in the *Mikra'ot Gedolot*.

SHIMON BAR YOHAI: Second-century Palestinian *tanna*, a student of Akiva's and one of the key halakhic decisors of his era. The *Zohar* is pseudepigraphically attributed to him.

SHIMON BEN LAKISH: Third-century Palestinian *amora*, also known as Reish Lakish. Widely known for his great physical strength (legend has it that he had been a gladiator) and remarkable learning. Talmud reports hundreds of his debates on *halakhah* with his brother-in-law Yokhanan bar Nappakha.

SHMUEL BEN MEIR (c. 1080–after 1158): Grandson of Rashi, older brother of Rabbenu Tam, an important Torah commentator whose work is based on *peshat*, drawing heavily on his extensive knowledge of Hebrew linguistics and the *targumim*.

SOLOVEITCHIK, JOSEPH B. (1903–1993): Twentieth-century Orthodox rabbi, one of the key thinkers of the Modern Orthodox movement and religious existentialism.

SOLOVEITCHIK, YOSEF DOV (1820–1892): First of the great *rashei yeshivot* of Brisk, Lithuania, and ancestor of Joseph Soloveitchik. Nicknamed Beis Ha'Levi for his highly thoughtful Torah commentary, which covers both halakhic and aggadic subjects.

TENDLER, ARON: Modern Orthodox rabbi, currently at Shaarey Tzedek in Los Angeles.

TUITO, ELAZAR: Professor in the Department of Bible, Bar-Ilan University.

TURNER, MASHA: Faculty member in the Department of Philosophy, Bar-Ilan University.

TZE'ENAH U'R'ENAH: Important commentary on Torah written for women in Yiddish by Ya'akov ben Yitzkhak and Ashkenazi of Yanof.

TZOHAR, YAEL: Contemporary scholar and faculty member of the Bible Department, Bar-Ilan University.

THE VILNA GAON (1720–1797): Eliyahu of Vilna, eighteenth-century Lithuanian rabbi, a.k.a the Gra. Among the greatest Torah scholars of his time, a child prodigy who went on to be the central figure among the *Mitnagdim/Opponents,* the Lithuanian rabbis who sternly opposed the Hasidic movement. Extraordinarily prolific author whose works include Torah commentary, halakhic writings, and philosophy.

WALFISH, ABRAHAM: Rabbi and faculty member at Yeshiva Har Etzion, Israel.

WAXMAN, CHANOCH: Rabbi and faculty member at Yeshiva Har Etzion, Israel.

WEINBERG, MATIS: Contemporary Orthodox rabbi and author of multivolume Torah commentary, *Frameworks.*

YALKUT SHIMONI: Twelfth-century collection of midrashim by Shimon Ashkenazi.

YITZHAKI, EPHRAIM: Contemporary scholar and professor in the Talmud Department of Bar-Ilan University, Israel.

YITZKHAK, RAV: Second-to-third-century Palestinian *amora* and a prominent teacher in the Talmudic period.

YOHANAN BEN ZAKAI: Perhaps the greatest of the first generation of *tanna'im,* founder of the yeshiva at Yavneh and the Sanhedrin, of which he was the first president.

ZOHAR: One of the central works of Jewish mysticism, authored by Moses de Leon but (falsely) attributed to Shimon bar Yokhai.

GLOSSARY OF TERMS

The following glossary owes a great deal to one assembled by Professor Robert Kraft of the University of Pennsylvania, which can be found at numerous Web sites.

ADONAI: "Our Lord," one of the commonly used names for the Deity.

AGGADAH: Heb., "telling." Nonhalakhic matter in Talmud and Midrash; includes folklore, legend, theology/theosophy, scriptural interpretations, biography, and so forth; also spelled *haggadah*, not to be confused, however, with the text of the Passover seder, which is also called "the Haggadah."

AKEIDAH: Lit. "binding." Biblical account of God's command to Avraham to offer his son Yitzkhak as a sacrifice, found in *Bereishit* 22.

ALEPH-BET (ah-lef bet): The Hebrew alphabet. The name is derived from the first two letters of the aleph-bet.

ALIYAH: Lit. "going up," "ascending." 1. Term used when a Jew is called to say a blessing before and after the Torah is read. 2. Permanent immigration to Israel. Literal meaning is "going up" or ascension; thus, immigrating to Israel is seen as a spiritual ascension. One who "makes" *aliyah* is an *oleh*, pl. *olim*.

AM YISRAEL: Lit. "the people Israel," usually used to refer to the Jewish people (the descendants of Ya'akov, aka Israel).

AMORA (pl. *amora'im*): Heb., lit. "speaker." Rabbinic Jewish teachers of the third and fourth centuries C.E. who produced the Gemara for the Babylonian and Palestinian Talmuds.

AMUD: Reading desk at the front (or center) of sanctuary at which the Torah will be read.

APOCRYPHA (adj. apocryphal): From the Greek, meaning "hidden away." It is used in a technical sense to refer to certain Jewish books written in the Hellenistic Roman period that came to be included in the Old Greek Jewish scriptures (and thus in the Eastern Christian biblical canon) and in the Latin Vulgate Roman Catholic canon, but not in the Jewish or Protestant biblical canons.

ARAMAIC: Semitic language, closely related to Hebrew, in which key Jewish texts, most notably the Babylonian and Palestininan Talmuds, were written. The lingua franca of the Middle East before the Arab conquest, it is still spoken in communities around the world.

ARK: From the Latin. The word has no connection with Noah's ark, which is *teivah* in Hebrew.

ARON HA'KODESH: Lit. "holy chest." Holy ark, usually found at the front of sanctuary, containing two or more Torah scrolls.

ASHKENAZIC: The term now used for Jews who derive from northern Europe and who generally follow the customs originating in medieval German Judaism, as distinct from Sephardic Jews, whose distinctive roots are traced back to Spain and the Mediterranean. Originally the designation *Ashkenaz* referred to a people and country bordering on Armenia and the upper Euphrates; in medieval times, it came to refer to the Jewish area of settlement in northwest Europe (northern France and western Germany). By extension, it now refers to Jews of northern and Eastern European background (including Russia) with their distinctive liturgical practices or religious and social customs.

BA'AL KRIAH: Lit. "master of the reading." One who reads or chants aloud from the Torah during services.

BA'AL TESHUVAH: Lit. "one who has returned." A formerly nonobservant Jew who returns to Jewish practice (in a traditionally observant manner, it is implied).

B'MIDBAR: Lit. "in the desert." The fourth book of the Torah, the book of Numbers.

BAR: Aramaic word meaning "son." See also *ben*.

BAR MITZVAH (pl. *b'nei mitzvah*): Lit. "son of the commandment." A boy who has achieved the age of thirteen and is consequently obligated to observe the commandments. Also, a ceremony marking the fact that a boy has achieved this age.

BAT MITZVAH (pl. *b'not mitzvah*): Lit. "daughter of the commandment." A girl who has achieved the age of twelve or thirteen and is consequently obligated to observe the commandments. Also, a ceremony marking the fact that a girl has achieved this age.

BAVLI: Jewish shorthand term for the Babylonian Talmud.

B.C.E.: Before the Common (or Christian) Era.

BEN: Heb. "son," "son of"; Aramaic, bar, ibn. Used frequently in "patronymics" (naming by identity of father); Akiva ben Yosef means Akiva son of Yosef.

BERAKHAH (pl. *berakhot*): A blessing. A prayer beginning with the phrase "Barukh atah . . ." (Blessed art Thou . . .).

BEREISHIT: Hebrew name for the book of Genesis, taken from the opening word of the book.

BET DIN: Lit. "house of judgment." A rabbinical court made up of three rabbis who resolve business disputes under Jewish law and determine whether a prospective convert is ready for conversion.

BET KNESSET: Lit. "house of assembly." A synagogue.

BET MIDRASH: Lit. "house of study." A place set aside for study of sacred texts such as the Torah and the Talmud, generally a part of the synagogue or attached to it.

BIMAH: Place at front of synagogue from which service is led, i.e., the pulpit.

BINAH: Intuition, understanding, intelligence. Also, in kabbalistic thought, one of the Ten Sefirot.

B'NEI YISRAEL: The Children of Israel.

BRIT: Heb. "Covenant." Used in Judaism especially for the special relationship believed to exist between God and the Jewish people.

BRIT MILAH: Lit. "Covenant of circumcision." The ritual circumcision of a male child before the age of eight days or of a male convert to Judaism. Frequently referred to as a *bris*.

B'TZELEM ELOHIM: In the image of God

CCAR: Central Conference of American Rabbis, organization of the Reform rabbinate.

C.E.: Common (or Christian) Era. Preferable to A.D., "Anno Domini," Latin for "Year of

Our Lord," because of its implication that Christ was the Son of God, a concept that Jews and Muslims (among others) reject.

CANAANITES: Ancient tribes that lived in Kina'an before the Israelites came.

CANTOR: From Latin, "one who sings." In Judaism, a reciter and chanter/singer of liturgical materials in the synagogue; also used similarly in Christian contexts (choir leader, etc.). Also called *hazan*.

CIRCUMCISION: See *Brit milah.*

COMMANDMENTS: See also *mitzvah.* According to rabbinic Jewish tradition, there are 613 religious commandments referred to in the Torah (and elaborated upon by the rabbinic sages). Of these, 248 are positive commandments and 365 are negative. The numbers respectively symbolize the fact that divine service must be expressed through all one's bodily parts during all the days of the year. In general, a *mitzvah* refers to any act of religious duty or obligation; more colloquially, a *mitzvah* refers to a "good deed."

CONSERVATIVE JUDAISM: A modern development in Judaism, reacting to early Jewish Reform movements in an attempt to retain clearer links to classical Jewish law while at the same time adapting it to modern situations. Its scholarly center in the United States is the Jewish Theological Seminary in New York.

DAYS OF AWE: Ten days from Rosh Hashanah to Yom Kippur, a time for introspection and considering the sins of the previous year. See also *Yamim Nora'im.*

DECALOGUE: A Greek term referring to the Ten Commandments (*Aseret Ha'Dibrot*) received by Moshe on Mount Sinai according to Jewish scriptures (*Shemot* 20:1–17; *Devarim* 5:1–21).

DEUTERONOMY: From the Greek, meaning "second [telling] of the Law," fifth and final book of the Penatateuch.

DEVARIM: The book of Deuteronomy.

DIASPORA: The dispersion of Jews throughout the world after the fall of the Second Temple (70 C.E.). Refers to all Jews living outside of Israel. Also known as the "Exile" (Heb.: *galut*).

EIN SOF: Heb. "without limit." In Jewish kabbalism, a designation for the divine—"the unlimited one."

ELOHIM, EL: Heb. general term for deity.

EMANCIPATION: In Jewish history, the nineteenth-century movement/events that led to Jews being granted full civil status in European societies.

ERETZ YISRAEL: Heb. "land of Israel." In Jewish thought, the special term for the Palestinian area believed to have been promised to the Jewish people by God in the ancient Covenant.

EREV: Heb. "evening." Usually the evening before a holiday, e.g., Erev Shabbat is Friday evening, Erev Rosh Hashanah is the evening before the day of Rosh Hashanah.

ESSENES: The name of a Jewish subgroup in the first century C.E. according to Josephus, Philo, and other sources.

EXODUS: From Greek, "to exit or go out." Refers to the event of the Israelites leaving Egypt (see also Passover) and to the biblical book that tells of that event. Hebrew name of the book is *Shemot/The Names.*

EITZ KHAYIM: Lit. "tree of life." 1. Hymn that is sung/recited as the Torah is returned to the ark at the end of *Seder Kri'at Ha'Torah*. 2. The wooden spindles on which the Torah scroll is mounted.

FIRST TEMPLE: Built in Jerusalem by Shelomo, destroyed by the Babylonians in 586 B.C.E., it housed the ark of the Convenant, and was the site of all the most important rites of pre-Rabbinic Judaism. See also Temple.

GABBAI: Layperson who assists prayer leader during Torah reading, calling to the *bimah* those who have *aliyot*.

GALUT: Heb., "exile." The term refers to the various expulsions of Jews from the ancestral homeland. Over time, it came to express the broader notion of Jewish homelessness and state of being aliens. Thus, colloquially, "to be in *galut*" means to live in the Diaspora and also to be in a state of physical and even spiritual alienation.

GAON (pl. *Geonim;* adj. geonic): Heb. "eminence, excellence." A title given to the Jewish head of the Babylonian academy and then to distinguished Talmudic scholars in the sixth to twelfth centuries.

GARTEL: See *Hittul*.

GELILAH: Act of dressing the Torah scroll after the reading from it at a service. One who performs this honor is called the *golel*.

GEMARA: Aramaic, "completion" or "tradition." Popularly applied to the Jewish Talmud as a whole, to discussions by rabbinic teachers on Mishnah, and to decisions reached in these discussions. In a more restricted sense, the work of the generations of the *amora'im* in "completing" Mishnah to produce the Talmuds.

GEMATRIA: An interpretive device in Rabbinic Judaism that focuses on the numerical value of each word.

GEMILUT HASADIM: Deeds of loving-kindness, one of the three pillars on which the rabbis said the world rests.

GENIZAH: Heb. "hiding." A hiding place or storeroom, usually connected with a Jewish synagogue, for worn-out holy books. The most famous is the Cairo Genizah, which contained books and documents that provide source material on Jewish communities living under Islamic rule from about the ninth through the twelfth centuries. It was discovered at the end of the nineteenth century.

GEZEIRAH (pl. *gezeirot*): A law instituted by the rabbis to prevent people from unintentionally violating commandments.

GNOSTIC, GNOSTICISM: Derived from *gnosis*, meaning "knowledge." Refers to various systems of belief characterized by a dualistic view of reality—the God who created the material, phenomenal world is different from (often antithetical to) the ultimate (hidden) God of pure spirit. Possession of secret gnosis frees a person from the evil material world and gives access to the spiritual world. Gnostic thought had a great impact on the eastern Mediterranean world in the second to fourth centuries C.E., often in a Christian form.

GOLEL: See *gelilah*.

HAFTARAH (pl. *haftarot*): Specific section of the biblical prophets read in synagogue services immediately after the corresponding Torah (Pentateuch) section called the *parashah*.

HAGBAH: The act of holding the Torah scroll aloft for the entire congregation to see (opened wide enough for four columns of writing to be visible). The one who performs this honor is the *magbiah*.

HAGGADAH: The liturgical manual used in the Jewish Passover seder.

HAKAFAH (pl. *hakafot*): Procession around the sanctuary with the Torah scrolls.

HAKHAM (pl. *hakhamim* or *hakhmim*; "the wise"): A Jewish title given to pre–70 C.E. protorabbinic sages/scholars and post–70 C.E. rabbinic scholars.

HALAKHAH: Any normative Jewish law, custom, practice, or rite or the entire complex. *Halakhah* is law established or custom ratified by authoritative rabbinic jurists and teachers. Colloquially, if something is deemed halakhic, it is considered proper and normative behavior.

HALF KADDISH: See *Khatsi Kaddish*.

HA'SHEM: Lit. "The Name." Used by traditionally observant Jews so as to not actually utter one of the Names of God.

HASIDIM, HASIDISM: Heb. "pious ones." The term may refer to Jews in various periods: 1) a group that resisted the policies of Antiochus Epiphanes in the second century B.C.E. at the start of the Maccabean revolt; 2) pietists in the thirteenth century, known as the Ashkenazic Hasidim, much involved in mysticism of the period; 3) followers of the movement of Hasidism founded in the first half of the eighteenth century by Israel Ba'al Shem Tov.

HASKALAH: Jewish rationalistic "enlightenment" in eighteenth- and nineteenth-century Europe.

HAVDALAH: Heb., "separation." The Jewish prayer ceremony using wine, spices, and candles at the conclusion of the Sabbath or a Festival. Smelling the spices signifies the hope for a fragrant week; the light signifies the hope for a week of brightness and joy. Brief group of prayers that mark the end of Shabbat or a Festival.

HERMENEUTICS: Principles of interpretation (from the Greek, "to interpret, translate"). The term is often used with reference to the study of Jewish and Christian scriptures.

HITTUL: The belt that holds a Torah scroll closed when it is not in use. Also called a *mappah* and, in Yiddish, a *gartel*.

HUC-JIR: Hebrew Union College–Jewish Institute of Religion, the rabbinical seminary of the American Reform movement.

ISRAEL: A name given to the Jewish patriarch Ya'akov by God (*Bereishit* 35:9). In Jewish biblical times, this name refers to the northern tribes (as distinct from Judea, the southern tribes), but also to the entire nation. Historically, Jews have continued to regard themselves as the true continuation of the ancient Israelite national religious community. The term thus has a strong cultural sense. In modern times, it also refers to the political state of Israel.

IVRIT: Hebrew (in Hebrew).

JEHOVAH: Mechanical attempt to represent the special name for deity, *YHVH*, the Tetragrammaton (Greek, meaning "four letters").

JTS: Jewish Theological Seminary, rabbinical seminary of the Conservative movement in the United States. (The West Coast equivalent is the University of Judaism, in Los Angeles.)

KHAG SAMEAKH: Hebrew greeting on a Festival, meaning "happy holiday." (The Yiddish equivalent is *Gut Yuntif.*)

KHAI: Lit. "living or life." Word often used as a design on jewelry and other ornaments. Donations to charity are often made in multiples of eighteen, the numerical value of the word; hence, double Khai would be thirty-six.

KHATSI KADDISH: "Half kaddish," omitting the final three verses, recited at several points in liturgy as a separation between sections of the worship service.

KHAVURAH: Lit. "fellowship" or "companionship." A small worship circle, usually egalitarian in nature, led by laypeople rather than a rabbi.

KHAZAN: See Cantor.

KHILLUL HA'SHEM (khil LOOL hah-SHEM): Lit. "profanation of the Name." Causing God or Judaism to come into disrespect, or causing a person to violate a commandment.

KHUMASH (KHUH mish): Lit. "five." A compilation of the first five books of the Bible and readings from the Prophets, organized in the order of the weekly Torah portions.

KABBALAH: A system of Jewish theosophy and mysticism.

KABBALAT SHABBAT: Opening section of Shabbat evening service, "welcoming the Sabbath."

KADDISH: Prayer that extols the greatness of God. Best known as the Mourners' Prayer, *Kaddish* is said at other times during Jewish liturgy; the shortened version, the *Khatsi* (half) *Kaddish,* occurs as a punctuation at various points in the liturgy to separate sections.

KADDISH D'RABBANAN: *Kaddish* prayer extolling our teachers, recited after learning in a group (which includes sections of the *Shakharit* service that are considered Torah study).

KAHAL: Heb. "congregation, gathering." Used to refer to the corporate Jewish community of medieval Europe.

KARAISM, KARAITES: Derived from *qara,* "scripture." Group that arose in opposition to Rabbinism in the eighth century C.E., and emphasized the written scriptures while criticizing the rabbinic use of Oral Law.

KAVANAH: Lit. "intention" or "direction." The focus and concentration that is essential to meaningful prayer.

KEDUSHAH: Prayer proclaiming God's holiness, recited on Sabbath and Festivals.

KEHILLAH: Heb. "community." Jewish sense of community, in a particular sense, within the larger *knesset Israel.*

KETER (pl. *katerim*): Lit. "crown." The ornament, usually silver, that covers the staves of the Torah scroll when it is fully dressed. See also *rimonim.*

KETUVIM: Heb. "writings." The third and last division of the Jewish Bible *(Tanakh),* including large poetic and epigrammatic works such as *Tehillim* and *Mishlei* and *Iyov* as well as a miscellany of other writings *(Shir Ha'Shirim, Rut, Eikhah, Kohelet, Ester, Danyel, Ezra-Nekhemyah, Divrei Hayamim).*

KEVA: Fixed, as in prayers that have been written down and whose order is specified in the prayer book.

KIDDUSH HA'SHEM: Lit. "sanctification of the Name [of God]." One who dies a Jewish martyr is said to have died *kiddush Ha'Shem.*

KIPPAH: A headcovering worn for worship, religious study, meals, or at any other time; also called a *yarmulke.*

KIRUV: Outreach.

K'LAL YISRAEL: The community of Israel, that is, the Jewish people.

KNESSET: Lit. "assembly." The legislative branch of the present-day Israeli government.

KNESSET YISRAEL: "Assembly of Israel," or the Jewish people as a whole.

KOHEIN (pl. *kohanim*): The priestly caste in ancient Palestine. In a traditional congregation, a *kohein* will be given the first *aliyah* when the Torah is read.

KOSHER: "Proper" or "ritually correct." *Kashrut* refers to ritually correct Jewish dietary practices. Traditional Jewish dietary laws are based on biblical legislation. Only land animals that chew the cud and have split hooves (sheep, beef; not pigs, camels) are permitted and must be slaughtered in a special way. Furthermore, meat products may not be eaten with milk products or immediately thereafter. Of sea creatures, only those (fish) having fins and scales are permitted. Fowl is considered a meat food and also has to be slaughtered in a special manner *(shekhitah)*.

LADINO: The colloquial language of Sephardic Jews, based primarily on Spanish, with words taken from Hebrew, Arabic, and other languages, and written in the Hebrew alphabet.

LASHON HA'RA: Lit. "evil language." Encompasses all forms of forbidden speech (gossip, slander, lying, etc.).

LEVITES: Descendants of the tribe of Levi, dedicated to the service of the *kohanim*, the priestly caste. In a traditional synagogue, a Levite will be given the second *aliyah* when the Torah is read.

LIBERAL JEW: When used in the United States, it means an adherent to any of the non-Orthodox streams of Judaism. In the UK, refers to member of the British equivalent of Reform Judaism in the United States.

LIBERAL JUDAISM: British denomination similar to Reform Judaism in the United States.

LITURGY (adj. liturgical): Rites of public worship, usually institutionalized in relation to temple, synagogue, church, kaba, or mosque locations and traditions, but also in other formalized observances.

MA'ARIV: Evening service.

MAFTIR: The "concluder," one who has the final *aliyah* during the Torah reading and who reads the *haftarah*.

MAGBIAH: See *hagbah*.

MAGEN DAVID: Heb., "shield of David." The distinctive six pointed Jewish star, used especially since the seventeenth century.

MAGGID: Heb., "a speaker." A kabbalistic notion of how the holy spirit is mediated to the mystic; later meant a preacher among the eighteenth century Hasidim (as Dov Baer, the Maggid of Mezritch).

MAH TOVU: Hymn that begins *Shakharit* services, five verses from *B'midbar* and *Tehillim*, beginning *"Mah tovu ohalekha Ya'akov mishkenotkha Yisrael/How lovely are your tents, O Jacob, your dwelling places, O Israel."*

MAPPAH: See *hittul*.

MASORETES, MASORETIC TEXT: Derived from *masorah*, meaning "tradition." The Masoretes were scholars in ninth century Palestine who sought to preserve the traditional text of the Bible (hence called the Masoretic text), which is still used in contemporary synagogues. The Masoretes were scholars who encouraged Bible study and attempted to achieve uniformity by establishing rules for correcting the text in matters of spelling, grammar, and pronunciation.

MAZEL TOV: Means "congratulations" and "good luck" in Hebrew and Yiddish.

MEFORSHIM: Torah commentators from the rabbinic period.

MEGILLAH (pl. *megillot*): Lit. "scroll." Refers to one of the five scrolls read on special holidays: Sukkot—*Kohelet;* Purim—*Ester;* Pesakh—*Shir Ha'Shirim;* Shavuot—*Rut;* Tisha B'Av—*Eikhah.*

ME'IL: The mantle that covers a Torah scroll in Ashkenazic practice.

MEKHITZAH: The wall or curtain separating men from women during religious services in a traditionally observant synagogue.

MELAKHAH: Work, any of the categories of labor forbidden on the Sabbath.

MESSIAH: Lit. "anointed one." Ancient priests and kings (and sometimes prophets) of Israel were anointed with oil. In early Judaism, the term came to mean a royal descendant of the dynasty of David who would restore the united kingdom of Israel and Judah and usher in an age of peace, justice, and plenty; the redeemer figure. The concept developed in many directions over the centuries. The Messianic Age was believed by some Jews to be a time of perfection of human institutions; others believed it to be a time of radical new beginnings, a new heaven and earth, after divine judgment and destruction. The title came to be applied to Jesus/Joshua of Nazareth by his followers, who were soon called Christians in Greek and Latin usage (from the Greek word for anointed one, "christos." Jesus is also *Messiah* in Islam (e.g., Qur'an 3:45).

MEZUZAH (pl. *mezuzot*): Lit. "doorpost." A parchment scroll with selected Torah verses (*Devarim* 6:4–9; 11:13–21) placed in a container and affixed to the exterior doorposts (at the right side of the entrance) of Jewish homes (see *Devarim* 6:1–4), and sometimes also to interior doorposts of rooms. The word *Shaddai* ("Almighty") or the letter *shin* usually is inscribed on the container.

MIDRASH (pl. midrashim): From *darash,* "inquire," whence it comes to mean "exposition" (of scripture). Refers to the "commentary" literature developed in classical Judaism that attempts to interpret Jewish scriptures in a thorough manner. Literary Midrash may focus either on *halakhah,* directing the Jew to specific patterns of religious practice, or on *aggadah,* dealing with theological ideas, ethical teachings, popular philosophy, imaginative exposition, legend, allegory, animal fables, and so on—that is, whatever is not *halakhah.*

MIKRA'OT GEDOLOT: The Commentators' Bible, a single volume that incorporates the text of the entire *Khumash* and the commentaries on it authored by numerous important medieval and early modern rabbis, including Rashi, Ibn Ezra, and others.

MIKVAH: A ritual bath used for spiritual purification. It is used primarily in conversion rituals and after a woman's menstrual cycles, but many Hasidim immerse themselves in the *mikvah* regularly for general spiritual purification.

MINHAG (pl. *minhagim*): Custom that evolved for worthy religious reasons and has continued long enough to become a binding religious practice. The word is also used more loosely to describe any customary religious practice.

MINKHAH: Afternoon service.

MINYAN: A prayer quorum of ten Jews over the age of thirteen; in traditional congregations, only men are counted toward a minyan.

MI SHEBEIRAKH: Prayer for the well-being of one who is ill, has just given birth, or is about to be circumcised. Requested by an individual and read following the blessing after reading the Torah.

MISHNAH: Heb., "teaching." The digest of the recommended Jewish oral *halakhah* as it existed at the end of the second century and was collated, edited, and revised by Rabbi Yehudah Ha'Nasi. The work is the authoritative legal tradition of the early sages and is the basis of the legal discussions of the Talmud.

MITNAGED (pl. *mitnagdim*): Lit. "opposer(s)." Traditionalist and rationalistic Jewish opponents of eighteenth-century Jewish Hasidism.

MITZVAH (pl. *mitzvot*): Obligation or commandment. Colloquially, a good deed.

MODERN ORTHODOX: A branch of Orthodox Judaism found primarily in the United States. Believers in *halakhah* and traditionally observant, they also accept the importance of secular study, modern dress, and so forth.

MUSAF: "Additional" service that follows immediately after *Shakharit* on Sabbath and festivals.

MYSTIC, MYSTICISM (adj. mystical): From Greek for "initiant" into religious "mysteries." A vaguely used term to indicate certain types of behavior or perspective that goes beyond the rational in the quest of what is considered to be the ultimate in religious experience (often described as union or direct communion with deity). See also Kabbalah, Gnostic.

NAVI (pl. *nevi'im*): A prophet. *Nevi'im* became a designation for a section of the *Tanakh* encompassing the books of the Prophets.

NAZIR, NAZIRITE: Member of an ascetic sect within Judaism who took vows of abstinence from alcohol, did not cut his hair, and was not permitted to come into contact with the dead. The vows could last anywhere from brief time to an entire life. Shimshon/Samson is the most famous Nazirite.

NER TAMID: "Eternal light" that hangs in front of the ark in a synagogue.

NIKUDOT: The "dots" and other markings that indicate vowels in printed Hebrew. Hebrew that includes these is called "pointed," while texts that omit them—like the Torah scroll—are called "unpointed."

NUSAKH: Musical mode in which Torah is chanted and/or liturgy is sung. There are at least eight different modes that have developed from geographically disparate Jewish communities. In addition, there are different modes for Shabbat and the Festivals, for Morning, Afternoon, and Evening services.

OMER: The sheaf of grain offering brought to the Temple during Passover, on Nisan 16; thus also the name of the seven-week period between Passover and Shavuot.

ONAH: Obligation of a husband to sexually satisfy his wife (see *Shemot* 21:10).

ORAL LAW: In traditional Pharisaic/rabbinic thought, God reveals instructions for living both through the written scriptures—the Pentateuch—and through a parallel process of orally transmitted traditions. Critics of this approach within Judaism include Sadducees and Karaites.

ORTHODOX: The most traditionally observant stream of Judaism. See also Modern Orthodox, Hasidim, Hasidism; *Mitnaged.*

OU: Orthodox Union, the largest umbrella group of Modern Orthodox congregations in the United States, also the largest kosher-certifying body in the world (their hekhher is a capital *U* inside an *O*).

PALESTINE: Greek form representing "Philistines," for the seacoast population encountered by early geographers. An ancient designation for the area between Syria (to the north) and Egypt (to the south), between the Mediterranean Sea and the Yardein; roughly, modern Israel.

PARASHAH (pl. *parashiyot*). Heb., "section." Prescribed weekly section of biblical Torah (Pentateuch) read in synagogue liturgy on an annual cycle.

PAROKHET: The curtain (as distinguished from the doors) in front of the *aron ha'kodesh*.

PARSHANIM: Classical rabbinic Torah commentators.

PASSOVER (Heb., Pesakh): The major Jewish spring holiday (with agricultural aspects) also known as *khag ha'matzot* (festival of unleavened bread) commemorating the Exodus or deliverance of the Hebrew people from Egypt (see *Shemot* 12–13). The Festival lasts eight days, during which Jews refrain from eating all leavened foods and products. A special ritual meal (called the seder) is prepared the first two nights, and a traditional narrative (called the *haggadah*), supplemented by hymns and songs, marks the event.

PASUK: A verse of Torah.

PENTATEUCH: From Greek for "five books/scrolls." The five books attributed to Moshe: *Bereishit, Shemot, Vayikra, B'midbar,* and *Devarim;* known in Jewish tradition as *Torat Mosheh* (the teaching of Moses), or simply the Torah.

PEREK: A section of the Torah portion; each Torah portion has seven of them.

PESHAT: Interpretative method of reading Torah based on the "plain" meaning of a text.

PHARISEES: Heb. *perushim*, lit. "separatists." The name given to a group or movement in early Judaism, the origin and nature of which are unclear. Many scholars identify them with the later sages and rabbis who taught the Oral and Written Law; Sigal and some others see them as a complex of pietistic and zealous separatists, distinct from the protorabbis. According to Josephus, the Pharisees believed in the immortality of souls and resurrection of the dead, in a balance between predestination and free will, in angels as active divine agents, and in authoritative Oral Law. In the early Christian materials, Pharisees are often depicted as leading opponents of Jesus/Joshua and his followers, and are often linked with "scribes" but distinguished from the Sadducees.

PIKUAKH NEFESH: The principle that saving a life takes precedence over almost all other ritual obligations and overrides all other prohibitions except idolatry, murder, and immoral sexual behavior.

PSEUDEPIGRAPHA (adj. pseudepigraphical): From *pseudos,* "deceit, untruth," and *epigraphe,* "writing, inscription." A name given to a number of intertestamental apocryphal writings that are implausibly attributed to an ancient worthy such as Adam/Khavah, Enokh, Avraham, Moshe, Yeshayahu, Ezra, and so forth.

QUMRAN OR KHIRBET QUMRAN: The site near the northwest corner of the Dead Sea in modern Israel (West Bank) where the main bulk of the Jewish "Dead Sea Scrolls" were discovered abound 1946. The "Qumran community" that apparently produced the scrolls seems to have flourished from the third century B.C.E. to the first century C.E., and is usually identified with the Jewish Essenes, or a group like them.

RABBI: Lit. "teacher" or "master." Ordained expert in Jewish worship and law. An authorized teacher of the classical Jewish tradition (see Oral Law) after the fall of the Second Temple in 70 C.E. The role of the rabbi has changed considerably throughout the centuries. Traditionally, rabbis serve as the legal and spiritual guides of their congregations and communities. The title is conferred after considerable study of traditional Jewish sources. This conferral and its responsibilities is central to the chain of tradition in Judaism.

RABBINIC JUDAISM: A general term encompassing all movements of Judaism descended from Pharisaic Judaism.

RABBINICAL ASSEMBLY: Organization of the Conservative rabbinate in the United States.

REBBE: The title of the spiritual leader of the Hasidim; see *Tzaddik*.

REBBETZIN: Yid. The wife of a rabbi.

RECONSTRUCTIONIST JUDAISM: Founded by Mordecai M. Kaplan (1881–1982), this represents a recent development in American Judaism, and attempts to focus on Judaism as a civilization and culture constantly adapting to ensure survival in a natural social process. The central academic institution is the Reconstructionist Rabbinical College in the Philadelphia suburbs.

REDACTOR: An editor, especially with reference to ancient books such as the Jewish and Christian scriptures.

REFORM JUDAISM: Modern movement originating in eighteenth-century Europe that attempts to see Judaism as a rational religion adaptable to modern needs and sensitivities. The ancient traditions and laws are historical relics that need have no binding power over modern Jews. The central academic institution of American Reform Judaism is the Hebrew Union College, and it is represented also by the Central Conference of American Rabbis. Umbrella group of member congregation is the Union for Reform Judaism (formerly the Union of American Hebrew Congregations).

RESPONSA (sing. *responsum*): Also called *teshuvot*, from *she'elot u'teshuvot* (questions and answers); answers to questions on *halakhah* and observances, given by Jewish scholars on topics addressed to them. They originated during the geonic period, and are still used as a means of modern updating and revision of *halakhah*.

REVELATION: A general term for self-disclosure of the Divine (God reveals to humans), which is often considered to be focused in the revealed scriptures.

RIMONIM: Lit. "pomegranates." Elaborate silver ornaments shaped like the eponymous fruit and adorned with small bells, like those on the hem of the priestly robes. Sometimes used instead of *keterim*. See *Keter*.

ROSH KHODESH: Heb. "head of the month." The New Moon Festival.

ROSH YESHIVA (pl. *roshei yeshiva*): Head of a Talmudic academy.

RRC: Reconstructionist Rabbinical College, rabbinical seminary of the Reconstructionist movement in the United States.

SABBATH: Heb. Shabbat. The seventh day of the week, recalling the completion of the Creation and the Exodus from Egypt. It is a day symbolic of new beginnings and one dedicated to God, a most holy day of rest. The commandment of rest is found in the Bible and has been elaborated by the rabbis. It is a special duty to study Torah on the Sabbath and to be joyful. Sabbaths near major Festivals are known by special names.

SABBATIANISM: A messianic movement begun in the seventeenth century by Shabbetai Tzvi (1626–1676), who ultimately converted to Islam.

SADDUCEES: Sect of the Second Temple period, allied with the priestly caste in opposition to the Pharisees.

SAMARITANS: Another of the numerous subgroups in early Judaism (see also *Sadducees, Pharisees, Essenes*) and residents of the district of Samaria north of Jerusalem and

Judah in what is now Israel. They are said to have recognized only the Pentateuch as scripture and Mount Gerizim as the sacred center rather than Jerusalem. There was ongoing hostility between Samaritans and Judeans. Samaritan communities exist to the present.

SANHEDRIN: From Greek for "assembly" (of persons seated together). A legislative and judicial body from the period of early Judaism and into rabbinic times. Traditionally composed of seventy-one members.

SECOND TEMPLE: Rebuilt after the Babylonian Exile, the Temple stood in Jerusalem until it was destroyed by the Romans in 70 C.E. See also *Temple.*

SEDER: Lit. "order." The ritual dinner held on the first two nights of Passover.

SEDER KRI'AT HA'TORAH: Service for the reading of the Torah.

SEFER TORAH (pl. *sifrei Torah*): a Torah scroll.

SEFIRA (pl. *sefirot*): Heb., "counting, number." In Kabbalah, the *sefirot* are the primary emanations or manifestations of deity that together make up the fullness *(pleroma)* of the Godhead.

SEPHARDIM: The designation *Sepharad* in biblical times refers to a colony of exiles from Jerusalem (*Ovadiah* 20), possibly in or near Sardis; in the medieval period, Sephardic Jews are those descended from people who lived in Spain and Portugal (the Iberian peninsula) before the Expulsion of 1492. As a cultural designation, the term refers to the complex associated with Jews of this region and its related Diaspora in the Balkans and Middle East (especially in Islamic countries). The term is used in contradistinction to Ashkenazic, but it does not refer, thereby, to all Jews of non-Ashkenazic origin. See also *Ashkenazic.*

SEPTUAGINT: Strictly speaking, refers to the ancient Greek translation of the Hebrew Pentateuch, probably made during the reign of Ptolemy II, Greek ruler of Egypt around 250 B.C.E. Subsequently, Greek translations of other portions of the Jewish scriptures came to be added to the corpus, and the term *Septuagint* was applied to the entire collection. Such collections served as the "scriptures" for Greek-speaking Jews and Christians.

SIDDUR: From Heb. "to order." Jewish prayer book used for all days except special holidays (see Seder). See also Liturgy.

SIDRA (pl. *sidrot*). Section of the Torah read during a particular week. See *Parashah.*

SIMKHAT TORAH: Heb. "rejoicing with the Torah." A festival that celebrates the conclusion of the annual reading cycle of the Torah.

SOFER (pl. *soferim*): Heb. "scribe." Used as a general designation for scholars and copyists in both Talmudic and later literature; a "scholastic," a learned researcher whose vocation was the study and teaching of the tradition. In early times the *sofer* was the scholar. By the first century he was no longer a real scholar but a functionary and teacher of children. Today it usually refers to one who writes a Torah scroll.

SYNAGOGUE: Greek for "gathering." The central institution of Jewish communal worship and study since antiquity (see also *Bet midrash*) and, by extension, a term used for the place of gathering. The structure of such buildings has changed, though in all cases the ark containing the Torah scrolls faces the ancient Temple site in Jerusalem.

SHABBAT: Heb. The Jewish Sabbath, beginning at sundown Friday night and ending at sundown the following evening. (In Ashkenazic pronunciation, it is transliterated as *Shabbos*, in Yiddish usually as *Shabbes*.) See also Sabbath.

SHABBAT SHALOM: A greeting given on Shabbat, meaning "[may you have] the peace of the Sabbath."

SHAKHARIT: Morning service.

SHALIAKH TZIBUR: Heb. "messenger of the community." The lay leader of a service (not an ordained rabbi or cantor).

SHALOM BAYIT: Lit. "peace of the house." The principle that domestic tranquillity should be undisturbed as much as possible.

SHAMAS: Lit. "servant.

1) The candle that is used to light other Hanukah candles.

2) The janitor or caretaker of a synagogue.

SHAVUOT: Heb. "weeks." Observed fifty days from the day the first sheaf of grain was offered to the priests; also known as Festival of Firstfruits. Holiday celebrates the giving of the Torah at Sinai.

SHEKHINAH: Jewish term for the Divine Presence; the Holy Spirit. In Kabbalah it often took on the aspect of the feminine element in deity.

SHEM HA'MEFORASH: Heb. "The Forbidden Name." The Tetragrammaton.

SHEMINI ATZERET: The Eighth Day of Assembly. Festival that immediately follows the seven-day festival of Sukkot (Tabernacles).

SHEMOT: Lit. "Names." The book of Exodus.

SH'MA: Heb. "hear." Title of the fundamental, monotheistic statement of Judaism, found in *Devarim* 6:4 ("Hear, O Israel, the LORD is our God, the LORD is One" / *Sh'ma Yisrael YHVH Elohenu YHVH ekhad*). This statement avers the unity of God and is recited daily in the liturgy (along with *Devarim* 6:5–9, *Devarim* 11:13–21, *B'midbar* 15:37–41, and other passages), and customarily before sleep at night. This proclamation also climaxes special liturgies (like Yom Kippur) and is central to the confession before death and the ritual of martyrdom. The *Sh'ma* is inscribed on the *mezuzah* and the *tefillin*. In public services, it is recited in unison.

SHOFAR: Ram's horn sounded at Rosh Hashanah morning worship and at the conclusion of Yom Kippur, as well as other times in that period during the fall.

SHUL: Yid. "synagogue."

SHULKHAN ARUKH: Lit. "the prepared table." Sixteenth-century compilation of Jewish ritual laws, put together by Joseph Caro, considered authoritative by most traditionally observant Jews.

TAKANAH (pl. *takanot*): A law instituted by the rabbis and not derived from any biblical commandment.

TAKHANUN: Prayer of supplication, requesting grace and forgiveness from God, recited daily in *Shakharit* Service, except on Shabbat, Festivals, and joyous occasions like weddings.

TALLIT: A large, four cornered shawl with fringes and special knots at the extremities, worn during Jewish morning prayers. The fringes, according to the Bible (*B'midbar* 15:38–39), remind the worshipper of God's commandments. It is traditional for the male to be buried in his *tallit*, but with its fringes cut off.

TALMUD: Heb. "study" or "learning." Rabbinic Judaism produced two Talmuds: the one known as "Babylonian" is the most famous in the Western world and was completed around the fifth century C.E.; the other, known as the "Palestinian" or "Jerusalem" Talmud, was edited perhaps in the early fourth century C.E. Both have as their common core the Mishnah collection of the *tanna'im*, to which are added commentary and discussion (Gemara) by the *amora'im* (teachers) of the respective locales. Gemara thus has also become a colloquial, generic term for the Talmud and its study.

TANAKH *(Tanakh):* A relatively modern acronym for the Jewish Bible, made up of the names of the three parts of *Torah* (Pentateuch or Law), *Nevi'im* (Prophets), and *Ketuvim* (Writings).

TANNA: (adj. tannaitic; pl. *tanna'im*): Heb. "repeater, reciter." A Jewish sage from the period of Hillel (around the turn of the era) to the compilation of the Mishnah (200 C.E.), distinguished from later *amora'im*. *Tanna'im* were primarily scholars and teachers. The Mishnah, Tosefta, and halakhic midrashim were among their literary achievements.

TARGUM: Heb., "translation, interpretation." Generally used to designate Aramaic translations of the Jewish scriptures. See also Septuagint (in a sense, Greek *Targums*).

TARYAG MITZVOT (or *Taryag*): The 613 *mitzvot* prescribed in the Torah.

TEFILLAH: Heb. "prayer." The Amidah, the standing prayer, is often referred to as Ha'Tefillah, "The Prayer."

TEFILLIN: Usually translated as "phylacteries." Boxlike appurtenances that accompany prayer, worn by adult males (and now some females as well) at the weekday *Shakharit* services. The boxes have leather thongs attached and contain scriptural excerpts. One box (with four sections) is placed on the head. The other (with one section) is placed (customarily) on the left arm, near the heart. The biblical passages emphasize the unity of God and the duty to love God and be mindful of him with "all one's heart and mind" (e.g., *Shemot* 13:1–10, *Shemot* 13:11–16, *Devarim* 6:4–9, and *Devarim* 11:13–21). See also *sh'ma*.

TEMPLE: In the ancient world, temples were the centers of outward religious life, places at which public religious observances were normally conducted by the priestly professionals. In traditional Judaism, the only legitimate Temple was the one in Jerusalem, built first by King Shelomo around 950 B.C.E., destroyed by Babylonian king Nebuchadnetzar around 587/6 B.C.E., and rebuilt about seventy years later. It was destroyed by the Romans in 70 C.E. The site of the ancient Jewish Temple is now occupied, in part, by the golden-domed Dome of the Rock Mosque. In recent times, *temple* has come to be used synonymously with *synagogue* in some Jewish usage (but never by Orthodox Jews, for whom the only "temple" is the Temple in Jerusalem).

TESHUVAH: Heb. "turning," "repentance." Turning away from sin, toward the good. It is the central goal of the days between Rosh Hashanah and Yom Kippur.

TETRAGRAMMATON: Greek, "four-lettered (name)." The four-letter "forbidden name" of God. See also Jehovah, *Shem Ha'Meforash*, YHVH.

THEOGONY: The study of the origins of God(s).

THEOLOGY: The study of God and the relations between God and the universe.

THEOSOPHY: Study of the nature of the Godhead.

TIK: The wooden case within which a Torah scroll is kept in Sephardic practice.

TISHA B'AV: The ninth of the Hebrew month Av. A twenty-five-hour fast day that commemorates the destruction of both the First and Second Temples.

TORAH: Heb., "teaching, instruction." In general, Torah refers to study of the whole gamut of Jewish tradition or to some aspect thereof. In its special sense, "the Torah" refers to the Five Books of Moses in the Hebrew scriptures (see Pentateuch). In the Koran, incidentally, "Torah" is the main term by which Jewish scripture is identified.

TOSAFISTS: Generation of Talmudic interpreters after Rashi. Best known as exponents of *pilpul*, hairsplitting dialectical exegesis of Talmud.

TOSEFTA (pl. *Tosafot*): Heb. "supplement." Tannaitic supplements to the Mishnah. Called *baraita* (extraneous material) in the Talmud.

TZADDIK: Heb. "righteous one." A general term for a righteous person in Jewish tradition. More specifically, the spiritual leader of the modern Hasidim, popularly known as rebbe.

TZEDAKAH: Heb., "righteousness," "justice." Term in Judaism usually applied to deeds of charity and philanthropy.

TZIZIT: Heb. "fringes." See *tallit*.

UNITED SYNAGOGUES OF CONSERVATIVE JUDAISM: Umbrella organization of Conservative congregations in the United States.

URJ: Union for Reform Judaism, formerly Union of American Hebrew Congregations, umbrella organization of Reform congregations in the United States.

UTJ: Union for Traditional Judaism, umbrella organization of Traditional congregations in the United States.

YAD: Lit. "hand." Hand-shaped pointer used while reading from Torah scrolls.

YAHRZEIT: Yid. "anniversary." The anniversary of the death of a close relative.

YAMIM NORA'IM: Days of Awe. Hebrew name for the High Holy Days (Rosh Hashanah, Yom Kippur, and the ten-day period that separates them).

YARMULKE: See *kippah*.

YESHIVA (pl. *yeshivot*): From the Hebrew meaning "seated." A Jewish rabbinic academy of higher learning. See also *Bet midrash*.

YETZER HA'RA: The inclination to do evil.

YETZER HA'TOV: The inclination to do good.

YHVH (Yahweh): The sacred name of God in Jewish scriptures and tradition; also known as the Tetragrammaton. Since Hebrew was written without vowels in ancient times, the four consonants YHVH contain no clue to their original pronunciation. They are generally rendered *Yahweh* in contemporary scholarship. In traditional Judaism, the name is not pronounced, but *Adonai* ("Our Lord") or something similar is substituted. In most English versions of the Bible the Tetragrammaton is represented by *LORD* (or less frequently, *Jehovah*).

YIDDISH: From German *Juedisch* or Jewish. The vernacular of Ashkenazic Jews; it is a combination of several languages, especially Hebrew and German, written in Hebrew script.

YOM KIPPUR: Heb. "Day of Atonement." Annual day of fasting and atonement, occurring in the fall on 10 Tishri (just after Rosh Hashanah); the most solemn and important occasion of the religious year.

ZEALOT: From Greek, "to be enthusiastic." A general term for one who exhibits great enthusiasm and dedication to a cause. Specifically, a member of an early Jewish group or perspective that advocated Jewish independence from Rome.

ZION, ZIONISM: (Mount) Zion is an ancient Hebrew designation for Jerusalem, but already in biblical times it began to symbolize the national homeland (see *Tehillim* 137:1–6). In this latter sense it served as a focus for Jewish national religious hopes of renewal over the centuries. Ancient hopes and attachments to Zion gave rise to Zionist longings and movements since antiquity, culminating in the modern national liberation movement of that name. The Zionist cause helped the Jews return to Palestine in this century and found the state of Israel in 1948. The goal of Zionism is the political and spiritual renewal of the Jewish people in its ancestral homeland.

z'L: Abbreviation for *zikhrona u'livrakha/may his memory be a blessing,* frequently placed after the name of someone who is dead.

z'MIROT: Shabbat table songs.

ZOHAR: "Book of Splendor." The chief literary work of the kabbalists. The author of the main part of the *Zohar* was Moses de Leon (twelfth century) in Spain, but it is pseudepigraphically ascribed to the Palestinian *tanna* Shimon bar Yokhai (second century C.E.).

BIBLIOGRAPHY

I have marked with an asterisk the books that I believe will prove particularly helpful to a beginner.

KHUMASHIM

There are probably at least a thousand translations of the Torah into English. I have listed a few that I found particularly helpful. It should be noted that many of the commentaries cited elsewhere in this bibliography include complete translations of the *Khumash* as well (particularly any edition of Rashi).

Adler, Elkan, and Solomon Schechter. "Genizah." *The Jewish Encyclopedia* (originally published in 1905, now available in its entirety at http://www.jewish encyclopedia.com).

Ben Yashar, Menachem. " 'And I Will Harden the Heart of Pharoah.' " *Lectures on the Torah Reading.* Bar-Ilan University, 1998 (Ramat Gan, Israel). http://www.biu.ac.il/JH/Parasha/eng/vaera/yashar.html.

*Berlin, Adele, Marc Zvi Brettler, and Michael Fishbane, eds. *The New Jewish Bible.* New York: Oxford University Press, 2003.

Cohen, Howard, "Reconciliation and Change." *A Reconstructionist D'var Torah,* December 15, 2000. http://www2.jrf.org/recon-dt/dt.php?id=22.

*Fox, Everett, comm. and trans. *The Five Books of Moses: Genesis Exodus, Leviticus, Numbers, and Deuteronomy.* New York: Schocken Books, 1995.

*Friedman, Richard Elliott. *Commentary on the Torah, with a New English Translation and the Hebrew Text.* San Francisco: HarperCollins San Francisco, 2001.

Hertz, J. H., ed. *The Pentateuch and Haftorahs.* 2nd ed. London: Soncino Press, 1979.

*Lieber, David, sr. ed. *Etz Hayim: Torah and Commentary.* Philadelphia: Jewish Publication Society, 2003.

*Plaut, W. Gunther, ed. *The Torah: A Modern Commentary.* New York: Union of American Hebrew Congregations, 1981.

The Torah: The Five Books of Moses: The New JPS Translation of the Holy Scriptures According to the Traditional Masoretic Text. Philadelphia: Jewish Publication Society, 1962.

Zlotowitz, Meir, trans. and annot. *The Family Chumash: Bereishit.* Brooklyn, N.Y.: Mesorah Publications, 1989.

OVERVIEW, BACKGROUND, AND REFERENCE

Agnon, S. Y. *Present at Sinai: The Giving of the Law,* trans. Michael Swirsky. Philadelphia: Jewish Publication Society, 1994.

*Alter, Robert. *The Art of Biblical Narrative.* New York: Basic Books, 1981.

Alter, Robert and Frank Kermode, eds. *The Literary Guide to the Bible.* Cambridge, Mass.: Harvard University Press, 1987.

Amsel, Nachum. *The Jewish Encyclopedia of Moral and Ethical Issues.* Northvale, N.J.: Jason Aronson, 1996.

Bamberger, Bernard J. *The Bible: A Modern Jewish Approach.* New York: Schocken Books, 1963.

Bark, Franziska. "The God Who Will Be and the Generations of Men: Time and the Torah." *Judaism* 49:195 (Summer 2000).

Ben-Sasson, H. H., ed. *A History of the Jewish People.* Cambridge, Mass.: Harvard University Press, 1976.

Bialik, Hayim Nahman, and Yehoshua Hana Ravnitzky. *The Book of Legend / Sefer Ha-Aggadah: Legends from the Talmud and Midrash.* New York: Schocken Books, 1992.

Birnbaum, Philip. *A Book of Jewish Concepts.* New York: Hebrew Publishing Company, 1964.

*Bonchek, Avigdor. *Studying the Torah: A Guide to In-Depth Interpretation.* Northvale, N.J.: Jason Aronson, 1996.

Borowitz, Eugene. "Freedom." In *Contemporary Jewish Thought,* ed. Arthur A. Cohen and Paul Mendes-Flohr, pp. 261–67. New York: Free Press, 1987.

Brams, Steven J. *Biblical Games: Game Theory and the Hebrew Bible.* Cambridge, Mass.: MIT Press, 2003.

Brown, Francis, with S. R. Driver and Charles A. Briggs. *The Brown-Driver-Briggs Hebrew and English Lexicon.* Peabody, Mass.: Hendrickson Publishers, 1997.

Buxbaum, Yitzhak. *Jewish Spiritual Practices.* Northvale, N.J.: Jason Aronson, 1990.

Carmell, Aryeh. *Aiding Torah Study.* Spring Valley, N.Y.: Feldheim Publishers, 1988.

*Cohen, Norman. *The Way Into Torah.* Woodstock, Vt.: Jewish Lights, 2000.

Donin, Hayim Halevy. *To Be a Jew.* New York: Basic Books, 1972.

Dorff, Elliot N. *Knowing God: Jewish Journeys to the Unknowable.* Northvale, N.J.: Jason Aronson, 1992.

Ecker, Ronald L. *And Adam Knew Eve: A Dictionary of Sex in the Bible.* Electronic ed., 2005. http://www.hobrad.com/and.htm.

Editors of *Commentary Magazine,* eds. *The Condition of Jewish Belief.* New York: Macmillan, 1966.

Eisen, Arnold. "Covenant." In *Contemporary Jewish Thought,* ed. Arthur A. Cohen and Paul Mendes-Flohr, pp. 107–112. New York: Free Press, 1987.

———. "Exile." In *Contemporary Jewish Thought,* ed. Arthur A. Cohen and Paul Mendes-Flohr, pp. 219–25. New York: Free Press, 1987.

———. *Taking Hold of Torah: Jewish Commitment and Continuity in America* (Bloomington, Ind.: Indiana University Press, 1997).

*Eisenberg, Azriel. *The Book of Books: The Story of the Bible Text.* London: Soncino Press, 1976.

Eisenstein, J. D. *Commentary on the Torah.* New York: Pardes Publications, 1960.

Etshalom, Yitzchak. "Parashat Mattot/Mas'ei." Siyyum on Sefer B'midbar, July 2001. http://www.torah.org.

Feiler, Bruce. *Walking the Bible: A Journey by Land Through the Five Books of Moses.* New York: William Morrow, 2001.

Frand, Yissocher, "When Do We Say 'It Was Good' About Division?" *Rav Frand on Parashas Bereishit,* October 15, 1998. e-mail list ryfrand@torah.org.

Franzel, Jordan. "Which Came First—the Doing or the Understanding?" *Torat Hayim*, 2000. http://urj.org/Articles/index.cfm?id=2744&pge_prg_id=32903&pge_id=3448.

Freedman, David Noel. *The Unity of the Hebrew Bible*. Ann Arbor: University of Michigan Press, 1991.

Freedman, David Noel, with Jeffrey C. Geoghegan and Michael M. Homan. *The Nine Commandments: Uncovering a Hidden Pattern of Crime and Punishment in the Hebrew Bible*, ed. Astrid B. Beck. New York: Anchor Bible Reference Library/Doubleday, 2000.

Gersh, Harry. *The Sacred Books of the Jews*. New York: Stein and Day, 1968.

*Gillman, Neil. *The Way Into Encountering God in Judaism*. Woodstock, Vt.: Jewish Lights, 2000.

Golan, Shimon. "A Candelabrum of Pure Gold." *Lectures on the Torah Reading*. Bar-Ilan University, 1998. (Ramat Gan, Israel). http://www.biu.ac.il/JH/Parasha/eng/teruma/golan.html.

Goodman, Roberta Louis. "The Tenth Plague—A Test of Whose Faith." *Torat Hayim*, 1998. http://urj.org/Articles/index.cfm?id=3035&pge_prg_id=32322&pge_id=3448.

Greenstein, Edward L. "Biblical Law." In *Back to the Sources: Reading the Classic Jewish Texts*, ed. Barry W. Holtz, pp. 23–103. New York: Summit Books, 1984.

Grossman, Yonatan, "The Census of the Leviim" *Virtual Bet Midrash*, 1997. http://www.vbm-torah.org/parsha.59/34bamid.htm

Guggenheimer, Heinrich W., trans. and comm. *Seder Olam: The Rabbinic View of Biblical Chronology*. Northvale, N.J.: Jason Aronson, 1998.

Hahn, Jerome S. *Bible Basics: An Introduction and Reference Guide to the Five Books of Moses*. Boca Raton, Fla.: International Traditions Corporation, 1996.

Hirsch, Ammiel, and Yosef Reinman. *One People, Two Worlds: A Reform Rabbi and an Orthodox Rabbi Explore the Issues That Divide Them*. New York: Schocken Books, 2002.

*Holtz, Barry W., ed. *Back to the Sources: Reading the Classic Jewish Texts*. New York: Summit Books, 1984.

Isaacs, Ronald H. *The Jewish Bible Almanac*. Northvale, N.J.: Jason Aronson, 1997.

———. *Miracles: A Jewish Perspective*. Northvale, N.J.: Jason Aronson, 1997.

Jeffrey, David Lyle, gen. ed. *A Dictionary of Biblical Tradition in English Literature*. Grand Rapids, Mich.: Wm. B. Eerdmans, 1992.

The Jewish Encyclopedia. Originally published in 1905. Now available in its entirety at http://www.jewishencyclopedia.com.

*Kugel, James L. *The Bible As It Was*. Cambridge, Mass.: Harvard University Press, 1997.

———. *The God of Old: Inside the Lost World of the Bible*. New York: Free Press, 2003.

———. "Torah." In *Contemporary Jewish Thought*, ed. Arthur A. Cohen and Paul Mendes-Flohr, pp. 995–1005. New York: Free Press, 1987.

Leibowitz, Yeshayahu. "Commandments." In *Contemporary Jewish Thought*, ed. Arthur A. Cohen and Paul Mendes-Flohr, pp. 67–80. New York: Free Press, 1987.

*Levenson, Jon D. *Sinai and Zion: An Entry Into the Jewish Bible*. New York: Harper-Collins, 1985.

Lichtenstein, Murray H. "Biblical Poetry." In *Back to the Sources: Reading the Classic Jewish Texts*, ed. Barry W. Holtz, pp. 105–27. New York: Summit Books, 1984.

Lipner, Pinchas. "Torah Study Builds Faith, Strength to Sustain Us Through Difficulties." *Jewish Bulletin of Northern California*, June 27, 2003.

Mihaly, Eugene. *A Song to Creation: A Dialogue with Text.* Cincinnati, Ohio: Hebrew Union College Press, 1975.

Musaph-Andriesse, R. C. *From Torah to Kabbalah: A Basic Introduction to the Writings of Judaism.* New York: Oxford University Press, 1981.

Neusner, Jacob, editor in chief, and William Scott Green, ed. *Dictionary of Judaism in the Biblical Period: 450 B.C.E. to 600 C.E.* Vol. 2. New York: Macmillan Library Reference USA, 1996.

Nulman, Macy. *The Encyclopedia of the Sayings of the Jewish People.* Northvale, N.J.: Jason Aronson, 1997.

Olitzky, Kerry M., and Ronald H. Isaacs. *A Glossary of Jewish Life.* Northvale, N.J.: Jason Aronson, 1996.

Pollack, Robert. *The Faith of Biology and the Biology of Faith.* New York: Columbia University Press, 2000.

Rabinovitch, Nahum Eliezer. "The Way of Torah." *Edah Journal* 3:1 (2003).

Rabinowicz, Tzvi M. *The Encyclopedia of Hasidism.* Northvale, N.J.: Jason Aronson, 1996.

Reed, Walter D., and Fay Sand. *Contract With God.* New York: Four Seasons Publishers, 1965.

*Robinson, George. *Essential Judaism: A Complete Guide to Beliefs, Rituals and Customs.* New York: Pocket Books, 2000.

Rosenberg, Joel. "Biblical Narrative." In *Back to the Sources: Reading the Classic Jewish Texts,* ed. Barry W. Holtz, pp. 31–81. New York: Summit Books, 1984.

Rosenberg, Shalom. *Good and Evil in Jewish Thought.* Tel Aviv: MOD Books, 1989.

Rosenzweig, Michael L. "Live History Data in the Bible, From Abraham to Joshua." *Judaism* 29:115 (Summer 1980): 353–59.

Sandmel, Samuel. *The Hebrew Scriptures: An Introduction to Their Literature and Religious Ideas.* New York: Alfred A. Knopf, 1963.

Twain, Mark. *The Bible According to Mark Twain: Writings on Heaven, Eden, and the Flood.* Ed. Howard G. Baetzold and Joseph B. McCullough. Athens: University of Georgia Press, 1995.

*Visotzky, Burton L. *Reading the Book: Making the Bible a Timeless Text.* New York: Schocken Books, 1996.

Wigoder, Geoffrey, and R. J. Zwi Werblowsky, eds. *The Encyclopedia of the Jewish Religion.* New York: Adama Books, 1986.

Yoder, Perry. "Biblical Hebrew." In *Versification: Major Language Types,* ed. William K. Wimsatt. New York: New York University Press, 1972.

Zakovich, Yair. *The Concept of the Miracle in the Bible.* Tel Aviv: MOD Books, 1991.

TORAH AND LITURGY, TORAH AS RITUAL OBJECT

Dobrinsky, Herbert C. *A Treasury of Sephardic Laws and Customs: The Ritual Practices of Syrian, Moroccan, Judeo-Spanish and Spanish and Portuguese Jews of North America.* Rev. ed. Hoboken, N.J., and New York: Ktav/Yeshiva University Press, 1988.

Elbogen, Ismar. *Jewish Liturgy: A Comprehensive History.* Trans. Raymond P. Scheindlin. Philadelphia: Jewish Publication Society; New York: Jewish Theological Seminary of America, 1993.

Fine, Steven. *This Holy Place: On the Sanctity of the Synagogue During the Greco-Roman Period.* South Bend, Ind.: University of Notre Dame Press, 1997.

Frankel, Ellen, and Betsy Platkin Teutsch. *The Encyclopedia of Jewish Symbols.* Northvale, N.J.: Jason Aronson, 1992.

Handelman, Susan. *The Slayers of Moses: The Emergence of Rabbinic Interpretation in Modern Literary Theory.* Ithaca, N.Y.: State University of New York, 1982.

Henkin, Yehuda. *New Interpretations on the Parsha.* Jersey City, N.J.: Ktav Publishing House, 2000.

Hirsch, Samson Raphael. *Horeb: Philosophy of Jewish Laws and Observances.* Trans. I. Grunfeld. New York: Soncino Press, 1962.

Hoffman, Lawrence A. *The Canonization of the Synagogue Service.* South Bend, Ind.: University of Notre Dame Press, 1979.

*Hoffman, Lawrence, ed. *My People Prayerbook.* Vol. 4: *Seder K'riat Ha'Torah.* Woodstock, Vt.: Jewish Lights, 2000.

*Kolatch, Alfred J. *This Is the Torah.* Middle Village, N.Y.: Jonathan David Publishers, 1994.

Latner, Helen. *The Book of Modern Jewish Etiquette: A Guide for All Occasions.* New York: Schocken Books, 1981.

Levine, Lee I. *The Ancient Synagogue: The First Thousand Years.* New Haven, Conn.: Yale University Press, 2000.

Milgrom, Abraham. *Jewish Worship.* Philadelphia: Jewish Publication Society, 1971.

Munk, Elie. *The World of Prayer.* 2 vols. New York: Feldheim, 1961, 1963.

Nulman, Macy. *The Encyclopedia of Jewish Prayer.* Northvale, N.J.: Jason Aronson, 1996.

Pinchas, Mordechai. http://www.bayit02.freeserve.co.uk/index.html.

Portnoy, Marshall, and Josée Wolff. *The Art of Torah Cantillation: A Step-by-Step Guide to Chanting Torah.* New York: UAHC Press, 2000.

Rubenstein, Shmuel L. *The Sefer Torah: An Illustrated Analysis of the History, Preparation and Use of the Sefer Torah.* New York: Zeirei Agudath Israel, 1976.

Sender, Yitzchak. *The Commentators' Siddur: Insights of the Sages on the Weekday Prayers.* Spring Valley, N.Y.: Philip Feldheim, 1995.

Sheffer, Shlomoh. "Parashat Shemot: The Commandment of Reading the Torah in Public." Bar-Ilan University, 1996. www.biu.ac.il/JH/Eparasha/shemot/sheffer.html.

Slotki, Israel W., trans. "Sefer Torah," *The Minor Tractates of the Talmud.* Vol. 2. London: Soncino Press, 1965.

Trepp, Leo. *The Complete Book of Jewish Observance.* New York: Behrman House/Summit Books, 1980.

THE WRITING AND EDITING OF THE TORAH

Akenson, Donald Harman. *Surpassing Wonder: The Invention of the Bible and the Talmuds.* New York: Harcourt Brace, 1998.

Barton, John. "The Literary History of the Pentateuch (Documentary Hypothesis)." http://www.ucalgary.ca/~eslinger/genrels/DocHypothesis.html.

Bigman, David. "Finding a Home for Critical Talmud Study." *Edah Journal* 1:2 (Sivan, 5761).

Cohen, Menachem. "The Idea of the Sanctity of the Biblical Text and the Science of Textual Criticism." http://cs.anu.edu.au/people/bdm/dilugim/CohenArt.

Eisenstein, J. D. *Commentary on the Torah.* New York: Pardes, 1960.

Freedman, David Noel. *The Unity of the Hebrew Bible.* Ann Arbor: University of Michigan Press, 1991.

Friedman, Richard Elliott. *The Hidden Book in the Bible: The Discovery of the First Prose Masterpiece.* San Francisco: Harper San Francisco, 1998.

*———. *Who Wrote the Bible?* New York: Summit Books, 1987.

Greene, Toby. "Ezra as Editor." *The Jewish Quarterly*, no. 189 (Spring 2003): 86–88.

Halivni, David Weiss. *Revelation Restored: Divine Writ and Critical Responses.* Boulder, Colo.: Westview Press, 1997.

Helfand, Jonathan. "Striving for Truth: Struggling with the Historical Critical Method." *The Edah Journal* 2:1 (Tevet, 5762):

Levy, B. Barry. "Text and Context: Torah and Historical Truth." *The Edah Journal* 2:1 (Tevet, 5762)

*Margolis, Max L. *Hebrew Scriptures in the Making.* Philadelphia: Jewish Publication Society, 1922.

Navon, Chaim. "Theological Issues in Sefer Bereishit: Lecture 5—Biblical Criticism." Yeshivat Har Etzion, 2004. http://vbm-torah.org/archive/bereishit/05bereishit.htm.

Reif, Stefan C. "The Cairo Genizah: A Medieval Mediterranean Deposit and a Modern Cambridge Archive." Paper delivered at 66th International Federation of Library Associations Council and Conference, Jerusalem, August 13–18, 2000. http://www.ifla.org/IV/ifla66/papers/058–145e.htm.

Rofé, Alexander. *Introduction to the Composition of the Pentateuch.* Sheffield, U.K.: Sheffield Academic Press, 1999.

Schniedwind, William M. *How the Bible Became a Book.* Cambridge, U.K.: Cambridge University Press, 2004.

*Shanks, Hershel. *The Mystery and Meaning of the Dead Sea Scrolls.* New York: Vintage Books, 1998.

Solomon, Norman. "Torah From Heaven: The Sherman Lectures 2001." www.art.man.ac.uk/RELTHEOL/JEWISH/sherman01.htm.

Vermes, Geza. *The Complete Dead Sea Scrolls in English.* New York: Penguin Books, 1997.

Weingreen, J. *Introduction to the Critical Study of the Text of the Hebrew Bible.* London: Clarendon Press, 1982.

*Zerin, Edward. *The Birth of the Torah.* New York: Appleton-Crofts-Century, 1961.

TORAH COMMENTARY

*Aminoah, Noah, and Yosef Nitzan. *Torah—The Oral Tradition: An Outline of Rabbinic Literature Throughout the Ages.* Trans. Haim Shachter and Larry Moscovitz. Jerusalem: World Zionist Organization, 1983.

Batnitzky, Leora. "Translation as Transcendance: A Glimpse Into the Workshop of the Buber-Rosenzweig Bible Translation." *New German Critique,* no. 70 (Winter 1997): 87–116.

Bertman, Martin A. "Buber: Mysticism Without Loss of Identity." *Judaism* 49:193 (Winter 2000): 81–92.

Bialik, Hayim Nakhman. "Halakhah and Aggadah." In *Modern Jewish Thought,* ed. Nahum Glatzer, pp. 55–64. New York: Schocken Books, 1977.

Bialik, Hayim Nakhman, and Yehuda Ravnitzky. *The Book of Legends/Sefer Ha-Aggadah: Legends from the Talmud and Midrash.* Trans. William G. Braude. New York: Schocken Books, 1992.

Buber, Martin, and Franz Rosenzweig. *Scripture and Translation.* Trans. Lawrence Rosenwald, with Everett Fox. Bloomington: Indiana University Press, 1994.

Casper, Bernard M. *An Introduction to Jewish Bible Commentary.* London: Thomas Yosseloff, 1960.

Cohn-Sherbok, Dan. *Fifty Key Jewish Thinkers.* London: Routledge, 1997.

Dan, Joseph. Introduction to *The Early Kabbalah.* New York: Paulist Press, 1986.

Epstein, Isidore. "Maimonides." In *Jewish Philosophy and Philosophers,* ed. Raymond Goldwater, pp. 41–81. London: Hillel Foundation, 1962.

Fine, Lawrence. "Kabbalistic Texts." In *Back to the Sources: Reading the Classic Jewish Texts,* ed. Barry W. Holtz, pp. 305–59. New York: Summit Books, 1984.

Finkel, Avraham Yaakov. *The Great Chasidic Masters.* Northvale, N.J.: Jason Aronson, 1992.

———. *The Great Torah Commentators.* Northvale, N.J.: Jason Aronson, 1990.

———. *The Responsa Anthology.* Northvale, N.J.: Jason Aronson, 1990.

Fishbane, Michael. *The Exegetical Imagination: On Jewish Thought and Theology.* Cambridge, Mass.: Harvard University Press, 1999.

Freehof, Solomon B. *A Treasury of Responsa.* Philadelphia: Jewish Publication Society, 1962.

Friedlander, M. *Essays on the Writings of Abraham ibn Ezra.* London: Publications of the Society of Hebrew Literature, 1877.

Gimani, Aharon. " 'They said to one another, "What is it?" ' . . . "That is the bread." ' " Commentary on *parashat Beshalakh,* February 23, 1998. http://www.biu.ac.il/JH/Parasha/eng/beshalah/gimani.html.

*Ginzburg, Louis. *Legends of the Jews.* Trans. Henrietta Szold. 7 vols. Baltimore, Md.: Johns Hopkins University Press, 1998.

Glatzer, Nahum. *Hammer on the Rock: A Midrash Anthology.* New York: Schocken Books, 1962.

Goldenberg, Robert. "Talmud." In *Back to the Sources: Reading the Classic Jewish Texts* ed. Barry W. Holtz, pp. 29–175. New York: Summit Books, 1984.

Goldwurm, Hersh, ed. *The Rishonim: Biographical Sketches of the Prominent Early Rabbinic Sages and Leaders from the Tenth-Fifteenth Centuries.* Based on research by Shmuel Teich. Brooklyn, N.Y.: Mesorah Publications, 1982.

*Green, Arthur. *A Guide to the Zohar.* Stanford, Calif.: Stanford University Press, 2004.
———. "Teachings of the Hasidic Masters." In *Back to the Sources: Reading the Classic Jewish Texts,* ed. Barry W. Holtz, pp. 361–401. New York: Summit Books, 1984.
Greenstein, Edward L. "Medieval Bible Commentary." In *Back to the Sources: Reading the Classic Jewish Texts,* ed. Barry W. Holtz, pp. 213–59. New York: Summit Books, 1984.
Hepner, Gershon. "Verbal Resonance in the Bible and Intertextuality." *Journal for the Study of the Old Testament,* 96 (2001): 3–27.
Heschel, Abraham Joshua. *Maimonides: The Life and Times of the Great Medieval Jewish Thinker.* New York: Doubleday, 1982.
Holtz, Barry W. "Midrash." In *Back to the Sources: Reading the Classic Jewish Texts,* ed. Barry W. Holtz, pp. 177–211. New York: Summit Books, 1984.
Kalmin, Richard. *Sages, Stories, Authors and Editors in Rabbinic Babylon.* Providence, R.I.: Brown University Press, 1994.
Kaplan, Aryeh. *The Light Beyond: Adventures in Hassidic Thought.* New York: Moznaim, 1981.
Katz, Michael, and Gershon Schwartz. *Swimming in the Sea of Talmud.* Philadelphia: Jewish Publication Society, 1997.
Kellner, Menachem. "Returning the Crown to its Ancient Glory: Marc Shapiro's The Limits of Orthodox Theology: Maimonides' Thirteen Principles Reappraised." *Edah Journal* 4:1 (Iyar, 5764).
Kolatch, Alfred J. *Masters of the Talmud: Their Lives and Views.* Middle Village, N.Y.: Jonathan David, 2003.
Langerman, Yitzhak Tzvi, ed. and trans. *Yemenite Midrash: Philosophical Commentaries on the Torah.* San Francisco: HarperCollins San Francisco, 1996.
Leeman, Saul. "Ibn Ezra on the Torah: Observations." *Jewish Bible Quarterly* 27:2 (Apr.–June 1999): 160–63.
*Lehrman, S. M. *The World of Midrash.* London: Thomas Yoseloff, 1961.
Leibowitz, Yeshayahu. *The Faith of Maimonides,* trans. John Glucker. Tel Aviv: MOD Books, 1989.
Levine, Nachman. "The Curse and the Blessing: Narrative Discourse Syntax and Literary Form." *Journal for the Study of the Old Testament* 27:2 (Dec. 2002): 189–99.
Liber, Maurice. *Rashi,* trans. Adele Szold. Philadelphia: Jewish Publication Society, 1910.
The Lookstein Center. "Nechama Leibowitz." http://www.lookstein.org/nechama_biography.htm.
———. "Nechama Leibowitz's Methodology: An Overview." http://www.lookstein.org/nechama_methodology.htm.
Mack, Hananel. *The Aggadic Midrash Literature,* trans. John Glucker. Tel Aviv: MOD Books, 1989.
Marantz, Haim. "Bearing Witness: Morality and Religion in the Thought of Yeshayahu Leibowitz." *Judaism* 46:181 (Winter 1997): 35–46.
Margolis, Max. *The Story of Bible Translations.* Philadelphia: Jewish Publication Society, 1917.
Nadich, Judah. *The Legends of the Rabbis: Vol. 1, Jewish Legends of the Second Commonwealth.* Northvale, N.J.: Jason Aronson, 1994.
———. *The Legends of the Rabbis: Vol. 2, The First Generation After the Destruction of the Temple and Jerusalem.* Northvale, N.J.: Jason Aronson, 1994.

————. *Rabbi Akiba and His Contemporaries.* Northvale, N.J.: Jason Aronson, 1998.

Neusner, Jacob. *Ancient Israel After Catastrophe: The Religious Worldview of the Mishnah.* Charlottesville: University Press of Virginia, 1983.

————. *Introduction to Rabbinic Literature.* New York: Anchor Bible Reference Library/Doubleday, 1994.

————. *Invitation to the Talmud: A Teaching Book,* rev. ed. New York: Harper and Row, 1984.

————. *The Midrash: An Introduction.* Northvale, N.J.: Jason Aronson, 1990.

Noveck, Simon, ed. *Creators of the Jewish Experience in Ancient and Medieval Times.* Washington, D.C.: B'nai B'rith Books, 1985.

Rabinowitz, Abraham Hirsch. *The Study of Talmud: Understanding the Halachic Mind.* Northvale, N.J.: Jason Aronson, 1996.

Resnick, Henry. "Conversations with the Talmud." www.huc.edu/kollel/talmud.

Rosenberg. A. J., trans. *Mikraoth Gedoloth—Books of the Bible.* Multiple volumes. New York: Judaica Press, 1995.

*Schwartz, Howard. *Reimagining the Bible: The Storytelling of the Rabbis.* Oxford, U.K.: Oxford University Press, 1998.

*Shinan, Avigdor. *The World of Aggadah,* trans. John Glucker. Tel Aviv: MOD Books, 1990.

Siegel, Eliezer. "A Page of Talmud." http://www.acs.ucalgary.ca/~elsegal/ Talmud -Page.html.

Sion, Avi. "Judaic Logic: A Formal Analysis of Biblical, Talmudic and Rabbinic Logic." Geneva, Switz.: Editions Slatkine, 1997; may be found at http://www.thelogician .net/3_judaic_logic/3_jl_frame.htm.

Sosland, Henry A. "Discovering the Netziv and His *Ha'amaik Davar.*" *Judaism* 51:203 (Summer 2002): 315–27.

*Steinsaltz, Adin. *The Essential Talmud.* New York: Basic Books, 1976.

————. *The Talmud: A Reference Guide.* New York: Random House, 1989.

Strack, H. L., and Günter Stemberger. *An Introduction to the Talmud and Midrash,* trans. and ed. Markus Bockmuehl. Minneapolis, Minn.: Fortress Press, 1992.

Zarum, Raphael. "What Makes a Good Torah Commentary?" *Le'ela: A Journal of Judaism Today* (June 2000).

WOMEN AND TORAH

*Adler, Rachel. *Engendering Judaism: An Inclusive Theology and Ethics.* Philadelphia: Jewish Publication Society, 1998.

Alpert, Rebecca. "What Gender Is God?" *Reform Judaism* 20:2 (Winter 1991).

Arts and Culture Staff. "Lysistrata in Sheital and High Heels: Have Men Hijacked the Mesorah?" *The Yeshiva College Commentator* March 18, 2005.

Baskin, Judith R. "Silent Partners: Women as Wives in Rabbinic Literature." In *Active Voices: Women in Jewish Culture,* ed. Maurie Sacks, pp. 19–40. Urbana: University of Illinois Press, 1995.

Baumel, Judith Tydor. "Torah for Everyone." *Ha'aretz,* March 9, 2004.

*Biale, Rachel. *Women and Jewish Law: The Essential Texts, Their History and Their Relevance for Today.* New York: Schocken Books, 1995.

Cantor, Aviva. *Jewish Women, Jewish Men: The Legacy of Patriarchy in Jewish Life.* San Francisco: HarperCollins San Francisco, 1995.

Carlebach, Julius. "Ze'enah Ur'enah: The Story of a Book for Jewish Women." *Le'ela*.

Chabin, Michele. "The New 'Poseks': Orthodox Women." *The Jewish Week*, October 8, 1999.

Cixous, Hélène. *Coming to Writing and Other Essays*, ed. Deborah Jenson. Cambridge, Mass.: Harvard University Press, 1991.

Elper, Ora Wiskind, and Susan Handelman, eds. *Torah of the Mothers: Contemporary Jewish Women Read Classical Jewish Texts*. New York: Urim Publications, 2000.

Forman, Lori. "The Untold Story of Eve." In *The Women's Torah Commentary: New Insights from Women Rabbis on the 54 Weekly Torah Portions*, ed. Elyse Goldstein, pp. 47–52. Woodstock, Vt.: Jewish Lights, 2000.

*Frymer-Kensky, Tikva. *Reading the Women of the Bible: A New Interpretation of Their Stories*. New York: Schocken Books, 2002.

*Goldstein, Elyse. *ReVisions: Seeing Torah Through a Feminist Lens*. Woodstock, Vt: Jewish Lights, 1998.

*Greenberg, Blu. *On Women and Judaism: A View from Tradition*. Philadelphia: Jewish Publication Society, 1981.

———. "Women and Judaism." In *Contemporary Jewish Thought*, ed. Arthur A. Cohen and Paul Mendes-Flohr, pp. 1039–53. New York: Free Press, 1987.

Greenspan, Frederick E. "A Typology of Biblical Women." *Judaism* 32:1 (Winter 1983: 43–50.

Gross, Rita M. "Steps Toward Feminine Imagery of Deity in Jewish Theology." *Judaism* 30:2 (Spring 1981): 183–93.

*Halevi, Shira. *The Life Story of Adam and Havah: A New Targum of Genesis 1:25–5:5*. Northvale, N.J.: Jason Aronson, 1997.

Hauptman, Judith. *Rereading the Rabbis: A Woman's Voice*. Boulder, Colo.: Westview Press, 1998.

———. "Some Thoughts on the Nature of Halakhic Adjudication: Women and Minyan." *Judaism* 42:4 (Fall 1993).

———. "Women and Prayer: An Attempt to Dispel Some Fallacies," *Judaism* (Winter 1993): 396–413.

Jachter, Howard. "The Parameters of Kol Isha." *Rabbi Jachter's Halacha Files*. www.koltorah.org/ravj, February 2, 2002.

Jelen, Sheila E. "Women Read Torah—A Review of *Torah of the Mothers: Contemporary Jewish Women Read Classical Texts*." *Tikkun* (September 2001).

Kimelman, Reuven. "The Seduction of Eve and Feminist Readings of the Garden of Eden." In *Women in Judaism: A Multidisciplinary Journal* 1:2. www.utoronto.ca/wjudaism/journal/vol1n2/eve.html.

Ostriker, Alicia Suskin. *Feminist Revision and the Bible*. Cambridge, Mass.: Blackwell Books, 1993.

———. *The Nakedness of the Fathers: Biblical Visions and Revisions*. New Brunswick, N.J.: Rutgers University Press, 1994.

Parker, Kim Ian. "Mirror, Mirror on the Wall, Must We Leave Eden Once and for All? A Lacanian Pleasure Trip through the Garden." *Journal for the Study of the Old Testament*, no. 83 (1999): 19–29.

*Plaskow, Judith. *Standing Again at Sinai: Judaism from a Feminist Perspective*. San Francisco: Harper and Row, 1990.

*Ronson, Barbara L. Thaw. *The Women of the Torah: Commentaries from the Talmud, Midrash and Kabbalah.* Northvale, N.J.: Jason Aronson, 1999.

Ross, Tamar. *Expanding the Palace of Torah: Orthodoxy and Feminism.* Waltham, Mass.: Brandeis University. Press, 2004.

Shkop, Esther M. "The Implications of Feminine Imagery in the Bible." *Tradition* 27:1 (1992): 42–47.

Student, Gil. "Sources Regarding Kol Isha." www.aishdas.org/student/kolisha.html 2002.

Swidler, Leonard. *Women in Judaism: The Status of Women in Formative Judaism.* Metuchen, N.J.: Scarecrow Press, 1976.

Trible, Phyllis. "Feminist Hermeneutics and Biblical Studies." *The Christian Century,* February 3–10, 1982.

Tuchman, Shera Aranoff, and Sandra E. Rapoport. *The Passion of the Matriarchs.* Jersey City, N.J.: Ktav, 2004.

Weisberg, Dvora. "Insiders or Outsiders: Women and Rabbinic Literature." *Judaism* 52:3–4 (Summer/Fall 2003): 203–15.

Weissler, Chava. *Voices of the Matriarchs: Listening to the Prayers of Early Modern Jewish Women.* Boston: Beacon Press, 1998.

Ziskind, Jonathan R. "The Treatment of Women in Deuteronomy: Moral Absolutism and Practicality," *Jewish Bible Quarterly* 27:3–4, Part 1 (July–Sept. 1999): 152–58; Part 2 (Oct–Dec. 1999): 231–37.

TROUBLING TEXTS

Benbassa, Esther, and Jean-Christophe Attias. *The Jew and the Other,* trans. G. M. Goshgarian. Ithaca, N.Y.: Cornell University Press, 2004.

Biale, David. *Eros and the Jews: From Biblical Israel to Contemporary America.* New York: Basic Books, 1992.

Bialinsky, Michael, and Jane Shapiro, eds., *Looking Within: Reading Sacred Violent Texts.* Jerusalem: Florence Melton Adult Mini-School, 2002. http://www.bjeny. org/pdf/judaic_curicula/Looking_Within_Reading_sacred_violent_texts.pdf.

Bloom, Jack. "Amalek and Us." *CCAR Journal: A Reform Jewish Quarterly* 48:2 (spring 2001): 51–55.

Bodoff, Lipmann. "The Real Test of the Akedah: Blind Obedience Versus Moral Choice." *Judaism* (Winter 1993).

Boteach, Shmuel. "Has *Halakhah* Become a Foreign God?" Oxford, U.K.: self-distributed e-mail, 1996.

Boyarin, Daniel. *Unheroic Conduct: The Rise of Heterosexuality and the Invention of the Jewish Man.* Berkeley: University of California Press, 1997.

Bregman, Mark. "Aqedah: Midrash as Visualization." *The Journal of Textual Reasoning* (June 2003).

Caudill, Gershon. "Homosexuality and Leviticus." http://home.earthlink.net/ ~ecorebbe/.

Cohen, Aryeh. "Teaching Troubling Texts." *Sh'ma: An On-Line Journal of Jewish Responsibility* (April 2001). http://www.shma.com/apr01/index.htm.

Conway, Daniel W. " 'Seeing' Is Believing: Narrative Visualization in Kierkegaard's Fear and Trembling." *The Journal of Textual Reasoning* (June 2003).

Drucker, Malka. "The Meaning of Amalek: Yesterday, Today, and Tomorrow." www .malkadrucker.com/amalek.htm.

Fornrobert, Charlotte Elisheva. "Cultivating a Multivocal Rabbinic Tradition." *Sh'ma: An On-Line Journal of Jewish Responsibility* (April 2001). http://www.shma.com/ apr01/index.htm.

Glowacka, Dorota. "Sacrificing the Text: The Philosopher/Poet at Mount Moriah." www.mun.ca/animus/1997vol2/glowack1.htm.

Greenberg, Steven. *Wrestling with God and Men: Homosexuality in the Jewish Tradition.* Madison: University of Wisconsin Press, 2004.

Haberman, Bonna Devora. "Difficult Texts." *Sh'ma: An On-Line Journal of Jewish Responsibility* (April 2001). http://www.shma.com/apr01/index.htm.

*Hartman, David. *A Heart of Many Rooms: Celebrating the Many Voices Within Judaism.* Woodstock, Vt.: Jewish Lights, 1999.

Heschel, Abraham Joshua. *God in Search of Man: A Philosophy of Judaism.* New York: Farrar, Straus and Giroux, 1995.

*Holtz, Barry W. *Textual Knowledge: Teaching the Bible in Theory and in Practice.* New York: Jewish Theological Seminary of America, 2003.

Ingall, Carol K. "Teaching Flaw and Holiness." *Sh'ma: An On-Line Journal of Jewish Responsibility* (April 2001). http://www.shma.com/apr01/index.htm.

Kahn, Yair. "The Books of B'midbar." *Virtual Bet Midrash.* http://www.vbm-torah .org/parsha.61/32behaal.htm

Kamenetzky, Mordechai. "The Rainmaker." *Drasha.* 5:2. http://www.projectgenesis .org/learning/drasha/5759/noach.html.

Katz, Claire Elise. "The Voice of God and the Face of the Other." *The Journal of Textual Reasoning* (June 2003).

Klepper, Deeana Copeland. "Shattering Innocence: Disturbing Texts and Children." *Sh'ma: An On-Line Journal of Jewish Responsibility* (April 2001). http://www .shma.com/apr01/index.htm.

Kula, Irwin. "Vayera." www.clal.org/wklysedra.html.

Ladin, Jay. "Akedah 5760." *Cross Currents* (Spring-Summer 2000).

*Laytner, Anson. *Arguing with God: A Jewish Tradition.* Northvale, N.J.: Jason Aronson 1990.

Levene, Nancy. "Introduction." *Journal of Textual Reasoning* 8 (1999). http://etext .lib.virginia.edu/journals/tr/indexpast.html.

Levinas, Emmanuel. "A Propos of 'Kierkegaard vivant.' " In *Proper Names,* trans. Michael B. Smith. Stanford, Calif.: Stanford University Press, 1996.

———. "Kierkegaard: Existence and Ethics." In *Proper Names,* trans. Michael B. Smith. Stanford, Calif.: Stanford University Press, 1996.

Lichtenstein, Aharon. "Chazal's Criticism of Moshe Rabbenu." The Lookstein Center at Bar-Ilan University. http://www.lookstein.org/articles/chazal_criticism .htm.

Litman, Jane Rachel. "Working With the Words of Torah." *Sh'ma: An On-Line Journal of Jewish Responsibility* (April 2001). http://www.shma.com/apr01/index.htm.

Littlestone, Lawrence. "After the Shop." December 30, 1998. http://shamash3.shamash .org/tanach/tanach/commentary/daf-hashavua/vayechi-5759.dafhashavua.98

Lopatin, Asher. "What Makes a Book Orthodox? Wrestling with God and Men by Steve Greenberg." *The Edah Journal* 4:2 (2004).

Magid, Shaul. "What Is 'Troubling' About Troubling Texts." *Journal of Textual Reasoning* 8 (1999). http://etext.lib.virginia.edu/journals/tr/indexpast.html.

Maimonides, Moses. *The Guide for the Perplexed,* trans. M. Friedlander. New York: Dover Publications, 1956.

Menken, Yaakov. "Eikev." *Lifeline,* August 2000. http://www.torah.org/learning/lifeline/5759/eikev.html.

Meskin, Jacob. "Textual Reasoning, Modernity, and the Limits of History: A Critical Essay." *Cross Currents* 49:4 (Winter 1999).

Mohrmann, Doug C. "Making Sense of Sex: A Study of Leviticus 18." *Journal of the Study of the Old Testament* 29:1 (September 2004): 57–79.

Navon, Chaim. "Lecture #5: Biblical Criticism." *Theological Issues In Sefer Bereishit.* http://www.vbm-torah.org/archive/bereishit/05bereishit.htm.

Plaskow, Judith. "Dealing with the Hard Stuff: Hard Texts in Scriptures." *Tikkun* (September–October 1994): 57–58.

Prosnit, James. "The Gift of Responsibility." *Torat Hayim,* Oct. 17, 1998. http://www.urj.org/Articles/index.cfm?id=3072&pge_prg_id=29218&pge_id=3450.

"Q & A About Being Gay and Frum." http://members.aol.com/GayJews/FAQ.html.

Rashkow, Ilona N. *Taboo or Not Taboo: Sexuality and Family in the Hebrew Bible.* Minneapolis, Minn.: Fortress Press, 2000.

Riskin, Shlomo. "Rabbi Riskin's Shabbat Shalom." *Divrei Torah.* http://www.ohrtorahstone.org.il/previousissues.htm.

Rose, Or. "Wrestling with Words." *Sh'ma: An On-Line Journal of Jewish Responsibility* (April 2001). http://www.shma.com/apr01/index.htm.

Schorsch, Ismar. "Chancellor's Commentary." *Divrei Torah.* http://www.jtsa.edu/community/parashah/archives/index.shtml.

Schulweis, Harold. "A Second Look at Homosexuality." http://www.vbs.org/rabbi/hshulw/homo.htm.

Signer, Michael A. "Rashi's Reading of the Akedah." *The Journal of Textual Reasoning* (June 2003).

Spiegel, Shalom. *The Last Trial: On the Legends and Lore of the Command to Abraham to Offer Isaac as a Sacrifice,* trans. Judah Goldin. Woodstock, Vt.: Jewish Lights, 1993.

Tendler, Rabbi Aron. "Bereishis." *Rabbi's Notebook,* 1998. http://www.projectgenesis.org/learning/rabbis-notebook/5759/bereishis.html.

Tuito, Elazar. "What's in a Name?—'And These Are the Names,' " *Lectures on the Torah Reading.* Bar-Ilan University, 1999. http://www.biu.ac.il/JH/Parasha/eng/shemot/tui.html.

Turner, Masha. "The Dreams in Joseph's Story." *Lectures on the Torah Reading.* Bar-Ilan University, 1996 (Ramat Gan, Israel). http://www.biu.ac.il/JH/Parasha/eng/vayeshev/vayesh.shtml.

Tzohar, Yael, "Joseph the Saint," *Lectures on the Torah Reading,* 1997, Bar-Ilan University, (Ramat Gan, Israel). Located at http://www.biu.ac.il/JH/Parasha/eng/vayeshev/tzohar.html.

Walfish, Avraham. "Acharei Mot: The Torah Reading of Yom Kippur." *Virtual Bet Midrash,* April 1997. http://www.vbm-torah.org/roshandyk/yk63aw.htm.

Waxman, Chanoch. "Each Man His Fire Pan: On the Deaths of Nadav and Avihu." *Virtual Bet Midrash,* April 2002. http://www.vbm-torah.org/vayikra.htm.

Yitzhaki, Ephraim. "Abraham's Tribulations." *Lectures on the Torah Reading,* Bar-Ilan University, Oct. 25, 1998 (Ramat Gan, Israel). http://www.biu.ac.il/JH/Parasha/eng/lekh/itz.html.

Zank, Michael. "Teaching the Bible as a 'Troubling Text.' " *Journal of Textual Reasoning* 8 (1999). http://etext.lib.virginia.edu/journals/tr/indexpast.html.

Zemer, Moshe. *Evolving Halakhah: A Progressive Approach to Traditional Jewish Law.* Woodstock, Vt.: Jewish Lights, 1999.

COMMENTARIES ON THE PARASHIYOT

Antonelli, Judith S. *In the Image of God: A Feminist Commentary on the Torah.* Northvale, N.J.: Jason Aronson, 1997.

Blidstein, Gerald J. *In the Rabbis' Garden: Adam and Eve in Midrash.* Northvale, N.J.: Jason Aronson, 1997.

Buber, Martin. *Moses: The Revelation and the Covenant.* New York: Harper and Row, 1958.

*Cohen, Victor. *The Soul of the Torah: Insights of the Chasidic Masters on the Weekly Torah Portions.* Northvale, N.J.: Jason Aronson, 2000.

Colodner, Solomon. *Concepts and Values.* New York: Shengold, 1968.

*Davis, Avrohom, and Avrohom Kleinkaufman, trans. *The Metsudah Chumash/Rashi,* 5 vols. Hoboken, N.J.: Ktav, 1991.

Edwards, Betzalel Philip, trans. and ed. *Living Waters: The Mei HaShiloach, A Commentary on the Torah by Rabbi Mordechai Yosef of Isbitza.* Northvale, N.J.: Jason Aronson, 2001.

*Fields, Harvey J. *A Torah Commentary for Our Times.* 3 vols. New York: UAHC Press, 1990–93.

*Goldstein, Elyse, ed. *The Women's Torah Commentary: New Insights from Women Rabbis on the 54 Weekly Torah Portions.* Woodstock, Vt.: Jewish Lights, 2000.

Gore, Norman. *Tzeenah U-Reenah: A Jewish Commentary on the Book of Exodus.* New York: Vantage Press, 1965.

Hirsch, Samson Raphael. *The Pentateuch,* trans. Isaac Levy. Multiple vols. Gateshead, U.K.: Judaica Press, 1973.

*Jacobson, B. S. *Meditations on the Torah.* Tel Aviv: Sinai Publishing, 1956.

Jacobson, Dan. *The Story of the Stories: The Chosen People and Its God.* New York: Harper and Row, 1982.

Katz, Mordechai. *Ulmode Ul'Lamed: From the Teachings of Our Sages . . .* Spring Valley, N.Y.: Feldheim, 1978.

*Kushner, Lawrence S., and Kerry M. Olitzky. *Sparks Beneath the Surface: A Spiritual Commentary on the Torah.* Northvale, N.J.: Jason Aronson, 1998.

The Language of Truth: The Torah Commentary of the Sefat Emet, Rabbi Yehudah Leib Alter of Ger, trans. and interp. Arthur Green. Philadelphia: Jewish Publication Society, 1998.

*Leibowitz, Nehama, *Studies in B'midbar: In the Context of Ancient and Modern Jewish Bible Commentary,* trans. and adapt. Aryeh Newman. Jerusalem: World Zionist Organization, 1981.

———. *Studies in Bereishit: In the Context of Ancient and Modern Jewish Bible Commentary,* trans. and adapt. Aryeh Newman. 4th rev. ed. Jerusalem: World Zionist Organization, 1981.

————. *Studies in Devarim: In the Context of Ancient and Modern Jewish Bible Commentary*, trans. and adapt. Aryeh Newman. Jerusalem: World Zionist Organization, 1981.

————. *Studies in Shemot: In the Context of Ancient and Modern Jewish Bible Commentary*, trans. and adapt. Aryeh Newman. 2 vols. Jerusalem: World Zionist Organization, 1981.

————. *Studies in Vayikra: In the Context of Ancient and Modern Jewish Bible Commentary*, trans. and adapt. Aryeh Newman. Jerusalem: World Zionist Organization, 1981.

Leibowitz, Yeshayahu. *Notes and Remarks on the Weekly Parashah*. Brooklyn, N.Y.: Chemed Books, 1990.

Levine, Dov, trans. *The Torah Discourse of the Holy Tzaddik Reb Menachem Mendel of Rimanoc, 1745–1815*. Hoboken, N.J.: Ktav, 1996.

Matt, Daniel, trans. *The Zohar*, 2 vols. to date. Stanford, Calif.: Stanford University Press, 2004.

Milgrom, Jacob. *Leviticus 17–22*. New York: Anchor/Doubleday, 2000.

————. *Leviticus 23–27*. New York: Anchor/Doubleday, 2001.

*Peli, Pinchas. *Torah Today: A Renewed Encounter with Scripture*. Washington, D.C.: B'nai B'rith Books, 1987.

Ronson, Barbara L. Thaw. *The Women of the Torah: Commentaries from the Talmud, Midrash, and Kabbalah*. Northvale, N.J.: Jason Aronson, 1999.

*Sarna, Nachum M. *Exploring Exodus: The Heritage of Biblical Israel*. New York: Schocken Books, 1986.

————. *Understanding Genesis: The Heritage of Biblical Israel*. New York: Schocken Books, 1970.

Scheinbaum, A. L. *Peninim on the Torah, Sixth Series*. Cleveland Heights, Ohio: Peninim Publications, 2000.

Schneerson, Menachem M. *In the Garden of Torah*. 2 vols. Brooklyn, N.Y.: Sichos in English, 1995.

Sperling, Harry, and Maurice Simon, trans. *The Zohar*. 5 vols. London: Soncino Press, 1984.

*Weinberg, Matis. *Frameworks: Exodus*. Boston, Mass.: Foundation for Jewish Publications, 1999.

————. *Frameworks: Genesis*. Boston, Mass.: Foundation for Jewish Publications, 1999.

————. *Frameworks: Leviticus*. Boston, Mass.: Foundation for Jewish Publications, 2000.

Weisblum, Moshe Pinchas. *Table Talk: Biblical Questions and Answers*. Northvale, N.J.: Jason Aronson, 2000.

*Zornberg, Avivah Gottlieb. *Genesis: The Beginning of Desire*. Philadelphia: Jewish Publication Society, 1995.

————. *The Particulars of Rapture: Reflections on Exodus*. New York: Doubleday, 2001.

As we have seen, there are literally nearly a thousand commentaries on *parashat ha'shavua* available through e-mail and on the Internet. At one time or another in the course of working on this book, I have subscribed to over a hundred such e-publications. Almost all such *divrei Torah* are archived online. Rather than try to list all of those or the specific *derashot* I read, I refer you to the sidebar "Torah on the Internet" (p. 258) for an introduction to the ones that I have found to be the most consistently helpful, provocative, and interesting.

A NOTE ON THE TYPE

The text of this book was set in Ehrhardt, a typeface based on the specimens of "Dutch" types found at the Ehrhardt foundry in Leipzig. The original design of the face was the work of Nicholas Kis, a Hungarian punch cutter known to have worked in Amsterdam from 1680 to 1689. The modern version of Ehrhardt was cut by the Monotype Corporation of London in 1937.

Composed by Creative Graphics, Allentown, Pennsylvania

Printed and bound by Berryville Graphics, Berryville, Virginia

Designed by M. Kristen Bearse

2/07